DISCARDED

The American Utopian Adventure
SERIES TWO

AUTOBIOGRAPHY OF ADIN BALLOU

Engraved by H.W. Smith

Adin Ballou

AUTOBIOGRAPHY

OF

ADIN BALLOU.

1803 — 1890.

CONTAINING AN ELABORATE RECORD AND NARRATIVE
OF HIS LIFE FROM INFANCY TO OLD AGE.

WITH APPENDIXES.

COMPLETED AND EDITED BY HIS SON-IN-LAW,

WILLIAM S. HEYWOOD.

"We spend our years as a tale that is told." — *Ps. 90:9.*

PORCUPINE PRESS

Philadelphia 1975

First edition 1896
(Lowell, Mass.: The Vox Populi Press — Thompson & Hill, 1896)

Reprinted 1975 by
PORCUPINE PRESS, INC.
Philadelphia, Pennsylvania 19107

Library of Congress Cataloging in Publication Data

Ballou, Adin, 1803-1890.
    Autobiography of Adin Ballou, 1803-1890.

    (The American utopian adventure : series two)
    Reprint of the 1896 ed. published by the Vox Populi Press, Lowell, Mass.
    "Published works of Adin Ballou": p.
    Includes index.
    1. Ballou, Adin, 1803-1890. I. Heywood, William Sweetzer, 1824-1903.
BX9969.B27A3   1975   288'.092'4 [B]   74-26603
ISBN 0-87991-033-X

Manufactured in the United States of America

INTRODUCTION.

By the Editor.

This volume is one of several prepared by its author and left in manuscript at his decease, the publication of which was duly provided for in specific clauses of his will. Its appearance has been considerably delayed by pre-existing engagements and more urgent duties on the part of him to whose supervision the matter was entrusted, and by other circumstances that could not be easily avoided or overcome. Its contents have been condensed somewhat from the original in order to bring them within desirable limits, but nothing has been eliminated that was deemed necessary to the completeness of the work as a portraiture of the man whose life, character, and career it was designed to outline and illustrate. Save in the particular indicated, the narrative, up to the time when the hand of the writer became incapable of further service by reason of the illness that terminated his mortal life, is given in his own way and mostly in his own language. The plan of the work, the arrangement of topics, its literary style and mode of expression, are distinctively his own, and bear the impress of his marked individuality.

The subject of the autobiography was no ordinary personage, and he played no unimportant part in the drama of human affairs during the eventful period in which he lived. Springing from humble and obscure conditions, without ancestral or social prestige or the favor of influential friends; without more than very meagre opportunities for self-improvement and for rising above the common level, he yet became a central figure in the community where most of his days on earth were spent, a great power for good in the world, a noteworthy man of his age. Wherever he was known, he was loved and honored for his elevated and pure spirit, for his many excellences of character, for his broad and disinterested philanthropy, and for his unremitting endeavors to promote the welfare and happiness of his fellowmen. Born in the early years of the nineteenth century and continuing until the opening of its last decade, he was not only an interested observer *of*, but an active participant *in*, those great progressive moral and religious movements which make that century memorable in the annals of the race. He appeared upon the stage of being when the stern dogmatism of the primitive New England theology was beginning to be permeated with the leaven of a more reasonable and a more liberal faith, and when the long-received beliefs of the fathers were made the themes of sharp and unrelenting controversy on the part of thoughtful religious people throughout the land. While yet a mere youth, he passed through certain profound spiritual experiences which gave bias and trend to his entire subsequent life — which foreshadowed as they, in large measure, shaped his whole earthly career. Very naturally, in his immature and receptive state of mind, he imbibed at first the dominant views of his teachers and elders upon religious subjects, concerning which he formulated for himself a definite statement of doctrine which, to his mind, was impregnable. But presently, by reason of questionings and doubts from within as well as from without, he entered upon and went through a most searching investigation which resulted, much to his own surprise, in a complete reversal of his own previously cherished convictions upon some of the most fundamental doctrines of theology, and caused him to adopt those representing more cheerful and inspiring views of God and man — of life, death, and immortality — in which he rejoiced with exceeding joy, and of which he became an earnest, eloquent, uncompromising, life-long adherent and champion. Passing over from his former conception of the sovereignty of God, as expressed in His inexorable will and irresistible power, to that of the fatherhood of God, expressed in His infinite goodness and love, his idea of the whole vast economy of being and of the overruling divine providence was correspondingly transformed, as was also his idea of human duty and responsibility. The new thought of the great Author of all being and Disposer of all events engendered new emotions, as it appealed to new motives in his breast, gave, in his estimate, a new meaning and purpose to existence, and required a new type of personal character and a new order of life among men. It brought into distinct and commanding prominence the humanitarian side of religion. Out of the fatherhood of God comes, by logical and moral necessity, the brotherhood of man and the whole vast round of sentiments and obligations incumbent upon the co-equal members of one great family.

The author of this book saw this and in the candor and loyalty of his mind and heart accepted it, and with it all the issues it involved bearing upon human conduct and character. He was thus not only predisposed but compelled to espouse and advocate every salutary moral reform, and to lend a hand to every activity and enterprise calculated to benefit and bless the world. Nay, more. Deeming the principles of the gospel of Christ, in which he was a most devout believer, and the spirit of brotherhood applicable to human life in all possible circumstances and concerns, and beholding the injustice and wrong, the suffering and misery inseparable from the existing social order, he devised and, with the co-operation of sympathizing friends, put in operation a scheme for the complete reorganization of society, by which all special reforms should be united in one great comprehensive movement for the suppression of the ills that afflict humanity and the promotion of the welfare and happiness of all the classes and conditions of people; by which all human interests and affairs should be brought into harmony with the divine law of love to God and man — an attempt, in short, to inaugurate the kingdom of heaven on the earth.

Of one whose life was consecrated to such purposes and spent in the pursuit of such objects as have been indicated, this volume treats with all needful particularity of detail, showing how he went on, step by step, in his course from childhood and youth to hoary age, animated and cheered by an unfailing faith in God and the eternal realities, and by the unbeclouded vision of a reign of righteousness, brotherhood, and peace, which shall some day come to emancipate, uplift, sanctify, and rejoice with exceeding joy, the children of men. And it is commended to those who would be glad to know something of such a man and of his varied and manifold experiences in the attainment of those qualities of mind, heart, and character which he so fully illustrated, and in the prosecution of the work by which his influence for good shall be felt by those coming after him unto many generations. It is commended, also, to his surviving relatives and friends, who hold his memory dear and who will be glad to have some memento bearing the impress of his own immediate hand, wherewith to be reminded from time of the lessons he was wont to give them while he was with them in the flesh, and to be kept in touch with his spirit and the purpose of his life. It is furthermore commended to the earnest and reverent students of sociological problems — to those who, in the present or some coming day, believe in the possibility of a divine order of society among men, and who are desirous of doing what they may to make that possibility a living and enduring reality upon the earth. In the hope that those to whom reference is made and many others disposed to peruse the pages that follow, may find in them a source, not only of pleasure and satisfaction, but of inspiration to noble living and to endeavors to advance the interests and subserve the ends which the author had so much at heart, this book is sent forth into the world and submitted to the considerate attention of all who seek to show forth their reverence and love for God by faithful service of mankind.

Of the two portraits herein found of the author of this work, the first is a steel engraving copied from a photograph taken when he was about fifty years of age, and represents him as he was in mid-life and as he is remembered by a few of his older friends and acquaintances; the other is a half-tone picture reproduced from a copy of a negative taken in 1888, and shows him as he appeared during the last years of his mortal pilgrimage.

The other manuscript volumes, referred to on a preceding page as awaiting publication, will be issued in the not far distant future. The first of them, "A Complete History of the Hopedale Community," will be put into the printer's hands at an early day and may be expected to appear in the autumn of 1897.

PREFACE.

The world worships success and despises failure. It judges of success and failure chiefly according to outward appearance — according to material manifestations and tangible results. It concerns itself little with causes, motives, preliminary conditions or noiseless agencies and operations. Its eyes are carnal not spiritual. It contemns the prophets of any given age while they are yet alive — perhaps crucifies, stones, or starves them — but builds the tombs and garnishes the sepulchers of those of a former age who have passed away, and whose testimonies and sufferings have immortalized their memories. So it has ever been; so it is still. Nothing else is to be expected.

I have not been a man of much popular success, but in several respects of failure. Not because my intentions, principles, ideals, objects and plans were reprehensible and unworthy of success, but because they foreran the conditions and means indispensable to its acquisition. My hopes were too urgent and sanguine; my standard and aim were set too high for immediate realization. So have I been defeated in some of my noblest schemes; some of my most disinterested and earnest labors have been expended in vain, and my way has been overshadowed with disappointment and grief. The world has judged and will for some time longer judge of me and of my undertakings after its own ancient fashion, and I complain not. In the wisdom of God all is for the best, and nothing true and good is forever lost. The final verdict is not rendered yet, and my case and cause are adjourned to a more auspicious future.

Times and generations are coming that will justly estimate me and my work, and assign both to their proper place in the providential plan for the progress and redemption of humanity. For them, as it has proved, have I lived and labored, rather than for my contemporaries. To them I appeal for vindication and approval; to them I bequeath whatever is valuable and worth preserving of my possessions — the fruits of my toil while yet a dweller in the tabernacles of earth and time.

I have been repeatedly urged by some of my relatives and friends who seem to cherish for me a very earnest regard and to have great confidence in me, to write my biography. In my less buoyant moods I have shrunk from the task, feeling for the time being that I preferred to be forgotten, if possible, by posterity and to have all my seemingly illusory theories and abortive projects buried in oblivion. But in more lucid and thoughtful states of mind and heart, under cheering inspirations from the spiritual world which have always prevailed against impulsive and momentary despondency and gloom, I have been more inclined to undertake the task desired of me. Yielding to such inclination, I have at length set myself about the work involved, with a view of carrying it forward to completion as rapidly as possible without interfering with other duties to which I am pledged, making due allowance for hindrances and delays to which my position before the public and wide acquaintanceship expose me continually. I do this partly because I think that in this way I can still render some benefit to mankind; partly because no one else, moved to tell the story of my life after my decease, has at hand the data I can command for doing the subject justice; and partly because, if nothing more comes of it, the narrative will afford my surviving relatives and friends, to whom I owe a great debt of gratitude for all their kindness to me, something of personal satisfaction and delight.

I have many memoranda preserved among my private papers and a carefully kept diary covering the greater part of my active life, as well as much private matter accumulated through a long term of editorial service, from which I can draw to aid my memory in giving definiteness and authenticity to the facts of which mention will be made. I shall proceed, therefore, in the preparation of a volume for the press, with an unwavering confidence in the accuracy of all the details essential to a trustworthy and desirable narrative.

CONTENTS.

CHAPTER I.
1803–1813.

Birth, ancestry, and family relationship — Place of nativity and vicinage — Unpromising infancy — Natural disposition and susceptibilities — Annoyances and casualties — Paternal discipline — Relation to employees — First appearance at church — Ancient burying ground — Early religious impressions — Prevailing indifference to spiritual things — Home and life there — Old-fashioned tavern — Military witchery — Intoxicating liquors — At school — Easy to learn — Episode in domestic affairs — Back again. — War clouds and the opening storm . . 1–26

CHAPTER II.
1813–1818.

Interest in public affairs — Opportunities for self-culture improved — A great "Reformation" — Parents and older brothers converted — Church of the "Christian Connexion" formed — Father made deacon and kept ministers' tavern — Personal experience — Baptized and received into the church — Self-revelation and self-conflict — A memorable year — Great September gale — General Conference — Death of brothers Cyrus and Arnold — Routine of employment — Intense love of learning — Hope for a collegiate education thwarted — Reflections — Singing-school privileges interdicted — Spiritual lapse and recovery 27–43

CHAPTER III.
1818–1821.

Increased responsibilities — Lurch into asceticism — A formulated belief — Final destruction of the wicked held and maintained — All forms of Universalism deemed anti-Christian — Several clergymen noticed — Eccentric Lorenzo Dow and his lesson — Informed upon political questions — Favorable school privileges enjoyed and much benefit derived from them — Important commission undertaken and executed with much difficulty — Marriage of cousin — One such occasion leads to another — Betrothal — Apologetic comments — Manager of ancestral estate — Disastrous business venture . . 44-60

CHAPTER IV.

1821-1822.

Life-plans presumably settled — Undreamed-of changes subvert them — A startling vision — Call to the Christian ministry — Conflicting emotions awakened thereby — Many reasons for not responding favorably to the mysterious message — Yet it seemed sacredly imperative and could not be denied — Yielding, therefore, the work involved was soon made manifest — Unpremeditatedly, announcement to preach was made and a text in due time given — The result — The evil of sin — Invitations to conduct religious services — First authorship — Teaching — A refractory pupil and an angry father — Wedding feast interrupted, but with a satisfactory issue — Housekeeping 61-76

CHAPTER V.

1822-1823.

Preaching in the general vicinity — Winchester's Dialogues read — Discussion with Universalist neighbors — Self-satisfied, but conscious of one weak point — Doubts concerning destiny of the impenitent wicked arise — Thorough search of the Scriptures resulted in the conviction that they teach Universal Restoration — After an agonizing experience accepted that doctrine and announced the change of belief — A stormy time followed — Denounced by relatives and friends, and excommunicated by the church — Entered Universalist fellowship, though not accepting the dogma of no future punishment — After another heart-searching experience fully confirming the new faith, began preaching it — Second visit to Boston — New friends under new auspices . 77-95

CHAPTER VI.
1823–1825.

Engagement to supply several pulpits — Disgraceful proceeding at Bellingham — "The furious priest reproved" — First born child — Candidacy in Boston — Ordained as a Universalist minister — Call to the pastorate at Milford received and accepted — Entered upon the work with diligence and zeal — A religious war of several years' continuance in the town — Causes and characteristics of the same — Incidents growing out of it — A stroke of good policy — A Free Mason and military chaplain — Teaching again — Religious condition of Milford Society 96-115

CHAPTER VII.
1825–1828.

Provision for a home — Ludicrous performances at a funeral in Franklin — More serious one near at hand — Personal bereavements — House completed and occupied — Celebration of American Independence, 1827 — Laughable incident — Received invitation to preach for Prince Street Society in New York city — Accepted, though under some misapprehension — After a brief candidacy was called to the pastorate — Removal to the new field of labor — Child lost and found — Work prosecuted vigorously, but with indifferent results — Expectations unrealized — New means of usefulness — Friendly messages and appeals from Milford 116-138

CHAPTER VIII.
1828–1329.

Return to former parish decided upon — Regrets of New York people expressed — Inquiries concerning a successor revealed a desire to obtain Rev. Hosea Ballou — Negotiations opened accordingly — Encouraging response received — Mr. Ballou's visit to the city to arrange details — Satisfactorily settled, then unsettled, and settled again with an *if* — Meanwhile the proposed return to Milford had been effected — Reflections on Rev. Hosea Ballou's proceedings — Some misapprehensions corrected — Universalism in New York — A singular marriage — A gloomy premonition — Treading the old paths — Visit from Origin Bachelor and a consequent theological debate — Birth of a daughter — Decline of wife's health and early death — Musings 139–156

CHAPTER IX.
1829–1830.

Field of service enlarging — A student in theology — The use of tobacco — Its final abandonment after a desperate struggle — Extracts from diary — Sudden and serious illness — Recovery gratefully referred to in the first sermon thereafter — A re-established home contemplated — Engagement of marriage with the daughter of a parishioner — Her qualifications for the duties of wife and mother — The nuptial vows sealed, Rev. Hosea Ballou 2d officiating — A Wrentham funeral — Consolatory discourse attacked by a local clergyman — Pastoral duties divided between Milford and Medway 157–169

CHAPTER X.
1830–1831.

Eventful year — Attitude of early Universalists on Future Retribution — Radical change on the subject — Existing dominant belief accompanied by a derision of Restorationism — The famous "Medway sermon" — Request for its publication granted and it was sent to the *Trumpet* office accordingly — Before appearing in print, it was severely criticised and disparaged by the editor, Rev. Thomas Whittemore — A new crisis reached. — Review of the situation resulting in a determination to repel the attack and defend the truth — A vigorous Reply to Mr. Whittemore was written but refused publication — The Milford Society and its action — An uncompromising Restorationist thenceforth — *The Independent Messenger* started — Bitter hostility of so-called ultra Universalists — Discharged from Milford and invited to Mendon — Fourth of July, 1830 — Birth of a second son — Renewed assault of the *Trumpet* and rejoinder — Restorationist brethren timid . . . 170–192

CHAPTER XI.
1831–1832.

Settled in Mendon — Condition of the parish — Revival of interest and continued increase in prosperity — Ecclesiastical gatherings — Massachusetts Association of Restorationists organized — Occasion of a fresh assault on the part of the *Trumpet* — Met with unabated vigor — Restorationism assailed from the opposite direction and defended no less vigorously — Rev. Amos A. Phelps — *Independent Messenger* moved to Boston — At the end of a year's service in Mendon was engaged for five years — Policy in regard to salary — Friendship with prominent Unitarians 193–214

CHAPTER XII.
1832–1833.

Installation by a council of Restorationists and Unitarians — Prevailing spirit of harmony and co-operation — Sermon of Rev. Bernard Whitman on Christian Union — Courage and independence of Unitarians who sympathized with Restorationists — Espousal of the Temperance Reform — Curious conduct of Rev. J. M. L. Perry at a public meeting in aid of the cause — Benefits derived from the position taken — Calls to lecture — Resolutions of the Providence Association — Extracts from diary — Anxiety and sorrow — Death of two children — Consolatory thoughts 215–233

CHAPTER XIII.
1833–1834.

Installation of Seth Chandler, former theological student — Whitman's "Letter to a Universalist" — Third son born, named Adin Augustus — Call to Watertown declined — Rev. Stephen Cutler and an unfortunate partnership — Review of Huidekoper's treatise on "The Destruction of the Wicked" — Discussion with Rev. Jonathan Farr — Abhorrence of the doctrine of endless punishment emphasized — Controversy with ultra Universalists continued — Challenge to a public discussion — Accepted by Rev. Daniel D. Smith — Report of what was said printed — Course of Mr. Smith and Universalists generally in regard thereto 234–252

CHAPTER XIV.
1834–1836.

Another student, Edmund Capron — Swords measured with distinguished champions of orthodoxy — Temperance

work — Attendance upon public occasions — Death of
Rev. Bernard Whitman — Family Bereavements — Settlement of father's estate — "Omega" to the controversy with former associates — A long silence ensued
concerning the main points in question, followed by an
almost unanimous adoption of the views held and maintained by the Restorationists — Warfare with advocates
of endless torments still raging — Debate with Rev. W.
P. Apthorp — Improved condition of Mendon parish —
Diary extracts 253-270

CHAPTER XV.
1836-1838.

Ordination of George W. Stacey — Interesting visit to Concord — Mendon pastorate extended — Endeavors to promote the Christian life of the people — Total Abstinence — The Anti-slavery movement — Its claims examined — Conclusions arrived at and stand taken — Fast
Day sermon, 1837, and its consequences — Fourth of
July oration — A vexatious episode — Blunder of Rev.
Mr. Grosvenor at installation of Rev. Thomas Edwards
— Ordination of Rev. Edmund Capron and death soon
afterward — Reform resolutions passed by Massachusetts Association of Restorationists — "The Touchstone" published — Personal religion — Murder of
Lovejoy — Dangerous illness of son 271-297

CHAPTER XVI.
1838-1840.

Personal memoranda — An unusual ceremonial — A parishioner elected to Congress — First Christmas celebration
in Mendon — Claims of the cause of Peace carefully
considered — Serious questions involved — Christian
Non-Resistance — The logical outcome of Restorationism — "Standard of Practical Christianity" — Opposition by conservative brethren — Death of father —
Quarterly conferences — On the Non-resistant platform
— End of the *Messenger* — A new organ provided
for 298-317

CHAPTER XVII.
1840-1842.

The Practical Christian — Groton Convention — Requirements of the adopted "Standard" — Truth is to be lived — A new civilization demanded — The Fraternal Communion — Other social experiments — Brook Farm. — Declaration of principles — Location of proposed Community selected and named Hopedale — Village site laid out — The outlook — Varied experiences — The Restorationist Association — Lectures — Afflictions — Letters of William Ellery Channing, D. D., and Rev. Paul Dean — Farewell to Mendon and removal to Hopedale — First religious meeting there — Visit of Frederic Douglass 318–338

CHAPTER XVIII.
1842–1845.

Man, a moral and religious being — Deductions from that postulate — Hopedale statistics — Valuable lessons learned — Rev. David R. Lamson and his co-incompatibles — The real trouble — Change of policy required and effected — Withdrawal of Mr. Lamson and his subsequent history — Lectures on Social Reform and kindred topics — Second Advent discussions — "True Scriptural Doctrine of the Second Advent" — Progress — Donation of Andrew H. Ernst of Cincinnati — Religious meetings — Difficulties and dangers — Heavy bereavement . . . . , ... 339–359

CHAPTER XIX.
1845–1852.

Personal reflections — Helpmeet in the household — Year of marked prosperity — Faint-heartedness, nevertheless — Withdrawal of Rev. George W. Stacey — Visit from Robert Owen, an English Communist — Reverses — The system simplified — Cemetery laid out — Small partnerships granted, with diverse results — Rectification of land titles — Resignation of Rev. Daniel S. Whitney — A new President — Death of Susan Fish — Death of the dear son, Adin Augustus — "Christian Non-resistance" published — Debates with Origin Bachelor and Rev. Thomas Williams — Spirit manifestations examined — Education of children — "Educational Home" — "Memoir of A. A. Ballou" — Work on Spiritualism — Henry C. Wright and Oliver Johnson — "The Practical Christian Ministry" — Demise of wife's mother — Preaching for Theodore Parker . 360–384

CHAPTER XX.
1852–1858.

Enfeebled condition of body and mind — Sympathizing friends — Visit to Troy, N. Y. — Lectures on Spiritualism — Opening of 1853 — Tragic death of Butler Wilmarth, M. D. — Inductive Communion — Inquiries answered and errors withstood — "Practical Christian Republic" — Work on "Practical Christian Socialism" published — Journey to the West, with notes by the way, visits to noted places, and interviews with distinguished statesmen — Year of prosperity — New Communities proposed — Explorers in Western fields — Lecture tours — Call upon Hon. Gerritt Smith — The fatal crisis — Resolution for the future — Commune No. 1 — Vision of Rev. Thomas L. Harris . . . 385–407

CHAPTER XXI.
1858–1862.

Promulgatory activities — Hopedale Home School — Lecture on the Bible — Pleasant memories — Hopedale church organized — Death of friends — The John Brown raid — Course of Anti-war Abolitionists condemned — Peace principles of the American Anti-slavery Society stated — Stirring meeting of Worcester South Anti-slavery Society — Position of William Lloyd Garrison criticised — Past and present utterances contrasted — Commentary on the Scriptures — Discontinuance of the *Practical Christian* — Kindly words from Rev. Thomas Whittemore and response — Promulgation Society formed — New house of worship — Remarkable spirit seances — Discussion with Miles Grant — Mutterings of coming war — Birth of granddaughter — "The Monitorial Guide" — The Lord's freemen . . . 408–435

CHAPTER XXII.
1862–1872.

Hopedale affairs — Business prospers, but Practical Christianity is in abeyance — Home School suspended — Discourses of William Lloyd Garrison — Discussion of objectionable points sought but declined — Reviewed in the pulpit — Case of conscription — Excursion and comments — Andrew Leighton of Liverpool, England

CONTENTS. xvii

— Discourses on "Human Progress in respect to Religion" — The Hopedale Parish formed — Its first pastor — The Worcester Unitarian Conference joined — Work for coming generations prosecuted — Sketch of Milford — "Primitive Christianity and its Corruptions," Vol. I. published — Long-standing misrepresentations corrected — Unitarians, Spiritualists, Special Reformers, etc. 436–463

CHAPTER XXIII.
1872–1882.

"Primitive Christianity" reviewed by Rev. A. St. John Chambre — Rejoinder — Ancient dogma rejected — Essay before Worcester Conference — Parochial Christian Union — Resignation of pastorate tendered and withdrawn — "Primitive Christianity and its Corruptions," Vol. II. in manuscript — Last scene in the drama of the Hopedale Community — Third volume of "Primitive Christianity, etc" prepared — The church as it is — "History of the Hopedale Community" ready for the printer — Engaged to write a complete history of Milford — Termination of the Hopedale pastorate — The narrative broken, with note by the editor — Celebration of the Centennial of American Independence — Letter from Mr. Garrison — Sermon before G. A. R. post — Serious illness of wife — Arranged to prepare a history of the Ballous in America 464–490

CHAPTER XXIV.
1882–1890.

The Ballou History — Family burial lot — Essays and Reviews — Tho town of Hopedale — Dedication of the town hall — Ex-Gov. John D. Long's oration and Mr. Ballou's correction of its disparaging statements and misapprehensions — Dr. Richard Eddy on the Restorationist secession — Count Leo Tolstoi's "My Religion" read and criticised — Letter to Tolstoi and response — Answer to the last. — Sermon of Rev. Lewis G. Wilson and *Arena* article — Deaths of William H. Humphrey, George Draper, and Ebenezer D. Draper — Relations of latter to the Hopedale Community and its founder — Death of brother, Ariel Ballou, M. D. — Work on auto-biography — Eighty-ninth birthday — Last public efforts — Funerals and marriages — Decline, illness, and death — Funera l. 491–527

APPENDIX A.
Tributes and testimonials 529–546

APPENDIX B.
Funeral sermon 547–560

APPENDIX C.
The Adin Ballou Lectureship 561–566

APPENDIX D.
Mrs. Lucy Hunt Ballou 567–572

APPENDIX E.
Published works of Adin Ballou 573–574

Index 575–586

AUTO-BIOGRAPHY.

CHAPTER I.

1803–1813.

Birth — Genealogical Relationship — Native Vicinage — Personal Characteristics — Incidents of Childhood.

I WAS born Saturday, April 23, 1803, in the town of Cumberland, Providence County, Rhode Island, on a farm inherited from my paternal ancestors, and lying, partly in the state named, and partly in Massachusetts. The dwelling-house and accompanying buildings were on the Rhode Island territory, about fifteen miles north-northwest from Providence, three in the same direction from Cumberland Hill, and four east of Woonsocket. The locality was then, as now, a comparatively obscure, rural one, remote from any populous center, and inhabited, chiefly, by plain, hard-working, economical tillers of the soil.

My parents were Ariel and Edilda (Tower) Ballou. The former was the son of Ariel, who was the son of James, who was the son of James, who was the son of Maturin Ballou, — the immigrant ancestor of the family and a co-proprietor with Roger Williams in the first settlement of Providence Plantations, in 1646. My mother was the eldest daughter of Levi and Mary (Whipple) Tower, natives of Cumberland, both of whom I remember well. She departed this life in my early youth; he, several years later. She was a woman of portly presence, natural dignity, strong common sense, and great benignity, without the slightest affectation. In her old-fashioned way she was at once commanding and genial. I have a vivid recollection of the affectionate hospitality which I always received from her in my childhood visits. My grandfather Tower was not her equal in all these excellent qualities, yet a respectable man and citizen. He had a tall, well-built frame, a somewhat excitable temperament, a mechanical genius for work in wood and metals, and a penchant for mineral discoveries and experimentation, though he gained thereby neither profit nor popularity.

My paternal grandparents, Ariel and Jerusha (Slack) Ballou, had both finished their earthly course before my birth. I have therefore no knowledge of them except what has come to me in scanty records and traditions. They reared a large family, and, from all I can learn, deservedly enjoyed the respect of the social circle in which they moved. My grandfather had the misfortune to be sadly crippled during the latter portion of his life, in consequence of mercurial medication injudiciously administered in a severe illness. He was long unable to walk, and could only move about in a chair specially fitted to his case. My grandmother on that side survived him many years. They have always been represented to me as industrious, frugal, sensible, worthy persons, ranking with the better class of their rustic contemporaries. Whether or not they were members of the Baptist church in their neighborhood I have never learned, but think it probable.

My father's children were eight in number: six by his first wife, Lucina (Comstock) Ballou, and two by his second, Edilda (Tower) Ballou. Those by Lucina were: Rozina, Abigail, Cyrus, Arnold, Sarah, and Alfred; by Edilda, myself and Ariel, M. D. Rozina married Nathan Arnold and died December 5, 1825, leaving one son and two twin daughters. Abigail married Davis Cook, both now deceased, having had numerous children and grandchildren.

Cyrus married Susannah Ballou, a third cousin, and died March 7, 1816, leaving two sons who have had children. Arnold married Lorinda Bates and died November 27, 1816. A posthumous daughter married and became the mother of several children. Alfred married Matilda Cook, both having recently deceased, leaving children and grandchildren. Ariel, my own younger brother, an eminent physician, married Hannah Norton and had several children, of whom only two daughters survive; their mother having passed away some years since. Of my own family I shall speak at length in due time and place.

As yet I have been unable to trace my ancestry further back than Maturin Ballou, who was at Providence, as stated, in 1646. I have a faint hope of ascertaining his birthplace and progenitors. I find his Christian name and surname both spelled with a various orthography in the old Rhode Island records, but his descendants have for a long time written the two as above. Tradition holds him to have been of French extraction, belonging to a Huguenot family and coming to this country from England, whither many of that persecuted sect fled some generations since. There is little doubt that such was the case, but for lack of reliable information I must be content to commence my pedigree with him.

[Later investigation convinced the author that his family was not of Huguenot descent, but sprang from one Guinebond Balou, who probably passed over from Normandy with William the Conqueror in 1066 and served as one of his marshals at the battle of Hastings. See introduction to "The Ballous in America."—Ed.]

I have often been taken or *mis*taken for a son of Rev. Hosea Ballou, a distinguished Universalist clergyman of his time, and have frequently been asked what our relationship was. He was a third cousin of my father, our common immigrant ancestor, Maturin Ballou, having had three sons, who lived to rear offspring: John, James, and Peter. His descent ran thus: Maturin^1, John^2, Peter^3, Rev. Maturin^4,

Rev. Hosea[5]. Mine was as follows: Maturin[1], James[2], James[3], Ariel[4], Ariel[5], Adin[6].

James Ballou[2], my great, great grandfather, settled in what was then Providence, later Smithfield, and now Lincoln, R. I., and founded a homestead, still owned, I believe, by one of his descendants. It was less than a mile southerly from the village of Manville, on Blackstone River, and about half a mile west of Albion. He was a very capable, enterprising man, becoming a great landholder in his later years. He had five sons, viz: James, Nathaniel, Obadiah, Samuel, and Nehemiah. He endowed them all with handsome farms, or at least with tracts of land that became handsome farms. To Samuel he gave his home place, and to Nehemiah an ample estate in what was then Gloucester, but is now Burrillville, R. I. Each of his three older sons, James, Nathaniel, and Obadiah, he settled on wild or nearly wild lands, purchased by him, on the northerly side of Blackstone, then called Pawtucket River, within the boundaries of territory for a long time in dispute between the three colonies of Plymouth, Massachusetts, and Rhode Island. Neither of the Colonies knew exactly where their respective lines were, but each laid strong claims to the section involved. After many years a settlement was effected, "Attleborough Gore," as it was called, being surrendered to Rhode Island, the Legislature of which, in 1746, incorporated it with its inhabitants as a township bearing the name of Cumberland.

In 1713 James Ballou[2] conveyed the lands specified by gift deeds to the three sons named, who soon after settled their families upon them — their several patrimonies lying adjacent to each other and constituting "The Ballou neighborhood," as it was for a long time designated. This was originally more than half a square mile in extent, and, with inherited rights in common lands adjoining, ultimately covered an area of nearly a whole mile square. All this section of country and its landmarks were familiar to me in my youth, and are still fresh in my remembrance. "Beacon Pole Hill" received its name from a tall mast with a crane attached, from which was suspended a kettle designed to be filled with tar or other combustibles and lighted on occasions, as an alarm signal during the Revolutionary War and as a summons for "Minute Men" from far and wide to reinforce the Rhode Island army. "Iron Rock Meadow" is supposed to have been originally a beaver pond. It contained forty acres and was the first purchase made by James Ballou, senior, in the vicinity. For many years it bore splendid crops of nutritious grass, which finally run out or was supplanted by a comparatively worthless kind. Its name was derived from "Iron Rock Hill," an elevation near by which is very much of a natural curiosity. It seems to have been raised to the height of a hundred feet or more by some volcanic upheaval, and is largely composed of a rich iron ore, with magnetic qualities, amalgamated with solid rock. Nothing of the kind is to be found within hundreds of miles of it.

A little north of this remarkable hill the early settlers built a small house of worship, known in all that region as the "Ballou Meeting House." It has undergone successive repairs from generation to generation, and though occupied only occasionally, in the mild season of the year, remains in its rude simplicity, an interesting memorial of the olden time and its characteristic piety. A few rods southeasterly from it is the ancient "burying ground," where sleep the mortal remains of the original worshippers and many of their descendants, some with sculptured monuments, others with common stones from the field, while many are scarcely marked at all amid the wild grass and brush. It is a place for the study of moss-covered inscriptions and for solemn meditation, especially to a Ballou of the lineage of James. There moulder the ashes of my older kindred, and there my father, in my early youth, erected a family tomb, one of the first two built in the enclosure.

"The Ballou Meeting House" was designed for and long occupied by a church of the order called "The Six Principle Baptists"—a small sect hardly known out of Rhode Island, and now almost extinct even there. Elder Abner Ballou, son of Obadiah, was long pastor of this church. He had considerable local celebrity in his day, passing away Jan. 4, 1806, and leaving behind him a venerated memory. In that old Meeting House, I first listened with awe to prayer and preaching from the lips of Elder Stephen Place — the successor, and I think the last successor, of Elder Ballou. In my youthful veneration I worshipped him almost as God, certainly as one of God's best human representatives. But as I grew older, my reverential estimation became modified somewhat by the criticisms of middle-aged people who knew him in the common walks of life, and who were not too good to reveal their discoveries that he was not wholly above the general weaknesses of human nature. How few of us escape this judgment of our more intimate contemporaries!

In this immediate vicinity the descendants of James, Nathaniel, and Obadiah Ballou multiplied greatly and for a long time constituted a majority of the population. At length they began to scatter by emigration, till now but few families of the name remain. One of the first to leave was James, a brother of my grandfather. He had many children, most of whom settled with him in Richmond, N. H. Among his sons were James, long famous in that region as an astrologer and fortune teller, and Silas, the rustic poet. Rev. Eli Ballou, of Vermont, is the descendant of another emigrant family in the line of Nathaniel, the second in age of the three Cumberland patriarchs. [See my History and Genealogy of the Ballous.]

But I return from this digression to the main thread of my story. It was in the Ballou neighborhood above described, about a mile north of Iron Rock Hill, that I was born, as stated, on an estate derived by inheritance from James Ballou, my great grandfather and a grandson of the common ancestor. It is now owned by the heirs of my brother Alfred. My father at the time was about forty-three and my mother thirty-two years of age. My mother informed me that my birth was one of uncommon peril both to her and me; that I was a lean, feeble, unpromising babe; that for several weeks I seemed more likely to die than to live; and that I was six months old before she could have me seen without some feeling of motherly mortification. Thenceforth, however, I grew healthy, ruddy, and handsome, so that she was no longer ashamed of me. On the contrary, to use her own homely language, "I was proud to turn you out in company by the side of anybody's baby, and often got complimented for your comeliness."

Nevertheless, my early childhood, as I learned from the same source, was subject to frequent attacks of illness, some of them quite severe, seriously threatening at times my life. Moreover, I seem to have been anything but a lymphatic, quiet, good-natured child. I did my part at fretting and crying, and was indebted to my kind mother's indulgence in carrying me about the house while at her work, for escaping my father's hand of discipline, after he deemed me old enough to behave better than I sometimes did. So she laughingly told me in after years. He was of the old school in regard to family government, and believed in suppressing bad humor occasionally with a little wholesome severity. I have no doubt I sometimes tried his patience when he was weary with toil, for he was a very hardworking man. Besides, I remember when quite a small boy scarcely three years of age, being called by the housemaid, "a little mud-wasp."

It did not mend my temper much that the older members of the household were roguish enough to take delight in hectoring me. They could excite my mirth or my irritability at very little cost to themselves, and they were fond of opportunities. While still a mere frockling their various pranks were often played upon me and became indelibly stamped on my memory. Among the worst I call to mind was that of being held under a bush covered with rose-bugs; the bush being meanwhile violently shaken till my hair, neck, breast, and, indeed, my entire body under my clothing, were alive with the hateful creatures. I had always felt and often evinced a great dread of these insects, and at the time referred to I screamed and ran for my mother's help in a very lively, and, to an observer, amusing manner. I was frightened and maddened to the utmost, while half a dozen of my tormentors shouted with merriment. It was exquisite sport to them, but intolerable vexation to me. Nothing malicious was intended by these mischievous teasings, but I am sure they made my excitable passions worse.

In those early years, I also had my full share of casualties. My father owned a saw-mill and I barely escaped drowning one day in its flume. My brother, Alfred, four years older than myself, persuaded me to attempt following him over a tottling plank or slab from one of the mill-doors across the flume to the dam beyond. The saw was running with my father in charge. I was a poor balancer and hence when part way over tumbled into the water. My father got the alarm just in time to save me. I was, at the moment, several feet under water and being drawn rapidly into the current that rushed through the open gate. The mill had a great "head and fall," so that in a single minute more I should probably have been carried through the wheel, a lifeless mangled mass of flesh and bones. I was not so far gone as quite to lose my breath, and presently was able to be led home. I still wore long clothes and remember the sorrowful figure I cut as I draggled along tremulously some twenty-five rods, muttering as I went incoherent denunciations against that "plaguy old slab and flume." I was welcomed to the fond maternal bosom as a child rescued from the very jaws of death.

Not long afterwards, while sporting with a playmate, I fell into a stone sluiceway which my father was building and broke my arm. Dr. Abraham Mason, our family physician, who resided at Cumberland Hill, was sent for to set the fractured bone. By the time he arrived the process had been rendered painful by inflammation and swelling. I could not easily endure the operation or soon forget it, though it was so successfully done that I wholly recovered in a few weeks. As I grew older and was put to business in and about the farm buildings, I experienced plenty of throwings from horses, kicks from skittish cattle, and other mishaps incident to boyhood in that sphere of life.

Notwithstanding my natural sensitiveness and susceptibility to irritation by small provocations, I was generally easily governed. I was neither turbulent nor stubborn, but yielded prompt submission to authority and responded heartily to kind treatment. I was readily persuaded by reasonable appeals, but stung to the quick by personal taunt and reproach. My mother said that she never used the rod upon me but once and then very lightly. It was before my remembrance, in my second year. I seemed to have been seized with a strange freak of destructiveness in the way of throwing things into the fire. She had chided me again and again for my misconduct, but in vain. When left to myself, article after article went rapidly into the flames. At length, as she told me, she "got a little tingler," and, upon a repetition of the offence one day, gave me a few touches with it. I hopped about, screamed loudly, and was effectually cured. When a half-grown-up boy, I used to see a checkered linen handkerchief about the house with one corner gone. I was curious enough to enquire after a time, how that came to be. "It is a piece of your work," said my mother, and then told me the story with good-natured glee.

My father was stern and authoritative in his discipline, yet I can recollect only one whipping from him. This I shared with my brother Ariel when we had become old enough to drop corn, etc., in planting time. We had driven the cows to pasture one morning and instead of returning directly home where we were wanted for service in the field, strolled off to an old well and amused ourselves for a long time in throwing stones into the water below. Hearing the old conch shell blown, which we understood to be an extra summons to the house, we hastened thither and were told by our mother that she did not know what would happen to us, "for your father has been calling you at the top of his voice, and as you did not come has gone planting alone quite out of patience with you." We hastened into the field, a few rods distant, where he was doing our proper work, with a few apple-tree sprouts stuck in his vest. He had not many words for us, but enough smart blows to make the impression that duty and business must take precedence of amusement in his family. There was no undue severity in this correction, but it was conclusive.

I generally found myself a favorite with my father's employes, indoors and out, of whom he had always more or less. I made myself agreeable, and sometimes serviceable to them, never having a particle of haughtiness or contempt to express towards them, even in childish ways, as of an inferior caste. In turn they liked me, and I received frequent acceptable proofs of their good will, either openly or slyly, from man-servants and maid-servants. Earliest of them all I remember Reuben Purchase, a sturdy, glossy-haired Indian, whose copper-color was slightly bleached with the blood of the white race. He took a great liking to me, called me *his* boy, carried me about pick-a-back with him into the fields or woods, and made quite a big pappoose of me. He must have been approaching middle age at the time, and had a family in the general neighborhood. He loved his mug of cider, and stronger drinks moved him occasionally. But he and I were on good terms and he gave me many a little token of his partiality. As I grew older I made successive friends in this line all the way up to manhood, and found my own trifling investments of kindness turn to good account in various ways, as, on a broader scale, I always have through life.

My first remembered attendance on public worship was soon after I donned boy's attire, perhaps as late as the summer of my fifth year. I was rigged out in a new suit of calico, the pants buttoned to the coat in the common fashion of that day, and was led by the hand of my mother a mile on foot to the "Ballou Meeting House." I began to feel of some consequence in the world, but was too bashful to put on pompous airs, and paid reverential attention to the services of the occasion. Elder Stephen Place, mentioned on a preceding page, was the minister. He must have been sixty years of age, had a venerable aspect, and spoke in those sanctified tones of the old-time preacher, which, somehow or other, had a very solemnizing effect upon the younger hearers. I recollect nothing that he said, but he filled me with sublime, though vague impressions of God, heaven, and hell, and made me feel for a long time afterward that he must be next to Deity. My parents were not then professors of religion and yet were partially religious. The ancient *Six Principle Baptist* Church was falling into decay, and the members were mostly elderly people. I recall distinctly their solemn countenances, whether in the "Deacon's Seat" or on the hard old pew seats — men and women occupying separate parts of the house, — those fathers and mothers in Israel of a generation long since passed away.

The old Burying Ground, too, was a place of almost dreadful solemnity to me. Thither the people resorted during the sabbath intermissions, between forenoon and afternoon services, and thither I was sometimes led in my childhood by the maternal hand. My mother and others would read the epitaphs, and I instinctively moved with cautious tread lest I should do sacrilege to the silent abodes of the departed. Death was a strange and awful mystery to me for a considerable time, notwithstanding the patient answers to my inquiries concerning it. But at length I imbibed the inculcations given me that the souls of the dead had been taken away by God into some region of happiness or misery; that their bodies were asleep in the ground; and that at the great "Judgment Day," or "morn of the Resurrection," all would be raised to life again, body and soul be re-united, every one be judged according to his works, and then each be consigned to heaven or hell forever.

These religious ideas took early root in a susceptible and fertile soil. I had little special religious instruction, no Sunday schooling, no catechising such as then prevailed in even the more popular churches — nothing in the way of spiritual culture but the suggestions which I incidentally stored up and the crude workings of my own busy mind. I had no doubt that there was a great and holy, yet awful, God in the form of a gigantic man, who was seated in a glorious chair above the blue arch of the sky. I imagined that he caused it to thunder by rolling a huge log with octagon corners from the convex center of the brazen firmament in various downward directions; that the sun, moon, and stars, the clouds, slorms, and winds were all managed at will from day to day by his immediate interposition; and that all human actions were accurately recorded in a vast book for final judgment at the end of the world. Thus, with what I was taught and what I invented through my imagination, "I spake as a child, I understood as a child, and I thought as a child," until old enough "to put away childish things." But neither then nor since have I lived without thinking, and thinking for *myself* in some fashion.

The remaining five years of this first decade of my life, as I call them to mind, witnessed very little religious interest in the Ballou neighborhood. Preaching in our Meeting House grew irregular, the old church became colder in zeal and fewer in numbers, and a large majority of our Cumberland people spent the Sabbath in labor or rude sports and games. What followed will be noted in the next chapter. I certainly was not brought up thus far in a manner to be much injured or benefited by my religious training. Yet I was drawn into no very vicious or immoral courses of thought or conduct. Perhaps my industrial education and activity were the strongest safeguard against harm of that sort.

Work was the fundamental law in my father's household. He led off and all his forces had to follow. He allowed no idling and but a small modicum of amusement. This was confined to homely and simple kinds, such as hunting, fishing, wrestling, jumping, ball-playing, quoit-pitching, husking bees, quiltings, and the like, with neighborhood parties for the young folks and games appropriate to indoor arrangements and furnishings. Even these were few and some of them far between, and none of them wholly unrestricted and free. Card-playing was utterly disallowed and anathematized. My father used to say that he once got bewitched with that sort of pastime, and, seeing its evils, forswore it forever. This was in his younger days. In my time, woe to every pack of cards smuggled by man or maid into his dominions. He had them in the fire instantly on discovery, and gave little quarter to the smuggler. Even simple countrified dancing was mighty scarce in my youthful days.

My father had over two hundred acres of land, including some wood-lots nearly a mile away; also a saw-mill, a cider-mill, a large stock of cattle, and of course, there was no lack of employment indoors or out. Plowing, planting, harvesting, and all the multiform activities of farm life, with accompanying incidentals, kept all hands busy through the year. My mother used to say, when we of the younger brood complained of being hurried up in the morning and kept snug at work through the day, "You have a much easier time than your older brothers and sisters had, for your father has grown in years and does not drive ahead as he did when I first came to live with him." We thought it might be true, but that was no great comfort to us, as we still deemed ours a hard lot in the labor line.

We had a large, comfortable domicile, plenty of wholesome food, decent clothing, and the ordinary necessaries of an agricultural family; but luxuries, fineries, and gentilities were afar off. Brown bread and milk or porridge, different kinds of meat, rye or barley cake, coffee, cheap tea, cider, etc., were the staples of table fare, with plenty of butter, cheese, apple sauce, and simple condiments. Cakes, pies, and other home-made delicacies had their occasions, but rarely was anything very rich or of outside manufacture furnished us. Our clothing was mostly of home production, spun and woven from flax and wool of our own raising—the woolen cloth being fulled and dressed at mills three or four miles distant. Some extra cotton and woolen stuffs from other sources supplemented what was made by the family, increasing rapidly as I grew up. In my early boyhood young women pulled flax and assisted sometimes in the hayfield, but this soon went out of fashion. The spinning wheel and loom were in vogue much longer, and their operations in my parental household were memorable.

We were shod in those days chiefly with leather tanned at an establishment two miles away, and made of skins from our own cattle or those obtained in barter for them. Once a year, not long before winter set in, a shoemaker came to the house with his kit of tools on his back to do the family cobbling. He had to stay several days, and to us, younglings, at least, he was an important personage. New boots or shoes, and especially calf-skin ones, which, however, were rare, inspired much interest, not only in anticipation and realization, but in the process of their manufacture. Wonderful manipulations were witnessed from the time of taking the measure of our feet to that of trying on the finished article to see if there was a good fit. Sometimes we were favored with a story or song, or whistled tune from the dignitary of the awl and lapstone as the work went on. This entertaining drama ended with a settlement between father and the craftsman, who usually received part or all his dues in some kind of farm produce.

As to places of dissipation, there was but one in the neighborhood. This was an old-fashioned tavern kept by Major William Ballou, a son of Rev. Abner, already mentioned. It was located a mile south of us and a short distance east of the Meeting House. And a sorry establishment it was, especially for the proprietor and his family. Rum-selling was too largely its business. The concomitants and pernicious consequences need hardly be mentioned. It was a resort for the vicious, profligate, and sottish of the surrounding country, although it had some respectable phases of use. But it ruined the Major and all his family. They began life at the top of our Cumberland society as to wealth and general good standing, but most of them ended at the bottom, intemperate, poor, and more or less degraded. But this dangerous resort was placed under a perpetual ban by my father so far as his household was concerned, or at least his children. We were kept entirely away from it, except on now and then a public holiday or a strictly business errand.

I shall never forget one occasion on which I was allowed to go there with older members of our family. There was a military training, a single company of militia under Capt. Amos Cook being out for regular parade. They had a kettledrum and fife for music, and their officers were arrayed in their accustomed toggery. I was perfectly bewitched with this, my first spectacle in the drama of war. I could not have been more than seven years old but I followed at the heels of this train-band all the afternoon, till compelled to go home. Swords, guns, colors, marchings, evolutions, and above all the music of that drum and fife (now disgusting to me), completely charmed me. If I had been of military age, and there had been a call to the wars, it would have taken neither the promise of a large bounty nor an eloquent appeal of patriotic oratory, to have made me "a brave soldier boy." I was effectually inoculated with the pro-war contagion, which fevered in my veins for long years afterward.

Recurring to the subject of using intoxicating beverages, I will remark that I was brought up to a very restricted indulgence but not to total abstinence. My father laid in a supply of ardent spirits for haying time and furnished them more or less on special occasions; but for common use, cider was the staple drink. I got lightheaded once or twice on the stronger liquors, of which I could bear but little. I had grown to man's stature, however, before I presumed to call for a glass of intoxicating drink at any public bar. Indeed I was a stranger to such places. Of cider, I was never fond, especially after it began to ferment or grow sour. But I had my fill of making it in my father's mill, and also of drawing and serving it, after it was stored in the cellar. This was boys' special business, and many a barrel had I to help empty, quart by quart. There must be cider on the table at meal-time, also in the mill or field or woods, wherever there were work-folks, at all seasons, and it was by no means to be omitted as a mark of hospitality to callers, whether they came on business or pleasure. Even the miserable sots of the general vicinity must not be denied it, unless absolutely intoxicated or dangerous. A few such there were who could pour down a quart at two or three draughts, and it is wonderful that they did not become twice as numerous as they actually were.

I will now take up the reminiscenses of my earlier school-boy days. The State of Rhode Island was very slow to adopt the common public school system of education. In my childhood the voluntary method prevailed. But every considerable section of territory had some kind of a schoolhouse and more or less schooling, both in warm and cold weather. The Ballou district was not an inferior one in this respect. It had wealth and intellect enough to erect a small building for educational purposes, and to secure competent teachers for summer and winter terms, which were of about three months' duration each. A female was employed for the former, and a male for the latter. Our neighbors in Massachusetts, who prided themselves on being better provided for in this respect than we, were prone to reproach us as ignorant and heathenish Rhode Islanders, which begat no very amiable feelings on our side the line. As a matter of fact we had in our particular district more and better schooling than the adjacent ones in our neighbor state, though neither had anything of this sort to boast of. Only the rudimental branches were taught and these but imperfectly, as compared with what is done at the present day.

There were eight or ten proprietors of our schoolhouse and they managed all school affairs. They provided for raising money, for boarding the teacher, a fortnight in one family and a week in another, as circumstances would allow, for supplying fuel and other incidentals, and appointed such committees to act for them as were deemed needful. They had their yearly meetings which were characterized by some tedious deliberations and sharp figurings. I frequently attended these gatherings after I was old enough to long for the school to open, but so much time was consumed in irrelevant talk and close reckoning that I often went home, discouraged and disgusted at the proceedings. But they knew what they were about and brought preliminaries to an issue generally on or before the first of December. The children of non-proprietors were provided for at a stipulated price of tuition per week; or, if their parents were quite poor, they might attend free, though this was of infrequent occurrence.

I think it likely that I was sent to the summer school earlier than I can now remember. I have a dim impression that I learned my letters of a school-ma'am when about three years old, but I recall distinctly the first master I had. It was when I was in my *a*, *b*, *abs*, and the shortest monosyllables. I was furnished with a new spelling book which was strongly covered with sheepskin by my mother that I might not soon injure it by careless usage. I was placed on the small boys' seat with others, a bashful, awkward little fellow, and ordered to keep still, but was very much at a loss what to do with myself or how to behave. For there was his majesty, the master, and a whole houseful of scholars, many of them men almost and women grown. And who was I! The scene comes to me afresh. I dropped my head, stuck one corner of my book in my mouth, and unconsciously began to gnaw it. I had already done some mischief of this sort when I was discovered by the teacher and reprimanded. But I seemed fated to round off those book corners. Nor was I cured of the fault for some days, though frequently threatened with something dreadful if I did not desist. At length, after much harm had been done, I was called up, ordered to take off my coat and roll up my shirt-sleeves, when the announcement was made that here was a boy with bad blood in his veins which must be taken out of him. The teacher then exhibited a fine sharp-pointed penknife as the lancet, and applied it to the skin of my arm with a slight prick. By this time the terror-stricken young culprit cried for mercy with such piteous penitence that, on solemn promise of amendment, he was spared further punishment and sent to his seat. He nevermore treated a book disrespectfully. But the nice new spelling book was irreparably damaged, and long remained a sad memento of my entrance upon my educational career.

Nevertheless, I soon began to love books, study, and learning, fondly. And from that time to the present, I have hungered and thirsted for knowledge with unsatisfied desire. My older brothers cared little for books till fifteen years of age, but I delighted in them from my sixth year. I liked to go to school, was easy to learn, had a good memory and an ambition to excel. I was generally docile, orderly, and disposed to be on the best of terms with my teachers, a point on which I seldom failed. The punishments I received were few and comparatively light. Most of them I incurred by yielding to the instigation of my roguish cronies who could easily make me laugh, or divert my curiosity, or swerve me into some infraction of the prescribed proprieties; into nothing very bad, but sufficiently out of order at times to require correction.

With my school-mates, I maintained, for the most part, genial and harmonious relations. In scholarship I kept up with my rivals and left the majority of pupils in the rear. At play most of my mates excelled me, and the dullest of them would often leave me in the lurch. I was no match for many at wrestling, running, leaping, snow-balling, etc., or any of the athletic exercises, unless it were some trial of mere strength, like lifting, pushing, or pulling. At skating, in which many of my companions were experts, and which I much admired as a beholder, I was nothing. Having once put on a pair of skates to try my capability, and suffered a fall backwards that made me "see stars," I renounced them forever. But in all matters where head work and tongue work came into requisition, I feared none of my associates. I was not fond of joking, punning, blackguarding, or hectoring in any way, and never begun at "cutting up" my playfellows. But if attacked, I could give back principal and interest. I asked nothing more of the bravest than that they should keep their hands off. Unluckily, in a few instances, some of the older and stouter of my assailants, when silenced in speech, made up for their intellectual defeat by a resort to brute force, when I went under. I soon learned what I have since found generally true, that the sauciest jokers and blackguards could bear the least of their own ammunition in return.

I was unhappy in but one of my childhood schools. That, I think, was a private one. It was taught by a worthy young lady, a niece of my father's first wife, on whose instructions I had already attended in our Ballou schoolhouse and whom I personally liked. But she was now teaching in her own neighborhood, in West Wrentham, Mass. I was yet too young to be worth much at work, and so was sent to her school by my parents with the best of motives. But it was a mile and a half away, and nearly all the pupils were strangers to me. We belonged to different clans, of uncongenial peculiarities. Some of the older and rougher ones, whom I dared not answer back, taunted me with being a "Rhode Island Yankee," and called me in derision the "high priest." I was not able to bear all this with undisturbed equanimity and patience.

Moreover, there was a weird-looking, yet harmless, old lady, known as "Granny Grant," living on the road to the school, for whom I had conceived a superstitious aversion. My head had been filled with all sorts of ghost and witch stories, causing me many strange, imaginary apprehensions. What should possess me but the notion that this woman was a witch. She had a sinister lop of one eyelid, an imperturbable face, and a queer voice, what little there was of it. She walked abroad with a staff, wearing an old-fashioned, hooded cloak, whether of drab or bright scarlet, I forget. She was frequently on the road, trudging slowly along, and answered to my ideal of a witch completely. I had a great dread of her, and avoided meeting her whenever I could, by making a circuit outside of the highway near her residence, always keeping a sharp lookout for her from every eminence.

These repellant circumstances rendered the Wrentham school decidedly unpleasant for me. I frequently loitered and was behind time, for which I was reproved by my teacher, causing me to feel deeply mortified before my sneering schoolmates. Finally, I brought things to a head by skulking nearly all one day in the vicinity of the schoolhouse; but, being discovered by some of the older pupils, I was seized and marched into the presence of the mistress, my captors in loyal triumph exulting over me as a doomed truant.

Fortunately, my judge dealt with me "more in sorrow than in anger." She deprecated my misconduct and said she should content herself with reporting me to my parents. She did so, and I was severely admonished. By this time I was sufficiently humbled and almost sick. My kind mother, after hearing my explanations, saw through the case, and had me remain at home a few days, till she could recruit my health and encourage me to brave out the undertaking. This being done, I resumed my school attendance and no further trouble ensued. But I could not love my associations, and derived little profit from that particular opportunity. Probably, however, my experience there was a wholesome discipline to me.

One other unpleasant affair I call to mind in this connection. It occurred one winter in our district school, when I was between eight and nine years old, I think. One Christopher Olney from Providence, or vicinity, was the teacher. He had been a brilliant student at Brown University, but falling into some bad habits was expelled. He was an excellent scholar and a genius at teaching. He delighted in his profession, won the affection of his pupils, and was remarkably successful, provided he let liquor alone. An appetite for the intoxicating cup was one of his fatal weaknesses, and made a wreck of him at last. I shall never forget the captivating assiduity with which he would drill me all through an evening. This was his custom with his scholars wherever he boarded, especially if they manifested any interest in their studies. We were mutually fond of each other and he would flatter me by saying he was proud of me. He was also fond of cider, and when he had finished an evening's tuition, would cry out with a significant shrug of the shoulders, "Now take the bright luminary, descend into the dark vault, and fetch me some *aqua vitae* in a minute." And many a time I did it, which was sufficient pay for his extra services.

Before my time, this teacher had taught the same school, and had given a dramatic exhibition in the old Meeting House at the close, which won popular admiration and fame in the vicinity. He now proposed to repeat the experiment, and began to prepare for it, the pupils all being expected to participate in the exercises of the occasion. To me was assigned the poetic effusion entitled "An Elegy to Pity," commencing:

"Hail! lovely power, whose bosom heaves the sigh,
When fancy paints the scene of deep distress."

I easily committed it to memory, but I was troubled because it must be spoken to begin with before the school, with the usual oratorical accompaniments as to gesture, emphasis, intonation, etc. I felt so diffident and awkward that I utterly shrunk from this first appearance on the stage, though it was only in the presence of my teacher, and school-fellows. I had to be literally broken in by force. In spite of their mutual kindly regard, the teacher and his pupil had a falling out on account of this, though but for a short time.

When the rehearsal took place, I was called, in my turn, to the floor. I was slow to respond. My heart palpitated, my knees grew weak, a strange mingling of dread and shame seemed to possess me, and I had to be hauled into my proper position. Even then I could not or did not speak. My master, not expecting such conduct from his favorite pupil, flattered, urged, commanded me to begin, but all in vain. He then used threats, which proved equally ineffectual. Finally, he resorted to a droll, ignominious kind of punishment, more mortifying and vexatious than painful, unknown to me elsewhere before or since. It was a mock shaving, after the fashion of a barber, with a wooden razor, amid the laughter of the whole school. As he proceeded to put me through this process, I became *stuffy*, but neither struggles nor cries saved me. It was a ludicrous conflict, but I was subdued, and made to blubber out my rudimental oratory with more spunk than elegance.

Thenceforth I progressed to my teacher's entire satisfaction. He was quick to make up with me, professed to be sorry for the shaving episode, and almost begged my pardon. I was easily conciliated, and our relations were thenceforward as amiable as ever. The unfortunate man fell into some of his dissipations soon after, the Meeting House exhibition was given up, and only an impaired school-house programme performed. But the teacher pronounced me the flower of the occasion, and lavished on me abundant commendation.

The round of school exercises in those days was comparatively simple, as the text books were few in number, and crude in method and arrangement. The teacher stuck closely to the letter of the books, seldom asking questions or submitting problems calculated to draw out the mind, or awaken and discipline thought. There was but little done by way of explanation or fresh analysis. What the books contained was deemed sufficient. Now and then a genius in the teacher's chair or among the scholars transcended this routine, but such innovations were rare in the sphere of my observation till I had passed my tenth year.

I learned to read and spell with ease, and in those branches excelled the majority of my school-fellows. Spelling schools on winter evenings were customary, exciting great interest and a spirit of wholesome emulation. As a result, good spellers were, I think, as numerous then as now. We had readers, writers, and arithmeticians of very respectable attainments, chiefly by reason of the few departments of study then pursued. I began grammar before I was ten years of age, and soon memorized Alexander's Elementary work, and could parse plain prose after the old fashion very well. But it was some time before I really understood grammatical principles so as to enjoy the study. When I did it became my delight. In penmanship and arithmetic, I by no means kept pace with my other acquirements.

Our school district was prolific in teachers of its own production. Many of the sons and daughters of the populous Ballou families, as they grew up, took their turns in their native school with good acceptance; also in other neighborhoods on both sides the state line. Yet only one of them, Barton Ballou, received a college education. I was withdrawn from summer school as soon as I was old enough to be of use on the farm, and I lost entirely the winter term next preceding my ninth birth-day. This happened by a somewhat strange transfer to a cotton factory, whereof I will give a brief account.

After the celebrated Samuel Slater, a native of England, had established cotton spinning by machinery at Pawtucket, R. I., his success excited others to ambitious enterprise in the same pursuit. Money was to be made, it was thought, at a fabulous rate, and capitalists, large and small, became adventurers in the business. Even staid farmers caught the fever and formed companies for purposes of cotton manufacture. One was started in our neighborhood with a capital of fifteen or twenty thousand dollars, in which my father became pecuniarily interested to the extent of two thousand dollars, a part of which he was obliged to borrow, much to his grief in the end. At the outset, however, everything was alluring and hopeful. The Blackstone (Slater's) establishment, then deemed gigantic, had already begun operations with a most promising outlook, and fresh adventurers were encouraged to push forward their projects with all possible speed.

Early in the year 1811, an eventful one in the history of our family, a factory was erected by the company formed in the Ballou district, on Mill river, just above its junction with the Blackstone, about three miles due west of our residence. It was in the same town and only a short distance from Woonsocket Falls, the village bearing that name being then exceedingly small, rude, and unimportant. Near the mill a tenement house was put up, the construction of which was effected by my father. The proprietors of the establishment called themselves the "Social Manufacturing Co." and their plant was known as the "Social Factory," afterward nick-named the "Pistareen Factory."

The grand climacteric of this whole scheme was that my father became one of the overseers of the mill and removed his family to one of the tenements in the house he had previously built. Renting his farm to my oldest brother, Cyrus, he transferred the rest of us to the new house late in the season, and the winter of 1811–12 was spent there. He had charge of the carding room and his children were distributed in various positions of service about the establishment. I became what they used to call a "cotton bug." In this way I lost the tuition of the schoolhouse for that term, but received another kind of education which was perhaps quite as valuable.

I was delighted with my new position for a time and rose rapidly from the roping to the throstle-frame. But when spring opened my confinement grew irksome, and I sighed for my accustomed outdoor life. Great, therefore, was my joy when it was announced that father was disgusted with his situation and had arranged to return to the old home. This took place in April, and my ninth birth-day found me once more a farmer boy.

For some time previous to this episode in our family history, the war-clouds had been gathering in the usually peaceful sky, and a rupture between England and the United States became more and more probable as the weeks and months went by. The early part of the year 1812 was replete with martial excitement throughout the land. The crisis came on the 18th of June when war was declared by the United States government against the mother-country. Hostile operations were soon after begun and continued through the year with varying results. The press teemed with the reports of what was going on; the Republican and Federal parties were in bitter contention for and against the war, and all classes of the people were greatly agitated. Military companies of volunteers were formed all over the land, and our own neighborhood and family were not disposed to shirk any duty in the existing emergency. My two oldest brothers became lieutenants in their country's service, and I, silly child, regretted that I was not old enough to be in the ranks. As the young duck takes to water at the first opportunity, so was I predisposed to patriotism, politics, and war, from the start. But more of this hereafter. I close the present chapter with the single remark that the routine of the year under notice, aside from what has been stated or hinted at, consisted of the ordinary experiences of a lad in my situation at that period of history, and these were continued to the end of my first decade, April 23, 1813.

CHAPTER II.

1813–1818.

INTEREST IN PUBLIC AFFAIRS — RELIGIOUS EXPERIENCES — FAMILY BEREAVEMENTS — HOPES AND AMBITIONS — REFLECTIONS.

BEFORE the date at which this chapter opens, I had, as already intimated, begun to take a lively interest in public affairs. The war with England was now going on. Napoleon Bonaparte was descending from the zenith of his glory and the civilized world was in great commotion. My father took the leading Republican paper of the state, published at Providence, and I read it with eagerness and delight. It was my oracle. The then Republican and Federal parties were hot and violent against each other, and, in our town, nearly balanced. My father had gone over from the latter to the former during the contest between Adams and Jefferson, and it was natural that I should be of the same political faith.

As the Republicans went all lengths for Madison and the war, also for Bonaparte and the French as against the British and their allies, my boyish sympathies ran strongly in the same direction. I not only read all I could find in the papers that related to the existing conflict, but the few books I could get hold of containing information upon the French Revolution, the rise of Bonaparte, his campaigns, and strangely varying fortunes.

For some years my young head was as well filled with these and similar themes, as, in my obscure position, it well could be. Still there was room for religion, as I shall presently relate; but my dreamy reveries of political and military glory were legion. I always contrived in my surmizings to have a good cause and a brave army. Then such grand battles were fought, such victories achieved, and such a noble use was made of success, as never took place outside of a prolific imagination. It is well that they all originated, were carried through, and had their historic fame wholly within my own boyish mind.

Doubtless some will query how it came to pass that a rustic farmer lad of my age should occupy himself with matters usually entertained only by those more advanced in life. I was undoubtedly unlike others in some respects. My mental as well as physical development was early and rapid in a marked degree, even though external incentives were comparatively few, and opportunities small. I was held closely to the ordinary routine of useful industry, according to my capability. I had barely common school advantages in winter, the weekly paper, and a very few books of any sort. To be sure, my father was a proprietor with others of a small library several miles distant which his family sometimes patronized; he had also a few volumes at home, and I could now and then borrow one of a neighbor. But the stock to which I had access was, all told, very scanty. Moreover, I was seldom brought into contact with persons above the common grade of country people. There were a few *Revolutionaries*, as they were called, in our neighborhood, to whose stories of adventure and perilous experience I delighted to listen. I was allowed to go to one or two town meetings a year and to general muster if not too far away; also, occasionally, to a Fourth of July celebration. These were about all the opportunities for self-improvement I enjoyed.

But of these I made the most, getting out of them everything that one intensely interested could. Every school privilege, every newspaper, every book, every story, every town meeting, muster, or public celebration, was eagerly grasped, sedulously improved, remembered, and turned to good account. I went nowhere to play or kill time. At town meeting, for instance, I was not among the boys, engaged in or witnessing the sports, but with the men where business was going on, scrutinizing all that transpired. In this way I was continuously gathering facts, suggestions, items of information, sufficient to keep my intellect, ambition, and imagination always active. I have learned by experience as well as observation that small resources and opportunities, made the most of, produce greater results than an amplitude, indifferently improved. It is not so much what we have as how we use it that determines attainment. When the old domestic lights were not available to read by in the evening, I could and did read by firelight rather than not read at all. I made good use of what I read by thoroughness and fertile reflection upon it. The text might be brief, the suggestions few, but the comments and amplifications of thought were manifold.

It was during the year 1813, if my memory is not at fault, that an extensive "Reformation," as it was called, or revival of religion, commenced in our vicinity. Elder Zephaniah S. Crossman of the *Christian Connexion* was the pioneer preacher and for a time almost sole manager of the movement. It spread over a region of country not less than fifty miles square, of which the Ballou neighborhood might be considered the center. My father, mother, brothers Cyrus and Alfred, and finally myself, became converts and were baptized by immersion. A large number of persons, nearly a hundred I should think, professed to have "experienced religion" during the three years of continued excitement.

A church of the order named was formed, of which my father was an active member and deacon. For a time it prospered wonderfully. Elder Crossman was not a profound man, but impulsive, magnetic, and insinuating. He did not deal so much in the terrific as in the pathetic and sentimental. He was full of touching anecdotes, illustrations, and appeals to the emotions of his hearers.

He could sing, pray, exhort, in a manner well calculated to enlist the sympathies and move the feelings of those who had been living in comparative indifference to spiritual things, and had little intellectual discipline or insight. His matter, manner, and measures were novel and temporarily effective, but wore out with familiarity. Hence the period of his success, remarkable while it lasted, was brief, like that of most sensationalists in any one locality. After a few years he lost his influence and finally abandoned the ministry. Many of his converts fell away and even the church he had established in our midst ere long began to decline, becoming finally extinct.

The "Reformation" took deep and lasting hold of my father, who, from the time of his baptism through several succeeding years, devoted his personal efforts and property with almost Pentecostal zeal to the cause he had espoused. He kept a sort of Ministers' Tavern, not only opening his house for meetings at all times, but furnishing free entertainment for itinerant preachers, friends from a distance, etc., who flocked in to help on the "work of the Lord," as was claimed, or, as one might be tempted to say, to obtain their full share of "the loaves and the fishes." For it is a fact which gradually became stereotyped on my mind that religion and moral reform are not apt to spoil people's appetites when hospitality is offered them without cost, however eminent they may be as saints, or contrite and under "deep concern of mind as sinners," or devoted to the good of humanity. At length my father's patience with this kind of visitors gave out, as his resources were likely to do, and he rebelled, shutting down almost entirely the gates of his long-continued, lavish generosity. This phase of the great revival is, one might say, a ludicrous picture to look back upon with experienced and critical eyes, but one of not infrequent occurrence in the history of religious excitements in this country.

But there is a better side to the movement which must not be ignored. Many persons who had been living on

FRUITS OF THE REFORMATION. 31

in ignorance and sin, regardless of all obligation to God and their fellowmen, were arrested in their worldly, carnal career and converted to a better life. A few, possibly, were disgusted with what was said and done, and hardened into scorners. Some, as stated, started off with good resolutions, but afterward fell back into their old ways. Yet a considerable number were really and lastingly benefited. Of these, I was one. True it is, we made a very crude beginning in what I now understand to be the real Christian life. But it *was* a beginning and one in my case, without which, I fear, I never should have been on my present religious plane. It was wrought out by solemn and rich spiritual experiences to which I look back with reverential gratitude to my Heavenly Father.

In another respect the revival was productive of good to the people affected by it. It was a wholesome agitation of thought. It moved the mental, as well as moral waters of the community. It awakened inquiry, investigation, and a progressive exercise of the understanding. It left people somewhat in advance, intellectually, of what they were before or probably would have been without it. This is undoubtedly true of all religious and moral excitements, none of them being utterly useless—all dross—though many of them have deplorable drawbacks and imperfections.

But to come back to my own personal experience, I remark that seeing and hearing so much of what deeply impressed others around me, and especially those in my father's family, it was impossible for me not to become seriously affected. I was too young, however, to have it suspected in those days that I could be converted like older persons. Children of my age were then regarded by many as incapable of being religious in the deeper, experimental sense of the word. Therefore, little notice was taken of me in relation to the matter at first, and no one seemed to think I was a proper subject of conviction, repentance, and faith. Yet I felt that I was so, and it grieved me that I was not treated accordingly. How often I longed to have some minister or church member say something to me which would open the way for me to make known my feelings and desires! Nevertheless, I gave close attention to the meetings, watched the proceedings, heard the preaching, praying, singing, etc., and noted carefully every form of religious demonstration that was made.

I was intensely interested in all these things. I longed to be a Christian, and prayed and wept in secret places, seeking to be humble and penitent enough to receive some heavenly assurance of acceptance with God. I felt the same sense of imperfection and sinfulness which others described in narrating their experiences, but still no sense of divine pardon or approval was realized by me. Neither had I any human advisor or comforter. At length, when only about eleven years old, I retired one day, deeply distressed in mind, to my chamber and threw myself on my knees, in agonizing prayer. I gave myself up to the All-Father in the name of my Savior with the profoundest consciousness of submission, to be dealt with and disposed of as divine wisdom and love should determine. That moment my burden was removed; a heavenly light beamed upon me, and an inexpressible peace was diffused through my soul. I arose from my knees, believing that I was approved by Christ as one of His disciples. I rejoiced with exceeding joy and felt that I was entering upon a new life. I have ever recurred to that blessed hour as the decisive beginning of my Christian pilgrimage. It gave bent and direction to my character and career thenceforward to the present time.

It was not long before the matter began to be known to the church, and I received the sympathy I had so longed to enjoy. The result was that I was recognized as a true convert to Christ when about twelve years of age, was baptized by Elder Crossman, May 21, 1815, and registered as a member of the church in regular standing. My case called out divers comments from

BEGINNING OF THE CHRISTIAN LIFE.   33

those who knew me, many deeming me too young to know what I was about, or to have any proper understanding of religious experiences, obligations, and professions. No doubt I was ignorant and of crude judgment, yet, I am sure, I was not far beneath the majority of those who have made a public profession of religion. I certainly knew that I was committing myself to Christian discipleship, and I think few of my seniors at the time acted more intelligently than myself.

If it be said that, according to my own showing, I mixed up my religion with politics, patriotism, and warlike reveries, it was in the same way that nominal Christians have been doing for sixteen hundred years — in the same way that a vast majority of them are doing now. My theology and ethics were not clear and consistent, but quite as much so as is the case with most members of the so-called Christian Church today, even in the most enlightened denominations. Whatever my folly or imperfection, I have never regretted the step I then took, but have been devoutly thankful to the author of all good that thus early in life I committed myself to His service under the leadership of Jesus Christ.

For a year or two after uniting with the church, I was a constant attendant upon its meetings and established ordinances, and in a few instances ventured to take part in some of the more private and social gatherings, but was usually a silent listener and learner. As time went on and the enthusiasm began to abate, I was gradually brought to realize that I had undertaken a more difficult task than at first appeared obvious. I had pledged myself to a Christian life without counting the cost. I had presumed that my "change of heart" went a great deal further than was actually the case. This arose partly from my own ignorance and partly from the extravagant representations of the older professors and of my religious teachers generally. The notion that "experiencing religion" was a miraculously radical change led me, as it has others, to conclude that if the conversion was genuine the natural propensities and passions would either be eradicated or so neutralized as to be harmless. The truth slowly forced itself upon me that the animal nature in my constitution remained essentially unchanged, and that what had been wrought in me was chiefly the germination of the spiritual element as a contestant against that nature for the throne of my being. Between these two forces or agencies there was to be a long and severe conflict — a warfare of many battles and of fluctuating successes and defeats. But it was a grand gain that the spiritual and divine had been born in my heart and had been unequivocally acknowledged as rightful heir to the kingdom.

The war indicated was not long in coming on. I had the same propensities and passions as before my conversion. If temporarily silenced by strong religious inspirations, they were awake and ready for action as soon as those influences subsided. This was proved in my subsequent experience. First, I was astonished at the strange coldness that crept over me — a sort of spiritual inertia, languor, listlessness, whereby I could neither pray fervently nor watch vigilantly. Then I was grieved to find my quick, irritable temper awake again and as sensitive and imperious as ever, gaining by degrees the mastery over me. It was a sad mystery how I, who had passed through such purifying seasons of thought, feeling, emotion, amounting almost to transfiguration could be plunged into such depths of an opposite character.

As time passed by, all my natural propensities took their turns at tantalization and taught me of what stuff I was made. In manifold forms each asserted its claim, and in every direction some sort of battle seemed inevitable between the contending forces within. The good and the evil alternately prevailed for a season and the

AN EVENTFUL YEAR. 35

warfare of a long life was inaugurated, as described by the Apostle Paul, in Gal. 5 : 17, and Rom. 7 : 18-24.

The year 1815 was one of memorable events in the affairs of the world. Peace was restored between the United States and Great Britain. Bonaparte was decisively crushed at Waterloo, and the old order of things was reinstated, as far as possible, on the continent of Europe. A thousand prophecies and interpretations of prophecy that had dazzled ardent, fanatical minds from the commencement of the French Revolution, vanished away or were indefinitely postponed, while the mysteries of Daniel's vision and the Apocalypse were bequeathed to another generation of expounders. Princes and nobles went into exile and those previously sent into retirement returned to the estates of their ancestors. Republican dreamers of equality and fraternity hid from the tempest of monarchical reaction and almost cursed their brilliant visions, so long cherished and now so apparently falsified. And yet there had been undoubtedly some progress made; some gain realized in behalf of justice and humanity. But at what cost of life, suffering, and treasure!

Among the more eventful local occurrences of the year was "the Great Gale," as it is called in New England annals, which swept through Rhode Island and Massachusetts with terrific force at the time of the autumnal equinox, September 23. I recollect being engaged near my father's saw-mill handling lumber with my brothers when the stocks of boards around us, piled up to season, began to be caught away by the rising wind and blown about strangely. We endeavored to pick them up and replace them for a while, but found ourselves borne along and almost lifted from the ground in spite of our utmost exertions. We were soon in danger of limb and life from the flying rubbish and lumber, and betook ourselves to a place of safety at the substantial farmhouse, which was built heavily and strong enough to resist the stoutest storm. The wind increasing, buildings began to be unroofed, smaller structures were moved out of place or completely demolished, apple and forest trees were upturned by the roots, and even the stoutest dwellings creaked and trembled before the mighty gusts that seemed to threaten destruction to everything that happened to be in their way.

The tempest, which began about 7 o'clock in the morning, reached its height at noon, when it was little else than a hurricane. Multitudes of people were filled with terror and consternation. I confess that I was, and hastening to my chamber, obtained what relief and composure I could from the unseen world by earnest supplication. I gained something of trust and calmness, but hardly enough to overcome all my fearful apprehensions, for there seemed to be no place of refuge from impending danger and my faith was not of the surest type.

When the storm subsided, the inhabitants of southern New England looked with amazement on the devastations it had caused. Inland the noblest timber lots were covered with prostrate trees and upturned earth, the finest orchards were laid waste, rail-fences, wood, and lumber were scattered far and wide, roads were rendered mpassable by accumulated debris, and incalculable damage had been done to buildings on every hand, many of the lighter ones being wholly destroyed. In seaport towns and along the shore, still greater havoc, if possible, had been wrought. The ocean rolled in upon the coast its mountainous waves, which, in thickly settled localities, inundated the wharves, streets, and exposed places of business, filled the cellars and lower stories of dwellings and warehouses near the water line, causing the occupants to flee for their lives, and destroying immense amounts of property that chanced to be within reach. The wind drove before it all sorts of sea-craft, even the largest vessels, sinking some, wrecking others, and landing many high on the beach, far away from tide-water. The remains of sloops and schooners, gradually dismantled and abandoned, appeared on the sand banks and along the coast for years, victims of the Storm-King's insatiate power. Such was the "great gale" of 1815, the like whereof has never been seen by New Englanders since the Pilgrims landed on Plymouth Rock.

Soon after this gale occurred, the *Christian Connexion* held one of their General Meetings at Assonet, in Freetown, Mass. Thither my father and other members of our church, including myself, went. The convocation continued for several days and was replete with religious interest and edification. Elders Elias Smith and Abner Jones, then at the head of the denomination, were present, as were also Elder Frederick Plummer, an eloquent revivalist; Elder Daniel Hix, the solid farmer preacher; Elder Benjamin Taylor, the John-like apostle; and a host of other zealous evangelists of that distinctive faith. Those were the palmy days of the "Christian" Order in this section of the country, and we had much stirring exhortation, preaching, and other religious demonstration. Enthusiasm ran high and hopes of a good time coming were in the ascendant. The gathering was refreshing to the assembled hosts and passed off, as a kind of Pentecost, to general satisfaction.

About this time the health of my brother Cyrus began to decline and in spite of all efforts to restore it he gradually sank into an incurable consumption. He was failing during the entire winter following and died on the 7th of March, 1816. This was the first event of the kind in our family after I was old enough to remember it, the one last preceding having been the decease of a sister in 1803, the year of my birth. My brother was deeply religious and had been much exercised by impressions that it was his duty to enter the gospel ministry. But fatal illness ended all expectations in that direction. He departed in sweet hope of a blessed future and with the most perfect composure.

I did not witness the closing scene, but my father, who was with him during the night of his departure, perceiving a change in the countenance of the sick man indicating that death was at hand, said to him as he lay quietly before him, "Cyrus, do you know that you are dying?" He answered distinctly, "No. Do you think I am?" "Yes," father responded, "it seems so to me." For a few moments the invalid was still; then of his own accord, said; "I believe I am dying. I feel differently from what I ever did before." "Are you afraid to die?" he was asked. "Oh, no!" was his reply. "I long to go and be with Christ; I am happy." He expressed a wish to be turned upon his other side, when, without a sign of pain, he breathed his last before the summoned family could reach the room.

This event could not fail to make a deep impression on us all. But to his youthful widow, left with two little boys, it was one of the heaviest of bereavements. My brother lacked a few days only of his twenty-seventh birthday, she being somewhat younger. Not many years afterward she married a second husband, who died in 1862, leaving her the second time a widow. She is still living in Franklin, Mass. Thus roll on the ceaseless wheels of time, bringing changes to all human fortunes, but the divine providence faileth not.

This year, 1816, was one of sore visitation to our family, inasmuch as death invaded it a second time before its close. My next older brother, Arnold, an intelligent, amiable young man in the twenty-fifth year of his age, was summoned hence before winter set in. He was not a professor of religion, though always reverential towards it. In comeliness of person, sedateness of mind, urbanity of disposition, and propriety of deportment, he was the flower of our domestic circle. Wherever known, he was universally respected and loved. I had a strong and peculiar affection for him, though he was eleven years older than I. My father, who was beginning to feel that it was desirable to arrange his temporal affairs for old age and death, leaned confidently on this son. His plan was to settle one-half of his real estate on him and the other half on me when I should become of age,—himself and my mother to be amply provided for by us, and suitable legacies to be paid in due time to the other children.

With this in view, Arnold, having married in April, brought home his young wife and entered at once upon the management of affairs. But in the autumn he was attacked by a fever which took on dangerous complications, and finally, in defiance of all medical skill, terminated his life on the 27th of November. He passed away in comparative unconsciousness and gave forth no memorable religious manifestations like those of Cyrus just recorded. And so another young heart was widowed, parental bosoms were deeply wounded, and the remaining family circle filled with mourning and distress. A posthumous daughter was born the following spring. By this second bereavement, my father's cherished plans and fond hopes went down to the dust.

The time passed over by the foregoing narrative, from 1813 to 1817, brings me to the fifteenth year of my age. It will naturally be imagined what the general routine of my employment and experience was during this period. In the summer I was at work, as a lad in my circumstances might be expected to be, and indeed all through the year except so much of the winter as I spent in school, of which I have spoken in preceding pages. And even while attending my usual three months' school, my time was much broken in upon by a variety of calls at home and abroad, incident to life on a large farm in those days, which, however necessary and unavoidable, resulted in serious hindrances to my educational progress.

Nevertheless, I made up, as far as I could, for deficiency of opportunities and systematic means of mental improvement in every possible way; so that I ripened in scholarship, such as mine was, every year, and stored up for future use all the fragments of general information that came within my reach. My thirst for learning grew with my growth, and before I was fifteen became intense, as is illustrated in the following incident of my experience. My father had in Providence a considerable number of special customers for butter and other products of his farm which he marketed there from year to year. Among these was Rev. Dr. Messer, president of Brown University, who would occasionally ask him as he went his rounds when he was going to send one of his sons to college, repeatedly urging him to do so. Upon his return home with reports of what Dr. Messer had said to him, I could not help having awakened in me the hope that somehow or other such a lot as was indicated might be mine. At length the hope became so strong and my desire in that direction so great that I begged my father to give me a collegiate education, proposing that the three or four hundred dollars it would cost in those days should be my sole inheritance out of his quite large estate, and confessing myself ready to quitclaim any right or title I might have to what might remain, for the sake of having this grand privilege granted me. So earnest was I in this matter that I believe I would have undertaken to crawl on my hands and knees to Providence, fifteen miles, if by so doing I could have secured my coveted object. My father was often moved in my behalf for the moment when I made my appeals to him, and would say he wished he was able to gratify me, but usually wound up with, "I am too much in debt." If I plead my case with great persistency and zeal, telling him how much better it would be for me to have the knowledge I would acquire than many times what it would cost in money, he would refer me to a distant kinsman who spent his little patrimony in getting a liberal education, but had been unsuccessful and poor all his days. In vain I endeavored to unclinch this nail; for the inexorable conclusion was, "I cannot send you to college as your all and have you basking about in learned poverty." And so all my aspirations of this sort perished in the bud.

WHAT IF CONDITIONS HAD BEEN DIFFERENT?

I have often in my later years pondered seriously over this matter and wondered what would have been my course and position in life if my ardent longing for a collegiate education had been gratified. In all probability they would have been radically different from what they have been and are. I should have been placed under influences quite dissimilar to those that have been brought to bear upon me, and at a period of life when I was supple and plastic and likely to yield to them. With my natural worldly inclinations and ambitions, heretofore adverted to, the chances are that I should have chosen the profession of law as most likely to open promising avenues to distinction and so-called success. Religion might have possibly become of chief importance to me; possibly literature. This would have depended much on my teachers and patrons, for I should have been easily led and molded by them. I should not have been drawn readily into the medical or clerical professions, as I had no natural inclination for either of them.

But whatever course or calling I had been persuaded to pursue, I should have become so trained and committed to it, as probably never to have broken away from its complicated attachments. In some popular, time-worn channel of respectability and renown, the current of my personal energies would very likely have flowed through life. The independent convictions, principles, and aims now so sacred to me, though so unpopular and in worldly parlance, impracticable, if not contemptible, would either have found no welcome to my mind or been suppressed within it by the imperious dictates of a temporizing policy. I have hardly a doubt of this. Was it then a blessing or a bane that I was denied the training and culture I so longed to secure? Thousands would doubtless deem it a great misfortune. But I have come to regard it a benefit to myself and mankind. At any rate it was ordered or permitted by Him who overrules all things that my most earnest youthful wishes should not be gratified, nor the crowning ambition of my early years be encouraged. And if there reigns a God worthy to be reverenced and loved by his rational creatures, it was somehow all for the best.

When I was about fourteen years old, one Samuel Forest opened a singing school in our neighborhood — a rather uncommon event in that locality. The young people generally were delighted with the innovation and I hailed it as offering me a desirable privilege. I was gifted with not more than ordinary musical capability and could hope for only moderate attainments in that department of culture, even by dint of proper training. I had learned to sing many current tunes by rote, imperfectly, but greatly needed tuition in the principles and rules of rhythm and vocalization. In this, again, I was completely thwarted. My father was conscientiously opposed to choir singing as a part of divine worship, especially by the "unconverted" or "world's people." A singing school led directly to this "public mockery," as he called it. If he allowed me to join such a school, he would be an encourager and partaker of the assumed sin. So he peremptorily forbade my attending it. I quietly yielded but with great regret, and never afterward found a favorable opportunity to acquire even the rudiments of a musical education. My two brothers were less submissive and went to the school in spite of the same paternal prohibition. But I never regretted my filial obedience, though I deplored my loss and could not quite endorse my father's scruples or *prejudices*, as some would call them. Yet when I have witnessed the levity and almost impiety of some talented occupants of singing galleries, I have been compelled to think their performances were little better than "public mockeries." But how much worse the shortcomings of the choir are in the sight of God than those of the pulpit and the press, I will not presume to judge. True worship is more sacred and rare by far than common minds have yet dreamed.

The winter before I was fifteen, Mr. Noah Cook, a young man from Mendon, Mass., taught our school and

I attended for the last time in our own neighborhood. He was a live, ambitious teacher and succeeded well. I liked him and made commendable improvement in my several studies. He thought well of me, and amid the rivalries of the schools on different sides of the state line, offered to present me as a grammarian against some that boasted much greater privileges than I enjoyed, and were prone to speak of those less favored than themselves with contempt. Nothing, however, came of it except a little sharpshooting to and fro across the border with the pen. Mr. Cook was not a religious man and my own spiritual tone was somewhat in decadence, for the revival had burnt out and the zeal of many waxed cold. In this state of things, the influence of Mr. Cook over me was not of the best since he introduced me to pleasure parties and social gatherings where, though nothing vicious or immoral occurred, there was little to stimulate the better purpose and higher life of the soul. I soon, under some compunction, abandoned these assemblages and devoted much of my spare time to religious study, meditation, and prayer until I reached the anniversary of my birth, April 23, 1818.

CHAPTER III.

1818–1821.

RELIGIOUS STATE — THE CHRISTIAN CONNEXION — THEOLOGY — LORENZO DOW — LAST SCHOOLING — MISCELLANEOUS EXPERIENCES.

WITH the opening of the sixteenth year of my life, I entered on a period of increased personal responsibility. My oldest surviving brother, Alfred, was absent from home most of the time for the next two years, partly at school and partly in a factory counting-room, and I became my father's chief deputy in the management of the farm and collateral interests. Indeed, he signified his desire and purpose to settle me on the ancestral estate as his successor and the stay of his old age, and I began to shape my expectations accordingly. When winter came around work took precedence of schooling, causing it to be postponed to another year. It was hoped I might then be compensated for the loss of my ordinary privileges in our own district by securing more advantageous ones elsewhere, and this proved to be the case.

As to my religious state, I recovered from what I regarded my backsliding in the course of a few months, abandoned ordinary social gatherings and places of worldly amusement, and devoted my leisure hours largely to religious exercises and duties. I studied my bible and books of devotion intently, prayed much in secret, had my seasons of fasting and self-examination, paid close attention to divine worship and subsidiary meetings, became clerk of our church, and gradually took on a phase of decided ascetism. I cultivated as stern a zeal for piety and

THEOLOGICAL BELIEF FORMULATED. 45

righteousness as my nature was capable of and subjected myself to a stricter self-discipline than at any other time of my life.

Meanwhile my theology assumed a definite and positive form, its essential features being such, substantially, as prevailed in the "Christian Connexion," whose leaders, though constantly denouncing creeds, had one, as a matter of fact, of pretty sharp points distributed through their preachings and published writings. I have generally found this to be the case with nominal anti-creedists, even down to nothingarians. By study and reflection, I had formulated the following items of doctrine in which I most firmly believed: *1. The Plenary Inspiration of the Bible; 2. The Pre-existant Divine Sonship of Christ; 3. The Personal Unity of God, the Father; 4. The Impersonal Agency of the Holy Spirit in working out the divine designs; 5. The Fall of Man in Adam and consequent universal but not total depravity; 6. The Indispensable Necessity of the New Birth; 7. Man's Free Moral Agency; 8. This Life the only Probationary State for Eternity; 9. The Resurrection of the Body; 10. The Final General Day of Judgment; 11. The Special Immortalization of the Righteous, both Body and Soul, at the Judgment Seat; 12. The Just Punishment of the Wicked, terminating in their utter destruction — absolute non-existence.*

The controversy between the Trinitarians and Unitarians in this country was inaugurated about this time, and the "Christians" took sides against the former, though they clung to a sort of high Arianism and rather stiffly repudiated those forms of Unitarianism which questioned the personal pre-existence of Christ. I embraced this view of the subject and thought myself strongly intrenched therein behind the word of God.

Another grand question then in dispute was that relating to the final destiny of the wicked. Elders Elias Smith, Abner Jones, and other influential leaders in our order had come out against endless punishment and in favor of absolute, final destruction or annihilation of the doomed impenitent. This obliged them to deny the innate immortality of the soul, and contend that no one could ever be rendered immortal except by the special will and gift of God. These doctrines I readily embraced and made myself an expert in their scriptural defense. They and kindred topics furnished my ever active mind ample themes of inquiry and speculation in the department of theology.

The Restorationists, as they termed themselves, of earlier times were only slightly known to me by general report, and it was a foregone conclusion that their distinctive doctrine could have no possible foundation in divine revelation. The Universalists, many of whom had rejected, as baseless, all belief in future punishment, were beginning to prevail in certain localities, and through their preachers and published expositions to make their influence felt in many places where they had no organized foothold. This was the case in our vicinity. We had several neighbors who professed to believe in the final salvation of all men, and ministers of that faith occasionally visited them, such visits growing at length frequent and conspicuous. But I regarded all persons of that way of thinking as anti-religious in spirit, anti-Christian in doctrine, and practically no better than Deists. And I think, even now, that many of them gave me too much reason for regarding them as I did, though my prejudices made me unjust to them in a greater or less degree. The Universalists of later times and especially of this day exhibit very great religious improvement, both in theory and practice, on their predecessors of that period.

Elder Crossman, the chief promoter of the great "Reformation" spoken of in the last chapter, had now lost prestige and standing in the church and was fast receding from the ministry. He at one time professed Universalism, then recanted, then vacillated for awhile between different forms of faith — finally falling into some irregularities which terminated eventually his labors as a religious teacher. Later in life he became a book-peddler. Elder Elias Smith, who had been regarded as one of the two chief apostles of the "Christian Connexion," went over to the Universalists, in whose fellowship, after some vibrations to and fro, he finally died. During his last years upon earth he devoted himself to the practice of medicine acording to the Thompsonian system of therapeutics, which he claimed to have essentially improved. These and other unexpected developments rather shook the structure of the "Christian" denomination, but by no means destroyed it. The disturbed elements resumed their equilibrium and other leaders, older and younger, arose and moved forward in the van of the host. Little did I dream when the defections referred to took place that I should ever find sufficient reason for changing my general theological ground as related to the doctrines involved.

Of some of the new preachers who came forward to fill the vacancies that had been made in our "Christian" ministry, I will make brief mention. There was Reuben Porter, Jr., a native of Coventry, R. I., who first visited us as a youthful exhorter before the *revival* had subsided. He afterwards prepared himself for the ministry and at length became our pastor, leaving us finally for other fields of service. He was a scholarly, pleasant, fluent preacher, popular for a time and much esteemed. But he was not profound and did not excel in intellect, piety, or weight of character. After a gradual moral decadence of some years, he acquired intemperate habits, becoming at last a confirmed sot. He came to a sad end, being found dead in the street of a village not far from the place of his nativity.

Elder Dexter Bullard was the next in order of our pastors, receiving ordination at Cumberland Hill. He was not a brilliant preacher, but a man of sound common sense, intelligence, candor, Christian principle, and moral integrity, sincere and faithful in all things. He married a respected cousin of mine, Julianna Sayles, had quite a numerous family of worthy children, most of whom settled in the West, whither himself and wife removed many years since, and where he died in 1865.

Among numerous itinerant preachers of our Order and one of the ablest and best of them, was Elder Benjamin Taylor of Swansey, Mass. He did not appear in our vicinity often, but was always welcome and his services were every way acceptable. He was not only a man of good natural abilities, but an upright, conscientious, exemplary Christian, combining zeal with knowledge and uncompromising fidelity to principle with a broad, deep charity. He was a John among our preachers, always entreating us to "love one another." Elder Mark Fernald of Kittery, Me. was also a visiting preacher of creditable ability and reputation, but somewhat ascetic in his habits, — a stern, blunt man, severe at times in speech, but possessing a kind heart and making himself useful in his sphere.

The celebrated and eccentric Lorenzo Dow, who belonged to no sect, but was a sort of Methodist comet in the ecclesiastical heavens, visited us occasionally during the two years of which I am now writing. I first saw him in Providence. His fame was widespread, and I had read with much interest his published autobiography. Learning that he was to be in an adjoining town, some of our people were anxious to see and hear him, myself being one of the number. I went to the house of a Methodist brother where he was stopping, but it was so thronged with callers that I barely got a glimpse of him. My only recollections of him are that he wore his hair and beard long (then an astonishing sight); that he was a lean, spare, dark-complexioned man; that his dress and general appearance were plain and simple, as of a pilgrim devotee; and that when he started for the chapel where he was to preach he could not find his hat and so went out bareheaded, but was soon supplied with the missing article by his consumptive-looking, devoted wife, Peggy, who came running after him with it in her hand, and shouting in shrill, tender tones, "Lorenzo, Lorenzo, here is your hat," which he rather indifferently accepted. Of his discourse, characteristic of him, no doubt, I, though hearing it, remember nothing.

After this he preached at different times in our neighborhood, stopping with us, and I became well acquainted with him, being charged with the duty of waiting upon him and of attending to his personal comfort, as occasion required. This I did with fidelity and discretion, carefully avoiding manifesting any surprise at his seeming eccentricities. He treated me not only with unaffected civility and kindness, but with confidential cordiality. It had been said that he was sometimes gruff and ungracious to those who served him, but I was led to believe that those complaining of such treatment provoked it by their ill-timed flattery and sycophantic fawning. He was a keen observer of human nature and scorned all affectation and obsequiousness.

We had unequivocal manifestations of his eccentricity amounting almost to breach of propriety or incivility sometimes during his several visits with us. Some of these may be mentioned. While preaching one evening in our large, old-fashioned kitchen, in his peculiar, impassioned style, an officious, elderly spinster, then an inmate of the family, disturbed him by repeatedly getting up and fussing with the fire,—picking up the falling brands, replenishing the fuel, and otherwise setting things about it to rights. Seeing her start for the third or fourth time on the same errand, he left the thread of his discourse and broke out in an imperative tone, "Woman, sit down, and don't be up trying to show off that new gown of yours any more." Spinster, in her fresh calico, subsided as if paralyzed and remained fixed in her chair till the meeting closed.

At another time he was seated with our family in the parlor after meeting, the center of a large circle, my mother being on his left and a worthy woman who was then working for us on his right hand. During a little lull in the conversation, he sat musing for a moment and then in suddenly broke out, saying to my mother, as he pointed to the woman, who was a stranger to him, "Who is this? Whom have you here?" My mother gave the woman's name. "What is she good for?" he continued. "Many things," replied my mother. "She is a good, honest woman, a member of our church, a devoted Christian, kind and helpful in sickness, and always quietly industrious." "Perhaps, but how about her temper? If one should tread on her toes, would'nt she feel something fluttering up in here?" shaking his skeleton-like finger significantly over his breast as much as to say, "Hasn't she a quick, irritable disposition?" This abrupt, queer incident took us all by surprise and shocked our demure servant well nigh into spasms. Meanwhile he looked the saint he was reputed to be.

The next day I was to take him in a sleigh (for it was winter) first to Cumberland Hill, where he was to preach at 11 A. M., and thence in the afternoon to Providence. Some delay about starting occurred, although there was ample time to reach the place of meeting in season for the service, at which he exhibited considerable uneasiness. When we were well seated in our vehicle and moving off at good speed, he turned to me and with a very earnest but kindly look, said, "Young man, I have a lesson for you. You may become a public character, perhaps a preacher. My lesson is this: *Always take elbow room.* Do you understand me? I mean keep a little ahead of your appointments. Be on hand some minutes before the set time. Make no one wait for you. Never be in a hurry at the last moment. Then you will not only avoid occasion for others to complain, but be in a calm, self-collected frame of mind to proceed with your own duties. Do you understand the lesson?" "I do," said I; "it is a wise and wholesome one; I thank you for it; I will endeavor to lay it up and profit by it." "So do," he responded, thus ending his admonition. I

INTEREST IN PUBLIC AFFAIRS.   51

have never violated his rule — "Always take elbow room," without perturbation, regret, and shame.

Arriving at the little "Catholic Baptist Meeting-house," so-called, in due season, the service was conducted in the usual form, the sermon being an exposition and application of the parable of the laborers in the vineyard, Matt. 20: 1–16, laying the chief stress on the words, "They received every man a penny." After the meeting I went on with him to Providence, where we parted, never to meet again in this world. From what I saw and knew of him I judged him to be a faithful, conscientious, Christian minister, notwithstanding he was so singular and erratic in many of his ways.

During the period of my youth now under review, though mainly occupied with manual labor on the farm and personal religious nurture and discipline, I kept myself posted in regard to public affairs and what was transpiring in the world at large, so far as the newspaper of the family and occasional conversation with well-informed townsmen could serve me in that direction. When the "Missouri Compromise" excitement prevailed, I recollect getting interested in it and being so patriotically devoted to the Union as to defend our Rhode Island congressman, who was severely denounced for voting in its favor. Without a particle of pro-slavery either in my nature or habits, I was at that time so utterly ignorant of the "peculiar institution" and its fatal evil tendencies, and so carried away with the cunningly-raised bugbear, "The Union in danger," that I readily took the wrong side from good motives — as many of my grave seniors then and afterwards did.

During this same period a cousin of mine, Otis Mason, some ten or fifteen years older than myself, taught what was called the "Academy" at Cumberland Hill. With him I fell into some intimacy and occasionally visited his school. At his solicitation I was induced to join a debating club connected with the institution, in which I a few times mustered courage enough to speak. There was a library in the same connection from which I took books to read at my convenience. By these means I made partial amends for the lack of regular educational advantages and gained some valuable intellectual culture which otherwise I should have missed.

Near the close of the year 1819, after the farming operations were for the most part suspended for the season, it was arranged that I should go to school ten weeks during the coming winter in the neighboring town of Franklin, Mass. The school was nothing but a rural district one, but it was to be in charge of one Caleb Ward Wilson of Mendon in the same state, a talented and successful teacher at that day, and was to have among its pupils some twenty or more young men and women who had attended sundry higher seminaries of learning under celebrated classical preceptors. So that the opportunity was an especially favorable one for me, much better than I had ever before enjoyed. I was to board in the family of my uncle, Daniel Sayles, a resident of the town, whose wife was a sister of my father. His oldest unmarried daughter, Avilda, had been an accomplished teacher, and his youngest daughter, Juliana, about twenty years of age, was an excellent scholar; while his sons, Orin and Ariel, about my own age, who had shared some superior educational advantages, were to be my fellow-students. These circumstances rendered the opening additionally desirable and promising.

When I entered the crowded school house at the beginning of the term, I felt not only rusty in scholarship but a little awkward from the consciousness of being surrounded by proud-spirited associates who could not easily suppress their prejudices against a green Rhode Islander. It was therefore prudent for me to be modest, — at least, not to expose my ignorance presumptuously or unnecessarily. Our teacher was really a superior one and handled his school in a manner worthy of his great reputation. In dealing with his large upper class, which made an imposing array upon the high seats, right and

AT SCHOOL IN FRANKLIN, MASS. 53

left, he treated them with marked respect, in consideration of their age and attainments, not only allowing but urging them to have opinions of their own, and to differ from him if their judgment so dictated, as well as from each other on all critical points, especially those of grammatical construction and analysis. Issue might be taken upon any question at any time and the parties involved might give reasons for their opinion, each one arguing in proper order according to his best judgment and ability. There were several in the class who deemed themselves well advanced in scholarship and capable of criticism, and there were some exciting discussions both among the pupils and between pupils and teacher. If he happened to make a mistake, which rarely occurred, he was manly enough not only to hear himself foiled in argument without wounded pride, but to yield the point with open-hearted frankness and promptitude.

For my part, I listened with thoughtful attention to all that was said and done for five or six weeks, but did not venture a word of my own — waiting to have my scholastic rustiness well scoured off and learn how bright and keen my fellow-pupils were before measuring lances with them. At length, finding that they were not altogether infallible, and thinking I was not wholly incompetent to cope with them in any case where our opinions might not concur, I cautiously submitted, now and then, some criticism of their conclusions. My bashfulness made this a severe trial to me — all the more so when I saw that I was regarded as one aspiring to a rank above my merits and antecedents. This, however, in the end proved to be an advantage to me, for it awakened in me a sense of self-respect and a determination not to be cowered into tame servility to those in no wise my betters.

So on one occasion I took the liberty of questioning the correctness of a certain analysis and the appropriateness of the rule given for it. My comrades stared with contemptuous scorn at what they assumed to be my presumption, and the teacher decided offhand against me. "But stop," he said in his usual courteous way, "we must hear the reasons for objecting to the view presented." And turning to me, continued, "How, sir, do you make out your case?" My face crimsoned with timid blood and my heart leaped into my throat, but truth and pride put me through the struggle. I stated my position so clearly and gave my reasons so conclusively that the teacher was himself convinced and immediately responded, "He is right after all, and I am wrong." This "put the boot upon the other foot," as the saying is, and my learned sneerers looked as crestfallen as if I had robbed them of their fancied preeminence by magic.

Such experiences, when looked back upon from the far-off summit of advanced age, seem of little consequence if superficially regarded, yet they were in fact of great account to the novices immediately concerned — means of discipline, of progress and lasting enjoyment. They, too, are texts in the volume of human nature on which we can profitably moralize. They remind us that no one ever rises above the level of his supposed-to-be proper sphere without a struggle. His progress is obstructed and resisted by adverse surroundings, by jeering contemporaries, or envious rivals, and he must fight and conquer or be ignominiously overcome. Even those who from natural relationship or friendly consideration ought to cheer on the struggling aspirant, often frown contemptuously on his efforts and dissuade him from pressing forward in the line of his nobler purposes and aspirations. As Eliab said to David in the Bible story of Goliath, "Why comest thou down hither, and with whom hast thou left the few sheep in the wilderness? I know thy pride and the naughtiness of thy heart. For thou hast come that thou mightest see the battle." The undaunted youth only answered, "What have I now done? Is there not a cause?" And he went on in his chosen way — went to conflict and to victory. *1 Sam. 17th Chap.*

AN IMPORTANT TRUST UNDERTAKEN. 55

Having gained my point and a reputable standing in the school and wishing to avoid all unpleasant rivalry or whatever would occupy an undue proportion of my time and energy, I betook myself to those studies necessary to a well-rounded development in which I was particularly deficient, and where there was little or no emulation. I had always the best understanding with this teacher, and profited greatly by his instruction. His school proved to be my college of graduation. I did not "finish" my education there, as some seem to do in regularly organized institutions of learning, but I never again was a student in any strictly educational establishment of any kind or name.

The same winter developed other interesting occurrences beside those connected with my school, some of which resulted in experiences of signal importance. It so happened that a mutual intimacy between Elder Dexter Bullard, already spoken of, and my cousin, Juliana Sayles, in whose father's family I was boarding, had ripened into a matrimonial engagement which was to be consummated by marriage before the school term expired. Preliminary to the legal solemnization of the union, there must be the usual *publishment* of the intentions of the parties on the part of the town clerk, either by "crying" the same in religious meeting on two successive Sabbaths, or by "posting" for two weeks in some place of public concourse. It was quite a desideratum with those immediately concerned to have this done as noiselessly as possible and to make it, since it must be known in due time, a surprise to outsiders, even to the family relatives. I was a special confidant in the matter, and to me was entrusted the necessary mission to the public official authorized to act in such cases, with the special charge to execute it with the utmost secrecy.

I was entirely ignorant of the details of such transactions and undertook the task assigned only for friendship's sake and with great reluctance. Having accepted the trust, I was confronted with the double problem of how to fulfil it and how to do this with the desired secrecy. I must not take any of my school hours nor absent myself from my meals, nor engage a horse with which to ride to the residence of the town clerk, which was three miles away, since either of these would excite suspicion and lead to a discovery of the whole plot. So after supper one evening I slipped quietly out of the house and by an unfamiliar, unfrequented road reached, after much difficulty, the place I was seeking. Unfortunately, the clerk was not at home, being engaged in teaching some distance away and not returning except on Saturday evening for the Sabbath. Not knowing that I could accomplish the object of my visit by leaving the proper details with his wife, to be attended to when he was advised concerning them, I retraced my steps to my uncle's, weary and disappointed, to report my ill-luck and to be told, to my great mortification, how easily all further trouble could have been obviated by the means just indicated.

I had not been missed or inquired for, and under a deep sense of humiliation, I resolved to try again on the ensuing Saturday evening, confident that I should then be able to make everything sure. I governed myself accordingly. But the gentleman I wanted to see had not arrived when I reached my destination. Nor did he come after long waiting till time and distance admonished me that I must be on my way to my boarding-place again. So I left my errand in writing with his wife, but by further blundering failed to mention the proper residence of the groom. This, however, I did not find out until I reached my uncle's and reported progress. The omission was a greater mortification to me than my former misadventure, and I was as vexed with myself as I was tired, but, as there was no time to be lost, I determined, weary though I was, to go over the ground again immediately and finish my ill-starred performance before the dawning of another day. So I actually trudged those six miles (out and in) once more, awoke the now returned and sleeping official, gave him the lacking data, got back home again unsuspected, in season to have a short nap before morning, judging myself amply qualified by experience to act as agent for a couple wishing to have their intentions of marriage published according to law. I never had occasion, however, to undertake another commission of this sort, but was paid for executing this one in the consciousness of having served my beloved employers satisfactorily and in the lesson it taught me of understanding my errands before trying to deliver them. Much of my wisdom I have purchased in the same costly way as my readers will not fail to see while tracing my subsequent history.

But something of greater consequence to me came from the event, one of the antecedent incidents of which has just been narrated. As arrangements for the approaching wedding were making, it was decided that I should be groomsman, and, after considerable canvassing of the claims and qualifications of several of the fair cousins of the bride on her father's side, of which I was more or less cognizant, that Abby, daughter of Smith Sayles of Smithfield, R. I., should be bridesmaid. Though she was a comparative stranger to me, I readily acceded to the wishes of my friends in this respect as in others where I could serve them. The marriage was solemnized as provided for, Feb. 1, 1820, and the foundation was laid for a long, useful, and happy union, under mortal conditions and in the order of the family, of two worthy, congenial, Christian souls.

One occasion of this sort often leads to another of a similar character. Very likely the arrangement concerning groomsman and bridesmaid in this case was entered into with some ulterior design respecting the parties brought together which did not appear to the casual observer, and which was not communicated to those more particularly concerned. Whether this were so or not, the acquaintance then formed between Abby Sayles and myself was by mutual agreement continued through occasional correspondence and personal interviews until it ripened, not many months afterward, into a definite hymeneal engagement, to be carried into effect at a then undetermined date of the future. So much was done in anticipation of marriage soon after I had entered upon the eighteenth year of my age.

To the wise and prudent reader this early pledge of marital purposes and fidelities on my part may be deemed boyish and absurd, bespeaking my folly and want of sound judgment. Perhaps so. I cannot blame those who pronounce such a verdict upon me, but rather confess that, from my present standpoint of rationality, I was unfit to take such a step — unqualified to assume the contemplated responsibility. But I had no one to admonish or restrain me and was not wise enough to see, much less realize, my deficiencies. It had already been planned that I should settle down with my parents on the farm, see them through life, and inherit their domain. On that score I was favorably situated as to then present conditions and future prospects. What better could I do than take to myself a wife! As to my affianced, I satisfied myself that she was every way worthy of my confidence and love. She was three years my senior, which, however objectionable in some regards, was really an advantage to me, her experience and more mature understanding acting as a counterpoise to my inexperience and unripeness. She was well qualified for the proposed relationship in all matters pertaining to domestic economy. She had been well trained to all womanly acquirements in a good home under wise parental influence, having a mother whose excellencies of character I shall never cease to love and revere. Her educational accomplishments, though comparatively small, were respectable for her rank and times. She was not a professor of religion, but eminently conscientious, virtuous, and exemplary. She was a woman of good sense, of sterling principles, and, above all, of an amiable disposition and an affectionate heart. The only serious drawback was her delicate health, which foredoomed our union to an early dissolution, as the sequel will show. That union, while it lasted, was a most cordial, harmonious, and happy one, and I trust it was best under the circumstances for both parties to it. And so, while I do not recommend my example to youths of my age and immaturity, I yet do congratulate any, young or old, who are fortunate enough to have entered a marriage relationship as well-matched, as rich in experience, as full of enjoyment, as abundantly blessed, as the one under notice.

Passing my next birthday, I settled down to the various duties of my position as manager and prospective owner of the paternal homestead, where I confidently expected to spend my days. During the year upon which I had now entered, one incident occurred which was especially trying to me at the time, being, as it was, my first business venture outside of the calling to which I had been trained from my early years. It was, under the circumstances, an unfortunate and discouraging affair, but it reminded me that it was not wise for me to assume responsibilities for which I had no qualification, either by native aptitude or acquired skill. My father had a tenant in a small dwelling-house on his premises who manufactured on a limited scale what were called cotton-plush waterproof gentlemen's hats. He suggested to me the idea of becoming at certain leisure seasons of the year a traveling salesman of his goods about the adjacent country, and made me believe that I could make handsome profits on them. In my condition this was desirable, and I eagerly caught at a proposition which promised to fatten my inconveniently lean purse. I therefore closed a bargain with him for a goodly stock of hats, procured an outfit of a suitable team, and made preparations for starting on an expedition for which, the more I thought of it and the nearer I came to it, the stronger was my conviction that I was in no wise capacitated. While meditating on what I had undertaken and apprehending probable failure, the particular kind of hat which I had to dispose of was superseded by a better one and became almost entirely unsalable at any price. So my ambitious plans in that direction proved an utter failure and my lean purse grew leaner instead of more plethoric thereby. With this narration I close the present chapter, as I do the record of the eighteenth year of my life.

CHAPTER IV.

1821–1822.

CALL TO THE MINISTRY — FIRST SERMON — CONNECTICUT CONFERENCE — AUTHORSHIP — TEACHING — MARRIAGE.

AT the opening of my nineteenth year, my general life work and field of activity seemed to be definitely marked out and permanently settled, as already indicated. I had entered upon my chosen vocation and my temporal interests had been satisfactorily provided for. The needful preliminaries to the founding of a home of my own had received due attention. My religious status, in respect to belief, practice, and associative position, was supposed to be fixed in essential respects for all coming time. Little dreamed I of the changes awaiting me — even of those close at hand.

It was early in the season that the first and most important of them occurred — the one that perhaps above all others turned my thoughts into new channels and caused me to recast the whole programme of my future career. I had retired alone to my chamber on a certain night, gone to bed, and fallen asleep. Not far from midnight I awoke to consciousness in a state of mind such as I had never before and have not since experienced. I was taking cognizance of myself and surroundings with feelings of inward exaltation as unimpassioned as they were sublime and strange, when I distinctly beheld a human form, clad in a white robe, standing just outside of a window in front of me opening to the south, some twelve feet distant. I gazed upon the unusual object with a sense of profound amazement, but without the least fear or trepidation. Scrutinizing the features of the apparent personage, a sublimated resemblance to my deceased brother Cyrus became perfectly distinct. As I continued looking, he (for the appearance had now assumed personality to me) slowly entered the window, which was closed, as if there were no obstruction and approached my bedside. His countenance was moderately luminous, but not dazzling. Every lineament was perfectly defined. His aspect was calm and benign, but impressively solemn. When almost near enough to touch me, he paused, fixed his eyes upon me for a moment, inclined slightly forward, pointed with his right hand directly at my forehead, and in the most significant manner, said: — "Adin, God commands you to preach the Gospel of Christ to your fellow-men; obey his voice or the blood of their souls will be required at your hands." I was filled with unutterable awe; my hair seemed to stand on end; I remained mute and immovable, but felt thrilled through and through with spiritual emotion, yet with no distraction of timidity or fright. The moment the words were spoken, the appearance turned from me, moved slowly back through the window, and vanished from my sight.

Memorable and ineffaceable vision! How often since have I yearned for similar ones to confirm or direct me in the path of duty, but without being gratified! How many times have I wondered at this manifestation and puzzled my rational powers to account for it; to make myself sure whether it was real or illusory, objective or subjective, divinely ordained and sent, or mysteriously originated in the wilds of my own imagination!

But in whatever way the light of eternity may answer these inquiries, the vision was irresistibly effective and powerful on my own mind and subsequent life. When my first emotions had subsided a little, I tried to make myself sure whether or not I was "in the body" and in the full possession of my senses. I soon succeeded in this so far as everything material and normal was concerned. Time, place, circumstances, and my own consciousness were unmistakable. The vision itself alone was mysterious. Could it be a dream or anything of similar nature? If so, it was radically unlike anything of the kind I had ever had before. After revolving the matter deliberately in my mind, I could not resist the conviction that, somehow or other, it was a reality and was fraught with divine significance and authority. Five years before, the spirit of my brother had left its earthly tabernacle, taking its departure from that very chamber. He had been profoundly impressed for some time that it was his duty to preach, but reluctantly shrank from doing so, and felt some compunction on account of such hesitancy. Had God sent or permitted him to incite me to the same mission?

All the day following my strange experience, I was quite unlike my ordinary self, and though I went about my customary labors, nothing seemed quite natural to me. I was in what is called a spiritualized or exalted condition. When this passed away, I was left to the most serious and trying reflections. What ought I to do? What *could* I do? What *must* I do? My cherished plans and expectations were threatened with annihilation in a moment and seemingly by a mandate from heaven. I shrank from communicating with any one and confined all my thoughts, reasonings, inquiries, and convictions entirely within my own breast. There it was that I must make the momentous decision forced upon me first of all for myself. So I pondered, prayed, and wept in secret for weeks.

My case was a peculiar one. There was not a single motive or inducement of a temporal nature in favor of my becoming a religious teacher — a preacher of the gospel. Moreover, I had no attraction or inclination to that profession whatever, but on the contrary, a strong repulsion from it. When I looked at the subject in a moral and spiritual light, the office of a true minister of

Christ appeared to be so pure, sacred, unselfish, and renunciative of all worldly ambition — so replete with humility, service, and earthly emptiness, that I felt myself utterly unfit for it and unworthy to assume it. When I looked at the ministry *as it was*, I saw that a large proportion of its functionaries, as I had known them, were deficient in mental power or marked by moral delinquencies, or compelled to frequent change of residence, alike annoying and vexatious, through ever recurring dissatisfaction and inharmonies. They were a pitiable class, I thought, in almost every temporal respect. Even the popular and petted few afforded me no encouragement to the step proposed to me. The good were so far above all the probable attainments I could ever make in the conditions of success that it was useless for me to try for them; the bad were so un-Christlike in essential characteristics that their presence in the pulpit was an abomination to me.

Besides, I had no clerical education and no prospect of any. There was no theological school or professor of divinity within my reach. If I became a preacher at all, it must be in the most unpopular denomination extant or in the world at large, without name or prestige — where I must work my way against wind and tide under adverse circumstances and on very humble fare. At the same time I was young, inexperienced, diffident, and certainly far too unspiritual to delight in those heavenly contemplations and anticipations which all true ministers of Christ feast on amid their labors for the souls redeemed through their instrumentality. Moreover, I had contracted marriage without the most distant thought on the part of either myself or my betrothed that she was to become the wife of a poor preacher, and to make her such without her cordial approval would be alike presumptuous and dishonorable. All these things taken into consideration made it impossible for me to decide upon the work of the ministry without an intense mental struggle. I could have been easily won to the profession of law, or perhaps to medicine; but preaching the gospel was utterly distasteful and fearful to me. There was nothing that could bring me to it except a most unwelcome sense of duty and the woe of disobedience to a call from Heaven — considerations I could in no wise ignore or escape. That vivid and awfully impressive vision hung perpetually in my memory and the solemn echoes of the closing words of my celestial visitant: — "Or the blood of their souls will be required at your hands" would not cease to reverberate in my mental ears. It was this that finally conquered me and determined my subsequent career. In regard to the result of my decision, I can truly say in the language of another, "Though I preach the gospel, I have nothing to glory of; for necessity is laid upon me, yea, woe is me if I preach not the gospel. For if I do this thing willingly, I have my reward; but if against my will, a dispensation is committed unto me." 1 Cor. 9:16, 17.

I have known of persons animated by a fervent aspiration to become preachers who qualified themselves for the profession with pleasing alacrity, and who were filled with delight when able to enter upon its appropriate duties. Alas! It was not my lot to know anything of such joys. On the contrary, I shrank from my call, as stated, to begin with, and often in my long life I have risen to preach with such reluctance, with such a sense of spiritual poverty and tremor (perhaps unsuspected by my hearers), that I would fain have vanished out of sight. Yet, when forgetting myself in my subject or borne along on some favoring breeze of inspiration, I have experienced unqualified enjoyment in prosecuting my mission. And now, after all I have passed through as a minister and as a man, I am so far from regretting my mysterious, imperative call to the work that I feel profoundly thankful that the dispensation was forced upon me. For it has laid me under a wholesome discipline and wrought in me a spiritual regeneration and growth of character of inestimable value. I can but hope it has done some, though I fear too little, good to those around me and to the world of mankind; to me it has been of unspeakable and, I trust, eternal benefit. God knew how to use and bless me against my own will and to him be praise, worship, and glory forevermore.

But to take up again the thread of my narrative. Having yielded to my inexorable convictions of duty, I communicated the conclusion I had reached to my intended wife. She was naturally astonished, but manifested no opposition or revulsion, and calmly acquiesced in the new phase of our probable future. I also opened my mind to my father, who was evidently pleased with the new aspect of things and saw nothing in my determination which need interfere with the plan previously arranged between us; his idea being that I might fulfil all stipulated obligations to him, reside on the old homestead, be pastor of our own little church, and make occasional preaching excursions abroad. How different was all this from what actually transpired with me during the long years that were then before me! To others I was entirely reticent concerning the change that had come to me until compelled to reveal it on the Sabbath before I first occupied a pulpit. That occurrence was another notable feature of this eventful year, — another crisis, and a most trying one, in my earthly career. How it came to pass is worthy of mention.

Our church had no pastor during the summer of 1821, and there was very little regular preaching in the "Ballou Meeting-house," but we held in lieu thereof a conference or deacon's meeting there from Sunday to Sunday. My father usually presided on these occasions and led off in the exercises, while the lay members followed in due form with prayer, singing, or exhortation, as they were moved by the Holy Spirit or a sense of personal obligation. I had refrained almost entirely from taking any active part in the proceedings, suffering as I did intensely from diffidence and dread of responsibility. On a certain Sunday, however, about the first of July, I was

THE FIRST SERMON. 67

inwardly impelled to rise at the close of the exercises and announce that with divine assistance I should preach in that house on the Sunday following, naming the hour. No language can describe the oppressive and almost suffocating sensations which at the moment agitated me. My knees smote together, my voice and even my whole frame trembled, and I sank back into my seat seemingly paralyzed, as soon as the words were out of my mouth. To the little congregation of men and women gathered there, my notification was like a sharp electrical clap from a cloudless sky — utterly unexpected and astonishing. They went their way in different directions and trumpeted the strange tidings far and wide on every hand. No alarm of war could have been more eagerly heralded abroad through all the surrounding region.

The die was now cast; the announcement was made and could not be recalled. I must stand up when the time came and at least *attempt* to preach. And I must speak from inspiration, as thoughts and words should be given me at the moment. A written discourse, or even an abstract on paper, was almost sacrilegious in my estimation. My education and all my conceptions of a truly God-called preacher prejudiced me against everything of the kind. I must speak right out of the heart and soul, even if I broke down in the effort. Happily, my text and subject were given me in a dream, which seemed to be in accord with my former mysterious experience. The text was: "Necessity is laid upon me; yea, woe is me if I preach not the gospel."—*1 Cor. 9: 16.* The subject was easily deduceable from that passage.

The momentous day arrived. The weather was fine and when the hour of worship drew near the ancient sanctuary was packed with expectant people — ministers, deacons, church-members, my young friends and acquaintances more or less interested in me and in the things of the religious life, with a mixed throng of outsiders drawn to the place by curiosity. I occupied the old-fashioned pulpit alone, wrought up to the highest pitch of conscientious purpose, anxiety, and self-consecration. I almost agonized in silent prayer when I saw the multitudes surging in. But confidence and assurances of help from above seemed to possess my soul as I rose to begin the service. I opened with prayer and proceeded in the usual order to the sermon, which was, of course, the chief matter of interest and concern. I talked for three-quarters of an hour, receiving the most respectful and profound attention. My youth, sincerity, and zeal no doubt atoned in good part for my lack of sound matter and coherency, so that those present departed with good impressions and an increased personal respect for me. Probably most of them were disappointed for the better by this my first effort at preaching. My discourse, little of which I now recall, must have been more hortatory than dialectical, and quite inspirational in some of its appeals. But whatever it was in substance and form, it discharged a solemn duty, as I then believed, and introduced me to a long ministry of religious teaching. I crossed the threshold of a public career whose varied experiences, often trying and repellant, have always seemed, like the first, providentially inevitable.

It is true that my subsequent change of theological faith from Destructionism to Restorationism naturally relaxed somewhat the intensity of my early concern about the ruin of souls, and the strain of my anxiety lest my unfaithfulness should occasion that ruin. But reflection has always impressed me deeply with the assurance that the wiles and dangers of sin are sufficiently dreadful to demand my most earnest efforts to avert them, however certain it may be that they are to be overruled, conquered, and finally terminated by the operations of omnipotent divine wisdom and love. Moreover, the ultimate triumph of good over evil cannot be rationally hoped for on the assumption that sin is not inherently malignant or hateful, or that its natural tendency is not poisonous and deadly, or that it works its own cure and must of necessity eventually extinguish or destroy itself. On the contrary, the only well-grounded expectation of its final extinction and of the deliverance of all sentient, moral beings from its miserable bondage, is the persistent, all-conquering will, wisdom, and grace of God, operating not only directly but through various intermediate instrumentalities and means, among which the faithful preaching of those great truths and duties embodied in the gospel of Christ is undoubtedly one, and a most important one. So if I am called to this work, I can not be excused, but "woe" is unto me still if I refuse to do it. My better hopes of the ultimate universal reign of holiness and happiness in the universe of the great Creator, supplanting those of only a partial victory of the right, good, and true over the wrong, evil, and false,— a victory darkly palled with despair of anything better than annihilation for countless incurable sinners, rationalizes my faith without changing my duty or excusing my neglect of it. Nay, rather am I encouraged and strengthened to greater fidelity by assurances of final success. My grand concern, therefore, is to stand fast in my lot and be faithful to my trust; otherwise just condemnation and punishment await me.

It was not long after my first attempt at preaching that I began to be called upon to speak at home and abroad, both on Sundays and week days, in public houses of worship and in private dwellings. I also was soon employed to conduct funeral services — a department of ministerial work which has commanded much of my attention and energy through my entire life. To enlarge my acquaintance with the denomination to which I was attached and its leading representatives, and to open the way to greater usefulness, I attended a meeting of what was called the Connecticut Christian Conference, which included the churches of the "Christian Connexion" in Rhode Island and Connecticut, held at Hampton in the latter State in the autumn of the same year. There I was received into the fellowship of the entire body of believers known by the general name of "Christians," as attested by a certificate of which the following is a copy:

"*To all whom it may concern:*—I hereby certify that Adin Ballou of Cumberland, R. I., is a member in good standing and fellowship of the Connecticut Christian Conference.
      REUBEN POTTER, JR., *Standing Scribe.*
"Cumberland, R. I., Sept. 1, 1821."

A few weeks later, the general conference of the denomination, including all subordinate local conferences, churches, and ministers, met at New Bedford, Mass. This, also, I attended, having for a traveling companion thither Elder Ebenezer Robinson, an enthusiastic young minister from Greenwich, Mass. On the way we visited Elder Daniel Hicks, a venerable farmer-preacher of our order in Dartmouth, Mass., with whom we spent the night, holding an evening service at his request in his meeting-house, with a goodly audience in attendance. At the conference there was a large representation of the talent and wisdom of the denomination — its greater and lesser lights shining with varied luster from pulpit and council room, much to my edification and encouragement and to the general satisfaction. Thence Brother Robinson and I walked to Boston — fifty-six miles — where we spent a few days and where we separated, not to meet again for many years — both of us meantime having changed our doctrinal views and ecclesiastical relations. This was my first visit to the Athens of America, then wonderful to me, but hardly to be compared in magnitude, wealth, and magnificence with what it is today.

About this time my ambition and zeal betrayed me into the folly of appearing in print as a polemic author against modern Universalism. Several of my neighbors were of this persuasion and a few of them great debaters in its support. They plied me with their publications to read and with their arguments to answer. Willing to investigate and hear all sides, I perused their books and tracts, and, confident of my ability to maintain my own cause and defend my convictions, I did not shrink from the controversy to which I was invited. I felt, too, that I was in the way of my duty and that I could do something to put down what I deemed a dangerous and rampant error. Having met and refuted to my own satisfaction my Universalist assailants at home, I deemed myself qualified to enter the lists against more notable champions of false doctrines abroad, should occasion and loyalty to truth seem to require it, as was not long after the case. Rev. Hosea Ballou of Boston, a distant kinsman of mine, was at that time the master spirit of Universalism in what was known as its "ultra" phase. He had been delivering in his church fortnightly lectures expository of his peculiar views, which had been promptly published and disseminated far and wide throughout the country. These were pressed on my attention by my Universalist friends and I had sharply combated some of the positions taken by this author, in conversational discussion. Among the lectures was one delivered in January, 1820, upon "The New Birth," from the text in John 3: 3: "Except a man be born again, he cannot see the kingdom of God," and this was handed me and commended as a masterpiece — conclusive and unanswerable. In that lecture the author gave some sharp thrusts at the prevailing theological notions of regeneration, and claimed that Christ in the passage under notice treated of a work "effected in the rational powers and faculties of man, by means of information which operates to change the sentiments and remove the errors of the mind, and, of course, the affections of the heart." And in illustration of that view the lecturer said: "The gospel as Jesus proclaimed it a system of impartial salvation to the world, is now performing the miracle of regeneration and thousands are born again from the partial systems and creeds of the church to the acknowledgement of the universal mercy and grace of Zion's King." Virtually and practically, this made the Christian new birth to be a turning from the old faith in endless punishment to a belief in Universalism. This was too much for me to swallow or patiently endure. So I must needs face Goliath in polemic battle array. I therefore wrote and published a "Review" of the "Lecture-Sermon," in which, after endeavoring to refute the author's reasoning, I gave my own exposition of the subject under consideration.

On general principles, this youthful exploit of mine was unwise, crude, presumptuous, and of little consequence. I was too unskilled in rhetoric to write for the press, too inexperienced in theological criticism to set up as a public reviewer, too immature in mental discipline to expound the great doctrine of regeneration, and too obscure and uninfluential an opponent to command the notice of my adversary or the community at large. And yet I am constrained to declare that, judged from my present standpoint, my pamphlet contained more truth and less error on the main question at issue than the sermon whose theory and reasoning it condemned. It is true that I was then a Destructionist theologically, and changed not long afterward to a Restorationist, but my views of spiritual regeneration were essentially the same after the change as before. I became a believer with Hosea Ballou in the grand idea of universal salvation, but never a convert to his peculiar ideas of regeneration, or to his favorite doctrine of no future punishment. The assumption that conversion from Partialistic dogmas to the Universalist faith is the new birth taught by Jesus Christ no more commends itself to my acceptance now than when I foolishly published my "Review" of the "Lecture Sermon."

When the winter of 1821-22 approached, I engaged to teach the school in my native district and did so, beginning at the usual date early in December. During the term my marriage was solemnized, to wit, on the seventeenth of January, 1822. Among all the pleasant and joyous experiences connected with my teaching and wedding were some exceedingly disagreeable and trying ones,

DISAGREEABLE SCHOOL IMBROGLIO.

one of which was of sufficient importance to justify a brief notice in this connection.

The school opened under favorable auspices and went on for a time harmoniously and prosperously. With one or two exceptions, the pupils were docile, teachable, obedient, and kind. There was the best feeling between them and their teacher; all were happy together and excellent progress was made in the studies pursued. But unfortunately an evil star after a while cast its baleful glare across my horizon. It was as unexpected as it was disagreeable and humiliating. A lad some twelve years old, of apparently defective organization and subject to half-insane fits of sullenness and ill-temper, of which I was ignorant at the time, who had given me no trouble, became suddenly refractory, stubborn, insubordinate, and difficult of control, requiring all the tact, ingenuity, and wisdom I could command, together with some more distinctively disciplinary and punitive measures, to bring him to a state of submissiveness — the whole ending by my sending him home full of rebellious anger and vengeful spite. To his parents he had a terrible "tale of woe" to tell, making them think he had been unjustly dealt with — outrageously abused indeed. His father, an ignorant, intemperate man, took up the matter with a firm determination to be revenged for my supposed ill-treatment of his boy. He made clamorous appeals in all directions for sympathy and for help to bring me to justice, but to little purpose. Even the greatly exaggerated and baseless stories of my alleged cruelty, savagery almost, failed to arouse any interest in his case except among people of his own stamp, and those "lewd fellows of the baser sort" to be found in every community, who are rife for mischief, and who delight in some sort of quarrel or tumult, the occasion of which matters little with them.

Of course I was to be prosecuted and made to suffer to the full extent of the law. An astute, unscrupulous Justice of the Peace was found to issue a warrant against me, the execution of which was entrusted to a constable of kindred spirit and character. And to crown all, the conspirators planned to have the warrant served on me on the day of my approaching wedding and while the nuptial festivities were going on; all of which was kept a profound secret from the parties immediately concerned. The programme thus arranged was punctiliously carried out. The memorable seventeenth of January arrived. The betrothed couple with a large company of their relatives and friends were at the residence of the bride's parents in Smithfield, R. I., where ample provision had been made for the occasion. The marriage vows were acknowledged, the marriage pledges were given and received, and the marriage union was declared to be legally consummated and recognized by Rev. Reuben Potter, Jr., who officiated at the nuptial altar. Everything proceeded joyously. Congratulations were extended to the bridal pair and the wedding feast was going on, when, lo! the ministers of the law appeared without previous announcement and demanded, "in the name of the State of Rhode Island and Providence Plantations," that I should accompany them as their prisoner to Cumberland Hill, three miles distant, to answer before Mr. Jillson, Justice of the Peace, for certain misdemeanors, specified in the legal document they carried, of which it was claimed I was guilty, and await his squireship's pleasure.

At first I was inclined to comply with the requisition without any delay. But upon taking counsel of some of our older and wiser guests who were amply competent to give it, I declined leaving the house. Whereupon the chief officer of the invading party grew pertinacious and intimated that he had the aid necessary to enforce his orders if they were not peaceably obeyed. I appealed to Hon. Thomas Mann, Judge of the Court of Common Pleas, one of those present, who gave the person clothed with a little brief authority to understand that he was exceeding his powers and had no grounds for compelling me to go with him, if I could only give bonds to appear before the justice named at a designated time, which I was entirely willing and ready to do. "You had better accept such guaranties," said the judge to the constable, "and go home." The latter, finding himself confronted by one greater in authority than he was, become at once supple and compliant, accepted the pledge, and with his fellow conspirators left; but not, however, till they had partaken of an undeserved portion of the wedding feast.

The issue of this tragico-comical affair was as complimentary to me as it was humiliating and condemnatory to my accuser and his abettors. I went, as agreed upon, before Justice Jillson, the constable and witnesses being present, but it was found that the charge against me was so groundless, so unsupported by requisite evidence, and so certain to be met by triumphant counter-evidence, that even he, the hitherto supple tool of the conspirators, refused to have the case come to trial, declaring that he would dismiss the complaint and consider the warrant annulled. The prevailing sentiment of the better citizens in the community was manifestly in my favor, deeming the proceedings against me malicious and shameful, and all parties to them worthy of abhorrence and contempt. This episode over, I took up again the duties of my position as teacher and carried the term of school through to a happy and successful conclusion.

So well pleased were my friends and the general public with the results of my labors in the schoolroom that I was immediately approached with a proposition to open a private school in the same place and continue it for a few of the following months. As circumstances seemed to render it expedient that I should abandon the plan of settling down upon the old homestead with my parents and succeed to my father's estate and occupation, that plan was now given up and the contemplated private school was started, specific charges being made per week for tuition. It was also deemed best that my wife and I should set up housekeeping on our own account, and we accordingly did so in a small dwelling owned by my father near the ancestral residence; my nineteenth birthday finding us happily installed in our new home. Our means were very limited, as my income was small, but our wants were comparatively few and our expectations in no wise extravagant, so that we probably enjoyed quite as much in our newly-begun domestic life as most of those at this day who start out under more auspicious worldly circumstances in general, and with abundant or perhaps princely resources at their command. I preached often here and there, but received little pecuniary compensation therefor; and teaching, my most productive source of supply, afforded me but a small revenue. Moreover, my *hat speculation*, before mentioned, had imposed a heavy financial burden on me, which was increased by the publication of my "Review." I was getting ahead in dear-bought experience certainly (perhaps in useful knowledge), but not in the means of maintaining a family. We were comfortable so far as present necessities were concerned and hopeful for the future. Nor were our hopes wholly profitless and vain. Even our annoyances and trials were not without profit to us.

> "There's a divinity that shapes our ends,
> Rough hew them as we will."

This is something more than poetry; it is a universal truth. I realize it in my own case. I hewed awkwardly, but Providence shaped results. So it was in my youth; so it has been through my earthly pilgrimage. I have been led by a way I knew not and in paths of dubious aspect, but thus far through every dark defile and fearful pass into bright and peaceful resting-places.

This chapter has detailed the experiences of only a single year; the next one will be scarcely less replete with incidents for a similar period.

CHAPTER V.

1822-1823.

FOUNDATIONS SHAKEN — INWARD CONFLICT — CHANGE OF VIEWS — ALIENATION — EXCOMMUNICATION — NEW FELLOWSHIP.

DURING the continuance of my school, which closed about June 15th, I preached on the Sabbath either in the "Ballou Meeting-house" near by, or in the general vicinity, not farther away than Providence on the south and adjoining Massachusetts towns on the north. My discourses, doctrinally, were along the lines indicated in a former chapter, and yet my mind began to be exercised with some doubts whether, after all, Destructionism, as the final doom of the impenitent wicked, was really taught in the Bible. Some time before this, my wife's mother, one of the best of women and a sincere Restorationist withal, had asked me if I would read Winchester's "Dialogues on Universal Restoration." "Certainly," said I, "and I am sure such a doctrine can be easily refuted." She made no reply, but smiled at my self-confidence and handed me the volume. I went through it carefully, but with the persuasion that it was full of error and would make little impression on me. I was surprised, however, to find it written in such a serious, religious, and candid spirit as to deeply interest and gratify me. Unlike most of the Universalist publications which had been urged upon my attention, there was not a sentence in it that seemed to denounce or ridicule what I called strictly religious convictions and feelings — regeneration, experimental piety, or consecration to God.

Moreover, I was struck with the moral grandeur of the author's distinctive doctrine and the force of his answer to some leading objections to it. Yet I was not convinced that he was right, nor consciously shaken in my own belief. His argument seemed to be spent chiefly against the dogma of endless punishment which I considered even then as indefensible as it was horrible. I flattered myself at the time that my own doctrine of the annihilation of those who died impenitent was so much stronger than that of never-ending misery or that of ultimate universal redemption that it must triumph over both in a fair contest. And I said so when I returned the "Dialogues" to my good mother-in-law. She was not disposed to debate the matter with me, but leave all to time and my own reflective mind. I now see what I was then unconscious of, that Winchester's ideas had imparted their leaven to my understanding too effectually to be wholly neutralized by my prejudices. And I would drop the hint to such religious inquirers as are determined never to embrace Restorationism that "Winchester's Dialogues" is too seductive and convincing a work for them to read, without jeopardy to their opposing faith.

The fact that I had published a "Review" of Rev. Hosea Ballou's sermon on the "New Birth," naturally opened the way for further discussions with my Universalist neighbors. Several of them were fond of and skilful in debate and they missed no good opportunity of testing my ability in the same line. And on my part, I never declined to take issue with them. Foremost among these disputants were Lewis Metcalf, Luke Jenckes, and Levi Ballou, the first two resident in Wrentham, Mass., the last in Cumberland; but all of them known by me from early childhood. They were elderly men, uneducated in the scholastic sense, but naturally strong-minded, shrewd, sharp reasoners, and well posted in all matters pertaining to Universalism. Winchester's opinions and claims they repudiated, cleaving with great tenacity and admiration to the new-school, no-future-punishment expositors and doctrinaires. I thought myself competent to battle with these men, especially on their own peculiar platform. They argued mainly from Scripture and reason, both of which I could use to their frequent perplexity and discomfiture. But I found that I had one weak point to defend and that was that an all-perfect God, infinite in power, wisdom, and love, who really willed the final holiness and happiness of all human kind, and raised up Christ to redeem all, must needs ultimately annihilate most of them as incurable sinners and so practically confess his impotency and utter failure in that important behalf, so far as they were concerned. My opponents pushed me hard on this point whenever they could. And all I could do was to contend that the Bible taught the doctrine and that it was the best thing God could do without depriving mankind of moral freedom — an evil out of the question. When brought fairly to bay this was my only refuge.

At length, however, I began to have some doubts whether, after all, the Bible did, on the whole, teach what I claimed, and also whether it were absolutely certain that God must destroy man's moral freedom if he finally by his saving might regenerated all who left this state of existence unreconciled to himself. These doubts were too slight at first to affect me much, and especially so long as I firmly held the opinion that man's earth-life was his only probation for eternity. This opinion my ultra-Universalist opponents did not attack with much force, for though they scouted it as groundless, their phase of Universalism led them to expend their strength in proving that the Bible taught no such thing as sinfulness and punishment after death under any possible circumstances. All this to me was labor lost, for I was just as certain then as now that if the Bible, particularly the New Testament, does not teach that a portion of mankind will wake up condemned sinners in the next life, it teaches nothing that common sense can understand. And I think now as I thought then, that many of the expositions whereby no-future-punishment Universalists explained away what are generally considered as threatenings of future retribution, are specious, unsound, and some of them absurd. I should never have been converted from my old belief by any such interpretation of the sacred record.

But it was impossible for me to get over the weak point mentioned to my own satisfaction, however successfully I could confute my adversaries on their distinctive ground. Recurring to Winchester's "Dialogues,": I felt all the force of their reasoning and felt it against the doctrine of annihilation as well as against that of endless misery; for though the former was incomparably preferable to the latter, it was an alternative involving in less degree the same principles, difficulties, and objections, and was bound to go to the wall when it came to be submitted to the tribunal of my more enlightened, rational, and moral understanding, as was the case at an early day.

I think it was in the month of June during the year now in review that the organization known as the "Southern Association of Universalists" held one of its sessions at West Wrentham, Mass. My friend, Levi Ballou, kindly invited me to attend its public exercises. I accepted his invitation, but heard nothing from the preachers on the occasion that made much impression on me or exerted any appreciable influence in the way of effecting a change in my theological convictions. I was introduced to several of the ministers, among whom was Rev. Hosea Ballou 2d, as he was then called. I had a conversation of much interest with him and took a decided liking to him at the time and thenceforth through life, though we did not sail in the same ecclesiastical ship except for a brief session. He was a candid and calm as well as a close reasoner and was more of a Restorationist than an ultra-Universalist in his views, though he remained in continuous fellowship with the new-school men of the sect. Albeit he argued with me as one holding the idea of future retribution as well as that of final restoration and begged me to remember that the denomination embraced both believers and disbelievers in that view of the divine government, not making either a test of fellowship. I must therefore ponder the arguments on both sides and if I could accept the doctrine of universal salvation, do so on grounds that seemed to me reasonable and satisfactory. Should I adopt Restorationist views, I should not be obliged to endorse the other, and should be regarded the equal in every respect of those differing from me by all intelligent believers in the final redemption of all men.

I returned home under some conviction that I might be in error concerning the consummation of all things, but by no means converted from my former belief. I felt, however, that I must thoroughly investigate the whole subject, and at once set myself about the task, becoming a very close and anxious student. I took my bible and went through it carefully from Genesis to Revelation, noting down under three distinct heads, viz: endless punishment, final destruction of the wicked, and universal salvation, every text which seemed to favor each doctrine or which I knew to be quoted as such. I also noted the passages supposed to teach that this life is man's only probation for eternity or that there is no change from sin to holiness after death. The result was that I found the smallest numerical array of texts under the head of endless punishment, the largest under the head of the destruction of the wicked, and the next largest in favor of the final salvation of all. To my astonishment the word "probation" was not in the bible, nor a single passage evidently intended to teach the doctrine that this life is man's only probationary state, and only about half a dozen passages from the letter of which that view could be plausibly inferred — none of these absolutely requiring such inference.

Respecting the texts seeming to favor endless punishment, I learned that their strength depended mainly on words often having a limited signification or on intensified forms of expression, employed in a figurative, impassioned sense, and that none of them were obviously designed to affirm that dogma as an article of faith; in fine, that they were highly-wrought, glowing descriptions of retribution in its general aspects, rather than positive and definite declarations of divine truth concerning it. The numerous passages apparently teaching the destruction of the wicked were also found to be of the intensive, figurative class, in which the mere sound of the words gave them force — words used elsewhere with a meaning altogether different from that of utter annihilation, and not one of them obviously employed to denote an item of doctrinal belief. The passages that seemed to favor universal salvation were of various kind. Some commonly used in that behalf had no force whatever; others might be construed so as to support either of the three theories under examination; but there were none which I could be certain were designed to assert the doctrine absolutely as divinely revealed truth. There were, however, a large number, the principles and spirit of which would consistently harmonize with no other view. These related (1) to the nature, attributes, and moral character of God; (2) to his will, purpose, and design towards mankind; (3) to the mission, office, exaltation, and triumph of Christ; (4) to the essence and spirit of God-likeness, *i. e.* the moral imitation of God as the only true personal righteousness; (5) to the aim or purpose of divine rebuke, chastisement, judgment, and retribution, as beneficent and reformatory; and (6) to a grand prophetic era, in which there shall be no sin, evil, pain, but God " be all in all." I perceived that these six classes of Scripture testimony were of a different nature and scope from those seeming to teach the other two doctrines. They were not incidental statements, descriptions, or representations of divine retribution, nor figurative, intensified, impassioned forms of phraseology, but were declarations of great truths to be religiously held, and of fundamental principles demanding the broadest application both in faith and practice. Their weight did not depend on mere sound of words, it was intrinsic. They did not express a simple, positive, theological conclusion in respect to God's final disposal of the human race, but they necessitated the conclusion that it must be a disposal perfectly benevolent, impartial, wise, and good; perfectly accordant with his own will and purpose; and perfectly triumphant through Christ over all opposing forces, hindrances, and obstacles. I saw, therefore, that it was not warrantable to construe even the most intense, highly-wrought representations of sin and punishment as finalities, or as frustrating the ultimate divine purpose, or as rendering in any way doubtful the absolute moral perfections of God.

I was now in a tight place, with a flood of light beaming on my mind and a host of new ideas taking possession of my understanding. The whole subject presented itself in an aspect original and astonishing. The plain, unavoidable issue came home to me: — Is the belief that God will finally blot out of existence all who die in sin reconcilable with the fundamental truths and principles unquestionably declared in those six classes of texts? And is any other belief than that He will sooner or later render all human beings holy and happy consistent with those testimonies? Regarded in the spirit of truth and unprejudiced reason, the case looked very much as if I must yield? But why had I not seen the subject in this light before? I had been as sincere and honest in my desire for truth in the past as now. Why had so many millions of pious and learned Christians in all ages of the church held the final loss in some form or other of all that die out of Christ? I was then ignorant of the fact that many eminent Christian Fathers, including the great Origen, were unequivocal advocates of universal restoration. [As he was also of the fact that of the six great schools first founded to promote the interests of Christian philosophy, four taught absolutely that distinctive doctrine. — *Ed.*]

Furthermore, if I became a believer in the final holiness and happiness of all mankind, I should have to avow and preach it. In that case I must renounce all I had thus far professed and contended for to the contrary. I should shock, aggrieve, and alienate my fellow-Christians, including my nearest and dearest friends. I should be denounced as a changeling and an apostate, as others had been. And with whom should I find myself presently in fellowship but those whom I had regarded as rejectors of experimental religion and whose phase of Universalism was radically repulsive to me? Then arose the strong internal suggestion: — "You are a victim of Satanic delusion and that makes universal salvation look probable to you. Take care how you advance." I trembled and shrunk backward. Objections and doubts rolled in upon me. I wept, prayed, and reviewed the ground I had gone over again and again till I was well nigh distracted. I could not eat, drink, sleep, or appear like myself. I grew pale and wore an anxious, sickly look, to the serious concern of my wife and friends, who knew nothing of the conflict that was raging within me. My solicitude, doubt, and fear brought me to a poise of suspense and disquietude hardly to be endured.

In this dreadful condition I wandered off by myself one day to a retreat out of human sight (I can never forget the place), and gave full vent to my emotions, bordering almost on despair. A voice came to me, saying: — "Kneel and pray." "Alas!" thought I, "for what shall I pray?" "For deliverance — for heavenly light and guidance. Pray that if this be a Satanic delusion it may be dispelled; but that if the Spirit of Truth is leading you into more glorious truth, you may not resist it; and that all doubts be banished from your mind." I did as directed, breathing forth my petitions with all the fervor of which I was capable. In a moment the heavens seemed to open above my head;

an inexpressibly sweet influence flowed in upon my soul; the whole subject became luminous, every doubt vanished, a vision of the final triumph of good over evil shone forth in majestic splendor, and my heart was filled with transports of joy. I was supremely blest and if I could have commanded an archangel's trumpet, the whole world would have heard the sublime gospel then and there revealed to me. My faith was conclusively sealed, and I have never since felt one serious doubt of the final universal holiness and happiness of all the immortal children of God. I returned to the house with a buoyant step and a joyful spirit, told my wife what had transpired, and she rejoiced with me.

A letter from Hosea Ballou 2d reached me about this time in reply to one addressed to him asking an explanation of certain of my strongest proof texts in support of Destructionism. But the work had been taken out of his hands and was already accomplished — more effectually than he possibly could have done it. His letter was an excellent one, but it would not have met my mental and moral wants as they had been supplied from the eternal world. It was valuable of its kind, as was also his then recently published discourse on Gal. 3: 8 — a copy of which he sent me. But neither of these would have overcome wholly my objections or removed my principal difficulties, because they did not deal so much with fundamental principles as they did in special expositions and polemic subtleties, some of which I should then have deemed unsound or at least inconclusive.

I had now a stormy scene to pass through with my brethren, relatives, and friends. No sooner was it known that I had embraced the doctrine of Universal Salvation than they were filled with astonishment and overwhelmed with grief. All the fair promise I had given of gospel usefulness was to their minds blasted in the opening bloom. My own father was first and foremost among the aggrieved. I expected he would be, and thought it my duty to be prompt and frank with him and let him receive the painful news from my own lips. It was the bitterest cup he had ever been called upon to drink. I have no doubt that my death would have been more endurable to him. I was his favorite son and had flowered out into a promising minister of the gospel, as he understood and prized it. Profoundly sincere and firmly established in his religious convictions, he was no less so in his prejudices against Universalism in all its forms. He had not a doubt that it was of the Devil nor that I was the deluded victim of his Satanic majesty's wiles. He remonstrated, rebuked, denounced, pleaded, and deplored, but could not move me. Finally, in his impatient vexation, he threatened to disinherit me if I did not renounce such a damnable error. This had no effect whatever upon me. I was so insensible to such a motive that it did not even disturb my equanimity, for I had counted the cost and had received a special assurance from above that I should never be forsaken. I therefore replied in perfect kindness that I had no claim to any of his property, that he had a perfect right to give it to whomsoever he chose; but of this I was sure that if I had no earthly father to provide for me, I had a heavenly one who would never fail me. He was sorely vexed by this answer and retorted, "You will find you have no father in heaven to do you any good in the way you are going." I merely rejoined, "I can trust him implicitly." This was the last in a series of conversational debates I ever had with him. He had said and done all he could to save me and now gave me up as hopelessly lost. He, however, became sorry for his passionate threat of disinheritance and some months after wished my ever kind mother to tell me he should never cast off a child of his for difference of opinion. Meantime, he stood aloof from me and did not become fully reconciled till ten years had elapsed. My mother did not accept my new faith and probably regretted the change, but treated me with unaltered maternal affection and kindness. On the other side, my parents-in-law rejoiced in my conversion to their own cherished faith, and gave me nothing but sympathetic encouragement.

My father next felt it to be his painful duty to have me publicly disowned by the church and formally deposed from its membership as dangerous to its welfare. He dissuaded all he could from holding personal discussions with me, as it would be of no use to me and might unsettle their own minds; for, he said, I was very adroit and seductive in argument. Most of my friends were thereby deterred from coming to see me at all, but good Deacon Nathaniel Aldrich, who was once a member of our church, but who seceded on account of his strong Calvinistic views, had so much concern for me that he resolved upon a personal interview. My father, who never liked him very well, when he announced his intention, advised against it and signified that it would be labor lost. Yet the deacon was not to be deterred from his purpose; so he called upon me and gave me the full benefit of his counsel. Finding that I was unconvinced by his argument, and unmoved by his solemn admonition, he said he must leave me with grief to my chosen delusion. He deplored my apostasy and consequent doom, but could do no more for my salvation. I had taken pains to draw out his Calvinism in its baldest form, and now that he was about to leave with such despairing professions of sorrow for my fate, calmly said:—"Why do you allow yourself to be so much distressed on my account? If I am one of the *elect*, you cannot doubt my final salvation; and if I am one of the reprobates, it will be for the glory of God and the good of the universe that I should be lost. Why do you distrust the sovereignty of God, the wisdom of his decrees, or the certainty that my destiny will be just what you should rejoice in, whether I am consigned to heaven or hell?" His only response was a sigh! He reported my case as hopeless to my father, who, after he left, said to my mother:—"Aldrich has been talking with Adin and he got his mouth shut up pretty quick, as I knew he would." Father abhorred Calvinism almost as much as he did Universalism, and probably derived more pleasure from the recusant deacon's discomfiture than he could have done from his success.

At length I was summoned to appear before the Church during the first week in August, 1822. The meeting was held in the same venerable house of worship in which I first heard preaching and where I delivered my first sermon. A full attendance of members was present and my father laid the case before them as one perfectly plain to them all and requiring no investigation or trial. To his heartfelt affliction and regret, I had become a Universalist. This I had openly avowed and persisted in, notwithstanding the most faithful admonition. The church could give no fellowship or countenance to that doctrine, my acceptance of it excluded me from the fold of Christ, and it was the solemn duty of the church to disown me. Discussions were unnecessary; action and record only were required. I asked the privilege of being heard in explanation and defence of my views, which I did not wish to disguise, but this was denied me, my father saying that he well knew my ability and skill at talking and should afford me no opportunity to unsettle and mislead the young and draw susceptible minds into my snare. The others concurring, I saw that the whole proceeding was a solemn farce and requested them to finish their work without the least delay. They did so and I became to them "as a heathen man and a publican."

Whether the Connecticut Conference, whose letter of fellowship I held, ever took any action on my case, I do not remember. Probably not, as my disownment by the Cumberland Church was deemed conclusive. For my part, I was so disgusted by that action that I did not care a straw for all the excommunications in the world. Good Elder Benjamin Taylor of Swansey was the only one of my old "Christian" brethren, who, to my know-

OBJECTIONABLE FEATURES OF UNIVERSALISM. 89

ledge, regretted and condemned the proceedings against me as utterly repugnant to the very foundation on which the denomination professed to stand, viz: "*No creed but the New Testament* interpreted by each individual for himself, and a practical Christian life." Father Taylor was right — consistent with the often-boasted platform of the order and with his own large soul. He said: " Our young brother Ballou should have been treated tenderly, reasoned with kindly, borne with patiently, without ever being censured, much less disowned, except for un-Christian conduct." If I had been so treated, I should in all probability have spent my days as a minister of the "Christian Connexion." For it was in some important respects an unnatural and most disagreeable transition for me to leave my old, fondly-cherished, ecclesiastical relations and become identified with the Universalist denomination as it was at that period of its history.

For while I had come to believe in what might be regarded the distinguishing doctrine of that body, there were many opinions, notions, theories, put forth and urged by its leading spirits as correlative deductions from, if not essential adjuncts of, that doctrine, with which I had not one particle of sympathy, but rather an instinctive repugnance to them. Those leading spirits were strongly opposed to the idea of any future disciplinary punishment; explained away, often by far-fetched interpretations, all the passages of Scripture which teach retribution after death; ridiculed revivals of religion; held all spiritual experience to be superstitious or fanatical; and expended nearly all their effort in proving, argumentatively, the naked tenet of universal salvation, as if that were the whole of the gospel of Christ. And this result was made to depend more on the arbitrary will and decree of God than on any searching process of regeneration whereby each soul must have a conscious struggle of choice or consent and be brought into a state of personal holiness. Death was to finish sin and the resurrection to inaugurate perfection of character and blessedness. These peculiarities of faith and practice were repulsive to my spiritual instincts and habits of thought. They had not exerted one particle of influence in aid of my conversion. During that whole experience, from inception to consummation, I had not had a single doubt that mankind would be called to judgment after death for the deeds done in the body; nor that most of the texts (not all), commonly understood to refer to retribution in the invisible world, did so refer; nor that death and the resurrection affected chiefly the mortal and immortal organisms inhabited by the soul in its different states of existence rather than its absolute moral character; nor that men must be born again out of animal selfishness into the love of God and man in order to enter the kingdom of heaven; nor that constant self-sacrifice must be practised as a necessary condition of true holiness and happiness, here and hereafter. The much-vaunted notion that the destruction of Jerusalem was the grand crisis of divine judgment and retribution to which Christ and the apostles chiefly referred in their warnings against sin, did not commend itself then any more than it does now to my understanding. In short, I was not converted to the no-future-punishment phase of Universalism, nor by any arguments therefrom derived, but to pure Restorationism by reasons which had no affinity with those upon which that phase of the doctrine was based.

But notwithstanding all this, I entered into the pale and fellowship of the denomination indicated — compelled to that alliance by stress of circumstances. I was driven out of the "Christian Connexion" by the honest narrowmindedness of its members. The vast majority of them could not at that time tolerate the doctrines I had espoused. One must believe in destructionism or in endless torment, else in their judgment he could not be a Christian. On this ground, in spite of their declaration against all creeds save the Bible as each individual understood it and their boast that their sole test of fellowship was a

Christian life, I was excluded from their Order. On the other hand, I was hailed and welcomed by the Universalists as a convert to their faith, although I scarcely held any views in strict accordance with what was generally believed among them except the single tenet of final universal holiness and happiness. I told them frankly how far I was in agreement with them and that on many points I differed from most of them. "All right," they said; "there are various opinions among our people upon those minor particulars, but we allow the largest liberty. Come with us, fear nothing, and feel at home." Thus behind me was the merciless outcry, "Begone from our midst," and before me a thousand greetings of hospitality and assurances of welcome.

As a religious outcast therefore, with no power to assume and maintain an independent position, I sought the only place of refuge open to me, and accepted the only proffered welcome and fellowship — casting in my lot with my new-found friends, — the Universalists. In doing so, I did not feel that I was compromising any moral principle, or yielding any point of honor, all necessary explanations, positions, and concessions having been interchanged and clearly understood. Still I was unfortunately situated, inasmuch as the masses of my new allies, like most masses, were too indiscriminating to appreciate my peculiarities, while I was so placed as to be perpetually tempted to yield my scruples and conform to the prevailing sentiment of the body with which I had associated myself. And this temptation was all the more seductive and potent in that so much geniality and kindness were shown me. With ample liberty to differ, and with so many expressions of cordial friendship, it was much easier to agree and conform than to nurse dissent. Such was the course things took with me, and ere long I became to outward appearance completely amalgamated with the Universalists as a sect. Whatever dislikes and misgivings I had at first gradually diminished by closer intercourse till they ceased almost to exert any perceptible influence over me. In this I gained social power, but probably lost some religious stamina and strength of moral purpose. But whether, on the whole, more were lost than gained to me and to the world remains to be seen in the light of the great future.

It may be asked what I was doing in other respects during this transition period. As soon as I began to doubt seriously the soundness of my theology, I suspended preaching altogether, and for a time gave myself wholly to study and investigation. This taxed my health and strength to the utmost. After passing the crisis and finding myself physically enfeebled, I began to have some anxiety in regard to my temporal affairs. My funds were low, I was burdened with debt, and the outlook, in a worldly point of view, was far from encouraging. I had many dark hours on this account, but in one of the darkest of them, when I was in secret deploring my dubious earthly prospects, a voice again came to me, saying: "Fear not, my child. I will never leave thee nor forsake thee." The effect was electrifying and rapturous. My soul was thrilled to ecstasy and I felt the most perfect trust in divine providence and the most heartfelt joy. The promise was soon after so fully verified to me, and has been through life, that I should deem myself basely ungrateful to doubt that it was from heaven. For I had hardly passed through this experience when an offer came to me from my uncle, Daniel Sayles of Franklin, Mass., already mentioned, to work for him during haying time according to my strength, it being mutually understood that I was unable to render full service and should receive pay accordingly. This tided me over the shallow waters and enabled me to provide for myself and family until I could begin preaching again under new auspices and with assurances of a remunerative income equal to my necessities. And this good fortune visited me at an early day.

After becoming fully established in the belief of the final triumph of the all-redeeming grace of God, I wrote to my friend, Rev. Hosea Ballou, 2d, in reply to his letter referred to on a preceding page, announcing the fact and giving somewhat in detail the circumstances attending the change through which I had passed. The substance of my letter he published in the "Universalist Magazine," Boston, of which he was one of the editors, the last week in August, 1822, I think (Vol. 4, p. 36), under the heading of "Another conversion in the ministry." This brought me before the public in my new ecclesiastical position, and advertised me far and wide among friends and foes as a Universalist minister. As a consequence, I immediately began to receive invitations to preach in the general region round about, which I was very glad to accept so far as health, time, and convenience would allow. My first discourse under new auspices was delivered in the Elder Williams meetinghouse, West Wrentham, Mass., to a crowded audience, it having been extensively notified that "Young Ballou would give on the occasion the reasons for his change of theological faith." I also preached at Bellingham, Cumberland Hill, Woonsocket Falls, Providence, and other places in Rhode Island and Massachusetts, not far distant from my home, and officiated at several funerals in the same general vicinity, not lacking for employment in my adopted profession.

During the autumn I made a second visit to Boston and its environs, being a guest for some days in the family of Rev. Hosea Ballou 2d, of Roxbury, where I was kindly received and treated with all the courtesy and hospitality I could desire. Nor ought I to say less of his great-uncle, often called "Father Hosea," and other clergymen of the denomination with their families to whom I was introduced. I was invited to preach in each of the Ballou pulpits and perhaps one or two others near by. Of my impressions of the younger Hosea and my attractions to him, I have already spoken.

"Father Hosea," with whom I also visited, was a very genial man in the midst of his large family, and fond of pleasantry in common conversation. He was then in mid-life, being about fifty-one years old. His oldest son was already a clergyman in Vermont, his second son just entering the profession; while the youngest was a little boy in his frock, running about the house. One of his daughters was married and the others were at home, gracing the domestic circle. He was a man of sensible, plain habits; living comfortably, but not extravagantly. He was a great lover of children, and governed his household admirably, with a gentle but commanding discipline. He had a large store of anecdotes, and although not a great talker knew well how to keep up conversational discourse and entertainment when surrounded by his friends. He was not, however, inclined to intrude his theological peculiarities upon his visitors, much less to indoctrinate his juniors with them. So during this visit not a word was said to me on the subject of no future retribution, which, if broached, might have raised a discussion between us.

This pleasant visit had an indirect but strong tendency to blunt my convictions and scruples, or as might be said, soothe my prejudices against ultra-Universalism. I was silenced, too nearly, by so much respect and kindness, and was drawn too far into acquiescence with men from whose teachings I was afterwards obliged strongly to dissent, much to my cost. And what was worse, I became infected with an almost groundless prejudice against Revs. Paul Dean, Edward Turner, Charles Hudson, and others — the defenders of Restorationism as opposed to ultra-Universalism. A controversy had already been opened between the parties representing these two *isms*, in which some personalities appeared. And these, which were of trifling importance as related to the real point at issue, were magnified by the ultra leaders and made to seem the fundamental reasons or motives of their opponents in inaugurating and continuing the controversy. In fine, the Restorationist champions were represented as mere ambitious factionists and mischief-makers in the order, with no honest, solemn convictions of doctrinal faith or of Christian duty. This was a gross injustice to them, as I afterwards learned, for which there was no reasonable excuse. Nevertheless, this visit had the effect of making me for a time a sharer in that injustice to my subsequent regret and sorrow, causing me to think ill of the Restorationist party and their proceedings, when I ought to have sympathized and acted with them — at least on the main question at issue.

Returning from Boston, I preached from time to time during the autumn as opportunity in the surrounding towns offered, and in the winter had charge of a school in West Wrentham, adjacent to my home. New religious friends flocked around me from all directions and seemed anxious to make up for the loss of old ones, deserving by numerous manifestations of regard and kindness to me and my wife an indelible record of heartfelt appreciation and gratitude. Olney Ballou, Levi Ballou, and Luke Jenckes, with their families, belong to this category, as do others of less prominence. My always first and foremost friend, my dear mother, never changed.

After the close of my school, perhaps in February, I received a request to preach one or two Sundays to the First Universalist Society in Boston. Their design seemed to be to hear different clergymen for short periods each, with a view of inviting the more acceptable of them to serve subsequently as candidates in anticipation of a call and settlement — their pastorate being already, or about to be, vacated by Rev. Paul Dean, who had filled it for several years most acceptably. I occupied the pulpit as desired, then gave way to others, but was afterwards asked to supply it for six months, of which note will be made in the next chapter.

CHAPTER VI.

1823–1825.

PREACHING — "THE FURIOUS PRIEST REPROVED" — CANDIDACY IN BOSTON — ORDINATION — FIRST MARRIAGES — SETTLEMENT IN MILFORD — INCIDENTALS.

MY twenty-first year opened with an arrangement to preach regularly in several different places once or more in each month, viz: — in West Medway, in Bellingham, and in different neighborhoods of Mendon, South Parish (now Blackstone), all in Massachusetts. I had warm friends and admirers in these several localities who were very desirous of sharing my ministrations as often as possible. My family residence still continued to be the tenement house of my father, already mentioned. In the place first named, the Universalists owned a small meeting-house jointly with the Baptists. In Bellingham Center our friends were striving to obtain the occasional use of the only house of worship there, the occupancy of which was in dispute between the town and the Baptist society. Pending the settlement of the matter, our meetings, by my advice, were held in the hall of the adjacent tavern. At South Bellingham, services were in a schoolhouse. In the factory village of South Parish, Mendon, now East Blackstone, we occupied a store-loft furnished by my friend Col. Joseph Ray and his partners. I also spoke in the hall of the Henry Thayer tavern (five corners), in Capt. Aaron Burdon's hall, Chestnut Hill, or in some schoolhouse in that part of the town. Occasionally I lectured in other neighborhoods of my general region. In the principal of these places, my friends con-

BELLINGHAM BAPTISTS AND UNIVERSALISTS.

tributed to my support at the rate of five or six dollars per Sunday. In others and for lectures a smaller sum. As I never dictated prices or compensation for my religious ministrations, what I received was freely given, was the better enjoyed, and was all I had any right to expect under the circumstances. In other respects I was encouraged and cheered by the cordial interest manifested in my public exercises as well as in my private welfare.

On the third Sunday in May, 1823, a somewhat exciting and memorable occurrence transpired in Bellingham Center which it may be well to record. The town claimed to own and have rightful control of the meeting-house, and had voted that the Universalists might occupy it one Sunday in each month. But the Baptists contended that it belonged wholly to them and were unwilling the others should use it at all. There had been much wrangling in the matter, and the case had been submitted to the courts for adjudication, but was not yet settled. So the quarrel was still on between the home parties when I engaged to preach there. I told my friends that I should avoid all proceedings which savored of trickery, force, or indecorum, and occupy the disputed pulpit as a gentleman and a Christian or not at all. On the third Sunday in April, large and excited crowds of both parties assembled to watch proceedings and see what would be the issue. The Rev. Abiel Fisher was pastor of the Baptist church, a man of large combativeness, pluck, and obstinacy, and he determined that the Universalists should not occupy the house on that day, though the town had assigned it to them. But he and his people could not enter it, inasmuch as it was locked and the selectmen had the keys. So he collected his congregation about the doors of the edifice and preached from the steps, both morning and afternoon. My friends, by my advice, demanded as their right a peaceable entrance to the building, but not being allowed it, retired to the hall before spoken of and held services there.

When the month came round again in May, matters were in a still more aggravated condition than before. During Saturday night some desperate Baptist entered the meeting-house by a back window which he found unfastened, wrenched off the lock from the inner door of the entry, and set free the corresponding outside door which was rendered secure by a cross-bar. Having done this, and, as he supposed, made access to the house easy for his Baptist friends on the following day, he withdrew. About this time, Mr. Foster of the public house, who had the keys to the place of worship in his possession, dreamed of what had been done; but upon awaking and thinking it over concluded it was only a dream and went to sleep again, when the same dream was repeated with the same result as before. But when it occurred a third time, he deemed it of enough importance to be looked into a little. He therefore arose, much excited, dressed himself, lighted his lantern (for it was not yet daylight), and went and examined the premises, to find that what he had dreamed was literally true in all its details. He immediately procured another lock for the inside door, replaced the bar to the outside one, and returned home to await further developments. As the hour of morning service drew near, the Baptist pastor and his flock collected about the house as four weeks before, those in the secret not doubting, probably, that they would obtain an easy entrance. Upon trying to open the supposed-to-be-unfastened door, they found, to their ill-concealed chagrin, that it was as firmly closed as ever. Nothing now remained for them to do but to go through the forenoon service outside again, I and my friends worshiping in the hall at the same time.

At the noon recess, several of the influential members of the Baptist society, becoming tired, if not ashamed, of such proceedings, approached some of my friends with assurances that if the house were opened in the afternoon we might occupy it in peace. But they either were unwarranted in giving those assurances or were deceived by their pastor. For when we approached the house, led by the selectmen with the keys, Mr. Fisher and his allies rushed forward and as soon as the door was unlocked both parties crowded in, filling the vestibule instantly, while considerable numbers remained outside. The padlocked inner door prevented further advance and I, who was directly behind the selectmen, requested them not to permit entrance to the audience room till the situation could be somewhat discussed. I then demanded of Mr. Fisher what such conduct meant. The town had voted us the house and we had been promised the use of it by some of his leading men for the afternoon. He was furious with rage, declared the town had nothing to do with the house, and silently ignored the action of those who had made pledges to us. I remonstrated calmly but firmly, maintaining our rights and declaring that I should do nothing in violation of the true Christian spirit and rules of propriety. God could not be worshiped acceptably in the midst of such confusion and strife. Some of his people made a proposition to withdraw and leave us in possession of the place; but he and his more zealous supporters would not hear to it, determined as they were to force themselves in if possible. I then said: — "Let the door be opened and if Mr. Fisher does not conduct himself decently, I certainly shall and will publish his doings to the world."

The door was then unlocked, the selectmen entering first, with me immediately in the rear. We proceeded slowly and becomingly up the central aisle toward the pulpit, but Mr. Fisher crowded in as quickly as possible and rushed at rapid speed by one of the side aisles to the pulpit stairs, which he reached about the same time the head of our column did, and bouncing up them cried out as he arrived at the top panting for breath, "Let us begin the worship of God by singing, etc." Some of his people had now entered their pews and, as the whole matter had been pre-arranged between pastor and flock, commenced singing. The whole scene was so ludi-

crous and withal such a mockery of public worship that
I remained but a moment in the pulpit, which I had
entered simultaneously with the breathless parson, then
signified my purpose to retire to Mr. Foster's hall, which
I did, followed by my part of the congregation.

What followed? Intensified excitement throughout the
community and in all the neighboring region. I at once
wrote and published a pamphlet letter to Mr. Fisher,
entitled "The Furious Priest Reproved," in which I
reviewed the whole case and characterized the proceedings in such terms of reprobation and censure as justice
demanded. The pamphlet had an extensive circulation
and a greedy perusal. By the affair I seemed to gain
reputation and influence, while my opponent suffered in
proportion. The question of the control of the meetinghouse was ere long decided by the court against the
Baptists and they abandoned it altogether, building a
new one for their own undisputed occupancy and use.
Mr. Fisher lost the respect and confidence of the people
at large, and a few years after left the place for a
more congenial home. In reading over, at this late period
of my life, my only preserved copy of my letter to him
and reviewing the whole strange scene it describes, I am
confirmed in the truth, justice, and rectitude of my
course, and can see nothing on my own part to be
ashamed of or to reproach myself for, though I am
obliged to regard all such religious squabbles as more or
less pitiable and much to be deprecated. With my
matured knowledge of human nature and of the workings of a perverted religious zeal, I make more allowances for my antagonist in this encounter than at the
time of it, having learned that *conscience* and *will* may
honestly fall into deplorable mistakes — mistakes oftentimes more to be pitied than blamed.

On Sunday, June 22d of this year, my wife brought
forth our first-born child, a son, to whom was given my
own name, Adin Ballou, Jr. This event was a joyous
one in our marital experience, though the constitution of

the mother was so frail that it taxed her physical energies to the utmost extent. The little one throve well as a babe and through its early childhood, awakening fond hopes in the parental breast for long years on its part, and great usefulness and honor in time to come. But these hopes were vain, for it was stricken with a fatal disease when in the tenth year of its age and was translated to the heritage of the immortals Feb. 10, 1833, as will be more fully noted hereafter.

In the month following, as foreshadowed at the close of the preceding chapter, I received an invitation from the First Universalist society in Boston, originally organized under Rev. John Murray, the reputed founder of that faith in America, to supply their pulpit six months as a candidate for the vacant pastorate. Rev. Paul Dean had, during his ministry, gathered about him a large congregation from which a colony of his devoted friends had gone out, erected and dedicated a new house of worship on Bulfinch street, and persuaded him to resign his position and take charge of the movement there. Those remaining in the old association, whose meeting-house was on Hanover street, had heard as many other preachers as they desired and voted to give me the proposed six months' probation. I shared the good will of surrounding Universalist ministers, and had been favorably heard for several Sundays by those now extending to me the offer as previously narrated; yet it was a somewhat presumptuous undertaking for me to engage in, considering the immaturity of my youth and the poverty of my qualifications. But I consented to make the trial. My friends in Medway, Bellingham, and South Mendon professed to be sorry to part with me, but acquiesced cheerfully in my decision and wished me success, it having been our mutual understanding that I was at liberty to accept any such call, should it come to me. My Boston candidacy began on the last Sunday in July, 1823, and continued till the third in January, 1824. During that period (my wife and child being with me a part of the time) I gained many ardent friends in the congregation and outside, and succeeded in my pulpit labors quite as much to my own satisfaction and that of my hearers as I had a right to expect, though I finally failed in the object sought. A single competitor entered the field, who, being in many respects my superior at the time, carried off the prize. This was Rev. Sebastian Streeter, who was willing to close his pastorate at Portsmouth, N. H., where he had been eight years. He was then at the zenith of his ability, experience, judgment, and pulpit eloquence, and he very naturally triumphed, receiving a considerable majority of the suffrages. Nearly one-third of the society adhered to me with considerable tenacity, but, of course, submitted to superior numbers. If my ambitious hopes were somewhat dashed, I had no right nor disposition to complain. I had much more reason for thankfulness than for murmuring, for I had gained many friends and the preference was, on the whole, wise and best for all concerned.

Just before entering upon my Boston candidacy, I had been proposed and formally admitted to the fellowship of the Southern Association of Universalists, assembled in semi-annual session at Stafford, Ct., though I was not personally present on the occasion. At the annual session, held in Milford, Mass., the next December, I was regularly ordained with the usual ceremonies, as is attested by the following certificate:

"This certifies that Brother Adin Ballou was ordained to the work of the ministry of reconciliation at the annual meeting of the Southern Association of Universalists convened at Milford, Ms., Dec. 10, 1823.   JACOB FRIEZE, *Clerk.*

During my six months' engagement in Boston, I solemnized the first three of my marriages, now (1882) numbering over one thousand. At its close, on the evening of the third Sunday in January, 1824, I preached my final sermon from the text: — " And now, brethren, I commend you to God and the word of his grace, which

CALL TO MILFORD ACCEPTED.

is able to build you up and to give you an inheritance among them that are sanctified."—*Acts* 20 : 32. Leaving the people with cordial good feeling and in a prosperous condition, I returned to my family. The call of the society, given soon after to Rev. Mr. Streeter, left me at liberty to find an available opening at my convenience and pleasure.

Several invitations were in prospect, but without waiting for a more desirable location, I accepted the one coming to me shortly afterward from the Universalist society in Milford, Mass., whither I removed my family about the first of April. This society had had two pastors before me, viz : Rev. Thomas Whittemore, then of Cambridgeport, for one year, and Rev. Jacob Frieze, who had just been called to Marlborough, for two years. Their salaries had been three hundred and thirty (330) dollars per annum, and mine was to be the same. The society was comparatively small and deemed this sum a handsome one, since it was the same paid by the Milford Congregational parish to their minister, Rev. David Long. The Methodist society in North Purchase, the only other one in town at that time was feeble and could not give their pastor anything like so good a pecuniary support. The whole population of the place scarcely exceeded twelve hundred and its since large and thriving industries were then in their incipient stages of development. Tenements were scarce and crowded and it was with difficulty that I could find a place suited to the needs of myself and family. I finally obtained one that served us for a while until we could do better. It consisted of two rooms and a few exterior accommodations, three-fourths of a mile east of the meeting-house, in the dwelling of Mr. Zebadiah Flagg, one of my people. The quarters were more limited than we had been accustomed to, but we made ourselves comfortable in them, and there we found ourselves domiciled on my twenty-first birthday, April 23, 1824.

My Twenty-second Year. I now applied myself diligently to my pulpit, pastoral, and miscellaneous duties, preaching often three times on Sunday,—twice regularly at home, and in the evening in some one of the neighboring towns; officiating at funerals within the same circuit, solemnizing marriages, and attending to incidental domestic affairs. My people received my services appreciatively and our mutual relations were pleasant and harmonious. Perley Hunt, Esq., Col. Ariel Bragg, Col. Sullivan Sumner, and others of prominent standing in the community were among the foremost of my people.

The town in which I was now located had been divided since 1819 into two very distinct and determined parties — the Parish party, so-called, and the Town party. The former consisted of persons attached to or sympathizing with the old or Congregational parish; the latter of Universalists, Methodists, and people having no religious affiliations — the promiscuous population. This division originated in conflicting claims to the old precinct meeting-house, or rather, perhaps, in a difference of opinion respecting the location of a new one. When the eastern part of Mendon was incorporated as the town of Milford in 1780, parochial affairs were assumed by the body corporate, and the existing house of worship was used for general public purposes. There was then only one religious organization in the place. In a few years the Universalist and Methodist societies were organized, while many persons signed off from the Standing Order or became indifferentists and refused to be taxed at all for the support of religious institutions, as formerly. This obliged the adherents of the old New England faith to reorganize, which they did under the name of the Congregational parish in 1815. Four years afterwards it was deemed advisable to build a new meeting-house, when a dispute arose whether the old site should be occupied by it or a new one selected, in which was involved the question of the ownership of the building. Those persons who favored the old site under the leadership of John Claflin, Esq., claimed that it belonged to the parish, while those who contended for a new site near where Dr. Fay's office stood, under the leadership of Peârley Hunt, Esq., claimed that it was the property of the town. Hence the names — Parish party and Town party. In the vote on the location, the Parish party prevailed, as they did finally on the matter of proprietorship before the courts, and proceeded to erect the new house accordingly. The minority of the parish then withdrew and joined the Universalists, the combined forces in due time setting about building a brick meeting-house, which they planned to be one foot larger on the ground than that of the parish, with a bell five hundred pounds heavier, and with a clock in its tower, which the other did not have. The Congregationalist house was dedicated Nov. 19, 1819; the Universalist, Jan. 10, 1821. By this time the conflicting parties were well-defined and belligerent to the highest degree. And the conflict thus inaugurated continued some fourteen years, entering more or less as a troublesome factor into all town affairs — into the consideration and decision of all public questions. Then a truce was sounded on both sides, a more peaceable era opened, and a growing spirit of mutual respect, unity, and co-operation sprang up, which has continued unto this day.

This conflict was at its highest pitch of intensity of purpose when I entered on my pastorate in 1824. I had no disposition to aggravate it and little power to mollify it. What I had, I found, after acquainting myself with the situation, must be exercised indirectly, prudently, and quietly. I took care not to add fuel to the flame, not to excite anyone by word or deed to greater partisan violence, but rather to moderate passion where I could, and above all, to set an example of courtesy, forbearance, and kindness in my personal intercourse with everybody. Two trifling incidents will illustrate my success in that direction.

I had been in town but a short time when a prominent leader of the parish, who enjoyed a joke and thought

the newly-come Universalist minister a proper subject for
one, was called upon by a colored wanderer from Connecticut and asked where he could get a night's lodging
gratis, as he had no money. "I belong to the hospital
at home," said he; "is there any hospital in these
parts?" "Oh, yes," answered the honorable wag,
"there is one down street kept by a Mr. Ballou." And
turning to his clerk, said: "Write this man a note of
introduction," at the same time dictating it as follows:
"Rev. Mr. Ballou: Please keep the bearer over night and
charge the same to him." No signature was appended.
After some trouble, the poor fellow found me in the
midst of a crowd on the common and handed me the
note. I saw that there was some trickery in the matter
and inquired who gave him the paper. "A fleshy man
they called the squire in the store near the other meeting-house. He said you kept a hospital and would let
me stay with you over night." "Well," I replied, "I
keep no hospital, as the squire very well knows. This
is an imposition on both of us. But you shall be cared
for. I cannot lodge you in my own house, but I will
pay for your entertainment with my good friend, Col.
Sumner, the tavern-keeper near by, and will introduce
you to him at once." He was astonished, but full of
thanks to me and indignant at the trickery played upon
him. He was well provided for 'till the next morning,
when he posted back to the squire and scolded him
sharply in his rude way for imposing on a poor wayfarer
and on so kind a gentleman as he found Mr. Ballou to
be. As the matter had already been pretty well ventilated in town and as several persons were listening to
the talk, the discomfited joker handed him a twenty-five-cent piece and told him to go along, which he at once
did, taking the road to Boston. I lost nothing by this
performance and never received another insult from the
Parish party.

A second incident, of an entirely different character, but
redounding equally to my credit, occurred not long after-

ward in connection with the annual town meeting in April. The ancient custom of opening the proceedings with prayer was still observed from year to year. Since the quarrel had been going on, the Town party being all the while in the ascendant in public affairs, Parson Long, the Parish clergyman, had not been invited to conduct that service, but it had been assigned to the Universalist and Methodist ministers alternately. At the time under notice, it fell to the former, and when the proper moment came, my friend, Col. Bragg, who was presiding, called upon me for the usual ceremonial. I was much surprised, being wholly a stranger to such a usage, and in no wise prepared for it. Moreover, it was as repugnant to my feelings as it was unexpected, for I knew in what an unprayerful, pugnacious state the minds of most of those present were, making the formality very much of a pious farce. My first impulse was to excuse myself outright, but I saw at once that this would hardly do. Instantly the thought flashed into my mind: "There stands Rev. Mr. Long, who would be glad of the chance; decline the honor and nominate him." In a moment this was done, and with proper deference to all present. Doubtless the moderator and people generally, as well as Mr. Long, were astonished; but the invitation was promptly accepted and the service satisfactorily rendered.

If I had carefully studied and devised a stroke of good policy, I could not have made a happier hit than was this unpremeditated act. It softened prejudice and won golden opinions in the Parish party, without disturbing the feelings of their opponents. I did not dream that it would have any effect beyond the passing occasion. But it did and much to my advantage. It not only pleased Mr. Long at the time, but secured his personal respect (which lasted, I believe, to the end of his days) and conciliated many of his people, who thereafter spoke of me as a gentleman and treated me accordingly. I never, before or since, received so much compliment and good will in return for so small an investment of makeshift civility.

During my first year in Milford, I ministered a considerable number of Sabbaths, either in person or by supply, to the society in Medway. This was pursuant to a mutual understanding between me and my people and was satisfactory to all parties concerned. I also made frequent exchanges with my ministerial brethren, some of whom occupied a high position and had an enviable reputation in the denomination. Among these were Revs. Hosea Ballou and Paul Dean of Boston, Hosea Ballou 2d. of Roxbury, and David Pickering of Providence, R. I. At the same time, my lectures and funeral addresses, which were then elaborate and carefully prepared sermons of an expository and argumentative character, were abundant at home and abroad.

In the summer of the same year I became a Freemason, passing through the first three degrees in Charity Lodge, Milford, of which I was, in orderly succession, a member, subordinate officer, and finally master. That lodge surrendered its charter and jewels a few years later to the Grand Lodge of Massachusetts, by reason of the violent anti-Masonic excitement which swept through the country, and other depressing circumstances. Before the close of 1825, I ascended through the Royal Arch degrees in Mount Lebanon Chapter in West Medway to those of knighthood in the Worcester County Encampment at Holden, since removed to Worcester and now known as the Worcester County Commandery. I had come to be much interested in the Masonic Order and its institutions, and especially in the broad fundamental principles of the fraternity therein represented. These commanded my reverence both in their theoretical and practical aspects, whatever might seem exceptional or doubtful in some incidentals. And although my interest abated somewhat in maturer age and under the pressure of more engrossing matters of thought and action, I still cherish a profound respect for the intrinsic essentials of Freemasonry, notwithstanding the furore of anti-Masonic denunciation which at one time threatened its existence.

There are few persons, institutions, or movements that have not their shady as well as their bright side. This has its defects and shortcomings in common with all human inventions. But its escutcheon is resplendent with "faith in God, hope in immortality, and charity to all mankind;" with "brotherly love, relief, and truth;" with "temperance, prudence, fortitude, and justice;" and with significant emblems of righteousness. It inculcates many great individual and social virtues, which, if they were faithfully practiced by its professors, would render it pre-eminently illustrious. But with all their failures, the Fraternity have not fallen so far below their acknowledged standard as has the nominal Christian Church. They have steered almost entirely clear of all mean proselytism, lust of dominion, monopolizing selfishness, and sanguinary persecution. On the other hand, they have done much to assuage intolerance, violence, and cruelty; to liberalize, genialize, civilize, and humanize mankind. The world has grievously needed the influence of the Order and still needs it. Therefore, it is not likely to be crushed out by its enemies nor to die out at any very early future of itself. When human society shall have fairly transcended it in absolute Christlikeness, doubtless its mission will terminate. Meantime, let anti-Masonic zealots demonstrate individually and socially that they have superseded its excellence and are therefore worthy to minister at its funeral.

On the 3d of August, 1825, my friend, Lebbeus Gaskill of South Mendon, colonel of the 2d Regiment, 1st Brigade, 6th Division Mass. Militia, did me the honor of placing me on his staff as chaplain. I received my commission as such Aug. 9th, and continued in the office till formally discharged July 13, 1837. I accepted the position with pleasure and officiated on various occasions to the best of my ability — always, I believe, to general satisfaction. Many a pleasant interview I enjoyed with my fellow-officers at their various meetings and refreshment tables. My first service in this new capacity was rendered at the autumnal muster of the regiment at Mendon on the ancient Hastings training field. An old Congregationalist deacon, not knowing me, was somewhat taken with my prayer and warmly commended it. But when told upon inquiry who I was uttered an exclamatory " Oh!" in blank astonishment and at once subsided. A prejudiced Calvinist, who knew me, commenting upon it, said it sounded more like an oration than a prayer, which was probably a fair hit; for a military prayer ought to be more oratorical than reverential to be in good keeping with its surroundings.

The reader may wish to know how I now view that military chaplainship and its duties. With little admiration and self-complacency, yet not with profound compunction and shame. For I was acting up to my then highest light. I had not at the time a thought or a scruple against war *per se* as un-Christian and wrong, and of course not against training and preparation for war. Like all others, I claimed to be opposed to wicked wars, under the presumption that there were sometimes righteous ones which I could approve. I simply acted according to my education and predilections. The all-important truth that Christ moved on a higher moral plane than that of civil society and national government as they now are and called his disciples to rise and act with him on his distinctive plane had not at that day shot its faintest ray into my murky understanding. I had no more doubt that civil government, backed by necessary deadly force, was consistent with genuine Christianity, and that Christian ministers and people ought to act in it in both political and military capacities than I had that they ought to be Christians. I took it for granted, as most good people do, that there is no plane or position distinctively higher than existing governmental civilization, which can be occupied to any practical advantage by eminently advanced minds, whether claiming to be Christians, or progressionists of some other name; as I also did that no Christianity can be organized above and in the lead of the prevailing civilization of the world. On this ground, Christianity must play the part of handmaid of such civilization, but attempt little or nothing more. On this ground, war must be provided for with all its requisites till the necessity for it shall cease by the universal prevalence of wisdom, righteousness, and love on earth—an era inconceivably remote under the reproductive genius of the politico-military system. In this view, chaplains of the army, navy, militia, etc., are as necessary, salutary, and respectable as voting citizens or any class of functionaries that co-operate in sustaining the existing institutions of civil society. So thinking in my youth, I acted accordingly. Besides, I had, as already indicated, the military, political, and civic instincts in my very nature, and it is no wonder that a regimental chaplaincy was congenial to my taste. The wonder is that such stock was ever fashioned into a conscientious, uncompromising, Christian, Non-resistant. But so it was and is.

I spent the winter months of 1824-25 in teaching what was known as the North Purchase school, two miles out of the village of Milford, in addition to my pulpit and pastoral labors. I had some eighty pupils under my care, ranging from those four and five years of age, just entering upon their educational tutelage, to grown-up young men and women, expecting to finish their common schooling with that term. My duties, so varied and multitudinous, kept my heart, head, and hands full, and I wrought persistently at my different posts of service. It was impossible for any one teacher to do full justice to such a throng of pupils as I had in charge, many of whom were poorly equipped and imperfectly classified. But all went prosperously on to the closing examination, which elicited flattering commendations from the superintending town committee. I won the respect, love, and general obedience of those under me and had little occasion to employ harsh corrections. One case of discipline which had passed from my recollection has recently been recalled by an elderly matron, then a little girl in the school. The peculiarity of it, reminding one of the methods employed by the philosopher, A. Bronson Alcott, in his far-famed Boston school, justifies a description of it in these pages.

It seems, according to my informant's statement, that I had among the rest a somewhat troublesome boy whose misbehavior evoked repeated reproofs on my part, but to little purpose. One day, after some fresh violation of the rules, I summoned him to my desk in unusually stern tones of voice, saying to him as he stood before me that I plainly saw that he meant to have some one whipped and the matter must be settled forthwith. "Now," said I, "here is my rod and I suppose it must be used or you cannot be cured of your misconduct. I cannot bear to whip you; perhaps it will do you more good if you whip me. At any rate, I have concluded to try it." Whereupon I took off my coat and having laid it aside, handed him the rod and told him to use it on me long enough to make him a good boy. Refusing to take it, I insisted that he should, inasmuch as it was necessary for him to do so in order to teach him obedience to the rules of the school. The boy broke down, wept bitterly, and promised that he would not repeat his offences. I then sent him to his seat amid the amazement of the whole school, and he gave me no further trouble. After the termination of my winter engagement, I gave myself with renewed zeal to the current duties of my home and pastorate, reaching while busily engaged in them the end of the twenty-second year of my life.

At this stage of my narrative, which finds me well settled under Universalist auspices in my new field of labor and active in my professional work, it may reasonably be asked: "What was the religious condition of your society in Milford at that time and what thus far were the fruits of your ministry as an ambassador for Christ?" Not very flattering in either respect to the ambition or reputation of a devoted, faithful, Christian pastor. In the estimation of so-called Evangelical religionists, I was not such a pastor, nor scarcely was I according to my own then best ideal, and much less according to my present theoretical standard. I was, however, sincerely desirous of preaching divine truth and of promoting human righteousness, as I then understood them, and current circumstances seemed to afford me favorable opportunities for doing so. And I have no doubt that in both of the particulars named, I exerted on the whole a salutary and effective influence. But I do not think my own intellectual, moral, and spiritual state was high enough to accomplish much in the way of raising the people of my charge to the true Christ-plane of thought and life. There was then no church organization among them, no meetings for social Christian culture, and no Sunday-school for the religious training of children and youth. Nor was there much, if any, perceptible desire for these institutions and helps to virtue and holiness. On the contrary, many were prejudiced against and adverse to them as savoring of "orthodox" superstition, craft, or bigotry. Even my own mind had been so repelled and sickened by the excommunicative and damnatory spirit of the dominant church religionists that I was in no haste to re-embrace their forms, modes, and expedients. Though in themselves good and perhaps necessary to human welfare, they had become so associated with irrational faith, terrorism, spasmodic emotionality, superstitious pietism, and sanctimonious cant, that I was not in a mood to separate them from their abuses and urge upon my hearers their right uses. I had swung off into a sphere of theological protest against the dogma of endless punishment and all kindred notions derogatory to the moral character of God. I was in the midst of a polemical war with vast hosts of bitter antagonists whose watchword was *No quarter to Universalists of any school.* I neither asked nor expected any, and fought accordingly. The whole denomination of which I had become a member was at that time in the same combative sphere — one not very conducive of personal and social piety of the constructive type. How it could have been otherwise in the then warlike stage of theological opinion is hardly conceivable. If we had been ever so devotedly intent on the cultivation of strictly personal religion, the whole solid phalanx of our opponents was inflexibly resolved that we could not and should not have anything of the sort except on their platform and after their fashion. For a person to repent, become regenerated, and enter into church relations while in full belief of universal salvation was in their view not only impossible, but absurd and ridiculous. Men must believe that God loved only his friends and hated his enemies, certainly in the next life, and that his merciless vengeance awaited all who died in their sins, else there was no adequate motive or reason for any one to try to be personally and experimentally a disciple of Christ. But that folly and bigotry was destined to be overcome by valorous conflict and give place to better theories and convictions.

I must also state that nearly all my congregation, seldom exceeding one hundred and fifty persons, had grown up as outsiders of the old churches; that some of them had been more or less skeptical with respect to revealed religion; and that as Universalists they were of the *ultra* school, with scarcely a Restorationist, properly so-called, among them. Even my own Restorationism had receded into the background, becoming faint and feeble in its abeyance to the then predominant no-future-punishment doctrine of the denomination. In view of such a peculiar and complicated state of things, the nature and success of my ministry in those days must be judged. The special reforms which afterwards agitated the pulpit and public mind — temperance, anti-slavery, peace, etc., — had not then been sufficiently developed to attract attention. So the old social habits, customs, and ideas remained undisturbed among the people of Milford, as elsewhere throughout the country. Nevertheless, all things considered, I cannot but persuade myself that my preaching, pastoral labors, and personal influence not only rendered no one morally and spiritually worse for this world or the next, but were salutary to some positive and appreciative extent and accomplished considerable good in the way of establishing religious opinions on a more rational basis than before in the community, commending practical Christian righteousness to my hearers as of inestimable worth, diffusing the spirit of charity and good will among the people at large, and making divine truth and love a power of redemption in the hearts and minds of men.

CHAPTER VII.

1825-1828.

PROVISION FOR A HOME — FUNERAL EXPERIENCES — BEREAVEMENTS — FOURTH OF JULY — CALL AND REMOVAL TO NEW YORK — EDITORSHIP.

THE labors of a duly settled minister of the Christian religion, though many and various, are much the same, generally speaking, from year to year, and to mention them in chronological order and detail would involve wearisome and needless repetition. Only those, therefore, of special interest and importance in themselves considered, or in their relation to the personality of the writer or to the thought and life of the world at large, will be chronicled at length or more than hinted at in these pages, although months and even years may be passed over without reference to anything transpiring in them. In a narrative like this one here given, the omitted particulars are so well known as to be easily supplied, if necessary, by the reader.

Passing over then the first half of the twenty-third year of my life, I come to the autumn of 1825, when I purchased of my friend, Col. Sullivan Sumner, an acre of land in the village of Milford, for the purpose of building upon it at an early day a suitable and permanent home. It was the lot on which now stands house No. 28 Main Street, owned wholly or in part by George B. Pierce. I soon afterwards planned a dwelling thirty-eight feet in length by thirty-two in width, two stories high and nine feet between joints, fronting the north, with a sufficient yard between it and the road. On the

BUILDING OF A HOME.

first floor were a parlor, dining-room, and kitchen of large size, with the needful halls, pantries, and other smaller apartments desirable for domestic uses; while on the second floor were two large chambers in front and one of still greater measurement in the southeast corner designed for a schoolroom. The remaining area was divided as necessity and convenience seemed to dictate. A contract for the erection of the structure above the underpinning was made with Col. Sumner, who was to have the whole completed according to specifications and ready for occupancy on or before the first of the following August. The cellar and foundations were to be otherwise provided for and made ready for the superstructure in due season.

This undertaking, entered upon with fond expectations, was rather a wild and extravagant one for a young minister with little capital, a meagre income, and no certainty of a permanent residence in the town. But various considerations weighed with me in deciding to enter upon it. I was very much in need of a more eligible and commodious residence than the one I occupied; the estate, it was said, would be salable at any time without loss; a part of it might be rented, if I desired; it was so arranged that I could open a select school in it and so increase my annual receipts; my principal creditor, Col. Sumner, was a very kind and indulgent man and would favor me in the matter of payment for the land and building, while other friends would give me an occasional lift; and, to cap the climax, I had a large amount of hope. So I went ahead with my project and took the consequences, some of which proved to be good, others indifferent, and yet others — the pecuniary ones — bad. None of my creditors' lost anything by the affair, though it was some seven years before the last installment of the indebtedness incurred was paid. Circumstances so changed that I occupied the premises only about half of that period. So far as they furnished me a home, they added to my convenience, comfort, and happiness; otherwise they occasioned me many outlays, anxieties, and vexations. I rented them at much disadvantage and finally sold them at considerable pecuniary loss. My experience, I think, was that of the general average in analagous cases. I do not advise others, though like myself well-disposed and over-hopeful, to follow my example.

Other occurrences of quite a different nature took place during the year 1825, which left a lasting impression on my memory. Two of these were connected with my funeral ministrations. The first to be mentioned is almost laughable in its leading incident. Mr. Darius Morse of Franklin, a Universalist in faith, invited me to conduct the services upon the death of his mother. The celebrated Dr. Emmons, then far advanced in years, was still pastor of the old church of that town, and they were few who dared dissent from his distinctive theological teachings. Mr. Morse was one of these, and so, when his mother passed away, he turned from the venerable champion of the ancient beliefs to one of the larger hope touching the plan and providence of God; but invited two of the elderly members of the Doctor's church, to which the deceased had belonged, to assist as bearers at the burial. When they learned that a young heretic was to officiate on the occasion, they refused to act as desired unless they could be roomed out of hearing of the preacher while the service was going on. Mr. Morse accommodated them by assigning them to a chamber in a remote part of the house. Thither they repaired in season to prevent contamination and there remained till all danger of that sort was over.

In untroubled ignorance of this arrangement, I went through with what devolved on me to do, opening with a brief invocation, then preaching a regular sermon from Isaiah 25 : 7-8, and closing with a funeral prayer and benediction, as was my custom in those days. When all was over, the two self-secluded bearers appeared to perform, with others, the duty belonging to them. Of their exploits I was informed not long after, as I was also in due time of the light in which their conduct was regarded, both by individuals in the community and by Dr. Emmons himself. Laughed at by those of less religious turn of mind, they repaired to the house of their pastor to tell him how bravely they had stood by their creed, and to obtain his commendation, as they no doubt believed they would. But Dr. Emmons was not the man to relish their sort of tactics. And so after questioning them closely and getting all the information he wanted in the matter, he exclaimed: "What! What! Shut yourselves up in a chamber during the services! I am ashamed of you! You'll make people think your own faith is pretty weak if you act so cowardly as that! I don't advise you to run after such preaching, but if you have to go to a funeral, don't hide away from it as if you were afraid to trust your creed in its presence." They undoubtedly retired from the interview with more mortification than comfort, well cured of all such errantry.

About a month after this ludicrous affair took place, another of a more serious nature and of more immediate concern to me transpired, which taught me a salutary lesson. Within my own proper field of pastoral labor there had lived a family, consisting of the two parents and several children, indirectly connected with my parish. The husband and father, though possessed of a handsome estate, was penurious and miserly, living shabbily himself and denying his family the comforts and even the necessaries of life. The wife and mother, a most estimable woman, discharged the duties devolving upon her conscientiously and faithfully for many years, but finally by overwork, privation, neglect, and abuse, broke down in health and became a victim of consumption. Under these distressing circumstances, her husband made less provision for her comfort and happiness than before. At length her parents took her home to care for and nurse during her evidently few remaining days on earth. I frequently called to see the suffering woman, as her life was slowly ebbing away. In one of my last conversations with her, after referring sorrowfully to the cold and cruel treatment she had received from her husband, she spoke of her funeral (at which I had already engaged to minister) as soon to take place, and expressed the hope that I would so admonish and reprove him on that occasion as to make him realize his blameworthiness and guilt. It seemed to be a charge given me on her dying bed and I promised to fulfil it. She soon passed through the gate of death and arrangements were made for her obsequies in the Universalist house of worship.

The occasion was one that imposed unusual responsibility upon me, as a discourse was expected suited to the well-known circumstances of the case. I therefore prepared myself with great care, writing out in full what I had to say, which I was not accustomed to do except in extraordinary emergencies. The manuscript I have preserved — the oldest of its kind that ever came from my pen. To indicate the fidelity with which I discharged the trust committed to me from a dying bed, I subjoin a few disconnected extracts. Taking a text from Job xxi: 23, 25, 26, I first unfolded the subject there brought to notice in its general aspects, and made an application of it to the life, character, and trials of the deceased in such a way as to commend and honor her name and memory. I then proceeded to address the mourners directly, and particularly the husband, who sat cowering among the family relatives in the midst of a large promiscuous congregation, gathered for various reasons, no doubt, from all classes of the town's population. The passages which I deem it proper to reproduce are as follows:

"I commence with you, my friend, who claim the first and nearest relationship—that of husband—to the deceased woman who lies in silence before me. I beseech you in the name of Almighty God to hear patiently the solemn admonition of one who feels for you nothing but kindness and pity such as cannot be uttered. You never injured a hair of my head personally, but by a strange course of conduct, to me altogether unaccountable, towards your deceased wife, you have inflicted a grievous blow on my humane feelings and thereby laid me under the painful necessity of counseling you in the name of Jehovah for your good this day. Friend, bear with me and pardon my plainness, for I must be no flatterer or hypocrite towards you; otherwise, my God, who hears me, would smite me with a just condemnation. I must tell you what you can but already know, that you have lost one of the best of wives —one of the most devoted and faithful of bosom companions. She lives no longer yours — no longer the victim of sickness and death, or, what is still worse, ingratitude. But though silent in death, she still speaks to you through me. She solemnly asks why you treated her as you did; why you neglected her after she had been so faithful to you; why you abandoned her in her last sickness and in the hour of expiring agony! Did she deserve all this at your hands? Was she unworthy to receive your kind attention; unworthy to be benefited by the abundance of your wealth; unworthy to die in your house and in your arms? . . . . . . Alas, my wretched friend, how can you answer these solemn questions? Have you done what you have in secret? No; but openly, before all the world, as it were, as well as under the inspecting eye of that God who is full of justice and judgment, who brought you into existence and has mercifully bestowed upon you all that you call yours, who has wept, if such a thing could be, at your doings, and whose warning voice has so often reproved you and called on you to turn from your errors.

"Let me ask you if a great sin lies not at the door of your heart, unrepented of and big with impending woes. Flee, oh, flee, friend, from them. Repent and seek shelter in the pardoning mercy of that God to whom thou art answerable, but who is a compassionate and sin-forgiving God. Bring forth fruits meet for repentance. Then God and good men will forgive thee. . . . . . Thou canst not undo altogether what thou hast done, but thou canst do what remains to be done. Break off thy inordinate love for the treasures of this vain and transitory world, for thou, too, must die and leave them all in a few more passing years. Let not another day go by before thou confessest unto God, unto thy father- and mother-in-law, unto all this circle of mourners whose feelings thou hast injured, and unto the whole public before whose eyes thou hast done this great wrong. Go and pay the uttermost farthing of the expense incurred by reason of the sickness and death of her whose remains we are about to house in the tomb. Take these motherless children and be both a father and mother to them. Withhold nothing from them that can tend to make them comfortable. . . . . . Let them be trained up in the nurture and admonition of the Lord — in the love of virtue and truth. Do all this, and the manes of thy departed wife will be appeased. God will smile mercifully upon thee, prosperity and happiness will attend thee, and all will believe thee to be a sincere penitent for sin, and a good man.

"O that God might sanctify unto thee this event of his providence for thy good! If thou turn unto him with thy whole heart, thou wilt be safe—thou shalt be blest before him. But if not . . . I can hold nothing before thee but the blackness and darkness of woe. For the chastising hand of God will lie heavy upon thee, and thou canst never escape till by salutary correction he has brought thee back to the ways of righteousness. Think, friend, seriously, of all I have said and lay up no hardness against me for uttering what has been so trying and painful to me, what I should never have said had I not felt that God had laid the duty upon me. It is my fervent prayer that thou mayst follow my counsels and enter into rest. I leave thee in the disposing hand of God. May he be gracious unto thee according to the multitude of his mercies."

I have made these quotations as a funeral curiosity and as suggestive of a lesson to be pondered and taken solemnly to heart. My whole discourse and especially the portion thus given was listened to with profound attention and mingled emotions that cannot be described. Many of those present expressed approval of my testimony as just, though some no doubt questioned silently the wisdom of it. One heart was deeply grieved by it, that of a sister of the inculpated man, who acknowledged the painful facts in the case and their wrongfulness, but pleaded that her brother was insane and so not responsible for his conduct. At first I could give no credence to this plea, but time proved it to be substantially true. His mental aberration, then unknown save by a few who were brought into close contact with him, increased as the years went by until he became a confirmed lunatic, not of the violent type, but of so pronounced and positive a character as to necessitate the appointment of a legal guardian to have constant charge of him and of his affairs. He lived, however, to a good old age, and when he at length passed away I was called upon to minister at his obsequies.

My course in this matter, which had been suggested and even enjoined by the suffering victim of neglect and abuse on her death-bed, and pursued under a profound sense of duty and with the conviction that some good would come of it to the offender and possibly to others, was subjected to a very careful and searching review on my part not long afterward, whereby I was brought to the conclusion that I had acted unwisely, and to no such salutary effect as I had anticipated. I therefore never again allowed myself on a funeral occasion to sit in judgment on sinful mourners, nor administer special personal rebuke even to notorious evil-doers. I had become convinced that such is not the time, place, and method for serving the cause of truth or promoting the moral and spiritual improvement of my fellow-men. Neither the guilty nor the innocent are made better thereby. Very likely, in my purpose to avoid a recurrence of the mistake I made in this instance, I may have gone many times to the other extreme and estimated the virtues of both the departed and their survivors too highly, without intending to justify or palliate anything wrong in human conduct or character. But a fault in this direction, especially when proceeding from kindness of heart, seldom does moral harm.

Three other deaths of more than ordinary personal interest to me occurred during the year 1825, subjecting me to a deep sense of bereavement and producing a lasting impression upon my heart and memory. The first of these took place March 27th, removing from the scenes of earth and time the oldest member and one of the leading supporters of my society — the venerable and worthy Wales Cheney in the 93d year of his age. He was a man of good common sense, rigid justice, true to his word, outspoken to bluntness, strictly temperate, exemplary in all his habits, scrupulously conscientious, a little eccentric in some of his ways, but of kind and generous sympathies. Both he and his son Alexander, who cared for him in his declining years, were earnest Universalists and steadfast friends of mine, and his decease was a great grief to me.

Near the close of the year my half-sister, Mrs. Rozina (Ballou) Arnold, the oldest of my father's children, died in child-bed at the age of 42 — a great and sad bereavement to her family and a large circle of relations and friends. She was a woman of many excellent qualities and a noble heart, but sensitive to adverse experiences and subject to great depression of spirit and over-anxiety amid the trials through which she was called to pass. The loss of a greatly beloved and tenderly cherished daughter just blooming into youthful womanhood in the summer of 1824 was a terrible affliction to her and nearly crushed out her life. She recovered in a measure from the shock which so utterly prostrated her, but not sufficiently to rally from the exhaustion incident to the birth of twin daughters a year and a half later — a few days after which event, in which she greatly rejoiced at the time, her spirit passed on to the unseen world. She was the fourth of my father's children to enter that world and shares the rest and reward that there await all true and loving souls. Clouds and darkness seemed to hover over her departure hence, and to her husband and little ones it was indeed shrouded in gloom, but divine love and wisdom meant it for good — sometime to be understood and gratefully acknowledged.

Still another visitation of a similar kind occurred about the same date as the one just named. It was the decease of Mrs. Joanna (Sayles) Sweet, wife of Jesse B. Sweet of Providence, R. I., a favorite sister of my wife, next older than herself. The two had grown up in loving intimacy from childhood, and their marriages were consummated not far apart. My wife felt this bereavement most keenly, as also did the whole family circle. The departed left infant children needing a mother's care and love. She was an amiable, excellent woman, whose spirit home must be a blessed one.

Little of a personal, professional, denominational or general nature transpired during the year 1827 that I deem worthy of record. During the spring and summer months my house, contracted for late the previous season, had been in process of erection, the foundations having been prepared, and the grounds put in proper order under my own immediate supervision, though I received substantial help in executing the work from kind friends who rendered me gratuitous service and from hired jobbers or day laborers employed as they seemed to be needed. Much of the work, however, was performed by myself at such times and in such a manner as my other regular duties allowed. I was naturally ambitious to have the oversight of these outside matters and to take an active part in carrying them forward to completion according to my own choice and taste. I had been brought up to rough manual labor such as is incident to the care and management of a large farm, and deemed myself competent to judge fairly well how the task in hand ought to be accomplished. The result justified myconfidence in my own ability in that direction—at any rate, I was satisfied and contented with what was done.

At length the house was finished, its surroundings were put in decent condition, and the premises were ready for occupancy. About the first of September, I and my little family were nicely settled in the new home and the machinery of our domestic life began to move under more agreeable conditions and with better prospects than ever before. I immediately opened a private school, as provided for in the original plan of my dwelling, and found myself encompassed and burdened with cares and duties many and various, which taxed to the utmost my time, strength, and energy of body, mind, and soul. I seemed to be firmly established in my lot and dreamed little of the changes that awaited me at an early day.

For the greater part of a year all things went smoothly on without jar or disturbance of any kind and without premonition or expectation of what was soon to come to pass. As the anniversary of American Independence, 1827, drew near, the Republican citizens of Milford resolved to celebrate the day in some becoming manner, and I was favored with an invitation to deliver the oration in my own church, more commonly known as the "brick meeting-house." Patriotism — civil, military, and religious — was then an essential part of my Christianity and I cheerfully accepted the proffered honor.

The occasion was one of unusual importance and one long remembered by those participating in it. Extraordinary preparations were made for it. Besides the oration, the dinner, and a grand military display, with martial music and other accompaniments, there was to be a formal presentation of a "splendid standard" by the ladies of the town to the long-famous Artillery Company, which had been organized in 1803 under Pearley Hunt, Capt., as a testimonial of respect and admiration. Announcement was duly made in all the neighboring towns of what was to be done and such a time was provided for and expected as Milford had never seen before.

Nor were the promise and anticipation unfulfilled. The day was ushered in not only by bells and cannon, but by a resonant and copious thunderstorm, the last of which, however, soon passed away, leaving as clear a sky and atmosphere as mortals could desire. The programme was carried out in full and every thing went off to universal satisfaction. The streets were thronged with people from all the surrounding region, eager to share in the festivities and keep in patriotic fashion the nation's holiday. The more formal proceedings began with the presentation of the flag. The company to be honored was out in full numbers and bright uniforms,

Capt. Clark Sumner commanding it, with Lieut. Isaac Davenport second officer, and John Corbett, Jr., third or standard bearer. A suitable platform had been erected on the common where the exercises were to take place, and where in due season the principal actors in the scene were gathered, surrounded by interested multitudes of people. A prayer having been offered, Miss Lucy Hunt, eldest daughter of Pearley Hunt, Esq., (with Miss Laura Ann Adams on her right and Miss Harriet Hunt on her left, all tastefully attired,) came forward bearing the elegant gift, and partially unfurling it, presented it with an appropriate address to 2d Lieut. Corbett. He received it with an appreciative response, at the close of which the band struck up one of their liveliest airs, amid whose inspiring strains and the plaudits of the delighted populace, the ladies were escorted back to Col. Sumner's hotel, whence they came.

A long civic procession was immediately formed, and began its march through some of the principal streets to the meeting-house, led by an imposing array of soldiery. The auditorium of the building was crowded to the full, many desiring entrance being obliged to remain outside. The oration, which was the principal feature of that part of the celebration, was delivered at the proper time, being preceded and followed by anthems, prayers, odes, and other customary accompaniments. There was nothing unique, profound, or eloquent about it, but it probably compared favorably with the old-style productions of that sort. A copy of it was asked for the press and the request being granted, a considerable edition was at once printed and widely distributed, a few numbers of which are still in my possession and will be preserved wholly or in part with a complete set of my published works.

The services at the church having been concluded, such of the audience as were disposed, with others of like mind, repaired in processional order to the dinner-tables — those for the ladies being spread in the hotel, the others under spacious tents or awnings outside where the post-prandial exercises were held. These were presided over, if my memory serves me, by Pearley Hunt, Esq., assisted by Newell Nelson, Esq., as toastmaster — most of what transpired consisting of regular and volunteer toasts, which, as they were announced, were washed down after the old ante-Temperance fashion, and responded to by cannonry and strains of martial music.

Without going into much further detail in regard to what took place on this occasion, I must speak of one laughable incident connected with the after-dinner festivities. Among those present was Mr. Timothy Walker, an elderly citizen of Hopkinton, who had distinguished himself somewhat during or soon after the war of 1812, by publishing several magniloquent letters to Gen. William Hull, of ignoble fame arising from his surrender of Detroit to the British. Opportunity being given for volunteer sentiments, Mr. Walker rose, saying to the toastmaster that he had one to offer which he hoped would be received without local offence. Whereupon Esquire Nelson in strong, sonorous voice, called out, "Citizens, please give attention to a volunteer toast from Mr. Timothy Walker, author of letters to Gen. Hull." Mr. Walker in sharp, age-cracked tones started off in a long sentiment, prepared no doubt with much care for the occasion. When about half way through it he paused for a moment to take breath. The director of the artillery, supposing he had finished, signaled the cannonier accordingly, when *boom* went the six-pounder and up struck the band, to the great merriment of those who understood the situation. But Mr. Walker, not in the least disconcerted, kept his standing, and when the music ceased cried out: "Mr. President and fellow citizens, you have been too fast for me; I hadn't got half through." This increased the mirth, which in no wise subsided when, re-announced by the toastmaster and given full sway, the speaker began anew and went through to the end as follows:

"*Party Spirit* — that wicked and baneful party spirit, by which empires, kingdoms, and republics have been overthrown, and by which too many of the good people of *this* town have been greatly led astray: may this noxious party spirit be torn up by the roots, transported to the island of Java, and there placed in battle array with the bohon upas tree, till it shall be demonstrated which is most poisonous to humanity, that deadly upas or party spirit." Then came another gun, more music, and deafening shouts of applause from the greatly amused assemblage. This closed substantially the more formal proceedings of the day.

Removal to New York. A few days subsequent to the Fourth of July celebration just described, I received an unexpected visit from Asa Holden, Esq., an entire stranger to me and a leading trustee of the First Universalist Society, Prince street, New York City. He had come as a special messenger to New England for the purpose of looking up a minister to fill the vacant pastorate of that body. I had been mentioned to him by some of my older clerical brethren and recommended as a suitable person for the position, and he had called upon me to engage my services at an early day as a candidate for it. There were good reasons why I should at once have declined the proposition. I had a nice field of usefulness where I was, and the unanimous good will of an increasing number of friends, though in a rural community, which could afford me but a moderate compensation for my labors. I was well established with my family in our pleasant new home, and it was annoying, if not unwise, to leave it without great certainty of a better location elsewhere. There was no such certainty in the case presented me, for the society in question had just been sadly weakened by a division which resulted in the withdrawal of a considerable number of its members. The famous Abner Kneeland had been its pastor, and being in that unsettled, transitive state of mind which not long after landed him in open infidelity, his preaching had so alienated from him a majority of his people that they voted his discharge from the pulpit. Thereupon his friends, considerable in number, seceded, hired a public hall, set up a rival organization, and employed him as their minister. All this must render my position in the Prince street pulpit, if I occupied it, not only a delicate and trying one, but one of problematical success. New York was not as sensational then as now, and not easily moved by aspirants for popular favor of my moderate type and caliber. But I was probably too ambitious, vain, and short-sighted to weigh all these considerations judiciously, and so was inclined to yield to the solicitations urged upon me. Nevertheless, I argued against the proposed change for some time with ambassador Holden, and requested him to consult some of my leading supporters, get their opinion, and learn their feelings about the matter,. which he consented to do. He was a stirring, sanguine man and made quick work of his conferences, returning very soon and reporting that the few he could find thought I was fully competent to fill the proffered pastorate, and had better go to it if called, though it would be a great loss to them. He represented in particular that such were the views expressed by Esquire Hunt, my most influential parishioner. I was rather taken aback by this statement, inasmuch as it caused me to infer that possibly there was a willingness to have me leave, founded as much on indifference to my continuance in Milford as on a conviction of my fitness for the prospective place in New York. I was therefore much more disposed by this representation to listen to these new overtures than before. I ascertained afterward, however, that Esquire Holden had no warrant for saying that any willingness existed that I should leave the Milford parish, though I was not informed of this till too late to profit by it. I suppose that his zeal to have me comply with his wishes either warped his veracity or caused him to misconstrue expressions which

VISIT TO NEW YORK.

seemed to favor his suit, though not intended to do so. Suffice it to say that I was persuaded to be a candidate for the vacant pastorate and engaged to preach as such the last two Sabbaths in July and the first in August. So much being settled, Brother Holden returned home with joy to report his success.

Pursuant to the above-named arrangement, I took my wife and little boy to Smithfield, R. I., about the middle of July to remain with relatives during my absence from Milford, and proceeded directly to New York to fulfil the terms of my candidacy there. A letter written to the former soon after my arrival detailed my experiences on the way and after reaching my destination to date, and also my first impressions of the people to whom I ministered and of the city. It has been preserved and the major portion of it may not be inappropriate to the purpose of this volume, nor uninteresting to its readers. I therefore give it insertion here:

"NEW YORK CITY, (Monday) July 23, 1827.

"DEAR WIFE: I embrace an early opportunity to write you a few lines agreeably to promise, and certainly according to inclination. Through the providence of God, I am well and hearty in the midst of this great and bustling metropolis. I did not arrive here till Sunday morning, just in time to attend divine service. The reason why was a disappointment at Providence. I reached that place about 10 o'clock on Friday morning. But on going to the steamboat wharf — behold, no boat was there! They told me none went on that day, but that a stage started soon for New London, where I could take a steamer for New York. On inquiry, however, I learned that the coach had gone, and of course I must wait till the next day and make the best of my ill-fortune. Meanwhile, I came across Brother Pickering, then pastor of the First Universalist church in Providence, who comforted and encouraged me, inviting me to spend the intervening time at his house, which I did very agreeably. I feel much indebted to him, for he was very kind. . . . He acted the part of an able and warm friend throughout, of which I shall speak more fully to you hereafter.

"On the passage, we had good wind, weather, and luck. The boat went much faster than usual, so that I reached the city in season for the morning service. Mr. Holden, to my great joy, was at the landing, looking with eager eyes for me. He received and welcomed me with great kindness, took me in a coach to a friend's house, not far from the church, etc. I was much fatigued, but preached three discourses notwithstanding.

"I am treated with much respect by the brethren here, who are plain, intelligent, kind people. There was double the number present at meeting I had expected, so that I was happily disappointed. I am also happily disappointed in the place. Those who have spoken against this city have misrepresented it. It is superior to Boston. The streets, if not so clean, are much more spacious and airy; the water is fully as good, if not better; and the people are less stiff and starched than in most large New England towns. But I can add no more now. As to my being settled here, I can say nothing yet, for neither party is fully prepared to decide. The probability is that it will depend on my consent and pleasure.

"Your affectionate husband,
"ADIN BALLOU."

The above language indicates that the candidate was rather captivated by his surroundings and prospects, and quite likely to take the new position. So it proved. After preaching three Sabbaths, I received and accepted the society's call on a salary, I think, of $800 per annum, to be raised as the society grew. During this visit I was pleasantly boarded in the family of Brother Sylvanus Adams, one of the trustees, and was introduced to most of the members. I also solemnized one marriage.

It being settled that I was to remove to New York, affairs made haste with me. My installation was arranged for the 26th of September, the Rev. Hosea Ballou to be invited to preach the sermon. But my pastorship was to date with and from the 16th of that month, the third Sabbath; and I was to make an exchange with Brother Hosea for that day and the Sunday following, arrangement for which was agreed upon and carried into effect.

I returned to my home in Milford, taking my little family from their three weeks' visitation with me, and set about the necessary preparations for removal. My friends seemed deeply aggrieved at my leaving them, but blamed the New York strategist rather than myself, as having seductively robbed them of their minister in an unfraternal manner. I was sorrowful for them and also for myself, fearing that I had done wrong and that the change I was to make might turn out an unwise one for all concerned. But the die was cast; nothing could be undone. I must go ahead and do my best.

On the five Sabbaths that remained before the close of my pastorate, I preached morning and afternoon in my own pulpit to interested and anxious audiences, and on successive days at 5 P. M. lectured in Blackstone, Hopkinton, and Bellingham. My afternoon discourse September 9 was in the nature of a valedictory, from the text: "Finally, brethren, farewell; be perfect, be of good comfort, be of one mind; live in peace and the God of love and peace shall be with you."—*2 Cor. 13: 11*. It was an affecting and impressive occasion. A large audience was present, composed mostly of deeply interested friends, though some outsiders were there, drawn by curiosity or otherwise. I could ask no more unmistakable demonstrations of personal respect and attachment, nor of regret at my departure than were there manifest. And it was substantially the same with friends in neighboring towns where I was accustomed to lecture and officiate at funerals.

On the third Sabbath in September I commenced fulfilling my engagement to supply the pulpit of Rev. Hosea Ballou in Boston, while he went on to occupy what was now mine in New York. I spoke in the morning in his School street church; in the afternoon in that of the First society, Hanover street, in exchange with Rev. Sebastian Streeter; and in the evening, by request of Rev. Hosea Ballou 2d, in his desk at Roxbury. The next Sunday morning I exchanged with Rev. Brother Thompson of Charlestown, and in the afternoon preached again in School street, thus concluding my engagement and with it my ministry in New England for the then present.

Meanwhile preparations had been going on rapidly for transferring myself, family, and belongings to the new home and field of service in the country's metropolis. Some household and other articles not likely to be needed had been disposed of at auction, and the rest were carefully packed and shipped in proper order. Our dwelling-house was put in good hands, to be rented or sold, as might be deemed most desirable. All things being ready, we left Milford on Tuesday, September 25, for Providence, where we boarded a steamer, expecting to reach our destination the next forenoon in time for the installation services at 3 o'clock P. M. But various things transpired to delay our boat, and we had a long, dismal passage, terminating about 5 o'clock, when we landed, in poor plight (by reason of seasickness, broken rest, etc.) for appearance before the public in any form. The installation had been postponed till evening and came off accordingly, though at a later hour than hoped for, and with much less than the customary display of parts. I have neither memoranda nor recollection of details further than that the sermon was by Rev. Hosea Ballou, who took for a text *Rom. 1: 14–16*. The subject of discourse was treated with the well-known ability of the preacher, a respectable congregation was present, and the exercises were appreciatively satisfactory. Thus my pastoral canoe was once more launched on the uncertain waters.

After temporary accommodation in the family of Brother Holden, we rented a tenement and set up housekeeping at No. 99 Thompson street, though it was some time before our domestic affairs were comfortably reconstructed so that we felt really at home. We were subjected to serious disappointment at an early day in our New York life, in that our matronly friend, Miss Joanna Cook, who had come on with us to be an assistant in household cares and a companion more particularly for my wife, became so decidedly homesick and otherwise ill that she insisted upon returning to the friends she left behind her, and did so within a month of our arrival. After her departure we supplied the place thus vacated as best we could—sometimes readily and satisfactorily, but frequently quite otherwise.

While getting settled in our new quarters we were one day thrown into a spasm of fearful anxiety and alarm by the sudden disappearance of our son, then a little over four years old, for whom a careful search of several hours throughout all the neighborhood and repeated calls in all directions proved fruitless and vain. I went hither and yon, hoping to find him in some of the streets or alleys; friends and neighbors were rallied to assist in looking him up; but the mystery grew deeper and deeper, and our apprehensions more and more distressing, till at length our good Brother Holden appeared, leading the tired and trembling wanderer into our presence. It may be imagined what relief came to our burdened hearts when we caught sight of him again and with what emotions of grateful joy we once more had him in our arms.

It seemed that he ventured some distance from our dwelling-place, lured by strange and pleasing sights — so far that when he came to himself and wanted to return, he could not find the way. Realizing very soon that he was lost, he began to cry and moan piteously, saying, "I want to go home." A watchman hearing him, took him in charge, and not being able to learn where he lived, carried him, agreeably to city regulations, to the public almshouse, where such stray ones are kindly taken care of until called for. When Brother Holden heard of his disappearance, knowing the course pursued in such cases, he at once repaired to the institution named where he found the lad a short time only after he had been brought in by the officer. The little fellow recognized Mr. Holden, whom he had seen repeatedly before, sprang to meet him, seized his hand eagerly, and was happy to be led by him back to the home from which he had thoughtlessly strayed and to the fond embraces of parental hands and hearts.

Having been duly inducted into my new field of labor, I addressed myself to my pulpit and pastoral duties with all the ability and zeal of which I was master, but with less evident success than I had hoped for. I had good friends who did what they could to assist and encourage me, but Mr. Kneeland and his adherents seemed to prosper, drawing into their support and fellowship many wavering and susceptible minds. My society had been seriously weakened by the division, and the faithful were anxiously looking for an increase of numbers and renewed thrift under my administration. But circumstances were unpropitious, and with all my diligence and zeal, I could not realize my own expectations, and what was a greater trial to me, I felt that I was not realizing the expectations of my people. After several months of earnest effort to little purpose, as I thought, I began to suspect that I was not the "right man in the right place!"

Still I persevered and cast about in my thought for some new means of usefulness and influence. In my anxiety and desire to accomplish the most I could for myself, my society, and the cause of truth, I devised a plan or scheme for starting and editing a small, semi-monthly paper to be called "The Dialogical Instructor," and made arrangements for carrying the project into effect. I secured a few personal friends as financial backers, and prepared and put to press my first issue, which bore date Jan. 5, 1828. This gave me my first experience in editorship, of which I have had much since that day.

My removal from Milford, though determined upon somewhat abruptly, and, as I afterward found, much against the judgment and earnest wishes of the principal members of my society there, awakened no unkindly feelings on their part toward me, and called forth from them no expressions of blame or condemnation. On the other hand, they still seemed to hold me in profound respect, manifested toward me a truly friendly spirit, and hoped the change would prove advantageous, both for me personally and for the cause of Universalism, which both I and they had so much at heart. This was evinced by the correspondence carried on between me and some of their leading representatives, which was always characterized by the utmost cordiality, frankness, and good will.

Somehow or other, perhaps by some casual remark of mine or by the general tone of my letters, or in some other way, it began to be suspected among my former parishioners ere many months had passed by, that things in New York were not going altogether to my mind; that my expectations were not fully realized; and that consequently there was a growing uncertainty in regard to what my future was to be. This suspicion appeared in letters of friends inquiring particularly into my pastoral affairs, whether or not I was satisfied with my position and work, etc., reminding me of my promise to return to Milford if all did not go well, and signifying that they all would be very glad to see me back again.

As early as Jan. 11, 1828, Esquire Hunt wrote me as follows: "We are one and all anxious to hear how you are situated, what society you have, of your prosperity or adversity. I wish you to write me plainly and truly. I have a letter from Esquire Holden, who states that he was mistaken in his communication to me respecting your wishing to be considered a candidate for their society, but quite the reverse; therefore he takes the blame upon himself. Please give my compliments to him and tell him I thank him for the pamphlets he sent me, but am sorry that he should be the means of separating you from our society. We are at this time without any meeting except visiting each other, — all waiting to hear from you."

It was evidently understood among my Milford friends that I was struggling against wind and tide, with little prospect of any change for the better. Probably I said as much as this in my letters to them from time to time. And so on Feb. 25, Mr. Hunt wrote me again: "You have the same opportunity, and I think, greater reason to return to Milford than you had to leave it; but you must and will be your own judge. Here are Milford, Bellingham, and Medway with meeting-houses; and Hopkinton, Mendon, Upton, Uxbridge, and many other societies you used to labor with, all destitute at this time. We, as well as our neighboring brethren, still feel anxious for your return. I do hope and trust you will not disappoint so many of your good friends here as to deprive them of your labors in the ministry without, after due trial and just experience, you are fully persuaded you can be far more useful in New York than in Milford." And once more, March 17th:—"Since I wrote you last I have not heard anything from you, etc. I am requested by the Universalist Committee to say to you that it is their desire you should inform them on what conditions you will return to Milford and settle with us for seven or ten years, provided there is a printing-office set up and a schoolhouse built for you. For our society still believe it is best for them, as well as yourself, that you should come back as soon as possible."

About the first of April I sent a response to these earnest appeals of Esquire Hunt, confessing that I felt somewhat disappointed by my New York experiences, that I appreciated the good feelings and wishes of my Milford friends, and that I might ultimately think it best to return; but that there was likely to be a severe struggle in my mind before I could decide to abandon my situation. At this point all correspondence was suspended for a few weeks, during which period thoughtful deliberation was going on with both parties concerned, in order that a wise decision might be reached in regard to the matter in hand. Meanwhile I was brought to the end of the twenty-fifth year of my life.

CHAPTER VIII.

1828–1829.

RETURN TO MILFORD — EXPERIENCE OF NEW YORK SOCIETY WITH REV. HOSEA BALLOU — REFLECTIONS — DISCUSSION WITH O. BATCHELOR — AFFLICTION.

THE urgent appeal from my former Milford society, quoted near the close of the last chapter, made a profound impression upon me, partly, no doubt, on account of the unpropitious circumstances in which I was placed. And hence, after much reflection, I concluded to signify to the trustees of my New York parish that I was not satisfied with the result of my labors in their behalf, and felt that I had better return to the place whence I came. They seemed to be astonished and sorry when I communicated my decision to them and expressed the hope that I would reconsider it. Finding me persistent in my purpose, they at length consented to give me up, provided I would assist them in obtaining another preacher of satisfactory talents and character. I replied that my influence was small in such matters, but what I had would be exerted to their advantage. On inquiring if they had any one particularly in view to succeed me, they named, to my great surprise, a no less distinguished personage than Rev. Hosea Ballou. I told them I had no faith whatever that he would entertain such a proposal as was suggested, but added that if his services could be secured it would be the making of the society and I would gladly do anything in my power to promote so desirable a consummation. They replied that they had good reasons for believing that he could be induced to come to New York, for he had signified as much when he was last in the city in a conversation with Mr. James Hall, an eminent Universalist merchant. I was still incredulous, thinking there must have been some misunderstanding on the part of the gentleman. They were sure there was none and asked me to open a correspondence with Mr. Ballou, which for want of faith in the thing I declined to do.

Thereupon Mr. Henry Fitz, chairman of the board of trustees (who were more confident than I), was delegated to address him upon the subject. An answer to his letter of inquiry was soon received, which we all understood to be favorable to the contemplated negotiation. I confessed myself happily disappointed and immediately addressed an urgent appeal to my venerated brother in the ministry to come to New York and take charge of the Prince street society. I had then unbounded confidence in him, both as to intellectual ability and moral integrity and honor. He responded, saying that in a few days he would see our trustees and confer with them face to face.

Mr. Ballou came on accordingly and a meeting was held when the whole matter in hand was thoroughly considered. During the interview, the reverend gentleman was asked what salary he should expect were he to take the position proposed. His reply was in substance this: "I am now very happily situated in Boston, my society there is large and respectable, I am in the midst of numerous friends, my children are settled at no great distance from me, my salary is ample— about $1600—as large as my supporters are well able to pay; all I need or would willingly receive. Now if I come to New York, the good of the cause, not pecuniary advantage, would be the chief inducement. I shall therefore ask only such compensation as to be no loser in a monetary point of view." Nothing could be more just, honorable, or satisfactory than this and the conference closed.

A full meeting of the board was soon after held for final action in the case. The whole ground was traversed again, all the circumstances of expense of removal, comparative cost of living, distance from friends, etc., were carefully and frankly discussed, resulting in an agreement that my honored kinsman should come to New York upon a salary of $1800 — the expense of getting his family and goods from Boston to be paid by the brethren here. In regard to the time when the new pastorate should begin, Mr. Ballou said he was not sure his Boston society would release him, but thought there would be no great difficulty about it, and if he was released, he could enter on the new engagement in a few weeks. The interview closed satisfactorily and the trustees were joyous for the future. The tidings of what had been done and of the new prospects opened to the society gave great satisfaction to the members and their friends, exciting the liveliest anticipations — alas, never to be realized.

Mr. Ballou was to preach in Philadelphia the ensuing Sunday and in my Prince street pulpit the one following. Before leaving my house for the Quaker City, having been my guest during his stay in New York, he began to think he had been too moderate in his demands upon the brethren here, telling me in private conversation that he deemed it very doubtful if his Boston friends would consent to his leaving them on the terms named. After a long talk with him with a view of finding out what offers would be necessary to induce his people to give him up, he told me that if $200 were added to the sum agreed upon, making it $2000, he had no doubt they would release him, though, he added, he could not be absolutely certain of it. On the strength of what he said, I promised to submit his new proposition to the trustees, hoping for the best.

I fulfilled this promise immediately after he started for Philadelphia, though it was an awkward and disagreeable task for me. The trustees were astonished at this new phase of the matter and some of them almost incredulous as to my having a correct understanding of Mr. Ballou's views and feelings; the increased demands, after what had been definitely agreed upon, being wholly unexpected, not to say exorbitant. But they were not long in finding out that even greater exactions were to be laid upon them and that if their object was to be attained, it would be upon still harder terms. For when the candidate returned and negotiations were opened anew, all former action was reconsidered and annulled, and an entirely new arrangement was consummated, to wit: The annual salary should be $2000, to be specially guaranteed by pecuniarily responsible individuals, the settlement to be for life, with the understanding that a colleague should be provided when necessary without reducing the salary more than $800 per annum, and all the expenses of removal to be paid. This being settled, an ardent epistle was sent by the trustees to the Boston society, beseeching them to concur in the contemplated change and a glorious consummation seemed now to be fully assured. All this transpired about June 1, 1828. The final outcome of this protracted effort to secure the pastoral services of the most distinguished preacher in the denomination with all the manœuvring and apparent craft connected therewith was that in due time word came from Boston announcing that Mr. Ballou's society there refused to release him on any terms, and therefore he could not remove to New York. The Prince street society were greatly disappointed, as well they might be, in thus having all their earnest endeavors prove fruitless and their plans for the future utterly frustrated; and they were thrown for the time being into a state of consternation, bewilderment, and almost despair.

While these things were going on with reference to my New York parish and its prospective pastorship, I had been negotiating with my old society in Milford for a return thither. In response to a letter written by me about the first of April, to which allusion has already been made, I received, after the lapse of a few weeks, the following communication:

"MILFORD, May 3, 1828.
"DEAR REV. RROTHER:—

"The Committee of the Universalist Society in Milford have had the pleasure of perusing your favor, through the politeness of Brother P. Hunt, to him of the 1st. of last month. We thought we discovered a willingness in you to take up your residence and preach with us once more on some conditions or other. There are certain facts connected with this business which we think it proper to state, viz: Our Society are more than anxious that you should come and will not be satisfied with an answer in the negative; yet with the present numbers they are unable to pay you more yearly than before. We do not doubt that some would give almost all they have. We should be willing to add to the amount as the Society increases. We have a desire, should you return, even in our present circumstances, that you should have a barn and a horse and chaise as soon as possible. Should you be so kind as to come back, we will build you a barn suitable for your use immediately, and give the old salary — prompt pay; also as much and as fast towards a horse and chaise as our means will admit. In fact, we will do all we can and more than we would for any other man. We understood you that there must be a conflict in your mind before you could decide. If it must be so, we hope it will soon begin, and soon end by your being placed in the bosom of your friends, where, if you have but a morsel of bread, you will eat that in love and quietness. All which we humbly submit for your candid consideration and for ourselves and Society anxiously await your answer.

"From your most devoted friend,
per order of the Committee,
"ARIEL BRAGG."

On the 12th of May I answered this letter, communicating my decision to comply with the committee's invitation and return to Milford in the course of a few weeks. To this Col. Bragg cordially rejoined a week later, expressing for himself, the committee, and society, the most fraternal love and satisfaction. So much being settled, the New York trustees, elated with the expectation of having Rev. Brother Ballou for a minister at an early day, consented to the removal of my family and effects to Milford as soon as I found it convenient, provided that I would supply the pulpit till my successor's arrival, which, it was understood, would be the first Sunday in July. During the week that he was in Philadelphia, therefore, we packed up whatever we desired to take with us to our old home, started it on its way, while we ourselves left in season to reach there before the following Sunday, when I was to preach again to the people of my former charge. Having stored my goods for a few weeks and placed my wife and child among friends, I returned the next week to New York to fulfil my engagement there and close up a few matters that remained unsettled. I had the good fortune to find an old friend, Mr. Noah Cook, who was ready to take my house off my hands for the remainder of the time for which I had rented it, in order to occupy it himself. It was also necessary to make some disposition of *The Dialogical Instructor*, which had reached its 13th number, and an arrangement was entered into with Revs. Thomas Whittemore and Russell Streeter, then about to start *The Trumpet and Universalist Magazine*, by which its subscription list was transferred to them.

I preached for the last time as pastor of the Prince street society June 29, 1828, giving my friends an informal farewell with the least possible ado. My position at the time was a somewhat anomalous and trying one. I had pledged myself to supply the pulpit there till my successor was ready to take my place, which, it was supposed, would be on the next Sunday. And now word had just been received that Mr. Ballou, who had been relied upon to follow me, was not coming at all. The people were perplexed beyond measure, inconsolable almost, by their disappointment, and nothing that I could say was likely to soothe their feelings. All my plans were laid with reference to the closing of my pastorate there and resuming the one at Milford immediately. No reasonable objections could be made to my leaving at once and I acted accordingly. And so on the first of July I bade my New York friends a final good-bye, taking a steamer to Providence, going thence to Smithfield where my family was, and proceeding with them to Milford. I was received with outstretched hands and warm hearts, and recommenced my pastoral labors the Sunday following, July 6, 1828.

In closing the record of my experiences in New York I deem it proper to indulge in a few reflections which they naturally suggest. The question has often arisen in my review of the matter just narrated whether or not there was anything wrong or dishonorable in the course I pursued with reference to it. I have never been able to see that there was, but have always felt myself justified and unworthy of blame at the bar of my own conscience and before my Maker. I have not, however, been able to render the same exculpatory verdict in the case of Father Hosea Ballou. I thought at the time and I still think in the serenity of old age that his treatment of the Prince street society was discreditable and blameworthy, derogatory to his character and standing as a man and as a minister of universal grace and salvation. It seriously shocked my previously entertained reverence for and confidence in him. Indeed, it destroyed much of these and they were never restored to me. There seemed a worldly shrewdness, a sort of mercantile foxiness in his conduct, which was repugnant to my notions of Christian duty and honor, and which I had thought to be morally impossible in *him*. My feeling in the matter was intensified by ascertaining soon after, on what I regarded good authority, that his manœuvre resulted in securing some hundreds of dollars addition to his yearly stipend from his Boston friends. Nor does the fact that this is the way of the world and of many clergymen render it less culpable in my judgment, or more innocent and Christlike. I do not censure Mr. Ballou for not going to New York. It would have been unwise for him to have done so on *any* salary. I censure him for demanding so much of the society there, repeatedly increasing his figures, and then accepting a premium for remaining in Boston, while making all the time the highest professions of disinterestedness and devotion to the cause of Universalism.

One good effect was produced by the revulsion that took place in my own mind at the transaction under consideration. My former great respect for Rev. Brother Hosea had drawn me far towards his peculiar doctrine that all sin, suffering, and punitive discipline end with man's earthly life; also into the evil persuasion that those Restorationists in the Universalist denomination who had publicly controverted that doctrine had done so not from honest convictions of truth and duty, but mainly from personal ambition, envy, spleen, and pique. I had never been converted to the no-future-punishment hypothesis, yet I was so strongly attached to the leading apostles and devotees of this hypothesis that I was silently acquiescing in it and as near embracing it as one could be who wished to find some convincing reason for doing so, but had wholly failed in the attempt. Moreover, by the same subtle influence, I had become greatly prejudiced against the "factious" Restorationists, as they were designated, which made the matter still worse. But here had come a shock to my feelings which suggested that I might have been too credulous and facile, and which led me to examine the ground on which I was standing and correct the mistakes into which I had been unwittingly led.

Another incident which occurred, I think, while the negotiations spoken of were going on, contributed largely to the same result. One day while Father Hosea was stopping at my own house, I tried to draw from him the main reasons for his distinctive view of the restriction of sin and misery to the present state of being. I addressed him in substance as follows: — "I am perfectly persuaded of the final holiness and happiness of all human souls; as I am that there can be no such thing as God's inflicting any vindictive, cruel, or useless punishment on men here or hereafter. But if there are those who leave this mortal state in a sinful condition, hating the Heavenly Father and one another, and dying perhaps in the very commission of some wicked act, how can they possibly enter into happiness in the next life without first experiencing more or less shame, sorrow, and penitence?" This was a question of profound interest to me, and I expected he would give me, in view of my youth and of our mutual relations to each other, his strongest arguments in support of his theory, and so do something to enlighten me on so vital a subject. To my utter disappointment, he waggishly evaded the issue and with a smile and a shrug, said: "So then, Brother Adin, you think they'll have to be smoked a little, do you?" I was profoundly in earnest, but he chose to be facetious and, as he thought, witty. I did not like it and concluded, after reflecting upon the matter, that he could not give even a plausible answer to my inquiry. Nor have I ever had occasion to change that opinion. This was the first, last, and only conversation we ever had upon the subject.

Not far from this time, Rev. Charles Hudson, an able exponent of the Restorationist theory of life, death, and destiny, published in book form a series of letters in defence of the doctrine of limited future retribution addressed to Rev. Mr. Ballou, which were of great value and had a wide circulation. Although designed especially for the latter's consideration, he, instead of giving them the attention they deserved, or which common courtesy even would have prompted, gravely announced to the Universalist public through its Boston organ, that he had not read the work and should not answer it, as he was told it contained nothing new upon the question involved. This did not tend to check the declining respect I had for him. It rather led me to decide that men and doctrines alike ought to stand or fall, not on mere assumptions, but on their respective intrinsic merits or demerits, as determined by an enlightened and candid judgment.

Passing from these more immediately personal matters, I am moved to remark that the general conditions and prospects of Universalism in the nation's metropolis, as I was obliged to see and study it while there, were at best somewhat dubious. Rev. Edward Mitchell, an eminent champion of the doctrine of the final redemption of all men, and his society worshipping in Duane street, were Restorationists and stood almost entirely aloof from the mass of those bearing the Universalist name. Moreover, he was far along in years, with failing health, and his people were not large in numbers. Rev. Abner Kneeland in his new movement was riding a high horse down hill into atheism, with a motley train of admirers at his heels. The Prince street society, of which he previously had charge, was greatly crippled by the withdrawal of so many who followed him in his wild career. Furthermore, with the exception of a few choice spirits, it was difficult to tell what the majority of professed Universalists believed or were aiming at—only that they had cut loose from the endless-misery sects and were adrift somewhere on the high seas of liberalism, with less of sound faith than of volatile skepticism. Of fraternal unity, co-operation, and fellowship, there was little. Thus my first favorable impressions proved illusory, and I left New York " a sadder, though a wiser man."

The prevailing aspects of moral and social order, or rather of disorder, in the city, did not brighten much upon closer acquaintance. The place was a Babylon, composed of all peoples and tongues, high and low, rich and poor, fortunate and unfortunate, in one vast whirl of good and evil enterprise, — a heterogeneous compound which I will not attempt to describe.

During my ministry there, I was called upon to officiate but a few times either on funeral occasions or at the nuptial altar, though I solemnized enough marriages to give variety and uniqueness to my experience. As the laws of the state then were, few restrictions or safeguards were established for the governance of those proposing to enter the marital relation; no publishments, no registration, no certificates of intention being required of the parties concerned. Those conducting the ceremonial—magistrates or clergymen—must do so on their own responsibility, at least so far as mutual fitness was taken into account. In my youthful inexperience, I made some grievous mistakes. In one instance, the groom proved to be an unprincipled bigamist. In another, when two couples came to my house for the ceremony, there had been a mutual unmarrying of parties previously united, and swapping of mates. On the following Sunday, as I descended the pulpit stairs, I was met by a finely appearing lady dressed in mourning, who claimed to be the sister of one of the brides, and who stated that the family were greatly troubled about the affair and desired me to call at their house, giving me the street and number, and assist in straightening things out. I took the matter under advisement, and after reconnoitering the place designated and its neighborhood, concluded that it was the more discreet course not to risk any intimacy with the inhabitants of the premises indicated, but leave them to adjust their affairs without my aid. These experiences led me to believe that matrimonial alliances were liable to more uncertainty and erraticism than I could at that early period comprehend.

A gloomy premonition. While fulfilling my engagement to supply the New York pulpit for a few Sundays succeeding the removal of my family to New England, I boarded with Mr. N. Rose and wife, members of the Prince street congregation and devoted friends of mine. During my sojourn with them I received in a dream one night a solemn premonition of coming bereavement. I saw, or seemed to see, as in a vision, the dead body of my wife lying before me, and near by a new-born, living infant. The impression was so distinct and dreadful that it awoke me in a "horror of darkness," and thenceforth the memory of it haunted me more or less ominously until some months later it was literally fulfilled. I concealed the dream in my own bosom, hoping it might be only a barren and harmless freak of the mind, yet fearing all the while that it would prove true, and watching sedulously the signs that might in any way foreshadow or indicate the fatal issue it portrayed.

About the first of July we were once more domiciliated in Milford, my opening sermon under the new arrangement being delivered on the morning of Sunday, the 6th of that month. As our own house had been rented to families that could not readily vacate it, we occupied rooms temporarily in an adjoining dwelling, but ere many months elapsed we were fairly established again in our old quarters, with none to molest or make afraid. A new barn was erected during the summer, and in due time a horse and chaise were added to our domestic equipment, not only that they might contribute to our personal convenience and pleasure, but that I might more easily and faithfully discharge the pastoral duties of my office — the people of my charge, though not very many in number, being distributed in all directions over a wide extent of territory. Moreover, the many calls I had for miscellaneous services of one kind or another within driving distance of Milford, rendered it a part of wisdom and economy for me to have means of conveyance of my own and be independent of neighbors, parishioners, etc., however kind; and of livery stables, however ready to serve me, for a consideration, in that respect.

Very soon after my return, I found myself not simply going my old round of ministerial duty, but more in demand and more actively engaged otherwise than ever before. I received several invitations to occupy vacant pulpits as a candidate for settlement over parishes of more distinction in various respects than that of Milford, but felt myself in honor bound under the circumstances to decline them all. I attended and participated in the services of numerous ecclesiastical gatherings,— ministerial associations and ordinations, dedications of houses of worship, religious conferences and the like, and made frequent exchanges far and near with my clerical brethren. At the dedication of the Universalist meeting-house in Pawtucket, R. I., in December of the year now in review, at which time Rev. Jacob Frieze was installed pastor of the society, I met my elder brother, Rev. Hosea Ballou, but nothing passed between us concerning the New York affair, neither on that occasion nor indeed ever afterwards.

Meanwhile, my wife's health perceptibly declined, necessitating the giving up on her part of all manual labor and the employment of domestic help continuously. Very naturally, my dream would often recur to me and with ever-increasing vividness, awaking anew in my breast and torturing me with the most fearful apprehensions. I could do no otherwise than maintain unbroken silence about it, suppress and conceal as far as possible my feelings, and await the issue with such calmness and composure as my reason, conscience, and faith in the infinite perfections of my Heavenly Father enabled me to command. Nevertheless, the cloud still hung in the sky above me, and sent its chilling shadows into my heart.

In the autumn of 1828, I was visited by Mr. Origen Bachelor of Providence, R. I., editor of a small periodical entitled *The Anti-Universalist*, which, as its name indicates, was devoted to the controverting of the doctrine of the salvation of all men in its every form and feature. He had been canvassing the town for subscribers, he said by way of introduction, and so dropped in on me. I acknowledged his courtesy in some general reply in no wise calculated to provoke discussion or suggest even religious conversation. But he soon broached his favorite topic of thought, rather in the spirit of controversy than of candid discussion, for he loved debate as he loved his victuals. As my disposition has been through life not to seek nor shrink from polemic warfare,

I met his assaults on my cherished faith promptly in a long and earnest argument. He was keen, forcible, persistent, and I was not slow to ward off his blows at every turn, and give, as well as receive, sharp shots of dialectic musketry. A severe toothache on his part and an equally severe headache on mine, brought the interview to a premature end, neither yielding a hair's breadth of ground assumed in the debate. But he conceived so much of a liking to me, as he said (with the notion, perhaps, of helping his paper), that before leaving he proposed a discussion of the subject at issue between us in its columns. I could not well refuse, and so consented to a public correspondence with him in a series of articles, *pro* and *con*, of a polemic character. To show how anxious he was for the fray, I copy the following letter received from him shortly afterward:

"Providence, Oct. 18, 1828.

"REV. MR. BALLOU: The public are on tiptoe with expectation. They feel great solicitude in relation to our proposed discussion. Already have some political papers noticed it and among the rest the *National Gazette*, Walsh's paper in Philadelphia. Some have subscribed for the *Anti-Universalist* solely on account of this expected controversy, and even some Universalists. What remains for me to observe is that after having excited public expectation, we proceed to gratify it without delay. Please, sir, forward me the introductory number as soon as possible. It is necessary that I receive it early next week in order to its insertion in our next.

"Very respectfully I am, etc.,
"ORIGEN BACHELOR."

Before this urgent prompting reached me, I had received an anonymous letter from a conspicuous Universalist layman in Providence, entreating me to have nothing to do with Bachelor and his *Anti-Universalist*. He said that "Universalists should treat that paper and its editor with silent contempt." "Its publisher and patrons aim merely to villify and abuse." "Your character may suffer by coming in contact with such a low and contemptible vehicle." "Saving a few bigots in this town, it is execrated by the whole community, etc., etc." Nevertheless, having committed myself as far as I had, and never fancying a dainty dignity that refuses to notice ungenteel opponents for fear of getting besmeared, I went ahead. Quite a long series of articles followed, the merits of which I can hardly pass judgment upon at this late day, the papers containing them having been lost or mislaid. Probably more good than harm was done, but not much of either.

During the ensuing winter I had charge of the school in North Purchase, the same taught by me the first year of my residence in Milford. I rode three miles to it in the morning, returning to my family at night, the health of my wife being such as to require more than usual attention and care. All my other duties were performed in regular order, and none of the interests entrusted to my keeping were consciously neglected or allowed to suffer detriment.

On the 30th of January, 1829, another child was born to us; a daughter who, notwithstanding the early loss of her mother and in spite of many threatened dangers, has survived to the present time — the only one of my four children now remaining in the flesh. The patient passed through the trying ordeal as well as could be expected in view of her previously debilitated condition, and for some days seemed so comfortable that I hoped for an escape from the portended fatal issue. It was not long, however, before there appeared in the case marked symptoms of failing vitality and strength, ultimating in what was called quick consumption in those times, from which there was no release except in death. Oh, the sad and anxious days and nights through which I then passed! My feelings can be imagined only by those who have been visited by similar calamities. Everything possible was done for the sick and suffering one. The best of nursing was secured and there was all needful kindly, sympathetic helpfulness on the part of the women of my congregation. Our family physician, Dr. G. D. Peck, in whom we had great confidence, called in as counsel Dr.

Daniel Thurber of South Milford, the most experienced, skilful, and eminent practitioner in our general region, so that there was no lack in that regard. But all in vain. Nothing could check the ravages of the destroyer.

When the fast-sinking patient became aware of her critical condition, she conversed with me freely about it and about her approaching dissolution. She desired me to pray with and for her (which I did as best I could with my anguish-stricken spirit and quivering lip), assured me of her unabated dying love for me, confided the children and her personal effects to my care, and expressed the wish that her body might be buried in some place where mine at last could rest by its side. She said but little about the future, but manifested an undoubting trust in her Heavenly Father and an assurance that all would be well with her spirit beyond the river of death. She was calmly resigned but could not talk at any length, her eyes and countenance telling what her organs of speech were unable to articulate. In just three weeks from the birth of her child she breathed her last and passed into the world of spirits, leaving me her lifeless body and a little infant just as had been shown me in that dream-vision some months before. Thus about seven years after marriage I was bereaved of a most affectionate, devoted, and exemplary wife, whom I had every reason to love, confide in, cherish, and hold in perpetual and ever precious remembrance. Our brief union had, I can but feel, the sanction of the Divine Father, as it certainly received abundant blessings from his guardian hand.

My beloved wife died the 20th of February, 1829, at he age of 28 years, 10 months, and 20 days. The funeral took place in the brick meeting-house on the 24th, having been postponed one day on account of a terriffic snowstorm that rendered the roads almost impassable. For this reason, but few relatives on either side were able to be present, but of sympathizing friends, parishioners, and neighbors there was a large attendance. The services, consisting of prayers and a sermon, etc., were conducted by Rev. Hosea Ballou, 2d, of Roxbury, for whom I cherished a peculiar fraternal regard, and were appropriate and consolatory. What was mortal of the dear departed was interred in the old burying-ground at Milford Center, and monumental stones with suitable inscriptions were soon after erected at the head of the grave. Some twelve years later the whole was removed to our burial lot in the Hopedale Cemetery.

A brief obituary notice from the pen of Rev. H. Ballou, 2d, as I suppose, appeared in the *Trumpet and Universalist Magazine* of March 7, 1829, from which I transcribe the following passages:

"Throughout her short but painful sickness, amidst the rapid decay of a quick consumption, she uttered no complaint; nor was she alarmed on receiving a tender intimation from her husband that her disease threatened to prove mortal. As her life wasted away, she maintained a steady and serene confidence in the Father of Universal Grace, and when the last hour arrived and the torpor of death came upon her, she bade her husband farewell with composure.

"From her childhood she was brought up in the doctrine of Universal Salvation; and in mature age her character, mild, benevolent, and conscientious, seemed to comport well with the sentiments she had received. Naturally attached to domestic life, its duties were the principal objects of her care and application; and if her religious professions were not loud and imposing, it was because her disposition as well as her belief inclined her to show her faith by her works."

My parochial and other duties, which had been somewhat interrupted by the sickness and death of my wife, were resumed after the funeral solemnities were over, and proceeded thenceforward with tolerable regularity. My thoughts were thereby turned away from the great sorrow through which I had passed, and I was somewhat relieved of the burden of grief and pain which otherwise would have seemed too heavy to be borne. At the same time I had the strongest reasons for gratitude to God, not only for spiritual consolation during all my afflictive experience from the great fountain of all good, but for a multitude of sympathetic demonstrations from my earthly friends. I remember "the wormwood and the gall" and also, I trust, "the wine and the oil" of those far-off days. The outlines of my troubled dream remain and of what it seemed to prognosticate, but the light and shade thereof grew more and more indistinct with the receding years.

Where, now, I can but ask, are the relatives and friends that then mourned with and comforted me? Nearly all gone over to the spirit continent, a scattered remnant only remaining, like myself, on these mortal shores, and we are awaiting the summons hence. But how has it fared with the departed? Are they lost in oblivion or only gone before? Not lost, but translated to immortal fields—their spirits rehabilitated in bodies and garments suited to their present mode of being—each one in proper order progressing towards a celestial destiny of ineffable good and glory; some more slowly than others, but all surely. They have greeted each other on the eternal shore and congratulated each other upon their triumphant deliverance from the power of death and the grave, and upon the unfolding goodness of the Infinite Parent in all the dispensations of his ever-faithful providence. So may they greet us and we them, as we in God's own time shall emerge from the shadows of earth into the glorious sunlight of immortality.

CHAPTER IX.

1829-1830.

ENLARGED FIELD — THEOLOGICAL STUDENT — SELF-CONQUEST — OVERWORK — DANGEROUS ILLNESS — HOME RECONSTRUCTED — FUNERAL EXPERIENCE.

AS I entered the 27th year of my life, I found new fields of service opening before me and new opportunities for advancing the cause of truth and righteousness, of which I felt myself to be the friend and champion. Not only did calls to lecture in surrounding towns on Sunday evenings and to officiate at funerals and on marriage occasions increase, but also invitations to preach in other pulpits than my own, both far and near; sometimes in exchange with a resident minister, and sometimes to fill a vacant place, in which latter case, if accepted, I had to provide for my own people as best I could. Moreover, I took about this time under my care and tuition a young man who had been living at Lowell, Seth Chandler by name, for the purpose of educating and training him for the work of the Christian ministry in the interest and fellowship of the Universalist denomination. He had in some way conceived a liking for me, and for some time a correspondence had been carried on between us in regard to his becoming my student. It resulted in an arrangement whereby his wishes were to be gratified, but sickness and death in my family had prevented it from being carried into effect. After the interruptions and changes occasioned by my bereavement had passed by, however, and I was fairly settled again in my plans and work, having secured board at the table of Mr. Adams Perry, Sr., to whom I had rented my house, Mr. Chandler came to Milford to enter upon his proposed course of study. This was in the month of June, 1829. He obtained an abiding place with Mr. Perry, so as to be with me as much as possible, receiving instruction from me and all the guidance and information I could impart to him in the way of equipping him for his chosen calling. This opened a new page of duty and responsibility for me to fill out. He was about 22 years of age, a young man of excellent principles and moral character, with respectable talents and a moderate preliminary education, yet of laudable ambition, willing and anxious for improvement. His general knowledge was somewhat extensive and he was well posted in the literature of Universalism. I put him under such drill as I thought suitable, finding him an apt scholar, but so sensitive to criticism that it took me some time to make my correction and discipline fit his peculiar organization. We soon, however, came to understand and to adapt ourselves to each other, and his progress was rapid and satisfactory to a high degree. He remained under my tuition and influence till he was ripe for the pulpit — some three years. Soon after closing his engagement with me he was settled as pastor of the First church and society of Shirley; a position which he held and honored through a long and useful ministry.

About this time I was much exercised respecting the pernicious habit of using tobacco, which I formed not long after I entered the ministry of the Christian Connection, by reason of the example and influence of the older clergymen with whom I was associated and for whom I entertained profound respect. In those days nearly all the ministers of every denomination were "hail fellows well met" in the filthy, harmful, and reprehensible practice of smoking, and many of them yet belong to the same shameful category. By continued indulgence I became a slave to the habit; so much so that I had a cigar or pipe in my mouth most of the time during my waking hours. I was so charmed and beguiled by what I was doing that I verily imagined that I could read, study, meditate, and write much better under the inspiration thus engendered than otherwise. At length my eyes were opened to the injury I was doing myself in this particular. There were unmistakable signs that I was undermining my health and waging war against my physical well-being. My reason and conscience were finally aroused and became faithful monitors and witnesses against me. I was convinced that I was abusing as well as defiling the temple in which God had for this present life installed my soul. Yet when I tried to escape from my thraldom, I found that in this as in other cases, my appetites, whether natural or artificial, when once enthroned were exceedingly pertinacious and obstinate. But could I not subdue them and reform? If not, I ought to be ashamed to preach repentance and reformation to others. And if I could but did not do this, I was no true minister of the cross. I pondered this aspect of the case; I prayed for divine help and at last resolved to place my tobacco and pipe on a shelf within reach and see how long I could let them alone. I tried this expedient and through grace from above strengthening me triumphed with comparatively little struggle. The harmful, dangerous appetite was broken and I have abstained from its indulgence for more than forty years. And now, whenever I see an old or young tobacco slave, I am profoundly grateful to God for my own emancipation, and prayerful that all other such sinners may experience the like deliverance.

As an indication of the multiplicity of my cares and labors at this period and of the extent to which I was unconsciously overtaxing my physical and mental energies, I take the liberty of making a few extracts from my diary for the year 1829:

"Attended and took part in the dedication of the new Universalist meeting-house in Marlborough, Mass., September 3. Remained there over the Sabbath and preached three times.

Also dedicated three children as a part of the afternoon service. Brother Chandler supplied the Milford desk for me. At home on the next Sabbath. Traveled the same week to Winchester, N. H., to attend the general convention of the Universalist denomination, before which I delivered a discourse on Wednesday. Much annoyed and displeased at that convocation by the interference of Rev. Hosea Ballou with an arrangement whereby Rev. David Pickering, of Providence, was to offer the principal prayer in connection with the preaching of a sermon by Rev. Paul Dean, of Boston. There had been some ill-feeling engendered between the objector and Brother Pickering by reason of the vigorous and unanswerable protest which the latter had made on different occasions against the former's pet hypothesis of no future retribution. The assignment of the part referred to was before the brethren for approval and seemed likely to receive it. Whereupon Rev. Hosea peremptorily said, 'If this convention has any regard for my feelings, it will not allow this man to pray before it.' This silenced all debate and secured unresisting submission at once! I resolved in my own mind not to attend another convention of that sort, and I never did.

"September 20th preached two discourses at Chestnut Hill, A. M. and P. M; another at 5 P. M. in Millville; and a fourth at 7.30 P. M. in Uxbridge. On the next Sabbath exchanged with Rev. Massena B. Ballou, of Charlton, Mass. On the following Wednesday preached three times at Chepatchet, R. I., being entertained at the residence of Mr. Sabin Smith. Thence home almost sick, having stopped on the way and spent an hour with my friend Clark Cook, in Mendon, who was confined to his bed with a fever. On Sunday, the 4th of October, I had arranged an exchange with Rev. Paul Dean, Bulfinch street, Boston, where I was expected to deliver three discourses, the last to be an anniversary one before the Sabbath School Association. But this expectation was not realized. My morning sermon was cut short and the services for the day abruptly closed by a sudden attack of illness which forbade all further effort on my part. I was much exhausted and feverish when the exercises commenced and I proceeded with difficulty. At length in the midst of my discourse my sight failed me and faltering, I summoned strength to announce my inability to go on further, then sunk back almost helpless upon the pulpit sofa. The congregation was much alarmed, friends flocked to my relief, and presently a devoted brother, one of my warmest adherents when a candidate for the pastorate of the First Universalist society in 1824, had me in a coach conveying me to his humble but most hospitable home. Arriving there, himself, wife, and the whole family did all in their power to soothe and recruit me during the ensuing afternoon and night. They besought me to remain with them, have a physician, and get better before attempting to return to Milford. But I instinctively felt that I must by all means get home. So with ardent thanks for their great kindness, I almost tore myself away from them the next morning and being lifted into my chaise, started on my journey. The day was cold and blustering, and when I had completed my ride of 30 miles I was chilled through and felt myself to be a sick man. I went directly to my chamber, utterly prostrated with what resulted in a severe and protracted lung fever."

I passed the night of October 5th in unalleviated distress, and on the morning of the next day sent for Dr. Peck, my regular physician, who at once saw what my disease was and said it must have its usual run. He, however, applied such palliatives and antidotes as seemed necessary to render me as comfortable as possible and secure a favorable issue. My brother, Ariel Ballou, Jr., then a student with Dr. Thurbur (before mentioned), at South Milford, was sent for to come and minister to me as best he could in various ways, since there was no one else on whom I felt at liberty to call in my emergency. He hastened to my bedside and proved a brother indeed, watching over me and attending to my wants with all vigilance and faithfulness, scarcely leaving me till the crisis was passed and I was out of danger. My theological student, Mr. Chandler, also favored me with much kind and efficient service. During my convalescence, I was cared for by my beloved mother whose presence was a comfort and support to me and whose experience enabled her to render me most valuable assistance; and by the daughter of one of my most respected and worthy parishioners, Miss Lucy Hunt, between whom and myself there had already sprung up a very strong and tender attachment — an attachment which some months later ripened into marriage, as will be noted in due time and place. Under the ministrations of such devoted, faithful, and efficient attendants, and of the most competent and scrupulous physicians, my disease was held much in check and successfully overcome, and my progress in the way of recovery, after my fever had passed its turning point, was rapid and sure, without serious hindrance or relapse. So that in five weeks from the day I was stricken down in Boston, I was in my own pulpit again engaged in the active duties of my ministerial office.

I however preached but one sermon on that second Sabbath in November, and that a written one — one of the few in those days which I committed to manuscript. In it I referred to my recent illness and recovery in terms which I am moved to reproduce in these pages. It was prepared specially for the occasion and had for a text Ps. 116:18: "What shall I render unto the Lord for all his benefits towards me?" After the introduction, consisting chiefly of the context with a few incidental suggestions, I came to my own case:

"My friends, I stand before you as one rescued from the cold prison-house of death. A few days ago it was by no means an improbability that the icy hand of the destroyer would soon be laid upon your minister and you be called to follow his remains in sad procession to yon dormitory of the dead. But the burning fever was arrested, the ravages of consuming disease were made to cease, and the dawn of returning health smiled calmly upon me. But by whom, above well-directed and kind human exertions, have I been restored to life and health? Who blessed the means used for my recovery, and whose hand hath brought me back from the borders of the grave? Do I not stand before you a monument of the unfailing compassion of Him that liveth forever and ever! Yes, it is of the mercy of the Most High that I am permitted again to utter my voice from this desk. I called upon him when sickness had almost swallowed me up and he hearkened to my supplication. He answered me with peace and returning strength; He lifted upon me the light of his countenance and the dark clouds were dissipated. He said, 'Let him walk again in the land of the living, for I will have mercy upon him.' And now, lo, I stand before you this day to make my grateful acknowledgements amid the congregation of my people for the loving kindness of God toward me. He hath restored me that I might watch over my tender children; that I might again bear testimony to the great salvation and proclaim the final redemption of a lost

DOMESTIC LIFE RE-ESTABLISHED.

world. He hath preserved me to come in and go out before you, my friends, and that I might take sweet counsel with you again on the shores of mortality. He hath restored me to the enjoyment of all that may reasonably be expected to fall to the lot of favored man, and I will venture to hope that many years of prosperity and usefulness yet remain to me in the appointments of indulgent Heaven. Oh, how great and precious are the blessings and benefits of our Heavenly Father! Let us all praise and magnify His name from henceforth even forevermore!

As winter came on, I found myself so fully restored to health and strength as to warrant me in engaging to assume charge of the school in the 1st district in town for the approaching term; a new schoolhouse having been recently erected and made ready for use only a quarter of a mile from my place of residence. This engagement I was able to carry into effect without detriment to myself, and to the satisfaction of teacher, pupils, parents; in fact, of all concerned.

Having closed my school and being comparatively free from outside responsibilities and labors, I turned my attention more immediately to the rehabilitating of my own home and the renewal of my own distinctive family life by entering a second time, as before intimated, into the marriage relation. The young lady spoken of on a preceding page and I had already become affianced to each other by mutual attraction and pledges of affection and constancy, and there seemed to be good and sufficient reasons why the formal and legal marital union should be consummated at an early date. I longed for the independence and freedom which exist only in one's own household. I yearned for the companionship, the sympathy, the sweet heart-repose which can be found only in the domestic circle. I sighed for my dear children, separated from me and from each other, and earnestly desired that they might be with me, under my constant supervision and care, where proper parental influence might be exerted upon them and where they might contribute more directly and effectively to my comfort and happiness. I was fully persuaded that she whom I had selected to be the partner of my future joys and sorrows was not only worthy of my confidence and love, but every way competent to fill a mother's place toward my little ones and to discharge a mother's sacred responsibilities. Though young in years and just ripening into womanhood, yet was she much more mature in experience and judgment than many farther advanced in life. She was sedate, modest, circumspect, sensible, and discreet in her general deportment, intelligent, thoughtful, well trained in household affairs, affectionate, kind of heart, and obviously disposed to solid usefulness. I was satisfied with her and she professed to be with me, and we were mutually agreed upon uniting our fortunes and our destinies at an early day.

The 3d of March, 1830, was finally determined upon as the date when our marriage should be solemnized and preliminary preparations were made accordingly. The ceremony took place in the meeting-house in which I ministered, in the presence of a large concourse of people. My favorite clerical brother, Rev. Hosea Ballou, 2d, was the officiating clergyman on the occasion. He preached an appropriate sermon and our choir furnished interesting musical accompaniments. Everything passed off pleasantly and satisfactorily to the wedded pair and to the whole congregation, and the day closed with a wedding banquet at the house of the bride's parents, at which there were present only the immediate relatives of the bride and groom and a few invited guests.

We very soon commenced housekeeping in the home that for more than a year had been so sadly broken up and troubled. My little boy, Adin, Jr., was immediately brought from his year's sojourn with my good friends, Clark Sumner and wife of North Purchase, but his infant sister had caught the whooping cough and could not safely join us for some weeks afterward. In due time, however, we were all together and the bark of our new domestic life, fairly launched upon the waters of time,

SCENE AT A FUNERAL. 165

glided calmly on towards the great future that stretched out before us.

Near the close of the 27th year of my mortal pilgrimage, on the 20th of April, I had a very singular funeral experience, which in itself and in its accompanying circumstances illustrates a certain type of religion and of religious sense of duty much more prevalent in my younger days than at the present time. A little daughter of my good friend Capt. Wm. Grant, of West Wrentham, was burned to death — an event which almost overwhelmed the family with grief and awakened heartfelt, sympathetic sorrow throughout the entire neighborhood. As on previous similar occasions in the household, I was summoned to officiate at the funeral. The principal services were to take place in what was called the Elder Williams meeting-house, which, though originally a Baptist sanctuary, had come to be owned in part and to be occasionally occupied by the Universalists of the vicinity, of whom my friend was one. The edifice was thronged with the relatives, friends, and sympathizing acquaintances of the deeply bereaved ones. The acting minister of the Baptist society at the time, a Rev. Mr. Reed, of English birth and training, had, out of courtesy, been invited to go into the pulpit with me and offer the concluding prayer. We were utter strangers to each other, and I suppose, from what transpired before the close of the exercises, he was as thoroughly prejudiced against my general religious faith as a man could be. In opening my discourse, which was in the form of a sermon, I took a text from *Lamentations 3:32, 33*: "But though He (God) cause grief, yet will He have compassion according to the multitude of His mercies; for He doth not afflict willingly nor grieve the children of men." The general drift of my remarks may be inferred from the passage quoted, what I said being based upon the infinite goodness of God and his unfailing kindness and love to his human offspring, whence might be deduced the consolatory lesson that under His divine government in the universe of souls, the trials, misfortunes, and afflictions to which we are subject in this mortal state must and will be overruled for good and made to work out the final holiness and happiness of those experiencing them. I illustrated my subject with appropriate examples and applied the lesson inculcated to the case of bereavement and distress which had awakened such widespread sorrow and called together so large a congregation.

Good Brother Reed was not at all pleased with my discourse, but deemed it delusive and dangerous. Therefore, instead of proceeding at once with his prayer when he arose to take the part asked of him, he stated that he had a burden of duty upon his mind which he could not forego, and that was "to protest against the sentiments that had just been expressed and to warn the people present of the danger involved in them." It can be imagined how such an unusual proceeding would, under the circumstances, affect the congregation. They were in a state of solemn, intense, yet measurably suppressed excitement. Nevertheless, they listened quietly while the reverend gentleman went on to state that the preacher had falsified and perverted the gospel, that he had flattered his hearers with the notion that God loves and is merciful to His sinful creatures, and applied the promises of grace to them without the condition of their faith and repentance, etc. "I tell you," he continued, "that as sinners you have nothing to expect from God but fiery wrath and indignation. You are His enemies and He is your enemy till you make Him your friend by turning to him with all your heart. Thus only can you secure His love and mercy, whatever may be your calamities, afflictions, sufferings, and bereavements." Having gone on in this strain for several minutes, he closed with a corresponding prayer.

I immediately responded. "Bereaved and sympathizing friends," I said, "it is very disagreeable to my feelings to hold a theological controversy on a funeral occasion, and especially one so sad and distressing as the present, but since it has been forced upon me by the extraordinary remarks of our reverend friend, you will pardon me a brief rejoinder. You are all my witnesses that I have not preached to you unbelief, rebellion, and impenitence before your Heavenly Father, nor underrated the necessity of faith, submission, and loving trust toward Him as indispensable to your welfare and happiness in this world or the world to come. But I have preached that God is your all-perfect friend, whether you are His friends or not, whether you love Him or not, whether you are thankful or unthankful, good or evil. And on the ground of His eternal goodness, I have counseled and exhorted you to obedience, penitence, and reconciliation to Him. On the ground that He first loved you, I have besought you to love Him and give Him the unreserved confidence of your hearts. The real point at issue between the brother and myself is whether God loves mankind because they first loved Him or the reverse. Whether God first is merciful and seeks after sinners, or they first seek after Him and implore His mercy in order to make Him good, kind, tenderly affectioned, savingly disposed to them.

"Now in this case our brother has much more important personages to contend against than I am. His quarrel is not with me but with Jesus Christ and his chief apostles." I then went on to quote the parables of the lost piece of silver, the wandering sheep, and the prodigal son, remarking that the lost sheep did not first return to the shepherd, nor the wayward boy's confession of penitence inspire his father's compassion and forgiveness. I also repeated such passages from the Saviour's lips as the following: "God so loved the world that he sent His only begotten son, etc." "Love your enemies, bless them that curse you . . . that ye may be the children of your Father in Heaven. For He maketh His sun to rise on the evil and on the good, and sendeth rain upon the just and the unjust." "Be ye therefore merciful as your Father in Heaven is merciful." "He is kind to the unthankful and the evil." Also from the words of Paul: "God commended His love toward us in that while we were yet sinners Christ died for us." "God, who is rich in mercy, for His great love wherewith He loved us even when we were dead in sins, hath quickened us together in Christ." And from John's Epistle: "Herein is love; not that we loved God, but that He loved us and sent His son, etc." "We love Him, because He first loved us." These and other texts of similar import which I quoted I accompanied with appropriate remarks as a sort of running commentary upon them, closing as follows: " I shall leave our friend to contend with and denounce the Saviour of the world, the great apostle to the Gentiles, and the beloved St. John. If he can silence them, he will have silenced me, for I have only echoed their testimony upon the matter in question between us. Even John Calvin, his great theological father, he opposes, for that distinguished champion of the old faith taught positively that the elect were chosen from the fallen race of Adam 'without the least foresight of faith, good works, or any conditions performed by the creature.' Yet here today, over this charred body, in the presence of these afflicted mourners, whom I have tried to console with words of hope and trust, he could not even pray without denouncing and warning this whole congregation against the doctrine on which all I had said was based, that God's aboriginal, perfect, unchangeable, eternal love, so clearly affirmed in the Christian Scriptures, renders Him the adorable refuge of all the afflicted, sorrowing children of men. His controversy is not primarily with me, but with the oracles of divine and everlasting truth." I then pronounced the benediction. My opponent left the house in agitated confusion, his own brethren and friends deploring his fatuity and want of wisdom, and the multitude rejoicing in the triumph of the truth.

Early in the spring of 1830, arrangements were made between the Universalist societies of Milford and Medway by the terms of which I was to divide my services between the two, preaching alternate Sundays in each, and during the summer delivering five o'clock lectures in each on the days I was absent at the regular hours of worship. Brother Chandler, who had been away teaching in the winter months, had rejoined my family and was making rapid progress in his studies, having already become an acceptable preacher in the pulpits of the general vicinity. My time was crowded with professional and other labors and responsibilities, the religious community was greatly agitated, and important developments were at hand.

CHAPTER X.

1830 – 1831.

EVENTFUL YEAR — CONTROVERSY WITH ULTRA–UNIVERSALISTS — JOIN PROVIDENCE ASSOCIATION — INDEPENDENT MESSENGER — CLOSE OF MILFORD PASTORATE — CALL TO MENDON.

I NOW enter upon a review of one of the most eventful and stirring years of my life-history — a year in which momentous questions were canvassed as never before, ecclesiastical changes made, and a new future opened to my advancing feet. All this came about by reason of the attitude of the Universalist denomination as a body, in respect to the dogma of no future punishment and my own growing convictions touching both that attitude and the dogma itself. I could in reason and conscience abide neither of them. Nor could I do otherwise than disapprove and scorn the contemptuous tone of the general Universalist press and pulpit towards nearly everything, however right and good in itself, which bore the stamp and characterized the action of the so-called evangelical sects. All such manifestations were an offense to me from the beginning.

Although the early advocates of the final redemption of all souls believed and taught that the consequences of sin extended into the future state of being, and although the Universalist Convention at Philadelphia, in 1791, emphatically disclaimed the theory that the good and the bad, the believer and unbeliever, are equally happy at the dissolution of the body, yet had it come to pass at the time of which I am writing that this latter view had gained overwhelming ascendancy among the class of Christians bearing the Universalist name. Those who were deemed leaders — the ablest and most aggressive preachers — were of that way of thinking, and more than nine-tenths of the laity were in sympathy with them; while the few Restorationists, as those of the opposition were called, especially if at all outspoken in their opinions, were scarcely treated with common civility. Their only chance for respectful consideration from the dominant party was to keep silence on the subject of difference and serve in the common ranks obsequiously. It was authoritatively proclaimed by those in the ascendant that not a single passage of Scripture, justly interpreted, taught the doctrine of sin, punishment, reward, or corrective discipline beyond this mortal life. Floods of absurd and wretched exegesis rolled forth and swept away assumptively every text which old-time Universalists, as well as believers in endless punishment, had always construed to teach future retribution. All believers in the final restitution of all things, ancient and modern, were claimed as Universalists, but those holding to retributive rewards and penalties beyond the grave were set down as crude in their notions on the subject, and not to be recognized as trustworthy expositors of the sacred oracles. The title, "American Universalists," was assumed for those who were deemed sound and consistent representatives of the doctrine and who were the only true Universalists in what had become the proper denominational forms of speech. The positive and proscriptive declaration was made that "*Universalists now know of no condition for man beyond the grave but that in which he is as the angels in Heaven.*" At the same time, limited future retributionism was odiously represented as " an old heathen notion," and " a remnant of superstition akin to the delusion of Salem witchcraft." In addition to all this, almost every conceivable form of derisive and censorious expression was bandied about, in public and private, at the more spiritual, devout observances, customs, and socially religious instrumentalities of the "*Orthodox.*" These were characterized and sneered at as superstitions, or hypocritical pretences, or inventions of priestcraft. There seemed to be an absolute infatuation in such matters among the prominent Universalists of that period. And that infatuation was accompanied by so much self-conceit, dogmatism, intolerance and scorn towards any in their own ranks who dissented from such invidious characterization, that if they had any staunch mental independence or honest convictions or sense of justice, it was impossible for them to be otherwise than repulsed and outraged thereby. Certainly I was.

The Medway Sermon. Under these circumstances, and in the state of mind indicated, I wrote a sermon on "The Inestimable Value of Souls," which I preached at Medway on Sunday, the 25th of April, 1830. It was prepared in no spirit of controversy, and with no design of antagonizing any of my Universalist brethren. But it proved to be the first gun of a protracted and somewhat violent war. My Medway friends, pleased with it, kindly asked it for the press. I consented to the request, and the manuscript was sent to the *Trumpet* office to be printed in pamphlet form, with little thought of the opposition it was destined to provoke. Its chief offense to those decrying it was that it interpreted and applied certain important passages of Scripture, in such a way as to derive from them support for the doctrine of future retribution, which was contrary to the *ex-cathedra* expositions of Rev. Hosea Ballou and kindred doctrinaires. Such interpretation and application were made innocently on my part, from honest conviction and incidentally to the main drift of the discourse, which was to advocate and defend the doctrine of Universal Restoration in opposition to that of endless punishment, my text being *Matt. 16:26*: "What is a man profited if he gain the whole world and lose his own soul? or what shall a man give in exchange for his soul?"

Though the sermon was sent to the *Trumpet* printing

office soon after it was delivered, with the expectation that it would be at once put to press and made ready for distribution at an early day, it yet suffered considerable delay and was not permitted to get into the hands of its readers until it had been heralded abroad and denounced by an extended notice from Rev. Thomas Whittemore, the editor of the paper mentioned. My self-constituted censor arraigned me as worthy of reprobation on six counts, which were substantially as follows: That I had inculcated the heathen notion of future rewards and punishments; that I had used certain texts of Scripture in support of that notion which leading Universalists and some others interpreted and applied differently; that I had done this without showing that they were in the wrong; that I had aggrieved and insulted some of my elder clerical brethren by saying that many divines, both orthodox and heterodox, tortured particular passages to no other purpose than to show their ingenuity; that I had injured and abused Rev. Hosea Ballou especially, by discarding his expositions and charging him with making "egregious mistakes;" concluding his arraignment by declaring that "I was far behind the orthodox in rescuing the sacred writings from perversion." He was moved to notice my errors and offences, he said, by a sense of duty "lest, if this sermon be read where the views of American Universalists are not known, it should be supposed they interpret the Scriptures in the same manner," and for the purpose of preventing the public from thinking that the sentiments of my sermon were embraced by Universalists generally.

The unreasonableness and injustice of all this carping criticism appear from the following facts: 1. The Universalist denomination had been founded and mostly built up by believers in a limited future retribution. 2. It still embraced a respectable minority who held to that doctrine. 3. There was no denominational creed or standard of faith giving the no-future-punishment view any precedence of its opposite. 4. It was acknowledged by all parties that the Restorationists and the Ultras, as they were respectively called, had co-equal rights in advocating and defending their distinctive views, without restriction or censure. 5. My Medway sermon contained nothing but what was perfectly consistent with these facts, professions, rights, and mutual understandings. Yet this editor, assuming to speak for the whole body of Universalists, took it upon himself to denounce me as a notable offender for advocating universal salvation on the old ground occupied by Murray, Winchester, Chauncey, and all the early champions of that form of faith.

By what had now transpired, I was unwittingly brought face to face with one of the leading spirits of the denomination to which I belonged and with whose distinguishing doctrine I was in hearty accord. In the ordinary discharge of my duty as a minister of Christian truth and an advocate of God's impartial and all-saving grace, I had provoked the hostility and the denunciatory judgment of the principal editor of the denominational organ, who, without doubt, in his attack upon me reflected the sentiment of a large majority of those holding the Universalist faith, and especially of those who had a controlling influence in its counsels and in the general administration of its affairs. And now what was I going to do about it? What could I do? I must either sit down quiescently under the denunciation launched against me and let everything go as it might chance to do, or I must stand up manfully in defence of my cause. Had no great principle been involved—nothing but merely personal considerations, it might have been politic for me to keep still and "crook the pregnant hinges of the knee where thrift may follow fawning." But as it was otherwise in my judgment, I was impelled to pursue a different course. If I were to act according to that impulse, I had nothing to expect but a bitter and unequal contest, in which the triumph of my cause, of which I was sure in the end, would cost me many

A NEW CRISIS CONFRONTED. 175

a pleasant friendship, ejection from my pastoral office in Milford, grievous aspersions of my motives, and numberless other discomforts and privations. Of merely temporal advantage there was nothing in that direction to gain, but seemingly much to lose. The main current of feeling and opinion in the Universalist denomination was unmistakably with my opponents. Few professed Restorationists were outspoken and resolute in behalf of their distinctive tenets. Nearly all the pulpits and periodicals were either positively ultra or in some sort of abeyance to that arrogant influence. And the dominant policy was to decry every independent-minded defender of future disciplinary retribution, as a factious, ambitious, mischief-making disturber of the order. As to honest conviction, devotion to principle, and conscientious love for truth and righteousness, they were all claimed for those who had transcended the old swaddling-clothes of infant Universalism. They might contemn and denounce the doctrines of their opponents on the issue under notice as an "old heathen notion," "the wildest of all reveries," or however else they pleased, and do so from the purest of motives, for they were not only honest and disinterested, but superiorily enlightened. So it verily seemed to them as it does generally to new-fledged speculatists, iconoclasts, and superficial radicals. They were honest and zealous, driving their chariot, Jehu-like through their eccclesiastical Israel, and evoking deafening shouts from their admiring sympathizers. And yet I could not then, nor can I now, see one single plausible, much less valid, reason for their peculiar assumptions.

A new crisis had now arrived in my career as a minister of the gospel of Christ, and my decision in regard to it must be made. For several days I had a painful mental struggle upon the question whether to keep silence or to boldly meet the issue that had so unexpectedly been forced upon me. Very grave consequences, I was aware, must follow either course. I contemplated them on either hand with dread. I had no personal grievances to redress, wrongs to avenge, ambitions to gratify. But I had a position to maintain, a cause to defend, a consistency of life, character, and teaching to preserve and make clear before God and the world. I was a sincere, firm, devoted believer in the doctrine of the final universal holiness and happiness for the entire human race. That doctrine was sacred to me as the apple of my eye. I could not deny it, hide it under a bushel, nor in any way ignore it. To me it involved everything in theology and ethics worth preaching or living for. I had come into the belief of that doctrine by a never-to-be-forgotten experience which affected and agitated me to the very depths of my being. I had continued in that belief at great sacrifice of personal friendship, of social advantage, of religious fellowship, of promised worldly success. I had been thrust out of the Christian Connexion on the urgent motion of my own father because that body could not tolerate my honest convictions in that respect, though professing to have no creed and to fellowship all who lived a Christian life, regardless of theological belief. I had come into the Universalist denomination at the earnest solicitations of some of its foremost representatives rather than by my own importunity. And when I frankly stated that I was a Restorationist and not an ultra-Universalist, so-called, I was assured of as hearty a welcome as if it were otherwise, and of being accorded an equal right to hold and preach limited future retribution with others cherishing different views upon that point. I believed this, joined the order, and found everything pleasant and cordial till I began to use my stipulated liberty of dissent from the prevailing orthodoxy of the denomination. Then, instead of kindly salutations and fraternal fellowship, there came coldness, detraction, harsh accusation, invective, denunciation.

Thus out of harmony and sympathetic union with my fellow-Universalists, whither could I look for that cordial,

FUTURE COURSE DECIDED UPON.

hearty friendliness and spirit of co-operation so much to be desired in the pursuit and promulgation of religious truth and the things of the religious life. I could not quietly withdraw from existing ecclesiastical relations and offer myself to one of the so-called evangelical sects, except by stealth and cowardice. They had their honest convictions, I had mine; and the two, on certain vital points, were fundamentally irreconcilable. They knew this as well as I. They must do their duty and I mine, each as we respectively understood it. They wanted nothing of me as I was, nor I of them as they were, except to wish them well and honor them for whatever good they might do. As to the Unitarian denomination in this country, it had, through its acknowledged leaders and advocates, manifested no approval of outspoken Restorationism at that day, though a few of its adherents professed a *quasi* belief in it. The general attitude of the body was one of aversion to that form of faith rather than of hospitality. I could not therefore, with honor, think of gaining entrance into that fold. Much less was I morally capable of accepting any form of philosophical materialism or of nebulous transcendentalism with its hazy dreams of the Great Absolute and of a doubtful immortality, even though I might be allowed to entertain and promulgate my views unchallenged and without hindrance of any sort.

There was for me no alternative so far as I could see but to remain where I was and either yield tamely and obsequiously with a padlock on my lips to the autocratic majority, or accept the issue which confronted me, and in an honorable, manly, Christian way defend myself, my views, and my line of action from the attacks of my adversaries. To my apprehension there was much more involved in the question that arose between me and my ultra brethren than one at first would be inclined to think. "Why," it might be asked, "inaugurate what promised to be a long and acrimonious conflict with your opponents about the time, place, and continuance of divine retribution — whether all before or partly after death — so long as you were agreed upon the great distinguishing subject of the final salvation of all the children of men?" To my mind the question between me and my assailants was not simply one of "time, place, and extent" of retributory visitation, but one of far more radical and vital importance — one comprehending, as it then was stated, interpreted, and applied, the moral nature and accountability of man; the intrinsic relation of the present state of existence to that which is to come; the equity and impartial justice of retribution for wrong-doing; and the correct exegesis and use of the Scriptures. It was not enough for me that the advocates of no future punishment professed the highest devotion to the doctrine of universal salvation if at the same time they held it and interpreted it in such a way as to annihilate or undermine the idea of the moral agency and personal responsibility of mankind; or virtually break the thread of continuity between this life and the next, and so make existence to consist of two lives instead of one and the same life extending through two stages of being; or misrepresent the divine government in its practical administration as absolutely just and righteous in all respects; or falsify and pervert the Hebrew and Christian sacred books by unwarrantable and absurd interpretations. It was on these grounds and for the reasons thus indicated that after deliberate, conscientious, prayerful, canvassing of the situation, I resolved to take up the gauntlet that had been thrown at my feet and enter at once upon the warfare that I could not in good conscience avoid or turn away from except in cowardly disgrace. I had consecrated myself to the unconditional service of God and His eternal truth. I was solemnly bound to maintain and defend what I sincerely believed to be the fundamental principles of moral order in the universe of souls. I was no less solemnly bound to stand up bravely for that freedom of utterance without which truth cannot be proclaimed or sustained against error, or divine principles be extended far and wide among men. I had no doubt that my cause was just and could be triumphantly vindicated on an open platform at the bar of enlightened reason. And in resolving upon a contest in its behalf, I was equally resolved that it should not be a half-smothered family quarrel, nor a series of sham fights, but one of open field, pitched battles. I had seen enough of cautious, politic, temporizing resistance to ultra-Universalism on the part of Restorationists. It had only irritated their opponents, excited their animosity, aroused their scorn, and provoked more aggravated aggressions. I therefore solemnly determined to proclaim and enter upon a square fight on all the issues involved, as the only just, honorable, and rational course to pursue. And having so determined, there was no longer on my part the least hesitation or vacillation. Whatever the consequences might be, the die was cast and cast irrevocably. There were to be no discharge and no retreat in that war.

The decision made, I sat down and wrote a detailed and exhaustive "Reply to Mr. Thomas Whittemore's Review of a Sermon delivered in Medway, Mass., by Adin Ballou." It was addressed "to the clergy and laity of the Universalist faith throughout the United States." In my opening paragraph I quoted verbatim the several definite charges made against me in the Review, as in substance presented on a preceding page, saying at the close, "A sense of duty to myself and the cause of truth requires that I should meet and repel these charges with a sober and dignified answer."

This I proceeded to do in an argument or series of arguments covering some fifteen large pages of manuscript, equal to about the same number of pages if transferred to this volume and hence too long for insertion in it. The final paragraph of the document was as follows:

"In closing this reply, it is incumbent on me to declare in the most solemn terms that I consider Mr. Whittemore's strictures upon my sermon an unjustifiable infringement of my inalienable rights, a deliberate violation of the obligations of fellowship, and a declaration of hostilities against both me and my doctrine. And I do furthermore solemnly declare that I consider myself outlawed and alienated from all fellowship with Rev. Thomas Whittemore and all persons who shall be found to have approved, justified, and encouraged him in this act of persecution. With these declarations clearly understood, I now submit this my defence to the candid contemplation of the clergy and laity of the whole denomination of Universalists, conjuring them to pass a righteous judgment upon my case and appealing to God in Heaven for the interposition of His justice and wisdom in bringing all difficulties to a happy conclusion."

The Reply was accompanied by this reasonable request:

"MR. EDITOR: I ask at your hands the justice to insert in your paper the following vindication of myself from your recent attack. I desire you to publish it immediately, or if you decide not to do so, to return it within four days.

"With regret.

"ADIN BALLOU."

Did Mr. Whittemore grant this request and publish my reply in the *Trumpet*? No. Did he open the columns of his paper to the free discussion of the points at issue? Never. Did he render any excuse, apology, or reason for not giving my article a place there, as he was desired to do? Not a word. Did he ever inform his readers that I had attempted an answer to his charges? No. What did he do? Returned my manuscript to me by mail in about a week without note or comment. And the most I ever heard from the *Trumpet* office on the subject was that he said my communication was "of a nature to disgrace me before the public" and he withheld it from his readers "out of compassionate regard for my reputation." This may have been more kindly meant than I was capable of understanding or being thankful for. However this may be, it was evidently deemed best that my article should be treated with silent contempt, presuming doubtless *that* would be the end of the matter. But I was not made of the stuff to cower and subside under such proceeding, as will appear in subsequent pages.

My next step in this matter was to present the controversy now inaugurated and my relation to it frankly to my society in Milford. I knew the majority in it were ultras or prejudiced strongly in that direction. The notice of my Medway sermon in the *Trumpet* had already aroused the more excitable of them to contemptuous remarks about my "purgatory," "little tophet," "hell junior," etc. I also knew that there were some solid, considerate members who were disposed to see me treated honorably, and a few who sympathized with my distinctive views. But I felt that I ought not to continue my pastoral relationship with my people without a fair mutual understanding. So on the second Sabbath in July, at my five o'clock service I laid the whole matter before my congregation in a discourse having for a text: "Men, brethren and fathers, hear my defence, which I make now unto you."—*Acts 22:1*. I distinctly stated my views, feelings, and course of action in the past; how the case now stood in consequence of the public denunciation issued against me on account of my honest sentiments, with no chance of exculpating or explaining myself allowed me; that I was determined to be henceforth an outspoken Restorationist at all hazards; that I knew the general predilection of my hearers for the doctrine of no future retribution; that I could not ask them to retain me as their minister contrary to their convictions and choice; that I should be glad to continue with them if they could bear with my honest independence and desired me to remain; but if otherwise disposed, I should make no complaint for being openly and honorably discharged at their discretion. The discourse was well received by the nobler-minded of the society, and my friend, Ariel Bragg, very kindly said to me that he saw no reason why my outspoken sentiments should render me less acceptable, useful, or desirable as their minister.

Others concurred. But a different class of minds went away with confirmed dissatisfaction which subsequently manifested itself in decided hostility, the results of which were soon to be made known to their associates and to the community at large.

From that day forth I stood before the public an independent, uncompromising Restorationist, in contradistinction from the ultra-Universalists on the one hand as well as from the advocates of endless punishment and the Destructionists on the other. For some months I continued preaching under prior arrangement, half the time in Milford and the other half in Medway—lecturing at convenient intervals in various other places. To complete my divorcement from the no future Retributionists, it was only necessary for me to unite ecclesiastically with the Providence Association, which was under their ban of outlawry on account of its declared opposition to their favorite dogma. This I did at an early day, casting in my lot with its Restorationist Separatists, for such they virtually were, and thus practically severing my connection with the General Universalist Convention.

A new movement had now actually begun among those rejecting the doctrine of endless punishment. An important desideratum as a means of promoting that movement was an organ of publication. Upon surveying the field and finding no one prepared to establish such an organ, I concluded to assume the responsibility myself, relying on such pledges of assistance as my sympathizing brother ministers were willing to offer. At a meeting of the Providence Association, held in Oxford, Mass., Aug. 19, 1830, the subject of a weekly periodical was introduced, discussed, and approved, and a title, suggested, I think, by Rev. Charles Hudson, *Independent Messenger*, was adopted. The following document, drawn up by myself, was then submitted to those present and duly signed:

"We, the subscribers, do hereby solemnly bind and obligate ourselves to Adin Ballou that, in case he shall within one year commence the publication of a weekly periodical to be called

INDEPENDENT MESSENGER FOUNDED.

the *Independent Messenger*, we will be responsible for the prompt payment of our respective subscriptions according to the number of copies noted opposite our several names.

PAUL DEAN, Boston, 100 copies; DAVID PICKERING, Providence, 100 copies; LYMAN MAYNARD, Oxford, 50 copies; CHARLES HUDSON, Westminster, 25 copies; PHILEMON R. RUSSELL, Halifax, 25 copies; SETH CHANDLER, Milford; 25 copies.

These 325 copies were all I could depend upon as a subscription list outside my own personal influence and exertions — not a large outfit for such an undertaking. Evidently the prospect was by no means flattering, but I was in earnest and not to be easily intimidated or discouraged. It was readily seen that the venture must be conducted with the most rigid economy or it would fail, and that right early. I therefore concluded to enlist a practical printer with an inexpensive establishment, form a co-partnership with him, and open an office in Milford, where the paper could be published, and more or less job work be done in order to reduce expense. An opportunity for such an arrangement soon presented itself. Mr. George W. Stacey, a young Restorationist brother, had been publishing *The Groton Herald* at Groton, Mass., in partnership with a Mr. Rogers, but the undertaking had proved unsuccessful and was to be abandoned. He had a fairly-equipped plant, was well recommended to me by those who knew him, and being approached with the proposition indicated, responded favorably. Articles of co-partnership between him and myself were drawn up and signed Sept. 24, 1830; the office and its belongings were removed to Milford, and business began about October 1, under the firm title, "Ballou & Stacey." This was the first printing establishment in Milford and was domiciled in an old building long since removed, situated between the Congregationalist meeting-house and Water street, fronting the parish common.

During the month of October I issued a prospectus of the *Independent Messenger*, to be published once a week on a neat, royal sheet of good paper at the price to subscribers of $1.50 per annum in advance and $2.00 after sixty days. The purpose and character of the new journal were clearly indicated in the opening paragraph, which is copied entire.

"Through the medium of this publication, we shall disseminate, illustrate, and defend the ancient doctrine of the "Restitution of all things;" explain, enforce, and vindicate the Holy Scriptures as the grand rule of Christian faith and practice; advocate the doctrine of limited future rewards and punishments; inculcate repentance towards God, faith in the Lord Jesus Christ, and good works among men; endeavor to promote piety, morality, charity, and social order; encourage free inquiry; contend for civil and religious liberty, and cultivate useful literature."

As was to be expected, the ultra-Universalists did all in their power to hedge up the way of this new venture and render it abortive. Not one of their periodicals (to my knowledge) gave my prospectus a favorable notice, several of them ignored it altogether, and one or two spoke in opposition to it. The old cry was raised in many quarters, "he is making difficulty in the order"; "stirring up disunion, discord, and strife among brethren"; "he cares nothing for doctrines or principles— it is all from ambition, envy, personal pique, and revenge." No means were spared to prejudice all susceptible persons against the proposed paper — to influence the public not to subscribe for it or in any manner countenance its publication.

Nevertheless, on the first day of January, 1831, I issued No. 1, Vol. 1 of the *Independent Messenger*. Its leading article was entitled, "An Epistle General to Restorationists," and occupied about two pages of the issue, beginning thus:

"To all sincere believers in the doctrine of Universal Restoration, whithersoever dispersed:—Wisdom and grace be with you from God the Father and His Son Jesus Christ.

"BELOVED BRETHREN:—Having been called by the God of our fathers to the defence of that ancient truth whereof He hath 'spoken by the mouths of all His holy prophets since the world began,' I deem it my solemn duty to submit to your consideration an undisguised exposition of the motives and feelings with which I enter upon so responsible an undertaking. In order to render such an exposition more clear and forcible, I have chosen to present a brief historical sketch of my life and experience during the last eight years."

I then proceeded to state and explain everything necessary to illustrate the whole case. And I did so with entire honesty and frankness from beginning to end. The article is too long to insert in this auto-biography, but I have taken care to collate it, with many kindred writings belonging to this controversy with the ultra-Universalists, in a volume which may, if deemed advisable, be published at some future day.

What was the effect of this *pronunciamento* on my part? It aroused the indignation of the Ultras in all directions. Its bold, trenchant, uncompromising disclosure of their aggressions and my expressed determination to resist them on every issue provoked their hostility to the utmost. But my onset was so unexpectedly impetuous and powerful that they were uncertain at first what course to pursue. But after taking counsel with each other, they decided that "their strength was to sit still" in their chosen retreats and operate in secret ways to my detriment. By this policy they hoped I might ere long exhaust my energies and resources, and retire from the field. But they were soon obliged to break their silence by the unanticipated effect of my frank and fearless utterance in another quarter. My statement commanded such respect from the Orthodox and more conscientious and devout liberalists of all shades, that they manifested at once their approval and gratification. The *Boston Recorder*, then the leading Trinitarian journal in New England, commended exceedingly my "Epistle General," and reproduced copious extracts from it in its own columns. This galled the editor of the *Trumpet* greatly and impelled him to speak out in the matter. But in doing so, he took pains to have it understood that he took notice of my slanders (as he characterized my declarations), not on my account, but solely because the *Recorder* had copied and indorsed them. The implication was that I was too insignificant and contemptible a foe to waste ammunition upon, but the *Recorder* was an old, respectable, and formidable enemy, with whom to do battle was honorable.

Meanwhile matters were ripening to a final issue in my society at Milford. The Ultras in it were much disturbed at my doings and resolved to get rid of me in a quiet way at as early a date as possible. So at a meeting held, without notice of what was designed, Jan. 22, 1831, it was "voted to dispense with the services of Rev. Adin Ballou as to supplying their pulpit in their meeting-house any more." This was objected to by some of my friends as having been done without any article in the warrant or other announcement providing for such action, and a motion to reconsider the vote was made, to be acted on at an adjourned meeting a week later. At that time it was readily "voted not to reconsider the vote dispensing with the services of Rev. Adin Ballou," and a committee was chosen to notify me accordingly. This was done immediately afterward by the chairman, Mr. Otis Parkhurst, causing my relations to the Milford people to come to a speedy termination. There was a striking and unpleasant contrast between this dismissal and the warm, urgent recall which brought me back to Milford from New York less than three years before. But circumstances alter cases, and I was prepared for anything that might arise.

Just at this juncture of affairs an incident occurred which I can scarcely regard otherwise than an ordering of divine Providence in my behalf, giving me renewed assurance that my heavenly Father had not forsaken me, but was opening the way before me to new fields of service and to larger opportunities of usefulness in the world than I had previously enjoyed. At about the same hour I was voted out of my Milford charge, the First Congregational parish in Mendon had taken action preparatory

OPENING OF MENDON PASTORATE.

to inviting me to its vacant pastorate; and the Milford committee had hardly discharged its duty of informing me of the act by which my labors in that town were to terminate, before a committee from Mendon waited upon me for the purpose of offering me the pulpit at its disposal. The offer was accepted, and the details of my removal to the neighboring town and of my entrance upon my new duties there were arranged to the satisfaction of both parties. Thus it came to pass that on the last Sunday of January, 1831, I closed my labors with the Universalist society in Milford, and on the following Sunday entered upon corresponding labors as pastor of the First society and church in Mendon. At as early a date thereafter as was practicable, my family and printing-press were transferred to my new field of labor, and I was fairly settled in my re-established home, in my editorial work, and in the activities of my ministerial office, at the expiration of the 28th year of my life, April 23, 1831.

Before proceeding to record the events and experiences of a new year, however, it seems advisable to go back a little in the order of time and briefly note a few facts that transpired during the period just passed in review, but that could not be mentioned in their proper place, chronologically considered, without abruptly breaking in upon the continuity of the narrative in hand. The first of these is that on the fourth of July, 1830, I delivered my second oration commemorating the Declaration of our National Independence. It took place in the manufacturing village (now town) of Blackstone, in the then South Parish of Mendon, before a large, respectable, and apparently gratified audience. An honorable committee of the citizens of the village and vicinity waited upon me after the exercises of the occasion were over, and solicited a copy of my address for the press. Their request was granted, and the production soon after appeared in print and was widely circulated in the general community. It may be found by interested parties in the library of the town of Hopedale, with most of my printed works, and will show my political and patriotic status at that date.

On the 28th of November, 1830, we had a son born to us, whom we named, in honor of his maternal grandfather, Pearley Hunt Ballou. He brought great joy into a household which was passing through trying experiences, and awakened many ardent and precious hopes for the future in the breasts of his parents and of all who held him dear. But his life was of but a few brief years' continuance here, being cut short by a fearful malady, which swept him and his elder brother into an early grave.

I have already spoken briefly of the effect produced by the issuing of the first number of the *Independent Messenger* upon my ultra-Universalist brethren and especially upon the editor of the *Trumpet*, who, after resolving evidently upon a policy of silence, was goaded to publish a rejoinder to my "General Appeal to Restorationists" by the use made of that article on the part of the *Boston Recorder* and other Orthodox journals of that day. It is worth while to state that the paper mentioned declared "the Restorationist ministers concerned in the new movement to be the most respectable of the Universalist clergymen" which was too bitter a pill for the Rev. Thomas Whittemore to swallow with composure. His equanimity was greatly disturbed, and he must speak out, as he did in an issue of the *Trumpet* January 29th, 1831, in which he opened fire, not on me, for I was beneath his notice, but on the Orthodox who had committed a grievous offence by quoting my slanders and misrepresentations, and so making them their own. What he had to say at the date named, however, was mostly explanatory and predictive of what was to come in the next issue of the paper, when big guns were to be leveled against the offending Orthodox brethren and their chief instigators, the leaders in the Restorationist movement; myself, puerile and unworthy of notice as I was, among the number.

The appearance of the next number of the *Trumpet*

and Universalist Magazine, to give the full title of the publication, was awaited with earnest expectation and fond desire, and when received its long editorial treating of the matter in hand was read with intense interest, but with equally intense repugnance and detestation. The article opened with dark assaults on the moral character of Revs. Paul Dean and David Pickering, two of our leading ministers, with scarcely less accusatory ones against Rev. Charles Hudson and other Restorationist divines. These assaults were not open, frank, specific allegations, but vague assertions, implications, insinuations, and threats of contingent exposure. I replied to them in the *Messenger* as follows:

"The aspersions with which they (the conclave which spoke through Mr. Whittemore) have endeavored to destroy the reputation of such men as Revs. Paul Dean, David Pickering, and Charles Hudson, will only rebound, and, like barbed arrows, pierce their own bosoms. These men will in due time reply to the defamatory charges with which they have been individually assailed. With regard to the vile insinuations against Brother Dean [who was then on a preaching tour in the Southern States] and the threat that certain 'certificates' now in the possession of Rev. Hosea Ballou, together with 'a full history of the faction from the beginning shall go before the public,' we feel authorized to speak in language that cannot be misunderstood. And therefore, in our own name, in the name of Mr. Dean, and of all independent Restorationists, we solemnly demand of Rev. Hosea Ballou and Thomas Whittemore, the immediate publication of said 'certificates,' and of all other documents alluded to as affecting the case now pending at the bar of public opinion. We know the purport of those wonderful documents and we also know that the private use of them by their very compassionate possessor has soured more minds against Brother Dean and injured his reputation more than their publication can ever do, allowing them to be as frightful as Mr. W. intimates. The friends of Brother Dean may rest assured that the papers referred to will prove, *upon explanation*, injurious chiefly to those who hope to turn them to the gratification of their revenge. Furthermore, we inform the public that we know of papers in safe keeping which relate to Rev. Hosea Ballou — papers which have, in a great measure, been hid from the public eye in order to save the subject of them from justly deserved reproach and blame. Should occasion require, these, under the hand of a justice, will be made known to the world."

This response was more than had been bargained for. It silenced the great gun of the enemy. No more was ever heard of those "certificates," nor of that "full history of the faction." Brothers Dean and Hudson waited for the threatened exposures before appearing in self-defence, but the occasion for such appearance never came. Brother Pickering submitted his case to the trustees of his society, who immediately demanded of Mr. Whittemore specific charges against their minister, if he had any, instead of the secret stabs with which he had assailed his character and reputation. He responded in a private letter, making no definite accusations, but only repeating the former vague insinuations. The trustees replied, telling him that he had no case, that his attacks were wholly unjustifiable, that they had full confidence in their pastor and were entirely satisfied with his character and conduct, closing with a request that the correspondence between them and him be published in the *Trumpet*. With his usual unfairness, he refused. It, however, appeared in the *Independent Messenger* of March 18, 1831. To this was added in the next number a communication from Brother Pickering in triumphant vindication of himself, which left nothing more to be said, and which silenced his accusers thenceforth and forevermore.

So much relating to the first part of the article of Rev. Thomas Whittemore, in response to my "General Epistle to Restorationists." The remainder of it consisted of a desperate cannonade designed to demolish my statements and professions in that "Epistle," against ultra-Universalism. His principal efforts were expended in an endeavor to nullify my testimony and make it appear unworthy of credence by representing and denouncing me (1) as a weak-minded young man, ambitious of a distinction wholly beyond my capacity to reach; (2) as the mere tool of certain unprincipled designing men, chiefest of whom was Paul Dean, who had flattered and cajoled me into joining their cabal in order that they might use me for the furtherance of their own perfidious schemes; and (3) as a pretentious, unscrupulous liar and hypocrite in a bad cause, incapable of speaking the truth in the matters at issue, and unworthy of belief or confidence. These several points he attempted by most fallacious and excruciating special pleadings to demonstrate, and to make it appear that I exemplified in my personality the compound qualities of both fool and knave. I found no difficulty in meeting the charges preferred against me, in defending myself at every point of attack, and in putting aside and shielding myself from all the enemy's vituperation. I suffered nothing but gained much by this encounter, both in my own self-respect and, so far as I could judge, in the esteem and confidence of the general public.

Another aspect of the case now in review ought not to pass unnoticed. While the boldness of my utterance aroused the indignation and provoked the animosity of my opponents of the ultra school of Universalists, it awakened the fears and apprehensions of some of the prudent, conservative, and politic of my Restorationist friends. One of the most respected and active of them immediately after the reception of the first issue of the *Messenger*, wrote me, chiding me somewhat for what he feared was my ill-timed though good article, and advising me that we must be " wise as serpents and harmless as doves." He also suggested that in order to mollify the sharpness of my rebuke and prevent needless ill-feeling, I insert an editorial in the next number something like the following :

"Our object is to defend our views rather than assail others. We intend to build up the cause of pure religion, not by a petty warfare with those who differ from us, but by presenting what we consider to be the truth. In our first issue, we felt it to be our duty to present to our readers a true, unvarnished tale of what we had felt, seen, and heard. Having done this, we shall not seek a controversy with the *Trumpet*, *Recorder*, or any of our neighbors. We shall commence no attack any further than it is necessary to vindicate our own sentiments. Being bent on truth, we shall not go out of our way to attack error, but if we are attacked, we shall endeavor to maintain our own ground."

Similar deprecatory expressions came from different sources, all kindly meant, and I could not do otherwise than give them thoughtful consideration. But they were for the most part lost upon me, for I viewed things from a standpoint quite different from that occupied by my kindly advisers and was in no mood to be governed by what seemed to them a wise expediency. So after duly canvassing the *pro* and *con* of their counsels, I decided to put them all aside and follow the dictates of my own best judgment and understanding — a conclusion which I never had reason to regret.

CHAPTER XI.

1831–1832.

MENDON PARISH — RESTORATIONIST ASSOCIATION — CONTROVERSY WITH THE ULTRAS CONTINUED — SYMPATHY FROM UNITARIANS.

AT the opening of the twenty-ninth year of my life, I found myself fairly well settled in the town of Mendon and busily engaged in the discharge of the duties incident to my new pastorate and in the management of the editorial and financial affairs of the *Independent Messenger*, most of which had, by force of circumstances and my own choice, been entrusted to my keeping. Myself and family were snugly domiciled in the dwelling-house belonging to what was then known as the Judge Rawson estate, located on high land overlooking the village from the west, near the junction of the Uxbridge and Chestnut Hill roads. Though not far from the center of the town, which was at that time one of the largest and most thriving in the southern part of Worcester County, and though pleasantly situated in many respects, commanding a fine view of the surrounding country, especially to the east and south, yet it seemed to us the most dreary and lonely abode we had ever occupied, contrasting most unfavorably with the comparatively new and attractive one we had left behind. The fact that we were the nominal owners of the Milford house and could in some proper sense call it our own, while the one we now occupied was the property of another, may account in some measure for the unhomelikeness and cheerlessness which characterized the latter and made it far from satisfactory as a permanent residence. Nevertheless, it was not in us to look backward with regret, murmuring, and complaint. The tide of events was onward and forward, and towards the future we were bound to press our way with courage and with hope.

The First parish and church in Mendon at the time I took pastoral charge of them, were in a depressed and unpromising condition. The church proper had been reduced by a recent secession to eight members, mostly superannuated persons, and the attendance on public worship was discouragingly small. Yet my predecessor, Rev. Simeon Doggett, was an educated, scholarly man with a benignant heart, who for sixteen years had sustained a generally respectable pastorate. But the Calvinists had come in with their fiery zeal and impassioned appeals, drawing many away from the staid formalities of the ancient sanctuary of the town. They had organized a new church, built for themselves a house of worship, gathered in a large congregation, and were in an apparently prosperous condition. Scattered through the territorial limits of the parish, however, were many heterogeneous elements which had drifted away from the established institutions of religion, but which, if they could be attracted to and combined with the substantial constituency that remained at the old center of church life, would presently change the aspect of things most essentially. And this was evidently the work for me to do — a work for which I deemed myself well equipped and qualified. I was of vigorous age, earnest zeal, and competent abilities, and was charged with doctrines and principles as positive and unequivocal as the most orthodox. To the task thus set before me I at once addressed myself and with most successful and gratifying results. Two discourses were preached every Sunday, which, with a reconstructed and active Sunday school, various special religious meetings during the week, and frequent parochial visitation, gave me enough to do in my proper ministerial field of service and yielded abundant fruit. My congregation increased greatly; the church membership soon began to be replenished, and the vacant places to be supplied, and an encouraging prosperity prevailed in all the borders of our Zion.

To these more strictly pastoral and home duties were added many lectures, funeral sermons, etc., outside my conventional field of service in the general vicinity. Moreover, my editorship and business oversight of the *Independent Messenger* occupied all the time I had to spare, keeping me in the harness oftentimes until midnight or the small hours of the morning. I was continually beset with controversial attacks from two classes of opponents — the ultra-Universalists, who were in determined hostility to the Restorationist movement, and the believers in endless punishment, who were equally in earnest against the views I sought to promulgate in the pulpit and elsewhere as opportunity offered. Moreover, I had an extensive correspondence with persons desirous of information upon various points of doctrine which I was known to hold and advocate. So that between open assaults on the one hand and professed inquiries after truth on the other, my pen had all it could do to answer the demands made upon it. But these demands were promptly and frankly met, as the preserved files of the *Messenger* duly attest.

All this work was done and all these calls were answered under circumstances that necessitated the most rigid economy and the most scrupulous care of my material resources and expenditures, with more frequent resorts to credit than I wished. My paper, the pecuniary responsibility of which I had assumed, was not self-supporting, and my salary for pastoral service was only about $400 for the year, with but little, if any, income from incidental sources. Such was the general condition of my affairs, financially considered, in the year 1831-32.

During this year, as in the preceding one, important events and interesting personal experiences marked my career. To these I must briefly recur, in the order which seems most advisable, though not always in precise chronological succession.

The annual meeting of the Providence Association of Universalists, with which I had become identified, was held in Westminster, Mass., then the pastoral home of our reverend brother, Charles Hudson, on the third Wednesday and Thursday of May. It was attended by the following ministerial brethren; Reverend Brothers Dean of Boston, Pickering of Providence, R. I., Hudson of Westminster, Maynard of Oxford, Wright of Attleboro', Russell of Winchester, N. H., Chandler of Medway, and myself. I was chosen moderator of the session, and Brother Maynard, clerk. Two full days were spent in profitable private consultation and public religious services, at which earnest discourses were preached by Brothers Chandler, Pickering, Dean, and myself, to good congregations, on which salutary impressions seemed to have been made.

Among the proceedings of the meeting in council was the passage of a resolution pledging cordial support to the *Independent Messenger* and recommending it to the patronage of friends and the public. Also was there provision made for the printing in the *Messenger* of a "Circular letter to our brethren scattered abroad," to be prepared by myself. A few extracts from it will show its character and spirit.

"To all their Christian brethren and especially those who cherish the hope of Universal Restoration, the Providence Association sends salutations of fraternal love, wishing you grace, truth, and peace from God the Father and Jesus Christ the Lord.

"We rejoice exceedingly in that divine goodness which hath shielded us from the fiery darts of the wicked and wrought our deliverance from the hand of them that sought our destruction. With deep-felt gratitude and joy, we announce to you that our most sanguine expectations have been more than realized in the success with which God hath crowned our cause."

"And now, beloved brethren, we exhort you to gird up the loins of your minds and take courage. With a cheerful and understanding zeal, persevere in the work of righteousness.

Be not carried about with every wind of doctrine; neither listen to those who turn the grace of God into a strife of words, but, setting your faces steadfastly Zionward, 'Let your light so shine before men that they, seeing your good works, may glorify your Father in Heaven.' Remember always that 'the grace of God which bringeth salvation to all men teacheth us that denying ungodliness and worldly lusts, we should live soberly, righteously, and godly in the present world.' We recommend that you be constant in your attendance upon the service of the sanctuary, that you confer often with one another, that you pray in your families and in social meetings with each other, but above all in secret — making supplication for us and for all men that the word of truth may have free course, and that the salvation of the human family may be consummated by the appointed means according to the purpose of God. Endeavor to become a peaceable, friendly, temperate, charitable people, that you may thereby adorn the doctrine of divine grace, promote the happiness of your fellow-men, secure your own eternal welfare, and enjoy the approbation of the Most High. And now we commend you to God and the word of His grace, which is able to build you up and give you a place with the sanctified forever. Farewell."

The second and most important of the ecclesiastical meetings of the year took place at Mendon, on the 16th, 17th, and 18th days of August. It commenced with a regular session of the same Association, which held council meetings and public services for two days, sermons being preached by Brothers Russell, Hudson, Dean, and Pickering to respectable and deeply interested audiences. On the last day of convocation, a certain number of us, members of that body, formed the *Massachusetts Association of Universal Restorationists*, thus consummating our separation from the Universalist denomination. The following is the document which announced to the world the step we had taken:

"Forasmuch as there has been of late years a great departure from the sentiments of the First Universalist preachers in this country by a majority of the General Convention, the leaders of which do now arrogate to themselves exclusively the name of Universalists; and whereas we believe with Murray, Winchester, Chauncey, and the ancient authors who have written upon this subject, that Regeneration, a General Judgment, Future Rewards and Punishments, to be followed by the Final Restoration of all men to holiness and happiness, are fundamental articles of Christian faith, and that the modern sentiments of no future accountability connected with materialism are unfriendly to pure religion and subversion of the best interests of society; and whereas our adherence to the doctrines on which the General Convention was first established, instead of producing fair, manly controversy, has procured for us contumely, exclusion from ecclesiastical councils, and final expulsion, and this without proof of any offence on our part against the rules of the order or the laws of Christ; it is therefore

"*Resolved*, that we hereby form ourselves into a religious Community for the Defence and Promulgation of the doctrines of Revelation in their original purity, and the promotion of our own improvement, to be known by the name of *The Massachusetts Association of Universal Restorationists*.

"*Resolved*, that the annual meeting of this body be holden in Boston on the first Wednesday and following Thursday in January.

"CHARLES HUDSON, *President*.
"NATHANIEL WRIGHT, *Secretary*."

Eight ministers and several laymen composed the convention that adopted the foregoing preamble and resolutions. These were originally drawn, I think, by Rev. Paul Dean, of Boston. They were unanimously adopted and sent out to the public as the climax of our independence and the herald of our cause. How they were treated by our former brethren of the ultra school will appear further on.

The third of our distinctive ecclesiastical meetings this year was a conference held in Medway village, so-called, on the second Wednesday and Thursday in October. A small society had been formed there, and had invited Brother Seth Chandler to become their minister. The principal object of this gathering was to confer the rites of ordination upon the pastor-elect and install him in his office. He had been my student in theology and I was much interested in his success. The occasion was a pleasant and edifying one. Four sermons were delivered at as many public services by Revs. George Blackburn, Paul Dean, Charles Hudson, and myself, respectively —

the last being an ordination sermon from *Acts, 20:27.* "I have not shunned to declare unto you the whole counsel of God." The ordaining prayer was offered by Brother Dean, the charge and delivery of the Scriptures by Brother Hudson, the right hand of fellowship by Brother Wright; all of which parts were printed with the sermon in an early issue of the *Independent Messenger.*

The controversy with the ultra-Universalists, the opening battles of which were portrayed in the preceding chapter, continued with more or less vigor during the present year. In the later spring and early summer months it assumed a guerrilla form of attack and was met at every point with promptitude and decisiveness. At any rate, if the assailants did not realize their discomfiture, they deemed discretion the better part of valor and withdrew at length from the field.

But after the organization of the Restorationist Association in August, as narrated, and the issuance of our "Proclamation of Independence" soon afterward, a fresh campaign was inaugurated against us by the editor of the *Trumpet*, which was carried on for several months with no lack of energy or intensity on either side. The renewal of hostilities occurred Sept. 17, when Mr. Whittemore opened fire upon us as set forth below:

"THE NEW SECT.

"The following article has been going the rounds of the Boston papers and we cannot permit its further circulation without exposing the misrepresentations of which it is composed." He then quoted our preamble and resolutions as herein before given, and proceeded to declare that nearly every statement of the former was a falsification of the facts of the case; a declaration which he attempted to make good by as groundless an argument as was ever framed in support of a weak and desperate cause. To the sophistry and special pleading of the *Trumpet* editorial, I immediately prepared a reply, taking up the several charges of misrepresentation one by one and answering them at length — said reply appearing in the two succeeding numbers of the *Messenger*, issued Sept. 23d and 30th, 1831, to the files of which in the Hopedale public library those interested in the details of the discussion are hereby referred.

Nevertheless, it seems desirable that I should give my present readers a general outline of the argument on both sides as it was carried on between Mr. Whittemore and myself, from which they may be able to judge, with a considerable degree of accuracy, what were the real merits of the case, and whether or not the Restorationists were justified in the course they saw fit to pursue and in the defence I was moved to make in their behalf.

Mr. Whittemore, in considering the first reason given by the Restorationists for the formation of a new order, to wit; " that there had been of late years a great departure from the sentiments of the First Universalist preachers in this country by a majority of the General Convention," did not deny the fact that such was the case, but asserted that it was not a reason for their separation and as a proof of the assertion said that " these men themselves have departed as widely from the early American Universalist preachers as any Universalists have ever done." To this I replied that " his assertion is a high and insulting charge of dishonesty" on their part, and that his assumed proof of such dishonesty " is his personal *ipse dixit* without one particle of evidence being adduced by him or anywhere existing in support of it." I therefore openly and emphatically denied the charge. I then quoted from my opponent's own work, " Modern History of Universalism," in which the author says of Winchester and Murray, the early Universalist preachers referred to: "They both held to the existence of misery in the future state "; and adds that the Restorationists entertain the same view, and furthermore that " they all believe, as Winchester and Murray did, that this misery will grow out of the sinner's unbelief, sin, and guilt, commenced in his life, persevered in through death, and remaining with him upon his entrance into the world to come." This, with those I represented, I declared to be an essential doctrine — a peculiar feature of the faith of the original Universalists, which separates them from modern ones generally and which ought to separate them entirely from the Universalist denomination as it then existed and was controlled. As to the Universalist leaders at the time of the controversy — Hosea Ballou, Walter Balfour, and Thomas Whittemore, who assumed to dictate the faith and polity of the denomination, they had renounced utterly this important theological position of their predecessors, as the author of the *Trumpet* article well knew when he penned it. To substantiate this statement, I presented, in full, passages from the writings of each of the men named, in which they repudiated unequivocally the views of Murray and Winchester, and other passages, in which they stigmatized those views as "Salem witchcraft delusions," "old heathen notions," etc. "Here, sir," I said, "your *ipse dixit*, omnipotent as you may imagine it, is overwhelmed with irresistible counter evidence. You have verified the ancient truth, 'The wicked is snared in the work of his own hands.'"

The preamble to the resolutions of the Restorationist Association further set forth that its framers "believe with Murray, Winchester, Chauncey, and the ancient authors who have written upon this subject, that Regeneration, a General Judgment, Future Rewards and Punishments, to be followed by the Final Restoration of all men to holiness and happiness, are fundamental articles of Christian faith." In noticing this declaration, Mr. Whittemore undertook to parry its force and make us appear guilty of misrepresentation and deceit by saying: "They (the Restorationists) do not hold to Regeneration as Murray did, nor to the General Judgment as he did, nor to future punishment as he did." To which I replied that whether this were so or not, the claim we made in our manifesto was not invalidated in the least. We did not profess to hold views upon the doctrines specified *pre-*

cisely as the fathers did. I said: "We intended to speak in general terms, not to split hairs, and we are well understood by those who care to understand us correctly. The preamble represents us as being in substantial agreement with Murray and others named upon certain great Christian truths which the leading Universalists of the present day and most of their followers either deny or virtually abandon and ignore, as no part of their theological system." And this point I went on to demonstrate by ample quotations and illustrations.

Our caviling critic referring to another clause in our preamble, said: "Universalists are represented as not holding to future accountability. This is a misrepresentation." In meeting this charge, I inquired how our statement was a misrepresentation. By the phrase " no future accountability" we meant what all the world must understand, *no liability after death to retribution for the deeds done in the body*, and in support of our declaration copied Mr. W.'s own words: " Universalists now know of no condition of man beyond the grave but that in which he is as the angels of God in Heaven," with references to similar testimonies from Rev. Hosea Ballou and Walter Balfour. " You may say," I continued, " that ' Universalists *do* hold to future accountability — they hold that people will be accountable in a future state for what they do in that state, though not for what they may have done in a former state.' This is a mere quibble, for it does not meet the case presented by us at all. It changes most essentially the meaning of the phrase, ' no future accountability' as we used it, and as the public generally understand it, and instead of making good the charge of misrepresentation against us, proves our censor guilty of misrepresenting us in his attempt to invalidate our testimony."

Again, the editor of the *Trumpet* said: " They (the Universalists) are represented as Materialists — another misrepresentation." " Another misrepresentation!" I exclaimed in my rejoinder. " These Restorationists must be horrid creatures!" I then produced extracts from the writings of Walter Balfour, one of the big guns among our opponents in those days as follows: "I deny that the soul is immortal." "All who have read my books will bear witness I have invariably contended it (the soul) means life." "How does the soul survive after men have killed the body? Have I not said until I am tired of repeating it, that it returns to God who gave it. But have you (Mr. Hudson) shown that the soul is immortal in the sense essential to your system; that it exists after death, in a state of consciousness, in happiness or misery? No, sir; this you have not done and I am confident you will never be able to do it." "Man cannot kill the soul or life. It is God only who can do this. He breathed into man at first the breath or life; at death the life or breath He gave returns to Him who gave it."—*Letters to Hudson*. "What then," I asked, "is rational man, on Mr. Balfour's scheme, but matter—mere matter animated with breath? Here, sir, is Mr. Balfour's Materialism, the Materialism deprecated in our preamble, the Materialism which you disavow as belonging to your sort of Universalism. I will ask if you, who deny future punishment, even the American Universalists (generally), do not stand on Balfour's ground? Is not his *your* favorite system? If not, why have you not, like honest men, disclaimed his tenets concerning the soul and concerning man's unconsciousness for a while after death? Why have you lauded the merits of his works with such unqualified praise? Say you in your *Trumpet*: 'These works are written in the spirit of candor, and are replete with forcible argument and sound criticism.'"

In his animadversion on this point, Mr. Whittemore referred to Rev. Hosea Ballou's "perfect distinction between the human spirit and body," upon which Mr. Hudson had formerly commented. To this I replied, "All that related to the *old* no-future-punishment scheme, as held before Mr. Balfour's *new* system came into vogue. That old system has been lost in silence since Mr. Balfour's has been promulgated. In fact, the two schemes are utterly irreconcilable. The essential doctrine of the former — the soul's immortality — Mr. Balfour sets down as *a mere heathen notion*. You knew all this, sir, when you wrote your charge of misrepresentation. Your allusion to writings against H. Ballou's old scheme of no future punishment had nothing to do with the present state of Universalism, unless you meant that the public should think that you and your confreres are still believers in the immortality of a distinct soul. But will you insinuate this? Will you revive the former views and discard Mr. Balfour's? Only be honest and consistent; you will then stand much better in the opinion of the public."

Upon the fourth reason given by the Restorationists for their action in forming an independent Association, which was that " our adherence to the doctrines on which the General Convention (of Universalists) was first established, instead of producing fair, manly controversy, has procured for us contumely, exclusion from ecclesiastical councils, and final expulsion, etc.," Mr. Whittemore made a two-fold accusation against those concerned. In the first place he said, "The General Convention never was established on the doctrine of punishment in a future state; the subject was left untouched and each member made up his mind as he understood the word of God." In my reply I stated that this declaration of my opponent implied that among those who founded the General Convention at Oxford, in 1785, were believers in the doctrine of no future punishment as well as Restorationists, which was not the case, and that the reason why the subject of future retribution was left untouched was because there was such entire unanimity in its favor that no one deemed it in any way important to include it in their platform. In support of my position I quoted largely from Elhanan Winchester, the leading spirit in the movement, who, upon learning that some persons professing to hold the doctrine of the final restitution of all things believed that all men would be happy at death, publicly preached against it, and not only disclaimed all fellowship with it, but denounced it outright as utterly intolerable and pernicious.

I furthermore stated that there was no evidence within my knowledge that John Murray (whose views upon the question of future limited punishment have been referred to) was any more ready to sacrifice his convictions in this matter than was Mr. Winchester. "There is scarcely room to doubt," I added, "that the founders and early members (whether clergy or laity) of the General Convention believed and took for granted as an unquestionable doctrine of revealed religion that those who left this life sinful and unreconciled to God must be miserable for a limited space beyond the grave. And for Mr. Whittemore to represent, even by implication, that it was otherwise — that ultra-Universalists as well as Restorationists were concerned in establishing the General Convention — was an act of dissimulation and Jesuitry unworthy of a man who stood before the world as a teacher of the principles and precepts of the Christian religion."

In order to show still more clearly the unreliability — not to say duplicity — of my reverend opponent, I reminded him that in his "History of Universalism," published the year before, he did not venture to date the difference between Universalists concerning future punishment earlier than "about twenty years since," and that Rev. Hosea Ballou, who was, in fact, the first great expositor of the modern ultra school, had affirmed, as quoted by Mr. Whittemore himself, that he was not fully satisfied that the Bible taught no future punishment until he examined the subject with Rev. Edward Turner of Charlestown. This examination took place in 1817. Previous to that date the doctrine of the Restorationists had been the recognized orthodoxy of the Universalist denomination, only here and there an individual claiming to hold to the idea of no future punishment, and then on his own personal responsibility. The charge that Universalists, as such, entertained that notion was denied by the Philadelphia Convention of 1791 (as I have before said) and denounced as an "unjust slander." "From all this," I observed, in closing this part of the discussion, "our readers can judge pretty conclusively whether the General Convention was established on the doctrine of future retribution, and whether the Restorationists are guilty of misrepresentation on this point or otherwise,— whether you (Mr. Whittemore) in charging them with misrepresentation have not stood forth *a false accuser.*"

In the second place, under the same general head, our editorial combatant stoutly denied the assertion of the Restorationist Association that their adherence to the views of the fathers had procured for them contumely, exclusion, and expulsion, etc. As a refutation of this denial, I brought to notice the declarations of our opponents in public print and elsewhere, which likened our views to the superstitions that produced the Salem witchcraft, to the Catholic notions of Purgatory, calling them "heathen chaff," "wildest vagaries," etc. Also the use of such terms as "Little Tophet," "Hell Junior," bandied about in connection with our names and convictions, and the sarcasm and ridicule with which Walter Balfour and others were wont to speak of us, and of the truths which we solemnly believed ourselves called of God to maintain, defend, and promulgate to our fellow-men. If such treatment was not justly characterized by the term "contumely," we knew of no way in which it could be properly designated. Our opponents might call it kindness, but we did not so understand the meaning of words and our readers would judge who of us were right.

As to our statement that we had been excluded and expelled from ecclesiastical councils, our contumacious censor affirmed that it was "a gross and wilful misrepresentation. Worse than anything that had gone before!" In rebuttal of this allegation, I cited and explained at length the refusal of the General Convention

INSTANCES OF EXCLUSION CITED.

at Winchester, N. H., in 1829, at the dictum of Rev. Hosea Ballou, to allow Rev. Brother Pickering to offer prayer introductory to the sermon of Rev. Paul Dean, although he had been formally assigned to the discharge of that duty; also the abrogation of my own right to a seat in the same body by a vote passed in September, 1830. Rev. Seth Chandler was denied recognition as a Universalist, though a member of the Universalist society in Lowell, which was in fellowship with the General Convention, though he commenced preaching as a Universalist and was admitted into the pulpits of the order as one of its ministers, and though Mr. Whittemore himself had enrolled him in the catalogue of ministers of the denomination in his *History of Modern Universalism*. The same was true of Philemon R. Russell. It was stated that he never belonged to the Universalist denomination *in any way*. But he received the fellowship of the Eastern Association bearing the denominational name, and as a member of that body belonged to the General Convention. No doubt if we had all obeyed the orders and conformed to the wishes of those who assumed to be our rulers, we should have been neither censured nor expelled. But we *were* censured and expelled, if there be any such thing in ecclesiastical parlance.

In June, 1830, several members of the Boston Association, with other ministering brethren, held a meeting of what was called the Southern Association, in Berlin, Conn., where a preamble and resolutions were passed to the effect that independent associations, such as the Providence Association, composed mostly of Restorationists, was known to be, tended to promote division in the order and must therefore be discountenanced, and that ministers connected with such associations ought not to be allowed a seat in the General Convention, unless they withdraw fellowship from the former. At a meeting of the General Convention in September following, the authors of the Berlin resolutions secured the passage of a vote excluding from a seat in that body all of us who were members of the Providence Association, so long as we retained such membership. The plea was that this organization held itself constitutionally independent of the General Convention. When those urging this plea were told that the Maine and New York conventions occupied the same independent position, they secured the appointment of committees to confer with those bodies and thus preserve friendly relations with them. But no committee was appointed to confer with our association for the evident reason that the managers in the matter did not desire to preserve friendly relations with us, but rather to break up our body, or failing in that, shut us out of the General Convention. We would not abandon our own fraternity and hence were cut off from the main body. It was said of us that we thus excluded ourselves from our former fellowship. Nevertheless, we maintained that by the carefully planned action of our opponents we were excluded from the Universalist Ecclesiastical Councils as we had affirmed, and we believed and felt that we had the support of the intelligent public in that position.

So ended, virtually, the direct controversy with our ultra-Universalist brethren growing out of the formation of the Massachusetts Restorationist Association, though the same ground essentially was retrodden by corresponding parties, at a meeting of the General Convention held in Barre, Vt., soon afterward. There our opponents put in ecclesiastical form, with slight modifications, the same charges, aspersions, and insinuations against the Restorationists previously set forth in the *Trumpet*. This reiteration of their special pleading and casuistry, was upon being made public, promptly repelled, partly by myself in the *Independent Messenger* of Oct. 14th and Nov. 18th, and partly by Brother Charles Hudson, in the same paper of Nov. 4th, Nov. 25th, and Dec. 9th, 1831.

As a further illustration of the disingenuous, contemptuous treatment shown the Restorationists by their former brethren in the fellowship of the Universalist denomination, I am impelled to state in passing to other topics that while the columns of the *Independent Messenger* were always open to our opponents, and while we invited communications criticising our distinctive views and exposing our fallacies of doctrine or argument, if any were thought to be found, never in a single instance were our refutory articles allowed to appear in their chief organ, the *Trumpet*, nor in any other of their publications. Neither justice nor magnanimity on their part gave us one solitary chance for self-defence in their columns, or for a frank and manly exposition of our views as in any way opposed to those of the leading influences of the Universalist denomination in doctrine and polity at that time. Whether or not this was fair, manly, and honorable, I left my readers then, as I leave my present ones, to judge.

I have already adverted to the fact that during this year (1831) I was beset with controversial attacks, not only from my Universalist opponents but from believers in endless punishment, each of whom I in proper time and place endeavored to repel and overcome. Most of the latter were merely newspaper thrusts and sallies to which I responded with such small shot as their unimportance required. A somewhat notable discussion, however, was carried on in the columns of the *Messenger* between an orthodox clergyman, who chose to write over the name of "Inquirer," and myself, the first onset being made by him. The wordy conflict continued through a series of fourteen articles in as many numbers of the publication, each of them being answered consecutively as it appeared. My inquiring assailant proved to be the pastor of the Congregationalist church and society in Hopkinton, a conscientious and zealous young man, who had been educated in Dr. N. W. Taylor's New School Theological Seminary at New Haven, Ct., and who felt himself called upon to defend against all adversaries the faith delivered to that sort of orthodox saints. His name was Rev. Amos A. Phelps, subsequently distinguished as an Abolitionist of the Liberal Party school.

The first noticeable event of the calendar year 1832 was the disposal of my pecuniary interest in the *Independent Messenger* to Brother E. M. Stone, who afterward became one of our most active and useful Restorationist ministers, and its removal with the allied printing establishment to Boston. This change, which was effected in the month of January, was deemed advisable by the concurrent judgment of those most interested in the paper and in the cause it was designed to promote, and my own convenience seemed to render it expedient. The office of publication was thenceforward for a considerable time at 40 Court street in the city named, at which place the printing was also done. No change, however, occurred in the character of the sheet, inasmuch as I remained its senior editor, with essentially the same assistants as before. Its financial affairs were in other hands and I was wholly relieved of its business management, much to my satisfaction, as I was thereby enabled to devote more time and energy to my proper ministerial and editorial labors.

About the same time the people of my Mendon parish, to whom I had been preaching and rendering other pastoral services for more than a year, initiated measures preliminary to a more formal and permanent relationship between me and them than had hitherto existed. My labors had been so satisfactory that at a meeting held to consider and act upon the continuance of them after the term of my engagement had expired it was unanimously voted to give me a call to a regular pastorate, according to ecclesiastical usages, and to have me publicly installed in that office. The parish committee were instructed to communicate to me what had been done, and take such other action as was necessary for carrying the wishes of their constituents into effect. The committee discharged the duty assigned them at once, so far as I was concerned, and to their letter informing me of the vote of the parish I made the following response:

INVITATION TO PERMANENT SETTLEMENT.

"MENDON, Feb. 6, 1832.
"*To the Committee of the First Parish in Mendon, etc.*

"GENTLEMEN: The undersigned, having received through you, as the organs of the First Parish in Mendon, a copy of the votes and doings of said Parish unanimously inviting him to settle with them in the work of the gospel ministry, begs leave to return the following answer, to wit: That the undersigned, grateful for the confidence and respect evinced toward him by the invitation of the First Parish in Mendon to become their permanent minister, and relying on the blessing of God to prosper his well-meant labors in their service, respectfully accepts their invitation on the terms expressed in their several votes, and will endeavor to discharge the duties of the station to which they have called him, according to the best of his ability. In communicating this answer, you, gentlemen, will please accept for yourselves, the thanks of the undersigned for the kind manner in which you have discharged the duties of your appointment, and rest assured of the sincere respect with which he remains the humble servant of yourselves and the parish you represent.

"ADIN BALLOU.

"To Messrs. WILLIAM S. HASTINGS,
"AMARIAH TAFT, } *Committee.*"
"JABEZ ALDRICH,

The terms of settlement were: For five years, commencing April 1, 1832, a salary of $400 per annum; the connection dissolvable at the expiration of said five years, or at any time thereafter by either party, upon giving the other three months' notice. To professionally educated people in more extravagant times, such a salary as was stipulated for me must of course seem a meager one. It was indeed small, and would have but poorly served my needs but for the most watchful care and economy in the management of my personal and family affairs. Not only was I fortunate in this respect, making me content with a moderate pecuniary support, but there were other reasons why I should not murmur, repine, or object to the compensation I received.

In the first place, I was in no proper sense a *professional* clergyman. For as Paul said of his message, "I neither received it of man, neither was I taught it but by the revelation of Jesus Christ:" *Gal. 1 : 12.* I have told in a previous chapter how and why I became a preacher of divine truth and righteousness; not of my own will, nor by my own free choice, but because a dispensation of the gospel was committed to me, and a sacred necessity seemed laid upon me. And when I was spiritually constrained to enter on this, to me, self-renunciative calling, I did so under an inward assurance that I should be provided for, so far as my material needs were concerned, without ever making my ministerial labor a salable commodity — wholly by the free-will offerings of those to whom I ministered. It has accordingly been the inflexible rule of my clerical life, now over sixty-seven years long, never to dictate or demand any given price for my services as preacher, pastor, or conductor of any religious exercises whatsoever, but to accept only what has been voluntarily offered me — not even exacting repayment for unavoidable cash expenses in any given case. Under this rule, I have never been called to suffer for want of the necessaries and comforts of life, nor to be a burden on the shoulders of charity, and I confidently trust I never shall be while my earthly life continues. Therefore when my Mendon friends named the salary specified above, I accepted it without hesitation or objection.

In the second place, had I demanded a larger sum, it would hardly have been granted me in the then existing circumstances of the parish. They had been long accustomed to paying but a small compensation to their minister; a recent secession of considerable numbers had sensibly reduced their financial resources, and new comers from the indifferent outside public could not be relied on to contribute generously to an experimental and possibly temporary pastorate. Under such a condition of things, a demand for an unusual amount in those days would have been dangerous if not fatal to the contemplated union, and to all the good results hoped to be gained by it. Hence both principle and policy dictated to all parties concerned moderation of pecuniary expenditures and obligations. And the end justified what was done in this regard.

Having formally accepted the call extended to me by the First Parish in Mendon, and arranged satisfactorily the terms upon which I was to become their duly settled pastor, the next thing to be done was to provide for a proper observance of the rite of installation. According to custom and the fitness of things the participating actors on such an occasion should be, as they usually are, persons largely in theological sympathy and spiritual fellowship with the one to be inducted into the pastoral office. I had broken away from the great body of my former Universalist brethren, and the sharp controversy I had carried on with some of their foremost men rendered it inappropriate, as well as repugnant to my feelings, that they should have seats in the installing council. But I had a goodly number of Restorationists whom it would be pleasant to have present on the occasion, and from among whom all the parts could, if deemed advisable, be filled. The parish, however, had been connected with the Unitarian body, and its leading members would naturally incline in that direction. Happily my course had attracted the attention of several prominent ministers of progressive tendencies in that denomination, and a strong friendship had sprung up between me and them. Among these were Revs. Bernard Whitman of Waltham, Samuel J. May of Brooklyn, Conn., Daniel Austin of Brighton, Charles C. Sewall of Danvers, all long since passed on to the heavenly world. The names of Bernard Whitman and Samuel J. May, I inscribe on these pages with most tender and reverential affection. I had exchanged and corresponded freely with both, and to some extent with others of the same household of faith, but these were especially congenial and dear to me. Between them and the Restorationist clergy there was so much in common and such sincere good feeling, that it was not difficult to secure an installing council that would be harmonious in itself and satisfactory to both me and my people. But before this could be fully accomplished and the services of installation take place, I had passed my twenty-ninth birthday, and the detailed account of that event belongs to the next chapter and |may be found on its opening pages.

CHAPTER XII.

1832–1833.

INSTALLATION — ESPOUSAL OF TEMPERANCE REFORM — REV. J. M. S. PERRY — MEMORANDA OF LABORS — FAMILY BEREAVEMENTS — REFLECTIONS.

THE necessary measures preparatory to my installation having been taken, as intimated on a preceding page, the event was auspiciously consummated on the 3d day of May, 1832. Letters missive from the First church in Mendon had been cordially responded to by the several Restorationist and Unitarian Congregationalist churches to which they were addressed, and their pastors and delegates in coequal numbers united in the exercises of the occasion. The subjoined notice of what transpired, from my editorial pen, appeared in the *Independent Messenger* of May 10 — Vol. 2, No. 18.

"INSTALLATION AT MENDON.

"The installation of Adin Ballou as pastor of the First Church and Congregation in Mendon was solemnized agreeably to public notice on Thursday last, the 3d inst. The preliminaries having been arranged in an orderly and harmonious ecclesiastical council composed of ministers and delegates from four Restorationist and four Unitarian churches, public services were rendered as follows: Introductory prayer by Rev. Samuel Barrett of Boston; reading of the Scriptures by Rev. Charles C. Sewall of Danvers; Sermon, by Rev. Bernard Whitman of Waltham, from *John 13:34* — 'A new commandment I give unto you that ye love one another'; Consecrating prayer by Rev. Charles Hudson of Westminster; Charge by Rev. Paul Dean of Boston; Right Hand of Fellowship by Rev. Samuel J.

May of Brooklyn, Ct.; Address to the Church and Congregation, by Rev. David Pickering of Providence, R. I.; Concluding prayer by Rev. Nathaniel Wright of Attleborough; and benediction by the Pastor installed. These services were accompanied and interspersed with appropriate and very delightful sacred music by the choir.

"It is not easy to speak of this occasion and its exercises in a manner corresponding to the deep interest and felicity excited in the minds of all present. Clergymen and Christian brethren of different names and religious opinions hitherto separated in a greater or less degree by sectarian walls of partition, took sweet counsel together, walked in company to the house of God, and there participated in a feast of intellectual dainties which caused all to *feel* and some actually to *exclaim*, 'It is good for us to be here!' All met on the level of enlightened Christian liberality, not to compare creeds and conform non-essential religious opinions to one standard formula; not to surrender the rights of private judgment or public profession of honest faith; not to discuss the relative value of sectarian names; not to concert measures of hostility against other Christian denominations; not to multiply causes of contention in the church of Christ — but to exemplify true brotherly love by Christian union on Christian principles; to enlarge and strengthen the influence of charity; to bear a united testimony against religious bigotry on the one hand and licentious skepticism on the other; to rally around the ancient standard of the 'Stem of Jesse'; and thus evince to the world that Christians may love one another in sincerity without agreeing precisely in all the items of their faith. Every exercise and indeed every circumstance of the occasion tended to the promotion of these happy results. Everything was done decently and in order, with cordial affection, in perfect harmony, with distinguished ability, and to universal acceptance. A pleasant day, a large congregation, and generous hospitality on the part of the society, were happy accompaniments to the ecclesiastical and religious felicities of the occasion. The very able and interesting sermon of Mr. Whitman will be published at the request of the Parish, and thereby, we hope, diffuse its truths widely among an inquiring religious public.

"Finally, we cannot but rejoice before God with humble thanksgiving for the blessings of this occasion, and while we exclaim in the language of Israel's royal poet, 'Behold, how good and how pleasant it is for brethren to dwell together in unity,' we shall indulge the precious hope that this is the opening dawn of a new and blessed era for liberal Christianity — the beginning of a union on truly Christian principles, which, while it effectually guards against mock religion and skepticism, will widen and extend itself over Christendom till all who truly fear God, love Christ, and work righteousness shall come into that unity of spirit whereof the bonds are peace."

Rev. Mr. Whitman's sermon was very scholarly, elaborate, and instructive. Its grand theme was *Christian Union*. It was published as stated, but owing to sickness and pressing avocations, he could not prepare it for the press till nearly a year after it was delivered. Meantime, he carefully revised and amplified it, so that when it appeared, it covered nearly seventy-eight pamphlet pages. There were appended to it Rev. Paul Dean's "Charge to the Pastor" and Rev. David Pickering's " Address to the People," both able and impressive utterances — all making eighty-four pages. It was intended to have Rev. Samuel J. May's "Right Hand of Fellowship" appear in connection with the other parts, but for some unknown reason the manuscript failed to reach the printers.

The sermon was planned to show: (1) What is *not* necessary for Christian union; (2) What *is* necessary for it; and (3) The great importance of laboring to promote it. These points were treated exhaustively and followed out to a practical application with devout earnestness. The preacher stated forcibly his own theological and ecclesiastical position, recognized clearly that of the pastor and his flock, and warmly congratulated all parties represented in our services on the exemplification of Christian union they were that day illustrating before the world. Copies of the pamphlet are preserved in the town libraries of Mendon and Hopedale.

It is proper to observe in this connection that in those days it required no little moral courage for Rev. Mr. Whitman and his Unitarian brethren to unite with the Restorationists in a public religious service like that of my installation — a courage now hardly conceivable as having any occasion for its exercise. But such occasion then existed and for two prominent reasons: (1) A large majority of the Unitarians at that time had a great dislike, amounting almost to contemptuous disgust, towards Universalists of every kind and name, few of them making any distinction between "ultras" and Restorationists, or if they recognized a difference, they had little respect for the latter so far as concerned any Scriptural authority for their distinctive belief. They insisted that though some mild form of endless punishment might or might not be true, the Bible, in their opinion, did not teach universal restoration but left the final destiny of the wicked in hopeless obscurity. Moreover, they generally believed that this obscurity was wholesome in its moral and religious influence upon mankind. Therefore, duty and expediency required them to preach the promises and threatenings of the sacred record according to the letter of the text as traditionally understood and not "to be wise above what was written"—at the same time explaining away or ignoring the letter of texts that plainly favored the doctrine of the final "restitution of all things." In this state of opinion, they deemed it sufficiently burdensome to defend their own special Unitarian tenets against the denunciations of the self-styled orthodox sects without fathering other heresies. And they were very sensitive about being charged by their theological enemies with any leanings toward Universalism. They were sure of being so charged if they affiliated with the Restorationists. They, therefore, dreaded and avoided all fellowship with them. (2) The Unitarians were largely a well educated class of people, and nursed the pride of having a highly educated ministry. But the Restorationists, tried by their standard, were "unlearned and ignorant"—only a trifle better schooled, perhaps, than the humble Nazarene himself and his original twelve apostles, without a D. D. among them, and little better than barbarians when compared with the graduates of Harvard College, and other polished literati. This was quite as objectionable to many of the "grave and reverend seigniors" of the denomination as our peculiar theology.

THE TEMPERANCE CAUSE ESPOUSED. 219

And I learned from my brave and kind Brother Whitman that, after the installation, he was sharply rebuked by one of his titled elders of the profession, for having assisted in introducing unlearned men into the clerical office. I mention these things to show that our Brothers Whitman, May, and others had to take up no little of a cross and incur considerable reproach from their more numerous and dignified associates for keeping company with us and extending to us the courtesies of ecclesiastical and Christian fellowship. Let them receive credit accordingly from all who honor courage, honesty, and fair dealing.

A somewhat memorable experience of the year in review was my open espousal of the Temperance Reform, all the more so by reason of the circumstances attending such action on my part. My neighboring clerical friend, Rev. John M. S. Perry, then pastor of the North Congregational church of Mendon (Orthodox), had become much interested in the cause, and, with a few of his people who sympathized with him, desired to inaugurate a movement for promoting its interests in our general vicinity. He accordingly came to me with a prepared preamble and pledge which he offered as a basis for a temperance society in the town. In the multiplicity of my cares and labors, I had not previously given the subject much attention and so begged leave for a little time to consider it and act advisedly in regard to his proposition. After due deliberation, I became satisfied that the reform was essentially a righteous one and greatly needed in the community. But I had good reason to anticipate that it would disturb the harmony of my congregation if I embarked in it with honest zeal, and perhaps alienate some of my parishioners and hitherto ardent friends. Many liberalists of that day looked upon the organization of societies like that contemplated as a scheme of the so-called Evangelicals for making sectarian capital and gaining to themselves some special advantage, and upon that ground regarded all such action with distrust. I had myself some reason in this case to suspect that my neighbors of the other church and society hoped the project might prove an apple of discord in my parish, whose rising prosperity they deprecated, and in that or some other way redound to their profit.

Nevertheless, I resolved (whatever might be the motives and wishes of Mr. Perry and his allies) (1) That I would not allow myself to turn my back upon so good a cause; and (2) That my evangelical co-workers should secure no sectarian ends by my espousing it. I therefore told my clerical neighbor, upon further consultation with him, that I would take hold of the work as he desired, but that the proposed society must be thoroughly guarded against all sectarian and partisan misdirection or entanglement, by specific stipulations to that effect in the preliminary papers about to be circulated. He rather coolly assented, and the documents were re-drafted in conformity with my wishes.

The next thing deemed necessary to be done was to hold a public meeting, and have an expository lecture given, presenting the whole subject clearly to the people. Upon broaching the question where and by whom this lecture should be delivered, Mr. Perry and his friends were prompt, decided, and urgent, that my church must be the place, and I the lecturer. Seeing their persistency, I accepted the responsibility thus thrust upon me, but gave my ministerial brother to understand that I should expect him to sustain me by going into the pulpit with me, offering prayer, and otherwise co-operating on the occasion. This I knew would pinch in the bud whatever religious exclusiveness he might cherish, and test his devotion to the temperance cause. To this arrangement he reluctantly consented. The time of the meeting was fixed on a given Sunday at 5 o'clock, P. M. The day and hour arrived, and, due notice having been given throughout the town, a large audience assembled, composed of Mr. Perry's people and my own with some outsiders. I remained in the vestibule of the church during the tolling of the bell before the opening of the service, waiting for my clerical brother that I might courteously direct him to the pulpit, as customary in such cases. But no such brother appeared. I at length ordered the tolling stopped, still remaining in the vestibule. After a little further delay he came in, when I cordially greeted him, and signified my expectation that he was ready to go with me and participate in the exercises of the occasion. He immediately began to make excuses, saying that his labors had been very hard during the day, and consequently that he was very much fatigued and unable to take any part with me, etc., etc. I declined to excuse him and insisted that he should accompany me to the desk, which he made a pretence of doing, many of the people hearing the conversation and watching us, as we walked up the aisle together, with interest and amazement. At length he suddenly broke from me, darted into a pew, took a seat, and I proceeded to the duty of the hour without him. I went through the various exercises by myself, according to my best judgment and with evidently good effect.

In answering the objections that were sometimes urged against temperance organizations, I at length reached the one, based on sectarian grounds, which made such organizations unworthy of liberal Christian support. I stated that however this might be generally or in other cases, it would not apply in the present instance. I then read the clauses in our plan of action, which explicitly declared that nothing sectarian or partisan should be allowed in our proceedings, following the same with very pointed and emphatic comments in explication and application of the same. In closing under that head, I remarked that if anything contrary to the stipulated unsectarian character of the movement had been manifested on the present occasion, I trusted the blame would be laid where it belonged. A thrill of suppressed excitement ran through the audience, which vented itself freely after the service was over. Mr. Perry's leading parishioner was mortified and indignant at his pastor's course, and administered to him a scathing rebuke for having done the worst possible thing to damage the cause of temperance in its local infancy. None of his religious friends approved his course, while mine, of course, denounced it. He was himself greatly surprised, abashed, and humiliated. The next forenoon he called on me, apologized for his conduct, and promised never to repeat it. And he never did. He was cured and I was amply vindicated. Our relations thereafter, while he remained in town, were pleasant and harmonious. He left his pastorate in 1835, and went with his wife as missionaries to Ceylon, where both ere long died of cholera, within an hour of each other.

At this point it seems proper for me to confess my great indebtedness to the temperance reform for the inductive lessons it gave me, and for its salutary discipline of my mind, heart, and character. It was to me a primary school from which I went forth to all my later moral and social reform attainments. I had been brought up a moderate drinker, regarding drunkenness — an abuse of intoxicating liquors — alone a sin. So I believed, so I preached, so I practised. And I deemed all temperance pledges and societies as supererogatory and useless. But I had come to a new view of the matter. The evils of intemperance were forced upon my attention wherever I went. Their terrors and the woes connected with them appalled me — wrung my very soul. And the great question how they could be removed confronted me whenever I thought of the matter, demanding, not only consideration, but decision and action. I was a rational and accountable being. I was more than that — a public moral and religious teacher. There was no justifiable excuse for neutrality upon a subject of such magnitude, upon a question so closely related to the welfare and happiness of multitudes of my fellowmen. I ought manfully to say *Yes* or *No* upon it; plant myself unequivocally and firmly on one side or the other; be for or against the reform. I thoroughly investigated the subject, weighing its claims in the scales of reason and conscience. I saw its merits and mastered its arguments. I became qualified to teach, defend, and successfully commend it to others, both by precept and example. I was rendered a better, a truer, a nobler man thereby. My whole being was enriched, my whole life was made a greater power for good for the stand I took at that early day in regard to this great movement.

Moreover, it suggested to me three great practical data in ethics, which have grown more and more important in my estimation ever since as means of promoting human progress and redemption. (1) That righteousness must be taught definitely, specifically, and practically to produce any marked results, not in vague generalisms. (2) That professed receivers and adherents of any given righteous cause must be unequivocally and uncompromisingly pledged to the practice of definitely declared duties pertaining to such cause, and not be left in a state of irresponsible non-committalism. (3) That such pledged adherents and receivers must voluntarily associate under explicit affirmations of a settled purpose to co-operate in exemplifying and diffusing abroad the virtues and excellences to which they are committed, and not act at random in disorganized and aimless individualism, often antagonistic to each other and detrimental to the interests involved.

Another great good which I derived from the temperance reform was that, under its influence, I was enabled to save myself, my family, and a multitude of friends (to say nothing of others whom I may have reached), if not from drunkenness, yet from all danger of it, and from innumerable foolish expenditures, wastes, and damages — pecuniary, physiological, and intellectual — while at the same time gaining more or less elevation of moral tone and character. My interest in it was a defense against many temptations in life and a help to many virtues, as well as a great means of usefulness to my fellowmen. I had no firmly rooted appetite for strong drink to overcome, and whatever inducements to break my pledge were presented to me after taking it were of a social and festive nature. It was the custom in those days, among family relatives and special friends when visiting or calling upon each other, to *treat* and *be treated*, as the phrasing was. A generous and warm-hearted hospitality demanded this, and even common civility, in some circles. To drink together was a badge or token of kindly regard. I remember visiting a venerable and much esteemed relative soon after committing myself to this cause and to abstinence from the use of all intoxicants. He knew nothing of the step I had taken in the matter, and, as he had previously done, brought out from his well-stored larder his choice liquors and concomitants for the usual treat. I, of course, had to decline his proffered glass. He was utterly astonished and deeply grieved, exclaiming, "What have I done that you refuse to drink with me?" I explained my position as well as I could, but he was hardly able to understand the reasons for my course. He looked so sorrowful that, but for my pledge, my good feelings would have impelled me to yield to his generous and kind-hearted solicitations.

Another result of my espousal and championship of the temperance cause, more trying and painful in many respects, though not without its salutary and helpful aspects, was the alienation of personal admirers, accompanied by a new baptism of vituperation and reproach. Some few of those who called me to Mendon, and who, up to this time, had been liberal in their plaudits and commendations, now turned their backs upon me as a disturber of their peace, and a meddler with what they deemed their personal rights. "Could they not eat and drink what they pleased without being called to account as sinners? Had they hired me to preach upon such subjects? No, indeed." And so they vented their indignation and spite upon me. These persons were chiefly wedded to the intoxicating cup. Only a few of them boldly gave utterance to their angry scurrility, but quite a number muttered their sullen dislike of my attitude in the matter. I knew what it was aforetime to be scorned and hated on account of theological and ecclesiastical offences, but now I must endure ill-will and denunciation as a moral reformer, seeking only the personal good of my assailants. I very likely needed this discipline, not only to wean me from the love of human praise, but to strengthen me to endure much sorer experiences of the same sort in the not far distant future. It was a wholesome medicine, which, though bitter to the taste, did me substantial good and resulted to my advantage. If I lost a few seeming friends, I gained many new and better ones. My heart was purged of some of its impurities, a wider sphere of usefulness opened before me, and multiplied opportunities were afforded me to labor for the uplifting and redemption of my fellowmen.

It was no sooner noised abroad that I had enlisted in this great reform and was prepared to devote myself somewhat to the proclamation and diffusion of its principles in the general community, and wherever an opening should be made for me, than I began to have calls to lecture upon the subject. These I was happy to answer affirmatively, so far as home duties and circumstances otherwise would allow, and was thereby enabled to gain and exert a moral influence in behalf of truth and righteousness, which I had not before possessed. As a further encouragement, I had the great satisfaction of seeing my ministerial brethren of the Restorationist faith engage in the movement and unite heartily in efforts to carry it forward to successful issues. At a meeting of the Providence Association, held June 6, 1832, which I had the pleasure of attending, the following resolutions were unanimously passed:

"*Resolved*, That this Association take a deep and lively interest in the great *Temperance Reformation* now in progress throughout the United States, and that while we congratulate the friends of this reformation everywhere on their success in this laudable and praiseworthy cause, we will not cease to co-operate with all our ability in the accomplishment of its grand and fundamental objects.

"*Resolved*, That we recommend our friends throughout the country to use their influence in arresting the progress of intemperance and in rearing up a generation who shall be temperate in all things."

As may be easily imagined, I had in those days no idle time. Besides my regular pastoral duties, — preaching twice each Sunday at home or on exchange, overseeing the Sabbath school, administering church ordinances in their season, and visiting among my people — I delivered frequent lectures at near or more distant places, ministered at many funerals outside as well as inside my parish, solemnized numerous marriages in my own and neighboring towns, wrote week by week important articles as principal editor of the *Independent Messenger*, attended various religious and reform meetings here and there, kept up an extensive correspondence, discharged the duties of a member of the town school committee, and, of course, took some care of ordinary domestic affairs. Little opportunity had I for rest and recuperation.

Perhaps the best possible inside view of my various activities at this period may be presented by quoting somewhat from the fragmentary memoranda I kept, and I therefore submit a few extracts:

Aug. 24, 1832. Hired my friend Lewis Boyden's horse and sulky and made a forenoon's inspection of the district school near Mr. Robert Allen's, taught by a Miss Morse. With only a single cracker for my dinner, I rode thence to the south-east part of Bellingham, near Franklin, to officiate at the funeral of friend Martin Cushman. He had been an eccentric man and somewhat misanthropic. He was quite intellectual, but had strong passions not easily controlled, which rendered him disagreeable to many people, and prompted him to frequent law-suits with his fellow-citizens. He had been an ultra Universalist in opinion, and held me in great esteem till I broke with my brethren of that school, when he repudiated me and denounced me outright. Yet when mortal sickness prostrated him he relented, became prayerful, and sent for me to visit

him, which I did, ministering in my way to his spiritual
needs. When near his end, he requested that I should attend
his funeral, and I was there on the date mentioned, accordingly.
I preached from 2 *Chron. 21:13*: "Let me fall now into the
hand of the Lord. etc." The house was small and could not
contain nearly all who had assembled, and so, the weather
being favorable, the services took place in the yard outside,
beneath some large shade trees. I spoke with a good degree
of spiritual freedom, unction, and effect."

"*Sunday, Aug. 26*. Usual services in the church. In the
morning gave an exposition of the first part of 7th chapter of
Matthew. Afterward attended the examination of the Sunday
School, which was good. Brother Fisher Ames Tyler addressed
the scholars. At night called on Mrs. Elizabeth (Mellen)
Torrey, widow of Stephen, aged 95 years, now nearing the end
of her mortal pilgrimage, and ripe for the heavenly granary.
Monday, 27th. At home. Prepared for the *Messenger* 'Review
of Rev. Lucius R. Paige's "Letters to my devoted friend, Rev.
Bernard Whitman,"' and wrote to the managing editor, Rev.
E. M. Stone. *Tuesday, 28th*. Attended a meeting of Revolutionary soldiers convened before our county judge of probate
to certify to their ages and war services, in order that they
might obtain pensions from the United States government.
Fifty applicants were present from Mendon and vicinity. I
dined with the company, and took home with me my venerable friend, Benjamin Pickering, who remained through the
night and most of the next day, in the evening of which I
went with wife and daughter to a considerable party at Mrs.
Mary (Hastings) Hayward's, widow of Caleb, formerly a prominent citizen of the town. *Thursday, 30th*. Took tea with others
at Col. Warren Rawson's. On returning home found my parents
awaiting us, having just arrived from Cumberland, R. I., for a
two days' visit. *Friday, 31st*. Went to Milford to invite my
wife's father and mother to come and double the parental company. They complied, and we had a memorable visit — one
never repeated in this mortal state."

"*Saturday, Sept. 1*. Letters received from two brother
clergymen requesting early answers had to be laid aside for a
less busy season. Rode 27 miles in the afternoon to Southbridge, where I had engaged to preach on the morrow.
Arrived at 6.30 P M., and stopped with Frederick W. Bottom,
Esq., by whom I was agreeably entertained. *Sunday, Sept. 2d*.
Preached three discourses to good acceptance: (1) A written
one from the text: 'Draw nigh to God, and He will draw
nigh to you'; (2) On universal restoration, *extempore*; (3) On
Christian charity and union. Full and attentive audiences.

Monday, 3d. Dined with my kind and cordial friend, Josiah Snow, publisher of the *Southbridge Register and Mirror*. He is a warm sympathizer and a zealous helper of the cause of universal restoration. Before starting for home, it was reported that a man in town had died of Asiatic cholera. Our whole country in a state of great alarm on account of this disease, which is causing many deaths in certain localities. Arrived home about sundown, finding Rev. James W. Hoskins, from Hampden, Me., with my family. He is an able and devoted Restorationist, and has, in my absence, supplied my Mendon pulpit acceptably. *Friday, 7th.* Troubled somewhat with sick headache, my frequent ailment. Off to Milford, with wife and two children. *Saturday, 8th.* Answered junior editor's letter, but sent no article for the *Messenger*. A call from friend Arnold Buffum, a pioneer Abolitionist, who proposed to lecture in our church tomorrow at 4.30 P. M. Went with him to consult Col. Rawson and Mr. Jabez Aldrich. Not much encouragement, but no opposition. Not a ripple of anti-slavery has yet reached Mendon. But friend Buffum thought it was high time to stir the waters, and he was not a man to be put off. So the appointment was made. *Sunday, 9th.* Preached A. M. and P. M., as usual, and announced friend Buffum's lecture. It came off accordingly. Important truths uttered to a very small audience, with no striking effect, and the contribution box circulated in vain. Evening rode to Uxbridge and solemnized marriage of Mr. Moses T. Murdock and Miss Dorinda W. Grout.

"*Monday, Sept. 10th.* A call from my ever estimable Christian brother, Rev. Samuel J. May, of Brooklyn, Ct. He brought with him Rev. Mr. Brooks, of Hingham, and we had a pleasant interview. *Tuesday, 11th.* Plenty of household duties, but the important event of the day was an unexpected call from my brother, Ariel Ballou, Jr., M. D., of Woonsocket, R. I., and his bride, Miss Hannah Horton, for marriage. He could wait for no preparation, and desired the ceremony to take place at once. We conformed to his urgency. The marriage was solemnized and they left within an hour. This was less agreeable to us than to them. Just at night had a call from Benjamin Davenport, Esq., one of my prominent parishioners, with a request from a niece of his wife, Mrs. Freeman Fisher, to have me come to Milford and christen a dangerously sick child. *Wednesday, 12th.* Went to Milford to find Mrs. Fisher's child a corpse. Just as safe in the Saviour's bosom as if formally baptized. Dined at Father Hunt's. Returned to Mendon. Mr. Smith Sayles and wife, my good parents-in-law by the first marriage, arrived from Smithfield. R. I., to make us a visit. Excellent relatives these, and worthy of our kindest attention. *Thursday, 13th.* Entertaining company, who left for home about 2 P. M. *Friday, 14th.* Funeral service of Mrs. Allen Chase in Bellingham.

"*Saturday, Sept. 15th.* Started with wife at half-past eleven A. M. for Brooklyn. Ct., to preach on the morrow in exchange with Rev. Brother S. J. May. Arrived at 8 P. M. and were quietly entertained by his family during our sojourn. *Sunday, Sept. 16th.* Preached A. M. *extempore* from Acts, 12:24-26: ' God, who made the world,' etc; and P. M., a written sermon from James, 4:8: 'Draw nigh to God,' etc. Before close of service published intentions of marriage for a couple, according to Connecticut law and usage. How much spiritual impression my performances made on the people, I know not — probably small. Took tea at 4 P. M. and departed for Thompson, Ct., where we spent the night. When nearing the place in the evening, we were suddenly surprised by the momentary flash of a brilliant meteor. *Monday, 17th.* Remained at Stiles hotel through the forenoon. About 11.30 o'clock, Brother May arrived on his return from Mendon, and we dined together and enjoyed a delightful conversational conference upon high and sacred themes. He is an advanced thinker, a whole-hearted philanthropist, and a most genial Christian gentleman. We parted at 2.30 P. M., he going home, and wife and I turning our faces towards Winchester, N. H,, where a conference of Restorationist ministers had been appointed for the ensuing Wednesday and Thursday. *Tuesday, 18th.* Left Leicester, our tarrying place for the night, early, and rode all day, reaching Warwick in the evening, and taking lodging in the public house. *Wednesday, 19th.* Off soon after sunrise, arriving at our place of destination about 8 a. m. The Universalist society there, one of the oldest of that faith in New Hampshire, was strongly inclined to Restorationism, having then for a pastor Brother Lyman Maynard, a member of our Massachusetts Association. Myself and wife were hospitably cared for in the family of Brother Asa Alexander, a devoted layman of the society. The conference opened auspiciously, and proved to be an interesting and profitable occasion. I preached on both Wednesday and Thursday mornings; Brother Charles Hudson, Wednesday afternoon; Brother Paul Dean, Thursday afternoon and evening. Exhortations followed the discourses of Thursday morning and evening, and appropriate devotional and musical exercises were enjoyed at every session.

Friday, Sept. 21st. Bade our Winchester friends a grateful farewell early in the morning and started for home with Brothers Dean, Hudson, and Stone. Dined at Templeton, having for a fellow guest at table a celebrated theological professor and D. D., who was remarkable for his eating powers and intemperate consumption of strong green tea, while descanting on the subject of temperance and exemplifying a coarse type of manners generally. His saintliness was quite below the standard of his reputation in Evangelical circles. Rode to Westminster in the afternoon and shared the kind hospitality of Brother and Mrs. Hudson for the succeeding night. *Saturday, 22d.* A good day's ride to Mendon, taking dinner at Worcester. A safe and enjoyable journey of a week was thus completed. *Sunday, 23d.* In my own pulpit again. Preached A. M., from Ps. 100:2: 'Serve the Lord with gladness,' and P. M. from Rom. 2:11: 'There is no respect of persons with God.' At 5 P. M. attended the funeral of Miss Polly Corbett at the house of her mother in South Milford, preaching from Ps. 124:8: 'Our help is in the name of the Lord, who made heaven and earth.'"

The foregoing passages from my journal, covering about four weeks of time, will indicate imperfectly to the reader the manner in which the wheels of my private and public life were kept in motion during the latter part of the year 1832, and there is no need of further particularization.

On the first Wednesday in January, 1833, the Massachusetts Association of Restorationists held its annual meeting in Boston. The occasion proved a busy one, several matters of importance coming up for consideration, in which I was much interested, and in the discussion of which I took an active part. The Annual Sermon, as it was called, was preached by me from Phil. 4:6: "Be careful for nothing, but in everything, by prayer and supplication, with thanksgiving, let your requests be made known unto God." I was housed and fed kindly by Bro. Dean, and the public services were held in his church in Bulfinch street. Several discourses were delivered to interested audiences, and the proceedings of private sittings were cordial and harmonious. The weather was remarkable for the season, being more like May than January. I returned home by way of Waltham, calling there on my excellent friend and brother, Rev. Bernard Whitman, with whom I had a brief, but most elevating and soul-satisfying interview.

DOMESTIC ANXIETY AND SORROW.

A dark cloud of anxiety and sorrow gathered without warning and hovered over our household towards the close of this month of January, 1833. Before the end of February its lurid bolts had bereaved us of two out of our three children. The scarlet fever, then nowhere prevalent in the vicinity, developed itself in our family and scathed, more or less severely, every member. On the 26th of January our eldest son, Adin, Jr., a lad in the tenth year of his age, was sent on an errand about a mile distant, and while away became so ill that he had to be taken in and put to bed by one of our kind, motherly parishioners. We received word of this in the early evening and I hastened to bring him home. We did not suspect anything serious, and the pressure of my various duties occupied my utmost attention. But my sick boy, instead of improving, became gradually worse. We summoned our family physician, Dr. John G. Metcalf, who at first thought the disease might be measles, but at length pronounced it scarletina or canker rash, though, so far as we knew, he had been exposed to neither. The case soon proved desperate and we were appalled at its aspect. Time had been inconsiderately lost and vigorous treatment delayed. In our distressed anxiety we called in the venerable and celebrated Dr. Daniel Thurber, but it was too late. The patient grew weaker and weaker in spite of all that was done for him, suffering intensely till relieved by death at half-past nine P. M., February 10. Before this occurred our other children and young housemaid had come down with the same malady, and we, the parents, were half sick, worn, and debilitated. The neighborhood was in a state of more or less alarm and the funeral must take place under forlorn and gloomy circumstances. We were favored, however, with all needed sympathy and assistance. The obsequies were sadly but consolingly solemnized on Tuesday, the 12th. Relatives from Milford, Cumberland, R. I., and Woonsocket, R. I., were in attendance on the mournful occasion, as also were a goodly number of our parishioners and personal friends. Rev. J. M. S. Perry, the Orthodox minister, and Mercy Thayer, a Friends Preacher, met with us, manifesting a sympathetic spirit. The religious services, consisting of discourse and prayers, were rendered by Brother Seth Chandler, then ministering to the Restorationists of Oxford. The day was stormy, neither parent leaving the house, but its duties and experiences transpired as favorably as could be expected. We were then hopeful of the other invalids, who seemed to be in a fair way of recovery.

But, alas, another bitter cup was awaiting us. In the evening of February 22, our other little son, Pearley H., aged two years and three months, who had been improving, apparently, up to that time, suddenly showed signs of a relapse. Medical aid was again called in and our best efforts were put forth to save him, but all in vain. Dropsy on the brain was soon developed, his case became hopeless, spasm succeeding spasm till the 27th of February, when he expired. He was a bright and loving child, but of slender health, and during this last painful illness, as well as before, gave forth very tender and affecting little utterances, which still linger in the memory of those who gave him birth. Another funeral darkened our home, drew around us condoling relatives and friends as before, and elicited needful religious consolation. It took place February 28, at 1 o'clock P. M., Rev. Samuel Clarke of Uxbridge being our religious counselor on the occasion, his words breathing the soothing perfume of comfort and Christian consolation upon all our hearts.

In recalling these trying experiences with their concomitants and disciplinary lessons, how many sacred memories enthrong us! What anxieties, cares, vigils, devoured our energies! What pains and distresses, sighs and moans, from the sick couches of our suffering ones harrowed our parental sensibilities! What pitying kindnesses flowed in upon us from helpful neighbors, friends, and relatives! What mercies, consolations, and sanctifications, distilled from Heaven, bedewed our stricken, aching souls! What a moral training for compassionate sympathy with other mourning families in after years! What longing aspirations swelled our breasts for perfect assurances of immortal life and blessedness! "Do the departed loved ones still live on?" we asked. Was it indeed true that they were "not lost but gone before"? Or must our hearts freeze amid the chilling blasts of doubt and scepticism? Nay, we believed that

> "Where immortal spirits reign,
> There shall we all meet again."

No other cases of scarletina occurred in our general neighborhood during the season. Those in our family were probably generated by local conditions, of whose deleterious influence we were then ignorant. The causes, preventives, and cure of disease will no doubt be better known in future ages than at present, and such knowledge will, I believe, deliver our human race from most of the ills to which it is now subject, and from most of the pain, suffering, and premature death that now afflict it.

CHAPTER XIII.

1833 – 1834.

WHITMAN'S LETTERS — INDEPENDENT MESSENGER — REVIEW OF HUIDEKOPER — ARGUMENT WITH REV. JONATHAN FARR — ORAL DISCUSSION.

THE pressure of duties and cares, though interrupted by the visitation of sickness mentioned at the close of the last chapter, continued unabated. Indeed, it seemed to increase as time went on, so that I had little opportunity to sit down and brood over our afflictions, desolating and painful as they were. Pastoral and other public labors incident to my ministerial calling, oversight of the town schools, editorial and correspondential writing, with more or less secular occupation, demanded constant activity on my part. Occasional calls for service abroad, as well as at or near home, came to me, and under circumstances that I could not very well refuse them, inasmuch as they usually related to the cause of universal restoration, of which I had become an acknowledged champion.

On the 25th of May, 1833, I attended the installation of Rev. Brother Seth Chandler, my former theological student, at Oxford, Mass., as pastor of the Universalist society there, one of the oldest of that persuasion in the country, having been established under the ministry of Rev. Adam Streeter, in 1785. A fraternal ecclesiastical council united in the services of the occasion according to the following order: Introductory prayer by Rev. Thomas J. Greenwood; Reading of the Scriptures by Rev. Charles Hudson; Sermon by Rev. Samuel J. May; Consecrating prayer by Rev. David Pickering; Charge by myself; Right Hand of Fellowship by Rev. Ebenezer Robinson; Address to the people by Rev. John Goldsbury; Concluding prayer by Rev. Nathaniel Wright; Benediction by the pastor elect. Proceedings in the council, composed of Unitarian and Restorationist clergymen, harmonious, the several exercises appropriate, hospitalities of the society generous, and the communion of saints pleasant. My accompanying delegate from the Mendon church was Mr. Stephen Albee, one of my life-long friends.

About this time, my esteemed brother, Rev. Bernard Whitman, published his able work, entitled, "Friendly Letters to a Universalist on Divine Rewards and Punishments." It was a duodecimo volume of 366 pages — candid, lucid, pertinent, conclusive, against the theory of no future retribution, and in support of the true Christian doctrine upon that subject. His sympathy and co-operation with me had procured for him the coarse denunciations of the ultra-Universalist press, which I promptly repelled through the columns of the *Messenger*. I gave in that organ the high commendation of the volume which it deserved, and did all I could to promote its circulation. Its opponents affected to despise it and to disdain answering it. They were politic enough to make no attempt to refute its conclusions. It was one among the effective efforts of those controversial days which gradually paralyzed the arrogant hypothesis that "knew of no condition for man beyond the grave but that in which he is as the angels of God in heaven." That hypothesis has for many years slumbered in an undisturbed tomb and many of the Universalist denomination to-day seem to have forgotten, if they ever knew, that it once claimed to be the orthodoxy of their order.

On the 30th day of June, the same year, we had born to us another son, whom we named Adin Augustus. The season of anxiety and sorrow through which we had a few months before passed seemed to have made its impress upon his very nature. His early infant wailings were like echoes of those moans of his languishing brothers, which still vibrated in the memories of bereaved parental affection. But these characteristics were slowly outgrown and he became a joyous child, a sprightly, winsome lad, a promising youth, and a model young man. But, alas, at that auspicious climax, as will be told in its season, he was translated to the invisible realm, whither the others referred to preceded him.

During the ensuing month of August, I received a call to the pastorate of a church and society of our faith in Watertown, Mass., which, though offering me sundry increased temporal advantages, I did not feel at liberty to accept. Immediately afterward I added to my already superabundant labors the care and responsibility of a private school opened in my own house. This enterprise succeeded very well with the exception of occasional interruptions caused by calls to funerals, etc., which I could not well decline, accomodating matters to them as well as I could, without serious inconvenience or complaint from any quarter. But the turn of a new leaf in the volume of my affairs obliged me to terminate the undertaking in October. For early in that month the *Independent Messenger* and its accompanying printing establishment came back into my hands. The Boston proprietor had become weary of the duties incident to its management, and urged me to resume them and so grant him the relief he desired. I was induced to yield to his wishes, partly, at least, by the offer of aid from a proposed co-partner, Rev. Stephen Cutler, of Cumberland, R. I., who would share the pecuniary burdens of the concern equally with me, and attend to all its business affairs, excepting those of editorship, which I thought I could execute without serious difficulty. I had reason to suppose that my contemplated co-laborer was competent and trustworthy, and the partnership was accordingly formed under the name of "Cutler and Ballou," Oct. 3, 1833. Four days afterward we went to Boston together, purchased the property in question, and completed all needful arrangements for its speedy removal to Mendon. This was effected October 18, and everything was soon in readiness for its designed use.

The experiment of forming a co-partnership in this matter proved to be a serious misfortune to me. Mr. Cutler, notwithstanding his pretensions and much show of ability turned out to be wholly unfitted for his new position in three months, and our relations were dissolved, everything pertaining to the affairs of the company coming into my hands for care and management. Nor was this all, nor the worst, of the matter. For by false representations on his part he had induced me to enter into bonds with him to his Cumberland creditors to the amount of several hundred dollars, most of which I was ultimately obliged to pay. I found him not only without business capacity, but destitute of capital and unreliable in moral integrity. So I gained nothing by my connection with him, but lost considerable of my much needed funds. The settlement of matters between us was long pending, the details and result of which restored neither my confidence nor my money. He came from the Baptists through the Universalist into the Restorationist fold, whence he returned to the bosom of the church from which he first set out, and in which he ended his career.

Thus it came to pass that at the close of the year 1833 I found myself more heavily burdened than ever before with professional duties, editorial responsibilities, and business demands and obligations incident to the management of a printing office. Moreover, I had become so involved financially by the transactions of the few preceding months that I was obliged to resort to my credit in order to keep the wheels of all the machinery under my care in good working order. I learned thereby how true was the saying "He who goeth a-borrowing goeth a-sorrowing," but happily I neither then nor afterward broke my bond nor my word to any one to whom I owed money, and so through life have I had all the accommodation of the kind indicated that I needed.

The third volume of the *Messenger* closed with the year specified. I had furnished many strong articles for its columns, most of which I deem worthy of continued preservation. The controversy with the ultra-Universalist brethren was prosecuted with unabated vigor on my part, and the dogma of endless punishment was opposed with some of the ablest argumentative expositions I ever wrote. My own doctrine of Restorationism I defended to my own satisfaction and that of my co-religionists, against all classes of assailants, and carried on interesting discussions with several doubting, but friendly querists.

Among the articles alluded to above was a series near the end of the year, in review of a then recently published essay of H. J. Huidekoper, of Meadville, Pa., on "The Final Destruction of the Wicked." The author was a learned, able, and candid Unitarian layman, born in Germany, but long a resident in this country and thoroughly Americanized, and a most excellent man. He was virtually the founder of the Unitarian society in the place named, and of the theological school there, now so widely known throughout the land. My friend, Bernard Whitman, knowing that I had been a convert from Destructionism to Restorationism, sent me a copy of the essay, with an urgent request that I should examine and answer it. I was glad to do so. When I had completed my review, I mailed the numbers of my paper containing it to Mr. Huidekoper, who, in due time, made a rejoinder, to which I in turn, replied. This discussion is preserved with other published writings of mine, as elsewhere stated.

During the same year, I was drawn into another friendly argument with Rev. Jonathan Farr, of Harvard, Mass., an intelligent and amiable clergyman, also of the Unitarian faith. It was upon the general subject of Restorationism and its correlative doctrines, and was carried on in the form of letters between us two, the opening one having been written by him. A few passages from my reply to his original communication will indicate the nature, drift, and spirit of the discussion, and so be of interest to the thoughtful reader:

"Permit me to say, kind sir, that I am exceedingly glad to find a Unitarian like yourself, at once well qualified by temper and talent, and willing to meet the Restorationists in a friendly discussion of the principal points which hinder their fellowship with the denomination you represent. It seems to be clear either that the Restorationists are carrying things *too far*, or that their Unitarian brethren are not carrying them *far enough*.

(1) "You say, 'The proofs which you bring in favor of a Final Restoration are very familiar to me. It may be prejudice, it may be ignorance, but still I am obliged to confess that the passages (of Scripture) which are so frequently adduced, do not to me seem to prove the doctrine in question. It seems to me that the doctrine is nowhere plainly taught in Scripture. From what I have read and heard on the subject, I have supposed that many who embraced the doctrine considered it rather one of inference than of revelation. It harmonized with their benevolent feelings and with their views of the goodness of God. I believe that many will own to you that this doctrine, important as it is deemed, is nowhere clearly, certainly, and directly taught in the gospel, and yet they receive it as reflecting more honor on the character of God and not inconsistent with his word.'

"I am willing to concede that some passages of Scripture have been adduced in support of our doctrine, which, in my judgment, have nothing to do with the subject. Can you tell me of a single doctrine in your theology of which the same is not true? Was there ever a cause so good as to avoid all unworthy support? Now I am willing to concede that there are no passages of Scripture which declare in so many unequivocal words that *all men will finally be restored to holiness and happiness*. But I contend that there are several striking passages which necessarily involve this meaning and which cannot be explained consistently with the rules of just exegesis without recognizing the support they give to our doctrine. I will quote you three from St. Paul, who, as apostle to the Gentiles, would, of all others, be most likely to inculcate the truth upon the matter in question: 'For it pleased the Father that in Him should all fulness dwell; and having made peace through the blood of His cross, by Him to reconcile all things unto Himself; by Him, I say, whether they be things on earth or things in Heaven.'—*Coll. 1 : 19, 20.* 'Wherefore, God hath also highly exalted Him and given Him a name which is above every name;

that at the name of Jesus every knee should bow, of things in heaven and things in earth, and things under the earth; and that every tongue should confess that Jesus Christ is Lord to the glory of God, the Father.'— *Phil. 2 : 9–11.* 'And when all things shall be subdued unto Him, then shall the Son also himself be subject unto Him that put all things under Him, that God may be all in all.'— *1 Cor. 15 : 38.*

"If these passages do not involve the doctrine of Universal Restoration, I grant it is not the doctrine of the Bible. I could name many others, but will not cover too much ground. These passages mean something. What is it? I have stated in general terms what *I* think they mean; you are confident they mean something else. You will now frankly explain what *you* think they mean.

"As to those Restorationists to whom you allude as acknowledging that our doctrine is not plainly revealed in the Scriptures, but who hold it rather as an indirect inference from their teachings, I think that either you have misunderstood what they mean by the term *inference*, or else, like the blind man at his first gaze, they 'see men as trees walking.' The light shines upon them through a dense mist, but it will by-and-by shine unobscured. I profess to regard the doctrine as essentially a *necessary* inference—first, from several very remarkable texts like those just quoted, to which I can give no tolerable significance without it; and second, from the fundamental truths of divine revelation, which cannot be carried out harmoniously to any other result. I consider this sort of inference the principal basis upon which the conclusions of human faith are founded. It is the ground upon which, in nine cases out of ten, civil, medical, and moral jurisprudence renders a verdict. In everything but religion the common sense of mankind is perfectly satisfied with this principle of attaining conclusions. But here, strange to say, the generality of minds is wholly unwilling to trust it.

"Ask one if God is benevolent, and he will say, 'Yes, God is love.' Ask him if God loves all his human children, and he will say, 'Yes.' Ask him if love seeks the highest good of its object, and he will say, 'Yes.' Ask him if pure misery, tending only to misery, is an evil to its subject, and he will answer, 'Yes.' Ask him if misery, gradually increasing and continuing to all eternity, would not be the greatest conceivable curse that one could experience, and his reply would be, 'Yes.' Ask him if perfect hatred could contrive a greater curse, and he would admit that it could not. Then ask him if the fact that 'God is love,' warrants the conclusion that he will so govern the moral universe as to render all finally holy and happy, and he will be off in a moment. He will see no necessary connection between the premises and the conclusion, but will tell you at once that God has no mercy for sinners except in this life; that all who die unsaved will be cast off forever as to any regard of their Creator for their welfare, and more likely than not will quote Scripture gravely to prove that God has threatened all this. At least, he will call upon you with an air of incredulity to prove from the Bible that God will not be malevolent after death; that he will not be cruel, that He will not be unjust, that He will not be the reverse of Himself, for it amounts to this. I have stood with astonishment to hear men lay down and define all the first principles of religion correctly, and then set themselves soberly at work to prove that God, the author and upholder of those principles, will so govern the universe as to violate every one of them. They will give just expositions of wisdom, benevolence, justice and mercy; they will urge them very powerfully upon the consciences of mankind; they are almost sure to decide upon the merits of human action agreeably to these first principles of religion; they revolt at everything in human laws and usages which looks like cruelty, injustice, malevolence, etc.; and yet, by holding the doctrine of endless punishment, they ascribe to the Almighty such horrible treatment of His creatures as finds no parallel in the annals of mortal tyranny and cruelty. Then, as if to cap the climax of inconsistency, they contend that this view of God's character and government is the only one that will sustain vital religion and save the world from utter moral corruption. What can be done with so much strange inconsistency? The Restorationists have made up their minds: first, to rejoice in all the good that men are doing, because good is from heaven and tends to human happiness; secondly, to labor with all their strength to remove from the character of Jehovah every imputation which tends to alienate the hearts of His creatures from Him, because they expect thereby to help forward the consummation of universal holiness and bliss.

(2) "You say again, 'I should be glad if our brethren of the Restorationist denomination could feel justified in giving their distinguishing doctrines a less conspicuous place — in dwelling on them with less frequency, and in considering them of less importance. They might insist on the doctrine of a future righteous retribution, without defining the duration of it, neither asserting nor denying its eternity in their daily instruction.'

"In reply to this, I shall speak for myself and endeavor to explain the principles by which I regulate my ministerial con duct. I consider it the great end of preaching to render men good that they may be happy. I regard all true moral goodness as divine — as learned and copied from God. When men love with such love as God exercises — when they are just as God is just — when they are merciful as their Father in heaven is merciful, *then* they are truly holy, truly good. Therefore I propose God as the perfect exemplar, and call upon mankind to strive with all their power to imitate Him. I tell them that this is the only genuine holiness and the only method of rendering themselves perfectly happy.

"Now, when I go forth to preach these truths, in what condition do I find the minds of my fellow-men? Are they believers in a God whose example it will do for them to imitate? Are they relieved of all notions of God which destroy the perfection of His character? No; the reverse of this. Trained from infancy to regard God as a great and terrible being — an omnipotent despot, who seeks only His own glory whatever becomes of His creatures, they have learned merely that He must be obeyed, because He cannot be resisted. They entertain no just idea of a benignant Father, who has no glory in view independent of the good and happiness of His children. They do not perceive that his parental solicitude for their welfare led Him to lay on them the restraints of the moral law; that He commands, rewards, punishes, and does all things which pertain to the administration of His moral government out of love to His creation. No; their minds are enveloped with a gross darkness which shuts out all the light of a truly religious appeal to their hearts. That veil must be rent away. That darkness must be dissipated, or there is no use in exhorting them to be holy, as God is holy.

"Besides all this, when I go forth to my ministry, I find my path hedged up before me. I find the most unjust prejudices against the truth as I understand it, reigning even in good minds. People will not suffer me to be silent concerning my peculiar views. Their religious teachers have set them all awry in regard to my heresy. I, therefore, upon entering the obstructed field, must clear away the hindrances, and after preparing men's hearts to feel the force of my preaching, bend all my efforts to their enlightenment and reformation. I do not then need to keep harping on the doctrine of final restoration. I have made myself understood. My hearers know I have discarded the doctrine of endless punishment and its concomitant notions. Then I can show them a perfect God at the head of a perfect moral government, accomplishing by a sure process perfect good. Then I can make them feel their obligations to love and obey such a God. I can make them understand that to be holy and happy, they must imitate this God. I can make them perceive the magnitude and utter inexcusableness of their guilt in disobeying this blessed Father of all men. I can warn them with tears to repent, and, like the prodigal, return to their Father's house. I can appeal to them as their own judge, and ask them how dreadful a punishment they will deserve if they contemn such a gracious Father's authority and counsels and mercies — if they abuse the infinite kindness of this greatest and best friend, and despise their own welfare. I can point them to the future and show them that they have no promise of finding anything but woe while they remain rebel sinners. They know that I do not limit punishment to this life nor to any definite period in the next, but leave all to the wisdom of our God, who will punish neither too much nor too little, but render to every man according to his deeds and moral needs.

"If this kind of preaching will not promote reformation of character and extend the empire of holiness over the human heart, my ministerial labor is vain. There are those who have sat under Unitarian preaching — under that very preaching which holds up a future retribution without either affirming or denying its strict eternity — and which, of course, the common mind regards as endless. These persons now sit under my preaching. Ask them whether, with my final restoration all understood, I do not preach as much punishment and make it as much to be dreaded as the Unitarians. Still, I perceive that many Unitarians hesitate to co-operate with me and my brethren because they consider us as offering up strange fire — as letting loose the restraints which they believe God has laid in the fear of endless punishment. Well, let them act conscientiously; we will not complain. Time will do us and our sentiments justice. We are willing and anxious to meet all Christians, however different from us in opinion, on a level of brotherly love, and while we claim and allow perfect freedom in matters of faith, to treat them as we wish to be treated. If we can have such fellowship and co-operation, we shall rejoice, not as a sect, but as Christians. If we cannot have such fellowship, we want none, for we are determined to be entangled with no yoke of bondage, but to 'stand fast in the liberty wherewith Christ has made us free.'"

Our controversy on these and kindred points was carried on to considerable length in the *Independent Messenger*, but, much as I desired it, nothing I wrote ever appeared in the Unitarian publication where Mr. Farr's first letter to me was found. Probably it was deemed impolitic by the "wise and prudent" manager of the paper to agitate such a theme at that date, but the denomination has since then gradually drifted out of its *quasi* indefiniteness into a more positive faith concerning the final destiny of the wicked.

My object in quoting so largely from my argument in this case is mainly to present a sample of the willingness, frankness, and independence with which I have always avowed and defended my convictions upon any subject when fidelity to myself and to the truth demanded it. I have seldom sought a public controversy with tongue or pen, yet never shrank from one when it was urged upon me. I have always believed in free discussion, especially when the parties thereto had co-equal rights and privileges, and have always been ready to give a reason for the hope and faith I had espoused.

Another motive prompts me to quote so freely from the columns of the *Messenger*, and that is to emphasize anew my abhorrence of the doctrine of endless punishment. This abhorrence does not arise chiefly from my sense of the injustice, cruelty, and worse than useless misery to which, it alleges, God will subject countless hosts of His sinful creatures through all eternity, though these are unspeakably horrible and revolting to me. But it arises rather from the destructive falsification of the Infinite Father's moral character which it necessarily implies, and which, were it true, would render the Divine Being unworthy of the reverence, homage, love, and imitation of any rational, right-hearted, moral creature on earth or in heaven. The doctrine blasphemes God, the Father; Christ, the Son; and the Holy Spirit of both. It assails the foundation principles of the only religion which seeks the universal highest good of all mankind. The longer I live, the more profoundly I loathe and eschew it. Many of its nominal adherents have been good men and women, not by its influence, but by other influences in spite of it; and never one such loved it or prayed in accordance with it, or acted from its dictates in the treatment of their fellow human beings. It has been modified, softened down, and reduced to its mildest possibilities in later days by those who could not wholly renounce it, but in doing this they have removed its original foundations and prepared for its final overthrow. Any form of it rests on a finality of incurable human wickedness and woe, which a God of love and all beings born of His spirit must forever deplore. It ought to perish utterly from the faiths of men, and it will, and the places that now know it will know it no more, while the earth wheels in its circling orbit around the sun.

While carrying on the friendly, argumentative correspondence with Rev. Mr. Farr, my controversy with the no-future-retributionists continued with unabated vigor. My course in this matter seemed unaccountable to many people in view of my well-known agreement with these antagonists as opponents of the doctrine of endless sin and misery. But I had my own distinctive faith (which was exceedingly dear to me) to defend against the attacks of both the ultra-Universalists and the champions of the last named doctrine, who vied with each other in treating that faith with misrepresentation, reproach, and abuse, and in seeking its extermination. Therefore, my hostility to both was justified, and I contended against both (not on personal grounds, but by reason of my abhorrence of the errors they maintained) conscientiously and with unflinching resolution. Both preferred controversy with each other rather than with the Restorationists, open debate with whom on equal terms they sedulously avoided, each seemingly conscious that more was to be lost than gained thereby. They were both brave to falsify and denounce Restorationism in private circles and in pulpits and denominational organs, from which all replies were uniformly excluded. Otherwise, their policy was "to sit still," in their dignity and self-satisfaction.

On the other hand, the Restorationists invited inquiry, argument, and the most searching scrutiny of their position and theories. They never shunned debate, free discussion, public exposition and rejoinder, when opportunity occurred, deeming such means of upholding and promulgating truth as not only laudable and effective, but indispensable almost to the progress and triumph of their cause. As an exponent and promoter of that cause, I desired nothing so much as a fair and open field for canvassing *pro* and *con* all the important points at issue between myself and those differing from me. Under this prepossession, I kept the columns of the *Independent Messenger* always free to opponents of my distinctive views, and to a full hearing on both sides of controverted questions. But, as I have already stated, my frank and friendly course in this respect was never reciprocated on the part of any of my assailants or co-disputants.

In consequence of this artful policy pursued from the beginning by my ultra-Universalist brethren, I was tempted to deviate from the general rule of my life in such matters, and to publish in my paper of Feb. 8, 1834, the following:

" CHALLENGE.

" 'Come, let us reason together.' Reverend fathers and teachers in the Israel of Universalism: I believe what you disbelieve — that the Holy Scriptures teach the doctrine of future righteous retribution. You consider my belief a relic of heathenism; I consider your disbelief a species of anti-Christian skepticism. A great controversy has commenced and will be prosecuted to an issue between yourselves and those who hold, with me, the doctrine of future retribution. Thousands of people need to be enlightened on the subject who cannot be induced to plod through the pages of elaborate works, but who would, nevertheless, be interested in an investigation carried on in the way of a public oral discussion. Now, therefore, I invite you to a friendly debate of the following question:— ' *Do the Holy Scriptures teach the doctrine of future rewards and punishments?* ' And I respectfully propose the following terms of arrangement, viz:

" (1) The discussion to be holden in some commodious hall or edifice n the city of Boston.

"(2) Thirty days' notice of its commencement to be given in the public papers.

"(3) Three moderators to preside, with full power to enforce the most wholesome and approved rules of debate, the parties respectively choosing one moderator each, and these two the third.

"(4) In the affirmative of the question, myself alone; in the negative, as many of your clergymen as you please.

"(5) The parties to occupy alternately thirty minutes space of speech.

"(6) Two experienced reporters to be employed, with full instructions to prepare for the press a faithful report of the whole discussion, as nearly verbatim as possible, without submitting any part thereof to the previous inspection of the disputants or any other persons.

"(7) The debate to commence on Tuesday and be continued, with suitable intermissions, till the close of Friday; and so on from week to week till the parties are mutually willing to terminate it, or till one of them shall absolutely decline its further prosecution.

"(8) All expenses properly incidental to the discussion (time, labor, and mere personal expense excepted), and all income arising from the sale of the Report, if any, to be equally shared by the parties.

"(9) The printing of the Report, whether by the affirmative or negative party, to be decided by lot, under the direction of the moderators.

"All which is respectfully submitted, with the humble hope that you will accept my invitation, proposals, and terms; and that by a friendly, fair, and full discussion of the question at issue, we may mutually contribute to enlighten and satisfy many thousand inquiring minds.

"ADIN BALLOU."

Two days after the publication of this challenge, I received a letter from Rev. Daniel D. Smith, accepting it on condition that the form of the question be so changed as to read: "*Do the Scriptures teach the doctrine that men will be punished and rewarded subsequently to this life (or after death) for the deeds done in this life?*" The writer also suggested the wisdom of having but one reporter instead of two, in order to reduce the expenses to the lowest possible figure. The letter was cordial, respectful, and friendly, and solicited an early response.

I replied at once, saying that I was happy to receive the acceptance of my challenge provided a specified change could be made in the wording of the question for discussion, to which change I cheerfully consented. I also yielded to my friend's proposition that but one reporter be employed, if we could find a person competent to fill the position. I furthermore, at his suggestion, named Tuesday, the 18th of March following, as the time for commencing the discussion, the place to be determined and made known at a later date.

So far everything was satisfactory and promised well for the fulfilment of my fondly-cherished desire. Shortly afterward, the standing committee of the First Universalist society of Boston generously tendered the disputants the free use of their church edifice on Hanover street, which offer was gratefully accepted. Other arrangements were speedily completed. Rev. Bernard Whitman consented to act as my moderator, Rev. Linus Everett as Mr. Smith's, and by their agreement Rev. Joshua V. Himes was the third, who was to occupy the position of chairman. The services of Richard Hildreth, Esq. of Boston, as reporter were happily secured, and everything was ready for the fray.

The discussion opened at 9 o'clock A. M. on Tuesday, March 18th, and closed on Thursday, March 20th, about 5 o'clock P. M, having been held for three successive days with two sessions per day of three hours each — in all six sessions or eighteen hours. Of its character and progress from beginning to end, I gave a description and estimate from my standpoint in the issue of the *Messenger* for March 29th, which I still believe to be truthful and just. I will not reproduce the article here, but refer the reader to the preserved files of the paper in which it appeared.

I may, however, observe that the discussion, so far as my own side was concerned, gave me unqualified and grateful satisfaction, as it did also the friends of the doctrine which I sought to vindicate and maintain. My

Restorationist brethren were enthusiastic in their commendation of my labors, and manifested their appreciation of what I had achieved for the cause of truth by presenting me on Thursday evening after the debate was concluded "Dr. Adam Clarke's complete Commentary upon the Scriptures," in six large, handsomely bound volumes.

As to my antagonist, I would state that although several Universalist clergymen disclaimed having counseled or encouraged him to enter the arena with me, yet he deserves the thanks of all Restorationists for doing so. He certainly thereby gave evidence of being an honest man in the matter, and though saying some things he probably afterwards had occasion to regret, yet I believe he did as well on the whole for his cause as any of his older and more experienced brethren could have done. If he made a poor fight of it, the fault was in his cause, and not in his lack of ability. In general he was calm and dispassionate, and preserved a respectful bearing. It was predicted, report said, that the disputants would soon lose their temper, become greatly irritated with each other, and finally outrageous. These prophecies, like many others of a like nature, did not come to pass. Alas, for the prophets!

The debate went on smoothly and in good order, with little hesitation or incoherency, during the first two days, but during the forenoon of the third day Mr. Smith showed signs of being weary of it and of wishing it were at an end. He complainingly remarked that he did not know but his opponent intended to keep him there till his locks were gray with age. I had compassion for him and when at noon some of his friends proposed to close the discussion with the afternoon session, I agreed to conclude my argument, if possible, before night, leaving it optional whether or not we should meet again the following day. He decided against doing so and the end came accordingly.

The conduct of Mr. Himes, who presided at all the sessions, and of our friend, Mr. Whitman, was such as became the dignity and responsibility of their position. With that of Mr. Everett, the moderator chosen by my opponent, I was not so well pleased. His manifest partisanship and desire for the success of his side of the case were apparent and provoked not a little unfavorable comment. As to the audience that listened to the discussion, it was respectable in numbers, general appearance, and deportment, throughout. Those comprising it were evidently interested in the subject under consideration and gave both the disputants candid, thoughtful, earnest attention. Everything in this particular was satisfactory and gratifying.

The lot to print the report of this affair fell to me, and an edition of 5000 copies in pamphlet form was mutually agreed upon and ordered. In due time it was issued, making an octavo work of 86 pages, and offered to the public. The Universalists did nothing to promote its circulation, but, on the contrary, all they could to discourage it. Their journals took no pains to advertise it and never recommended their patrons to read it, that they might be informed in regard to the merits of the discussion or to the nature and force of the arguments on either side of the question at issue. Even my co-equal disputant, Mr. Smith, notwithstanding the definite terms on which we entered the field of conflict, when he found that the report was not likely to redound to the honor and glory of himself and his cause, slunk dishonorably out of his engagements, refused to bear his equal share of the burden of disposing of the work, and to crown all left me to shoulder nearly all the pecuniary cost of the undertaking, including the expense of its publication and the payment of Mr. Hildreth's large bill for reportorial labors. I bore the wrong patiently, met all incurred obligations as soon as I was able, scattered copies of the pamphlet often gratuitously up and down the country, my Restorationist associaties and sympathizers co-operating with me in this distribution. What I lost in dollars and cents, I gained in a knowledge of no-future-retribution ethics, in the later satisfaction of learning that the leaders of "the order" were convinced that nothing could be gained for their *ism* by denouncing Restorationism and suppressing free discussion, and finally in seeing their peculiar dogma give way in their own denomination to the faith it was my privilege and duty to uphold, disseminate, and help to make perpetual among men.

But few additional events occurred during the then current year worthy of mention. I was present at several ecclesiastical convocations, such as are likely to be held at irregular intervals under the general administration of the affairs of a Christian denomination, participating more or less in the public exercises incident to them. Among these was the meeting of the Providence Association in Westminster, Mass., on the 11th and 12th of September. At that gathering, Brother Hudson's house of worship, which had been removed from its original site a mile and a half away to the central village and thoroughly renovated, was dedicated anew with appropriate services. On the same occasion Brother Edwin M. Stone, a native of Beverly, was ordained as a Christian minister and an evangelist of our Restorationist faith. He continued in our fellowship until the disbandment of the Massachusetts Restorationist Association in 1841, then entered the Unitarian denomination, under whose auspices he labored acceptably as pastor in various places,— the last years of his life being devoted to the work of the "Ministry-at-Large" in Providence, R. I., in which he rendered most important service.

On the 26th of the same month I again officiated as chaplain at a regimental muster in Uxbridge; the last time, if I remember rightly, that I appeared before the public in that capacity, though it was some years later that I became a convert to peace principles and received my official discharge. I dined, as was customary, with the officers:—Col. Peter Corbett, Lieut-Col. Horace Emerson, Major Putnam W. Taft, etc., at several of whose funerals I subsequently ministered. Having at that time become a devoted temperance man and so keenly observant of the evils of intemperance, I was enabled to see how many of the numerous attendants, as usually is the case on such occasions, needed salvation from inordinate artificial appetites and bad habits engendered thereby. I had been diligent in this field of reform for some time and measurably successful, but the field was of vast extent and I had gathered only a few sheaves into the granary of redemption.

CHAPTER XIV.

1834–1836.

EDMUND CAPRON — TEMPERANCE WORK — DEATHS — OMEGA OF CONTROVERSY — REV. MR. APTHORP.

IN entering upon the thirty-second year of my life, I found myself charged with extraordinary labors, cares, and responsibilities. In addition to those usually incumbent upon one occupying the position I did in the general community as a minister of the gospel and an expositor of divine truth, I had on my hands the entire proprietorship of the *Independent Messenger* printing establishment, the oversight of its weekly publication, its sole editorial management, and just at this time, the special burden of getting out 5000 copies of the Boston Discussion Report. Moreover, in order to render myself still further useful to our Restorationist cause, I received into my family and under my tuition, another theological student, Brother Edmund Capron, a very worthy and promising young man, anxious to devote himself to the work of the Christian ministry under the auspices of the Massachusetts Association. He was an earnest, faithful student, and successful in his endeavors to qualify himself for his chosen vocation. He remained with me until he had essentially completed the course of instruction requisite therefor — some two or more years.

The files of the fourth volume of the *Messenger*, then being issued under my sole care and supervision, bear witness to the industry, vigor, and zeal with which I continued to expound the doctrine of Universal Restoration, and defend it against all classes of assailants. I had still the leading Universalists of the ultra school to combat on the one hand, and the dogmatic champions of endless punishment on the other. Among the latter with whom I measured swords were such notables as Rev. Dr. Nathaniel W. Taylor, of New School Divinity fame; Rev. Dr. Bennett Tyler, of Old School Divinity fame; and President Charles G. Finney, D. D., of Oberlin Seminary. My opponents of this class had the great advantage over me of access to many journals through which to reach the public, all closed against me, and of a vast multitude of sympathizing partisans; while I had but one small paper of limited circulation, with comparatively few supporters. But I had the strong consciousness and assurance that I was the advocate of divine truths which must at last prevail, and I wrote and wrought accordingly.

I had at this time become actively engaged in temperance work, delivering lectures at numerous points and attending meetings and conventions held in the same behalf. I also attended ecclesiastical gatherings, taking part in several, some of which were noteworthy by reason of the prominence in the religious world subsequently attained by the principal participants. I take the liberty of mentioning a few of these.

On the 14th of May, 1834, I was present at the installation of Rev. Orestes A. Brownson, as pastor of the First Congregational church and society in Canton, Mass., in the exercises of which I had been assigned an important part. The council was composed mostly of members of the Unitarian denomination, the sermon being preached by Rev. George Ripley of Boston, from Heb. 13:8: "Jesus Christ, the same yesterday, today, and forever." Mr. Brownson was a ripe scholar, an able preacher, and a writer of rare ability. But in theology, metaphysics, ethics, and ecclesiasticism, his convictions, positions, and associations underwent strange vicissitudes. Soon after his settlement at Canton, he became a Transcendentalist, subsequently espousing the "Workingmen's Movement" (of which he was for awhile a distinguished champion), and later went over to the Roman Catholic church, resting there from his religio-philosophical journeyings, and rising to eminence as the author of several works devoted chiefly to the defence of the doctrines, polity, and traditions of the papal hierarchy. Rev. Mr. Ripley afterwards acquired a wide notoriety as the leader of the "Brook Farm" community, and later still, as literary editor for a generation of the *New York Tribune*.

The installation of Rev. Philemon R. Russell as pastor of the Liberal Congregational church and society of West Boylston, occurred on the 24th of May, the council consisting equally of Unitarians and Restorationists. The Restorationists having part in the proceedings were Rev. Paul Dean of Boston, who preached the sermon; Rev. Seth Chandler of Oxford; and myself, who gave the charge; the Unitarians were Rev. Joseph Allen of Northborough; Rev. Mr. Osgood of Sterling; Rev. John Goldsbury of Hardwick; and Rev. Ebenezer Robinson of Hubbardston. Mr. Russell was a zealous, enthusiastic man, with considerable natural and acquired ability, and much executive push. But his pastorates among us, of which there were several, were all brief. Either he did not wear well, or was himself a lover of change. After a time he left our body and joined the "Christian Connexion." Later, he espoused "Second Adventism," becoming its ardent advocate. When that illusion subsided, he abandoned the pulpit and rostrum, devoting himself thereafter to secular pursuits. in which he acquired a handsome property, ending his days at length in comparative wealth.

On Wednesday, June 18th, Brother David R. Lamson was ordained and installed pastor of the First church and society in Berlin, Mass., with a union council as before. Rev. Joseph Allen of Northborough, delivered the sermon, and Rev. Charles Hudson of Westminster, gave the charge. Of Mr. Lamson's ability, character, and life career, I shall have occasion to speak at a later period of this narrative.

Another union installation occured a week later, June 25th, when Rev. William Morse, recently of Quincy, was inducted into the office of pastor of the Second Congregational parish in Marlborough, Mass. I officiated in the opening exercises; Rev. James Walker of Charlestown preached the sermon; Rev. Paul Dean offered the Consecratory Prayer; Rev. Joseph Allen gave the Charge; Rev. Charles Hudson extended the Right Hand of Fellowship; Rev. Isaac Allen of Bolton addressed the society; and Rev. Mr. Sweet of Southborough made the final prayer. A fine day, harmonious communion of souls, able and impressive services, hospitable entertainment, and all the incidents of the occasion remarkably pleasant. Mr. Morse was well qualified for his office in all respects and had a satisfactory pastorate in Marlborough of ten years. He was subsequently settled in Tyngsborough and afterwards supplied in Chelmsford, going thence to Franklin, N. H., where he finally departed this life at the ripe age of more than fourscore years.

I participated in one other ordination during the year 1834, that of Rev. Richard Stone at West Bridgewater, Mass., on the 20th of August. I was the only Restorationist member of the council, being invited through the influence of several lay friends in the parish, all the others being Unitarians. The introductory prayer was offered by me; Rev. Jason Whitman, brother of my dear friend, Rev. Bernard Whitman, and secretary of the American Unitarian Association, delivered the sermon, and neighboring Unitarian clergymen took the several other parts,— all the exercises passing off pleasantly and auspiciously.

The semi-annual meeting of the Massachusetts Restorationist Association was held at Attleborough, on the 10th and 11th of September. Twelve of our ministerial fellowship were present, seven of whom preached during the several sessions of the convocation, which closed with great solemnity and sanctifying impressiveness by the administration of the ordinance of the Lord's Supper. An affecting incident of this gathering was the mutual farewell interchanged with our beloved brother, Nathaniel Wright, for some years secretary of the body, who had just closed his Attleborough pastorate and was about to remove to the far-off West. A testimonial of personal and professional regard for him was presented by Rev. Brother Dean, and adopted with hearty unanimity. Brother Wright spent the remainder of his earthly life in the town of Tremont, Ill., where he soon after located, and rarely made visits to his native state. How long or how successfully he prosecuted the work of the ministry in his new home I am not informed, but remember that later in life he was drawn into secular pursuits, attaining therein considerable success.

Death of Rev. Bernard Whitman. This faithful minister of Christ, this child of God and brother of man, this eminent champion of Christian liberty, truth, justice, and charity, this uncompromising opponent of bigotry, pseudo-liberality, and infidelity, passed through the shadow of death to the realm of the immortals on Wednesday, Nov. 5, 1834, at the meridian age of 38 years, 4 months, and 27 days. He was the thirteenth child of Deacon John Whitman, of East Bridgewater, Mass., who lived to be 103 years old. Though he inherited a strong constitution from his father, yet by overwork and exposure his native energies became early enfeebled, and he fell a victim to consumption, which resulted fatally, after several months of suffering decline, in his pastoral home at Waltham, Mass. Hewing his way through a forest of difficulties up to a well-equipped manhood, he had been an indomitable worker for religion and human progress, and had devised a host of plans for future usefulness which he longed to carry into effect; yet he bore his wasting sickness with Christian meekness and resignation, passing peacefully away from earth and leaving behind an admirable example of patient faith and of triumphant assurance of a welcome to the angelic mansions. Whether I regarded him as a personal friend, as a sympathizer with our Restorationist movement, or with reference to those public relationships which he sustained with honor to himself and spiritual profit to mankind, I felt it a sacred privilege to rank myself among his mourners and to welcome to the columns of the paper under my charge at the time numerous commemorative obituary testimonies celebrating his translation to the higher life.

Notable Family Bereavements. Two deaths in our respective domestic circles threw their shadows across the threshold of our home during the closing month of this year (1834). The first was that of an estimable and noble-hearted sister of my wife, occurring on the second day of December; the other that of my beloved and revered mother, which took place on the 27th. The *Independent Messenger* paid tender and affectionate tribute to each of them in turn as follows:

"In Milford, on the 2d inst., after a distressing illness of several months, Miss Chloe Albee, daughter of Pearley Hunt, Esq., in the 20th year of her age. Under this bereavement, the surviving family mourn the loss of a most worthy, kind-hearted, and estimable daughter and sister. Endowed with those better feelings which adorn human nature, the deceased endeared herself most to those who knew her best. She was rich in the noblest of social affections and virtues. To sympathize with and aid others and render them happy by helpful ministrations, was her delight. She has vacated a sphere of kindness in the midst of her family connections which they will long contemplate with sincere grief. She leaves many friends, too, and no enemies in the youthful circle in which she was accustomed to move. They will all miss one from their number who was among the first in that substantial worth which ensured lasting esteem," etc.

"In Cumberland, R. I., on the 27th ult., after a prostrating illness of eight days, Mrs. Edilda Ballou, wife of Deacon Ariel Ballou and mother of the editor of this paper, in the 64th year of her age. Though this obituary notice is inscribed by the hand of filial affection, let it not be regarded as the exaggeration of bereaved fondness. It registers in general terms the excellence of a woman mourned by all who knew her as 'full of good works and almsdeeds.' Her memory challenges not the honors rendered those who have moved in the fashionable walks of life. She was born and bred in the midst of the constant domestic cares belonging to the household of a New England farmer. Her mind, gifted with sound native sense and a strong thirst for improvement, was always restricted to scanty means, and, of course, gathered up only the fragments of general knowledge. These she employed to the great end for which she lived, the happiness of those around her. Here centered the distinguished virtues that adorned her character. She was naturally kind, sympathetic, generous, unassuming; by Christian grace eminently contrite, devout, meek, and charitable. She had that mind which was in Christ Jesus — the mind that sees itself largely in others, which loves to serve rather than be served, to give rather than receive, to suffer rather than see others suffer; which places its own chief good, glory, and happiness in the welfare of others. Poverty, sickness, sorrow, and misfortune never appealed to her in vain. Without the least seeming desire to show herself, she fed the hungry, clothed the naked, visited the sick, entertained the stranger, comforted the despondent, and pitied all the unhappy. Her religion and morality were of the same stamp.

"The good she loved of every name,
And prayed for all mankind."

The death of my mother was soon followed by a general settlement of my father's estate. He was too old and infirm to bear the burden of managing his large farm, especially now that his faithful companion had passed away. So he summoned his three sons to the parental home and desired them to come to some terms of agreement satisfactory to all concerned. We met, conferred with each other and with him, and soon arrived at an amicable understanding. Whereupon, specific legal writings were drawn and in due time executed.

Another important change in matters of interest to me occurred about the same time. I had assumed duties and obligations which I learned were too onerous for me to bear for a great length of time, and some kind of relief was not only desirable but absolutely necessary. After careful deliberation, I concluded to unload myself essentially of the burden of the *Independent Messenger*, the entire responsibility of which, pecuniary, editorial, managemental, etc., rested upon me. And as a practicable way out of the difficulties besetting me, I conceived the project of making the proprietorship of the paper and its correlative printing-house a joint stock concern, and of distributing the labor of furnishing matter for its columns among a staff of editors. Having duly digested the plan and brought it into proper form, I announced it to the public and appealed earnestly to my clerical and lay brethren to aid me in adopting it and in carrying it out to a successful issue. They responded promptly and cheerfully, and a joint stock company was soon organized, Rev. Paul Dean (whom I always found to be the soul of honor in such emergencies) taking the leading part in the contemplated enterprise. About the middle of March, 1835, circumstances under the new arrangement rendered it expedient to remove the *Messenger* and its appurtenances and belongings once more to Boston, the reasons for which, with sufficiency of detail, were given to the public in its issue of the 14th of the month. Thenceforward, it was published at the corner of Tremont (Court) and Howard streets, its printing and the general supervision of all business matters pertaining to it being entrusted to Messrs. H. B. and J. Brewster. Its editorial staff was Rev. Paul Dean, resident editor; Revs. Charles Hudson, William Morse, Philemon R. Russell, and Adin Ballou, corresponding editors.

For greater convenience and comfort to myself and family, I, in the spring of 1835, relinquished the tenement we had occupied since coming to Mendon four years before, which was quite out of the village, and hired what was then known as the Dr. Thayer house, at the very heart of the town, where we remained for seven years, or until I closed my official labors with the First church and society there. The location and internal arrangements of the building were much more pleasant than those we vacated and much better suited to the needs and circumstances of a clergyman's household.

Several public occasions occurring during the year 1835 in which I was a more or less active participant, are worthy of brief mention. The first was the dedication, January 13, of the new, commodious, and elegant church edifice of the First Congregational parish in Uxbridge, Rev. Samuel Clarke, pastor. The day was charming and a large congregation attended the services. The sermon was by Mr. Clarke, with a text from Exodus, 12 : 26 : "What mean ye by this service?" The venerable Aaron Bancroft, D. D., of Worcester, offered the prayer of dedication. Everything passed off harmoniously, pleasantly, and auspiciously. The officiating clergymen, with the single exception of myself, were of the distinctively Unitarian faith.

I shall do little more than make note of the several convocations of our Restorationist brethren during this year (1835), without entering much into details concerning those participating in them, the exercises, etc. The first was a special conference held in Mendon on the 7th and 8th of May. In addition to the usual public religious exercises, there were sessions of a semi-business character, at which affairs pertaining to the *Independent Messenger* transfer were canvassed and adjusted. Brother Dean, in his editorial comments on the meeting, characterized its religious features as "happily calculated to excite and perpetuate a healthy tone of devotional feeling." On the 3d and 4th of June, the annual meeting of the Providence Association took place at Providence, R. I., a full attendance of ministers and laymen being present. Important business was transacted, interesting and impressive religious services, including the administration of the Lord's Supper, were held, to the edification and spiritual profit of the participants. The Massachusetts Restorationist Association met at East Medway, September 2d and 3d, the occasional sermon being delivered by Rev. Lyman Maynard, then of Amherst, N. H., from 2 Cor. 4 : 42 : "Therefore, seeing we have this ministry, as we have received mercy, we faint not; but have renounced the hidden things of dishonesty, not walking in craftiness, nor handling the word of God deceitfully; but by manifestation of the truth, commending ourselves to every man's conscience in the sight of God." A special sermon was preached by myself from Acts 3:19: "Repent ye therefore, and be converted," etc. Rev. Orestes A. Brownson, before spoken of, was present and took an active part in the exercises of the occasion. An interesting feature of one session was the approbation and reception, as members of the body, of four young ministers — William H. Fish, Edmund Capron, George W. Stacey, Henry B. Brewster — the first and third of whom were long and successfully engaged in the work to which they were then consecrated.

The controversy with our ultra Universalist brethren was prosecuted vigorously by me till February 7 of this year, when I voluntarily closed it, so far as the public press was concerned. My determination (which was arrived at after a careful survey of the whole matter) I announced through the columns of the *Messenger* in an article entitled ." Omega," some extracts from which I submit to my present readers:

"Omega, the last letter of the Greek alphabet, was anciently employed to denote the end of any matter or thing. And I use the word to indicate that with this writing I terminate all newspaper controversy on my part with Universalist editors and their adherents, relating to the doctrine of future retribution. My opinions and feelings in respect to that subject are well known. My stand has been taken; my testimony has been recorded; my course for the future is marked out. I am inflexible.

"As I have believed, so have I spoken. I have opposed what is called Universalism as now interpreted with an indefatigable and uncompromising zeal. I have challenged its advocates to discussion and met them whenever I had an opportunity. I have reasoned against, repelled, and controverted whatever in Universalist doctrine, spirit, or practice, I deemed essentially erroneous. I have regarded, and still regard, their prominent tenets, their style of preaching and writing, their tone of feeling towards other denominations, and the general drift of their sectarian policy, hostile to genuine Christianity. If I am wrong in this, God enlighten and forgive me.

"But while there is a time to speak and to act, there is also a time to pause, to be silent, to cease from contending, even for 'the faith once delivered to the saints.' After one has said and done enough in the way of opposition and reproof, after he has been wrongfully accused, without stint or limit, and conjured again and again to let the subjects of his reprobation alone, it is time to suspend his labors and leave his antagonists to themselves. I feel that such a time has come with me in relation to the leaders of the Universalist denomination. They may believe, write, publish, manage, in their own way. But from me, so far as concerns newspaper controversy, they shall hear no more. The residue of my life shall be devoted to other matters.

So I thenceforth let them alone. What was the sequel? A notable change in a few years began to take place in the doctrines, spirit, preaching, writing, and general policy of the denomination, ultimating in a complete revolution in regard to every one of the points at issue at the time of the Restorationist secession and subsequent controversy. There was a radical reform both in theory and practice, which saved the denomination from its downward trend and led it upward and onward to its present condition of commendable excellence, usefulness, and prosperity. If its leaders in 1830 had stood where their successors now do, as evidenced by the action of the Universalist ministers of Boston and vicinity in 1878, there would have been no secession and no controversy.

But though my warfare with my Universalist brethren had come to an end, it was not so with that carried on between me and the advocates of endless punishment. That continued without abatement. My antagonists were numerous, persistent, and unrelenting. They represented the great mass of the nominal Christian church in all its popular denominations. To Restorationism they were unanimously and implacably opposed and neither truce nor quarter was to be expected from them. They were sincere and believed they were doing God service in trying to crush out what they regarded as a great heresy. But I was no less sincere and as confident and determined as they. They had great external advantages over me, but I had one condition of success not shared by them; I understood both sides of the question between us. I had been through the mill of investigation thoroughly and knew all the arguments they could command. In fact, I could defend their case at any moment as well or better than themselves, but they knew not the strength of Restorationism till discussion revealed it to them,— sometimes to their manifest confusion. So this particular conflict went on from month to month, through the columns of the *Messenger*, through written correspondence, through sermons, special lectures, personal conversation, and public oral debate.

An instance of the last named method occurred in my own town. Rev. W. P. Apthorp, provisional minister of the "North Mendon Congregational church" (orthodox), deemed it his duty to attempt the conversion and salvation of some of my deluded(?) hearers by visiting, catechising, and warning them against my dangerous views. On the street and in their houses, he improved convenient opportunities of pushing his crusade. He was not a man of large mental or moral caliber, but made up for other deficiencies by zeal and self-assurance. He had a professional outfit of theological scholarship after the fashion of his sect, was thoroughly imbued with the animus of his creed, and cherished an ignorant contempt for Restorationism. He soon learned that those he undertook to proselyte were not to be seriously affected by his endeavors. They received his exhortations and warnings calmly and intelligently. Some of them suggested that he had better call on me, get acquainted, and inform himself of my doctrines before arraigning and denouncing them. This he at first disdained to do, intimating that he knew all he wished to in that direction.

After receiving the same suggestion repeatedly, he finally said he intended making me a visit, signifying to one of my good women, whom he had plied his arts upon in vain, that he should do so on a specified evening. She informed me of his intentions, and asked the privilege of being present, which I cheerfully granted. When the time came, he appeared without previous announcement on his part,— a gentleman parishioner having come in incidentally a little before him. I greeted him cordially, told him I was happy to see him, as I had heard of his conversations with several of my people, and referred to some of his reported sayings. He seemed a little embarassed, but I soon put him at his ease and our conversation went on freely. He at first affected the role of an inquirer concerning my views and opinions, but soon assumed the attitude of a disputant. At the close of our interview he was not satisfied with the situation in which he had left his doctrine and solicited another opportunity to explain it. This I consented to and an evening was agreed upon when he was to call again. Meanwhile the matter was noised abroad in town, awakening considerable interest, resulting, when the time arrived, in my house being crowded with eager listeners.

At the end of the second evening's disputation, he was no better pleased with the aspect of his case than before, and hence must meet me again. The hotel-keeper of the village, one of his parishioners, seeing how my family was incommoded by the large company present, kindly offered his hall to us for the third conference and we went there accordingly, having a larger auditory than before. The discussion was chiefly conversational but waxed warm. At the close my antagonist was still dissatisfied and demanded further opportunities to defend himself and his cause. I agreed and it was arranged that we meet in his house of worship to accomodate the still increasing crowd. It was also decided that the disputants occupy ten minutes alternately in orderly discussion, and that the inn-keeper should act as moderator of the occasion. At the end of this fourth interview, Mr. Apthorp had not succeeded, as he thought, in doing full justice to his subject and requested another. I was quite willing to grant him all the time he wanted and consented to his wishes. By this time his friends began to think it was best for the discussion to be brought to an end, as no advantage was likely to accrue to himself or them by continuing it, and so advised him. He prudently yielded to their judgment and accordingly announced when we again came together that the debate would close with that session. It fell to my lot in the order of speaking to make the last address, and I took good care it should be conclusively my strongest. It told with such effect that Mr. Apthorp, greatly excited, sprang to his feet, exclaiming, "I cannot leave this subject so; I must discuss it further; I will meet Mr. Ballou again next Tuesday evening." But his brethren suppressed him and his appointment was reluctantly and sullenly relinquished.

The dates of our several meetings were October 13, 15, 16, 20, 22, 1835. In the discussion, which was chiefly a scriptural one, I rested my cause on the answer which the bible furnishes to these inquiries: — What is the character of God? For what end did he create man? For what end did he reveal the moral law? For what end was Christ sent into the world? For what end did he teach, suffer, and die? For what end has he been exalted to the Mediatorial throne? Finally, what do the holy prophets and apostles predict will be his success in accomplishing his undertaking?

My opponent conceded that the bible taught that the character of God was essentially and perfectly benevolent; that he created men for happiness; that the revelation of the moral law was designed to discipline man for holiness and bliss; that Christ was sent into the world to restore it; that he died for all men; that he was exalted to the Mediatorial throne to reign over and subdue all things unto himself; and that many of the prophetic and apostolic predictions of his final triumph were in their literal sense favorable to the doctrine of universal restoration.

While conceding all this in a certain way, he yet sought to disprove that doctrine by the help of what he called a *double sense* in the scriptures, and qualifying reservations. Being a "New School" man, he was neither a Calvinist nor Arminian all the way through, but by turns both, as best served his purpose. He steered as clear as possible from committing himself unqualifiedly upon any of the points raised, except that of believing in the absolute endless duration of punishment. To maintain this position he adduced the principal threatenings of scripture, emphasized their phraseology — such as the terms *everlasting*, *unquenchable*, etc., alleging that they ought to be understood in their most literal sense, and that from this point of view we ought to interpret all the rest of the bible, and to understand the nature of the divine benevolence.

The discussion of the entire five evenings centered in and was an elaboration of the several points thus indicated, the details of which need not be given. It began, progressed, and terminated just I could have desired. It did great good in the community and justified my conviction that such public debates subserve the triumph of truth. Moreover, it left me and my people free in the exercise and enjoyment of our own chosen faith. Neither I nor they were ever afterward troubled by the intermeddling of proselyting adventurers.

An extended report of this debate from my pen in the *Messenger* called forth a rejoinder by Mr. Apthorp which was followed by one article each from me and him respectively — the last appearing Jan. 15, 1836, when the whole matter passed into history. Not long after he left Mendon and nothing further is known of him.

During the autumn of 1835 I conducted another private school, carrying it through to a successful issue before winter set in. I also gave instruction to a young theological student, Brother Cyrus Morse, whose health, however, soon failed, obliging him to relinquish his studies and causing his death a few months afterward; his fond hopes of Christian usefulness in the world thus vanishing forever. He found a loving home in the family of

Brother E. D. Draper in Rogerson's Village, Uxbridge, where he received the kindest of ministrations and where he breathed his last on the ensuing 28th of March. He bore his illness with patience, meekness, and resignation, and departed in the full assurance of a blissful immortality. Appropriate funeral services were held in the Unitarian church, Uxbridge, in which I was assisted by the pastor, Rev. Samuel Clarke, and Rev. Mr. Ellis, Methodist minister at Rogerson's Village. I had a written sermon from the text: " Rejoice with them that do rejoice and weep with them that weep." — *Rom. 12 : 15.*

The year 1836 came in with a special greeting of appreciation from the ladies of my pastoral flock, who presented me with a fine blue broadcloth cloak. The garment was a very elegant and substantial one, of ample proportions, and is still extant, though in a somewhat modified form, but is capable of much service yet. Accompanying it was a paper, still preserved, containing the names of the forty-five donors with the amount of their respective offerings appended, and certifying that the gift was made " as a testimony to the esteem and respect we entertain for his individual and pastoral character."

Rev. Brother David Pickering having recently resigned his pastorate in Providence, R. I., and removed to New York city, I went by special invitation of the authorities of the church and society left without a minister, to supply the pulpit and administer the communion on Sunday, the first day of January. Three services were held—morning, afternoon, and evening, according to the custom in those days in large towns and cities. That society, after a time, renewed its connection with the Universalist denomination, and I never again occupied its pulpit in the order of ecclesiastical fellowship. Nor did I ever again meet Brother Pickering. He left the ministry a few years later, settled in western New York, where he encountered a series of adverse experiences, from which he happily emerged, removed thence to Ypsilanti, Mich., and there died Jan. 6, 1859, aged 70. He was largely a self-made man, of superior natural ability, an eloquent speaker, an author of considerable note, and a distinguished minister of liberal Christianity.

In the early part of April, my aged father, Deacon Ariel Ballou, then in the 79th year of his age, came to reside in our family. He was quite worn out with the continuous hard labor of a long lifetime, had various infirmities otherwise incident to old age, and was evidently nearing the grave. He remained with us only a few months, enjoying himself tolerably well, and seeming to take great delight in his little grandson, about three years old. Though I had departed widely from the strict path of doctrine in which he had trained me, thereby incurring his displeasure at the outset, yet he had laid aside all his unkindly feelings, and was pleased (when his health and strength would permit) to attend public worship, and apparently was able to extract considerable edification and spiritual profit from my ministrations.

I had now been the incumbent of my Mendon pastorate about five years. My church and society, which were in a greatly depressed condition when I assumed charge of them, had gradually improved, until they had attained a degree of prosperity unknown for a long time before. The Sunday School had taken to itself new life and was steadily increasing in numbers, discipline, and influence. I sought to elevate its religious tone and character by preparing a little manual of several opening and closing exercises in the form of a brief liturgy, with responsive readings and hymns — simple and impressive, such as any denomination might adopt and use to their moral and spiritual advantage.

I close this chapter with the following extract from my diary:

"*April 23, 1836.* My thirty-third birthday. Went into serious scrutiny of last year's experiences, my present spiritual condition, and what improvements I ought to make in the future. As on preceding birthdays, I had to lament many shortcomings, form many resolutions of amendment, and implore divine strength to act more worthy of my high calling. My ideal is always far above my highest attainments, and (what is humiliating) I stand convicted before my own internal judgment seat of repeating sins against even former lower ideals. But I desire not to let down the divine standard to my frailties. Therefore will I welcome every bright ray of light, and strive on and hope on, ever girding up my loins with the encouraging assurance: 'My grace is sufficient for thee; for my strength is made perfect in weakness.'"

CHAPTER XV.

1836–1838.

ORDINATION, ETC — MINISTERIAL WORK — REFORM MOVE-
MENTS — PERSONAL EXPERIENCES — ECCLESIASTICAL
AFFAIRS — RELIGIOUS LIFE — THE HOME.

ON the 4th day of May, 1836, I, in company with Mr. E. D. Draper as lay delegate with me, attended the installation of Brother George W. Stacey as pastor of the First Congregational church and society in Carlisle, Mass. He, as will be remembered, had formerly been associated with me in the printing of the *Messenger*, and becoming deeply interested in personal religion and in the principles of Restorationism, had resolved to devote himself to the work of the ministry under the auspices and as a member of our Massachusetts Association. His theological studies had been directed by Rev. Paul Dean, and he was deemed duly qualified for the office to the duties of which he had been called.

The installing council met as per request, and organized by the choice of the venerable Dr. Ripley of Concord, moderator, and Rev. Lyman Maynard of Amherst, N. H., clerk, after which the customary preliminaries for the public service of the occasion were harmoniously settled. Rev. David Damon of West Cambridge offered the Introductory Prayer, and Rev. Mr. Andrews of Chelmsford read the Scriptures. The Sermon was delivered by myself from Matt. 5:48: "Be ye therefore perfect," etc. The Ordaining Prayer was by Rev. Paul Dean; Right Hand of Fellowship by Rev. William Morse; Address to the People, by Rev. Dr. Ripley; and Concluding Prayer by Rev. William White of Littleton. Arrangements having been made with Brother Stacey for an exchange of pulpits, I remained at Carlisle through the three intervening days. On Thursday he took me to the then new but already wonderfully precocious city of Lowell, 9 miles distant. It was well started on its prosperous career, exhibited signs of great thrift, was growing rapidly in all directions, though, of course, buildings, streets, etc., were for the most part in a coarse, unfinished condition; all of which gave place in due time to that order, neatness, symmetry, magnificence even, which have commanded my admiration in my later visits there.

The following day we walked five miles to Concord, chiefly for the purpose of visiting Dr. Ripley abovementioned, a remarkably vigorous old man, 85 years of age. We were greeted with a most cordial welcome and received unstinted attention, courtesy, and hospitality. He conducted us before dinner to different parts of his estate, pointing out the several localities on and near it where occurred incidents connected with one of the first battles of the American Revolution. The spot where the firing and slaughter begun was shown us, as was also the place where the two British soldiers that fell in the encounter were buried,— a monument to whom, he said, had been contracted for and was soon to be erected there. A few years before Dr. Ripley had written an authoritative account of the Concord fight on the 19th of April, 1775, which was printed in pamphlet form, and a copy of which he presented each of us.

After a sumptuous dinner, presided over by his accomplished niece, his wife having been some years in the immortal realm, he took us about the town, going through the more important public buildings and acquainting us with whatever he thought would interest and instruct us. We were much impressed when in the county jail, by his conversation with, and advice to, the prisoners there. Some of them seemed more unfortunate than criminal, and only one or two appeared hardened and calloused through vice. One was held in confinement under the old barbaric law for a debt of twelve dollars, which he promised to pay his creditor if allowed twenty-four hours time. This he alleged was brutally denied him, and "Now," he said, defiantly, "I shall stand it out." We also went with our guide to call on his colleague, Rev. Mr. Goodwin, an intelligent, amiable, refined and scholarly gentleman, but a suffering invalid. He was in the morning of life, had just launched upon what promised to be a career of pastoral usefulness, and was cheered by the affectionate confidence of his people. But all hopes of such a nature were soon blasted, for about two months later his spirit was translated to the home of the redeemed. Returning to the hospitable mansion of our kind father in Israel, we were once more regaled at his table with a generous supply for our bodily needs and with pleasant and profitable conversation, after which, as the shades of evening came on, we retraced our steps to Carlisle. A memorable visit.

On Saturday, Brother Stacey left with his family for Mendon, while I was entertained at the house of his worthy deacon, John Green, the only surviving male member of the First Church after the orthodox secession of some years before,— an intelligent, devout, substantial citizen of the town. On Sunday I preached *extempore* in the morning from Acts 17:25, and in the afternoon from Phil. 2:5. At 5 P. M. I gave a temperance lecture in the meeting-house with apparently good effect. Rev. Dr. Ripley and Rev. Mr. Andrews of Chelmsford, who had exchanged pulpits that day, met at Deacon Green's on their return home and attended the lecture, giving it and the cause their encouragement. The Doctor remained over night and on Monday morning, after a delightful interview, we parted in gospel love to meet no more on earth. Five years afterward, in 1841, he entered his heavenly rest, aged about 90 years. I came home *via* Boston the same day, reaching my family at 9 P. M., after an absence of just a week.

Pastorate Extended. On the following Saturday, May 14, I was waited upon by two of my parishioners, Jabez Aldrich and Benjamin Davenport, a committee of the society, who presented me with the following document: "At a parish meeting holden May 2, 1836, *Voted* unanimously, that we cordially approve the conduct and pastoral services of the Rev. Adin Ballou during the four years that he has officiated as the minister of this parish, and we earnestly hope and desire that he may continue with us for another term after the expiration of his present contract. Therefore, *Voted*, that Jabez Aldrich, Benjamin Davenport, and William S. Hastings be a committee to wait upon the Rev. Mr. Ballou and ascertain from him upon what conditions and for what time he will engage to officiate as minister of this parish from and after (the expiration of) his present contract and to report at an adjourned meeting."

I promised an early answer in writing, which I soon forwarded to the committee. The substance of it was that I gratefully appreciated the confidence reposed in me by the parish, and should be happy to renew my engagement for the term of five years, from and after the first of April, 1837, on condition that my annual salary be raised from four to five hundred dollars. The proposition was acceptable to the parish, and a mutual agreement was in due time ratified.

The days through which I was passing at this period of my life were days of intense intellectual, moral, and religious activity. I zealously and scrupulously endeavored to improve my understanding in useful knowledge, to discipline my spiritual capabilities into true Christian holiness, to promote personal religion among my people, and to help forward the great moral reforms which had begun to command public attention. I read advanced books of the best quality, I studied the ancient languages somewhat, and in all possible ways sought to invigorate and enrich my mind. For religious quickening and culture, I familiarized my mind with Thomas à Kempis and other devoutly-minded authors, and subjected myself to strict rules of prayer, watchfulness, and self-examination. In trying to increase experimental piety among those to whom I ministered, I gave special lectures to the children and youth of the Sunday School, exhorting them earnestly to be conscientious, reverent, and prayerful, and to seek communion with their Heavenly Father and His son Jesus Christ; while with the adults, I labored to bring them into the church through serious convictions, conversion, and consecration, by preaching, social religious meetings, and personal counsel, and thus have them committed to acknowledged principles of righteousness and to a truly Christian life. So I pushed religion as urgently as I could, after the old methods modified by my revised theological views. The recent fashion of bringing people into the kingdom of heaven by social festivities and amusemental gatherings had not then been invented. My vineyard was not preeminently feasible and productive, nor was I the most skilful of husbandmen; but I did what I could. As to the great moral reforms, only three had yet been born — Temperance, Anti-slavery, and the Peace Movement, others having only an embryotic existence. The first two assumed so much importance and entered so largely into my personal and ministerial experience during the period covered by the present chapter, that they require special consideration.

Total Abstinence. The Temperance Reform in its first phase I had earnestly espoused, as heretofore set forth, and was its ardent advocate; but it had taken on a new and more radical character about the time now in review. The disuse of distilled liquors alone, which was the original basis of the movement, while those resulting from fermentation were allowed, had proved insufficient to overcome or essentially lessen the evils against which warfare was waged. Drunkards were multiplied by indulgence in the milder intoxicants — wine, beer, cider, etc. And sharp discussions had arisen among temperance reformers upon the question of putting these under the same ban as so-called ardent spirits. This was strongly opposed by a considerable party of those who clung to the use of them. Nevertheless, logic and the permanent success of the cause imperatively demanded *total abstinence* — abstinence from the use of *all* intoxicating beverages. I was fully convinced of this, as was a large majority of the adherents and advocates of the reform. The only practical course for the more radical party was to leave the conservatives in a peaceable manner and start a new movement whose central principle should be the entire disuse of all that can intoxicate, forming societies in accordance with that principle to carry forward the work. And this was what was done in many localities throughout our general vicinity. We organized under the new regime in our town, the organization being entitled "The North Mendon Young Men's Temperance Society," for which I, with others, labored energetically. This society prospered, as did similar ones in surrounding towns. Those remaining attached to the old system did little thereafter to make converts to it, and finally allowed it to die out.

My position in reference to this great reform has been the same from the beginning until now. I never placed the duty of total abstinence from all intoxicating liquors on the ground that it was a sin *per se* to use them moderately — like murder, robbery, etc.; but only as a wrong done to humanity and an offence against sound morality, when social conditions and dominant circumstances rendered it dangerous as a habit or as an example to others. Such conditions and circumstances then, as in later days, existed in a marked degree. The sale of all kinds of strong drink had become general and civilization was greatly demoralized by personal indulgence and social custom. Drunkenness increased to an alarming extent, and poverty, disorder, crime, and misery prevailed on every hand. The evils consequent upon the use of alcoholics came to be intolerable. Something must be done.

After much study and experimentation, a remedy for the deadly contagion and the ruin it wrought was discovered, viz : — *Total Abstinence.* It was demonstrated that intoxicating beverages were not necessary for persons in health, that they were more or less perilous to those using them, and that the utter renunciation of them was not only a cure for, but a safeguard against, the manifold evils of intemperance. We who made ourselves sure of this worked on the lines thus indicated for the cause, and looked for its early triumph. But appetite, interest, fashion, and habit, have proved stronger with vast multitudes of people than reason, philanthropy, or religion, down to this year of grace, 1889. Yet I swerve not one iota from my original temperance principles, convictions, faith, and hope. The cause will some day triumph, and the blessings it has in store for a humanity redeemed from its curse will be enjoyed. "Fly swifter round, ye wheels of time, and bring the welcome day."

The Anti-Slavery Movement. Strange as it may seem to most of my readers, I was more than thirty years of age before the thought entered my mind that I was in any way responsible for chattel slavery in my country. I had no pro-slavery in my constitution, training, or habitual feeling. I had by nature no prejudice against color, no spirit of caste, and no disposition to estimate any of my fellow-men higher or lower in the scale of being on account of nationality, race, birth, rank, wealth, sex, or any standard but personal merit and demerit. I was a born Democrat, and never had to take up any cross in order to treat any one kindly and justly, as I would be treated. Of other sins and shortcomings I had enough, but none of this sort. The wrongs, abominations, and outrages of chattel slavery were out of my sight and so out of my mind. A thick veil of reverent patriotism in those early days shut out the vision of many things I afterward came to see. I was brought up to idolize my country, its constitution and laws, as a rich and sacred patrimony, earned and consecrated by the heroic blood of Revolutionary sires, whom I was accustomed to glorify as the wisest and noblest of mankind. The National Union they had formed was sacred to me, to be preserved inviolate and transmitted as an invaluable heritage to posterity.

But all this self-complacent regard for the fathers and their work was destined to be sadly disturbed by the outcry of the Abolitionists that slavery as it existed in the land was a monstrous national sin of which we were all more or less guilty, and that immediate emancipation of the bondmen was an indispensable duty to God and man. That outcry grew louder and louder and was echoed by multiplying voices on every hand. It called in question the sacred guaranties of our fathers and laid violent hands on the ark of our national covenant. My blind patriotism was shocked and I deplored the agitation that had been raised. I did not desire to see the agitators harmed, nor to have their rights of free speech abridged, nor to oppose them by any other means than those of calm reason and earnest persuasion.

But presently their opponents of various sort began to assail them, not only with hard words but with threats of violence, and from threats they proceeded to flagrantly abhorrent deeds. Prices were set on the heads of their leaders, their meetings were broken up, their lecturers maltreated, their printing presses demolished, and their editors murderously hunted down and killed. While such outrages were being enacted it became impossible for honest, conscientious people not to think upon the subject lying back of them all — back of the agitation provoking them, and not to investigate it; and equally impossible after such thought and investigation to be indifferent to or remain neutral upon it. At any rate, so it was with me. I yielded to the necessities of the case; I did a vast amount of solid, earnest thinking, more, perhaps, than in any equal portion of my life, and from indubitable evidence I came to the following conclusions, to wit:

CONCLUSIONS CONCERNING SLAVERY.

(1) That slavery was what John Wesley had characterized it, "The sum of all villainies"; that what I had regarded as its abuses were its natural fruits; and that from its inception to its consummation it was utterly wicked.

(2) That as it had to begin by violence and cruelty, it must be maintained by the same means; and that the enslaved must be kept in ignorance and held in bondage by brute force, or they would, out of their natural love of liberty, of themselves go free.

(3) That our Revolutionary fathers (whom I had been taught to revere) notwithstanding their sacrifices for their own liberty, inflicted on their fellowmen, as Thomas Jefferson said, "a bondage, one hour of which was fraught with more misery than ages of that which they rose in rebellion to oppose." Also that, by certain guaranties of the United States constitution, they rendered all co-governing citizens of the country more or less responsible for the sin of American slavery.

(4) That the slave power had acquired such influence in Church and State, in commerce and finance, as to vitiate deplorably the whole moral status of the nation — millions being so perverted as to think wrong is right and right wrong; evil good and good evil.

(5) That Church and State, though nominally separate from and independent of each other, were yet so sympathetically and practically in harmony, as far as regarded subserviency to the slave power, the support of the guaranties of the constitution to oppressors, and the imposition of unrighteous obligations in the interest of injustice and tyranny upon all citizens, as to demand withdrawal from both on the part of every enlightened, conscientious opponent of the gigantic crime, and entire separation from the fellowship of those who, with happy accord, were accustomed to treat the Abolitionists and their allies as *pestilent fellows*.

It took me some time to learn these important lessons, but when I had mastered them, I wondered that I had not seen, appreciated, and accepted them long before — especially in view of the theological progress I had made and the ethics logically derived therefrom. For the universal Fatherhood of God, and the universal brotherhood of man, which were among my settled fundamentals of religion, ought to have made me a thorough-going Abolitionist the moment the question of chattel slavery was presented to my thought and conscience for consideration and moral judgment. They ought also to have made me understand and take home to myself, theoretically and practically, the several lessons just enumerated. Such, however, was not for a long time the case.

Nevertheless, light came to me before the spring of 1837, and both truth and duty in regard to the great national sin were clearly revealed to my mental and moral understanding. Of the essential wickedness of slaveholding I was thoroughly convinced, as I was also thoroughly convinced that I was under solemn obligations as a teacher of religion to make open proclamation of my views and to do what in me lay to oppose and overthrow the monstrous wrong. But such a course was obviously against my temporal interest, ambition, and comfort. Abolitionism was an element of discord in every social body it had entered thus far, and threatened to become more so as time went on. How would it affect the new Restorationist denomination I had worked so hard and spent so much to get launched? There were serious reasons for apprehending damaging consequences if it was allowed to come within the borders of our body. Though small, it contained both conservative and radical minds, equally honest and nearly equal in numbers. We were well agreed in regard to our theological and ecclesiastical tenets and policy. We had all committed ourselves to the growing temperance reform. But radical Anti-slavery — Abolitionism was a very different thing to deal with. It struck at what we all had been accustomed to deem venerable, sacred, and patriotic in our national life, at solemn covenants of the

Federal compact, at time-honored customs, at commercial interests, at political and religious affiliations and preferments — at a multitude of concerns affecting our personal, social, ecclesiastical, and civil well-being and happiness. It had already provoked popular prejudice and violent outbreaks in different denominations. What would it do to our little branch of the Christian church? We shall see.

And there were with me matters nearer home to be considered — questions to be answered, problems to be solved, difficulties to be met, trials to be borne. Were I to pursue the path that duty pointed out to me, what results to me personally and as a minister would be likely to ensue? Probably more or less disaffection towards me in my parish, withdrawal of support, loss of friends, perhaps ill-will, animosity, and bitter hate. Such had been the consequences to me hitherto of departing from the old ways, of adopting new truths, of proclaiming new principles of faith and conduct, of espousing unpopular causes, and going forward in the path of reform. Was this to be forever my fate? Why not remain quiet, let needed changes come without worrying myself to hurry their advance, thus giving Providence a chance to work out the problems of human progress and destiny without any of my aid? Worldly prudence and personal ease obviously dictated this policy. But duty would not be compromised with after this fashion and the voice of conscience said: *Follow thy highest light; be faithful to thy best convictions; bear witness to the truth; stand up for the right; be no laggard in the strife for God and man.* I heard, trembled, hesitated, and by divine grace obeyed.

So on the 6th of April, 1837, our annual State Fast-day, I preached my first distinctly outspoken anti-slavery discourse in my Mendon pulpit from Isaiah 58:5, 6: "Is it such a fast that I have chosen? A day for a man to afflict his soul? Is it to bow down his head like a bulrush and to spread sackcloth and ashes under him? Wilt thou call this a fast and an acceptable day unto the Lord? Is not *this* the fast that I have chosen? To loose the bands of wickedness, to undo the heavy burdens and to let the oppressed go free, and that ye break every yoke?"

The doctrine of this text I applied faithfully to the great system of American oppression, setting forth the manifold evils it represented and engendered and the manifest duty of all good men and women in regard to it. What were the effects? Such an excitement among the people at large as the staid old town of Mendon had never experienced before. The unanimity of my parishioners in my favor, so emphatically declared within a year, vanished in a moment. A dozen families were irreconcilably disaffected, and at once left my congregation; some of them previously among my best friends and largest contributors to the parish treasury. Many hard things were said and some discreditable ones done. I tried to appease the malcontents by all honorable means, but in vain. In the midst of the commotion I gave up my pastorate; but at the earnest request of numerous devoted parishioners, who approved in the main my course and who assured me that more new members were ready to come into the society than there were old ones likely to depart, I ere long recalled my letter of resignation.

This seemed to irritate those who had seceded and inflame their ire against me. One of the wealthiest of them, to whom I had become indebted for pecuniary aid in some former time of need, in order to make me sensible of my dependence on him and humiliate me as much as possible, sent me, immediately after this occurrence, the following significant note;

" *To Adin Ballou:*
"Sir: I request you *forthwith* to pay me what you are owing me, or procure a satisfactory endorser therefor.
"Yours, etc.,
" ———— ————."

I made known the position in which I was placed to some of my friends, who were ready to stand by me to the end and to help me in the emergency where I found myself, and within twelve hours after the imperative demand was made upon me, my disgruntled creditor was paid in full, and he never troubled me afterward. Such experiences are not pleasant, but they come sometimes and have to be endured. Happily, the main body of my people remained faithful to me, though probably some preferred that I should have kept silent on the subject of slavery, and the losses of hearers and pecuniary support occasioned by my fidelity to principle in this particular were soon more than supplied by new-comers, my congregations being larger than ever before. So I lost nothing in the end on that score. None of the seceders were happier for going away, and some of them ultimately returned to their ancestral religious home.

My labors were considerably increased by reason of the position I had taken with respect to the anti-slavery reform. I not only felt called upon to awaken interest in and secure co-operation for the much-maligned and struggling cause in my own town and its immediate neighborhood, but I was soon in considerable demand as a lecturer, platform-speaker, and general helper of it in more remote and distant places. Its leaders were kindly disposed towards me and glad to welcome me as a fellow-laborer with them in their public gatherings, and interested personal friends were solicitous to have me heard upon the great question that was agitating the public mind, in their respective localities.

On the 4th of July of the same year as that in which the incidents narrated above took place, I delivered an elaborate and carefully prepared anti-slavery address in my Mendon church to a large and deeply interested concourse of people, deeming this a most appropriate and profitable way of celebrating the anniversary of American independence. The production was very long and as complete in form and argument as I could possibly make it. It was printed and had an extended and influential circulation in this country; also reprinted in England and spread broadcast throughout the dominion of Queen Victoria, then just entering upon her long and illustrious reign.

After the delivery of this discourse, on the evening of the same day, we formed a strong anti-slavery society in Mendon, as auxiliary to the American society organized in Philadelphia four years before, and entered upon active work in behalf of universal freedom. Later on, we established an anti-slavery library, and these two instrumentalities wrought effectually for many years in the community to keep alive an interest in the cause, to disseminate the truth upon the subject for which they stood, and to hasten on the day when at length liberty should be "proclaimed throughout the land to all the inhabitants thereof."

A vexatious episode. In addition to my multiform legitimate labors and responsibilities as a man and a minister of religion, I became about this time very unwisely involved in a matter wholly extraneous and foreign to my proper line of activity, from which I derived only trouble, perplexity, vexation, and a fool's tuition. Two Mendon citizens, both professing at the outset to be my friends, fell into a controversy in regard to the boundary line between their two wood-lots, lying side by side. They had referred the case to the courts, but before it came to trial obtained leave to withdraw it and submit it to the judgment and decision of three mutually-agreed-upon arbitrators. Both wished me to act as chairman of this private board of judication, each choosing one of the other two. To this I foolishly consented. I and my associates had several meetings, canvassed the matter submitted to us, but accomplished very little; for, in spite of all the records we could find and of all the evidence brought before us, the true line of division seemed to us exceedingly obscure and uncertain. At length I unearthed the minutes of a long-forgotten survey which appeared to be well attested and conclusive both to me and my two comrades, and we decided pursuant to its plain statements. But our decision did not satisfy the chief claimant, and he declined to accept it, asking for another hearing, at which he said he could bring additional testimony in his favor and so cause us to change our verdict. So urgent was he that, upon my strong plea for him and against their own judgment, the others yielded, and another hearing was granted, though not till he solemnly promised that if he could not convince us that we were in error, he would freely quitclaim all right and title to the land we had assigned to his competitor. At the new hearing he failed utterly in presenting evidence calculated to induce us to change our opinion, and we therefore re-affirmed our former finding. This greatly incensed the dissatisfied contestant, who angrily refused either to abide by our decision or to fulfil the pledge to quitclaim the land in question which he had solemnly given at the last meeting. And no argument or appeal on the part of the referees could make him yield one iota of his dogged and injustifiable determination. I was personally greatly humiliated and chagrined, not only because it was by my efforts that this additional hearing was granted, but also because by having it we had passed the date at which our decision was to have been reported to the court under its rescript and thereby rendered ourselves censurable at its bar.

But this was only the beginning of sorrows experienced by me on account of this case. For this man, who, under professions of the greatest friendship, had enticed me into the position of arbitrator, and in whose behalf I had yielded my own best judgment and persuasively and appealingly had induced my coadjutors to yield theirs also, became my bitter and relentless enemy from that day on. He dogged my footsteps for years with false accusations, calumnies, and scurrilous epithets and insinuations, letting no opportunity slip for annoying and tormenting me by attempts to blacken my character and injure my reputation. I was harassed by lawyers whom he had suborned for that purpose; I was summoned before a private council to answer libellous charges; I was browbeaten, threatened, denounced, anathematized, and maltreated in a multitude of ways by this man, whom I had always dealt kindly and justly by and whom I had never wronged or harmed, till his health failed him in his old age and his power of abusing me had gone forever. I never met a person who so baffled my understanding — who was such a moral puzzle to me. With respectable natural qualities, good judgment, executive ability, and some commendable traits of character, he yet allowed himself to be so mastered by self-interest and self-will that his conscience seemed utterly paralyzed and oblivious to all considerations of justice and equity; to all claims of truth, honor, and the eternal law of God. And yet when confronted and brought to bay by those whom he had abused and persecuted (for I was not the only one thus treated) he would assume the most guileless and inoffensive air, and the tears would course down his cheeks as if he were the victim of the most bitter injustice and cruelty. At such times I would look at him in amazement, doubtful whether to count him honestly insane or a brazen pretender. I never quite satisfied myself in regard to the matter, but concluded finally to refer such an enigma to Him who knoweth all things and who judgeth righteously. I have ever regretted the injustice done to the other party in this unfortunate affair by my improper and mistaken indulgence of his grasping and unscrupulous competitor, whereby the first verdict of the board of referees was withheld from the court beyond the time fixed for its return, thereby failing of judicial ratification and enforcement; as I have also the trouble and expense to which he was put in consequence. But it is due him to say that he never to my knowledge or from trustworthy report uttered against me one word of reproach, complaint, or blame. Such is the difference in men.

And now, to go back somewhat in the order of time, I will mention the more significant ecclesiastical and religious happenings of the two years in review. And I begin with the annual meeting of our Restorationist Association held at Millville (then Mendon South Parish, now a part of Blackstone) Sept. 14 and 15, 1836. As usual, I was present at this meeting, participated in its proceedings, and took a lively interest in all that was said and done. It organized by the choice of Rev. Charles Hudson, moderator, and Rev. Alanson St. Clair, clerk. An extract from the report of its transactions in the *Messenger* will indicate its spirit and character:

"During its session it was agreed that henceforth at each meeting there should be selected a subject for an essay or dissertation at the next session, and a person appointed for its preparation; that letters of license be given to Brothers Emmons Partridge, and Daniel S. Whitney as preachers of the gospel; and that the superintendents of the Sabbath schools connected with our churches be requested respectively to make returns to the annual meetings of the association. There were six public services attended, at which discourses were preached by Brethren George W. Stacey, Lyman Maynard, Alanson St. Clair, Edwin M. Stone, Paul Dean, and William Morse. In the council, harmony of sentiment and action with the best feelings prevailed. In the public services, solemnity, fervency, and deep attention, characterized the speakers and the hearers. And the season will be long remembered as one of refreshing and joy from the presence of the Lord. The following address to the churches was ordered:

"ALANSON ST. CLAIR, *Clerk.*

"'MILLVILLE, Sept. 15, 1836.

"'BELOVED BRETHREN: We desire to impart unto you the spirit and joy of this happy occasion, that your joy may be full, your gratitude ascend to God, and your praise be given to the Redeemer of the world. We desire you to realize more fully what heavenly peace there is in believing; what hope there is in Christ; what bright prospects are opened to you in the gospel! It is yours to know the fellowship of the saints; to taste the heavenly gift, and to press toward the mark for the prize of your high calling; to grow up daily into a holy and happy meetness for the kingdom of God, and to let your light shine before men.

"'It has pleased God greatly to bless you in the views which He has given you of the character, design, and tendency of Christianity — the great instrument by which He will overthrow idolatry and error, and enlighten and reconcile the world to Himself; in your views of that divine providence under whose superintendence all things shall be conducted to a happy issue, and of that destiny assigned to all men and all holy intelligences, of glorifying God and enjoying Him forever.

"'These pure and lovely sentiments which God has committed to you in trust have been believed and proclaimed by holy prophets, early Christians, and many great and good men in all ages. They, at this moment, have the sympathy of many devout souls in this and distant countries, some of whom express that sympathy freely and others are only waiting to judge the tree by its fruits and to see whether these views will make you good, active, zealous, spiritual Christians. The eyes of thousands are turned on you to observe the result of the experiment now making — the effect of your doctrine on your lives.

"'Brethren, how high and solemn are the responsibilities under which we act; to God, to our fathers, and to the world! Leave to others the question of your success. It is yours to work and trust the reward to God, to be given in His own time. Let us forsake the vanities of the world, abandon all narrow and selfish feelings, and adorn the doctrine of God our Saviour in all things, regarding alike a good profession and a good life as twin cherubim in the service of God. It behooves us to be valiant for the truth in which the glory of God and the good of man are concerned; but to be mild, gentle, and charitable to those who dissent from us; to guard the truth from being mixed with the error of no future responsibility — no future hopes or fears on the one hand, and on the other from the soul-chilling error of endless torments, which, as far as it extends, annuls the merits of Christ and defeats the gospel of His grace.

"'Let then the heavenly spirit of Christ dwell richly in your hearts by faith, and let your light shine before men in acts of justice and mercy, in deeds of piety and benevolence. Honor the name, word, and worship of God; bless and cherish the social, moral, and civil relations of life, that the truth of God be not blasphemed.

"'Finally, brethren, consider that in the order of His providence and grace, God gives His kingdom to those who will best improve it, and lets His vineyard to those who will render Him the fruit in His season. Remember, also, that Jesus, our Great Master, sought His glory by saving the world, and that we can never gain His kingdom but by that piety and benevolence which delight in doing good to mankind. By thus living may we obtain an abundant entrance into the everlasting kingdom of the King of Kings, to share His grace and see His glory.

"'PAUL DEAN.'"

Though out of the line of my ecclesiastical fellowship, I attended, on the 28th of December, 1836, the ordination of Rev. Thomas Edwards and his installation as pastor of the "North Congregational Church in Mendon," which was established a few years before by those who had withdrawn from the old "First Church," over which I now presided. Rev. Dr. Jacob Ide of Medway preached the sermon of the occasion, the other exercises being rendered by clergymen of neighboring towns. I was interested in the several utterances, many good things being said and fewer offensive ones than I anticipated. A serious blunder was made by Rev. Mr. Grosvenor of Uxbridge — a young man to whom was assigned the part of extending the Right Hand of Fellowship to the minister-elect. In doing this, he emphasized the fact, as he claimed, that the church he represented was 106 years before a colony from that of the new pastor, when in truth neither his church nor the other was 10 years old; both being recent seceders from the original churches of their respective towns. Whether this fiction was due to the young man's ignorance or unscrupulous sectarian assumption I know not, and it matters little at this late day, but it indicates a habit of those times prevalent among certain persons who withdrew from the established churches on account of their liberal tendencies and founded new ones on a more rigid theological basis. Mr. Edwards, who was an Englishman by birth, remained in Mendon till February, 1840, and proved to be an agreeable clerical neighbor.

My young student friend and brother, Edmund Capron, having completed his preparatory studies and passed a satisfactory examination before an ecclesiastical council convened at Millville, Mass., May 3, 1837, was on that day ordained and settled as minister of the Restorationist society in that flourishing village. As his pastor, instructor, and spiritual guide, I was invited to deliver the ordination sermon, which I did from 1 Tim. 1 : 5 : "Now the end of the commandment is charity," etc. The other parts were taken mostly by ministers of our association, Rev. Samuel Clarke of Uxbridge being the only outsider. Everything passed off creditably, harmoniously, auspiciously, eliciting reciprocal congratulations from all concerned. A second service was held in the afternoon, when Brother E. M. Stone preached, and in the evening the newly-ordained pastor and Miss Abby Pitts, daughter of the late Esek Pitts, Esq., were married, most of the council, with family relatives and friends, being present.

Brother Capron entered upon his work in this new field of labor under most happy circumstances and with great promise of usefulness and honor. But alas for him, for his most amiable and fitting companion, their friends and the world, the auspicious aspects of the situation proved deceptive and vain. In the early autumn of this same year, a fearful pestilence swept through Millville, carrying off many lamented victims, he being among the number. He was stricken with the prevailing disease in the midst of his labors, and in spite of the best of medical skill, tender nursing, and yearning prayers, after a distressing illness of two weeks, on the 24th of September, he passed away, leaving his wife a heart-broken widow and his devoted flock pastorless. He was in the 29th year of his age. Then was there mourning indeed in that newly-founded home of his and in that Zion of our faith. Then I wept with them that wept, as once I had rejoiced with them in their joyfulness, and from the same pulpit where, a few months before, I had discoursed amid most cheerful, inspiring surroundings and abundant demonstrations of gladness and delight, I now ministered Christian consolation to a great concourse of sorrow-stricken sufferers and their sympathizing neighbors and friends. So are sunshine and shade, smiles and tears, joy and grief, mingled in the experience of mortals here below. A few extracts from the published obituary of this beloved brother will indicate his state of mind in view of his approaching dissolution:

"Though enduring great distress of body, he remained calm, patient, resigned in spirit to the last. As he drew near the end his mind became clearer and stronger, and the sun of his Christian hopes shone in a cloudless sky. Being asked if he remained firm in his distinguishing religious doctrines, he answered with cheerful promptitude, 'Yes; they give me happiness in death. How can one die happy without such hopes?' Having expressed his satisfaction with and gratitude to his physician and attendants and taken leave of his heart-riven consort and relatives, endeavoring to comfort them in the extremity of their anguish, he commended himself to his Redeemer and fell asleep without a struggle. Neither his strength of reason, of speech, or of Christian confidence failed him to his expiring moment. All who witnessed his exit were deeply impressed by such manifest triumphs of mind over the elements of mortality, and can testify to the blessedness of his death."

The annual meeting of the Massachusetts Restorationist Association for the year 1837 was a memorable one, and marked an epoch in the history of that body. It was held in Milton at the Railway Church, so-called, on the evening of September 29, and through the two following days. The first session was devoted mostly to business pertaining to the proceedings of the occasion and to the polity of the association; the six other sessions were given up to public religious services, after our usual custom. Sermons were preached by Revs. David R. Lamson (Occasional), Charles Hudson, Lyman Maynard, Philemon R. Russell, Paul Dean, and myself.

In council, William H. Kinsley and Alexander T. Temple were admitted to fellowship; I was appointed to prepare a dissertation on "The Intermediate State"; Revs. Charles Hudson, E. M. Stone, and William Morse were chosen a committee to present an address on the Sabbath; reports on Sunday schools were made; and a resolve was passed approving and recommending the

"Restorationist Tract Society," recently established. Thus far all went off harmoniously and to united satisfaction. But the harmony was sadly disturbed, if not fatally injured, by the introduction of three resolutions which I had drafted, on Total Abstinence, Moral Reform, and Anti-slavery, respectively. These were met and opposed by an influential minority of our members, and a very unpleasant discussion followed, which made me regret that I had introduced them; not because there was anything improper in them, but because my brethren were not far enough advanced to appreciate and endorse them. They evidently deemed them wholly uncalled-for, if not wrong in principle and detrimental to the growth of our denomination in the existing state of public sentiment. In this respect I saw that they were wise and prudent for the time being; but I was looking beyond immediate outward success, and had an ambition to build up a church that would lead, not follow public sentiment in true righteousness. This, I saw reason to fear, was a task too onerous to be accomplished. The association, as a body, was not ready to take so radical a position as the resolutions involved, and the discussion upon them was closed by an agreement that those who pleased might sign them on their individual responsibility without in any wise committing their contesting brethren to them, and that they should be published in our journal accordingly. This was subsequently done, as follows:

"*Whereas*, it has pleased God in these latter days to awaken the special attention of this people to the prevailing vices, iniquities, and corruptions of the age, and to incite them to extraordinary efforts for the reformation and improvement of their fellow-men,

"*And whereas*, the benevolent and purifying truths held by Restorationists urgently demand their zealous co-operation in every Christian enterprise for the reformation of the vicious, the recovery of the outcast, the deliverance of the oppressed, the maintenance of virtue, and the promotion of human happiness; Therefore, *Resolved:*

"(1) That the undersigned cherish a hearty interest in the cause of temperance, as based on the salutary doctrine of total abstinence from all intoxicating liquor.

"(2) That we cherish a hearty interest in the cause of moral reform, as judiciously prosecuted against all manner of libertinism, lewdness, impurity, and connubial faithlessness.

"(3) That we deeply deplore the existence of slavery in the metropolis, territories, and states of our country, as a foul reproach to the nation; that we are constrained to express our unqualified reprobation of any and every form of bondage which empowers one man to hold and treat another as mere property; that we deem the laws, customs, and usages which support or countenance the system of American slavery utterly sinful in the sight of God, utterly anti-Christian, and utterly hostile to the moral and religious welfare of mankind; and that we cordially approve of all laudable efforts for the promotion of immediate emancipation throughout the United States and the world.

"(4) That we do earnestly and affectionately recommend to all the ministers, churches, and people of our fellowship prayerfully to consider their duty in respect to these great enterprises; to give them their unequivocal and uncompromising support so far as they conscientiously can, and by no means to speak or act in a manner calculated to obstruct their progress.

"ADIN BALLOU, CHARLES HUDSON, GEO. W. STACEY, A. T. TEMPLE, LYMAN MAYNARD, ALANSON ST. CLAIR, WM. H. KINSLEY, DAVID R. LAMSON, WM. SPARRELL, LEONARD BULLARD, EBENEZER D. DRAPER; Members of the Massachusetts Association of Restorationists, met at Milton, Mass., Sept. 29, 1837."

In the line of religious controversial writing during the two years now being traversed, I did considerably less than previously. A few articles of mine appeared in the *Messenger* in support of Restorationism as against endless punishment, and I also preached a few special discourses of the same nature. My "Omega," noticed in a former chapter, had foreclosed all further newspaper discussion with the ultra-Universalists, but at the urgent request of my faithful friend, Samuel W. Wheeler of Providence, R. I., I prepared a concise statement designed to present in vivid contrast the two systems of doctrine represented by myself and them respectively. It so pleased him that he caused it to be printed in pamphlet form at his own expense and to be widely circulated. The publication was entitled, "*THE TOUCHSTONE: Exhibiting Universalism and Restorationism as they are,— Moral Contraries. By a Consistent Restorationist.*" It is the only one of my works, I think, not bearing my name.

Soon after this pamphlet was given to the public, it was noticed at some length by the editor of the *Christian Advocate*, a leading Methodist organ, who endeavored to disparage it, and to show that there was no essential difference between the two parties which it put in contrast. I publicly answered the article, exposing its absurdities, and showing that the disparity claimed by me was greater than that existing between the Methodists and Calvinists, the latter of whom the former had been bitterly denouncing for a hundred years. Believers in endless torments had a special interest in taking the position indicated, lest that some of their number who had a strong prejudice against the Universalists should be won over to Restorationism. But "truth is mighty, and will prevail." Restorationism will some day be the common orthodoxy of Christendom and all controversy regarding it will cease.

Before bringing this chapter to an end, I desire to enlarge upon and emphasize one feature of my ministerial work at which I hinted in one of its opening paragraphs. I have always realized more or less vividly the importance of awakening, cultivating, and promoting the distinctively religious life — personal piety and holiness in those to whom I preached, so that while honoring and exemplifying ordinary morality of all kinds and the external decencies of good society, they should not rest contented with such attainments of virtue as a sufficient equipment for eternity, or even for this world, without a spiritual force behind them generated by the proper activity of the religious faculties. Christ taught and insisted upon an inward experimental piety or sense of divine realities in each individual soul, which derives constant inspiration from the Heavenly Father and

WARFARE WITH EXISTING EVILS.   295

manifests itself in the outward conduct by fruits of righteousness and true holiness. And his ministers should teach, act, and live accordingly. To this phase of ministerial work and to the development of the corresponding side of the Christian character and life, I addressed myself with unfaltering energy and zeal, as it has been my aim to do through life.

But my efforts in behalf of personal religion were more or less interfered with, and the work I would gladly have done in that direction hindered by reason of the calls increasingly made upon me in the interest of the two great reforms — Temperance and Anti-slavery — whose importance and claims I was by no means disposed to forget or ignore. With respect to them, as with respect to spiritual concerns, "Necessity was laid upon me; Yea, woe was mine," if I did not do what I could to carry them forward on their mission of uplifting and redemption to a successful issue. The victims of strong drink, the wrecked characters, the ruined homes, the wretchedness and suffering of wives, mothers, and children, all resulting from the indulgence of perverted appetites and the use of intoxicating liquors, made appeals to my reason, conscience, and heart, which I could not and must not resist nor suffer to go unanswered. Moreover, the aggressions of the slave-power and the outrages committed by the myrmidons of tyranny and oppression, together with the wailings of the suffering bondmen, were continually forced upon my attention, urging me in the name of God and humanity to "cry aloud and spare not; lift up my voice like a trumpet and show the people their transgressions and the house of Jacob its sins." The pro-slavery murder of Rev. Elijah P. Lovejoy in Alton, Ill., in November, 1837, which startled the conscientious, liberty-loving people of the North by its bloodthirsty atrocity, occasioned numerous demands for commemorative addresses, and for instruction upon the lessons to be derived from the event, of which I had a prominent share in my general neighborhood. All these things made it difficult for me to provide for personal Christianization as I felt I ought to do, and to so divide the word of divine truth that none of the great interests of the heavenly kingdom should suffer detriment by any neglect or unfaithfulness on my part. Yet I realized in some good degree the diversified responsibilities resting upon me, and endeavored by help from on high to acquit myself acceptably in respect to them all, beginning with the least and reaching out unto the greatest. True Christianity I felt then as now, requires a loyalty on the part of all its subjects and professors at once particular and universal — a righteousness starting in the utmost recesses of the individual soul and extending through the family and neighborhood into general society and seeking the holiness and happiness of all mankind; yea, of all moral intelligences in all states of existence. It aims at the rectification of the minutest violations of the divine law, as it also does of the more flagrant wrongs, the giant crimes of individuals, families, communities, states, nations, races. It never overlooks or passes by the least or greatest duties — the particular or universal good.

The multiform interests that I had at this date come to represent before the general public, theologically, morally, and socially, not only increased very largely my correspondence (which laid an extra tax upon my time and energy) but also added greatly to the number of visitors calling for purposes of consultation and advice respecting ways and means of advancing those interests and making them serve most effectually the beneficent ends contemplated by them. My home became a sort of cabinet or place of resort for all kinds of reformers in which to discuss the various schemes proposed for the bettering the condition of mankind, and formulate plans for carrying such as were approved into effect; as it was also for a considerable swarm of inquirers into the principles and methods of human melioration and redemption. By unavoidable necessity, this made it at the same time a kind of public hostelry, in which entertainment of suitable sort — food, and not infrequently lodging — was to be provided. Myself and wife endeavored to act the parts of host and hostess with proper civility and liberality, showing due hospitality to all, though at considerable expense of money, time, and strength. The chief burden of it all, however, fell upon her, who, at the best, was illy fitted to bear it, but who nevertheless discharged the duties and endured the trials thus thrust upon her with a patient, unmurmuring, heroic diligence and fidelity, worthy of record and of grateful commemoration.

In the autumn of 1837, the more strictly private cares and labors of our household were very much augmented and intensified by painful anxiety and fear on account of the dangerous sickness of our little son, Adin Augustus, who was brought to the brink of the grave by scarletina. He had been with us on a preaching visit to Hillsborough, N. H., and the returning journey (made in great haste, and probably without sufficient precautions against exposure and fatigue) seemed to overtax his rather delicate constitution, rendering him an easy prey to this insidious and debilitating disease. He was in imminent peril of his life for several weeks, but happily, after a long period of convalescence, recovered, bringing the thirty-fifth year of my life to a close under circumstances calculated to awaken in the hearts of all the members of our household the most profound emotions of gratitude and joy.

CHAPTER XVI.

1838 – 1840.

PERSONAL MEMORANDA — NOTABLE EVENTS — NON-RESISTANCE ESPOUSED — STANDARD OF PRACTICAL CHRISTIANITY — QUARTERLY CONFERENCES — CHANGES.

AS time passed by and I came to understand more fully the practical meaning and value of the theological and ethical principles I had deliberately and conscientiously espoused, and their adaptability to human conduct in all the departments and relations of life; and furthermore, as the absolute necessity of applying those principles as ruling forces to human conduct everywhere in order to secure the welfare and happiness of mankind became impressed upon my mind and heart, I found myself morally and religiously bound to recast in some important respects both my preaching and practice, so as to bring myself into harmonious accord with the new responsibilities thereby imposed on me. Some of the changes I then felt impelled to make have already been noted at length, as others will be farther on. Meanwhile, the more common and uneventful course of my life, after passing the thirty-fifth milestone, moved on (according to my diary) as follows:

"*Thursday evening, April 26th.* Lectured in a school-house at West Medway, Mass., upon 'Universal Restorationism,' from Job 32:10. *Sunday, 29th.* Preached at home A. M. on 'The Fidelity of Christ as a Teacher,' from Mark 12:14; P. M. on 'The Sunday School,' from Prov. 22:6. Also presided at the election of Sunday school officers for the coming year. *Monday, 30th.* Ministered at funeral of Mrs. Otis Scott (South Mendon), preaching from Ps. 103:8, 9. *Sunday, May 6th.* At home. Preached A. M. from Matt. 19:14; P. M., from I Cor. 7:31. Lectured at 5 P. M. in school-house at North Bellingham. Text, Luke 6:36. *Tuesday, 8th.* Attended funeral of a third cousin, Charles Ballou, Woonsocket, R. I., preaching from Ps. 39:4. *Wednesday, 9th.* Attended Young Men's Temperance Union meeting afternoon and evening. Home past 11 o'clock. *Sunday, 13th.* At home. Communion day. Preached A. M. from Gal. 5:1; P. M., from Luke 17:17. Lectured at 5 P. M. in New England Village on Matt. 24:46. Great attention and interest. *Sunday, 20th,* At home. Preached A. M. from Ezek. 36:37. Doctrine—'The promises of God to men are coupled with the requirement that they pray, seek, strive after, and fit themselves for, his gracious gifts'; P. M., from Luke 9:55. Subject, 'Christ forbids the imprecation of the divine vengeance on enemies and the retaliation of injuries.' 5 P. M. Lectured at North Bellingham on Matt. 25:46: 'The severest threatenings against evil-doers are not in contravention of the sublime, far-reaching promises of God.'

"*Thursday, May 24th.* Participated in the installation of Rev. Brother Lyman Maynard as pastor of the Second Congregational church and society in Hingham (South Hingham), an occasion of much spiritual interest and edification. Rev. Paul Dean preached the sermon and I offered the consecratory prayer. Unitarian and Restorationist clergymen united cordially in the other parts of the service. The congregation was large and attentive; the several exercises were replete with ability, solemnity, and appropriateness; and every aspect of things was auspicious. In the evening, by particular request, I preached from I John 4:21, endeavoring to demonstrate that true piety and philanthropy are inseparable excellences of pure Christianity.

"*Sunday, May 27th.* Exchanged with Rev. Paul Dean, Boston, preaching A. M. from Ezek. 18:23, and P. M. from Matt. 25:19. Lectured in evening from John 3:3, on 'Regeneration, or the need of being born out of the animal life and earthly loves into the spiritual life and heavenly loves.' *Sunday, June 3d.* At home. Preached A. M. and P. M. from the same texts as in Boston a week before. At 5 P. M. lectured in Baptist meeting-house, West Medway, from Matt. 12:31, 32; the text being left in the pulpit by some unknown person with the accompanying request that I speak upon it, which I was happy to do. The subject to be considered was 'The sin against the Holy Ghost,' or 'The unpardonable sin.' I discussed it under several heads: (1) What is the Holy Ghost? It is the manifestation of God's presence as a spirit, adapted to the comprehension of finite minds and revealing to them what is absolutely true, right, and good. (2) What is the peculiar nature and wickedness of sin against the Holy Ghost? It is the known transgression of the divine law, ascribing to Beelzebub what one understands belongs to God, or putting that which is false, wrong, wicked, with evil intent, into the place of what is true, right, and good. This is wilful blasphemy. (3) What is the nature and effect of forgiveness? It is the merciful softening of the rigors of a just penalty for wrong doing by reason of the ignorance, frailty, or otherwise excusable characteristic of the offender, whereby he is exempt from more or less of the punishment which would ordinarily be visited upon him. (4) When is a sin not forgiven? When, by reason of its perverse and heinous character, he who commits it is condemned to suffer its entire punishment under the awards of absolute and unrestrained justice. (5) Can one thus unforgiven and punished to the full extent of the penalty for his wrong doing ever be redeemed from his iniquity and reconciled to God? Without doubt. Numerous instances of that sort are given in Scripture, to which I referred my hearers. If a man subject to the full penalty of the law is either by his suffering or in any other way made humble, penitent, and contrite — if he be brought by whatsoever means into a state of submission to the divine will and of trust in the divine mercy, God's favor will not be withheld from him, nor the smiles of His approbation be denied him. Neither reason nor scripture furnish any ground for believing otherwise, nor for believing that those who thus suffer will never abandon their sins and turn to God in true penitence and faith, but much to the contrary. The text, therefore, has a meaning perfectly consistent with the doctrine of the final triumph of good over evil and of the ultimate redemption of all mankind. The people were interested, instructed, and many of them, I think, convinced.

"*Sunday, June 10th.* At home. Communion service. I preached A. M. from John 13:17; P. M., I had a funeral discourse commemorative of the venerable Abigail Russell, the oldest of our church members, who departed this life May 30, in the 93d year of her age. She was a woman of excellent abilities, moral qualities, and social charms. She had been many years a widow, bore the increasing infirmities of old age with uncommon cheerfulness, and was held in high esteem by all who knew her. She was the mother of Hon. Jonathan Russell, who was distinguished as a member of the United States Commission which negotiated the treaty of Ghent, whereby peace between this country and England was secured at the close of the war of 1812-1815. At 5 P. M. on the same day I delivered a temperance lecture at Holbrookville, in

Northbridge. On the next Thursday evening, June 14th, I gave an anti-slavery lecture in Upton, and on the following evening, the 15th, at East Medway.
"*Sunday, June 17th*. Exchanged with Rev. Luther Bailey of East Medway. Preached A. M. from Ezek. 18:23; P. M., from Heb. 12:6; 5 P. M., a lecture appointed at Baptist meeting-house, West Medway, was postponed on account of rain. *Sunday, 24th*. At home. Preached A. M. from Luke 6:33. A sermon strongly impregnated with the doctrine of peace and non-resistance, the truth of which was rapidly growing to prominence in my mind. P. M., 2 Kings 8:13. The exclamation of Hazael, servant of the king of Syria to Elisha, the prophet, upon being foretold of his own murderous cruelty to the Israelites when he should ere long rise to the throne. Moral: Few people know what powers of evil slumber within them, or suspect how wicked they may become under a change of circumstances, especially if elevated to positions of great worldly wealth and power. 5 P. M. Lectured in Farnumsville, Grafton, from Gal. 5:13: Lesson—'Prove by your lives that your liberty is not license; that your faith works by love, purifies the heart, and blesses mankind.' *Thursday, June 28th*. The ordination and settlement of Brother Wm. H. Fish at Millville, as successor of the lamented Rev. Edmund Capron, took place. The ecclesiastical council, consisting of eight ministers and two laymen, met at the residence of Col. Moses Buffum in the morning, and after organizing, arranged the usual preliminaries of the public service, which was held in the house of worship commencing at 2.30 o'clock, P. M. At that service Rev. Wm. H. Kinsley offered the Opening Prayer; Rev. Isaac A. Pitman read the Scriptures; Rev. Charles Hudson delivered the Sermon from II Tim. 2:15: 'Study to show thyself approved unto God, a workman that needeth not to be ashamed, rightly dividing the word of truth.' The Consecrating Prayer was by Rev. Samuel Clarke; Charge, by myself; Right Hand of Fellowship by Rev. A. St. Clair; Address to the Society, by Rev. Paul Dean; Concluding Prayer, by the same; and Benediction by the new pastor. The whole ceremonial passed off satisfactorily, and a good degree of prosperity prevailed under the leadership of Brother Fish for some years. After the dissolution of the relation thus formed, by reason of changes incident to a manufacturing community in these later times, the church and society became extinct. The worthy pastor then ordained has done much general missionary work since, has had various settlements under Unitarian auspices, and still survives at this writing (1889), venerable in age and highly esteemed by all who know him. Through more than half a century of faithful

service, he has proved true to his ordination vows and to the principles he then professed, 'a workman needing not to be ashamed,' 'a good minister of Jesus Christ.'"

After the manner set forth in the preceding pages, I went on from week to week through the year and through the several years then passing, usually preaching morning and afternoon each Sunday, and delivering a lecture later in the day, with a lecture or two, or some ecclesiastical or reform convocation or funeral at which I always delivered a sermon, on intervening days. It is not desirable that I detail these labors in their order further. I will only, in passing to other matters, speak of certain special utterances of mine showing the state of my mind at the time and the general drift of my thought, theologically, morally, socially, etc., upon questions arresting the attention of the public on every hand.

"*Self-sacrifice.* Text — *Gal. 6:14*: 'God forbid that I should glory, save in the cross of our Lord Jesus Christ,' etc. Self-sacrifice is the heavenly genius of pure Christianity. Jesus was the prince of self-sacrificers. The genius of the world is self-gratification, which degrades and disappoints all its votaries. But as self-sacrifice exalted and glorified Christ, the Saviour of all lost souls, so it ennobles and glorifies all his faithful disciples. There is nothing else worthy to be gloried in. Let us learn, like Paul, to glory in nothing else and to seek nothing else as our highest good.

"*God's moral attitude towards sinners.* Text — *Ezek. 18:23*. 'Have I any pleasure at all that the wicked should die,' etc. God's infinite desire is that all sinners should turn unto him and live, a desire which has given His beloved Son to the world to regenerate it and subdue it unto himself, and which will never rest satisfied till it be fulfilled; — till through mercies and judgments, universal righteousness, peace, and joy prevail: till the divine 'kingdom come and the divine will be done on earth as it is in heaven.' Let us cherish to the utmost the same desire, praying, laboring, and hoping confidently for the same glorious consummation.

"*God's Repentance.* Text — *Jonah 3:10*: 'And God saw their works that they turned from their evil way; and God repented of the evil he said he would do unto them and did it not.' A merely human manner of expressing the principle on which God invariably acts in forgiving sinners when seasonably and heartily penitent; because he delighteth in mercy and in the restoration of the lost. Let us therefore repent early of our own sins, and in imitation of our Heavenly Father delight in forgiving those who trespass against us, as soon as they manifest sincere sorrow therefor.

"*The fountain of living waters.* Text—*Jer.'2 : 12, 13:* 'Be astonished, etc., for my people . . . have forsaken me, the fountain of living waters, and hewed them out cisterns, broken cisterns that can hold no water.' God is indeed the fountain of living waters to his moral offspring. If they forsake him, expecting happiness in following their own flattering devices, whether as individuals or nations, those devices will prove to be broken cisterns that can hold no water of happiness. They utterly disappoint all who trust in them. All sin is suicidal to him who commits it, as it is contemptuous and rebellious towards the Great Creator.

"*Evil-doers left to themselves.* Text—*Ps. 81 : 12:* 'So I gave them up to their own hearts' lusts,' etc. Thus God dealt with ancient Israel when they would not hearken to His voice, and thus He sometimes deals with people of these days — with individuals and nations — when they wilfully cling to their iniquities in spite of wholesome counsel and reproof. Then they make haste to be miserable and wantonly prepare for themselves bitter punishments; as it is written, 'Thine own wickedness shall correct thee and thy backslidings shall reprove thee!' Woe unto them that mingle wormwood and gall in the cup of their own sinful intoxication! Yet thanks be to God for overruling even this unto good.

"*Prayer.* Text—*James 5 : 16:* 'The effectual prayer of a righteous man availeth much.' That extraordinary results in the physical world even, are recorded in the scriptures as having taken place in answer to prayer, we all know. Modern rationalism doubts the record and the possibility of any such answer to prayer on the ground that God governs the universe by fixed laws and never by special interposition. But there may be and probably are spiritual laws regulating the uses and effects of prayer, as there certainly are regulating the exercises and effects of human will-power. The so-called laws of nature or of God are not arbitrary rules by which the Supreme One is obliged to administer His government in the realm of matter, but orderly methods according to which men have learned that He usually acts. He is not a bondservant of law beyond His own control, but a free moral agent, operating according to His own choice and judgment. He may therefore modify or direct the movement of His laws in such a way as to answer prayer, not only in an ordinary, but in what seems to us an extraordinary manner. Otherwise, our petitions are superfluous and absurd. Let us pray fervently for what we think is best and reverently leave our Heavenly Father to answer as he deems fit. I cannot distrust the good effect of fervent prayer.

"*The Resurrection of Christ.* Text — *Luke* 24 : 39. 'A spirit hath not flesh and bones, as ye see me have.' We are taught to believe in Christ's corporeal resurrection — that His spirit, which had not flesh and bones, re-entered and re-animated his crucified body, which had flesh and bones. This was an extraordinary manifestation of superhuman, God-given power, exercised in fulfilment of Christ's promise to His disciples for the confirmation of their faith. We are called upon to believe that the grosser elements of His body had been eliminated, leaving the organism so etherialized that he was able to render it visible or invisible, tangible or intangible to the external human sense, at will. Is this miraculous? Certainly, as we use words. We must believe in miracles of some sort if we believe in the credibility of the New Testament and in the claims of Christ to divine power as the Son of God, according to that record. Otherwise, we put ourselves outside of Christianity."

But I have made selections enough to serve the purpose for which I have quoted them, and now turn for awhile to more miscellaneous topics and events. On Wednesday and Thursday, Sept. 19 and 20, 1838, the Massachusetts Restorationist Association held its annual meeting in Brother Paul Dean's church, Boston, a preliminary session for more distinctively business purposes occurring on Tuesday evening, with a public service in the church afterward, at which a sermon was delivered by Rev. Matthew Harding, temporarily in our fellowship. Discourses were preached as usual with accompanying devotional exercises on Wednesday, and a praise service took place in the evening. Thursday morning was devoted to Sunday School interests, and an association for the special furtherance of those interests was formed. At 3 P. M. I read my announced dissertation on "The Intermediate State." At 6 P. M. a prayer-meeting was held in the vestry, and at 7 in the audience room. Brother Charles Gallagher, who had pursued his preparatory studies with Rev. Sylvanus Cobb, Universalist minister at Malden, well known in after years, was ordained as an evangelist, the sermon being preached by Brother William Morse and the charge made by myself. The entire proceedings of the convocation passed off effectively and to the gratification of all, no further inharmonies arising in respect to the widely agitated reform movements of the time.

A somewhat unusual ceremonial — unusual in the ranks of liberal Christians — was observed on the 30th day of September at South Wilbraham, whither I had gone on a Restorationist missionary tour at the request of friends residing there. Having preached both morning and afternoon, I baptized by immersion, in the presence of a large concourse of people, two worthy disciples of our Restorationist faith, Joshua Stanton and John Calkins, who thus desired to testify before God and men their belief in the principles which that faith stood for, and their consecration to a Christian life such as those principles required and were calculated to produce. The service was simple but reverent and impressive, and seemed to have a deeply religious effect upon those who witnessed as well as those who participated in it.

At the November election in 1838 Hon. William S. Hastings, a leading citizen of the town and one of my most devoted and reliable parishioners, standing by me through all the excitement growing out of my espousal of the anti-slavery cause, was elected a member of Congress on the Whig ticket over his Democratic competitor, the distinguished Alexander H. Everett, a minister to Spain under President John Quincy Adams. Mr. Hastings was eminently worthy of the honor thus conferred upon him, and proved to be so well qualified for the position that his constituents re-elected him in 1840 for a second term, during which he died.

First Christmas Celebration. I presume that the reputed anniversary of the Savior's birth was never celebrated in my ancient Mendon parish, nor elsewhere in the vicinity, until the year 1838. Traditionary prejudice, an inheritance from our Pilgrim and Puritan ancestors, was strongly against it. But I suggested and encouraged a change from the long-prevailing custom, to which my people readily consented. Our sanctuary was accordingly appropriately and gracefully trimmed and well lighted for the evening of December 24, when I delivered a specially prepared discourse to a large and deeply interested congregation. My text was Isa. 9:6, 7: "For unto us a child is born, unto us a son is given," etc. Since that time celebrations of the event have prevailed more and more in the churches of this general region and indeed throughout the land, the descendants of the founders of New England of all shades of belief, vieing with their Episcopalian and Roman Catholic brethren in making them attractive, significant, and impressive.

Early in the year in which the occurrences just noted took place, my attention was called to the claims of the cause of peace as opposed to the great war system of the world, in the more radical form it had lately assumed under the name of "Non-resistance." This resulted in part, I suppose, from the general influence upon me of the two great reforms in the promotion of which I had become actively and earnestly engaged, and in part from the testimonies and appeals of those who had come forward as adherents and champions of the new movement, some of whom I knew to be persons of high character and of a generous, noble, philanthropic spirit. I did not have to consider the subject a great while before I saw very clearly that something of the kind had a basis in the scriptures of the New Testament and in the suggestions of an enlightened and spiritualized understanding. But I did not feel quite satisfied with the form in which its advocates presented it to the public, nor with the sweeping conclusions which they declared it logically and morally involved and even necessitated. And yet when I came to investigate the matter thoroughly in all its relations to and bearings upon human conduct, I was convinced that they were right and I wrong. I was also convinced that if its professed friends and receivers were consistent they would have to withdraw from all governmental society constitutionally committed to the war principle or to the use of deadly force in any case. As logical consistency was a part of my religion, I should be opposed to acting inside of any government as a co-ordinate factor therein while abjuring all responsibility for the execution of its constitutional provisions, among which was the carrying on of war and the visiting of penal vengeance upon offenders. I must be honestly inside or outside of all such governments. Here I paused and pondered.

Ought I to take a stand outside of the body politic as represented by the state and nation, and have nothing whatever to do with the administration of public affairs? This question was a serious one with me at the outset, and it was some time before I could answer it to my satisfaction. I went over all the arguments *pro* and *con* that had ever been presented to me or that I could frame out of my own earnest thought, but without definite result. I finally looked to Christ to see if he did not provide a way of escape from my difficulty. I found that he nowhere inculcated, by precept or example, the duty of managing political concerns, of directing matters of state, of exercising the functions of citizenship in the existing governments of men. His kingdom was "not of this world." This fact he magnified and emphasized. And to the spirit and laws of the heavenly kingdom he enjoined uncompromising fidelity, even unto death. In subordination to that kingdom and as its earthly representative, he instituted a voluntary, fraternal association — the church — in which there were to be no titled magistrates or crowned sovereigns, but only chieftains and rulers who were *the servants of all*. And this association was to transcend the righteousness of this world, rise above and supersede all human governments, abstain from all carnal strife with and violent resistance to established civil authority, even when tyrannical and cruel, submitting rather to its exactions meekly and thus proving itself true to the principles of Christ's gospel in the spirit of holy martyrdom. When I came to see and comprehend this, I stood in awe of its sublime wisdom and goodness. I bowed before it in adoring reverence; I yielded to my highest convictions; I became a Christian Non-resistant.

But I did not become a blind, irrational one. It seemed to me clear that true Christian Non-resistance was not mere *passivity*, nor sheer tameness and indifference in respect to evil-doers, nor simple abstinence from physical force in the treatment of violent and wicked men, but abstinence from every kind of *injurious* and *unbeneficent* force whatsoever — from every act, word, feeling, towards evil-doers which harms their bodies, minds, or spirits, or disregards their highest good and happiness as individual and social beings, for time and for eternity. All rebukes and restraints, all preventives and resistances of wrong doing, which do not in any way harm but benefit those subjected to them, which are accordant with true friendship and good will towards them, are not only consistent with *Christian* Non-resistance, but are absolutely dictated by that godlike love out of which it springs. Such Non-resistance is not abject submission to injustice and wrong — it is not recompensing evil-doers with evil-doing, with harm, detriment, injury. It is radically different from the maxims, customs, usages, and laws of the different nations of the earth, whether savage or nominally civilized, and though greatly stigmatized and flouted by the worldly wise, is yet in my judgment an essential article in the orthodoxy of primitive Christianity, as it is a conclusion of the most enlightened reason.

In embracing this doctrine, it was a great satisfaction to me to know that it was logically and morally in harmony with my Restorationist theology and even requisite to its practical exemplification in individual and social life. It only required me to love my enemies and treat them in all regards as my Heavenly Father does, seeking their highest welfare in all my dealings with them, now and forever. Nevertheless, to my deep regret and sorrow, I found that this doctrine was offensive to some of my Restorationist brethren who were wedded to the popular opinion and practice upon the subject it involved, and I was the more grieved in that the new step I had taken seemed likely to break that bond of fellowship in which we had labored and sacrificed so earnestly and happily together for a common great and noble cause. But I could not be false to my honest convictions, nor refrain from acting according to their dictates. An irresistible spiritual impulse within me seemed to set all ecclesiastical and worldly prudence at defiance. Under its guidance I called around me the few brethren who had manifested a sympathy with my views, and after much prayerful and deliberate conference we adopted and published the subjoined statement, to wit:

"STANDARD OF PRACTICAL CHRISTIANITY.

"Humbly desirous of promoting Christian piety and morality in their primitive purity, the undersigned do solemnly acknowledge the Principles, Sentiments, and Duties declared in the following Standard, viz:

"We are Christians. Our creed is the New Testament. Our religion is love. Our only law is the will of God. Our grand object is the restoration of man, especially the most fallen and friendless. Our immediate concern is the promotion of useful knowledge, moral improvement, and Christian perfection. We recognize no Spiritual Father but God; no master but Christ. We belong to that kingdom of 'righteousness, peace, and joy, which is 'not of this world'; whose throne is holiness, whose scepter is truth, whose greatness is humility, whose pre-eminence is service, whose patriotism is love of enemies, whose heroism is forbearance, whose glory is self-sacrifice, whose wealth is charity, whose triumphs are salvation. Therefore, we can make no earthly object our chief good, nor be governed by any motive but the love of *Right*, nor compromise duty with worldly convenience, nor seek the preservation of our property, our reputation, our personal liberty, or our life, by the sacrifice of Conscience. We cannot live merely to eat, drink, sleep, gratify our sensual appetites, dress, display ourselves, acquire property, and be accounted great in this world; but to do good.

"All that we are and have, with all that God shall ever bestow upon us, we unreservedly dedicate to the cause of universal righteousness, expecting for ourselves in the order of divine providence only a comfortable subsistence until death, and in the world to come eternal life.

"Placing unlimited confidence in our Heavenly Father, we distrust all other guidance. We cannot be governed by the will of man, however solemnly and formally declared, nor put our trust in an arm of flesh. Hence we voluntarily withdraw from all interference with the governments of this world. We can take no part in the politics, the administration, or the defence of those governments, either by voting at their polls, holding their offices, aiding in the execution of their legal vengeance, fighting under their banners, claiming their protection against violence, seeking redress in their courts, petitioning their legislatures to enact laws, or obeying their unrighteous requirements. Neither can we participate in any rebellion, insurrection, sedition, riot, conspiracy, or plot against any of these governments, nor resist any of their ordinances by physical force, nor do anything unbecoming a peaceable submission to the existing powers; but will quietly pay the taxes levied upon us, conform to all innocent laws and usages, enjoy all righteous privileges, abstain from all civil commotions, freely express our opinions of governmental acts, and patiently endure whatever penalties we may for conscience' sake incur.

"We cannot employ carnal weapons nor any physical violence whatsoever to compel moral agents to do right, or to prevent their doing wrong — not even for the preservation of our lives. We cannot render evil for evil, railing for railing, wrath for wrath, nor revenge insults and injuries, nor lay up grudges, nor be overcome of evil, nor do otherwise than 'love our enemies, bless them that curse us, do good to them that hate us, and pray for them that despitefully use us and persecute us.'

"We cannot indulge the lust of dominion, nor exercise arbitrary authority, nor cherish bigotry, nor be egotistical, nor receive honorary titles, nor accept flattery, nor seek human applause, nor assume the place of dignity. We cannot be pharisaical, self-righteous, nor dogmatical. We cannot do evil that good may come. We cannot resent reproof, nor justify our faults, nor persist in wrong-doing.

"We cannot excommunicate, anathematize, or execrate an apostate, heretic, or reprobate person otherwise than withdrawing our fellowship, refusing our confidence, and declining familiar intercourse.

"We cannot be cruel, even to the beasts of the earth. We cannot be inhuman, unmerciful, unjust, unkind, abusive, or injurious to any being of our race. We cannot be indifferent to the sufferings of distressed humanity, nor treat the unfortunate with contempt. But we hold ourselves bound to do good, as we have opportunity, unto all mankind; to feed the hungry, clothe the naked, minister to the sick, visit the imprisoned, entertain the stranger, protect the helpless, comfort the afflicted, plead for the oppressed, seek the lost, lift up the fallen, rescue the ensnared, reclaim the wandering, reform the vicious, enlighten the benighted, instruct the young, admonish the wayward, rebuke the scornful, encourage the penitent, confirm the upright, and diffuse a universal charity.

"We cannot go with a multitude to do evil, nor take part with the mighty against the feeble, nor excite enmity between the rich and the poor, nor stand aloof from the friendless, nor abandon them that take refuge with us, nor court the great, nor despise the small, nor be afraid of the terrible, nor take advantage of the timid, nor show respect of persons, nor side with a friend in what is wrong, nor oppose an enemy in what is right, nor forbid others to do good because they follow not us, nor set up names and forms above personal holiness, nor refuse to co-operate with any man, class, or association of men on our own principles in favor of righteousness, nor contemn any new light, improvement, excellence, which may be commended to our attention from any direction whatsoever.

"We cannot make a trade or emolument of preaching the gospel, nor be supported therein by unwilling contributions, nor keep back any truth thereof which ought to be declared, nor consent to preach anything more or less than God directs us, nor encourage religious devotion in mere worldly show, nor pursue any course of conduct whereby the *money,* the *smiles,* or the *frowns* of corrupt men may overule the divine law and testimony. We cannot surrender the right of serving God according to the dictates of our own conscience, nor interfere with others in their exercise of the same liberty.

"We hold it impossible to cherish a holy love for mankind without abhorring sin. Therefore, we can give no countenance, express or implied, to any iniquity, vice, wrong, or evil, on the ground that the same is established by law, or is a source of pecuniary profit to any class of men, or is fashionable in high life, or is popular with the multitude; but we hold ourselves bound so much the more to testify plainly, faithfully, and fearlessly against such sins. Hence, we declare our utter abhorrence of war, slavery, intemperance, licentiousness, covetousness, and worldly ambitions in all their forms. We cannot partake in these sins nor apologize for them, nor remain neutral concerning them, nor refrain from rebuking their various manifestations; but must forever abstain from and oppose them.

"We cannot promote our own advantage at the expense of others by deceiving, defrauding, corrupting, degrading, overbearing, or impoverishing them. We cannot take away their good name by defamation, nor by retailing the scandal of their enemies, nor by spreading abroad evil reports on mere hearsay authority, nor by wantonly publishing their failings. We cannot be busybodies in other people's affairs, nor talebearers of domestic privacy, nor proclaimers of matters unsuitable for the public ear. We cannot rashly judge men's motives, nor raise evil suspicions against them, nor join in condemning the accused without a hearing, nor delay reparation to the injured, nor make any one's necessity our advantage, nor willingly render ourselves burdensome to others, nor cause any one a single unnecessary step for our mere gratification; but we will always deem it 'more blessed to give than to receive,' to serve than to be served — sacrificing *nothing* of *holy principle*, though, if need be, everything of personal convenience.

"We cannot live in idleness, nor be careless or extravagant, nor on the other hand avaricious, parsimonious, or niggardly. We cannot indulge a feverish anxiety in any of our temporal concerns, nor fret ourselves under disappointment, nor repine at anything that marks our lot. We cannot be austere, morose, or rude; nor capricious, ungrateful, or treacherous. We can not practice dissimulation, nor offer fulsome compliments, nor use a flattering courtesy. We cannot follow pernicious fashions, nor encourage theatrical exhibitions, nor join in frivolous amusements, nor countenance games of chance, nor array ourselves in costly apparel, nor wear useless ornaments, nor put on badges of mourning, nor distinguish ourselves by any peculiar formalities of raiment or language.

"We cannot indulge to excess in eating, drinking, sleeping, recreation, labor, study, joy, or sorrow, nor permit our passions to tyrannize over our reason. We cannot harbor pride, envy, anger, malice, wrath, ill-will, sullenness, or peevishness; nor cherish any unholy lusts, imaginations, or tempers.

"We cannot swear by any matter of oath, nor make any rash vows, nor offer any extraordinary protestations of our innocence, sincerity, or veracity; nor utter any blasphemy, imprecation, falsehood, obscene expression, foolish jest, or profane exclamation.

"We cannot enter into the state of matrimony without grave deliberation and an assurance of divine approbation. We cannot neglect or abuse our families, nor evince any want of natural affection towards our bosom companion, our aged parents, or our helpless offspring. We cannot imbrute our children by disregarding their education, nor by setting them an evil example, nor by over-fondness, nor by harshness and severity, nor by corporeal punishment, nor by petulance and scolding.

"We cannot neglect our brethren in their adversity, nor call anything our own when their necessities demand relief, nor be silent when they are unjustly accused or reproached. We cannot speak of their faults in their absence without first having conferred with and admonished them; nor then if they have promised amendment.

"We cannot over-urge any person to unite with us, nor resort to undignified artifices of proselytism, nor seek debate with unreasonable men, nor protract a controversy for the sake of the last word, nor introduce sacred subjects for discussion in a company of scorners. Yet we will hold ourselves ready to give an answer to every one that asketh of us a reason for our faith, opinion, or conduct, with meekness, frankness, and patience.

"Finally, as disciples of Jesus Christ, before whose judgment seat all must appear, we acknowledge ourselves bound by the most sublime, solemn, and indispensable obligations to be perfect as our Father in heaven is perfect, in all possible respects; and whereinsoever we come short thereof to take shame to ourselves, confess our sins, seek divine pardon, repair to the utmost our delinquencies, and bring forth fruits meet for repentance. And for all this, our sufficiency is of God, to whom be glory, world without end. Amen.

"ADIN BALLOU, DAVID R. LAMSON, DANIEL S. WHITNEY, WM. H. FISH, *Ministers.* CHARLES GLADDING, WM. W. COOK, *Laymen concurring.*

This "Standard," when originally presented to the public, was accompanied by numerous references to those passages of scripture which were understood to teach the truths and duties set forth in its specifications. Also by an explanatory statement indicating the relation, practically, which those accepting it stood to existing churches, ecclesiastical bodies, and moral and social reform associations, and to the persons and parties composing them, all professedly working to the same great end of human elevation, redemption, and happiness. Furthermore, there was appended to it a series of resolutions taking strongly radical ground against the giant evils of human society — war, slavery, intemperance, licentiousness, covetousness, and sectarian bigotry — and in favor of their opposites, together with one recognizing, commending, and rejoicing in the many indications of a better time coming to the world — an era when sin and misery shall be known on earth no more forever.

Whether we who put forth this manifesto fully understood what we were saying and realized our responsibilities, I have now serious doubts. And these doubts are confirmed by remembering how little we accomplished, and above all how far we fell short of our sublime ideal. Nevertheless, I believed when we adopted it that the principles, sentiments, and duties it embodied and inculcated were substantially true and obligatory, and I have never changed my mind, except with respect to a few comparatively unimportant declarations and phrases. I know that as a whole, it is not in accord with the popular Christianity of Christendom, but I am confident that it is in accord with the Christianity of the New Testament. And I am no less confident that it is indispensable to the regeneration and absolute happiness of mankind. If this made me a fanatic in 1839, I am a still greater one in 1889, though doubtless a wiser one by disciplinary experience.

The adoption and publication of the "Standard" widened the breach already opened between the conservative and progressive wings of our Restorationist body and hastened its dissolution. The former retained their places in the old order of society while the latter were impelled forward, entering alliances and taking up activities looking to a more Christlike type of civilization and leading more or less directly to the movement which two or three years later culminated in the Hopedale Community.

It may be proper to mention the fact that in connection with the consideration and adoption of the pronunciamento to which attention has just been directed, our Brother Daniel S. Whitney, another student of Rev. Paul Dean, was ordained as an Evangelist, himself preaching the sermon, the other ministering brethren present taking part in the service. He was afterward settled as pastor at Middlesex Village, West Boylston, and Berlin, and later became a participator in the enterprise at Hopedale alluded to.

I had but just passed the thirty-sixth anniversary of my birth in April, 1839, when I was summoned to the dying bed of my venerable father, who was nearing his end on the ancient homestead where he and all his children were born. I watched anxiously with him through one long night, but he was too far lost to the things of time to know me. The following day, April 28, his spirit was released from its mortal thraldom and ascended to the realm of the immortals. His age was 81 years, 2 months, and 7 days. His funeral was solemnized May 1, with becoming ceremonial. He was an honest, conscientious man, served his day and generation well, and merited the grateful remembrance of his children.

The Massachusetts Restorationist Association held its annual meeting for this year on the 17th and 18th of September, with Brother Lyman Maynard's parish at South Hingham. Rev. Paul Dean was chosen moderator, and Rev. Edwin M. Stone, clerk. Sermons were preached by Brothers Daniel S. Whitney, Edwin M. Stone, William Morse, and myself, with a closing address by Rev. Paul Dean. Discussions in council were pleasant, notwithstanding honest differences between the two wings. I remained at South Hingham over Sunday by exchange with Brother Maynard and preached morning, afternoon, and evening.

Quarterly conferences, as they were termed, had been started under the auspices of our association, and were kept up with a considerable degree of regularity during the period covered by this chapter, and thenceforth in subsequent years. They were welcomed wherever we had a foothold, were occasions of exceeding interest, and accomplished much good. I took care to attend them all and to render them as profitable as was in my power. To increase their efficiency as a means of awakening and deepening the religious life, I made a compilation of about a hundred of the most reverential and inspiring hymns I could find, interspersed with a few original ones, which I had printed and put in a form convenient for use at these gatherings and at other times, and they proved most serviceable. Several of the brethren were men of deep and vital religious experience and of fervent piety, and their ministrations in that regard were highly appreciated and beneficial. These conferences, under the circumstances, were replete with salutary preaching, counsel, and devotional exercises, and gave our cause a decidedly spiritual as well as intellectual character. They helped to nourish the divine life in us all.

My first appearance before the general public in my new role as a Christian Non-resistant was at the annual meeting of the New England Non-resistant Society, which was held in Boston on Thursday and Friday, the 24th and 25th of September, 1839. It was a most remarkable occasion — remarkable for its numbers, considering the unpopularity of the cause it represented, for the variety of its personal elements, for the free, unfettered utterance of diversified opinions, and for its uncompromising testimonies. Though not a member of the association, I was permitted to participate in its discussions, making an address on "Non-resistance in its relation to human governments," which received high commendation. It was published in the organ of the society and in tract form, and had a wide circulation among reformers and in the general community. I deem it one of my best expositions of the subject upon which it treats and will try to have it preserved for the benefit of posterity. Of the society itself, its work, and ultimate extinction, I shall speak more fully hereafter.

The *Independent Messenger*, which was started under my superintendence in 1831 as the organ of the Restorationists, was suspended at the close of the year 1839, with the promise of an early resumption, which, however, was never fulfilled. It had passed into the hands of parties alien in no small degree to the spirit and purpose of its founders and incompetent to give it much vitality on any basis or in any behalf. It had no sympathy and no encouragement for a progressive Christianity, on which account the reformatory wing of our body lost all interest in and withdrew all support from it. This, with other considerations, resulted in its speedy demise.

But those composing this wing, and especially the subscribers to the "Standard," were unsatisfied with the idea of having no organ through which to make known their principles, purposes, and doings to the world. They also felt the necessity of some bond of union among themselves — of some organization on their own ground, and accordingly formed an incipient one in the early months of 1840. This being accomplished, they then, though weak in numbers and in pecuniary resources, proceeded to lay plans and provide means for the publication of a small semi-monthly periodical, to be called *The Practical Christian*, the chief responsibility of its editorship and general management being assigned to me. The first number appeared April 1, 1840, just before the thirty-seventh anniversary of my birth, and thenceforth it was regularly issued for twenty years.

CHAPTER XVII.

1840-1842.

THE PRACTICAL CHRISTIAN — COMMUNITIES — BROOK FARM — HOPEDALE — REFORM LABORS — LETTERS — CLOSE OF MENDON PASTORATE — REMOVAL TO HOPEDALE.

FOR several years I had been comparatively free from editorial and other journalistic cares and responsibilities, but resumed them again, as before indicated, about the time of the opening of the period which the present chapter passes in review. The *Practical Christian*, our new periodical, of which I was given charge by my sympathizing associates, was but a small folio of four pages and could contain only a moderate amount of reading matter. Though it named "Mendon, Mass.," as the place of publication, yet for the first two years of its existence it had to be put to press at the nearest printing-office, either in Worcester or Woonsocket, R. I. It was devoted chiefly to the various reforms to which our section of the Independent Restorationists had professed adhesion, as set forth in the "Standard"; but it did not ignore our common Restorationist theology, inasmuch as all connected with its management believed and felt that that theology was the only basis upon which all reform, all true practical Christianity, logically rested. Both were therefore expounded and defended as inseparable counterparts and complements of each other. According to this view, which implies the vital relation existing in the nature of things between faith and works, theory and practice, fundamental principles and right action, belief and life, the *Practical Christian* was conducted during its entire existence.

Christian Union. An interesting religious movement bearing this designation originated in central New York a few years previous to the date of the occurrences just narrated. Its rallying cry was " Union of all Christians : Away with Sectarianism." Among its progenitors and leading promotors was a no-less-distinguished personage than Gerritt Smith, a world-renowned philanthropist, who, a few years before, had distributed a hundred thousand acres or more of his vast landed possessions among free negroes and other poor people, whereon to build homes for themselves and earn a livelihood. It had come to have so much of a foothold in central and eastern Massachusetts that in the summer of 1840 a general convention of its friends and those sympathizing with its declared sentiments and objects was called to meet in the town of Groton on the 12th day of August. One Rev. Silas Hawley seemed to be its chief representative in this part of the country and a prominent mover in getting up the Groton convocation. The call for it was addressed " To all the friends of the Redeemer and of Reform." Our little group of Progressives, though doubtful of a cordial welcome on account of what might be regarded as their theological heresies, were in a mood to hope something from such an ostensibly well-meant and philanthropic enterprise, and resolved to lend it, in a general way, their sanction. The meeting was accordingly announced with favorable comments in the *Practical Christian*, and immediately after a pleasant conference of our own in Southborough, most of us repaired to Groton — myself and wife among the number. We were kindly received, respectfully treated, and so far had no cause of complaint.

But such a heterogeneous gathering assembled as can hardly be imagined, made up, as it was, of Christian Unionists proper, Perfectionists, Transcendentalists, Comeouters, and nondescript eccentrics of widely varying types and peculiarities. The whole number of enrolled members of the convention was about 275. Dr. Amos Farnsworth (residence unknown) was chosen president, and Edmund Quincy of Dedham, Oliver Johnson of Boston, and Lucius M. Burleigh of Plainfield, Ct., secretaries. The parties interested in calling and providing for the meeting found themselves so involved with erratic and chaotic opinionists that they had hard work to control the proceedings or utilize the occasion to the advantage of their special cause. Many unacceptable subjects were introduced and warmly discussed; generally, however, in good temper. There was a large number of earnest talkers who dispensed profitable thoughts and suggestions as well as unprofitable ones, but few satisfactory conclusions were reached. Finally, as I recollect, the Christian Unionists succeeded in making their favorite and distinctive affirmations. These in condensed form were that Sectarianism is abhorrently anti-Christian and that the divided branches of the professed Christian church ought to come at once into harmonious fellowship. How this was to be done was not stated, nor was it found practically possible to realize it, even among those present. Could it have been accomplished there and extended thence throughout Christendom, it would have produced little improvement in the popular theology or ethics, or in the characters and lives of men. Names and externals might have been changed, but not *evil things*. I tried to be just and generous to these self-styled reformers, but was obliged to conclude that their aims and claims were comparatively superficial, and that, whatever their merits, we of the Practical Christian household of faith could derive no special edification from them.

Soon after the publication of our "Standard of Practical Christianity," my mind began to be exercised with the question of how it could be actualized. How could the principles and sentiments it contained be made the basis of individual and social life? I could not suppress this inquiry on my own part and my brethren were burdened with the same problem. To treat our declaration of principles and duties as a mere speculation or rhetorical flourish would be alike false to our highest convictions and "disobedient to the heavenly vision"—it would be both inconsistent and wicked. We must not only preach but live by what we had received as truth, or else renounce it honestly as impracticable. Conscience and a proper self-respect forbade its renunciation. There was no honorable retreat for us; we must go forward. But if we went forward, to whom could we look for co-operation and support? With whom could we affiliate in carrying our declared theories into effect? We had broken with the existing social system in three fundamental respects — in respect (1) to the non-resistance of evil with evil, (2) the serviceship of superiors, and (3) the fraternization of property. And we could not suppose for a moment that those who believed in and were a part of the existing order of society would encourage and aid us in preaching what was in its very nature opposed to and subversive of that order, or in any attempts we might make to establish and build up one that was radically different from it and designed in due time to supersede it in the administration of human affairs. We had nothing whatever to hope for from that quarter, either in the way of maintaining our ministry in the promulgation of the principles we had avowed, or in any effort we might put forth to apply and carry out those principles to their logical and moral results in life's varied interests and concerns. We must therefore depend on ourselves under divine providence and on the converts we could make to our cause in both its theoretical and practical aspects.

Here, then, we took our stand. For us there was no other alternative. Upon the Practical Christian platform which we had adopted and given to the world, we must try to build a new civilization radically higher than the old, which should hold inviolate the distinctive principles of truth and duty just enumerated and declared by us to be essential to the realization of a divine order of human society founded on the great ideas of the fatherhood of God and brotherhood of man. Could we hope to succeed in such an enterprise as this? We were credulous enough to believe that with the favor of heaven we might. At least we must try, however we might fail. In the light of a bitter experience our presumption now seems almost insane. But we were honest and conscientious, and perhaps our endeavors were necessary and useful, all things considered, as contributing to the final solution of the great social problem which still confronts the Christian philosopher and philanthropist.

As to the course we were to pursue in order to realize our purpose, we were for some time much in doubt. We were new converts to our own principles and ideas — novices even in our theoretical positions, and wholly inexperienced in everything like the practical workings of what we vaguely contemplated as the ultimate outcome of our movement. Moreover, we had nothing to guide us or help us in the experience of others. Nothing like what we were to undertake had been attempted before since the world was made. We were pioneers in the field of social reconstruction and must work our way along with such wisdom as we possessed; slowly, cautiously, as best we could, until the end we sought was gained or failure obliged us to relinquish our efforts in that direction.

For a few months, my coadjutors and myself as their leader entertained and discussed somewhat indefinitely the plan of purchasing a common farm, settling upon and running it as a means of mutual physical self-support — making it a sort of missionary post whence our preachers might go forth to localities where an opportunity was offered us, like the apostles of old, and proclaim an untrammeled gospel as we understood it in its application to all the affairs of life. This plan, after much consideration, grew into the more ample one of a community, which should be composed of a considerable number of persons sympathizing with us and representing a variety of interests pertaining to the welfare and prosperity of society. Having deliberated sufficiently, as I thought, upon the subject, I issued in the *Practical Christian*, the

15th of September, 1840, an article entitled "Communities," in which I announced and explained our private discussions and the result to which they brought us, viz: *The desirability of establishing a colony of persons pledged to the principles of our standard, for mutual encouragement and support in proclaiming and exemplifying those principles before the world.* In that communication I endeavored to answer many questions which would naturally be asked by persons of a practical turn of mind concerning such an undertaking, even going so far as to present a *suggestive constitution* for its general management. I also, in closing, set forth what I thought would be the advantages of the proposed scheme, as follows:

"Such a community would furnish a happy home to many pure-hearted Christians now scattered abroad, insulated from each other, ignored or maligned by a corrupt church, and oppressed by the unregenerate world. It would enable them to secure, with less severe toil and more certainty, a comfortable subsistence for themselves and their dependents. It would render it much easier for them to reform many pernicious habits of living and to promote the true physical health and comfort of themselves and families. It would remove them from the dominion of many corrupt and demoralizing influences to which they are now exposed. It would enable them to set up and maintain a purer religious worship, a holier ministry, a more salutary moral discipline, and altogether a better spiritual state of things than they now enjoy. It would enable them to send forth true-hearted religious, moral, and philanthropic missionaries into the surrounding world for its conversion; men and women who would not be bribed or frightened into subserviency to popular iniquities, and who, when weary, might return, like Noah's dove, to the window of a peaceful ark and find repose. It would enable them more effectually to prosecute every branch of moral reform and human improvement by means of the press, of well-ordered schools, and of teachers qualified to go out and inculcate our holy principles wherever people might welcome them. It would enable them to bring up their children 'in the nurture and admonition of the Lord,' free from those loose and corrupting influences so prevalent elsewhere. It would enable them to establish asylums for the orphan, the widow, and the outcast, in which they might be duly cared for and directed into the paths of life. In fine, it would be a powerful concentration of moral light and heat, which would make 'Practical Christianity' known and felt by the world."

Blessed dream, aspiration, and hope! But whose realization was too liable to be frustrated and indefinitely postponed by the frailty, inconsistency, and backsliding of its professed devotees!

Nevertheless, the undertaking was urged ardently and carried forward to very promising attainments. Its development was the theme of my profoundest study and my most constant efforts. All ordinary duties were performed with my accustomed fidelity, but more or less subordinately to the actualization of this darling project, which commanded the best energies of my primal manhood, and which, if we had possessed sufficient pecuniary means, I flatter myself would have risen to a triumphant success. But we were continually dependent on the will of those who could not love the cause as I and some of my early fellow-laborers did — albeit the former wrought well for it while their devotion lasted. It may have been, however, on the other hand, that had I chanced to have been wealthy by some fortuitous combination of causes, I should not have possessed the mind and heart to enlist in such a philanthropic, disinterested, and noble enterprise.

Little more was published concerning our proposed movement until, by patient elaboration, I had matured what I deemed a suitable constitution and submitted it to the careful consideration of those most interested, in a series of meetings held for that purpose. Meantime, my wife, who at first demurred at embarking in such a responsible and uncertain experiment, gave her adhesion to it and several others pledged it their encouragement. In fact, matters progressed so rapidly that at a quarterly conference held at Mendon in January, 1841, a definite organization with a general constitution was effected, under the name of "The Fraternal Communion." This provided for the establishment of local communities wherever feasible, and one was immediately formed by those present who were ready to unite for practical operations. This body was first called "Fraternal Community No. 1," afterwards "The Hopedale Community." It consisted of about thirty persons at the outset and its affairs were placed in charge of a provisional committee consisting of Adin Ballou, E. D. Draper, Nathan Harris, Wm. H. Fish, Henry Lillie, David R. Lamson, Daniel S. Whitney, and George W. Stacey, who received such instructions as seemed needful to insure the practical realization of their aims at the earliest possible date. Among the duties with which these persons were charged was that of collecting "such information as they may be able, respecting the location of the proposed community, the form and construction of buildings, the internal economies of communal and boarding establishments, hospitals, etc; respecting agriculture, manufactures, and education; and any other matters likely to promote the prosperity of our enterprise." One hundred dollars were appropriated for the use of the committee, as they were expected to go to work at an early day. This imposed heavy responsibilities upon me as chairman of the same. What came of all this will be recounted in due time.

Other Socialistic Experiments. A remarkable wave of social inspiration, aspiration, and experimentation swept through our country during the year 1840, resulting in numerous attempts similar to our own not long afterward. One of these was made at Northampton, Mass., under the leadership of George W. Benson, previously of Brooklyn, Ct., which had a character and form of organization peculiarly its own. Another, called the North American Phalanx, located in Monmouth County, N. J., was based upon principles first promulgated by a French philosopher and philanthropist, Charles Fourier, and introduced into this country by Albert Brisbane, Park Godwin, Horace Greeley, and others. Several were started under various auspices in the Western States, most of which were of a temporary duration. Rev. George

Ripley, a Unitarian clergyman of the transcendental
school, whose name appears in a preceding chapter, and
a few sympathizing coadjutors projected the Brook Farm
experiment in Roxbury upon a plan of their own devising, though, in some of its later phases, it possessed
many characteristics of the Fourier System.

It is a somewhat singular fact that our "Fraternal
Communion" originated altogether independently of the
general agitation referred to, and of the movements mentioned, as it did in utter unconsciousness of the existence
of any published expositions of the general subject of
social reconstruction. It grew primarily out of New
Testament Christianity as we understood it, as a practical issue of its essential spirit, principles, and precepts;
though our general reading and acquaintance with what
was going on in the world soon advised us of the
broader field of discussion and experiment which others,
in this and foreign lands, were occupying. When this
occurred, we availed ourselves of the opportunity of
examining their theories and suggestions, hoping to get
some light not before obtained upon the problem we were
earnestly trying to solve. But to little profit. For after
comparing the various schemes accessible to us with our
own, we preferred the latter with the peculiarities which
distinguished it from each and every other brought to our
notice.

A very kindly feeling sprang up between us and our
Brook Farm neighbors, and there was much friendly conference and correspondence between us, looking to a
union of the two movements. Mr. Ripley and his associates were very cordial and earnestly urged us to join
them at West Roxbury. The temptation was strong for
us to do so. We were few, poor, and comparatively
unlearned. They were more numerous, rich, and scholarly. In these respects they could be of great service to
us and our children. On the other hand, we could be a
help to them in more ordinary ways. But there were
serious, insuperable objections to anything of the kind

proposed. Their transcendentalism and individualistic independence made them quite averse to our views upon historic and authoritative Christianity, to our positive ethical position on several important points of doctrine and duty, and to our uncompromising religious and reform pledge. On our own ground, which we had carefully and conscientiously chosen, we were equally averse to their extreme views of personal liberty and their non-committalism. Such being our incompatibilities, neither party being able to yield to the other without giving up some things it regarded as most sacred in principle and most vital to success, we wisely decided to close all negotiations in peace and mutual good will, and go our own respective ways.

In proceeding to get ourselves into proper working order, it seemed desirable to abridge and modify somewhat the fundamental basis of our association as expressed in the constitution of our "Fraternal Communion." Our prolix "Standard of Practical Christianity" was consequently condensed into the following "Declaration," to be openly made by each individual entering our membership:

"I believe in the religion of Jesus Christ as he taught and exemplified it according to the scriptures of the New Testament. I acknowledge myself a bounden subject of all its moral obligations. Especially do I hold myself bound by its holy requirements never, under any pretext whatsoever, to kill, assault, beat, torture, rob, oppress, persecute, defraud, corrupt, slander, revile, injure, envy, or hate any human being — *even my worst enemy*; never in any manner to violate the dictates of pure chastity; never to take or administer an oath; never to manufacture, buy, sell, deal out, or use any intoxicating liquor *as a beverage*; never to serve in the army, navy, or militia of any nation, state, or chieftain; never to bring an action at law, hold office, vote, join a legal posse, petition a legislature, or ask governmental interposition *in any case involving a final authorized resort to physical violence*; never to indulge self-will, bigotry, love of pre-eminence, covetousness, deceit, profanity, idleness, or an unruly tongue; never to participate in lotteries, games of chance, betting, or pernicious amusements; never to resent reproof or justify myself in a known wrong; never to aid, abet, or approve others in anything sinful; but, through divine assistance, always to recommend and promote with my entire influence the holiness and happiness of all mankind."

As chairman of the provisional committee of Fraternal Community No. 1, I proceeded, as soon as practicable, to the discharge of the duties assigned us, with such assistance as my colleagues could conveniently render. I wrote a full exposition of our constitution, which need not be inserted here, but which was published and will appear in full in my proposed "History of the Hopedale Community."

The second meeting of our newly-formed association was held in Boylston, then the parochial home of Brother George W. Stacey, April 28 and 29, in connection with our regular quarterly conference. Interesting friendly letters which I had received from Rev. Dr. William Ellery Channing, Edmund Quincy, Gerritt Smith, and other notable philanthropists were read; the provisional committee made a report of their doings which was accepted as satisfactory, and the members were discharged from further service. No selection of a location for a Community home had been made, but much needful preliminary information had been obtained, and our prospects were full of promise. Several new members were admitted to our fellowship and fraternal enthusiasm waxed ardent. The respective officers required by the constitution, composing an executive council, were chosen, I being president, and were to serve till the first Wednesday in January, 1842, — the day and month designated for the holding of the regular annual meeting of the body. The Community was now properly organized and made ready to start out on its chosen mission.

The third meeting took place in connection with the quarterly conference at Millville, Brother Wm. H. Fish's parish, August 26 and 27 following. The executive council made a cheering report of progress in the march of affairs. Localities for the Community had been examined and one selected as decidedly preferable to all others. This was a farm in Milford containing 258 acres, which had a considerable stream of water called Mill River running through it, with a good fall for mill sites, and other natural advantages suited to our prospective needs. The land, however, was much run down in culture and the buildings were correspondingly dilapidated. It had long been known in the vicinity as the "Jones Farm," deriving that name from an early proprietor, and was sometimes called "The Dale," by reason of its situation. It had been offered for sale on moderate terms and was likely to find a ready purchaser. It seemed so well suited to our purposes that I, on my own responsibility, fearing the chance of obtaining it might be lost, had closed a bargain for it on the 30th of June, two months before. The council had examined the estate critically, approved of my action, and concurred with me in recommending its purchase by the Community. The recommendation was accepted, and our whole proceeding was unanimously and joyously ratified by our constituency. This included the christening I had given the domain, "Hopedale," — a name which united the high expectations we cherished for the future of our movement with the previous appropriate designation of the pleasant valley in which those expectations were to be realized. All our members hailed the name with delight as most happily chosen and befittingly applied.

At this meeting, important resolves were passed, by-laws, rules, and regulations were adopted, and all necessary preparations authorized for taking possession of our new home at the earliest possible date. Groups of friends soon after made pleasant excursions to Hopedale, and all were enthusiastically impatient to inaugurate the contemplated undertaking there. In the opening autumn I decided upon the general outlines of a village site and had it surveyed and laid out by my ever kind friend, Newell Nelson, Esq., who had previously taken the measurement of the fall in the river with a view to its subsequent utilization for mechanical purposes, his services being rendered gratuitously as a token of his good will towards me and the cause. In October, Brother Henry Lillie, one of our council, settled himself and family in a part of the ancient Jones domicile accorded to him by the resident tenant, Cyrus Ballou, a nephew of mine, through whom, as agent, I had purchased the premises. About the first of December, Mr. Ballou, by mutual arrangement, moved out of the house altogether, and Brother Nathan Harris with his wife and four children took possession of the rooms thus vacated.

The fourth meeting of the Community — its prescribed annual meeting — convened in Mendon, Jan. 5 and 6, 1842, the quarterly conference being held under the same auspices. The occasion was one of great religious interest and edification. While the exercises pertaining more directly to the conference were unusually earnest, impressive, and refreshing, the proceedings of the Community were eminently cheering and satisfactory. Not a jar of discord or distrust broke the happy unanimity of spirit, action, purpose, and hope that prevailed. The report of the executive council was encouraging, and called forth many expressions of gratification and delight. Eight new members were received into our fellowship and three persons became probationers for future consideration and approval, if deemed worthy. Official servants for the ensuing year were elected as follows: Adin Ballou, *president;* Wm. W. Cook, *secretary;* David R. Lamson, *auditor;* Lemuel Munyan, *intendant of finance and exchange;* Ebenezer D. Draper, *intendant of agriculture and animals;* Henry Lillie, *intendant of manufactures and mechanical industry;* Dr. Butler Wilmarth, *intendant of health and domestic economy;* Daniel S. Whitney, *intendant of education, arts, and sciences;* William H. Fish, *intendant of religion, morals, and missions.* For other particulars, see "History of the Hopedale Community." Provision was made at this meeting for the settlement of at least ten families on or near the Hopedale territory the following spring and early summer.

THE BEGINNING AT HOPEDALE.

The new social experiment was now fully organized and put in the way of speedy actualization. Thenceforth there was a steady rush of activities till we took full possession of our Community home about the first of April, 1842, and, of course, no cessation thereof occurred afterward. The number of persons anxious to commence residence and occupation with us at Hopedale was quite in excess of our domiciliary accommodations, as it was also of our means of profitable employment. Important expectations were sometimes disappointed as a consequence, and even honest pledges, it was found, could not always be fulfilled. Our pecuniary obligations, which were heavy considering our circumstances, had to be provided for and reputably met, as they were then and forever afterward. Before the close of March seven families and one unmarried member, aggregating twenty-eight persons, occupied the "old house," forming a unitary household, over which myself and wife presided by unanimous consent. We boarded at common tables and lodged in small but distinct apartments, too small and cluttered for comfort, yet passably endurable. Our faith, hope, and zeal enabled us to bear many privations, inconveniences, trials, vexations, disgusts, with reasonable patience and composure. Under ordinary circumstances, they would have seemed simply intolerable. We gradually settled into our respective places, took up our several lines of duty, and the wheels of our unique social mechanism revolved with something of their intended regularity, quietness, and efficiency.

From the details of our new life at Hopedale, I now turn to other items of personal experience.

The Massachusetts Restorationist Association gradually declined in interest and usefulness from the time when our reform wing began to push their convictions of duty beyond the approval of their more conservative brethren. These, however, tolerated and endured us until we promulgated our "Standard of Practical Christianity," when they honestly gave us up as impracticable fanatics, with whom they could go no further. I knew that I was largely responsible for what so disaffected and disappointed them. It was strange almost to myself that it was so — that I, who had devoted myself so ardently to the cause represented by that association as if it were a finality, should have come to be so transcendentally interested in moral reform, even to the extreme of social reorganization, that I was ready to give that body up or let it cease to be. How did all this come about? I had not repented of my protest against ultra Universalism; I had no regrets for helping to form the Restorationist Association; I had not renounced or come to undervalue my Restorationist theology. On the contrary, I regarded that theology as dearer than ever before, and felt that every one of my reformatory advances was in strict logical consistency with its fundamental truths. Nor was I in any way disposed to fall out with any of my brethren of the Restorationist faith and play the eccentric, but the opposite was true, and nothing troubled me so much as to alienate myself from their fellowship and approbation. The fact is, I felt impelled from step to step in my course, often reluctantly on my part, by a power within and above me which I could not resist and which then seemed and still seems divine. The truth involved in the great philanthropic movements I had engaged in had been revealed to me and I could not but act in accordance with it. My own avowed religious principles and ideas — the universal fatherhood of God, the universal brotherhood of men, the all-redeeming grace of Christ, the final redemption of all men — these all, in their practical application, tendencies, and results, not only suggested, but required, *necessitated* the course I felt myself sacredly bound to pursue. Logical and moral consistency, supplemented by an agency higher, mightier than my own, determined my action, even to the extent of Non-resistance and Practical Christian socialism, and I could do no otherwise than I did. "Woe was me if I did not preach that gospel" and order my life accordingly.

END OF RESTORATIONIST ASSOCIATION. 333

The Restorationist Association held a meeting with Brother Charles Hudson's parish in Westminster, Oct. 14 and 15, 1840. This was not long after the more advanced of us had taken our stand in favor of a new social order, and this fact may have had something to do in giving tone and character to our proceedings, though no direct reference was made to our action in that respect. Brother Lyman Maynard was moderator and I was scribe of the ministerial council. Public exercises took place in the church, at which sermons were preached by Brothers Wm. H. Fish, Norwood Damon, Lyman Maynard, and myself, and were accompanied by customary singing, prayers, and exhortations. In council, an interesting discussion took place upon the general question whether or not combinations of persons have any moral authority or right to do what their members as individuals cannot rightfully do. Brother Hudson read a carefully prepared dissertation on "Expediency," which was also fully discussed. These discussions naturally called out the ethical differences between conservative and reformatory brethren, but they were all conducted in an amicable manner. Indeed, the entire meeting was a remarkably pleasant, edifying, and satisfactory one, both to the ministers and laity present. I was appointed a committee to select a place for the next annual gathering and notify the brethren accordingly, and was also requested to write a dissertation for the occasion. But this convention at Westminster proved to be the last one ever held. I notified another, as provided for, to convene at Millville, Aug. 26 and 27, 1841, when our Practical Christian quarterly conference was to meet. But only one or two of the conservative members were there, and no organization of the association was deemed advisable. No arrangements were made for another gathering of that body, and so, at ten years of age, it fell quietly asleep to wake no more.

The quarterly conferences, so frequently spoken of, occurred regularly during this period of 1840-42, under the auspices of our Fraternal Communion, and were characterized by great fervency of spirit and unabated interest. They took place mostly in central and eastern Massachusetts, and were the most soul-stirring and religiously profitable gatherings it has been my privilege to attend during my long life of four score years and more.

At the time of which I am now writing, I was much engaged in connection with my regular ministerial duties in Mendon and their collateral activities, in giving lectures upon humanitary subjects about the country, sometimes far from home, and in attending reform anniversaries in Boston, and conventions held in the same interest at various points elsewhere. On these occasions, especially when I had the exercises in charge, it was my custom to extend to any persons present differing from me an opportunity to state their views, and to invite questions and objections that I might answer them. This often gave much additional interest and effect to the proceedings. A memorable instance of this kind occurred at Concord, Mass., in February, 1841. I had been engaged to lecture there before the town lyceum on the subject of Non-resistance. A large audience, including many of the literary and professional elite of that community honored me with their presence and with a respectful hearing. At the close of my regular address, the usual privilege being granted, I was plied with a goodly number of the hardest questions their sharpest critics could devise. I was favored with a good measure of spiritual inspiration, answered their inquiries as successfully as I could, kept all in good humor, and at the close was cordially congratulated by the venerable and Honorable Samuel Hoar, father of the present Senator George F. Hoar, who, though not a Non-resistant, was an advanced International Peace man, and gave me his best wishes for the conversion of the people at large from their idolization of brute force to a more kindly and humane attitude of mind and heart. This visit to Concord was memorable to me as furnishing the only opportunity I ever had of a personal interview with the distinguished Ralph Waldo Emerson. It was a pleasant one, being devoted chiefly to a free conversation between us upon questions of reform, but fruitful of no important results.

Two severe bereavements threw their shadow across the pathway of my mortal pilgrimage in the early part of 1841. The first was the death, at Milford, January 7, of Rev. John Dale. He was an Englishman by birth, and for a time a devoted Methodist clergyman, who, emigrating to this country, was brought into contact with our little band of Practical Christian Restorationists, finally adopting our views and dying in the full hope of a blissful immortality, not only for himself but ultimately for all mankind. Besides being a most excellent man, he was a valued personal friend, and his demise was a great loss to me, as it was to the cause of pure and undefiled religion. The second afflictive visitation referred to was the decease, on the 27th of February, of the mother of my first wife and grandmother of my now only surviving child, Mrs. Abigail (Scott) Sayles, wife of Smith Sayles of Smithfield, R. I. She was one of the best of women and all my recollections of her are precious.

Before closing this chapter, it seems fitting that I should refer somewhat particularly to two remarkable letters relating to the movement of which I was the reputed leader, that came to me during the year 1841. One of these, already referred to, was from Rev. William Ellery Channing, D. D., of Boston, then at the height of his fame as an able and eloquent divine and as the foremost champion of the great revolt which sprung up a few years before against Calvinism and all allied forms of theological belief. It is not necessary to insert it here, but I desire to say that it was an admirable communication — worthy of its illustrious author! Friendly, kind, candid, breathing noble aspirations, sentiments, and benedictions, and replete with wise suggestions. I appreciated it highly at the time of receiving it, and more highly after serious experiences in Community life. It may be found in full in "Channing's Memoirs," prepared by his nephew, William Henry Channing, Vol. 3, pp. 119-212; and will appear in my history of the Community.

A few months later there came to hand an elaborate letter on the same subject, though of a very different character, from Rev. Paul Dean, formerly of Boston, but at the time preaching at Westminster as successor of Rev. Charles Hudson. Preceding pages have shown the close and sacred relationship in which I long stood to Brother Dean in the Restorationist movement, and how we drifted apart by reason of my espousal of the great reforms. The Community enterprise completed the estrangement between us. He was fatally grieved and perhaps disgusted that I should go to such extremes, and I suppose gave me up as hopelessly bewildered if not fatally demented.

Brother Dean, unlike Dr. Channing, never dreamed of an ideal Christian community in which the members, "instead of preying upon one another and seeking to rise above one another after the fashion of this world, should live together as brothers seeking each other's elevation and spiritual growth," to be established by human thought, effort, and co-operation, in the spirit of Jesus Christ. He looked for the kingdom of God to come on the earth in the old miraculous way and traditional millennial form. Until it should so come, society must go on with some gradual improvement perhaps, but substantially in the future as in the past. He was entirely sincere in this view, and had not one particle of faith in the so-called "Fraternal Communion" I had devised and was about to inaugurate. He *knew* all such schemes were but *bursting bubbles*, people universally being too selfish, weak, capricious, untrustworthy, to do right and live together voluntarily in any such way as that proposed. With such views and feelings, he wrote his letter as a warning to me and a final protest against my absurd undertaking. Two or three brief letters respecting the publication of this lengthy missive and an open reply to it from me, to which he seemed to object, closed all correspondence between us. We never met but once afterward — at the funeral of a mutual friend in Roxbury, in 1857. He died three years later at Framingham, aged 77 years, 6 months, and 21 days.

From the time when it was decided that an attempt should be made to put our new social theories into practical operation at Hopedale, the general expectation and understanding among our members were that I and my family would be among the earliest to locate there. As I had led off in avowing and promulgating the principles of a reconstructed order of human society and in formulating plans and methods of action in accordance with those principles, so must I lead off in the work of carrying the plans and methods devised into effect. Hence, as the date when we were to come into complete possession of the purchased property drew near, and when actual operations under Community auspices were to begin, which was the date of the termination of my pastoral engagement at Mendon, I made all necessary arrangements for removal thither. I preached my valedictory discourse to an overflowing house on the afternoon of March 27, 1842, from II Cor. 13 : 11 : "Finally, brethren, farewell. Be perfect, be of good comfort, be of one mind, live in peace; and the God of love and peace shall be with you." It was published in the *Practical Christian* of June 25, Vol. 3, No. 3. The occasion was a profoundly interesting, impressive, and affecting one, — one long remembered by those participating in it. Thus closed my ministry of eleven years and two months as pastor of the First church and society in Mendon. Thenceforth my story hails from Hopedale, where I at once located.

The first public religious meeting on our new domain was held the Sunday following that just spoken of, April 3, in our ancient domicile, about 120 years old. It was a day of sacred meaning and solemnity, inasmuch as on that day we dedicated ourselves anew and our domain to the service of God and humanity. There were twenty-eight of us residents on the premises, who, with a considerable number of friends from the neighborhood, made a very respectable congregation. Our enthusiasm ran high, notwithstanding our temporal poverty, limited circumstances, and uncertain outlook for the future. In the morning I preached an earnest discourse from Ps. 133 : 1 : "Behold how good and how pleasant it is for brethren to dwell together in unity." In the afternoon Brother Daniel S. Whitney as chief speaker, resumed the joyful strain while I added my exhortation. We were all happy, little dreaming that we were ever to be otherwise, although even then disappointment and sadness awaited us at no great distance ahead.

Thursday, April 7, was the annual State Fast Day. A public meeting convened, agreeably to custom in general society outside. No sermon was delivered, but we had several excellent addresses. The great pleasure was given us of entertaining for the first time Frederick Douglass, the famous fugitive slave, and of being more than entertained by his stirring words. He remained with us some days and did much during his stay to break into floating fragments much of the pro-slavery ice of Milford and vicinity. Memorable times those!

I have no memorandum of what transpired at Hopedale on Sunday, April 10, but a week later I preached in the morning, ministered at a funeral in Mendon early in the afternoon, and at 4 o'clock attended a temperance lecture there delivered by the celebrated John H. W. Hawkins of Washingtonian reform movement distinction. An ample delegation from Hopedale swelled the large concourse of people present, and a lecturer could never have been more triumphantly eloquent. Our Community having undertaken with its infant hands to encourage and help all efforts to uplift humanity was called upon to appear at the front on many similar occasions in our general neighborhood.

CHAPTER XVIII.

1842–1845.

COMMUNITY EXPERIENCES — ORGANIC CHANGE — MISSIONARY LABORS — PUBLIC DISCUSSIONS — LIFE AT HOPEDALE — BEREAVEMENT, ETC.

MAN is naturally a religious being and also a responsible moral agent. As a religious being, he instinctively looks up to, reverences, adores, worships some kind of deity, power, or authority, which to him is supreme, absolute, and irresistible, and which he must submit to and obey or suffer loss. As a moral agent, he is conscious of an essential difference between right and wrong, good and evil, and of an inherent ability, to an indefinite extent, to choose, follow after, and act the right and good as against the wrong and evil, thereby fulfilling his duty in the varied relationships of life, and finding satisfaction and happiness. Man may be ignorant or enlightened, ill-disciplined or well-disciplined, of lower or higher attainments in every conceivable degree, but there is one irrevocable necessity laid upon him — he must be faithful to his duty in order to secure the benefits and blessings which duty brings. He must do this for himself under the divine law of personal responsibility. What is right and good is always best, regardless of circumstances or consequences, both to him who acts and to all beside. This was my doctrine and that of my associates when we adopted our "Standard of Practical Christianity" and inaugurated the Fraternal Community movement. It is mine still.

Again. Man as a religious being and moral agent acts more or less in three general spheres or departments of effort and responsibility, viz: — The individual, the social, and the civil or governmental spheres. All we think, say, and do, which relates to our own personality without regard to others, belongs to the individual sphere. All we think, say, and do, in concurrence with any number of our fellow human beings in the ordinary course of life, belongs to the social sphere. And all that we think, say, or do, as subjects, citizens, or officers of any kingdom, state, or nation, belongs to the governmental sphere. It follows, therefore, that there are individual duties, virtues, sins; social duties, virtues, sins; and governmental duties, virtues, sins. In each sphere our religious and moral obligations are the same. Right and wrong confront human beings at every step. To be perfect, one must think, say, and do what is right in each and all the spheres of responsibility named. In human life, strange inconsistencies, in these particulars, are exemplified. One may be very saintly in his personal character and in his ordinary social relations with his fellow-men, but a barbarous sinner in his governmental capacity — perpetrating the most abhorrent acts of tyranny and cruelty. Or he may be above reproach in his social life, but individually immoral and untrustworthy. So we have a very mottled righteousness, often among would-be saints. In our Fraternal Community No. 1 we sought to be all-sided saints,— bound to obey the law of divine righteousness as individuals, in social life, and in all governmental concerns. This was right, even though it should serve on trial to expose our frailities and imperfections.

As was stated in the last chapter, twenty-eight persons were located upon the Hopedale territory before the first of April, 1842 — myself, wife, and two children among the number — all residing as a unitary household in the one dwelling house there and adjusting themselves to each other as far as they could, and to the unique circumstances in which they were placed. At the expiration of three weeks, when I entered upon the fortieth year of my life, domestic affairs had assumed a good degree of regularity, order, and efficiency, considering the crowded condition in which we found ourselves and the limited culinary appliances and utensils with which we had to do. My wife had been seasonably appointed director of house-keeping by the executive council, and she had for chosen assistant, our good sister, Anna T., wife of Ebenezer D. Draper. Two most excellent and capable women they were, admirably fitted for the positions they occupied, and they executed the trust reposed in them most quietly, promptly, and successfully.

Before the month closed, great progress had been made in outside matters. A practical division of industrial operations had been arranged, and each one assigned to a position of responsibility, entered upon his or her duties with commendable fidelity and earnestness. A small building, 32 feet long by 14 1-2 wide, a story and a half high above the basement, was nearly completed — the first building erected by the Community. It contained six rooms; two on the main floor for a printing office and school, with two dormitories above and two apartments for whatever use they might be needed in the basement. A larger two-story dwelling house had been voted, but it was found that a mechanics' shop, in which a portion of our water power could be utilized, was indispensable, and that, therefore, first received attention. It was the second structure we put up and served a most important purpose in our earlier years. Our agricultural interests were judiciously provided for, the months of April and May being spent in preparing the soil and putting in the seed for an autumn harvest. When June opened we had on the farm 13 cows, 4 yokes of oxen, 2 horses, and 6 swine. We had also 17 acres of land under cultivation, and everything in this department of activity promised well for the future.

At the same time, as the weeks passed by and as our industrial and general business affairs developed, we were learning some very suggestive and valuable lessons by experience. Novelty wore off and enthusiasm cooled down. We began to see that we had undertaken more than we were aware of, and had not fully estimated our difficulties. We were greatly overcrowded by numbers, new comers frequently appearing and almost forcing themselves upon us; and as greatly pushed for want of money and means to do with. All meant well in the main, but none of us had any wisdom, strength, or patience to spare, and some of us too little of these requisite qualities for our common use. We had been led to hope for funds which did not come, and some which we had received were unexpectedly withdrawn. We had made a fine show of our plans for a new social state on paper, and had published them far and wide through the land. The rich and well-to-do derided our scheme and clutched their treasures the closer; the poor, needy, and homeless eagerly applied for a share in our privileges. Moreover, less than a third of our reliable associates had sufficient money at command to meet their own family expenses — much less to help in housing and furnishing subsisting employment to others. I, as the leader in this undertaking, ought to have been wise enough to postpone practical operations till there had been accumulated a common fund sufficient to give a comfortable home and fairly remunerative employment to those who might be enlisted under the banner of our new social state. But I was in too much haste to see the realization of my theories and plans. My hope was too large and my economic judgment too small. Two fundamental duties required by the Gospel of Christ, which I had not then discovered, would have simplified and benefited the whole movement, viz : — The limitation of property expenditure to the demands of personal and domestic well-being, and the devotion of surplus means (riches) to the welfare of humanity. These two duties will be taught, insisted upon, and sacredly guaranteed in the regenerate Christian church and in the order of society which such a church shall evolve on earth.

TRIALS AND DISCOURAGEMENTS. 343

In addition to the evils and hindrances adverted to — insufficient household accommodations and the virtual abandonment of family life, the lack of needful funds and the continual pressure of applicants for residence and membership with us, the enforced denial of whom caused disappointment and sometimes embittered feeling — in addition to these, we were troubled with too much hard work and wearisome anxiety on the part of those burdened with official responsibility, and with a growing preponderance of material interests over those of a moral and religious nature, which subverted the cardinal principle, process, and object that our movement was designed to embody and represent. Moreover, as we went on, we found increasing in our ranks the number of those who were evidently more anxious to secure "loaves and fishes" for themselves than to build up that "kingdom of heaven" on the earth which alone insures the highest rectitude and good of all classes and conditions of people.

Not that anything transpired among our early Hopedale settlers grossly aggravating or flagrantly improper and wrong. But the conditions and circumstances of the situation were such as to give my weak heart some serious aches and discouragements. I was loaded down, overborne almost, by unavoidable cares and responsibilities. I had the general management of our social organization on my hands, its extensive correspondence, much of its incidental writing and considerable physical labor connected therewith, besides attending to the editorial and publication departments of the *Practical Christian*, preaching, lecturing, ministering at funerals, etc., as I was often called to do. Moreover, there were specialties devolving upon me still more difficult and wearisome: to preside over frequent, long-drawn-out discussions, reconcile incompatibilities, settle disputes and misunderstandings, regulate the children and youth, maintain order in the dwelling-house and on the outside premises, preserve harmony and good feeling among all classes, and keep up the general courage and hope. I was so favored as to enjoy the confidence of old and young, and was held in such general respect as to give me authority and render me a successful counsellor and mediator amid my associates of every condition in life. The younger inmates of our domicile I found to be deferential and obedient, tractable, pleased to improve themselves, and willing pupils in the school of good manners, and the ordinary moralities of life. I was told beforehand that in this unitary household of ours and other close relations, the greatest trouble would be with the women; that they could not or would not work together without contention and quarrelling. But I am happy to record that these evil predictions proved false. Their leaders were eminently discreet, unassuming and judicious, and the rank and file were peaceable and uncomplaining. If there were frictions among them, they were successful in oiling the machinery among themselves, and no whisper of discontent or murmur ever reached the president's ear.

I wish I could say the same of our men. But this would be contrary to the facts in the case. We had not been together two months before an instance of incompatibility between two of our mechanics had, by fostering indulgence, become so unpleasant and offensive that my kind interference was required to restore good feeling and reconcile the parties involved. I but partially succeeded, as the two, of widely different constitution and temperament, could never perfectly harmonize. One of them, inveterately disposed to sarcasm and cutting remarks, soon after left us and that trouble ended. It was the first difficulty of the kind we had encountered, and being so trifling and so unnecessary, mortified me exceedingly. It was, however, followed by others, equally causeless and equally trying. They were all small matters to begin with, but rose to importance by dwelling upon and magnifying them. For the most part they arose, not from any evil intention or purpose of wrong, but from some peculiarity of judgment, idiosyn-

DEFECTS IN THE SYSTEM. 345

cratic opinion, or question of expediency exalted into the place of a supposed ethical principle, made more aggravating by protracted discussions at meal-time or in Community meetings. One of them grew to such proportions and had such a bearing upon our constitutional polity as to require special attention and finally a change in our fundamental laws and the methods of their administration. It deserves a brief notice.

A small minority of our members, under the leadership of Brother David R. Lamson, conceived the notion that our joint stock proprietorship, which constituted the basis of our industrial and financial operations, tended to produce an aristocratic spirit among us to the degradation of the poorer members, and that this tendency ought to be counteracted and overcome by a closer approximation to a system of common property. From this view I and a large majority of my associates strongly but kindly dissented. This called forth argument on the part of its friends, which was met by counter argument. The discussion *pro* and *con* waxed warmer and warmer until it became apparent to me and my friends that there were some serious defects in the system under which we had started out, though not of the nature charged. It was not working as smoothly and to such harmonious, beneficent, and happy results as we had anticipated, but on the contrary, was producing irritation, division, alienation, and dissatisfaction to a serious extent.

It was not, however, closer affiliation that was needed to remedy the existing difficulties as the dissentients claimed, nor the merging of all personal interests in the common welfare, nor the absorption of the individual in the community, but a more practical recognition of every one's inborn rights and obligations; more opportunity for personal seclusion, activity, and development; more individual freedom, enterprise, and responsibility. Above all, there should be in our organic social scheme a true and clear distinction made between rights and privileges, between benefactions and debts, between the dictates of charity and those of strict justice. Beneficiaries should not be allowed the claims of exacting creditors, much less usurp pre-eminence over their helpers. Nor must the weak, incompetent, and irresponsible be permitted to hamper or overburden those who were straining every nerve of their superior ability for the common welfare. Probably no one of our fraternity was conscious of practising or engendering any of these evils. Nevertheless, I knew they were actually doing so, however good their motives, however unconscious they were of harm. I knew also that thereby they were imperilling the cause we all professed to hold dear, and I determined to rescue it if possible — to save it from impending destruction.

This I saw could be done only by amending the constitution, by making some radical changes in the organized policy of the undertaking, by striking out such portions of our plan of administration as were calculated to produce the disabilities and unfortunate conditions under which we were laboring, and substituting those of an opposite character, tendency, and legitimate result. To the task thus set before me I then addressed myself, and in due time prepared and brought before my constituency the amended charter of our enterprise. There were seven distinct changes proposed by me as necessary in my judgment to meet the exigencies of the case and put the Community on a sure foundation for the years ahead. And I urged the adoption of the amendments under which those changes could be made substantially for the following reasons, viz: —

(1) They restore a large amount of individuality to the members of the Community, leaving every one at liberty to form with others a unitary household and invest his capital and labor in the joint stock operations, or to dwell in his own house and transact business by himself, as may please him; in either case

ADVANTAGES OF PROPOSED CHANGES. 347

acknowledging his obligations to the great principles and objects which the body represents.

(2) They make the Community to combine all the advantages of a well-ordered village of free-minded, conscientious individuals, and of a close co-operation of capital and labor without the disadvantages of either. They adapt the Community organization to the wants of all classes of Practical Christians without imposing excessive burdens or restraints upon any, and thus give the idea of associative life the vantage ground of a fair experiment on its own merits.

(3) They prevent all unreasonable dependence of any upon the more provident in the Community, quicken industry, induce economy, promote self-reliance, and make the just distinction between alms and wages, gifts and debts.

(4) They place all the members of the Community, whether they have much or little in the joint stock, on a common level as regards reciprocal obligations and responsibilities. Justice is the same to all and charity is to be exercised by all. None can hide within the mass nor screen themselves behind constitutional prescriptions from voluntary contributions to support schools and relieve the needy. Every one will appear in his own true light.

(5) They will disencumber capital of its present great risks and dangerous liabilities, give it moderate but sure profit, and at the same time secure to labor its just compensation.

(6) Finally, they simplify the whole social machinery of the community, make the experiment perfectly safe on a large or small scale, and render the mutual relationship at once more pleasant, more just, and more practicable to all free, honest, uuselfish minds.

It required all the ability and influence I could command to obtain the adoption of the proposed amendments; but I succeeded in my endeavors, though so much to the disappointment and grief of the minority that six persons gave up their membership in the organization, while several candidates for membership, who had leanings towards a common property financial policy, lost all interest in the movement. I lamented this, but saw no way to prevent it and save our undertaking. Most of those who sent in their resignations on the impulse of the moment, afterwards relented and became reconciled to the new order of things. But their chieftain and oracle, Brother Lamson, was permanently alienated. He soon after consorted with the Shakers, but finding himself after a little time no more at home with them than with us, returned to general society, giving up the ministry and locating at West Boylston, where he died, July 2, 1886, aged 80 years. His wife, an estimable woman, shared his varied fortunes sympathetically while she lived, preceding him but a few years to the world of spirits.

The lessons taught us by the experiences just narrated were more or less depressing to us all. I felt them deeply as did those of my associates who stood by and preserved the imperilled ship. The charm of our early enthusiasm had vanished, but our principles and objects remained sacred in the shrine of our devotion. We therefore girded up the weakened loins of our minds and resolved to push forward our renewed undertaking. We had done as well as could have been expected in our more material affairs,— the harvest from garden, orchard, and field, was fairly good, our little school was well started, several kinds of mechanical activities were in operation and others prospectively near, the mill-dam and attached shop were almost completed before winter set in, and the inmates of the "Old House", reduced somewhat in numbers, had been reorganized into six distinct families and made reasonably comfortable.

The annual Community meeting occurred Jan. 4, 1843. In my address as President, I reviewed the operations of the year, noting especially the changes that had been made and prophesying a happy future. Several new members united with us, among whom was my worthy third cousin, Amos J. Ballou, an experienced and successful farmer, who was at once chosen intendant of agriculture and animals. The other requisite officers of the body were elected, business matters were discussed, suggestions made, and plans for the coming season considered, and we entered upon our respective duties and labors with fresh zeal and determination.

Although largely engrossed with cares and activities relating to the internal order and welfare of the young Community, I yet performed much external service. I not only continued my general efforts in behalf of religion and reform, but I made special lecturing excursions for the purpose of promulgating our own distinctive Practical Christianity. In the early autumn of 1842, I gave four evening addresses in the Unitarian church, Grafton, upon "The Fraternal Communion, its principles and objects," to fairly sized and interested audiences. Soon afterwards I lectured twice in the Baptist church at New England Village, two miles north of the center of the same town upon "Christian Non-Resistance," and "The Inviolability of Human Life." I had a few choice friends in these places, and it was through their active influence and generosity that my labors were introduced and provided for. Respectable audiences, including ministers of different denominations, listened attentively to my testimonies, and many strong prejudices were no doubt meliorated though few full converts were made.

I next visited Providence, R. I., on a similar mission. This, my little native state, had been for some time in a ferment with the famous Dorr agitation. The mass of the people were in a belligerent mood, but there was a remnant ready to welcome the principles of peace. My ever firm and faithful friend, Samuel W. Wheeler, stood in the van and effectively favored my ministrations. I was happy to meet Elders Benjamin and James Taylor, McKenzie, and Cheney, on terms of general accord. The two first named were ministers of the Christian Connexion whom I knew in my youth but had not seen for many years. They were men of great hearts. Elder Benjamin was the one who, at the time of my excommunication from the Christian church in Cumberland, protested against the act as contrary to the avowed principles and policy of the denomination. I was also greeted cordially by a goodly number of friends of various persuasions, callings, and stations, who received my word gladly. I delivered three discourses in Elder James Taylor's new chapel, Pawtuxet street, to appreciative audiences:— the first on Christian Non-resistance; the second on the relation those accepting that doctrine should sustain towards existing human governments; and the third on slavery, intemperance, licentiousness, and other social evils. Later, I lectured upon the same themes in Hampton, Ct., West Wrentham, Upton, Medway, Wrentham Center, Northbridge, and Leominster, Mass.

These efforts of mine evinced my zeal and industry in promoting what I sincerely deemed the cause of truth and righteousness. I trust they did some good in enlightening the minds, rectifying the hearts, and elevating the conduct of men; though very little compared with what they would have done if the Hopedale Community had been loyally sustained by those who earlier and later rallied around its standard, but who subsequently forsook it. For the seed of truth must not only be sown and nurtured, but harvested into preservative granaries. In our case it was all important to demonstrate *practically* that our divine principles could be permanently lived out in a higher order of social life. And this must be done *voluntarily* — not by mere human law or compulsion, but by human agreement, fellowship, and co-operation. Those who would not or could not support our movement from honest choice and of their own free will, were sure to fall out by the way and go to their own place in compulsory society. Unfortunately, these predominated at last and failure was the final issue.

Second Advent Discussion. In the winter of 1842-3, during the widely prevailing excitement concerning the speedy coming of Christ and the accompanying end of the world, I was drawn into a discussion of the subject with some of its leading advocates. They had invaded Millville and set up their proselyting machinery with a bold flourish of trumpets, challenging any body and every body to meet them in public debate. Brother William H. Fish, our minister there at the time, asked Mr. Mayers, their leader, if he was willing to publicly discuss the matter with me, to which he replied in the affirmative with great self-assurance. I was at once communicated with and consented to the proposed meeting. Upon going to Millville to make needful arrangements with the challenger for the conflict, I found his bravery giving way somewhat to discretion, cunning, and strategy. He was not quite ready to champion his cause against me but must send off for an expert debater in his stead, which necessitated a delay of some days, my actual competitor appearing at length in the person of a Mr. Follett of Worcester. Revs. M. W. Burlingame, a Free Will Baptist, and Mr. Holbrook, Orthodox Congregationalist, were made moderators of the meeting at which the discussion was carried on. A full report of what was said and done was inserted in the *Practical Christian*, Vol. III, of which only a brief comment can be given here.

In the first place, Mr. Follett and his friends were over-cautious, timid, and non-committal, even in regard to points upon which they had been making the most positive statements and concerning dates which were blazoned on their grand pictorial chart hanging in full view of the crowded audience. They had demanded beforehand a statement of my several positions and line of argument, which I willingly furnished them, desiring to treat them fairly and candidly in all respects. In the discussion they dodged some of the main points at issue, prevaricated, and flatly refused to defend several of their fundamental assumptions. It was soon apparent that they were sick of their own bargain. I gave them but one cause of complaint, viz: just and unanswerable criticism of their fallacious assertions and specious argumentation. In the second place, they became so tired of the contest that they caused it to be brought to a close without allowing me half the time virtually pledged me for the presentation of my side of the case. But I good-naturedly excused them on the ground that their weakness compelled a retreat on their part. The result was that their efforts in Millville, begun with such bombastic pretensions, came to a premature and inglorious close. The comment made by one of their local sympathizers upon the affair was, "If the Lord begins any good work in these parts, the devil presently sends Adin Ballou to kick it all over." Truly, "If they have called the master of the house Beelzebub, how much more those of his household." — *Matt. 10:25.*

A kindred discussion grew out of the preceding one. Before leaving the pulpit where the speaking occurred, Rev. Mr. Burlingame, one of the moderators, signified a desire to meet me the next week at the same place to debate the question whether or not the second advent predicted in the scriptures is a yet future event, himself taking the affirmative, in opposition to views presented by me in my argument with Mr. Follett. He had no ambition to defend the damaged cause of the Millerites, but was sure that Christ was to appear again upon the earth, substantially as set forth by my opponents, though at an indefinite date, and he lamented that the public mind should be turned against that theory by any exposure of the assumptions of those who fixed that consummation in the autumn of 1843. I cheerfully accepted the challenge and it was arranged that we should meet Thursday, February 23, at 2 o'clock P. M., each party to have half an hour alternately till 5 o'clock and then fifteen minutes in which to conclude his argument. The affair came off accordingly in the presence of a crowded assembly. The question was phrased thus:

MORE CONCERNING THE SECOND ADVENT. 353

"Did the second coming of Christ, predicted in the scriptures, take place about the time of the destruction of Jerusalem, or is it yet in the future?" This form of it gave me the affirmative and, of course, the opening speech. Mr. Burlingame and his assistant, a Mr. Snow, had the negative. Messrs. Amos W. Pitts and Francis Kelly acted as moderators. My leading opponent requested me to furnish him some days in advance a definite statement in writing of my doctrine, the principal positions I should attempt to maintain, and reference to the more important proof-texts of scripture I proposed to use. I did so, but neither asked nor received anything of the kind from him.

My views upon the subject in question I stated and explained plainly and fully in my opening speech. The audience, composed of persons of various opinions and prejudices, listened eagerly to what I had to say, and I could see that my doctrine was new to most of them and that the general feeling was against the possibility of my maintaining it by any fair show of proof and argument. But my convictions were the result of a thorough study of the New Testament, and I knew them to be more accordant with the teaching of that book than any that had ever been brought to my notice. As the discussion proceeded, I had the satisfaction of seeing the tide of feeling turn in my favor, especially when the weakness of my opponents in trying to refute my positions became apparent. The debate went through and closed according to programme. Finding it impossible to say all I desired in the time allotted me, I proposed another session, but was overruled by the opposing party, who was evidently glad to end the discussion as soon as possible. I, however, notified the congregation that I should conclude my argument on the following Sunday in Brother Fish's church, and did so. The challenger and those sympathizing with him gained nothing by their venture, but they made the best of their discomfiture, virtually confessing the weakness of their cause by warning their adherents

23

to keep away from me and my dangerous teachings. I soon after published an ample pamphlet on the subject, entitled, "*The True Scriptural Doctrine of the Second Advent; An Effectual Antidote to Millerism and All Other Kindred Errors,*" which may be found among my numerous publications. To the general positions and explications contained therein, I have ever since adhered, although on critical revision I might make some modifications and qualifications, but none of vital importance.

The details of progress in Community affairs being given in full in my history of the undertaking still at this writing in manuscript, I will offer in these pages only an outline of what transpired from time to time with the passing years. The new order of things, already sufficiently portrayed, contributed at once to our prosperity. During the year 1843 nine half-acre house lots were sold to members for $100 each, whereby our treasury was to that extent replenished, and on three of these were dwelling-houses erected — one two-story double tenement structure by Amos J. Ballou and Edmund Price, one story-and-a-half cottage by George W. Stacey, and a similar one by myself, in which I and my family have ever since resided. Our mechanic shop was completed and supplied with labor-saving machinery so far as the main floor and basement were concerned, while the second story was divided in such a way as to accommodate our printing office in the southerly part and our school and Sunday meetings in the northerly. Desirable improvements were made in respect to our barns, of which there were three, standing separate from each other. They were brought together, placed over good basements, put in proper condition within and without, and made neat and convenient for use in the agricultural department. The principal streets of the village site were opened, partially graded, and designated by appropriate names. Late in the autumn ground was broken and a beginning made for a school-house, to be used also temporarily as a chapel, with a basement designed to accommodate a

Community store. It was to be surmounted by a cupola or belfry, so constructed as to furnish the needful conveniences for a public clock. It was completed in the spring of 1844 and immediately occupied. Originally twenty-six feet square, it was some years afterward doubled in length to serve the growing needs of the place in those respects for which it was first designed.

Meantime the major portion of our industries was organized and carried on under general joint stock arrangements in distinct branches, and the minor portion by individual members on their own responsibility. We had common farming, gardening, carpentering, printing, hat making, tin and sheet-iron working, boot and shoe manufacture, transportation, etc., all, of course, on a small scale, giving manual employment to our men, while our women were engaged in household and kindred duties. All our residents were busy people, idlers and dawdlers not being encouraged or even tolerated. New members took the places of seceders, a considerable number of probationers were received among us, and a few families, not of our way of thinking, were allowed to reside in our midst as temporary inhabitants of the place, enjoying its educational, social, moral, and religious advantages, and engaging in its industrial activities to a greater or less extent. Every vacant tenement on the premises was filled and a few in the vicinity were hired for the accommodation of persons more or less closely connected with us.

In the spring of the year now in review, the Community received a valuable donation from a sympathizing and generous friend in Cincinnati, Ohio, Andrew H. Ernst, Esq., who, with his excellent wife, *nee* Sarah H. Otis of Boston, had long stood in cordial Christian fellowship with me as Restorationists and well-wishers to our social reform enterprise. He was a practical horticulturist, having extensive nurseries at Spring Garden, on the outskirts of the then queen city of the West, and his gift consisted of more than three hundred young apple trees of several choice varieties, carefully selected and packed, and forwarded to us by the most available and rapid means of transportation. They were received in good condition and gave us great joy, but it was our misfortune not to have in proper state of preparation sufficient ground upon which to set them, so that a considerable portion of them were virtually lost. Those that we had a suitable place for were planted with due care and judiciously trained, thriving well and becoming fruitful bearers at an early day. Some of them still remain, large, flourishing, and productive, on my own homestead.

Regular religious meetings, two always on Sunday and sometimes three, with a social conference on Thursday evening, were established early in our Community life, and creditably sustained from week to week for many years. These were generally led by one of our approved public speakers or preachers, who usually gave a formal discourse, although in the absence of such, some layman or lay-woman, of whom there were several among us competent for the task, conducted the service. At the same time those of us who had formally entered the Christian ministry preached either statedly or occasionally at various places within a convenient distance of home, some of which we regarded as distinctive missionary stations for the inculcation and dissemination of the spirit and principles of Practical Christianity. Vigorous quarterly conferences of two or three days' continuance were held at these stations or wherever we had friends to invite us. Besides devoted attention to these religious gatherings by our ministers and people at large, we took active part in mass meetings, conventions, and celebrations held for the purpose of promoting the cause of temperance, anti-slavery, non-resistance, social reform, or whatever promised the improvement of our kind. A more industrious propaganda of regenerative religious and moral principles than this little cluster of Hopedalians existed nowhere else probably on the face of the earth.

But we labored all the while under great disadvantages, having to provide for our own material subsistence as well as for our distinctive social reform enterprise, besides helping along those other activities which have just been named. I stood in the fore front of those industries upon which we relied for means wherewith to live and lend aid to every good word and work, and though weighed down with home duties and cares, yet found time for considerable active effort abroad in behalf of truth and humanity. In October, 1843, I was chosen president of the New England Non-resistance Society, which imposed a new tax upon my time and energy. The Washingtonian Movement, which led to a conflict between the friends of moral suasion and those of legal coercion as methods of promoting the temperance reformation, and the division arising in the Abolitionist ranks upon the question of political action, both appealed to me through the issues raised, in a form and with a force which I could not wholly ignore, my feeling and conviction from the beginning being unequivocally in favor of moral and religious effort rather than legal and political, in carrying forward the work of individual and social regeneration upon the earth. I also took a decided stand and wrote against the ultra anti-Sabbatarians of those days, setting forth and promulgating what I deemed true and rational views upon the observance of the first day of the week under the Christian dispensation. The consideration of these great practical questions filled, in my thought and action, the place previously occupied by more strictly theological discussions.

The growth and general prosperity of the Community during the year 1844 was all that its friends could have reasonably expected. But it was not exempt from more or less internal friction. The great difficulty against which Dr. Channing warned us,— that "of reconciling so many wills, of bringing so many individuals to such a unity of judgment and feeling as is necessary to the management" of Community affairs, was always present with us, and was aggravated in our case by the preponderance of minds more or less deficient in mental and moral discipline. All meant well, and had sincere reverence for our "great principles,".as we termed them, but all had not a nice sense of order, justice, and fitness of action in little things, nor patience and forbearance with what crossed their feelings, habits, and tastes. On this account our membership was occasionally reduced by voluntary withdrawal, our doors always swinging outward as well as inward to those who at any time cast in their lot with us.

Another difficulty encountered by us was that of steering the vessel of our social system safely between the Scylla of organic arrangements and the Charybdis of individual license. If we adopted rules and regulations seemingly necessary to good order and permanent success, we were in danger of overriding personal rights or at least of making somebody unhappy. And if we relaxed in favor of greater individual liberty, there were some to jeopardize our enterprise by unjust usurpation or uncomfortable eccentricity. In seeking to find the happy and safe middle passage, we veered first one way and then the other a little too far, like unskilled craftsmen in that kind of seamanship. Nevertheless we came to our annual meeting in January, 1845, with a good showing for the preceding year, and started out anew with unfaltering courage, hope, and zeal, believing and feeling that better days than we had yet seen were before us. Detailed information concerning Community affairs other than what pertained more particularly to myself, I remand to the pages of my history of the movement.

A heavy bereavement befell our family in the sudden decease of my wife's honored father, Pearley Hunt, Esq. of Milford, March 29, 1844, in the 73d year of his age. He was an estimable man in public as in private life, dear to his own family and a great loss to the town and general community. His memory is very precious to both my wife and myself on account of his tender affection and innumerable kindnesses, from infancy in her case and from first acquaintance in mine. His paternal interest in our temporal welfare and comfort culminated in liberally assisting us to establish the home wherein we have dwelt since September, 1843. We therefore hallow his memory. From a brief obituary in the *Practical Christian* of April 13, I make the following extracts:

"The deceased has been long and extensively known in this general vicinity as an enterprising merchant, an influential public-spirited citizen, and a civil magistrate, in which several positions he has sustained his responsibilities with more credit to himself and less censure, with more favor and less hostility, with more friends and fewer enemies, than ordinarily falls to the lot of men passing through such varied scenes and manifold duties of public activity. In the more private relations of life, he was a man in whom the best domestic and social affections predominated — kind, provident, indulgent, generous, and faithful as a husband, father, brother, friend, and neighbor. His funeral was attended by a large concourse of people with every becoming demonstration of respect."

CHAPTER XIX.

1845–1852.

COMMUNITY AFFAIRS CONTINUED — LABORS ABUNDANT — SPIRITUALISM — PUBLICATIONS — CHILDREN — EDUCATIONAL HOME — GREAT SORROW.

IN the present chapter I propose to include as many of the experiences and events of my life during the period covered by it as space and convenience will allow. Much of my time, strength, and active effort was given to the affairs of the Community, of which I continued president until January, 1852, eleven years from the date of my first election to that position. I shall only glance in the briefest possible manner at what transpired in this sphere of activity, inasmuch as it is presented in full elsewhere, as I have before stated, with all the needful accompanying circumstances.

As the projector and practical head of the social experiment at Hopedale, I had from the outset an intense ambition to have it succeed, to actualize my ideal of a civilization based upon and fashioned after the true practical Christianity of the New Testament. In this ambition I was unconscious of a single selfish motive. I desired no good for myself which I did not believe would be equally good for all my associates, and indirectly for the whole human race. I sought no salary and no emolument whatever, and never received pecuniary support beyond the cost of a workingman's board — probably less than that. I never coveted a particle of authority or power which did not clearly seem to me to be respectful of every other person's rights and promotive of the general welfare. To domineer and dictate was abhorrent to my nature, habits, and moral principles. I loved to see every one do his or her duty willingly — from choice and not from compulsion, from inward conviction and not merely to please me. And I was always as happy to follow another's nominal leadership as to be followed, if I was sure that I was being led right. For these characteristics I claim no credit. They were born in me and cost me no effort or self-crucifixion. My errability and besetting sins were always enough in other directions to need the cross of humility and self-denial, and to make me a contrite suppliant and penitent before the divine mercy seat.

My companion in the household was, by my position, largely burdened with domestic labors imposed upon her by a constant influx of what might be called Community company; that is, visiting inquirers of all varieties, who for years made our humble home their hotel *gratis*, no public place being provided for the hospitable entertainment of such till 1847, and then not entirely to our relief. But she bore her toils with womanly fortitude and patience, receiving no other reward than the consciousness of duty well performed and of faithfully sustaining her husband in meeting his dubiously chosen responsibilities. I sometimes reproached myself for having drawn her into such hardships, for she had ordinary family cares enough for her health and strength, and servants other than ourselves were seldom at command had we desired them. But all this seemed inevitably involved in what I had undertaken, and if its exactions were seriously regrettable we were consoled with the thought that they were less severe and wearisome than is often the case in families of "high life" under the domination of style and fashion. Be this as it may, such were the personal and domestic circumstances amid which I performed the duties of my official position in the Community.

Nevertheless, I kept up a courageous and cheerful heart. The cause I had espoused was dear to me and worthy of all the trials I endured in its behalf. I rejoiced in all its prosperities and sorrowed in all its adversities. I watched for its welfare in all directions, and vindicated it against all its assailants. I deprecated its imperfections and aberrations, and to the utmost of my influence quieted its internal disharmonies. I devised, drafted, and revised most of its constitutions, by-laws, rules, and regulations, and prepared for the press nearly all its published documents. In fine, I served the Community to the best of my ability — not as infallible and sinless, but with upright intentions and without hope of earthly reward. And it is with great pleasure that I record the treatment I received in return from a large majority of its members and dependents. It was emphatically kind, courteous, and deferential throughout — one of confidence and loyalty. There were occasional crises of dissatisfaction, unrest, and threatening commotion when mine seemed to be the only voice that could calm the disturbed elements and restore the desired harmony. Seldom in times of confusion and distrust did my earnest appeal to the heart, conscience, and reason of those involved fail to win a gratifying response. For this, I devoutly thanked my Heavenly Father, from whom descendeth "every good and perfect gift."

The year 1845 was one of marked prosperity with us in nearly all respects. Unbroken health prevailed on our domain, and general success crowned our various industrial and other activities. Our numbers and village homes increased on the whole, though we lost a few members by withdrawal. Notable among these was Rev. Brother Geo. W. Stacey, one of the original subscribers to our constitution — an ordained preacher with whom I had been in very close and confidential relations and from whom I had counted much in carrying forward the work of social reconstruction on the principles of Practical Christianity. The reasons for his abandonment of this work were given in full in the columns of our Community paper. They seemed to me specious and unsatisfactory, as I endeavored to show in the same issue of the publication as that in which they appeared. There is no occasion for reproducing the *pro* and *con* of the case here, or to comment on it farther than to say that in closing his public pronunciamento, the departing brother declared that he still cherished a deep and unwavering faith in the heavenly principles which drew him to Hopedale, and at the same time professed for me personally the most sincere and unabated respect and love. Much as I differed from him and deeply as I regretted the step he felt impelled to take, I certainly could cherish only the kindest feelings towards him and the best wishes for his future prosperity, welfare, and happiness. He located in the neighboring village of Milford, soon became interested in town affairs, was honored by his fellow citizens with various public offices, including that of representative to the General Court, and maintained a reputable standing in general society. He was successful in business and real estate transactions, acquiring a handsome property, most of which he left to his heirs. He continued faithful to the anti-slavery cause to the end, and also to temperance, being for several of the last years of his life a devoted political Prohibitionist. But for Christian Non-resistance and social reform he had no further testimony. He is still living at an advanced age, but without serious decline of that physical, mental, or moral energy which characterized his earlier life. *

In the late autumn of 1845 our Community was honored with a visit from the celebrated English Communist, Robert Owen, widely known among social reformers for his practical efforts in his native land to realize his ideal of a reconstructed civilization upon principles which seemed true and sacred to him. Though his views differed radically from ours in many particulars, yet he was no less welcome to our domain and hospitality on that account, and the interview with him was cordial, agreeable, and gratifying.

---

* Rev. Geo. W. Stacey died a few years after this was written.

As already indicated, the annual report in our Community affairs in January, 1846, was highly favorable and encouraging, and I, in my official address, indulged in glowing representations of our condition and prospects. My rose-colored prophecies for the future were not destined to fulfilment. The very year upon which we then entered reversed our good fortune with sickness, several deaths, and general decline of business prosperity, causing much regret and discouragement. In 1847 matters went from bad to worse till, amid the increasing confusion and dissatisfaction, I myself well nigh lost heart and hope. At length we reached a crisis which obliged us to drop the existing industrial arrangements, again alter our constitution, and swing back still farther toward individualism. In doing this, we did not change our declaration of principles, our cardinal objects, or our integrality of joint stock property. But we greatly simplified our organic system of operations, and seeing little prospect of a Fraternal Community No. 2, concluded to call our association thenceforth "The Hopedale Community." About this time the lot of land across the river, which had been designated for burial purposes, was properly surveyed and laid out under my general direction by my friend David Davenport of Mendon, a gentleman every way competent for the task, who rendered his valuable services without compensation. Thus were made the beginnings of the present beautiful Hopedale Cemetery. Our village, with territory adjoining and the inhabitants thereof, was also, after protracted importunity, set off by the town of Milford as an independent school district; the final vote being large and cordial in behalf of the project, a result with which I was much pleased.

Immediately after the modification of our system just mentioned, we sold or rented most branches of our secular business to individuals or to small partnerships of ou. members. This worked well enough in cases where the party in control had a scrupulous conscience and good practical judgment. In other cases, risks were incurred, foreign help, which proved unsatisfactory, was hired, and poor work was turned out. This injured our credit in the business world and involved us in manifold troubles which necessitated an early resumption of management on the part of the Community. While this experiment was going on, we made a very important rectification and consolidation of all our land titles under the professional guidance of our kind friend, Ellis Gray Loring, Esq., an eminent conveyancer of Boston, who also generously made us welcome to his services. This was deemed desirable and necessary even, to render us and those coming after us absolutely secure in our real estate possessions to the latest generation.

Admissions to and withdrawals from our membership were comparatively numerous during these years, but the former greatly exceeded the latter, causing a steady increase of adherents and a growing expansion of all our varied activities. I regretted the departure of any of our number whose character and standing among us were above reproach, and especially of any who had embarked with us full of hope and zeal at the outset, and upon whom I had confidently relied as co-workers in making our movement a success. It was so in the case of Brother George W. Stacy, mentioned a few pages back. It was so with Rev. Brother Daniel S. Whitney, who resigned his membership with us in a letter dated March 29, 1850. The missive, which was a lengthy one, giving his reasons in full for his act, appeared in the *Practical Christian* of the next issue with a rejoinder from my pen. Like Brother Stacey, he made no charges against his associates for "dereliction from principle or duty," but rather against "the industrial organization," which he deemed productive of many evils too grievous to be borne, and which, to use his own words, "cost more than it was worth." As regards the principles underlying the movement, he said, "I most thankfully accept them as the truth of God. They are alike needful in their spirit and power to redeem mankind individually and socially."

Nevertheless, he could go back into the prevailing order of society in which those principles are systematically and persistently set at defiance and openly violated, and, without any scruples apparently, engage in the support and management of a government whose fundamental law in various particulars he had often declared to be hostile to and subversive of the government of God — "a covenant with death and an agreement with hell." I was never able to see the consistency or wisdom of all this, but somehow, he, like Brother Stacey before him, did, and acted accordingly. He became much interested in local and general politics, was for a long time an active member of the Republican party, but for some years past has been in close affiliation as ally and adviser with the political Prohibitionists or Third Party men. He had the distinction of representing the town of Boylston, where he located after leaving Hopedale, in the State constitutional convention of 1853. Subsequently taking up his abode in Southborough, he for many years held the office of postmaster in that town, where he still resides. His interest in temperance, peace, woman's rights, and other specific reforms on the basis of the existing social order, remains unabated.*

The affairs of the Community went on prosperously, though without any noteworthy event or occurrence, through the year 1851, and my heart rejoiced again in the hope that all serious troubles were over and that the future of our cause and movement was secure against all hindrances and adversaries. Under this inspiration I wrote and presented my address at the annual meeting in January, 1852, in which I magnified our good condition and prospects as the result of our many and varied studies, experiences, and labors, and declined being con- considered a candidate for re-election to the office of president, which I had held from the beginning. I was so fully assured that the Community was well and permanently established that I thought I had better retire

---

* Rev. Daniel S. Whitney departed this life in 1894.

and let it be put in charge of a new executive head who might not only safely direct its activities but perhaps impart new energy to them, though I soon doubted the wisdom of my course. In view of my contemplated action, I made my address essentially a valedictory. It was so regarded by my associates, who, after its delivery, "*Voted*, that a copy of it be requested for record, for publication in the *Practical Christian*, and for separate distribution; also that a committee be appointed to prepare a response thereto," to be presented at an adjourned meeting. All was done as provided for, the response, which was unanimously adopted, being as follows:

"DEAR BROTHER BALLOU: Though your resignation of the presidency of the Hopedale Community, tendered at the late annual meeting, was not unexpected by any of our fraternity, it was nevertheless received with much general reluctance and a most sincere wish that you might change your purpose and still continue in the position which you have so long filled with great ability, fidelity, and usefulness. But we know that the duties of the office have been many and arduous, absorbing so much of your time and energy that there was left to you little leisure for study and other pursuits in which you have a deep interest; and we did not feel, therefore, that we could justly insist upon your longer acting in a capacity imposing such demands upon you. Whilst, then, we have submitted to your desire and decision, we have deemed it a duty and a pleasure to express the deep sense of obligation and of gratitude which we cherish towards you for your important services in our common cause. This, we, the undersigned, most cordially now do as a committee of the Community and in accordance with a vote . . . unanimously passed immediately after hearing your able, interesting, and excellent farewell address. Of that address, we deem it unnecessary to say anything at length, as it will go forth into the world to speak for itself. You know that it was appreciated and heartily responded to by all who heard it, and that they were prompted by its impressiveness and its intrinsic worth to call for its publication. To you such a response from your co-laborers must be of far greater value than any eulogy our feeble words could pronounce, and those outside our fellowship yet in sympathy with us, will judge of it by its own character and therefore pass upon it a sentence of approbation.

"We will only add that though you are succeeded in the presidency by one competent and worthy to occupy that position, being a pioneer and a constantly devoted and generous laborer in the cause of Christian Socialism, we shall still regard you, as you will naturally be regarded by the world, as really the leader in our enterprise, to whom we shall constantly look with fraternal sympathy, confidence, and hope, certain of all the aid you can render us whenever needed and called for. We therefore take an affectionate leave of you as our *nominal* head, wishing you continued health and prosperity, both temporal and spiritual, and what will be still better to you, success in all your philanthropic and Christian labors; and after this earthly life, a still higher and broader mission of love and usefulness, in association under the Infinite Father with the good and faithful who have gone before us and whose rest is unwearied activity."

WM. H. FISH,
EDMUND SOWARD. } *Committee.*

These days of exultation, hope, and mutual congratulation were followed by a season of profound bereavement and lamentation. On the 21st of January, Miss Susan Fish, one of our worthy and highly esteemed members, was taken from us by death, to the deep regret and sorrow of all who knew her; and on the 8th of February ensuing, our beloved son, Adin Augustus Ballou, followed her to the world of spirits. This was a vast, irreparable loss to us all. He was the star of love, hope, and trust to his family, to the Community, and to a large circle of admiring friends. I shall recur to this sad affliction further on.

What I have thus far recorded in this chapter pertained almost exclusively to what transpired in connection with my relation to the Community. Its remaining pages will be devoted to matters of a more strictly personal and domestic nature. As to myself, I not only performed a large amount of mental, moral, and physical service for the cause in which I was engaged within our own borders, but no small amount in a general way for the public at large in the capacity of religious teacher, moral reform lecturer, writer, and controversialist. By definite arrangement with my associates. I preached at home, as a rule, two Sundays in a month at a morning service, and also elsewhere at convenient localities in the vicinity in the afternoon or evening. On the remaining Sundays I was employed in ministerial duties farther away, at distances so great usually as to necessitate my leaving home on Saturday and returning on Monday. These outside labors were with rare exceptions among friends personally interested in the principles of Practical Christianity and in movements for the bettering of the condition of their fellowmen. I, of course, had no access to wealthy and fashionable parishes, and but rarely to those of humbler rank in so-called "liberal denominations." But many of the common people, some of whom, for one reason or another, were outside of all ecclesiastical organizations, heard me gladly. Wherever I thought it practicable, I attempted to form some sort of association on the basis of our "fraternal communion," but with little success. I procured, when I could, subscribers to the *Practical Christian*, sold books, and circulated freely tracts which had been prepared as expositional and illustrative of our distinctive principles and objects. Of full and devoted converts to our "Standard of Practical Christianity," I made but a small number. There were good and sufficient reasons for this. Many who acknowledged the absolute truth of that "Standard," shrank from espousing it on the ground that it was too high, too good for them to think of attaining it or of ordering their lives by it. Others had, for various reasons, left old religious bodies and were determined not to jeopardize their much prized liberty by entering new ones. They were not only "Comeouters," but "Stayouters." Still others were wool-dyed indifferentists to all positive religion and clear-cut principles of righteousness. I could transiently interest such as these while exposing the errors and sins of existing society, but they cared little for definite constructive methods of personal or social regeneration. Nevertheless, I sowed the divine seed diligently, taking no thought as to whether it fell "by the wayside" or "on stony places" or "among thorns" or "into good ground"; but being willing to accept such results as the "Lord of the harvest" might find in his reckoning.

My labors in behalf of specific reforms continued abundant throughout the whole sphere of my personal acquaintance and public activity. Generally, I spent but a day or two in response to any given call for service of this sort, but at two different times I went out under the auspices of the Anti-slavery Society as lecturing agent for a term of several weeks; once to Eastern Pennsylvania, where I had a very pleasant campaign in 1846, and again to Central New York in 1848.

In the former of these years I prepared a small volume of 240 pages, entitled, "*Christian Non-resistance in all its Important Bearings. Illustrated and Defended.*" It was published by my good friend, James Miller McKim of Philadelphia, and re-published some years later by friends of the cause in England. It was critically reviewed, with some pretty sharp animadversions in the *Christian Examiner*, a Unitarian quarterly, in its issue of January, 1848. The reviewer was my former ecclesiastical brother, Rev. Charles Hudson, then a representative in Congress from the Fifth Massachusetts District. He caused his article to be struck off in a pamphlet form and sent me a copy. I honored it with a thorough examination and reply in the columns of the *Practical Christian*, which may sometime be given a wider circulation.

Respecting oral debates, I held several of interest and importance during the period now in review. One of these was with Mr. Origin Batchelor, an able Calvinistic layman fond of controversy, a zealous but fair opponent whom I had encountered before, as may be remembered, and whom I afterward met in verbal conflict on different occasions. On the 21st and 22d of October, 1845, by mutual pre-arrangement, we discussed at Norton, Mass., the following question: "Ought Christians to participate in any government whose constitution authorizes the destruction of human life under any pretext whatsoever?" The disputation was well conducted before attentive and deeply interested audiences.

During the same year I had two rather curious rencontres with Rev. Thomas Williams, a venerable Hopkinsian clergyman, sometime of Providence, R. I., who was also addicted to polemic controversy, though not in forensic form. He was encouraged to lecture in Uxbridge by Rev. Mr. Orcutt, pastor of the Trinitarian church there, upon "The divine ordinance of civil government and the punishment of crime." I had many friends in the place who were specially invited to be present. They accepted the invitation on condition that the lecturer allow questioning and criticism by some competent person after he had closed his formal discourse. This was promised and I was sent for to be present and avail myself of the proffered opportunity. I responded favorably and was an attentive auditor with many others on the occasion. The address of Mr. Williams was very long, continuing till 10 o'clock (it being given in the evening), which left me little time for any suitable rejoinder. I used what I had, however, faithfully, spite of discreditable artifices to prevent me, and my questions and criticisms did good execution in behalf of the truth.

Not long afterward, I had another contest with the same reverend lecturer in Upton, upon the same general subject. He seemed dissatisfied with the result of the Uxbridge interview and desired an opportunity to retrieve himself before the public. The subterfuges employed to get me to Upton and then to deprive me of a fair chance to defend my beleaguered views at the meeting were worthy of the cause which inspired them.

Besides these and other oral discussions upon some phase of the subject of Non-resistance, I was drawn into many similar or kindred written ones in the *Practical Christian*, as will be found by consulting its files. Indeed, I was very unfortunate in respect to my differences from both the extreme conservatives and the extreme radicals around me. I was either too fast or too slow for nearly all with whom I had to deal. Very few, even of my professed friends could keep exact step with me. Nevertheless, I managed, as I stated in our little periodical, "to respect myself and maintain a cheerful countenance." I was entirely confident that "my leading objects, principles, and positions, however unpopular now," were "approved of God and will be approved by future generations." "Pursuing the tenor of this humble but ever blessed path of wisdom and peace," I said, "I shall not be ashamed of my testimony, nor terrified by popular opposition, nor discouraged by seeing only 'here and there a traveler.'"

Spirit Manifestations. For a considerable time I received the newspaper reports of the mysterious phenomena which first appeared at Hydeville, N. Y., and thence spread into Rochester and elsewhere in 1848-9, with great incredulity. I made no haste to investigate the alleged occurrences, though I was soon impressed from what I could learn that there was some unaccountable reality about them. Previous to 1840, I had become so infected with modern Sadduceeism as to presume that I had outgrown the traditions of my childhood and even a part of my own profound spiritual experience. Demons, ghosts, haunted houses, etc., I supposed had been remanded by liberal learning and philosophy to the limbo of exploded superstitions. I had no doubt, however, that the soul or spirit was the essential entity of every human being, radically distinguishable from the material body; that it survived physical dissolution in a conscious state of existence; and that every individual commenced the super-mundane life at the same intellectual and moral point of development attained in the earthly life. But in respect to the power of departed spirits to manifest themselves to those still in this mortal state, I was exceedingly skeptical — groping in mental darkness. The bible in its literal form plainly taught that doctrine, but

I had been persuaded that all passages of such a nature could and should be otherwise explained. There was a long catalogue of books published at different dates during past centuries testifying to the reality of inter-communication between this and the unseen world, but I was ignorant of them and their contents. Animal magnetism, clairvoyance, and other psychological phenomena had arrested my attention and excited my wondering consideration, without suggesting the possibility of departed spirits having anything to do with them or being capable of acting upon principles which those realities illustrated.

In 1841 I had an opportunity of testing the alleged claims of the so-called "divining rod" as an indicator, in the hands of certain persons, of subterranean springs and water courses. I entered upon the investigation of those claims thoroughly unbelieving; I pursued it with great patience, care and thoroughness; I came out of it an unqualified believer. By my experience in that matter, I was led to conclude that " there are more things in heaven and earth than are dreamed of " in our common mundane philosophy, and was admonished never again to allow my self-conceited wisdom to flatter me that I had outgrown all the knowledge of the ancients.

This experience, supplementing my general faith in the superiority of mind over matter, predisposed me to the courteous and hospitable treatment of the purporting spirit manifestations when they appeared in our village and at my own doors in 1849 or 1850. I then determined to satisfy myself what the credible facts of the phenomena which challenged my conscientious consideration were. I ardently desired to know the truth and the whole truth in this matter, and to avoid all delusion. I felt that I had enough common sense, intellectual discernment, and honesty of purpose, to do justice to the proposed investigation and to accept the issue. Great prudence, caution, candor, and acumen were demanded, in order to reach a result that could be relied upon as final and unquestionable. Whatever of these capabilities I possessed, I exercised through a long series of seances held under circumstances that precluded all possibility of deception, trickery, or mistake. By such means, I arrived at the following conclusions: (1) That inter-communication between the spirits of those gone before to the unseen world and those still in the flesh was a reality; (2) that many cases of communications from the departed were clear and reliable, though the personal identity of those producing them was often uncertain; (3) that both *high* and *low* spirits, morally considered, were capable of producing manifestations; (4) that there were frequently equivocal and unreliable communications, due sometimes to the untrustworthiness of those making them and sometimes to the imperfection of the medium or the mesmeric influence of others consciously or unconsciously exerted; (5) that some professed mediums were deceivers and not to be trusted; (6) that all purporting spirit communications must be subjected to rational and moral criticism, like those made by persons in the flesh. To this extent and with these qualifications I became at that time and have ever since remained a Spiritualist. I avowed myself such and defended my position unequivocally, both in speech and through the public press.

Domestic labors and responsibilities of a general nature underwent little change with us from year to year. But during the period traversed by this chapter our two children were coming rapidly on towards maturity, and their training for the duties of the not far off future and for honorable usefulness in the world was a matter of increasing interest and solicitude on our part. We desired to educate them physically, industrially, mentally, morally, religiously, and socially, in such a way as to enable them to answer the great ends of existence, and they were good subjects for such an education. It was no part of our ambition to secure for them classical and professional distinction on the basis of our common civilization, but to qualify them for solid service in the better order of society we were endeavoring to institute. This

EDUCATION OF CHILDREN.

included the scholastic acquirements of real value taught in the public schools of Massachusetts. Beyond these we did not care to push them, leaving what more of erudite knowledge might be desirable to their own genius and self-exertion as opportunity should offer or occasion require.

Our eldest surviving child, Abbie, was early qualified to teach primary rudimental classes at Hopedale. But to enlarge her scholarship, make her acquainted with the best methods of imparting knowledge, and prepare her for efficient service in the higher grades of instruction, we sent her to the State Normal school, then located at West Newton under the very competent preceptorship of Rev. Cyrus Pierce. Thence, after a regular course of tuition, she graduated reputably near the close of .1847. Early the next year she entered upon a long series of valuable labors at the head of our public district school, and later as co-principal of a private seminary known as the "Hopedale Home School." Her success was eminent and surpassed only by her usefulness. She became an influential member of the Hopedale Community, having been admitted to our ranks Aug. 24, 1850, and has never swerved from the principles then professed. May 11, 1851, she was married to Rev. William S. Heywood, the event being solemnized at the close of the regular Sunday service in our chapel with my paternal benediction and amid the congratulations of a friendly congregation. The groom had studied with me for the Practical Christian ministry and been approved and ordained to his chosen work May 25, 1849. He was received to Community membership October 17 of the same year, and for fourteen years was one of our regularly appointed preachers. Subsequent changes at Hopedale, hereinafter to be detailed, necessitated his leaving the place with his family in 1863, soon after which he entered the Unitarian fellowship, under whose auspices himself and wife have been serving God and humanity in different localities unto this day, Sept. 2, 1889.

Our son, Adin Augustus, the inestimable treasure of our hearts and golden staff of our earthly hopes, was destined to an early translation from mortal conditions of existence to the abodes and societies of the angelic realm. We gave him the best common school privileges at our command till he was over seventeen years of age, and then much better ones in the State Normal school at Bridgewater, whereof that excellent scholar and disciplinarian, Nicholas Tillinghast, was principal. Meanwhile the influences of home and of the Community had been happily of a nature to develop his intellectual and moral capabilities in the right direction, and to these, as to all positive endeavors to call forth the best that was in him, he responded heartily and nobly. Though not physically strong, he yet enjoyed tolerable health which seemed to improve as he grew in years. He had an active, elastic mind, and a genial, cheerful temperament, which combined to render him a universal favorite among his associates, young and old. At ten years of age he entered the Hopedale printing-office, becoming expert enough at fourteen to assume charge of it as foreman. At the same time he planned, edited, and published on his own account a miniature semi-monthly paper for young people, which he facetiously entitled "*The Mammoth.*" It had quite a run among his friends as long as he chose to continue it.

On the 8th of August, 1850, he entered the Bridgewater school, as stated, where he prosecuted his studies through the regular year's course and an additional supplementary term. He then stood so high in the estimation of the principal and his associates that he was cordially invited by the proper authorities to take the position of junior assistant teacher in the institution. He accepted the invitation and entered upon the duties of the position full of enthusiasm and hope, Dec. 5, 1851. Here I turn aside for a moment from what was soon to transpire at Bridgewater to affairs relating to our son at Hopedale.

He had become so thoroughly inducted into the principles and life-work to which his parents were devoted that he was ready to consecrate himself to the same before entering upon his new responsibilities in the Normal School. He was accordingly proposed and admitted to membership in the Community, November 22. This consummation was an inexpressible satisfaction to me and scarcely less so to many others. I had watched the indications of his maturing ambition with anxious solicitude lest the temptations of the prevailing civilization should allure him from the struggling cause of Christian Socialism so dear to my heart. Nothing was more natural to one with his abilities and opportunities than to yield to such temptations, but whether he should do so or not depended on his own free choice. If he could not espouse the cause to which I had devoted my life of his own accord and with a full heart, he would be worth nothing to it, even though its nominal adherent. But he did so espouse it, to my great joy, and I could implicitly trust his fidelity. I had been deserted by coadjutors whose defection sadly disappointed me, and I longed to have their places filled with others whose congeniality, mental breadth, moral stability, and judicial competency should not be swerved from our holy standard by petty inconveniences and vexations. He was, I felt confident, by nature, by culture, and by divine grace, one of this reliable type.

Moreover, at the time when he took his stand for what I deemed right and good, I was maturing a favorite educational scheme to be put in operation in connection with our Community, and had organized an association for its actualization. It had been publicly announced and had awakened much enthusiasm among our friends at home and abroad, and all eyes were turned to him as the leading teacher and manager of the institution, soon, it was hoped, to be established. He himself entered most earnestly into the project and was looking forward with intense interest, as his letters testify, to the time when everything should be in readiness for him to assume a position which was full of attractions to him as opening a career of great service to truth and to humanity. A prospectus of the contemplated establishment, which was to be called "The Hopedale Educational Home," setting forth with considerable minuteness of detail its leading characteristic features, its special advantages, its claims upon the rationally religious and reformatory public, and making an urgent appeal for funds, was issued and widely circulated among our friends scattered abroad. To it was appended the constitution of the body organized to prosecute the undertaking and carry it forward to a successful issue, the first section of Article I, indicating its character, reading as follows:

"The grand aim and work of this association shall be to educate the young who may be intrusted to its charge for that purpose; to develop properly, thoroughly, and harmoniously all their natural faculties, moral, intellectual, and physical; to give them, if possible, a high-toned character based on scrupulous conscientiousness and radical Christian principles, a sound mind, well cultivated, stored with useful knowledge and capable of inquiring, reasoning, and judging for itself; a healthful, vigorous body, suitably fed, exercised, clothed, lodged, and recreated; good domestic habits, including personal cleanliness, order, propriety, agreeableness, and generous social qualities; industrial executiveness and skill in one or more of the avocations necessary to a comfortable subsistence; and withal practical economy in money matters. In fine, to qualify them, so far as a comprehensive and thorough education can do it, for solid usefulness and happiness in all the rightful pursuits and relations of life."

This circular, which was issued while Adin Augustus was with us just before taking up his duties as teacher at Bridgewater, was the last work done by him in the printing office — the last manual labor indeed that he ever performed. Little did any of us dream at the time he was thus engaged what an overwhelming storm-blast was gathering its ruthless forces to paralyze our affections and blight our fondly cherished hopes. Yet so it was. Two months later, Feb. 8, 1852, the shadow of death settled

GREAT HOPES DESTROYED.

down in thick darkness upon our beloved one, and all the brilliant prospects which clustered around his mortal personality vanished forever. After a few days of suffering from an insidious attack of typhoid fever, which his overtaxed energies were unable to repel, he expired at Bridgewater in the arms of his agonized parents, and his pure spirit was translated to its immortal mansion. Only his lifeless body and hallowed memories of him remained to the saddest of mourning circles. None doubted his blessedness in the heavenly realm; but oh, how desolate the places he had beautified and cheered on earth! The void was great and dreary and could never again be filled. Down into his grave went all the cherished plans whose fruition depended so largely on his earthly life, genius, and ministry. Alas, so willed our Heavenly Father, in all-wise love, no doubt, but to the shrouding of our brightest and fondest anticipations for this world. I need not here repeat the story of his life, character, sickness, death, and funeral. For lo, it is written in full in the truthful volume of one hundred and ninety-two pages which I published a year afterward, entitled "Memoir of Adin Augustus Ballou. By his Father." Read that, all ye who have sympathizing hearts and bless his precious memory.

The shock of our bereavement almost crushed the fondly doting mother, and was all that my own stronger energies could endure. Neither of us ever entirely recovered from its desolating effect. We have been comforted and sustained down to a favored old age, but our consolation and strength have descended from the invisible world. To that fountain of all good we looked for help and received it. Having become convinced of the reality of communications from departed loved ones, we availed ourselves of favoring opportunities of hearing from our beloved son. He came to us presently with messages of soothing assurance, intelligence, and counsel, and our broken hearts were anointed, alleviated, and made glad.

This tragic experience and the resulting circumstances just narrated hastened the preparation for the press of a work which I had for some time contemplated upon the general subject of spiritualism, as my investigations and studies had caused me to understand and believe it. The volume was published during the ensuing summer with the following title; "An Exposition of Views Respecting the Principal Facts, Causes, and Peculiarities Involved in Spirit Manifestations," etc. It had a wide circulation among believers and students of psychical phenomena, and a second edition considerably enlarged was issued a few years later. It was also re-published in England, where it commanded the attention not only of professed Spiritualists but of scientists and savants who were not too wise in their own conceit to candidly examine the subject of which it treated. So far as I am personally concerned, I abide confidently by the views and statements presented in that work, though not by all the expectations then entertained of early good results from the movement it aimed to interpret, explain, and set before the public in its true light.

I have now come down in the order of time to the date at which I propose to bring this chapter to a close, but there are a few additional incidents and events of a personal significance and interest deserving of record which I have thus far omitted to mention, and which I will briefly notice in the order of their occurrence.

The New England Non-resistance Society, of which I was many years president, took measures in 1845 to resuscitate its suspended organ, the *Non-resistant*, in order to impart new vigor and efficiency to the cause it represented. An arrangement was made whereby the periodical in pamphlet form was to be printed at Hopedale under my editorial charge. The experiment was attempted in good faith, but failed for lack of adequate support, and subscribers who had paid for the publication were supplied to the extent of such payment with our own *Practical Christian*. This paper three years later was adopted by the society mentioned as its organ, at least in part, and to indicate the change made it was given the title, "*The Non-resistant and Practical Christian.*" Very naturally, I was the responsible managing editor, although most of the matter for the new department was furnished by Henry C. Wright, lecturing agent for the society concerned. He had just returned from Europe, and entered upon the duties of his office with vigorous enthusiasm. Hopedale was his nominal center of operations, though he was there but little. He traversed the country on his mission in all directions and his correspondence, presenting an account of his labors, with comments and reflections thereon, filled the columns assigned him and gave variety and interest to the paper's contents. His zeal and activity were pre-eminent, his devotion to the cause unquestionable, his pen prolific, but his discrimination and soundness of exposition did not always command my admiration or satisfy my judgment.

It is proper to mention in these pages a brief connection which my friend, Oliver Johnson, at one time sustained to myself and our Community. An organization called "The Practical Christian Ministry," composed of our properly constituted preachers and lecturers, had been formed, to the membership of which this brother was admitted Sept. 23, 1848. He was a devoted Abolitionist, a teetotaler, peace man, and general moral reformer on Christian principles, and also an able and acceptable public speaker and writer. While in our fellowship he occupied pulpits that were open to us, filled lecturing appointments as one of our approved ministers, and assisted me in editing the *Practical Christian*, making himself in these and other ways very useful to us and our cause. But our field was too narrow for his talents and aspirations, and after a few months he left for a broader one in which he felt that his time and endowments could better serve his Maker and his fellowmen. Originally an Orthodox Congregationalist layman, a printer by trade, and sometime publisher of the *Christian Soldier*, he became an early convert to anti-slavery through Wm. Lloyd Garrison, and subsequently to the whole reformatory gospel, of which he was a staunch apostle and defender, as editor or sub-editor of various progressive publications, to the end of his days. Most of his later life was spent in New York city, where he died Dec. 10, 1889.

The decease of my wife's mother, Mrs. Chloe (Albee) Hunt, widow of Pearley Hunt, Esq., occurred Sept. 15, 1849, at the house of her daughter, Mrs. Diana (Hunt) Cook of Milford, inflicting a heavy bereavement upon our household, as did the decease of her husband five years before. Her many estimable qualities justly commanded the veneration and love of her children, grandchildren, other relatives, and friends. Her prayer that she might be spared a long and distressing sickness was graciously answered. She experienced but a few hours of pain and sank gently and without a murmur into that sleep which knows no waking here below. She had passed the allotted time of the psalmist, being in the 76th year of her age.

On the 11th of April, 1852, just before entering the 50th year of my life, I preached by particular request of a few friends to Theodore Parker's congregation at the Melodeon in Boston, upon the subject of Christian Non-resistance. I always felt that it was a mistake for me to have undertaken this service. The circumstances were unfavorable in many respects, and thwarted my best expectations concerning it. I was still suffering from the shock of our great sorrow. I was mentally and physically enervated and depressed, and had but indifferent command of my thoughts and energies. My voice was sensibly impaired and incapable of filling the vast auditorium in which I spoke. Moreover, the large audience present, with a few exceptions, not only had no sympathy for or interest in my doctrine, but was evidently disappointed, if not disgruntled, at not being privileged to hear the silvery tones and eloquent sentences of their favorite preacher, nor did it fail to manifest a general uneasiness and discontent thereat. To make the matter worse, the introductory exercises, including one of Mr. Parker's long prayers, were so protracted that I did not begin my discourse till half past eleven o'clock. I was therefore in the midst of my argument when the hour of twelve struck, causing considerable numbers of those present, eager perhaps for their dinner, to leave the house, creating thereby much confusion. Mr. Parker, who was very kind and courteous, entreated all to wait patiently and hear me through, but to little purpose. Seeing and comprehending the situation, I cut short what I had intended to say and hurried on to the end that I might as soon as possible relieve those to whom I was proving myself a burden and a bore. I felt at the time, as I have felt ever since, that I brought my wares to an unappreciative market, and that I gained no credit for myself or my cause. I cannot refrain from mentioning a peculiarly interesting incident that occurred in connection with this service. I read for a scripture lesson the 12th chapter of Romans in full. Upon taking my seat by the side of Mr. Parker, he smilingly whispered in my ear, "I never read publicly the words 'If thine enemy hunger, feed him; if he thirst, give him drink; for in so doing thou shalt heap coals of fire on his head.' They seem vindictive to me." I marvelled greatly at his sensitiveness on this point, especially in view of his known hostility to the doctrine of Christian Non-resistance which I was there to advocate.

In the afternoon, at Mr. Parker's social conference, the previously announced theme for consideration was set aside and the subject of my crippled morning's sermon was offered for consideration. About one hundred and fifty persons were present, among whom were William Lloyd Garrison and other able Non-resistants. Mr. Parker and one or two others freely stated their objections to the doctrine, whilst Mr. Garrison and the rest of us defended it and answered the objections to the best of our ability. It was a free and fair discussion, a respectful and courteous spirit characterizing the disputants and the entire meeting. Taken as a whole, this effort on my part was one of the most disappointing and unsatisfactory of my iife.

CHAPTER XX

1852–1858.

AT HOME AND ABROAD — TRAGEDY — PRACTICAL CHRISTIAN REPUBLIC — WESTERN EXCURSION — GERRITT SMITH — COMMUNITY CRISIS — COMMUNE.

I ENTERED upon the fiftieth year of my life enfeebled somewhat in body and mind, as I was sadly depressed in spirit by the heavy bereavement that had befallen our household. That visitation came so unexpectedly, seemed so untimely, and prostrated so many cherished hopes, that though divine support and consolation were all we could reasonably pray for, it enveloped us in a very dark cloud of disquietude and grief. I could not wholly throw off the burden that weighed so heavily upon me and hence performed the tasks incumbent upon me with depleted vigor and zeal. The enterprise contemplated by the Educational Home Association, upon which I had lavished so much thought and labor and in which centered so many and such glowing anticipations on my part and on the part of our ascended son, was paralyzed by what had transpired and ere long was abandoned altogether. The "staff of accomplishment," so far as its practical realization was concerned, was gone, and though advised by devoted friends to push the project forward, I had no heart to struggle further in its behalf. My Sabbaths were all occupied at home or abroad in the exposition, defence, and diffusion of my long-entertained moral and religious convictions of truth and duty which were as dear and sacred to me as ever, if not more so, but it was a long time before I could discharge the obligations under which they placed me with that elasticity, fervor, and enthusiasm which formerly inspired me and fitted me for the work I felt called upon to do. My friends, of whom I had many scattered far and wide over a large territory, were kind and sympathetic towards me, giving me ample opportunity to visit them and to preach my Practical Christian gospel in their respective neighborhoods. I have many pleasant memories of these missionary excursions enjoyed during the period of which I am writing, one of which gave me unusual satisfaction at the time, as it gives me much delight to recall it now that so many years have passed away since it transpired.

The last Sabbath in September, 1852, and the two ensuing days I spent in Troy, N. Y., where there was quite a circle of persons sympathizing with me in my general theological and reformatory views as I had published them to the world. Conspicuous among these was Thatcher Clark, formerly of Medway, in which town I had known him many years before. He had for a long time been a sort of disciple of mine, a liberal patron and gratuitous distributor of my writings. He had often in correspondence urged me to visit his adopted city and address such free-minded seekers after truth as he might induce to hear me. When I finally yielded to his wishes, I was cordially welcomed and hospitably provided for by him and his family, and during my stay in the city of his adoption made many new acquaintances, who manifested a genuine interest in my mission, entertained me genially, heard my messages gladly, and purchased my writings with a liberal hand. In a commodious hall belonging to Brother Clark, I addressed every way respectable audiences three times on Sunday, and also on Monday and Tuesday evenings. My themes of discourse in their order were (1) "The theology, piety, and morality of the sermon on the Mount"; (2) "The Infinitarian Philosophy," as I termed it, or the doctrine of the absolute illimitableness of God in all his attributes of space, duration, worlds, beings, and variety of conditions; (3) "The kingdom of God *on earth*"; (4) "Spirit Manifestations";

(5) "The Christianization of human society." I was heard with uniformly profound attention, encouraging me to hope for a reasonable amount of good fruit from the seed sown.

As already stated, I had at this time become so firmly convinced of the truth of spirit communication, that I had not only been prompted to publish a volume devoted to its defence and elucidation, but to preach and lecture upon it as I found opportunity, and to co-operate in various ways with its accredited advocates and promoters for its promulgation in the community and world. I attended and took part in conventions held in its behalf, wrote for papers devoted to its extension, and consented for a time to be accounted an agent of the Spiritualist Association. I continued this open and active support of the cause for several years or until I came to feel that my unwavering loyalty to Jesus Christ and His religion, which I never gave up or kept in abeyance even before a spiritualistic assembly, made me an unwelcome coadjutor. I then quietly withdrew from the ranks. But I have never repudiated my deep-seated convictions on the subject, nor declined to express them at proper times and on proper occasions. Nor have I ever cherished any sympathy with the skepticism and contempt shown in high places towards spiritualistic phenomena, but deem most of such contempt and skepticism unreasonable, absurd, and pitiable. There are falsities, errors, and follies connected with nominal Spiritualism with which I have no sympathy, but I am well assured that there is in it a considerable percentage of phenomenal reality and philosophical instruction which no wise mind can reject or despise. Such a mind will select the gold and cast the dross away.

No remarkable developments in Community affairs occurred during the year 1852. There was a small deficit in our industrial operations, which was satisfactorily adjusted. In all other respects, our experiment was eminently encouraging. Our numbers increased, our business interests multiplied, our intellectual, moral, and religious instrumentalities were healthfully vigorous, and our organic arrangements seemed ripening into well-assured solidity and permanence. There were still frictions and difficulties to be overcome, but no dangers to be feared, save from our own frailties and imperfections. We owed more money than was wise through unavoidable necessity, but our pecuniary credit was above suspicion and bound to remain so. We had only to keep the faith, abide steadfastly by our principles, and persevere to the end, and all would be well.

The year 1853 opened auspiciously and all hearts were gladdened by the outlook. But another great and lamentable bereavement befel us ere we had gone far on our way. Bro. Butler Wilmarth, M. D., a prominent member of our fraternity, on his way home from a Hydropathic Medical Convention in New York city, was one of the victims of the memorable railroad disaster which occurred at Norwalk bridge, Conn., the 6th day of May. As soon as his body was identified and his place of residence ascertained, the former was transmitted to Westborough where he had an institution for invalids, and thence to Hopedale where he received well-deserved funeral honors. He was a pillar in our social edifice, honored and beloved by us all and by a multitude throughout the general community in which he had practiced his profession. The depth and extent of mourning for him can be but faintly imagined. His grave is a marked one in our little cemetery among others of our sainted dead. During the ensuing year, Rev. Brother Wm. H. Fish prepared an excellent memoir of him, which was published with a good steel engraved likeness in a duodecimo volume of two hundred and fifty-six pages.

Aside from this afflictive visitation the year was eminently a successful and gratifying one. So hopeful were we for the cause of social reconstruction that schemes were devised and projects contemplated for founding offspring communities in the distant west, several states offering apparently favorable opportunity and inducements in the way of men and means for enterprises of that sort. Some of these seemed near ripening to a practical consummation a year or two later, but proved to have too little vitality to grow into permanent and self-sustaining movements.

In addition to my ordinary routine of labors which continued essentially the same from year to year, I had caused to be instituted not long before the time of which I am now speaking what was called "The Inductive Communion," which was designed to indoctrinate our young people in the principles and methods of social reform, and prepare them for the assumption in maturer life of the responsibilities and duties which they involved and required. This was under my immediate charge for many years, and, meeting as it did every Monday evening, required no little study and effort on my part to make it subservient to the general good of all connected with it. As editor of *The Practical Christian*, I was much occupied in replying to querists and opponents on various points of theology, ethics, and social economy. Standing also, as I did, between extreme radicals and equally extreme conservatives, I was obliged to contend right and left against what seemed to be pernicious errors in both directions. This was especially true on the radical side. All sorts of reformers were abroad, with whom we were in much sympathy as to their main object, but whose notions and declarations on collateral questions of truth and duty often tended, in my judgment, to nothingarianism and social anarchy. Of the pernicious errors from this source that I had to withstand were an incoherent Transcendentalism, which made every individual his own prophet, priest, king, and God; a rabid anti-bibleism, which treated the scriptures of the two Testaments indiscriminately as a jargonic mass of pseudo-sacred rubbish, of no divine authority whatever; and a gross anti-Sabbatarianism, which left no use for any sort of Sabbath, even for the moral and religious improvement or physical comfort of needy humanity. All such views, in my opinion, were false in principle, prejudical to human welfare and destructive of the growth of Practical

Christian Socialism, and I therefore opposed them with all the vigor at my command. A truly hallowed production of my pen in 1853 was the "Memoir of Adin Augustus Ballou," our departed son, already mentioned, which came from the press in September. It was eagerly sought for and read with deep and tender interest by all who had known him and by many beside, both old and young. It has the charm of a novel, the impressive force of a truthful biography, and the moral influence which excites aspiration for a type of life far above the popular level.

My health and strength, mental and physical, after a few months were so far restored that I felt ready to undertake the elaboration and completion of a project for a confederacy of communities, which I had long contemplated. I was prompted to do this by the unprecedented prosperity of our Hopedale enterprise, the consequent probability of an early colonization of some of its members in some western state, and the general increase of interest in Social Reform movements throughout the length and breadth of the land. I therefore spent much time in the autumn and winter following in devising and putting in proper form a general plan for the formation and government of such a confederacy, which I entitled "*Constitution of The Practical Christian Republic.*" This I submitted to my brethren of the community for their examination, criticism, emendation, and perfecting, before giving it to the public. After long and patient consideration of it, article by article and section by section, resulting in sundry alterations and amendments, it was finally approved and adopted, each part by itself, and as a whole, May 7, 1854. By this action a definite public policy and the line of confidently expected progress for the future were clearly sketched and authoritatively prescribed. The accepted constitution was framed on the most inclusive and comprehensive plan and sought to make provision for a wide diversity of methods and operations in the direction of social reorganization. It granted the privilege of forming, as conviction, inclination, or circumstances might suggest, four different kinds of

Fraternal Communities, under the same general head and as co-equal parts of the same general system, to be denominated respectively Parochial, Rural, Joint Stock, and Common Stock Communities. All the details of organization and administration usually embodied in documents of a similar nature, were set forth according to the light I then had, and to the best of my ability.

This being accomplished, I felt the importance, as the new constitution was sent out into the world, of having it accompanied with some explanation or elucidation of its distinctive characteristics and methods of operation; and this feeling grew upon me until I resolved upon preparing and having published a complete exposition of what I deemed the true system of human society, comparing it carefully with the prevailing system and with certain proposed new ones that were claiming the attention of philanthropists and reformers in both our own and foreign lands. I then addressed myself to the assigned task, devoting my time and strength, so far as they were not demanded by more urgent duties, for several months to the preparation of such a work. As a result, there issued from our Community press near the end of 1854 an octavo volume of six hundred and fifty-five pages, entitled "*Practical Christian Socialism*: *A Conversational Exposition of the True System of Human Society*. In Three Parts, viz: I. Fundamental Principles; II. Constitutional Polity; III. Superiority to Other Systems."

The book was written and put in print in very great haste and under many embarrassing circumstances, occasioning numerous defects and errors when considered from a literary point of view, which more time and care would have prevented and which I afterwards had reason to regret. Moreover, I have come to see, by profounder study of the subject, that I could amend what I have written on certain points of theory and practice, as I have amended them in some of the later fruits of my pen. But I still adhere to the grand essentials of the work and am sure that in coming time social reformers will find it rich in suggestions and a helpful guide in any proposed organization of society on a sure and enduring basis.

Meanwhile there occurred an interesting and noteworthy episode in the story of my career,— an exceptional ripple in the usually quiet current of my life. It comprised the experiences of a five weeks' tour with my wife through several of our American States and Canada, taken by the invitation and at the expense of our generous brother, E. D. Draper, who, with his wife, Anna T. Draper, accompanied us. Little time or inclination have I ever had for traveling farther than duty called me for missionary or reformatory purposes, and this was the only extended excursion ever made by me as a release from ordinary cares and labors, or from readily accessible means of recreation. It afforded me, however, great pleasure and satisfaction, and brought me into contact with phases of human life and character I had never met before, and with personages whose acquaintance I was happy to make,— some of them being distinguished as friends and champions of truth and righteousness in some one or other field of progressive, philanthropic, humanitarian effort. A few of the salient points of this expedition I am prompted to record.

We bade adieu to our relatives and friends in Hopedale, with tender emotions and amid a shower of good wishes, on the morning of the 8th of May, 1854, proceeding *via* Springfield, where we spent the night, to New York city. We were kindly and courteously welcomed to the great metropolis by our friend, Morgan L. Bloom, to whom and his accomplished wife we were indebted for many attentions during our four days stay there. We filled up the time pleasantly and profitably by visiting places of instructive interest, attending public convocations of various character, holding interviews with old or new-made friends, and seeing many of the sights of this modern Babylon. A very unusual experience with us was the going to the theater, where we witnessed and heard the admirable play of "Uncle Tom's Cabin" which had been repeated from the same stage more than three hundred times. We also attended the annual meeting of the American Anti-Slavery Society, went to an exhibition of the Five Points Reformatory Mission and to the then far-famed Crystal Palace, finding at each of these places something attractive and morally profitable. We availed ourselves of the opportunity of taking a brief trip to "The North American Phalanx," the Fourierite Community in Monmouth County, N. J., where we were courteously received and hospitably entertained by President Sears and his asssociates — gentlemen and ladies all. We were shown the premises generally, with the buildings and appurtenances thereto belonging, and the different departments of domestic, industrial, social, and educational activity. We were greatly pleased and edified, leaving the place well stored with topics for salutary reflection and practical use.

May 13 we extended our journey to Philadelphia spending the Sabbath in quietude there and devoting Monday to the famous Fairmount Water Works, Laurel Hill Cemetery, and other celebrated localities in and about the city. On the 16th we proceeded through Baltimore to Washington taking rooms at Beers' well-known Temperance Hotel. There we remained four days, dividing our time between the various imposing public buildings, congressional proceedings, and personal interviews with the great champions of freedom then in vigorous conflict with the slave power over the infamous Kansas-Nebraska bill, which was on its final passage in the House— American tyranny thereby driving its triumphal chariot furiously over the forms of its temporarily vanquished opponents. I had brief conversations with Charles Sumner, Joshua R. Giddings, and Gerrit Smith, neither of whom had I met before, and with Thomas Davis of Providence, R. I., a former acquaintance,— all unsuppressable Anti-Slavery members of the National Legislature and worthy of their great reputation.

On Saturday, May 20, we left Washington on our way westward by the Baltimore and Ohio Railroad, whose mighty and amazing constructions awaken wonder and admiration in the minds of all beholders. We stopped over Sunday at Cumberland, Md., resuming our journey early Monday morning and proceeding to Wheeling, Va., where we took a steamer to Cincinnati, Ohio. Arriving there early on Wednesday we were soon conveyed to Spring Garden, a semi-suburban part of the city, and to the residence there of our long-tried, faithful, and estimable friends, Andrew H. Ernst and his wife, Sarah H. (Otis) Ernst, formerly of Boston. This was our objective point and the western limit of our pilgrimage. Mr. and Mrs. Ernst welcomed us with the warmest cordiality to the unstinted hospitality of a home abounding with every convenience and comfort that ample wealth could furnish or appreciative visitors enjoy. Our sojourn lasted eight days, during which we received all the attention that could possibly render it pleasant and memorable. We were taken to numerous places of interest and instruction in and about the city, and introduced to many distinguished and excellent people; in fine, were filled to the brim with experiences and recollections calculated to gladden and enrich a lifetime.

During our stay in Cincinnati, I was exceedingly happy to renew a former slight acquaintance with Rev. Abial Abbot Livermore, pastor of the Unitarian church of the city, and to expand it by two or three delightful interviews. I met him at a Sabbath-school picnic on Saturday, May 27, when he informed me that an arrangement had been made for me to occupy his pulpit the following day. This I accordingly did, gratified as I was at the fraternal courtesy of my clerical brother and with the opportunity of preaching to his people the gospel of a pure and practical Christianity. Such a gospel in essential respects they have from Brother Livermore. For his is an enlightened, liberal, reformatory, Christian soul. He bears faithful testimony against all manner of wickedness in high places and in low places, and in favor of truth, righteousness, and human improvement in all things. He is the author of a valuable

Commentary on the gospels and the two following books of the New Testament, of an excellent Prize Essay on the Mexican War, and of other meritorious works. He was formerly pastor of the Unitarian church in Keene, N. H., and for some twenty years now past has been the able, revered, and beloved president of the Theological School at Meadville, Pa.

We spent a delightful afternoon on Wednesday, May 31, at Rev. Mr. Livermore's with our fellow-travelers, Brother and Sister Ernst, and Rev. Daniel Parker, an old Restorationist and Practical Christian friend from New Richmond, Ohio; and also enjoyed the services and festivities connected with the marriage of one of Brother Ernst's daughters the day following. On Friday morning, June 2, we took leave of our kind and beloved host and hostess, and turned our faces homeward. The former we never met again and the latter only two or three times in her subsequent widowhood. They both with Brother and Sister Draper are at home in the world of spirits, while wife and I survive them until now (Dec. 1889), but must soon rejoin them in the better land.

From Cincinnati we journeyed *via* Cleveland to Buffalo, N. Y., and took lodgings there. The next day, Saturday, we proceeded to Niagara Falls, engaging rooms at the Clifton House on the Canada side, where we were quartered till Monday. Meanwhile we traversed the enchanted country thereabouts and filled our souls with the majestic wonders and glories displayed on every hand, making our stay one ever to be remembered and enjoyed. Thence we went to Queenstown, lingering *en route* for an hour or two at the awful whirlpool, and from Queenstown crossed the then longest suspension bridge in the world to Lewiston, N. Y. Boarding a steamer we sailed across Lake Ontario to Ogdensburg and thence to the semi-antique city of Montreal, passing, as we entered St. Lawrence river, through the midst of the far-famed Thousand Isles and all the loveliness of scenery they enshrine, and, farther on, the fearful rapids, which seemed ready at any moment to engulf our floating palace and all it contained in one common doom. But brave hearts and skilled hands had our fortunes in their keeping, and we all came into quiet waters at length without injury or harm.

At Montreal everything was novel and strange to us—had a decidedly foreign aspect. The style of architecture, the appearance of the streets, the manners and speech of the people, soldiers taking their rounds, Catholic priests in long black robes, Sisters of Charity gliding about, the great cathedral with its ponderous bell, penitential confessions, and spectacular performances before its altars, all told us how unlike ourselves these northern neighbors are and how little we had yet known of the peculiarities and diversities of human life and its manifestations. Leaving Montreal by the Grand Trunk railway, we whirled rapidly through the wild and picturesque landscapes of northern New Hampshire and western Maine, arriving at Portland in the evening of June 9. Thence the next day we journeyed to Boston, spending the night there, and going to our Hopedale home on the 11th, where we received most cordial greetings from all our relatives and friends. We had been gone thirty-three days and had been greatly favored and blessed in all our wanderings and visitations. We returned glad and grateful that we had been preserved from all harmful casualties and had found refreshing and new life to both body and spirit. All were well and prosperous in our beloved dale, and we at once resumed the places and duties to which we were accustomed and from which we took leave of absence more than a month before.

The year upon which this pilgrimage was made, 1854, was the palmiest in the history of the Hopedale Community. It throve in all its departments, operations, and interests. Materially, socially, and religiously, its progress was most satisfactory. It was much the same through the succeeding year, 1855; no serious reverses or drawbacks occurring to diminish the fruit of our labors in any field of effort, to awaken distrust of the success of our undertaking, or chill the ardor of our fondest hopes. So well assured were we of the soundness of our position as Christian Socialists and of the not far distant triumph of our cause that a re-awakened interest was generated in the subject of founding new communities in the virgin territory of some of the western states, and steps were taken looking to the practical realization of the involved idea and purpose. Offers of a domain of considerable size were made us by a gentleman in Wisconsin who had been converted to the doctrine of social reconstruction by my writings (though not fully to Christian Non-resistance), and who was desirous of having that doctrine put to the test of practical experiment in his vicinity with himself as a coadjutor. Numerous articles appeared in the *Practical Christian*, mostly over the signature of Brother Wm. H. Fish, urging a movement in the same behalf on general principles, without indicating any particular locality, and calling for the names of persons ready to enlist in it. As a result of this renewed agitation of the matter, several of our own Hopedale brethren left home in the autumn of 1855 for the definite purpose of securing lands and taking the initiatory steps towards the realization of the object which commended itself to so many minds and which now seemed near achievement. Their objective point was the state of Minnesota, then rapidly filling up with new settlers, as offering the most advantages for the proposed undertaking. A series of unavoidable misfortunes prevented them from doing anything towards the accomplishment of their purpose until the following spring, when lands were secured and a settlement was made. This was done by individuals of the party on their own personal responsibility and in their separate behalf, though with a view of future consolidation and communitization, under one of the forms prescribed in the constitution of the Practical Christian Republic. This, however, never came to pass. Events that were even then ripening to a disastrous culmination at Hopedale, as will soon be narrated, not only put an end to all efforts in that direction, but postponed the whole great question of social regeneration and the work of building up on the earth a new and divine order of human society according to the New Testament ideal, to an indefinite future.

While these things were transpiring, I was devoting my time and energy to the advancement of the principles and cause I held dear, at home and abroad, wherever I could get a hearing. Rarely, if ever, did a Sunday pass by when I was not engaged in two or three religious services and rarely a week in which I did not lecture upon some theme pertaining to some one of the great reforms with which I had become identified and to the bettering of the condition of my fellowmen. Many were the localities I visited in Massachusetts, Rhode Island, and Connecticut, as fields of missionary labor for one or several days at a time; some of them regularly and others as mutual convenience would permit. In June, 1855, I spent ten days at Mystic, Ct., by invitation of Rev. S. S. Griswold, a Seventh-day Baptist minister of catholic spirit, preaching and lecturing there and in the vicinity with scarcely an intermitting day. In October I journeyed as far away as Pennsylvania and New York on a distinctively missionary tour which was made memorable by interviews with two or three distinguished personages of that period of American history. I first went to Philadelphia where I visited Passamore Williamson, a devoted Abolitionist, arbitrarily incarcerated in Moyamensing prison for alleged contempt of court in refusing to testify against certain fugitive slaves, of whose experiences he was accused of being conversant. He was in good spirits and in no wise humiliated or intimidated by his pro-slavery assailants and persecutors. I also by invitation dined one day with the celebrated Professor Robert Hare, a recent convert from stiff, scientific scepticism to modern Spiritualism and faith in immortality. He was kind, polite, affable, and we naturally fell into a friendly conversation upon the subject to which both of us had given considerable attention. It was only good manners for me to allow him to lead off in the talk, to assent to his views when I could, and to dissent, when I must, with all the deference my conscience would allow. He was honestly blunt in contemning Moses and the prominent Old Testament characters generally, as unprincipled and cruel, Christ and His Apostles as foolish and impracticable enthusiasts, and all the alleged spirit manifestations of the past as unreliable and of little or no account. But those of the present day, he claimed, are scientifically demonstrated to be true and so worthy of hearty acceptance. The reader can judge how his assertions and animadversions struck me. He was a Spiritualist, as I was, but of a very different type from myself. I puzzled him with some Socratic questions which he failed to answer to my satisfaction. All passed off pleasantly and we parted courteously.

After a four days' sojourn in Philadelphia, where I addressed public audiences some half a dozen times, I went *via* New York city and Albany to central New York, visiting my old, honored, and beloved friend and brother, Rev. Samuel J. May, at Syracuse. I remained with him over the Sabbath, preaching to his people in the morning and giving them a lecture on Christian Nonresistance in the evening. The day following I made a detour to Peterborough for the purpose of calling upon the distinguished reformer and philanthropist, Gerritt Smith, who kindly welcomed me to his commodious and hospitable mansion. I found him, true to his reputation, a man of dignified personal presence, thoroughly educated and devoutly religious, a devoted moral and political reformer, the heir to a princely estate, eminently charitable to the poor, a generous donor to public institutions, an outspoken friend of the suffering classes, a liberal entertainer of thousands, with wife and children to match. The special object of my visit was to solicit a loan or donation in aid of our Practical Christian Republic, having then in prospect the purchase of new Community domains.

He listened to the presentation of my case and appeal respectfully and kindly, but all his disposable funds were at that time pledged to other important objects of a humanitarian character, chief among which was the endowment of a university wherein should be taught his own peculiar views of "Righteous Civil Government," one of his leading hobbies. Hence all he could give to my movement was five dollars. I thanked him and left somewhat disappointed, though I had undertaken this suit rather on other people's judgment and faith than my own. Experience, not in this case only but generally, has taught me that rich people must not be expected, much less depended upon, to contribute largely to the building up of such a kingdom of God on the earth as is proposed in my Practical Christian Socialism. I soon after returned to my Hopedale home to prosecute the labors devolving upon me nearer at hand, and to share at an early day the bitter disappointment and grief resulting from the utter wreck of the most sacred hopes of my life, all the more bitter and crushing because so sudden and undreamed of when it occurred.

The Fatal Crisis. As I have already stated, the affairs of the Community were apparently in a highly prosperous and encouraging condition through the years 1854 and 1855, and I flattered myself with the idea that all was well for the future beyond doubt or peradventure. So I felt when we convened in annual meeting Jan. 9, 1856. The financial statement of the treasurer was not ready in all its details, but the general declaration was made by him that the joint stock operations had suffered no detriment and that the industrial and financial outlook was bright and encouraging. I was greatly pleased with this assurance and my gratification was enhanced by the concluding sentences of the address of our president, Brother Ebenezer D. Draper, as follows:

"We may rejoice together in considering the degree of harmony that exists at the present time in our Community; greater, I think, than ever before. And I hope and believe that with our past experience and present advantages, we shall continue to increase in love and wisdom and so become more and more a light to those around us, proving to the world that Christian Socialism opens a more excellent way in which men may live together as brethren, and that it gives us, as it will all who yield to its saving power, peace and good will to one another and to the whole human race. May the good God prosper and bless us all."

After such an assuring benediction, which set the bells of gladness ringing in all our hearts, what but a thunder clap from a clear sky could fill us with greater consternation than the announcement of the same president, only six weeks later, that the financial condition of the Community was so desperate and hopeless that he and his brother, George Draper, had decided to withdraw their investments from the joint stock capital. What had happened to cause such a reversal of the representation made at the annual meeting? We were then told that the deficit in the entire operations of the previous year was only $146.15 — an insignificant sum. But a more critical examination of monetary affairs disclosed the fact that the 4 per cent. dividends due to the joint stock had not been reckoned, and that the natural depreciation in the value of buildings, machinery, etc., had also been overlooked; which, with sundry other omissions, made our actual loss some ten or twelve thousand dollars — an ominous and, as was thought, insurmountable burden!

As soon as this state of things became known, a Community meeting was called and continued by adjournment through several sessions. Earnest and pungent discussions were carried on, and the feelings of many members were greatly disturbed. If there were blame anywhere in the management, it was found difficult to locate it. Evidently there had been lack of business ability or gross neglect somewhere, and, failing to discover where it was, it was natural and easy to attribute it to the system, and this was the culminating accusation. In making it, the lead was taken by George Draper who had been with us but two years, and who, from the beginning, had only dubious faith in Community life. He was a natural born man of the world, given to money-making, impatient of high ideals, but thoroughly honest in his opinions, upright in his dealings, and of unquestioned integrity and honor. He was moreover inflexible of will and purpose, and when once determined upon an object, he pursued it without hesitation or prevarication. So thoroughly persuaded was he in his own mind that our socialistic scheme was impracticable and the cause of all our troubles, and so persistent was he in attempting to bring his brother, our president, with whom he was closely associated in business, over to the same conclusion, that he at length, though with much difficulty, succeeded. This accomplished, the doom of the Community was irrevocably sealed.

Our fate was in the hands of these two men. They were in possession of three-fourths of the joint stock, and the withdrawal of their share would so cripple our movement financially, that it would be absolutely impossible for it to go on. The rest of us were poor, having no means to purchase their interest in the property, and though our credit was good and might have been used to meet the emergency, to have so used it would have been fool-hardy and perilous — would have been to load ourselves with a burden which all could see would not only crush us to the earth but defraud those who might befriend and help us. This therefore was not to be thought of for a moment. The only alternative was to yield to the inevitable and make the best of it.

As soon as this was settled in my mind, my first care was to see to it that in the final adjustment of affairs with the Draper brothers, provision should be made for the full payment, principal and interest, of all just demands against the Community. This was accordingly done, to the satisfaction of all parties, and no creditor of ours ever lost a dollar by his confidence in us. Then there came under my general direction and by my hand a radical change in our Community constitution, whereby our industrial arrangements were all abolished, our real and movable property was made over to the proper claimants or otherwise disposed of, and the organization itself reduced to the form of a religious society — a mere shadow of its former self. This being accomplished, many members withdrew and went to localities more favorable to self-support or to the realization of their best purposes in life for themselves, their families, and their fellow-men, while new comers multiplied as convenience, business interests, or general worldly considerations, influenced them. But never afterward did a single person settle in Hopedale from any regard to its original moral, social, and religious principles, spirit, purpose, and aim.

My distress and mortification at this issue of our Community enterprise — at this overthrow of my most cherished hopes and plans for the regeneration and progress of individual and social humanity, were inexpressible — almost unendurable. I felt like one prematurely consigned to a tomb. My darling expectations were blasted, my noblest ambition was crushed. I had been disappointed and deserted before, yet I could fall back on remaining resources sufficient to sustain me and urge me forward in my work. But now my calamity was greater than ever — overwhelming and irreparable. Nothing remained but to submit with the best grace possible to a deplorable failure, and in after years to search out the errors and mistakes which had caused it, and, having found them, to maké such record of them as should render them serviceable as admonitions and warnings to philanthropists and social reformers in coming generations. This I resolved to do, and by the preserving and helping mercy of God, have lived to accomplish it, as witnesseth my "*History of the Hopedale Community*" and my third volume of "*Primitive Christianity*;" both of which works I leave in manuscript for my successors to publish and give to the world.

While the occurrences just narrated were taking place, but before any serious results were apprehended, I became involved, much to my subsequent discomfort, in an undertaking of a more secular nature though not disconnected with our Community system. Hoping to strengthen our common bond of union and aid the common cause, as well as to secure better employment for a portion of our members not adequately provided for in that particular, I devised a plan for the formation of what was called a *Commune* within the pale of our general jurisdiction. This new body was to have certain specified franchises and privileges of its own for the associate use of those disposed to join it in the management of such kinds of industry as might by common consent be established. The plan received the sanction of the parent body, signatures to its compact or constitution were obtained, and *Commune No. 1* was organized and equipped for its designed work. It embraced some half a dozen members and their families, mine included. In order that the venture might be well inaugurated, I accepted its presidency and fathered its financial obligations. Two or three kinds of business were begun, chiefest of which was the manufacture of a patent tackle block for the lifting of heavy bodies in warehouses and on board vessels. Our required financial output exceeded our calculations and available resources, and we found ourselves at the start heavily burdened with debt. Just as we were getting under tolerable headway, though our principal article of production did not find the market we anticipated, the Community crisis burst upon us, producing confusion in our ranks and in our arrangements; and our infant Commune was strangled in its cradle. The upshot of the whole matter was that I had to shoulder a large percentage of the incurred liabilities, which in due time were honorably met and cancelled; though it was many years before I outgrew all the losses sustained by this fruitless effort to help some of my less fortunate associates. So it was that another of my favorite projects vanished before my eyes.

The Hopedale Community, though it had been transformed into a mere religious body, still bore its old name, retained a few nominal guaranties against ignorance, poverty, and vice, and struggled on in its dismantled state as best it could. It kept up its public and social meetings with a good degree of regularity and zeal, and even its quarterly convocations for a time. Its declaration of principles remained unchanged, and some flickering hopes that possibly it might be resurrected lingered in the breasts of its more devoted friends. Its educational activities were not permitted to languish, but its membership diminished, residents uncommitted to anything it had formerly stood for were peopling its surrendered domain, and it had no recognized part or lot in promoting the growing industrial prosperity of the village whose foundations it had laid in toil and 'tears. If its missionaries went abroad to proclaim the gospel hitherto represented by it, their words were shorn of much of their power by reporting the failure of their efforts to actualize that gospel in the manifold relations of life at home.

Personally, I was hedged in on every side by circumstances that I could neither destroy, overcome, nor escape. I could not go back on my record so long as I was unconvinced that I had been in the wrong, nor could I cease from my ministrations in behalf of what, notwithstanding all disappointments and failures, I still believed with all my heart was true and right. I must go forward in the same course as before, not utterly cast down but upheld by an invisible guardianship which has never forsaken me.

Arrangements were made whereby I came into entire control of the *Practical Christian*, assuming all the pecuniary responsibility of its publication, and conducting its editorial department essentially on the lines previously followed and in such a manner as in my judgment would most effectually serve my Maker and my kind. Funerals and weddings distributed over a wide extent of territory and occurring with unabated frequency, still commanded considerable of my time and attention, while calls and opportunities for preaching and lecturing on Sunday and during the week came from far and near, leaving me no time for idleness or ennui. I was still devoted to all the great reforms of the age and stood ready to champion them on moral and religious grounds, although the Hopedale apostacy had cut the nerve of my missionary zeal in behalf of Christian Socialism — the one great comprehensive reform which included all the rest. I found ample field for the expenditure of whatever ability I could command in expounding the distinctive characteristics of pure and undefiled religion, in showing their applicability to all human affairs in individual and social life, and in urging them upon the attention and acceptance of those who would listen to my appeals — thus broadcasting the seed which should in some coming day yield a harvest of good both in an improved personal character and in a higher order of society. If I could not attain to all I had calculated upon and striven after for so many years, I trusted that somehow or other in the economy of God I could be a sort of modern John the Baptist, preparing the way for a better future and making ready for the coming of the divine kingdom, perhaps after my earthly labors were over.

Moreover, in those days my views upon Spiritualism were in good demand and I was always ready to give a reason for the faith and hope that were in me upon that subject, endeavoring to set it forth and defend it on rational and scriptural grounds and so to save it, if possible, from over-credulity, which encouraged fraud and humbuggery on the one hand, and from anti-Christian and super-Christian radicalism on the other, which was equally hostile to what I deemed the truth and equally offensive to me. The readiness with which some people swallowed without discrimination whatever assumed to be a revelation from the spirit world was hardly less unreasonable and deplorable than the flippancy and irreverence with which others ignored the claims of pure Christianity and scorned to recognize the beauty, power, and glory of the principles and precepts of the religion of the New Testament.

It may not be out of place to note in this connection an interview I had in the autumn of 1856 with Rev.

T. L. Harris, a sometime Universalist minister, but for many years a Spiritualistic seer and lecturer of wide repute, and the founder of a Community of Spiritualists at Mountain Cove, Va. It occurred during a six days' preaching and lecturing visit I made with my wife to the town of Southold, Long Island, upon invitation of friend Joseph H. Goldsmith, whose acquaintance I formed during my brief pastorate in New York city twenty-eight years before. His father, Zaccheus Goldsmith, was an intelligent, upright, noble-minded man, a Christian philanthropist, and an earnest Abolitionist as early as 1795. The son had imbibed most of the same spirit and was ready to welcome my views upon religious, moral, and social theories and to aid me in promulgating them in his general neighborhood. At the time of the visit spoken of, Mr. Harris was boarding with a Mr. Richmond a few miles away, who asked us to spend an afternoon at his house that we might see the widely known prophet of the new dispensation. It was a deeply interesting and enjoyable occasion. The most memorable incident of it was the description of a vision seen by Brother Harris, which, aside from its poetic beauty, was sublimely grand and holy, and agreed so closely with my highest aspirations, convictions, and inspirations, that I could but accept it as substantially true. The interview gave me unqualified satisfaction, and I returned to my Hopedale home greatly strengthened, encouraged, and blessed. Events from 1858 onward will constitute the subject matter of another chapter.

CHAPTER XXI.

1858–1862.

PERSONAL LABORS — THE BIBLE — HOPEDALE CHURCH — JOHN BROWN — COMMENTARY — CLOSE OF PASTORAL LABORS — COMMUNITY AFFAIRS — DISCUSSION.

THERE is little to be said concerning Community affairs during the four years whose transactions and experiences the present chapter purports to put on record. The sanguine hearts of its disappointed devotees still clung to the dubious hope that it might be made a rudimental seminary for preparing men and women to be founders and co-operators of more permanent movements elsewhere, the character and purpose of which should be similar to what its own originally were. Its regular weekly, monthly, quarterly, and yearly meetings were continued in vigorous activity, and its semi-monthly organ, the *Practical Christian*, went its regular round as in former days. Its promulgatory publications and other instrumentalities for reaching and enlightening the public mind upon the great moral and religious truths and duties which it still represented were not suffered to decline, while its common and higher grade schools were reputably sustained under teachers of its own rearing.

The Hopedale Home School, though a private enterprise, reflected honor upon its proprietary principals, patrons, and the Community under whose approving auspices it was originally started. It was established and first opened to pupils in the spring of 1855 by Morgan L. Bloom and wife from the city of New York, but a year later passed into the hands of my son-in-law, Rev. Wm. S. Heywood, and his wife, Abbie B. Heywood, whose management rendered it eminently serviceable in its proper educational field to many youthful aspirants of Hopedale and vicinity, and to the children of progressive and reformatory families in other and sometimes far distant localities. It was in operation some seven or eight years, acquiring an enviable reputation for scholarship and moral standing and leaving behind it, when it came to be closed, a fragrant and enduring memory.

My labors during the year 1858 were expended mostly near home. On twenty Sundays I ministered in Hopedale; on twenty-three in Milford by special arrangement with a society of Spiritualists there; the other nine in places more or less distant where I had friends desirous of hearing me. My themes of discourse were generally drawn from my favorite field of Practical Christianity, though a considerable number of them pertained to some phase of the subject of Spiritualism, there being then a large demand for utterances of that sort. But my kind of Spiritualism in no wise conflicted with my theological and ethical system, long well known to those familiar with my preaching and writings. I never allowed my views upon any one great topic belonging to the realm of truth and duty to contradict or undermine those I entertained upon any other. And there was a corresponding harmony and consistency in all my testimonies. Christ, as the great teacher of truth, righteousness, and love—the Prince of Peace, never resisting evil with evil but overcoming it with good — was always the central figure on my banner, and I always abjured all carnal weapons as instruments or agencies for building up the kingdom of heaven on the earth, many distinguished personages to the contrary notwithstanding.

Views upon the Bible. About this time an unusual interest was awakened in our populous town of Milford and vicinity upon the subject of the inspiration and authority of the Hebrew and Christian scriptures. It was the result of certain bold discussions and criticisms which were started and continued for some time in a series of meetings instituted by an association formed for the purpose of examining the claims of those writings and matters akin thereto. Several Spiritualistic lectures, treating more or less freely and iconoclastically the sacred volume, increased the popular feeling. The Milford Bible Society, to counteract what its members thought to be the harmful tendency of these public utterances, inaugurated a course of Sunday evening lectures to be given at the town hall by able clergymen in defence of the so-called doctrine of Plenary Inspiration. In the midst of the prevailing excitement, *pro* and *con*, I was called upon for a presentation of my views upon the book in question, which were understood to differ somewhat from any of those that had been advocated and urged upon the attention of the public.

In answer to this call I prepared with much care and comprehensiveness an address which I delivered to a very large and deeply attentive audience in the town hall on the evening of Sunday, Jan. 16, 1859. It was entitled "The Inspiration of the Bible." It was received with more favor than I could reasonably have expected under the circumstances and seemed to meet a general want in the community. Its publication was earnestly solicited, in response to which a large edition was issued and a wide circulation secured.

In order to give my present readers some definite idea of the ground I took, defended, and illustrated in that discourse, I present herewith a liberal extract from the pages of the published pamphlet. After distributing the general mass of the professed friends and admirers of the book into five different groups under a system of classification distinctively my own, I proceeded as follows:

"I must differ more or less from all these specified classes and offer you views not in entire accord with any of them. For many years I have believed that the fundamental principles of the bible are absolutely divine, but that its explicative ideas and language are properly human. To explain, justify, and illustrate this view is the principal design of the present lecture.

"What do I mean by the phrase 'fundamental principles of

the bible?' To answer this question I must state definitely my general estimate and appreciation of the Bible. I hold that its essential excellence is solely of a spiritual and religious nature. It sets forth, commends, and insists on certain great spiritual and religious truths and certain great spiritual and religious duties which are indispensable to human well-being and happiness in both the present and future states of existence. These great truths man must receive into his understanding either by knowledge or faith, and cherish them in his soul with a profound love and loyalty or he cannot be eminently and permanently blest. Also, on the basis of these same truths he must perform and habitually practice the corresponding spiritual and religious duties or he can never be eminently and permanently blest. These truths and duties are the fundamental principles of the bible.

"The bible is not to be regarded as an encyclopedia of universal knowledge. It is not of authority in the physical sciences. We are not to consult its pages to learn astronomy, geology, chemistry, anatomy, natural history, physiology, agriculture, etc. These we can study better elsewhere. Nor are we to go to the bible to acquire a knowledge of mathematics, logic, grammar, music, statuary, painting, etc. It settles no questions of such a nature. Casually, incidentally, and fragmentarily, it affords us somewhat that may be of service to us in those departments of inquiry, but nothing authoritatively important. Its grand object, use, and excellence are purely of a spiritual and religious character. We are to go to it as spiritual and religious beings to obtain help in the knowledge and practical application of the fundamental principles of true religion. In respect to these, it is of inestimable value, because all the physical and merely intellectual knowledges in the universe, if we were masters of them, would be insufficient to render us eminently and permanently holy and happy; whereas, these essentials of true religion would do so with or without much proficiency in the things of the physical and intellectual life.

"Next, what do I mean when I assert that 'the explicative ideas and language of the bible are properly human?' I mean that there is a radical difference between its fundamental principles and the forms of speech in which they are expressed and made intelligible to the human mind. Every essential principle of religious truth and duty existed before the bible was written; yes, before it was revealed to the understanding of man. It existed intrinsically from eternity and will exist to eternity, independently of all human knowledges, ideas, and writings. God himself is from and to eternity the same, whether known or unknown by His creatures; so are the great principles of true religion. The bible did not originate them. They do not depend on the bible, but the bible depends on them. They emanated from and are co-eternal with God. If the bible had never existed, they would exist; if every copy of the bible were annihilated, not a particle of those divine essentials would cease to be. By some means they became known to the writers of the bible and were therein recorded. Thus they became known to millions more. I hold that those who first had knowledge of them obtained it by divine revelations and inspirations. How did God give them these revelations and inspirations? This is purported to have been done in several ways:

" (1) Through angels and spirits; by sensible manifestations and communications, oracular voices, signs, and tokens.

" (2) Through the opened spiritual senses of persons in visions, dreams, and trances.

" (3) Through strong impressions, suggestions, and convictions, divinely produced upon the soul.

" (4) Through special divine quickenings and intensified activities of the intuitive, rational, and religious faculties.

" (5) Through that common and universal influx from the unseen world which operates more or less on all moral agents according to their various degrees of susceptibility.

"Now let us consider certain facts necessarily attendant upon all divine revelations and inspirations.

" (1) They were not mentioned in any book of the bible till after they had taken place. They came to pass and were recorded some time, sooner or later, afterwards.

" (2) They were given to *human beings* and had to be adapted to their finite capacity and comprehension. It was impossible in the nature of things to make mankind fully understand and comprehend them at once, in all their bearings, whether receiving them at first or second hand.

" (3) They were given at particular times, and not equally at all times. Angels and spirits did not come frequently and regularly. Oracles, signs, tokens, visions, dreams, trances, strong impressions, and high inspirations, occurred only on special occasions, and at divinely-appointed seasons. Prophets, sages, and apostles, were wonderfully illumined for a while and then left to themselves. Some who were heavenly-minded and wise under certain circumstances, were, under others, carnally-minded, sensual and foolish. For instance, Solomon.

" (4) After receiving divine revelations and inspirations, so as to see and partially comprehend central facts and fundamental principles, the patriarchs, prophets, and inspirees exercised their own powers of thought and judgment as to

BETWEEN TWO EXTREMES. 413

details and clothed essentials more or less with explicative ideas which were after the manner of men. Thus the absolutely divine became clothed with human habiliments and sometimes obscured by error.

" (5) When the bible inspirees came to express and record their experiences, it could be done only in human speech. God never invented a peculiar language to be exclusively used in the bible. The Hebrew, Chaldaic, and Greek, used to record the divine revelations and inspirations of the Old and New Testaments, were substantially the same inside and outside the sacred volume. They had to be such as the people, whose instruction was designed, could understand.

" (6) Many ideas, opinions, sentiments, and particulars, which appear in connection with the fundamentals of the bible, were obviously written by prophets, legislators, kings, priests, apostles, and evangelists, simply from their own minds — not from absolutely divine inspiration.

" Such are my general views of the subject and I am confident I can fully sustain them by adequate proofs and illustrations."

These extracts will indicate where I then stood and where I still stand in my reverence for the Hebrew and Christian scriptures; between the Plenary Inspirationists on the one hand and the sweeping deniers of its divine authority on the other. Of the latter there were in those days several varieties, some of whom stood in the high places of religious, moral, and philanthropic reform. I did not question the sincerity of such, but I did question their knowledge, judgment, and inevitable influence. Of one thing I was certain that the leaven of their doctrines was a fatal poison to the Practical Christianity and to the new social order I desired to build up, inasmuch as whoever received these doctrines became straightway his own lord and master — an individual sovereign and hence incapable of co-operating harmoniously with others in the reconstruction of society and the establishment of the kingdom of God on the earth. I therefore withstood and protested against all such denials of bible authority, as the files of the *Practical Christian* abundantly show.

Among the pleasant memories of those days is that of a visit from our highly esteemed friend and sympathizer in every good word and work, John Child of Philadelphia.

I became acquainted with him and his estimable wife, Rachel, in 1846, when I first shared the hospitality of their delightful home. They were Hicksite friends in religious conviction and association, largely philanthropic and eminently intelligent, upright, and noble hearted. Rachel had departed to her heavenly mansion and her venerable survivor cheered and gladdened us, as stated, in the summer of 1858.

Another happy event, the flavor of which still lingers in our hearts, was a reception given us by our Milford friends to whom I was then ministering regularly twice a month, with the concurrence of a few Hopedalians, in our home chapel early the following spring. It was a simple, unpretentious occasion, but rich and fragrant in all that renders such gatherings valuable. Its material, moral, and social components were excellent and were accompanied by substantial and abiding tokens of respect, affection, and gratitude, of which both myself and wife were appreciative recipients.

The Hopedale Community, with its environing population, fell away from the high moral level formerly maintained and slowly descended the plane which inclined towards the old social state — a retrogression to which it was doomed by the revolution of 1856. The village it had founded amid toil and trial prospered externally under the control of its temporal lords, with many demonstrations of successful business enterprise. But the personally religious life of the people as manifestly declined, notwithstanding the maintenance of the usual appointments of public instruction and worship, and this decline prompted a few of the more spiritually minded and zealous of our number to propose the formation of a church, distinctively so-called. The proposition met with considerable favor and an organization with appropriate covenant, declaration of principles, and rules of discipline was effected Jan. 29, 1860; impressive ceremonies giving importance and sanctity to the event.

The new movement started out favorably and promised success, but predominating influences were against it.

Many prominent reformers and progressives, disgusted by the hostility of the church *as it was* to all philanthropic activities, had come to distrust and condemn all religious bodies as such, and hold them in great disesteem. This leaven had pervaded Hopedale to a considerable extent and was a potent though silent obstacle to the growth and prosperity of the new association. Moreover, the animating spirit of the place was more ambitious to obtain wealth and worldly distinction than it was to gain "the kingdom of God and his righteousness." Under these circumstances "The Practical Christian Church in Hopedale" died an early death. Other instrumentalities for the special promotion of personal religion languished and finally ceased to be, the weekly Sunday-school and service of public worship only remaining as permanent institutions of faith and piety.

On the 13th of February, 1860, my devoted friend mentioned in a former chapter in connection with our visit to Cincinnati in 1854, Mr. Andrew H. Ernst, departed this life at his beautiful home at Spring Garden in that city in the 65th year of his age. He was born in Korningen, Germany, came to this country when a young man, and distinguished himself by remarkable intelligence, enterprise, and noble-minded characteristics. He was in religious faith an ardent Restorationist and made himself known to me soon after I started the *Independent Messenger* in 1831 as a cordial sympathizer and patron, remaining my steadfast and generous Christian friend as long as he lived. His second wife, whom he left a heart-stricken widow, stood in the same kindly relation to me for many years.

Rev. Samuel Henry of Thorndike, Mass., died March 17 of the same year. Not rich in earthly goods, he yet was rich in the wealth of Practical Christianity and fruitful in all good works. Originally a Methodist, he became finally an independent Practical Christian — a reformer on all the lines of human regeneration. He was widely known, truly revered, and bore the name of "Father Henry." I had met him on several occasions, carried on frequent correspondence with him, and held him in profound esteem.

The John Brown Raid and its Concomitants. The year of my life on which the events just narrated occurred is memorable for the culmination of the career of the famous John Brown. It is not needful for me to tell who John Brown was, what were his distinguishing characteristics, how he undertook to overthrow the system of American slavery, or what the end to which he came at last. All these things are written in the history of those times and every one is more or less familiar with them. It *is* needful, however, and important as a part of my personal record, that I make note of my own attitude in respect to the foolhardy undertaking by which he fell under condemnation of the judicial authority of the state of Virginia as a capital malefactor and was made to expiate his offence upon the gallows. For the same reason, it is needful and important that I shall speak at some length of the controversy that sprung up between me and certain of my anti-slavery coadjutors on account of their abandonment of their former professed Non-resistant principles in the approval they gave of the course which John Brown pursued and in the eulogies they lavished upon his name and memory.

I was not surprised that the *pro*-war Abolitionists of the country should many of them be roused to vehement laudations of the hero of Harper's Ferry, to fierce denunciation of his captors, and threats of vengeance against all pro-slavery tyrants. But it was hard for me to understand how professing *anti*-war Abolitionists of long standing should so forget or ignore their former protestations against the use of violent means for carrying forward their work and freeing the bondsmen, as to be swept into the same foaming vortex of blood and death. As for me, I remained unmoved, except by sorrow for such a deplorable exhibition of mistaken ambition to promote a good end by evil means, and pity for the sufferer who had rashly plunged into a lion's den. My brethren exclaimed " Behold his religious sincerity, his noble motives, his self-sacrificing devotion to the cause of the oppressed, his matchless heroism in behalf of human rights and liberty! How can you restrain your sympathy and admiration, even if you cannot approve his methods and means! Above all, how can you deprecate and censure his courageous and disinterested acts!" I replied, "Because the great points at issue are not his religious sincerity, his worthy motives, his self-sacrificing devotion to the cause of the slave, or his heroism in behalf of human liberty. These might all be excellent in the abstract, and doubtless were to his own consciousness. But what were his methods, measures, deeds? Were *they* Christian or anti-Christian, right or wrong, good or evil, praiseworthy or reprehensible?" These were the questions I had to settle according to my own judgment when viewed from my own Non-resistent stand-point, and, having settled them, then I had to speak out my honest convictions without fear, favor, or compromise. This I did adversely to the truly great emancipator, and to the disgust of the whole school of red revolutionary Abolitionists as well as to the declared regret of most of my old associates on the anti-slavery platform. But how could I do otherwise without recreancy to my own publicly avowed fundamental principles; — principles dearer to me than mortal praise, earthly advantage, or life itself?

I was solemnly committed and pledged, as were all my fellow-members of the American Anti-Slavery Society, to certain distinctive methods for advancing the cause it was founded to promote, as follows: — " Our principles forbid the doing of evil that good may come and lead us to reject and to entreat the oppressed to reject the use of all carnal weapons for deliverance from bondage; relying solely upon those which are spiritual, and mighty through God to the pulling down of strongholds." *Declaration of Sentiments.* " But the society will never in any way, countenance the oppressed in vindicating their rights by resorting to physical force." — *Art. 111. Constitution.* This is Christian anti-slavery — the kind to which

I had subscribed and considered myself bound by solemn pledges. John Brown publicly repudiated and denounced this kind of anti-slavery — setting it at defiance by resorting to rifles, pikes, and bowie knives — a course of procedure which I abominated, and I spoke, argued, and acted accordingly.

For a long time before the attack upon Harper's Ferry took place the war spirit had been entering more and more into the discussions of the great question of the country, inflaming the public mind and preparing for bloody things to come. Against this aspect of the case I had protested with voice and pen as I had opportunity, though without abating one jot or tittle of my deep seated and ineradicable hostility to the gigantic system of American oppression. My testimonies had called forth numerous criticisms and expostulations from some of my highly esteemed friends, to which I in turn replied. In the midst of the discussion thus inaugurated and carried on, came the startling intelligence of the event referred to and of the discomfiture of the chief actors in it, which increased the prevailing excitement to an intensity unknown before. The raid of Brown occurred on the 17th of Oct. 1859, and on the next Sunday, Oct. 23, a special meeting of the Worcester Co. South Division Anti-Slavery Society was held at Worcester for the purpose of considering and taking action upon the matter. By reason of the recent decease of its president, Effingham L. Capron, I, as first vice president, was called upon to act as moderator of the proceedings. I had no doubt it was intended on the part of its projectors that the meeting should conduce not alone to more active hostility to the slave power, but to the diversion of the society from its hitherto peaceful channels of operation into those of violence and blood, by eulogizing and glorifying John Brown and his daring exploit. I determined to meet this aspect of the case at the outset and put myself on record against the scheme, though I had little hope of preventing its consummation. I did so by introducing a series of resolutions re-affirming the peace principles announced in the original organization of the society and insisting on a faithful adherence thereto. These resolutions I defended and illustrated in several speeches during the day against a considerable array of opponents, among whom several of my old Non-resistant brethren stood conspicuous. Though my arguments could not be answered, I was overborne by numbers, my resolutions being laid upon the table and others passed in their stead almost unanimously. The gist of the adopted ones was contained in the last, to wit: —

"*Resolved*, that as Abolitionists we have no disclaimers, no apologies to offer for the recent attempt of certain anti-slavery men at Harper's Ferry to break the rod of the oppressor by the same means by which our revolutionary fathers secured our national independence. On the contrary, while in the absence of all reliable information we are unable to judge of the wisdom of their measures, we are prompt to avow our cordial sympathy with the spirit and our devout admiration of the heroism of that valiant little band who preferred to die struggling for their country's freedom to living in a land where education is a crime, where marriage and the family relation are trampled in the dust, and where a million women are daily offered in the market for purposes of prostitution."

I contrasted this resolution, when it came to be discussed, with the anti-slavery declaration and constitutional pledge of 1833 and chose to abide by the old platform, leaving the new heroes of the cause to glory in the sword on their own responsibility. But where were my high-professing Non-resistant brethren? Alas, they were shouting with the rest for John Brown and his insurrectionary methods. He had captured them though himself a captive wounded and helpless at the feet of the slave power. Brother Stephen S. Foster at the Worcester meeting and elsewhere could stand shoulder to shoulder with Andrew T. Foss, Charles L. Remond, Thomas W. Higginson, and others, whose voice was still for war, exclaiming, "I am a Non-resistant, but not a fool," and so incite men on to deeds of blood and death. And — must I write it! — even Brother Wm. Lloyd Garrison, the man who penned the declaration and constitution referred to — who penned the "declaration of sentiments" adopted by the Peace Convention of 1838, whence sprang the New England Non-resistant Society — this man became more than an apologist, he became a eulogist of the blood-shedding hero of the Harper's Ferry tragedy.

At a great meeting held in honor of John Brown in Boston on the evening of the day of his execution, Mr. Garrison spoke, as reported without subsequent contradiction, thus :

"Mr. Garrison then paid a tribute to the courage and character of Captain Brown. His mission, the speaker alleged, at Harper's Ferry was peaceful. He did not mean to shed blood. And if he had weapons of war, they were only to be put into the hands of slaves that they might defend themselves in retreating to Canada. 'The men,' he said, 'who decry Brown are dangerous men, the old tories of the Revolution.' He would that we had the spirit of the Revolution that it might make the Commonwealth too hot to hold them. The speaker was a peace man and therefore disarmed John Brown. He was also a Non-resistant, but he was emboldened to say, 'Success to every insurrection against slavery, here and everywhere.' His heart was always with the oppressed, therefore 'Success to revolution.' It was the way to get up to the doctrine of Non-resistance."

Such language did not sound much like what he uttered in September, 1838, viz :

"The history of mankind is crowded with evidences that physical coercion is not adapted to moral regeneration; that the sinful disposition of man can be subdued only by love; that evil can be exterminated from the earth only by good; that it is not safe to rely on an arm of flesh — upon man, whose breath is in his nostrils — to preserve us from harm; that there is great security in being gentle, harmless, long-suffering, and abundant in mercy; that it is only the meek who inherit the earth.

"We advocate no jacobinical doctrines. The spirit of jacobinism is the spirit of retaliation, violence, and murder. It neither fears God nor regards man. We would be filled with the spirit of Christ. If we abide by our principles, it is impossible for us to be disorderly, or plot treason, or participate in any evil work; we shall submit to every ordinance of man for the Lord's sake; obey all the requirements of government,

FIDELITY TO PRINCIPLE VINDICATED.

except such as we deem contrary to the commands of the gospel; and in no wise resist the operation of law, except by meekly submitting to the penalty of disobedience."

In these paragraphs we have the pure doctrine and spirit of Christian Non-resistance. I love it with all my heart. But what concord is there between the sentiments they embody and those of the previously quoted speech? I see none at all. I was therefore grieved and disturbed by the speech, dissenting from it and remonstrating against it in the columns of my paper. My old friend's response was brief and decisive. He had "spoken deliberately" and "had nothing to take back." My "animadversion was uncalled for" and I had "no occasion for being disturbed." Of course I had nothing more to say, but I was in no wise satisfied with his curt rejoinder, having no sympathy whatever with those professed Non-resistants who vied with avowed pro-war men in paying homage to one whom I could regard only as a well-meaning, misguided, unfortunate zealot. So much for the John Brown episode and my position in reference to and controversy with the Abolitionist leaders concerning it. Further details may be found in the columns of the *Practical Christian*, Vol. xx.

But what became of the bellicose John Brown Non-resistants? They gradually declined in numbers from that time on and in a few years essentially disappeared. There was no further use for their kind of peace doctrine and they did nothing to propagate or preserve it. The slaveholders took the insurrection business into their own hands, leaped into the vortex of civil war, and gave these professed peace men the opportunity which many of them seemed to covet of helping on the compulsory abolition of the system of American oppression. Some of them went into the Federal army, others encouraged their sons to enlist, while the more masterly by pen, oratory, and various expedients, urged the war-chariot on its bloody way to victory. And when the victory at length came, they had been converted to the doctrine of the rightfulness of forcible resistance of evil, or to some indefinite conservative peace policy, or to silent indifference upon the whole subject. Scarcely a survivor of the anti-slavery insurrectionary Non-resistants was to be found. Had Jesus Christ and His apostles undertaken to abolish slavery and other evils in the Roman empire by similar means, we should probably never have heard of their doctrine of universal love and good will, nor of them either. Their religion and reformatory methods were of a higher order — "not of this world."

Scripture Commentary. As my peculiar views upon the character and authority of the bible and of Christ, when compared with other religious teachers, ancient and modern, became more widely known through the tract before spoken of and otherwise, I was importuned by some of my warm friends to prepare a commentary on the New Testament scriptures, insisting that such a work would be a valuable contribution to the sacred literature of the world and of great use to multitudes who in all directions were breaking away from the old bibliolatry and seeking some satisfactory interpretation of the early records of the Christian faith. Upon careful deliberation I concluded to assume the task to which they urged me, making due announcement of my determination in the columns of my paper. Pursuant thereto, I commenced the undertaking in the spring of 1858, my "General Introduction" and "Preface to Matthew's Gospel" being published in No. I, vol. xix of the *Practical Christian*, issued May 1 of that year. I continued the work through that volume and far into Vol. xx, when adverse circumstances led me to abandon it, having gone as far with my exposition as the 12th chapter of Matthew, where it came to an abrupt and final termination.

The same circumstances and the generally discouraging aspect of the cause of Practical Christian Socialism occasioned by the growing unrest of the country as it went hurrying on to the great rebellion, led me early in 1860 to advise the discontinuance of the *Practical Christian* at the close of Vol. xx, which would occur the following April. The paper had never been self-supporting pecuniarily, and although it was in that respect in as good condition as ever before, its future prosperity and usefulness were unpromising. The changed condition of things at home in regard to the paramount object for which it was started and the changing condition of things abroad in regard to its distinguishing reformatory principles, seemed to justify the proposed step in the judgment of its more responsible patrons and supporters, and the career of our little semi-monthly sheet came to an honorable close with No. 26, Vol. xx, April 14, 1860. This was a cause of regret to a large number of subscribers, who, whether they could practically accept and live up to all the high moral and social requirements of the publication or not, nevertheless felt that they were founded in the truth and ought to be promulgated as far and wide as possible, as they also felt that they and their families had been greatly benefited by the little visitant and needed its stimulating influence to keep them from falling utterly away from their high ideals of personal and social excellence. A considerable number of letters from different parts of the country expressed a grateful appreciation of the high character and wholesome influence of the *Practical Christian* upon themselves and the community and a sense of loss in the thought that they were to see it no more, together with sentiments of kindly regard for its editor. The press, also, especially the progressive journals, philanthropic and religious, added testimonials of the same general character. Among these was one so unexpected and remarkable in certain ways that I cannot deny myself the satisfaction of giving it in full to my present readers. It was from the pen of Rev. Thomas Whittemore, D. D., editor of the *Trumpet and Universalist Magazine*—the same redoubtable dialectician and antagonist with whom in earlier days I had so often measured swords in the conflict between the Restorationists and ultra Universalists. We had years before buried the last remnants of strife on honorable terms of his own proposing and sealed the same in a friendly and cordial personal interview, and the green grass had already covered the grave. His parting salutation was as follows:

"We deeply regret to learn that the *Practical Christian*, hitherto published by the Hopedale Community and edited by Rev. Adin Ballou, is about to be discontinued.

"We have always felt a love for this publication. We did not agree with every word it uttered, but we found little in it to disapprove. It has done us good and had we obeyed all its precepts we should have been a better man. We still hope the publication may be continued, but if it must be closed, here is a farewell hand to Brother Ballou. By his practical Christianity he has won us over to himself. In the days of the Restorationist controversy, thirty years ago, we were bitter to each other, but the bitterness has all gone from his heart and ours. He believes as he did and we believe as we did; but both have learned the law of love. We both believe the great fact of the restoration of all things, a point on which Brother Ballou has never wavered for a moment.

"One word as to the Hopedale Community. So far as we know, they are a band of brothers and sisters who seek to honor God by good lives. They are good citizens; they live quietly and peaceably, and the Lord blesses them. Often when we have been in Milford, we have desired to visit their houses, but we felt (perhaps more than we ought) that in their sight we were a heretic, and they would not receive us. Never have we had an unkind word from them, however. Perhaps it was a mere suspicion on our part. We will yet go to Hopedale. We should love to live where practical Christianity reigns." *Trumpet of Jan, 28, 1860.*

This generous, whole-souled tribute was copied into the the last number of the *Practical Christian* with the subjoined response: —

"Thank you, Brother Whittemore. You speak good words. They reach our heart. We reciprocate them. Welcome to Hopedale and our humble home always. *Editor Practical Christian.*"

Although this little unpretending sheet — *The Practical Christian* — was suspended at my suggestion and with my hearty consent and approval, yet the consummation of the

PROMULGATION SOCIETY ORGANIZED.   425

act gave me not a little pain. It was a child of my own begetting, born out of a profound, over-mastering love for the truth and for humanity. For twenty years it had been an instrumentality by which I had been able to serve the truth and humanity according to the dictates of my conscience and judgment. It had for that period been a medium through which I could hold communication with my friends scattered abroad and the public at large upon the most important questions that can enlist the attention of the wise and good, and disseminate far and wide those ideas and principles of morals and religion, those views of Christ and Christianity, which I believed and felt to be founded in the nature of things and the will of God, and to be indispensable to the progress, elevation, regeneration, and happiness of mankind. And I had experienced unspeakable comfort and delight in employing it to the ends indicated and in seeing it made serviceable to their accomplishment. How could I give it up without a pang! How could I be denied the satisfaction I had for so long time derived from it and not feel a sense of loss and heaviness of heart!

I tried, however, to keep up good spirits and to hope it was all for the best, to be proved so in due time. To supply the place of the little messenger and keep open communication with the world, as well as to mitigate what I was obliged to confess was a misfortune if not a calamity, I recommended the formation of a society whose office and mission it should be to publish and circulate leaflets, tracts, and other printed matter, in exposition and illustration of the distinctive principles which constituted the basis of our former social experiment, and which, notwithstanding our failure to carry them out to their final practical results in personal life and a new order of society, we still professed to believe in and hold dear. My recommendation was favorably received by a goodly number of my Hopedale friends who were ready to co-operate with me in the proposed plan. A society was accordingly formed and an organization effected, Feb. 6, 1860, which bore the name of

The Practical Christian Promulgation Society. The Hopedale Community made over to it the assets of the *Practical Christian* with certain bequeathed funds, to which special contributions were from time to time added. It went on prosperously for a few years, was instrumental in distributing a considerable amount of wholesome literature, most of which was the production of my pen, for I could not give up the idea of keeping the doctrines and ideas for which I had done so much before the world, but it at length lapsed into a moribund state and finally died out and was numbered with its predecessors.

An event of much importance in the history of Hope dale during the year 1860 was the erection of a new house of public worship of respectable dimensions and many conveniences on an eligible lot which in early Community days had been set apart for the purpose. The structure was completed in the autumn and dedicated with appropriate exercises on the 15th of November. Two sessions were held with a crowded auditorium during the day, Brother Wm. S. Heywood preaching from the first great command in the morning, emphasizing the value and importance of piety, and I from the second in the afternoon, urging the value and claims of morality and philanthrophy as essentials of a true personal character and of a perfect order of society. A third service was held in the evening at which there was a good attendance with exercises of an informal and miscellaneous character. There was no lowering of the standard of a true Practical Christianity in the utterances of the occasion and no discordant notes marred the harmony of its proceedings. Besides our own home speakers, clerical and lay, who participated in the exercises during the day or evening, were Revs. John Boyden of Woonsocket, R. I., Samuel May of Leicester, Robert Hassall of Haverhill, and George Hill of Milford, our near neighbor. Our beloved Joshua Hutchinson of Milford, N. H., the sweet singer of the notable "Hutchinson Family," had charge of the music and took part in it, charming his auditors with his delightful strains. It was a day long to be remembered.

A remarkable spiritual seance at which I was present was held about this time at the house of my old friend, George W. Burnham of Willimantic, Ct., whither I had gone on one of my incidental preaching excursions. There were some twenty or twenty-five reliable witnesses to the singular phenomena, the most striking of which occurred in connection with a little girl medium only nine years of age. She was seated in front of a heavy cooking stove, upon which she rested the tips of her fingers. Questions both audible and mental were put to what purported to be disembodied spirits, all of which were answered promptly and intelligently and to the astonishment and satisfaction of the entire company by the raising and lowering of a portion of the stove nearest to her, which came down with a thud sometimes that jarred the house. A skeptical friend, an educated professional gentleman to whom I related this experience, said that while he did not doubt my conscientious veracity, he was sure I must have been deceived, for such alleged phenomena were flatly contrary to the laws of nature and therefore impossible. Yet I knew them to be genuine realities beyond all doubt or peradventure. Nature has many grades of expression and all her laws are not in schoolbooks nor in libraries of the literati. Whatever may be true of spiritualistic credulity, materialistic assumption and incredulity often outmatch it. I know how to estimate and eschew both.

In the autumn of 1860, after unprecedented excitement that convulsed the nation from center to circumference, Abraham Lincoln was elected president of the United States on a platform that pledged him and his party to a firm, unfaltering resistance to the aggressions of the slave power hitherto unchecked and defiant of justice and the fundamental principles of a republican form of government. The public mind continued to be greatly agitated even after the election was over, and greatly confused in regard to the nature and extent of those aggressions and what was to be done by the victors now that they had gained the ascendancy. In order to throw some light upon the vexed problem and clear the airs of the fogs and vapors that bedimmed them, I prepared a lecture entitled "Violations of the Federal Constitution in the Irrepressible Conflict between the Pro-slavery and Anti-slavery Portions of the American People," which I delivered many times to large and deeply interested audiences and which was afterwards printed and circulated very generally throughout the community.

I also during the same autumn held two public discussions with the celebrated Second Adventist, Miles Grant,— one at Holden, which continued through five sessions of three hours each, and one at Worcester where there were four sessions of three hours each. The question debated at the first was "Has man an immortal entity?" I taking the affirmative and my opponent the negative sides respectively. At the second, the question in dispute took the following form: "*Resolved*, that immortality is a gift from God dependent on character," the order of discussion being reversed. Proper decorum prevailed on both occasions, large audiences were present, and a lively interest was manifested in the arguments presented. The doctrine advocated by Elder Grant was that man has no undying element in his native constitution, all human beings becoming utterly unconscious at death; that all will be restored to consciousness at the general resurrection, when God will render the righteous immortal by special gift and annihilate the wicked by what is termed "the second death." The doctrine I maintained was that the human soul is by nature immortal; that at physical death all human beings enter a state of moral discipline suited to their different characters; and that all will be raised through successive stages of regeneration to final holiness and happiness. The debate was conducted throughout in a mutually amicable temper and my antagonist complimented me as the fairest and most agreeable opponent he had ever met. As usual, both parties claimed the victory in the argument and retired self-satisfied.

Time went on. The mutterings of coming war were heard in the distant Southland, and near at hand were there declarations and pledges of resistance to the uttermost should violent measures be inaugurated. The shattered ark of the covenant of our fathers was approaching new perils which would try it as never before. At length the outbreak came. Rebellion raised a bloody hand against the Republic and must be met. Political and martial patriotism was ringing ardent appeals in all directions and Christian Non-resistance seemed to some minds akin to passive treason. Still the majority of our members were loyal to our original standard and clung to the hull of their half-wrecked social ship. They tried to stop its leaks and keep it afloat for some possible future use. But no expedient could avail to prevent downward tendencies and open withdrawals from our ranks. On the 9th of June, 1861, Brother George Draper, one of our most influential associates, sent to the recorder of the Community a letter resigning his membership, "having become satisfied," as he says, "that I am not in spirit or feeling or practice or purpose a Non-resistant." Yet he expressed a desire to do all he could to perpetuate what he believed Hopedale to have been and to be, "the most desirable village to live in on earth." He did not denounce the principles on which Hopedale was founded and by which it had been made what it was as wrong, but as "impracticable under existing circumstances." A great crisis had arisen in the country and it could be successfully met only by resorting to the sword. Several other members shared his sentiments and followed his example. Others left us for other reasons, reducing our numbers to less than fifty persons, who remained faithful to their ideals and determined to die an honest death when their hour should come.

In the spring of the year upon which the civil war broke out, a society of what were termed Rational Spiritualists was organized in Milford for the purpose of establishing regular Sunday services, a Sabbath-school, and other activities conducive to the moral and religious edification and improvement of the people. I was engaged to preach under its auspices at least once a month and oftener if I could, and to procure supplies for the rest of the time. For a while the experiment went on prosperously, but before a year expired it came to an end, either because my Spiritualism was too rational and Christian to suit the prevalent taste or because modern Spiritualism lacks the genius of organization and cohesive unity. Probably both these considerations operated to bring about the issue designated, causing me to betake myself to other fields of service.

An event of special interest to me and mine this year was the birth of a granddaughter, Lucy Florence Heywood, in the Home School mansion on the 28th of July. She proved to be the only child of our only surviving child, Abbie Ballou Heywood, wife of Rev. Wm. S. Heywood, who was at the time joint occupant with me of the Hopedale pulpit. She was well born in respect to all native endowments and capabilities, has been liberally educated, being a graduate of Smith College, Northampton, Mass., in the class of 1884, and has served as assistant teacher in the High School at Sandwich in this state. She is still living at this writing, April 5, 1890, a cherished blessing to all her relatives and a large circle of devoted friends.

During this year I prepared and caused to be issued from the Hopedale Press, owned and operated by Brother Bryan J. Butts, a small liturgical volume of three hundred and thirty-six pages, entitled "The Monitorial Guide." It was designed to aid in the intellectual, moral, and spiritual quickening and culture of both youth and adults in the principles and objects of the Practical Christian Republic by using it in inductive conferences

INTERVIEW WITH DEPARTED FRIENDS. 431

and other socially religious gatherings subordinate to that more comprehensive and definitely organized body. Its value was satisfactorily tested in the Hopedale Inductive Communion for several years before its dissolution, with which event it dropped out of sight. It has merits which some future generation may recognize and render serviceable in the great work of making the world better.

About this time occurred some of the most wonderful and convincing phenomena purporting to be produced by the denizens of the spiritual world in which I was ever privileged to participate. I had heard much through the public press and otherwise, especially through the personal experience of Brother E. D. Draper and wife, of the unique mediumship of the celebrated Charles H. Foster, then holding seances and astonishing multitudes of witnesses in Boston. Myself and wife had become so much interested in the reports received that we decided to visit Mr. Foster and see and judge for ourselves in regard to what transpired. We accordingly appeared at his boarding-place, No. 75 Beach street, one autumn morning and there awaited developments. We were ushered into a plainly furnished room, where we found the medium to whom we were absolute strangers, and were asked to sit by the side of a common table, on which there were slips of writing paper, several pencils, and a card with the letters of the alphabet in distinct type upon it. Being previously advised, we had written the names of quite a number of our departed relatives and numerous questions in fine script before leaving home, and rolled the paper on which they were inscribed into compact wads or balls, bringing them with us as means of testing whatever might be subjected to us for consideration and judgment. These were all placed before us, by the side of the other articles mentioned.

A few minutes elapsed when distinct raps were heard as if under the table, and the medium, after a few convulsive motions of the countenance said, "There is a band of bright spirits present, intelligent, affectionate, and unusually desirous of communicating with you. I perceive near *you* (pointing to my wife) a noble spirit, deeply interested in you, as if closely related." Then this spirit purported to say through the medium, "We rejoice to meet you in the presence of one through whom we can make most unmistakable manifestations of ourselves. And to convince you beyond a doubt who *I* am, I will cause my name to appear on the medium's arm at full length. Whereupon Mr. Foster bared his arm and then the name PEARLEY HUNT was distinctly seen, as if written with red ink in a hand which we at once recognized as that of the father of my wife when he was in mortal form. She at once, deeply affected, exclaimed, "O! that is my father." Further communications were received from him, partly in response to questions and partly of his own motion, but all strikingly characteristic of him, when he shook hands with us through the medium and departed.

Then came a wholly unexpected but scarcely less impressive and satisfactory interview with my wife's spirit mother, who spelled out her name CHLOE HUNT, at her own suggestion, by my pointing to the letters of the alphabet in their order, the right ones being designated by distinct rappings when they were reached. In the course of the interview this communicator said, "It was I who spoke to you in the garden." This was an explanatory answer to a question wife had addressed to our son, Adin Augustus, in one of the small wads lying on the table before us. It related to an incident that occurred more than a year before when she thought she heard the word "mother" one day when she was among her vegetables and flowers. This utterance she had always attributed to Augustus and had directed an inquiry to him on this occasion accordingly, — an inquiry, which her mother had now voluntarily answered. Here was strong presumptive proof that we were dealing with real invisible entities, as convincing as it was unanticipated and unsolicited.

Then occurred a manifestation which professed to be from our dear son himself. He was announced by the medium as a very bright and beautiful spirit, around whom everything was pleasant and cheerful, as indicating great affection and joy, — "the one," it was said, "you are most anxious to communicate with." He then extended to us through his interpreter most hearty congratulations accompanied by enthusiastic shaking of hands and expressions of intense pleasure that he had an opportunity of making us certain of his presence and identity. After referring to certain matters spoken of in the little balls before us and treating them satisfactorily, he continued: — "Now I will sensibly assure you that your son is indeed personally present with you by displaying my initials on the medium's arm." This was instantly done, the letters A. A. B. appearing in the exact shape familiar to us in his earthly life-time — the final curve of the B descending considerably below the line on which the other letters rested, as was his wont to make it. He then wrote with the medium's hand a somewhat lengthy message, subscribing what he had written with his well-known signature, "Adin Augustus Ballou," the same characteristic distinguishing the initial of the last name as before. Numerous questions were put to him which he answered intelligently and satisfactorily. This feature of the seance was profoundly impressive and convincing. Similar interviews, though not all of them so directly personal and affecting, were held with my venerable sainted mother, whose hands I was told were raised as if invoking a blessing upon me; with our beloved Brother Butler Wilmarth M. D., one of the victims of the Norwalk bridge disaster of ten years before; with my much esteemed friend E. N. Paine, formerly of East Blackstone; and with David Stearns Godfrey, a resident of Milford in his earth-life, from whom I had received many tokens of appreciative regard and to whom I was bound by very tender ties of confidence and affection. Referring to one of my last interviews with him in the flesh, when we had conversed freely upon the subject of spirit-communion and when he pledged me that he would report himself to me in due time and give me a certain test-word as a sure token of his identity, I asked him if he was ready to name that word, according to our agreement, of which I had never spoken to a living human being. He said that he was, and asked me to call over the letters of the alphabet. I did so and he by loud raps indicated the letters that spelled the word "*Portrait*," which was correct. He then dashed off through the agency of the medium, "True! True! True. I have tried since I left earth to give you the test agreed upon. It is now done. Take courage for all is well, PORTRAIT."

To conclude this remarkable demonstration or series of demonstrations, I requested the spirit relatives and friends present to give us their farewell benediction by a united succession of raps. This elicited a memorable response that seemed to carry inspiration with it, thrilling all our hearts. So closed the most remarkable and satisfying spirit seance at which I was ever a personal witness and participant, the descriptive account of which, as above given, is strictly and reliably true.

There will be plenty of skeptics with whom what I have recorded will have no weight. For such I do not write. They are resolutely determined not to be convinced of the truth of these things. They discard all the testimonies of sacred and profane history concerning the manifestations of angels, spirits, and demons from the unseen world made to mortal human beings, ancient and modern alike. I am a believer in such manifestations on rational and moral grounds, not holding a traditionary faith in the marvels of the bible while contemning those of other records and especially those coming in later days, nor on the other hand magnifying the latter as wonderful outgrowths or indications of human progress, to the disparagement of all the sacred writings of times long since past and gone. Nor do I exalt any modern spiritualistic revelation or philosophy above those principles of truth and righteousness declared to be essential to human welfare and happiness in the gospel of Jesus Christ.

An interesting and happy achievement in my life career was attained about the time when this chapter closes, to wit: My deliverance from the bondage of pecuniary indebtedness. As a result of my ambition to possess and enjoy a comfortable home, to encourage and relieve the needy, to accommodate and help real or supposed friends, and above all to further enterprises calculated to improve the condition of my fellowmen, I had been more or less financially involved from my first starting out in life. I was a borrower and therefore often a sorrower. But I was never a beggar, a defaulter, or a dependant on alms. My obligations were always faithfully kept, my word was sacred, and my credit beyond suspicion from first to last. And now, after all my struggles, disappointments, losses, I became "the Lord's freeman," owing "no man anything but to love one another." Thanks be to God, whose I am and all I have forevermore.

CHAPTER XXII.

1862–1872.

GARRISON'S DISCOURSES — CONSCRIPTION — HOPEDALE PARISH — PERSONAL LABORS — WORK FOR THE FUTURE — RELATION TO VARIOUS BODIES.

THE Hopedale Community, at the time of the opening of the present chapter, was little more than an ordinary religious society, though still maintaining nominally its originally adopted principles of Practical Christian truth as founded in the will of God and in the constitution of the moral world, and as applicable to all human affairs in all the relations of life. It continued to hold fast its primary guaranties against the evils of ignorance, poverty, vice, and crime, but the chief instrumentalities or means organically provided for in its distinctive industrial and social system by which those guaranties were to be made good had been essentially abandoned. Practically, we were no longer the vanguard and illustration of a new order of society, but only a quiet, peaceful, well-governed neighborhood of the old order, to the habits, practices, customs, and prevailing spirit of which our village was becoming year by year more fully and more complacently conformed.

The institutional routine of religious observances along the former lines and much in accord with the former spirit of the place was pursued with commendable regularity and to general satisfaction. Rev. Wm. S. Heywood and myself were the accredited ministers of the church, each rendering about an equal amount of service, only

PRACTICAL CHRISTIANITY IN ABEYANCE. 437

now and then a Sunday being assigned by definite arrangement to special invitees. Neither of us had abandoned the theological, ethical, and social theories adopted intelligently and conscientiously many years before, and our testimonies in no wise belied or undervalued our still cherished convictions. But the trend of things was manifestly against us and our teachings—to other issues than those we deemed of supreme moment and sought diligently to promote and secure.

The business interests of the village prospered exceedingly, its population increased, and wealth rolled in upon its leading citizens. Money-making, political engineering and advancement, and martial patriotism absorbed the thought and energy of the populace, while Practical Christianity, as a motive power in the individual community, state, and nation, fell proportionally into abeyance. Newcomers to the place cared little or nothing for the distinctive Christian principles of the men and women who founded it, while a goodly number of those who still cherished them and sought to honor them were obliged, under the newly-established regime, to seek employment and a home elsewhere. So it was that the Community, as an organic body, grew weaker and weaker in membership and in moral power from year to year, while the influence of the pulpit, Sunday-school, and conference room became more and more neutralized by prevailing indifference or hostile influences outside.

With the opening and progress of the civil war, causing in all directions great financial embarrassment and uncertainty, the patronage of the Hopedale Home School, which for several years enjoyed much well-deserved popularity, declined to such an extent, especially in respect to its boarding department whence its chief support was derived, that it was deemed advisable to close it permanently. This was accordingly done, much to the regret of its many friends in the vicinity and elsewhere, in the year 1862. The following spring its proprietors and principals disposed of the property and a few months later removed to West Newton. They have since resided in Scituate, Hudson, Holyoke, Boston, and Sterling, their present home (1890), in all of which places Mr. Heywood has labored as a settled minister in the fellowship of the Unitarian denomination.

A somewhat serious occurrence took place among us in July, 1862, the main features of which, as they concerned me personally, I cannot permit to sink into oblivion. By invitation of the committee of the Community on pulpit supply, my old-time friend and co-laborer in the antislavery cause, William Lloyd Garrison, delivered two discourses on the first Sunday of the month named in our Hopedale house of worship. He made use of the occasion to express and defend opinions on several important points of a religious nature which he must have known to be radically opposed to the faith and practice on which I had tried to build the Hopedale Community and was still trying to found the Practical Christian Republic. I and my friends had always held him in high regard as a distinguished philanthropist and treated him with fraternal deference, and I did not see why, under existing circumstances, he should raise controversial issues between me and him. I was present and listened with close and thoughtful attention to his disquisitions, but received no hint that he desired or expected me to say anything in defence of those views of mine which he vigorously assailed, though, of course, without reference to me. His utterances pleased all present who disliked my teaching upon the topics treated but naturally grieved me and those who revered the principles I maintained exceedingly. By reason of the seriousness of the case when considered in all its bearings, I deemed it my duty, without in any way impugning my friend's motives, to procure if possible a public discussion of the particulars upon which I took issue with him, in presence of our congregation, that they might better understand the merits of the whole case. How I succeeded will be learned from the following correspondence:

"*To Ebenezer D. Draper, Jerome Wilmarth, and Nancy W. Lewers, Committee:*

"DEAR FRIENDS: Our respected friend, Wm. Lloyd Garrison, who occupied the Hopedale pulpit last Sunday under your auspices, in the frank expression of his honest convictions, felt it his duty to teach the people, as I understood him, substantially as follows, to wit: —

"(1) That there is no divine authority whatever for setting apart the first day of the week as a sabbath or as time to be sacredly devoted to religious uses of any kind.

"(2) That to thus set it apart and to teach people to respect it as in any sense holy, is unwarrantable, superstitious, and pernicious.

"(3) That all such sabbatizing sprang from and is sustained by priestcraft for the mere advantage of a clerical or priestly class.

"(4) That all such sabbatizing, with its usual public religious exercises of prayer and other demonstrations of so-called worship, is essentially pharisaical.

"(5) That it is untruthful, improper, superstitious, and pernicious to call the bible a holy book, because it was written nobody knows when, by nobody knows whom; because it settles nothing in theology or ethics, proves all sorts of conflicting tenets, and carries with it no divine authority whatever — though nevertheless, it is worth more than all other books in the world.

"(6) That all authority to determine what is true or right in religion is vested absolutely in each human individual for himself — never to be overruled by the claims of any other person or persons as divinely inspired, commissioned, or authorized.

"(7) That Jesus Christ Himself is not to be regarded as an infallible and perfect religious teacher.

"(8) That it is wholly by or from human nature that we must finally settle all ethical questions.

"(9) That Non-resistance is in no way necessarily connected with or dependent on the teaching, example, or official authority of Jesus Christ.

"(10) That although Non-resistance holds human life in all cases inviolable, yet it is perfectly consistent for those professing it to petition, advise, and strenuously urge a pro-war government to abolish slavery solely by the war-power.

"Now it is well known to the people of Hopedale that my preaching and practice have always been to a greater or less degree contrary to these positions. It is also well known that a considerable number of persons in the village are opposed to my faith and practice on these points, and were delighted with friend Garrison's exposition of the subjects they involve. In view of all this, I deem it not only due to my self-respect but an imperative religious obligation to put myself in a way to be converted by fair argument to Mr. Garrison's views or by such argument to defend and sustain my own. I therefore respectfully request you to engage the service of our friend for some forthcoming Sunday or other day as soon as may be convenient, with the full understanding that he and I shall hold a free public discussion of the aforesaid and other collateral topics, to be continued through not less than two nor more than three sessions of two hours each, the parties to occupy uninterrupted equal portions of time. Your prompt attention and reply to this request will greatly oblige your brother and servant, ADIN BALLOU.

"Hopedale, July 9, 1862."

The committee at once forwarded my letter to Mr. Garrison and in due time received the following response:

"BOSTON, July 11, 1862.
" *To Ebenezer D. Draper, Jerome Wilmarth, and Nancy W. Lewers, Committee:*

"DEAR FRIENDS: The letter addressed to you by my friend, Adin Ballou, which you have kindly sent to me for my consideration, gives me very great surprise. It seems that he found several things in my discourses last Sunday at Hopedale from which he so strongly dissents and which he deems so heretical that he feels constrained to invite me (through you as a committee) to a public discussion of these controverted points at the same place as soon as may be convenient!

"In reply I beg leave very respectfully to say that I decline the invitation thus given; —

" (1) Because there seemed to be no reason why my friend Ballou should not have interrogated me, as did others in the audience, in order to a clearer elucidation of my views—as he was present at both meetings and expressed no dissent from anything I advanced.

" (2) Because I shall be too busily occupied for a month to come to attend to a discussion of this kind, even if I had (as certainly I have not) the inclination to do so.

" (3) Because my worthy friend gives me altogether too much credit and underrates his own efforts as a religious and ethical teacher for so long a period in his chosen Community, in declaring that he deems it not only important to his self-respect, (?) usefulness, and happiness, but 'an imperative religious duty' (!) to put himself in a way 'to be converted by fair argument to friend Garrison's views or by such argument to defend and sustain his own!' This magnifying the influence of my two impromptu discourses on his part is the more remarkable inasmuch as he says in his letter, 'It is well known to the people of Hopedale that my preaching and practice have always been in greater or less degree contrary to these (recited) positions.' Does he not discredit both his preaching and his practice by virtually admitting that my two poor discourses may measureably nullify their efficacy if not soon controversially replied to? I cannot permit such unnecessary depreciation of himself on the one hand, nor such absurd exaggeration of myself on the other. Besides, my friend Ballou has the field at Hopedale all to himself in the future as he has long had it in the past, and I am well content to leave [in his hands the 'considerable number of persons' in your village, who, he says, 'were delighted with my sentiments.'

"(4) I have [never yet consented to an appointed public discussion with any person on any subject and am too much of a non-resistant to accept any such challenge. Indeed, I have an unconquerable aversion to any set disputation after the manner of belligerent theologians, and believe little or no good ever resulted from it. It tends to beget partisanship rather than conviction, and it is something quite different from a general free discussion meeting.

"Finally, allow me to express my regret, and I will add my surprise, that my friend Ballou did not seek to have a frank interchange of views with me, socially, before I left Hopedale. Perhaps he could not possibly command the time on Sunday evening for that purpose. If so, I shall have no cause for surprise — only for regret that I was deprived of the pleasure and edification of such an interview.

"Thanking the committee for their kind overture, I remain,
"With warm regards, yours truly,

"WM. LLOYD GARRISON."

Under the circumstances in which I was placed by this letter, what could I do? If I remained silent, it must be inferred that I acquiesced in friend Garrison's doctrines or that I felt unable to refute them. If either of these inferences were true, I ought to renounce many of my fundamental positions as a religious teacher, social reorganizationist, and Christan Non-resistant; or, at least, to modify radically much of my theory and practice. Inasmuch as I was not converted to Mr. Garrison's views, but had good and sufficient grounds for rejecting them, I saw no other alternative but to *review* and *expose* both his objectionable affirmations and his reasons for declining to meet me in a fraternal public discussion. This I decided to do, and gave ample notice that my discourses of Sunday, July 27, would be devoted to that service. I therefore addressed myself to the task sat before me. In order to do justice to my subject in all its phases and bearings I had to go over considerable ground, only a brief abstract of which can be transferred to these pages.

" *Texts.* ' I also will show mine opinion.' *Job, 32: 10.* ' Come now, let us reason together.' *Isa. 1: 18.* ' He that is first in his own cause seemeth just, but his neighbor cometh and searcheth him.' *Prov., 18 : 17.* ' How can two walk together except they be agreed?' *Amos 3: 3.*

" *I. Friend Garrison's reasons for declining a public discussion.* I will not consume space by repeating them in full but refer to them by numbers as they appear seriatim in Mr. Garrison's letter, giving my several responses in their proper order.

" (1) I clearly understood every affirmation made by friend Garrison and needed no information as to his meaning on any point. But I wanted the reasons and proofs of what he assumed and an opportunity to test their validity and conclusiveness. To have asked for these and had my request granted would have turned the occasion into a critical debate and prevented the speaker from presenting his views fully, distinctly, and fairly. As to dissent, there was neither freedom nor opportunity to express any intelligibly and effectively. Our committee had said that Mr. Garrison wished me to be present and participate with him in the exercises of the meeting; but he offered no space of time, for me to do this, nor so much as hinted that he would be pleased to have me express my opinions counter to his own, though he well knew from what I had publicly said and written that I differed essentially from him in many of his declarations. He apparently desired to occupy all the time at his command, and I therefore felt at no liberty to claim any hearing that would have abridged his opportunity. A full and fair discussion at some other time was the desideratum needed. This I respectfully asked for, but it was refused; whether reasonably or otherwise, I leave others to judge.

" (2) The discussion would have been willingly deferred on my part to any more distant day mutually convenient. But if there was no 'inclination,' on his part, of course no convenient later day could be fixed upon between us.

" (3) The fallacy of this special pleading will be made obvious by considering the following facts: 1. Mr. Garrison was a talented, eloquent, and effective public speaker. He had a wide reputation not only for his ability but as a reformer and philanthropist. He was held in high esteem by our Community, myself included. He was invited to our pulpit as an honored friend and left free to choose his own theme of discourse. He delivered his two 'impromptu discourses,' consisting largely in broad, sweeping assertions and not in critical and discriminating reasonings, in his own off-hand but earnest, emphatic, impressive way. Much that he said was subversive of the fundamental principles and organic policy of our Practical Christian Socialism, and of such a nature as to produce doubt, distrust, and alienation respecting those principles in all susceptible minds, especially of the young, unstable, and inexperienced. The positive declarations of such a man, though impromptu, would naturally do more to undermine the social structure I was endeavoring to build up than years of constructive effort could replace. I therefore deemed it important that he who had been instrumental in creating doubt and uncertainty among those whom I had been trying to train to a high ideal of moral and social excellence, should be held answerable for his utterances in a fair discussion before the people whom he had previously addressed. 2. I was a religious teacher and social reformer. I had left the general prevailing order of civilization because in many of its distinguishing features it was largely wrong and anti-Christian. My new order was based upon and illustrated higher and diviner principles of truth and righteousness. In the construction of such an order of social life, all the natural factors of human society must be included and harmonized, and all that is necessary to both private and public welfare must be provided for. The individual, the family, and the community must conform to such regulations, customs, and courses of life as the highest wisdom shows to be morally right and practically advantageous to all conditions and classes of people. The Hopedale Community, while aiming to realize this Christ-like ideal, had never attained thereunto even in its best estate, and at the time of these 'impromptu' discourses had sadly fallen away from what it had at one time achieved. Moreover, the village was rapidly filling up with a population who preferred the old order to the new, thus helping to hasten the utter overthrow of all my cherished plans and aspirations for the enlightenment, moral renovation, and social regeneration of mankind. Nevertheless, in the midst of all this discouragement, I was still trying to hold up the true standard of personal and social righteousness in hope of a better future. Now friend Garrison was troubled with none of my scruples concerning organic society and with none of my constructive responsibilities. He was pre-eminently an Individualist rather than a Socialist of any kind. His mission was to destroy evil customs, institutions, and isms, and let good ones grow up as best they could. Mine was not only to overthrow what was wrong and prejudicial to human well-being and happiness, but to build up what was right and helpful of mankind. He magnified personal liberty as the right of all men, seeming to think if this were secured all other blessings would follow as a matter of course. I always insisted that personal liberty must be inseparably conjoined with personal obligation, duty, and responsibility, on the basis of the divine moral law. In religion, he discarded creeds, covenants, churches, and all external observances as useless and pernicious. On the contrary, I always insisted upon a co-ordinate unity of the human reason and emotional sentiments as expressed in religious beliefs, observances, confessions, and institutions founded in the essential truth of things and calculated to foster and promote high types of individual and social life, confident that without such, mankind will have false, absurd, and mischievous ones, or else sink into debasing irreligion or lawless, irresponsible nothingarianism. The differences between Mr. Garrison and myself thus indicated I earnestly desired to have considered in an orderly, candid, friendly discussion, testing them by the standard of reason and the moral law in the presence of the people; leaving nothing to anyone's *ipse dixit* or personal assumption. This was what I asked for, but I asked in vain.

" (4) Considering the friendly relations in which Mr. Garrison and myself had for many years stood before the public and the uncalled-for assault he had made upon some of my cherished opinions, I could hardly be ranked, I think, among 'belligerent theologians' in seeking the proposed discussion. The abuses of appointed set disputations afford no just ground for the alleged 'inconquerable aversion' to them, since they have the great advantage over casual and random debates that ample time is allowed for the presentation of conflicting views and that the parties concerned are given a co-equally fair opportunity to be heard. They are indeed 'quite different from a general free discussion meeting,' for in such a meeting the lions of the occasion and the expressed impatience of their partisan admirers leave little chance for modest and over-awed dissenters to give a full and fair presentation of their views. I have listened to many discussions of this character which yielded little profit to candid, truth-seeking hearers.

"Finally, I invited Mr. Garrison to call on me the Sunday evening after the objectionable discourses were delivered and he promised to do so, but failed to keep the promise. He left for Boston early Monday morning, sending in to me the apology that he was detained by pressure of company at the house of his host. There was therefore no opportunity for an interview at that time. For if, instead of waiting for him at my own home, as courtesy required, I had gone to the place where he was stopping, he could not, without manifest incivility, have turned away from his numerous other visitors for any protracted and satisfactory interchange of views with me.

"*II. Objectionable Doctrines of Friend Garrison Reviewed.* (1) Concerning the Sabbath. If what he states is true, then the Hopedale Community, in assuming that the first day of the week is a divinely-sanctioned day of rest and in some proper sense holy time, has acted without the warrant of reason, morality, or religion. The observance of that day by its members has been superstitious and pernicious, and their religious exercises and formalities, under the name of worship, have been pharisaic and hypocritical. Its ministers have been conducting these exercises and formalities for the advantage of their own priestly class.

"To this serious charge, I, for myself and associates, plead 'Not guilty.' We believed, as Christ taught, that the Sabbath as an institution coming down from the earliest ages of human history 'was made for man and not man for the Sabbath'; that it was established, not because one day is in itself holier than another, but for the benefit of mankind; that it is sacred only in the sense of being devoted to good uses; and that the right keeping of it includes not only attention to distinctively religious offices and ceremonials but also to the doing of all necessary, healthful, humane, and beneficent work. Needless secular business and ordinary amusements on that day were discountenanced by us, and general attendance upon the services of the house of worship was expected and provided for. In all this there was not one particle of priestcraft, superstition, or unreasonable strictness. By it the highest good and happiness of individuals, of families, and of the Community, were conserved and promoted. Such observance of the day was productive of salutary and desirable results and found in such results its complete justification. That the day may be abused, perverted, and made to serve selfish, partisan, and reprehensible ends is conceded, but it is no more just to denounce it on that account than to arraign and condemn anything else essentially right and good because human ignorance, folly, hypocrisy, and selfishness have sometimes falsified and dishonored it.

"(2) Concerning the Bible. Friend Garrison says 'that it is untruthful, improper, superstitious, and pernicious to call the bible a holy book, because it was written nobody knows when by nobody knows whom, settles nothing in theology or ethics, proves all sorts of conflicting tenets, and carries with it no divine authority whatever. Nevertheless, it is worth more than all the other books in the world.' What consistency is there in these statements? How can the bible be worth more than all other books if so destitute of all authenticity, homogeneity, and authority? The truth really is that no books of equal antiquity are so well authenticated as those comprised in the volume under notice. From the nature of the case more or less obscurity hangs over their date and authorship, yet this does not invalidate their claims to our confidence and regard, as it does not disprove or depreciate the essential truth they contain, the great principles of righteousness they declare and magnify. That truth — those principles — culminate in the New Testament, and the New Testament centers in the person of Jesus Christ, whose authority as teacher and exemplar determines the absolute religion of the bible. The bible, as Jesus interpreted, applied, and left it, does, as I understand it, determine what is fundamental in theology and ethics, affirms no conflicting tenets, and carries with it all the divine authority needful for the practical uses of life,— authority which He claimed to have derived from the Father.

"Friend Garrison asserted that 'Jesus Christ Himself is not to be regarded as an infallible and perfect religious teacher.' Then He was a false witness concerning Himself and a pretender, for He said, 'I do nothing of Myself, but as My Father hath taught Me I speak.' 'He that sent Me is with Me; the Father hath not left Me alone, for I do always the things that please Him.'—*John 8: 28, 29*. This was His uniform claim through all His ministry — a claim I feel bound in reason and conscience to admit. I do not believe he was a mere visionary or an arrogant pretender but an infallible and perfect religious teacher. And among all those who have asserted the contrary I have never found one who could fortify and maintain their assertions with good and sufficient reasons.

"3. Concerning Human Nature as Authority in Religion. But while friend Garrison denied that the bible carried with it any divine authority and regarded Christ as an imperfect religious teacher, he could set human nature on an infallible throne.

(See Nos. 6 and 8 of my letter on page 439.) Then no human being needs any inspired teacher, prophet, Christ, or God even, outside of himself. Then it logically follows that there is no absolute, universal, eternal, religious truth and righteousness which all men are in duty bound to seek out and obey, but each one's intuitions, opinions, conclusions are equally true to those possessing them; and all religious and ethical theories are equally authoritative to those professing them. The bible settles nothing; Christ is no reliable teacher; human nature settles everything! And what a mighty, endless babel of theories, doctrines, ideas we have in the world, all equally right, good, and true to those who entertain and cherish them! I prefer the theology and ethics of Jesus Christ — one universal fatherhood over all, one universal brotherhood uniting all, one universal law of duty for all, love to God and man — these I prefer to the theology and ethics of human nature as illustrated in all ages of the world's history. I cannot believe in the self-sufficient divinity of human nature as it ever has been and now is; my faith centers in universal divine principles, revealed from heaven through many media, but most clearly and perfectly through Jesus Christ.

"4. Concerning Non-resistance. Under this head I will first notice the declaration that 'Non-resistance is in no way necessarily connected with or dependent on the teachings, example, or official authority of Jesus Christ.' Then according to the theory just noticed, it must be connected with and dependent on the teachings, example, and inherent authority of human nature; that is, of such individual human beings as fancy it to be the outgrowth of their own personal intuitions, the number of which is not one in ten thousand of the race of man. To the masses of our kind — the uncounted multitude — Non-resistance is simply *nonsense*, as has been repeatedly affirmed by men standing high in public esteem and in the annals of reform. That is the manner in which human nature *as a whole* settles the ethics of Non-resistance. It pronounces against it in terms most emphatic and with a verdict overwhelming so far as majorities are concerned. Yet the testimony of Christ by both precept and example is equally emphatic and overwhelming. Which of these — human nature or Christ — speaks in this case with the greater authority? Which is most worthy of homage and reverence? Let professed Non-resistants answer.

"And now let us see how the elect few who derive their faith in Non-resistance from human nature — that is from their own human nature — settle the question with themselves and determine their duty in reference to it. Mr. Garrison is a competent representative of all such and it is but just that he be heard in their behalf. He says, — 'Although Non-resistance holds human life in all cases absolutely inviolable by professed Non-resistants yet it is perfectly consistent for them to petition, advise, and strenuously urge a pro-war government to abolish slavery by the war power.' Now the war power assumes that it is right to wound, mutilate, slaughter, any number of human beings who resist the authority of any state or nation, or who seek by violent means to prevent the execution of its will. And to ask a government to use the war power for the accomplishment of an object confessedly good, is to ask it to do what Non-Resistance teaches is essentially wrong. Can such a course be justified upon sound ethical principles? What one does by another he does by himself. This is true both in morals and in jurisprudence. And what one requests, advises, urges another to do, he is personally responsible for, if the thing be done. And to petition the government to abolish slavery by the exercise of the war power, is to become morally involved in the bloodshed and death resulting from such action. It is to adopt the Jesuitical maxim, 'The end sanctifies the means,' which is false in morals and suicidal in policy. Any worthy cause which is carried forward on that principle cannot long survive; will soon die by its own hand or the hand of its own advocates, as did that phase of Non-resistance. It has been silent in its grave ever since it thus lent itself to the work of human destruction for the promotion of human liberty.

"True Non-resistance—Christian Non-resistance—is of another type, of a higher genus. It came down from heaven. It was born, not of *human* nature but of the *divine* nature—of the pure wisdom and love of God. Human nature was constituted with a capacity for understanding, reverencing, cherishing, and exemplifying it, but not without more or less of self-crucifixion and help from on high. Jesus Christ did not originate this sublime doctrine, but He taught it and clearly illustrated it, enabling His disciples to comprehend and proclaim it to their fellowmen. As He taught and illustrated it, there was in it no inconsistency or self-contradiction. He did not preach one thing and practice another. He did not theorize beautifully about love and good will to all men, even to the worst of offenders, and then when a storm of wrath and war, engendered by human folly and transgression arose, straightway advocate the resistance of evil with evil, or ask and urge others to wield the battle axe and 'let slip the dogs of war,' in order to gain some greatly-to-be-desired good and help bring His righteous kingdom in. His kingdom was not of this world and could not be advanced after the fashion of this world's red revolutionary reformers, but rather by the regeneration of individual men through repentance for sin unto good works, and the love of righteousness whereby they would be brought into true relations with each other — into that state of unity, harmony, and brotherhood in which all should strive together for the universal good and happiness, blessing and cursing not. The banner of love, beneficence, forgiveness that He as 'Prince of Peace' flung to the breeze and called his followers to rally under and maintain as they went forth to the conquest of the world, has long been dishonored by His nominal church, which prostituted it to the service of the war power and of sword-sustained human governments. But the end is not yet. There will surely be some day a new and regenerate Christian church which will re-affirm, exemplify, and triumphantly glorify the original righteousness of the divine kingdom in this regard, and so truly honor Him whom it professes to believe in and serve. Here I rest my faith and close my defence of the truth as it has been made known to me against the detraction and false assumptions of my honored friend, William Lloyd Garrison."

A Case of Conscription. At this point I must put on record one special exploit of the high-pretending warpower of the United States government which we were counseled to summon to our aid in seeking the overthrow of slavery. In August, 1863, under a law authorizing the conscription of soldiers for replenishing the depleted ranks of the army, one of the loyal members of our Community, John Lowell Heywood, was drawn for the required service. As he could not conscientiously respond in person to the demand made upon him nor employ a substitute to fill his place, it was deemed advisable, after considerable hesitancy and discussion, that the prescribed commutation equivalent of three hundred dollars should be paid by him and such of his friends as might be moved to assist him in the crisis, rather than that he should be made to suffer the penal infliction provided for those who, under such circumstances, refused to join the forces then in the field. This was accordingly done. I have since feared that we acted wrongfully in the matter, feeling that it would have been more consistent with our principles and a more effective testimony against the wicked exactions of the government to have allowed the law to have taken its proper course and dealt with our unresisting brother to the full extent of its despotic and inexorable requirements. I do not recommend a repetition of our course in future cases of a similar sort, although in the unprecedented pressure of events I advised the payment of the money. It was done, however, under public protest formally presented to the military authorities at the time, a copy of which, prepared by myself and approved by the Community, I take the liberty to submit to my readers and to coming generations as follows:

"To the governmental authorities of the United States and their constituents, the undersigned, John Lowell Heywood of Hopedale, in the town of Milford, in the eighth congressional district of Massachusetts, respectfully maketh solemn declaration, remonstrance, and protest, to wit:

"That he has been enrolled, drafted, and notified to appear as a soldier of the United States, pursuant to an Act of Congress approved March 3, 1863, commonly called the Conscription Law.

"That he holds in utter abhorrence the rebellion which the said law was designed to aid in suppressing and would devotedly fight unto death against it if he could conscientiously resort to deadly weapons in any case whatsoever.

"But that he has been for nearly nine years a member in good and regular standing of a Christian Community whose religious confession of faith and practice pledges its members 'never to kill, injure, or harm any human being, even their worst enemy.'

"That in accordance with his highest convictions of duty and his sacred pledge as a member of said Community, he has scrupulously and uniformly abstained from participating in the state and national governments under which he has lived — not only foregoing the franchises, preferments, emoluments, and advantages of a constituent co-governing citizen, but also the privilege of righting his wrongs by commencing suits at law, and of calling on government for protection against threatened violence — in order thereby to avoid making himself morally responsible for their constitutional *dernier resorts* to war, capital punishment, and other kindred acts, and also to commend to mankind by a consistent example those divine principles which prepare the way for a higher order of society and government on earth.

"That, nevertheless, it is one of the cardinal Christian principles to respect existing human government, however imperfect, as a natural outgrowth and necessity of society for the time being, subordinate to the providential overrulings of the supreme divine government, and therefore to be an orderly, submissive, peaceable, tribute-paying subject thereof; to be no detriment or hindrance to any good thereby subserved; to countenance no rebellion, sedition, riot, or other disorderly demonstration against its authorities; to oppose its greatest abuses and wrongs only by truthful testimony and firm, moral remonstrance; and in the last resort, when obliged for conscience' sake to non-comply with its requirements, to submit meekly to whatever penalties it may impose.

"That with such principles, scruples, and views of duty, he can not conscientiously comply with the demands of this Conscription Law, either by serving as a soldier or by procuring a substitute. Nor can he pay the three hundred dollars of commutation money which the law declaratively appropriates to the hiring of a substitute, except under explicit remonstrance and protest that the same is virtually taken from him by compulsion for a purpose and use to which he could never voluntarily contribute it, and for which he holds himself in no wise morally responsible.

"And he hereby earnestly protests, not only for himself but also in behalf of his Christian associates and all other orderly, peaceable, tax-paying, non-juring subjects of the government of whatever denomination or class, that their conscientious scruples against war and human life-taking, ought, in justice and honor, to be respected by the legislators and administrators of a professedly republican government; and that, aside from general taxation for the support thereof, no person of harmless and exemplary life who is conscientiously opposed to war and deadly force between human beings, and especially no person who for conscience sake foregoes the franchises, preferments, privileges, and advantages of a constituent citizen, ought ever to be conscripted as a soldier, either in person or property.

"Now, therefore, I, the said John Lowell Heywood, do pay the three hundred dollars commutation money to the government of the United States, under military constraint in respectful submission to the powers that be, but solemnly protesting against the exaction as an infraction of my natural and indefeasable rights as a conscientious, peaceable subject. And for the final vindication of my cause, motives, and intentions, I appeal to the moral sense of all just men, and above all to the inerrable judgment of the Supreme Father and Ruler of the universe.

"Subscribed with my hand at Hopedale, Milford, Mass., this 18th day of August, A. D., 1863.

"JOHN LOWELL HEYWOOD."

The arrangement by which I was to supply the pulpit at Hopedale one-half the time continued till the close of the year 1865, my other Sundays being occupied elsewhere, usually in neighboring towns or localities not very far from home. The month of September of the year mentioned, I spent in part at Southold, L. I., with my esteemed friends, Joseph H. Goldsmith and wife, and in part with the family of my equally esteemed friends, Dr. Henry T. Child and wife, in Philadelphia, preaching and lecturing upon my favorite themes several times during each week as opportunity offered. The kindness and hospitality of these friends at this and other times are among the most cherished memories of my life.

While on this visit to Philadelphia, I was privileged to attend a most wonderful musical exhibition given at Concert Hall by the then celebrated "Blind Tom," as he was called — a rustic negro formerly a slave but recently set free by the famous "Emancipation Proclamation" of President Lincoln. There was nothing in the performer's external appearance to indicate unusual powers of any sort, but that he was a prodigy in his art no one who saw and heard him could question. He was but a youth, less than twenty years of age, and had received nothing that could be termed a musical education. But as a pianist his accomplishments were marvelous, while his vocal renderings were scarcely less than that. He surprised and delighted his auditors by his execution of popular airs as well as pieces of his own composition. Two of the latter — one entitled "The Thunder-storm," and the other, "When This Cruel War is Over"—were of surpassing excellence. Some of his feats with voice and instrument were as unique as they were astonishing. He imitated the common music-box with unaccountable precision; produced "Yankee Doodle" in a reversed position, his hands being behind him; and, to crown all,

A MEMORABLE INCIDENT. 453

played one tune with his right hand, another with the left, while a third was sung by him — all going on simultaneously. Here were modern miracles indeed! I could but think that "Blind Tom" was a medium for some musical genius of the unseen world.

A year later, in September, 1866, I repeated the visits to both Southold and Philadelphia, accompanied by my wife, to the great satisfaction and enjoyment of both of us. A peculiarly interesting incident occurred at the former place. By special invitation I attended a temperance meeting in the Presbyterian church one evening, and made a brief address in connection with other speakers. During a little pause in the proceedings, a stranger came forward unannounced and delivered a most charming speech. The audience was greatly pleased and when he closed called for the unknown man's name. With modest reluctance he at length said, "Andrew Leighton of Liverpool, England." I was surprised beyond measure, for I had corresponded for some years with Andrew Leighton and had longed to see him but never expected to enjoy that privilege. And now, without any forewarning or intimation that he was within three thousand miles of me, he was standing in my very presence. The reader can judge of the fervor of the greeting we gave each other at the close of the exercises, which took place immediately, and of the mutually gratifying interview we had afterward at the house of friend Goldsmith. It seemed that Mr. Leighton had been called suddenly to America for business purposes. Determining to see me, he went to Hopedale to learn of my absence and whereabouts. Hurrying on to Southold, he traced me to the temperance meeting, heard me speak, and finally made himself known in the way indicated. He proved to be a very intelligent, large-minded, companionable gentleman, well informed upon subjects in which I was interested, and ready in conversation, which he enlivened with choice anecdote, poetry, and song. He remained with us only about twenty-four hours, which he rendered memorable by the richness and variety of his communications and the warmth, generosity, and nobleness of his spirit. He left Southold for Boston and I never saw him more.

During the then current year I was occupying the pulpit at Hopedale three-fourths of the time, being the only regularly-employed minister of the Community, which still had a name to live and still continued to make provision for the moral and religious activities of the place. My son-in-law with whom I had been so long associated in the work of the ministry there, had withdrawn entirely from the field, having been settled as pastor of the First church and society of Scituate, Mass. At the opening of the year 1867, I was invited to preach at home all the time, my salary, which had been five dollars per Sunday in 1864, eight dollars in 1865, and twelve dollars in 1866, being fixed at fifteen dollars, or seven hundred and eighty dollars for the year — no provision being made for a vacation.

On the 26th of May and 9th of June, 1867, respectively, I delivered two carefully prepared discourses in the Hopedale church which were deemed worthy of publication. They were entitled "Human Progress in Respect to Religion." The first was upon "The Tendency of the Age to Dispense with the Specialties and Personal Responsibilities of Religion"; the second on "The Ultimate Convincement of Progressive Minds in Favor of the Pure Christian Religion and Church." These discourses were put into tract form and distributed far and wide in the general community. There was urgent need of the lessons and admonitions which this tract contained in 1867; there is no less need in 1890, and I apprehend this will be the case far on in the indefinite future.

As time advanced, the disproportion between the number of members of the Community resident in Hopedale and the number of persons who were not members was continually increasing, until it came to pass that the latter were greatly in the majority. And yet these had no voice in the management of the general affairs of the place, and especially of those pertaining to moral and religious culture and to the institutions and activities by which the moral and religious interests of the people at large — non-members as well as members — were to be fostered and perpetuated. There was seen to be an inequality — a wrong in this state of things which ought to be remedied. Those outside of the Community, technically speaking, were practically as much concerned in the moral and spiritual interests of the village — in public and private virtue and piety — as those inside, and should, as a matter of right, be privileged to act in reference to them — should be allowed to co-operate with their fellow residents in guarding and promoting them. This was recognized and conceded on all hands, and it was generally felt that some change was needed to meet the requirements of the case — some new method of administration so far as related to the things mentioned.

Hence, after due deliberation and conference, and with the consent of all interested parties, there was organized in the month of October, 1867, what was called "The Hopedale Parish," whose membership was composed of persons outside as well as inside the pale of the Community — of all in the place who desired to unite and work together, as set forth in the constitution, for the moral and religious education and improvement of all classes of the population and for the public welfare and happiness. This being done, the Community, in its distinctive capacity, transferred its powers and responsibilities in the matters indicated to the Hopedale parish, which at once assumed them and entered upon the discharge of the involved trust. Everything was settled to the satisfaction of those concerned, and the regime then established has continued to the present day, as it is likely to continue indefinitely in days and years to come.

This being accomplished, largely through my agency and by my advice, the next question of importance to me was "What am I now to do?" — a question which pressed heavily upon my mind and heart. I pondered it seriously and prayerfully before answering it and deciding upon my future course. My high convictions of truth and duty and my manner of life for many years had unfitted me to resume the pastoral office under the auspices of any denomination involved in the maintenance of the existing order of society; and I saw no opportunity of renewing the Community experiment elsewhere with the least hope of success. Moreover, my surviving friends in the village and what remained there as the result of my long-continued struggles, seemed to deserve my sacred regard; so that when the unanimous desire of the parish, including the new as well as the old settlers, was expressed that I should be their sole preacher for the immediate future, accompanied by an urgent invitation to that effect, I deemed it wise and right to accept and occupy the field of service thus opened to me. This was done with a full and fair understanding that I was to be as independent, outspoken, and free under the new system as I always had been under the old — as true to my own convictions and to the Master in whom I believed and whom I professed to follow. Not the slightest intimation was given me then or ever after that I would be expected to change or suppress any of my long-cherished ideas, principles, or peculiarities. And though the wind and tide were so obviously against me — so decidedly favorable to the established order of civilization that I had little to hope for a truer, a more Christian one, yet I felt that I could do something to preserve the fruit of my labors from utter extinction in the locality where they had been chiefly expended, or at least be able to transmit the memorials of them to coming generations. I thought that in addition to my covenanted pulpit work, which I was bound to perform faithfully, I might command the time and means of writing a truthful history of a frustrated experiment in behalf of a regenerated form of human society, set forth the causes of failure and show how they might be avoided, for the benefit of social reformers

UNITED WITH WORCESTER CONFERENCE. 457

in some age yet to be. And I furthermore thought that I might find time and opportunity to prepare a series of carefully studied expositions of my highest and best ideas concerning some of the great questions of morals and religion relating to the progress, welfare, and happiness of mankind, for future examination and use. This I finally resolved to do, hoping thereby to be of substantial service to the world after I had passed to other spheres of being — leaving behind me some of the fruits of my inspiration and endeavor which would prove my life-work less a failure than otherwise it might appear to be.

Three months after the inauguration of the new ecclesiastical regime, in January, 1868, the Hopedale parish, with myself as pastor, was formally admitted to "The Worcester Conference of Congregational (Unitarian) and other Christian Societies," at a meeting convened in the neighboring town of Westboro'. Our application had been fraternally received at a previous session and we were cordially welcomed to the fellowship of the body. As the Unitarian polity imposes no creed, covenant, or stringent conditions of affiliation upon either its individual members or associated co-laborers, recognizing only a general loyalty to Christ and his religion on the common basis of the fatherhood of God and brotherhood of man, we entered this new alliance on easy and satisfactory terms — neither giving nor exacting specific pledges of any kind. I was personally in no wise embarrassed thereby. I was not required or expected to renounce or modify any of my favorite beliefs, nor did I expect or require others to renounce or modify any of theirs on my account. There was mutual freedom, tolerance, friendliness. On many points of theology and morality there was entire harmony, theoretically, between me and my new allies. Among both clergy and laity of the conference I had many old acquaintances — some of them temperance, antislavery, and peace reformers — between whom and myself there existed sincere respect and confidence. So the dominant condition and aspect of things was pleasant to me and promised a chance for me to infuse wholesome leaven into the general body to which I became attached, without compromising myself or my sacredly cherished principles. At any rate, we could work harmoniously together for the common good and aid each other in promulgating among our fellowmen the distinctive doctrines and ideas of a rational, liberal, practical Christian faith. Such were the reasons for the step thus taken as they lay in my own mind, and if the good resulting from it did not realize all I desired, probably I could not have done better. I have always been treated with the utmost kindness and hospitality by my Unitarian brethren and sisters, and they have listened to my testimonies with attentive and gratifying interest, even when they could not accept them in all their bearings and applications.

I had been invited by the proper conference authorities to deliver an address at the opening session of the meeting referred to, which was held on the evening before our parish was admitted to membership. I accepted the invitation, presenting my views of the objects, principles, and methods which I believed all followers of Christ ought to co-operate in maintaining, prosecuting, and carrying out to their legitimate practical results. My effort was appreciated beyond my highest anticipations. Not only was the usual vote of thanks accorded me, but a copy of my discourse was requested for publication in the *Christian Register*. I cheerfully granted the request, furnishing the desired copy for the editor, who accepted it and gave it a place in his issue of Feb. 22, 1868. It was entitled, "The World's Need of the Church," and was designed to be, as I believe it was, a systematic, comprehensive, and incontrovertible vindication of the church of Christ as a redemptive force in human society; as an institution established in the nature of things and ordained of God for the enlightenment and regeneration of mankind.

I was now in full charge of the Hopedale pulpit and of the general moral and religious activities connected therewith, to the duties of which I addressed myself with diligence and zeal. I labored assiduously both at the sacred desk and in the Sunday-school to impart a high order of instruction to old and young, — sound, uncompromising Practical Christianity, amply illustrated and judiciously applied. I could not have striven harder if I had served a very large, sympathetic, enthusiastic congregation in one of our prosperous cities. Instead of this, I had but a small audience, respectful indeed, yet only partially sympathetic and responsive to my utterances, with little manifestation of interest and zeal in the work I was trying to do. I preached and taught the gospel of the new life, individual and social, for I could preach and teach no other. But more than half my people were committed to the old milito-political dispensation of the unregenerate world, and the minority, holding still to their former faith in something better and more Christ-like, were powerless against the receding tide. The currents of the home, the school, the market, the shop, the street, were against me for the most part, and were augmented by the dominant forces of the great world outside, neutralizing nearly everything I had to say or do. I was often made to feel that I was trying with all my heart to promote what most of those before me deemed impracticable and were invincibly pre-committed to disregard. But I did not see what I could do different or better. So I kept on, often with a sick and fainting heart.

In this condition of things, I was more and more impelled to contemplate the future, and to live and labor for coming generations. I gave up expecting to accomplish much for the reformation of my fellowmen in my natural lifetime and was led to devote more and more of my energies and pecuniary means to the benefit of my successors. Omitting no known duty arising from day to day and from year to year, I yet worked steadily as much as I could for the days and years ahead. To this end I busied myself in collating for preservation such of my published writings as I deemed worthy, adding thereto from time to time such new matter upon important subjects as I was able to prepare.

In 1868, by special request of Mr. C. C. Drew, publisher of the Milford directory, I wrote for his work a rudimentary sketch of the town's history, including an appropriate notice of the Hopedale Community. This was the crude beginning of my voluminous "History of Milford," given to the public some years afterward. During the years 1869-70, I prepared with great care and put in manuscript a series of twenty discourses, which I first delivered from my pulpit, and, two years later, pursuant to my original design, caused to be published in a 12mo. volume of three hundred and thirty-one pages. The work bore the following title: "Primitive Christianity and its Corruptions: Department of Theological Doctrines, etc." It was intended to be the first of three volumes on the same general subject — the other two to be made ready for the press subsequently as opportunity offered — the second to treat of "Personal Righteousness," and the third of "Ecclesiastical Polity." These were written in due time, as will be noted hereafter, and are still in manuscript. I have provided for their publication after my decease.

In 1871 I had occasion to correct a long series of misrepresentations which had appeared from time to time in the periodicals of the Universalist denomination concerning the Restorationist secession of 1831. The last appeared in the *Universalist*, the Boston organ of the sect, January 21. The entire list had been characterized by a disregard of facts and by gross disparagement and contempt of the seceding brethren. I had read many of these offensive diatribes with disgust and indignation, but kept silent, hoping they would die without special contradiction. But this fresh outburst of perversion and abuse led me to think that my hopes were vain, and to fear that these manifestos were likely to become chronic falsifications of history and go down to the unsuspecting future as trustworthy recitals of what had transpired. I determined, therefore, if possible, to correct them, especially as I was one of the few survivors of the maligned party, and master of all the facts of the case. I accordingly solicited the privilege of making the correction in the columns of the paper in which the offence was last committed. The favor was granted and I furnished two articles reviewing the whole matter and giving a brief but effective statement of it which seemed to be accepted as satisfactory—which, at any rate, silenced our detractors forever. The articles appeared in the issues of the *Universalist* for February 11 and 25 of the year mentioned.

In connection with the various labors thus noted, I kept up my usual round of weddings, funerals, and friendly visitations in my larger parish of the neighboring towns, and rendered many miscellaneous services as speaker at home and abroad on occasions of a religious, reformatory, secular, and commemorative character, to which I can only incidentally refer. My correspondence was still large, and I was still beset by visitors from near and far for conversation and counsel upon matters of religion, philanthropy, and reform, including inquirers after the way of a better social life. I generally attended the three sessions per year of the Worcester Conference with my six parish delegates, and frequently took part in the exercises. As a religious body, the Unitarians in some respects were quite below my ideal of Practical Christianity. I had no affinity with the extreme radicals among them and disliked their general indifference to questions of personal, moral, and social regeneration, as I did their invincible attachment, in common with all the sects, to the institutions and customs of governmental civilization as it now is. But they were an intelligent, tolerant, and courteous people, having among them truly elect souls, with whom I could heartily sympathize and co-operate for good and noble ends. I was furthermore in full accord with them in their great central idea of love to God and man as the sum and substance of the religion of Christ. For this reason I could not coalesce with the so-called Evangelical sects, whose dogmas of limited probation and endless punishment are virtual denials of the universal divine fatherhood — self-evident theological barbarisms which logically destroy the moral character of God and poison religion at its fountain head. Such dogmas I hold in inconceivable abhorrence.

In respect to the Spiritualists as a body, I had become weaned from my former attractions to them and ceased to attend their general public convocations. Not because I had discarded one particle of the Spiritualism I had ever believed in and advocated, but because I adhered inflexibly to Jesus Christ as my religious Lord and Master, superior to all spirits or spirit-mediums of ancient or modern times, and maintained that His expositions of truth and righteousness were divinely authoritative. The leaders and zealots of the spiritualistic gospel gave me to understand that they wanted nothing of this Christly supremacy. I therefore declined to urge it upon their devotees, and having no relish for *their* supremacy quietly withdrew from their active fellowship and went about my Father's business.

As to special reformers, they had mostly fallen away from my high ideals of Practical Christianity. The Non-resistants, with few exceptions, had failed in the hour of trial and yielded allegiance to the war-god when with his battle-axe he cleft asunder the fetters of the slave. The American Peace Society protested that it stood only for international disarmament and arbitration, not for extreme disuse of injurious force. A more radical movement, The Universal Peace Union, was started, but with some objectionable complications; yet I took an interest in it, lent it moderate support, and rejoiced in whatever of good it was able to do. Anti-slavery had become apotheosized by its war-power triumph and rested from its labors. All that could be done in its behalf was to carry relief to the freedmen, to which I contributed by words and deeds. The temperance cause called for devotees, and I gave it the support I could without involving myself in its reliance upon penal laws, arbitrary exactions, and final resort to violence. The same was true with the cause of women's rights. When it became chiefly absorbed in the question of suffrage and the use of the ballot-box, I shrank back somewhat from it, yet never abandoned the fundamental principles of justice and equity upon which it was based, nor withdrew my admiration from its more essential and distinguishing characteristics. Finally, the working people's movement flung its standard to the breeze and called for recruits to its heterogeneous ranks. I was interested in its objects and professed claims, as I had been in similar movements in America and England for many years, and I studied and watched it with sympathetic desire and hope. But I found in it little of the spirit of fraternity, of co-operation between the strong and the weak; little of the spirit of Christian brotherhood. It sought to level down but not up. Its trust was in legislation and governmental coercion. The sword was its *dernier resort*. It belonged to a moral and social sphere and to a field of reform from which I had withdrawn forever. So with nothing but the best of wishes for this and all other efforts to do good in the world, though by ways and methods which neither my judgment nor my conscience could approve, I addressed myself all the more devotedly to my own proper mission, that of preparing the way for future generations to dwell together as co-equal brethren and sisters of a common family, — the loving children of the one heavenly Father. Thus I reached my birthday in the year 1872.

CHAPTER XXIII.

1872-1882.

PRIMITIVE CHRISTIANITY — MILFORD HISTORY — RESIGNATION
OF PASTORATE — EDITORIAL NOTE — CENTENNIALS —
G. A. R. SERMON — SHADOWS.

NEAR the close of the last chapter I spoke of the preparation in 1870 of the first volume of my comprehensive work on "Primitive Christianity and Its Corruptions," to be completed in two additional volumes at some convenient subsequent date. In that initial number of the series, which was entitled "Theological Doctrines," I undertook to show how, from a very early period in its history, the Christian church, through ignorance, bigotry, and other agencies incident to an undeveloped, barbarous age of the world, had been diverted from the simplicity that is in Christ and led to adopt doctrines and beliefs which were not only an offence to enlightened reason and a quickened moral sense, but a travesty on the gospel as Jesus taught and exemplified it. I also endeavored to show that many of these early perversions of Christianity had come down to our own times and were still exerting a pernicious influence upon the faith and life of mankind — dishonoring the character of the heavenly Father and vitiating the primary conditions of human welfare and happiness. The only formal literary notice worthy of consideration which this book received appeared in the Universalist quarterly for April, 1872. It was from the pen of Rev. A. St. John Chambre, a courteous, scholarly, conservative clergyman of ritualistic tendencies, then in the ministry of the denomination indicated, but since gone over to the Episcopalians. He saw little in my performance to approve, but much to condemn. He animadverted somewhat severely upon my spiritualistic interpretations, my rejection of the dogma of "the Immaculate Conception," and other points definitely taken by me. I could not regard his strictures as just, discriminating, or valid, and they therefore brought conviction neither to my understanding nor my moral sense. I prepared, not long after, a critical rejoinder to his article, but as there was no good opportunity to give it to the public, I stored it away for future use. Most of the topics deemed objectionable by my reviewer are treated in some other connection in this narrative and I need not advert to them here. One of them, however, not mentioned elsewhere, I will briefly notice — the doctrine of "the Immaculate Conception." I had been led to set aside the accounts in the gospels of Matthew and Luke on which that doctrine assumes to be based, with extreme reluctance — not at all from a general sweeping disbelief in miracles, as they are termed, but solely on the ground of irreconcilable contradictions in the accounts themselves, which render them of doubtful origin, and of the utter silence of all the other New Testament scriptures concerning the matter. If it were true that Jesus was born as the popular creedists claim, not in the regular order of nature, but by supernatural intervention, and if this view is of the importance in the Christian economy of redemption attributed to it, then the fact that it is not once mentioned nor even alluded to by the other evangelists or by St. Paul is most surprising and utterly inexplicable. It is much more satisfactory to my reason and moral judgment to regard the passages relating to it as interpolations, agreeably to the conclusions of some eminent biblical scholars, or as erroneous interpretations of the actual facts in the case, than to accept the prevailing views of the nominal Christian church. And this I say while fully persuaded that the main body of the New Testament is entirely trustworthy as to the essential truth of the statements therein made. My only exceptions are a very few passages obviously self-contradictory or uncorroborated by collateral testimony in the record. Most of what ultra modern critics discard as untrustworthy in these scriptures I adhere to with unwavering confidence. I am particularly desirous of being understood correctly in this matter of faith in the reliability of the New Testament records.

At the regular meeting of the Worcester (Unitarian) Conference held at Brookfield in May, 1872, I, by invitation, read an essay upon "The Relation of the Intellect and Emotions Respectively to the Development of the Religious Life." The wording of the subject enabled me to present to the assembled representatives of the thirty or more societies of which the conference was composed, my favorite idea that true religion requires the co-ordinate and harmonious exercise of the various faculties of the human understanding and those of the emotional nature usually termed the sentiments. The purport of what I said may be deduced from my opening sentences: — "If we should find a person intelligent and rational, honest and conscientious, benevolent, considerate, and kind unto others; reverential toward God and divine things, devout, spiritually minded, exemplary in all the duties of true morality and piety, we should say the religious life was well developed in such a person. If we could find a whole society or denomination exhibiting generally these characteristics, we should pronounce the same verdict upon those composing it, collectively considered. On the other hand, if we should find individuals, societies, and denominations intelligent and rational, with a decent morality and ordinary philanthropy, but lax and indifferent in respect to religious duties and especially to devotional exercises, we should say there was an imperfect development of the religious life. Or if we should meet another class, very devout and zealous according to the fashion of their sect, yet unintelligent, contemnors of human reason, bigoted and superstitious, not over moral in their common life, denouncing homely good works as of little worth in the sight of God, we could justly affirm the same concerning them. They, with the others, would exhibit a very one-sided and defective religious development." These thoughts were elaborated, illustrated, and applied along the lines indicated, giving the reader a general conception of my effort on the occasion, concerning which I need not enlarge.

In my endeavors to discharge the duties devolving upon me as pastor of the Hopedale parish and as in some sense the guardian of the moral and religious interests of the people of the village, I was led to see the need of some more definite, positive, direct methods of culture and inspiration than the ordinary exercises of public worship and the Sunday-school afforded, and of a closer personal relation between me and the objects of my charge than as yet, under the new dispensation, had been enjoyed. With a view of supplying that need, I made a serious attempt early in 1873 to establish a "Parochial Christian Union," which I hoped might grow into an institution of permanent value, mentally, morally, religiously, and socially considered, to our entire population. I flattered myself with the idea that something of the kind would bring different classes together for purposes of self-improvement, developing in them the spirit of mutual helpfulness and aspirations after a higher and a better life. I therefore drew up a well-devised constitution as a basis of co-operative action, and calling those together who felt as if they could be interested in and profited by such a movement, went so far as to organize a small body of volunteers under its provisions. A few meetings were held and some steps were taken to put its proposed methods of study and discipline into practical operation. But it did not strike the popular mind favorably, it received no encouragement from influential quarters, and it had too small a number of competent adherents to work its machinery with satisfactory results. After a brief trial the effort was given up. There was no doubt of the intrinsic importance of the objects contemplated and no defect appeared in the plan or proposed methods of operation, but like many of my previous devices for doing good, it looked well on paper but failed when an attempt was made to put it to practical use, for want of appreciative, capable, and faithful devotees. Disappointed once more, I turned from special activities calculated to benefit and bless those living in the present time, to work with renewed diligence and zeal for what I believed might benefit and bless unborn generations.

Soon after my discomfiture in this every way laudable and praiseworthy undertaking, I, in the month of April, 1873, resigned my position as pastor of the Hopedale parish and congregation. I did this partly because of that discomfiture, which made me feel that the dominant influences of the place were against me, neutralizing my labors and thwarting my plans for carrying forward the work to which I was called, and partly because I had reached the age of 70 years and might be expected to give way to a younger man, whose matter, manner, and method would be more acceptable to the people generally than mine. Much to my surprise, not only was my resignation not accepted, but was met with a remonstrance so unanimous, positive, and urgent that I immediately recalled it and settled down for another term of service in my accustomed place — a term which as the issue proved, was to continue for seven full years more. But I never afterward ventured far out of my conventional routine of prescribed pulpit and Sunday-school labors — never renewed my endeavors to institute any new methods of moral and spiritual instruction and quickening, or any special social machinery for advancing the cause of virtue and piety, but going my own narrow round of official duties, left my parishioners and their dependants to their already established usages and to such other training and discipline as might please them.

I was now at greater liberty than ever before to go on with the work upon which my heart was so much set — that of putting my thoughts and ideas upon matters pertaining to human progress and redemption into proper form for preservation and transmission to those who might appreciate and use them after I should have passed beyond the scenes and cares of earth and time. I had already begun to elaborate and prepare for the press a second series of discourses upon "Primitive Christianity and Its Corruptions," which was to be published as Vol. II. of my comprehensive work upon that general subject and to bear the specific title of "Personal Righteousness." This series, the several parts of which were preached as sermons to my Sunday congregation, was carried through to completion during the year, the more important events and occurrences of which, so far as concerned me personally, I am now recapitulating. It was composed of twenty-eight discourses, each declaring and elucidating some important point of Christian duty as related to the individual man, woman, or child, the whole making a manual or study of the special topic of which it treats, symmetrical in statement and exhaustive in argument and illustration. In it I was careful to set forth, defend, and apply to human character and life the distinctive morality of the New Testament scriptures, and to show the corruption of the same in the theory and practice of the nominal Christian church. I was especially careful to emphasize and magnify those sublime duties of piety and morality which have been most perverted and disregarded by professing Christians, and which really constitute the transcendent excellence of Primitive Christianity, as compared with all other moral and religious philosophies and systems of the world.

It has been already stated that in 1868 the Hopedale Community, by its proper officers, transferred all its parochial prerogatives and responsibilities — the care of the moral and religious interests of the village — to the newly-formed parish, which at once entered upon the discharge of the trust thereby imposed upon it. Five years later, in December, 1873, the trustees of the Community, as the custodians of its remaining possessions, conveyed to the same authorities all their right, title, interest, and control in, unto, and over Community Square and its appurtenances, the meeting-house standing thereon, and the Hopedale Cemetery, to be held, cared for, and used by them and their heirs and successors after them forever. There was still in the trustees' hands the "Soward fund," so called, amounting to eight hundred dollars, the income of which was to be expended for the mental and moral improvement of the young through the agency of the Sunday-school. This fund was made over to the parish in December, 1875, which was the final transaction pertaining to Community affairs — the closing act of the drama of our new social state. Thus was the Hopedale Community laid in its tomb and consigned to the keeping of history. A few devoted survivors still live to hallow its name and memory, but the multitudes who once knew it heed not its ashes nor the memorials of its checkered career.

The third and closing volume of my work on "Primitive Christianity and Its Corruptions," was chiefly prepared during the year 1874. It was entitled "Department of Ecclesiastical Polity," and consisted of twenty-five chapters devoted to organic church life and its bearings upon sociological problems. Its grand aim was to show what the primitive church, as instituted by its great Founder, really was; when and how it became deteriorated and despoiled of its original character; and by what means it can be regenerated, reconstructed, and perfected. The general drift and purpose of its contents may be gleaned from a few considerations derived from well known facts of Christian history.

The New Testament scriptures nowhere assert or assume that Christ came into the world in order to prosecute his saving mission to mankind by raising up and establishing a church on the low moral level of carnal respectability, which merely educates and ornaments the intellect, animal propensities and powers, without transcending their instinctive selfishness and brutality. Refined, cultivated, polished, genteel selfishness and brutality are selfish and brutish still — often intolerably so, in utter hostility to the principles and spirit of the gospel. Jesus sought to lay the foundations of a church which should be "the light of the world" and "the salt of the earth," composed of those who were "wise as serpents and harmless as doves," who were "not of the world," but "chosen out of the world" to redeem the world. But if the light "be hid under a bushel" and the "salt have lost its savor" — if the members of the church bearing his name illustrate in their individual and social life no higher virtue and piety than prevail elsewhere, must not moral darkness, corruption, and iniquity still reign?

What, then, are we to think of the nominal church of Christ as it is and has been ever since its union with and practical surrender to the organized civilization of the world under Constantine the Great in the fourth century? Giving it all the credit which truth and justice demand, yet, as a whole, has it been essentially "of the world," with the same general admixture of good and evil, of righteousness and unrighteousness, which have characterized the unregenerated governing classes of society from generation to generation down the stream of time. Its worthiest and most Christlike representatives in all ages have been individuals, groups, and small sects — mostly persecuted heretics or schismatics — who went to the fountain head of Christian knowledge to learn what truth and duty are and taught and lived what was there revealed to them. It is these who have kept Christianity in its primitive purity alive in the world, preserving it from utter perversion or absolute extinction.

It is, however, claimed by some that the church is greatly improved in these later days, having put away many of the follies, absurdities, barbarities, iniquities, which it tolerated and fostered a few centuries ago. Perhaps so. But tried by the standard presented us in the precepts and injunctions of Jesus, what is it now? Do its leading denominations and their adherents scrupulously exemplify almsgiving, prayer, religious duties and observances in a way "not to be seen of men?" Do they render no idolatrous worship to the god Mammon, covet no property advantage over their fellows, and bestow their superfluous wealth on needy, suffering humanity for its relief and moral elevation? Do they heed scrupulously the Savior's counsel, "Be ye not called Rabbi, for one is your Master, even Christ," and not only refrain from all efforts to obtain self-exaltation and positions of superiority over their fellows, but use whatever gifts or opportunities they may have that others do not possess, not for their own emolument but for the good of those less fortunate than themselves? How much regard do they pay to the command, "Swear not at all, but let your communication be Yea, Yea, and Nay, Nay"? Do they renounce all resort to injurious and deadly force in their treatment of offenders, love their enemies, bless those that curse them, and continually endeavor to overcome evil with good? It is true that many members of the church at large are personally meek, generous, upright, charitable, and faithful to most of the sacred trusts of life, as is the case with some of the unchurched and irreligious; yet vast multitudes of them — making up its average constituency and determining its predominating character and polity — are grossly recreant to their acknowledged Lord's most sacred, important, and vital principles, precepts, and commands, making solemnly pertinent His condemnatory words, "Why call ye me Lord, Lord, and do not the things that I say?"

To meet the exigencies of the case thus indicated and the needs of the world, I, with much painstaking and deliberate thought, made ready for publication the volume mentioned, believing and feeling that I was thereby rendering some effectual service to the cause of truth and righteousness and storing up for future use counsel and admonition calculated to aid in the ultimate enfranchisement of humanity and in the building up of God's kingdom on the earth.

This being accomplished, I set myself about writing a detailed and authoritative "History of the Hopedale Community" from the first inception of it in 1840 to its final extinction in 1875, through all its multiform phases and vicissitudes. I felt that although the undertaking, begun in all sincerity and faith, had met with disappointing and, in some respects, humiliating failure, it would be a great misfortune to have its experience lost to the annals of human progress and reform. I felt, furthermore, that no one was so familiar with its doings and endeavors, its records and relics — with all its affairs from first to last, as myself; and that if I did not prepare a memoir of it and provide for having it put in permanent form no one else would do it, and the whole nobly conceived undertaking with all the aspirations, hopes, struggles, achievements it represented, would fall into oblivion and be irretrievably gone from the knowledge of men, or remembered only as another token of human conceit, folly, and fanaticism. Unwilling that such a fate should swallow up a movement characterized by so much that was unselfish, exalted, and Christlike; by so much that promised only good and happiness to mankind; by so much worthy of grateful commemoration, I devoted what time I could command aside from that necessarily taken up with other duties during the year 1875, to the preparation of this work, bringing it to completion in the January following. What I then wrote and regarded as final has been supplemented by a brief addenda, compiled from data not then in my possession, the whole going to make a volume of considerable size, and one which I trust will prove suggestive and helpful to social students and reconstructionists in coming time.

At the urgent solicitation of the authorities and leading citizens of the town of Milford, I entered into an engagement in the spring of the just-named year to write a comprehensive history of that municipality, and soon after took such preliminary action as seemed necessary to the successful prosecution of the undertaking. It proved to be a tedious and withal somewhat irksome task — a long-drawn-out performance of literary plodding and drudgery. I spent all the time and labor upon it which I could spare from other imperative activities during the next six years, receiving, as I proceeded, much valuable assistance from my wife. My cares and responsibilities in regard to it were much increased toward the last by my consenting to act as chairman of the town's publishing committee, making it incumbent upon me to look after many of the details incident to the passage of the work through the press. It was finally completed in all its parts in 1882 and given to the public, with whom it won well-earned credit as well as encomiums from those competent to judge concerning that kind of production. It made a royal octavo volume of eleven hundred and fifty-four pages, crowded with historical, genealogical, and biographical matter, the collection, arrangement, and writing of which required immense toil, carefulness, and patience. This achievement was not in the line of religious and moral reform, and so not altogether to my taste and pleasure. It was rather a business affair, entered upon mainly from the motive of a moderate monied compensation to be added to other small earnings and savings with which to provide for the printing and distributing of more important but less remunerative works directly promotive of human regeneration, elevation, and happiness. It served this purpose to a reasonable extent, was useful and gratifying to the general public, compromised none of my conscientious scruples, and, on the whole, added to my personal influence in fulfilling my recognized mission on the earth.

I continued to discharge the duties of my position as pastor of the Hopedale parish and allied congregation down to April 23, 1880, — my 77th birthday — when I finally resigned and closed my labors in that capacity, though still remaining in service as minister-at-large in the general community. This I did, not because I was made to feel that I was no longer wanted as religious teacher and guide, for I was always listened to with respectful attention, even by those who professedly and practically could not accept or conform their lives to my most pronounced testimonies, and treated with the utmost kindness and cordiality in all my relations to and intercourse with my employers and the people at large. Nor was I ever, even by intimation, restricted in my freedom of preaching, illustrating, or applying the gospel as I had received and understood it. But I felt that at the age I had attained it were better for all concerned that I should be released from the routine of ministerial service which I had been following under then existing auspices for thirteen years and under varying conditions for nearly sixty years; and also that my hold on the faith and conscience of my parishioners was too weak to bring them into working harmony with my highest convictions of Christian duty or to do them much good on the worldly plane of individual and social life which they occupied and to which they were determinedly committed for the rest of their mortal days — my preaching and the plain requirements of the sermon on the Mount to the contrary notwithstanding.

I was honorably discharged from the pastoral office, agreeably to my expressed desire and purpose, and through the influence of my ever kind friend, George Draper, was made the recipient of an annuity of four hundred dollars, to continue in quarter-yearly payments to the end of my natural life. This annuity, though coming nominally from the parish by a formal vote, was nevertheless contributed by Mr. Draper until his decease, and by the executors of his will afterward, agreeably to a provision specifically made in that instrument. This regularly received stipend, together with my small incidental earnings, funeral and marriage fees, and the savings of more recent years, augmented by the co-operation of a remarkably prudent wife, gradually overcame the pecuniary losses which still followed me, enabled me to meet all my financial obligations, placed me beyond beggarly dependence on others, and insured me a competence for more unproductive years. It also furnished me with means to answer the calls of incidental charity, to contribute to worthy causes, and to reciprocate some of the manifold expressions of respect and love shown me, without fear of coming to want or subjecting myself to special acts of self-denial as in former times. And what was to me best of all, it gave me an assurance of having something beyond the supply of my earthly needs for the promulgation of those divine principles which I had labored so disappointedly to make subservient to the uplifting and happiness of mankind, after I should have passed away. This was to me a token of the good providence of my Heavenly Father which awakened in my soul sentiments of profound gratitude and joy. It fulfilled not only the assurance of Christ that they who seek first the kingdom of God shall have all needful temporal things added to them, but the promise repeatedly made to me in moments of deep despondency and gloom by the voice of the Spirit speaking to my inner consciousness and saying, "I will never leave thee nor forsake thee"; "My grace is sufficient for thee." Blessed be the name of the Lord and His faithfulness forever and ever. Surely my soul shall love and trust Him even in the valley and shadow of death.

[NOTE. At this point of the narrative recorded in these pages, reached on the 12th of July, 1890, the strength of the writer, which had been perceptibly failing for some months, so far gave way as to oblige him to lay aside his pen for needed rest. He did this reluctantly and with the earnest hope that a few days' respite from labor would revive his energies sufficiently to enable him to resume his work and carry it through to completion—a consummation he ardently desired to accomplish with his own hand. That hope, alas! was vain. Instead of the anticipated restoration, he sank slowly into that confirmed but painless illness which three weeks later terminated in death. This event left the story of his long, busy life to be finished by another, who, while he assumes the task with a sincere desire to discharge the trust imposed on him faithfully, yet feels his inability to fill the place of the autobiographer or do justice to that part of his career, small though it be, which remains to be delineated.

Happily, however, he himself, although too weak to wield the pen, was for some days so far in possession of his mental powers as to be able to specify the more important things he wished to have mentioned in what was still to be written, which, with the aid of an elaborate diary, will enable his representative not only to carry out the general purpose of the work and so preserve its essential unity, but do it largely in the original author's way and even in his own language. For much of what follows is quoted from his exact words and what is not is dictated by a careful study of what he has left on record of himself. Such being the case, the auto-biographical character of the book is preserved, although it will necessarily lack many observations and reflections which the one of whom it treats would have introduced; much to the regret of his surviving friends and to the loss of the reading public. With this note of explanation and an appeal for the kindly indulgence of all concerned, the narrative proceeds to the end.— *Editor*.]

As no reference has thus far been made to a memorable occasion in the annals of the town in which the autobiographer had been a resident for nearly sixty years and to the prominent part he took therein, it seems to be the first duty of his deputy to take appropriate notice of the same and make record accordingly. On the 4th of July, 1876, the one hundredth anniversary of the signing of the Declaration of Independence was patriotically observed in all the larger municipalities of the land. The citizens of Milford made arrangements for contributing to the general demonstration of festal joy, resulting in what the *Journal* characterized as " the most imposing and successful celebration ever witnessed in the vicinity." Mr. Ballou, who had already begun to collect material for his history of the town, was very properly honored with an invitation to deliver the principal address of the day. The invitation was accepted and the involved duty faithfully performed. The orator, in what he had to say, reviewed briefly the circumstances attending the early occupancy of the territory then known as the " Easterly Precinct " of Mendon; the privations, struggles, and sacrifices of the pioneer settlers; the incidents connected with its incorporation; the inception and growth of its various industrial, educational, social, moral, and religious interests and institutions; as he also portrayed its general position and importance in the community at large and in the state and nation. Giving due credit to all who had in any way aided in promoting the common prosperity, and bringing to notice many things in the endeavors and achievements of its population worthy of grateful commendation, he, with characteristic regard for great principles of moral and social order, pointed out existing evils and defects, declared what in the body politic ought to be outgrown or overcome, and closed with a few eloquent and incisive sentences setting forth the only adequate remedy for whatever was working or threatened peril and disaster to the public or private well-being and happiness. In his peroration he referred a second time to the courage, integrity, and faith of the founders of the town, proceeding thence to say:

"Let us emulate their real virtues, their fidelity to their light and privileges, and their indomitable energy in overcoming the difficulties of their lot. They exterminated the wolves and rattlesnakes that infested this territory and turned its rugged forests into fruitful fields. Be it ours to subdue our own wild animal natures — the ravenous lusts and venomous propensities and crude passions of the carnal man. Let us dwell less in the basement and more in the upper story of our natures. If we cannot wholly shun or remove the temptations which are incident to material, intellectual, political, or social progress, let us manfully resolve to overcome them by the cross of rational and Christian self-denial. Herein lies the remedy for the present threatening distempers of our whole nation."

After indicating in a few terse passages the lofty and splendid attainments of personal and social excellence to which men are summoned "as children of the All-Father and sympathizing fellow-members of the great human family," he concluded as follows:

"This is the sublime march of moral progress that opens before us. It comes next in order to the splendid material, intellectual, and political progress we this day celebrate. Say not it is impossible, unattainable. I tell you it is the will of God — our duty, our privilege, our destiny. Therefore, let us gird up the loins of our solemn resolve, of reason, faith, hope, charity. Our fathers were the heroes of the past; let us be the moral heroes of the coming age. Let gratitude and a sense of responsibility inflame our ambition to achieve a glorious and God-approved future."

The oration was listened to with rapt attention and received from various quarters appreciative commendation "both for the matter embodied in it and its eloquent delivery." It was published in full the following morning in the *Milford Journal* and subsequently given a place in the voluminous history of the town.

At the time of the centennial celebration of the incorporation of Milford, June 10, 1880, Mr. Ballou excused himself from participation in the public exercises of the occasion, save as a silent and deeply interested listener and observer. He, however, contributed to its success so far as to loan his manuscript history, then nearly ready for the press, to the accomplished and patriotic orator of the day, Gen. Adin Ballou Underwood, from which to obtain data for his able, eloquent, and highly acceptable address.

As has been repeatedly intimated in other chapters of this work, Mr. Ballou, through his espousal of and labors for the anti-slavery cause, became early acquainted with the great champion of universal liberty, William Lloyd Garrison, between whom and himself a friendship was formed as lasting as life. Not that he was in any sense a blind follower or partisan adherent of that distinguished agitator, for he differed very radically from him in some important particulars, as has been before shown; but that he believed in the man — in the purity of his motives, in the disinterestedness of his purpose, in the intrinsic excellence of his character, and in the grandeur of the work he was commissioned to do for God and humanity. Frequent correspondence was carried on between the two while the conflict with the slave system was going on, and occasional missives passed to and fro ever afterward. Some time in 1878, the year before Mr. Garrison's decease, Mr. Ballou seems to have sent him congratulations and kind wishes on some noteworthy occurrence in his life, possibly a birthday, to which in due time came a response, accompanied by a picture of the eminent civilian and philanthropist of Great Britain, George Thompson, M. P., whom Mr. Ballou had met personally on some of his visits to this country. The letter was greatly prized by the recipient and will be read by the friends of both him and its author with interest.

"Roxbury, Mass., Nov. 23, 1878.

"DEAR FRIEND BALLOU: Receiving your postal card with its good wishes is next to seeing you face to face, which it would give me very great pleasure to do, including your estimable wife. The days of 'auld lang syne' can never be forgotten by me, when we were working actively together for the promotion of temperance, justice, and freedom to the southern bondmen, non-resistance, and practical righteousness in all its bearings. Your labors and testimonies were of invaluable service in enlightening the understanding, quickening the conscience, melting the heart, animating the spirit, and giving a powerful impulse to the various philanthropic and reformatory movements against which all 'the powers of darkness' were fiercely arrayed. Yours was the standard of immutable truth and absolute right, unflinchingly maintained by you through trials and privations of no ordinary kind. I contemplate your whole life admiringly. It has been unreservedly consecrated to the service of God and your fellowmen, with patience, fortitude, courage, exemplary self-abnegation, and in the spirit of all-embracing love. You have labored 'in season and out of season' for the good of others, for the reconstruction of society on the basis of mutual rights, interests, responsibilities, and duties after the exact pattern of the golden rule; for noble conceptions of the fatherhood of God and the brotherhood of man; for the largest freedom of thought, inquiry, and speech in matters of religious faith and worship; and for the arrival of that blessed period when all wars shall cease throughout the earth and the kingdom of peace be established thereon.

"Nor have you labored in vain. On all these subjects great advances have been made in public sentiment since you began to bear those testimonies which can never return void, and which, from your life and pen, have exerted a widespread influence, multiplying converts and shaping human destiny. Let this be comforting to you, even though your aspirations and efforts have failed to accomplish much that you had hoped to realize before seeing the 'last of earth' and entering into rest. You will pardon me for this expression of my feelings.

"I was sure you would feel gratified in receiving the very striking heliotype of dear George Thompson, representing him, as it does, almost in his prime. His was a most desirable translation. With kind regards to your wife, I remain

"Yours in warmest fellowship,

"Adin Ballou.   WILLIAM LLOYD GARRISON."

It is a noteworthy fact in the experience of Mr. Ballou that by his high personal character, his kind and courteous bearing, and recognized purpose to be impartially just and honorable in his treatment of all classes and conditions of men, he was able to gain and retain the confidence and regard, not only of those who were in hearty accord with him in his distinctive principles and views, but of those opposed to him in those respects — of those who were sometimes brought into emphatic condemnation by the practical application of his principles and views to human conduct in the various interests and relations of life. This was strikingly illustrated in the incident now to be narrated. In the spring of 1879 he was invited, agreeably to the prevailing custom in town, to take his turn with other resident clergymen in addressing the Maj. E. F. Fletcher Post, G. A. R., of Milford, on the Sunday preceding the approaching Memorial Day, when the members as a body would attend the church in Hopedale, where he was at that time the regular minister. The invitation was accepted and a sermon was delivered as proposed on the 25th of May, a large congregation besides the soldiery being present. To show how he acquitted himself on that occasion — how he could be true to his own avowed principles as a radical peace man and at the same time address a company of men whose organic existence not only implied the rightfulness of armed resistance to enemies of the public order and welfare, but was based upon the fact that those men had been personally engaged in the work of human slaughter — to show how he could do this without compromising himself and yet secure the approbation and continued regard of his military hearers, liberal extracts from his discourse are subjoined:

"Render, therefore, to all their dues; tribute, to whom tribute is due; custom, to whom custom; fear, to whom fear; honor, to whom honor." — *Romans, 13: 7.*

"Christ, His apostles, and the primitive Christians took no part in civil government, in war, in military affairs, or in politics, claiming to stand on a higher moral plane and to lead mankind, by precept, example, and voluntary association, into a state of universal brotherhood and peace. But it was one of their settled principles to pay due respect to civil and military rulers in their sphere, to be no detriment to civil society, as it necessarily existed for the world's general good under divine providence, and scrupulously to fulfill their own grand mission by peaceably showing a more excellent way of social order. I have been endeavoring to stand faithfully and consistently on this primitive Christian platform for over forty years, and today I most firmly and sincerely believe it to be the highest which any human being can occupy. Now you, military gentlemen, have honored me with an invitation to preach you a sermon appropriate to the Sunday next preceding your annual decoration of the graves of your comrades who died in defending the national union in the late gigantic civil war. You do not expect me to be disloyal to my own long-declared standard of Christian righteousness, but you have a right to expect me, in accordance with a sacred principle of that standard, to render to yourselves and those you represent due honor. I intend to do so; how, then, shall I do it?

"In the first place, how am I to determine what honor I owe you? By what moral standard must I measure your deserts? There are three moral standards by which all men may be justly tried: — first, the highest conceivable absolute standard of righteousness, which I hold to be that taught and exemplified by Jesus Christ; second, the commonly acknowledged civil and moral standard of one's age and country; third, the moral standard which an individual himself professes to be governed by.

"This third standard may agree with the first or with the second, or, on peculiar points, may differ from both. It is strictly the standard of the individual whose highest convictions of duty it declaratively expresses. No moral standard measures any one's strict moral deserts in a particular case, because personal circumstances always affect each individual's merit or demerit. But any moral standard determines what shall be considered right or wrong in human conduct under that standard, and generally, to some extent, the merit or demerit of actions. Now, for myself, I accept what I have called the absolute standard of Christian righteousness as my own. You must, therefore, measure my conduct by that standard, giving me the benefit of palliating circumstances wheresoever I fall short of my own acknowledged duty. But I cannot justly measure your conduct by this standard unless you acknowledge it to be yours, which I take for granted you have not done. I presume your standard is the second one stated, viz: 'the commonly acknowledged civil and moral standard of your age and country.' Therefore, I must measure your conduct by that standard, and give you the benefit of all mitigating circumstances wheresoever you may have fallen short of your acknowledged duty. Thus I shall obey the precept of my text, rendering to you your dues, and so honor to whom honor.

"Under your standard, patriotism is an indispensable duty. If not the highest, it is one of the highest civil and moral duties. Such you doubtless regard it. Patriotism requires you to stand by and maintain by force of arms and sacrifice of life, if need be, the existence, integrity, independence, laws, government, and honor of your country. The army, navy, militia, and warlike resources of every country are pledged to all this. All war rests for its justification on the rightfulness of self-defence by deadly force whenever endangered by enemies. It is deemed not only rightful, but an absolute necessity in the last extreme. The principle is the same for individuals, families, communities, and nations. And whoever holds this principle at all, as a part of his moral standard, is logically bound to hold it equally sacred in respect to individuals, families, communities, and nations.

"Granting this civil and moral standard of your age and country, which makes patriotism by deadly force in the last extreme an indispensable duty, to be the one by which I must measure your conduct, gentlemen, my duty is clear. You have, under that standard, done great and noble service. So did your comrades, whose graves you annually decorate with flowers, and whose deeds you are in various ways endeavoring to commend to posterity as worthy of patriotic imitation. There are three classes to whom honor is due for services rendered and burdens borne for their country, to make it triumphant in the last memorable conflict. First, the soldiers who fought its battles amid such peril of life, limb, health, and home comforts — many myriads of whom went down to an untimely grave. Second, those who sympathetically contributed so much of personal attention in the hospitals and on the sanitary commission for the alleviation of soldiers' sufferings — in which the women of the country exhibited such patriotic devotion. And third, the mass of citizens and people who furnished warlike supplies and have borne the inevitable burdens of consequent taxation. Foremost of these classes, by common consent, the post of honor belongs to the soldiers — and foremost among these to their dead and crippled living. Your fellow patriots have appreciated the services of their warriors none too highly, but far better than such services were ever appreciated before, since war on earth began. They have relieved, honored, and compensated them incomparably more justly than in any past generation a nation ever did those of its fighting defenders. Still, there remains, as results of the war, a vast amount of privation, loss, and suffering, which can only be compensated in some general way by national good. Go, then, as you have done for many a year in the vernal season, and commemorate the fame of your fallen associates with your wonted floral tokens. Go and teach posterity to serve and die for their country in like manner so long as they profess to be governed by the same civil and moral standard. And I, too, will accord to the dead and living the tributes and honors which fidelity to their own highest acknowledged standard of duty merits.

"But while I am bound to render these dues to others, I am no less solemnly bound to be true to my own highest convictions, under that absolute standard of righteousness which enjoins pure good will to all mankind, friend and foe, and which requires me to lay down my life rather than intentionally kill, injure, or harm any human being."

The preacher then went on to re-affirm his own long-maintained views upon the subject of war and peace, declaring his unfaltering conviction that the principles involved in the Christian doctrine of perfect love to all human beings are true and invulnerable and will sometime prevail throughout the world, and that his own well known course of theoretical and practical fidelity to them will at length be vindicated in the entire deliverance of mankind from bloodshed and slaughter, and the universal reign of amity and brotherhood. He concluded as follows:

"I have respect enough for you, military gentlemen and sympathizers, to believe that you understand my position, my ideas, my sentiments, and my exposition of the subject discussed. I trust, therefore, that our respect for each other is mutual and will remain forever steadfast. I have always found those who had most distinguished themselves on the field of battle and won laurels in war most ready to deprecate its horrors. For they have seen and felt them. No great military chieftain loves war for its own sake. Such define it only as a necessity, and as the least evil in extreme cases, because the world is not yet wise and good enough to do right without martial compulsion. Well, then, if this is your best thought and highest conviction, my friends, fight when you must, as you have done, on the side of justice, freedom, and human rights; and I will be one to render you due honor—judging you by your own acknowledged standard of civil and moral rectitude. In turn I trust you will reciprocate these sentiments and bid me do my duty as I understand it; bid me be true to my highest convictions; bid me be faithful to my acknowledged standard; bid me serve my country and humanity in the most excellent way I can, conscientiously; bid me do what little I may in my generation to fraternize our race, what little I can to render war morally avertable, to spare you and the soldiers of the future the sad necessity of sacrificing life in suppressing the violence of public enemies, and of weeping with widows and orphans over the graves of fallen comrades. And thus if our paths of duty diverge in some important respects, may we all unite in the one holy prayer of faith, hope, and charity: ' Thy kingdom come; Thy will be done on earth as in heaven'; singing with the poet:

> "Let love and truth alone,
> Hold human hearts in thrall;
> That heaven its work at length may own
> And men be brothers all."

Early in the year 1881 the subject of this life-history passed through one of the most notable and trying experiences of his whole mortal career — one which his own graphic pen and that only could adequately describe. It was occasioned by the serious and well-nigh fatal illness of his devoted wife, from which she recovered in a marvelous manner as if by some special healing agency or power from on high. As far as possible, he will be permitted to tell the story of the occurrence himself, liberal notes concerning it being taken from his diary.

The first indications of the existence of the insidious disease (pneumonia), he speaks of in his record of Thursday, January 6, as follows: "Wife very busy upon a letter to Abbie. Four o'clock finished it and I carried it to the P. O. at once. She had written it seated by the north side of the sitting-room, complaining of feeling cold. She ate but little supper and soon began to be sick at stomach, vomiting and shivering with increasing chills. I was much alarmed and gave undivided attention to her." He assisted her in retiring early and administered such palliatives or remedies from the household stock as seemed advisable. "But she passed a miserable night, and I an anxious one," "praying for relief but fearing the worst."

"The next day, Friday, she seemed in the way of recovery," and so continued until towards noon on Saturday, when unfavorable symtoms appeared and the family physician, Dr. Jerome Wilmarth of Upton, was immediately sent for. He "came promptly, examined the sick woman, pronounced one lung partially congested," and prescribed accordingly. The night following "she rested better than I feared."

Nevertheless, in spite of the acknowledged skill and tireless attentions of the doctor, the best of nursing, and the utmost solicitude and tender watching of relatives and friends, the invalid gradually lost strength and vitality for the week following, when she seemed past all power of recovery. On Thursday, January 13, the anxious husband writes: "Dr. comes; gives no hope of dear sick wife. Oh, my sad heart!"

On the next morning the diary reads thus: "Wife is much flushed with fever. Dr. pronounces her no better." And in the evening, after a second call, "He left, saying she was worse and sinking." The husband and all the household felt that she could not survive till morning. He retired to his chamber to get what rest he could, having been promised that he should be notified upon the slightest indication of the apprehended change.

"But before this," he says, "I had free though brief interchange with wife in which she spoke beautifully of her faith in the future, her resignation and confidence, and also about what I should do when she had gone, etc. She said she should be as near me and as much with me as permitted. All this was a great satisfaction to me, for I could not bear to have her leave me under a mental cloud. At the same time she expressed an intuitive hope that she might be spared a little longer." About this time the night-watcher, Mrs. Dutcher, brought in a beautiful bouquet of flowers. "She was delighted with it. She brightened up instantly and seemed almost transfigured. At length I retired. I kissed her goodnight and went to my bed-chamber groaning in spiritual prayer and dreading a summons to see her expire before morning."

Happily this was not to be. The diary contains an account of what transpired. "In the morning daughter Abbie, who had been summoned to the parental home some days before, came to surprise me with the news that her mother had passed a remarkably comfortable night and that her symptoms were better. What trembling, hopeful thanksgiving went up from my soul to heaven!" "Up a little past 7. Everything indicates that wife is really better. But I must wait and see if Dr. confirms it." "At length he comes, expresses a happy surprise to hear so good reports of the patient's comfortable night, examines her, and declares her to be decidedly better. Blessed be the Most High God whose holy angels have done what unaided man could not do. I will hope reverently, with unspeakable thanksgiving, for brightening prospects."

Nor did he hope in vain. The crisis had indeed passed and the course of the stricken one was thenceforth onward and upward to health and strength again. Her recovery was necessarily slow, but sure, with few if any, reactionary and discouraging indications. Not many weeks elapsed before she resumed the general charge of domestic affairs, finally regaining in large measure her accustomed health and strength, though not her former power of endurance, and these were continued to her until near the end of her mortal pilgrimage, which occurred somewhat suddenly at last, after two or three premonitory attacks, on the 7th day of August, 1891.

About a fortnight after the crisis just mentioned took place, the convalescent, remembering that the anniversary of the birth of her devoted daughter, who had been with her during most of her illness, was drawing near, conceived the idea of having the event celebrated in some appropriate way, and, quite contrary to the judgment and advice of both her nurse and husband, formed plans for carrrying that idea into effect. The result can be best learned from the diarist's own words, penned January 30, 1881, to wit: — "This is daughter Abbie's 52d birthday, and wife insists on giving her a surprise by inviting in her kind watchers, making a parental present, etc. I had doubted the propriety of this proceeding, fearing wife could not stand the excitement. But she was not to be overruled and I consented. It was a most extraordinary occasion. She had ordered preparations made for a collation. . . I had written a congratulatory note . . and enclosed a present, half from her purse and half from my own, to be given her, the daughter, during the exercises. The convalescent, chief of the occasion, was bolstered up in bed and all of us (thirteen in number) either seated or standing near. She opened the proceedings with a very affecting speech, considerably and pathetically broken by uncontrollable emotion. The whole company was affected to tears and sacred impressions were made. I followed with an address and the final presentation of my note and its contents. Daughter Abbie was deeply moved and made suitably appreciative response. Then came reciprocal congratulations, etc., succeeded by a repast, wife partaking with the rest. It was a solemn, loving, sacramental communion, at once tender, joyous, never-to-be-forgotten."

GRATITUDE FOR WIFE'S RECOVERY.

This little episode, instead of overtaxing the sick woman and hindering her progress healthward, as was feared, seemed to inspire her with new courage and to contribute substantially to her ultimate recovery. She improved rapidly thereafter, and at an earlier day than seemed possible was able to take her accustomed place again in the domestic and social circle. Gladder or more grateful heart never beat in human breast than that of Mr. Ballou at the *denouement* of this semi-tragedy — at the providential averting of this threatened disaster to his home and happiness. He ever afterward felt that on the memorable night of the 14th of January, 1881, when mortal help and hope failed, help from the unseen world was granted to save the dearest one on earth alive to him, that she might still share with him the cares and burdens of his lot, shed light and cheer upon his onward way, aid him in the prosecution of the work he had in hand, and by her kind and gentle ministry comfort and gladden his last hours in the flesh, and finally smooth his passage to the tomb. He was never able to speak of this trying experience afterward without deep feeling and some expression of the gratitude which the memory of it kept ever alive in his soul.

Little more occurred during the decade covered by the present chapter that requires extended notice. Most of the time, as it drew toward its close, Mr. Ballou gave to the completion of his "History of Milford," which was published early in 1882. To gratify his prevailing tastes, however, and further the supreme object of his life, he would snatch a few hours now and then from the swiftly passing days to prepare some paper or article upon some of the great themes he deemed important to mankind — " salting down " his views, as he was accustomed to say, for coming generations. In addition to the more elaborate volumes mentioned in preceding pages, he prepared in 1880 a review of an "Exposition of Matt. 16:26 by Rev. Hosea Ballou, 2d, D. D.," a theological dissertation, and also a critique upon the same author's interpretation of the text, "Resist not evil," the true meaning of which he felt had been perverted or misapprehended by his esteemed kinsman. He also about the same time reviewed a pretentious pamphlet entitled "Be Thyself," by William Denton, a popular lecturer upon scientific, reformatory, and religious subjects, and prepared an essay upon "The Importance of Definiteness in Religion," a favorite theme with him.

It may be stated in this connection that all through the daily chronicles of Mr. Ballou, especially during the later years of his life, there are to be found comments and criticisms of greater or less length called forth by current events, topics of the times, utterances of the pulpit and press, which may some day be gathered in a volume and given to the public. The nature of such a work can be determined by referring to some of the more important themes discussed, to wit: "The Relation of Science and Religion"; "The Assassination of President Garfield"; "Anti-Christian Spiritualism"; "Judge Wait's 'Christian Religion'"; "Proceedings of Unitarian Conferences"; "Tendencies of Unitarianism"; "The Office of Conscience and Reason"; etc.

On the 22d of April, 1882, the day before he entered upon the eightieth year of his age, Mr. Ballou made an arrangement with his brother, Ariel Ballou, M. D., and Hon. Latimer W. Ballou, a distant kinsman, both of Woonsocket, R. I., whereby he engaged to compile and edit an elaborate "History of the Ballou Family in America" on the one part, while they, on the other, became jointly responsible for the cost of publishing the same and for the payment to him of a moderate compensation for his services. Of the details of this contract and other matters pertaining to its fulfillment, due notice will be taken in the next chapter.

CHAPTER XXIV.

1882–1890.

BALLOU GENEALOGY — TOWN OF HOPEDALE — DR. EDDY —
TOLSTOI — BEREAVEMENTS — AUTO–BIOGRAPHY —
ADVANCING YEARS — ILLNESS AND DEATH —
FUNERAL.

THE history of Milford was completed early in the year 1882, and at the date of the opening of this chapter had been widely distributed throughout the town and vicinity. Mr. Ballou was therefore relieved of all responsibility relating to the preparation and printing of the volume, although, as a member of the publication committee, he was not wholly free from the obligations he had assumed in regard to it for several years afterward. He hoped and fully intended, when it was off his hands, to devote himself to his auto-biography and to such other writings as he ardently desired to execute before his decease, and while in the full strength and exercise of his powers of both body and mind. He did not care to enter again upon any line of work outside of his own chosen pursuits or engage in any undertakings which should divert his time and energy from carrying his determined purpose into effect. It was not of his own motion or choice, therefore, that he entered upon the task of compiling and editing an extended genealogy of the Ballou family already spoken of, but by the most urgent solicitation of his highly esteemed kinsmen, Dr. Ariel and Hon. Latimer Ballou, who were deeply interested in the matter and quite willing to meet all needful expenses that might be incurred, and who felt that he, of all the men they knew, was the one to have the matter in charge.

The contemplated work had been begun many years before by Ira Ballou Peck of Woonsocket, R. I., a member of a collateral branch of the family, long and meritoriously engaged in historical and genealogical labors in other fields of inquiry. He had collected a considerable amount of information pertaining to the immigrant Maturin Ballou and his descendants, but advancing years and lack of encouragement on the part of those more immediately concerned induced him at length to desist from further efforts in that behalf. What he had done having been brought to the notice of the gentlemen mentioned, they negotiated with him for the transfer of all the materials in his possession to them, with the understanding that it should be used and disposed of in such a way as to best secure the end which both he and they desired to have accomplished. This being done, they made the contract with the subject of this biography referred to near the close of the last chapter. The terms of that contract were that they should deliver up to him all the data — letters, family registries, copied records, transcriptions, and papers of every kind — received from Mr. Peck, and assist in obtaining further information of the same sort; and also assume all pecuniary obligations incident to its preparation and publication, including the payment to the compiler, once in three months, of a salary equal to thirty cents an hour for time actually expended; excepting such sums, not exceeding ten per cent of the aggregate amount, as he, of his own free will, might be pleased to contribute to the undertaking. [In the several settlements, it may be said, he voluntarily made a reduction of fifteen per cent. instead of ten, the limit formally agreed upon.] On his part, he was to collect, collate, arrange, and put in proper form whatever material, within reasonable bounds, could be obtained in order to make the work comprehensive, thorough, and symmetrical; prepare it for the press; superintend the printing, proof-reading, binding, and, in fact, everything necessary to its completion, making of it a volume well-proportioned and attractive in appearance, acceptable to his employers and to its patrons, and every way worthy of an honorable place in the historical and genealogical literature of the age.

Certain preliminaries being attended to, such as issuing circulars asking for information, looking over the medley of material furnished him for the purpose of ascertaining to what extent it could be made to serve the end in view, formulating plans for systematic labor, etc., he entered upon his task with great earnestness and zeal, and pushed it forward towards accomplishment with all possible dispatch. Yet, as for many years before, the time he was called upon to attend funerals, entertain visiting friends, and answer demands of various kinds at home and abroad, greatly interfered with regular consecutive work and desired progress. But he toiled on amid a multitude of delays, annoyances, and discouragements for six long years, when he had the satisfaction of seeing the end of his labors in that direction, and of feeling that his efforts were crowned with success. He had produced a volume of huge size, "much larger than any of us anticipated," the preface states, "containing more than twelve hundred octavo pages, over nine thousand names, and numerous artistic illustrations, printed and bound in creditable style." It was a monument of painstaking research, of unwearied toil, of scrupulous attention to details, reflecting great credit upon its author and upon all who aided him in bringing it to a successful issue.

It is eminently fitting and proper, as it is an act of simple justice, to state in this connection that Mr. Ballou was greatly assisted in the arduous task of producing this volume by his devoted, faithful, efficient wife, Lucy Hunt Ballou, whose services in looking over the manuscript copy and preparing it for the press, in helping to "correct the proof," in working upon the index, and otherwise, were of indispensable value. Without her aid, it would have been far more difficult, if not impossible, for him to have done the work with that thoroughness and accuracy which now characterize it, and which have evoked from many quarters appreciative commendation. To her effective co-operation, he himself bears willing and grateful witness on the pages of the book itself.

The Family Burial Lot. In the early days of the Hopedale Community, the founder, in concurrence with his wife, whose judgment and wishes he was accustomed to consult upon all matters of common interest, had selected in the public cemetery a family burial lot, to which was transferred soon after all that remained of the mortal bodies of his first wedded companion and two sons, previously interred elsewhere; in which was deposited, some years later, the manly form of his beloved Adin Augustus, and where he and the still living partner of his household expected in their turn to sleep the last sleep of earth and time. The exact localities of the remains of the departed had been marked by appropriate head-stones suitably inscribed, that of Adin Augustus being the most elaborate and artistic, as it was the most modern of them all. It had, however, been for some time the desire of both Mr. and Mrs. Ballou to have erected in the center of the lot a more substantial and imposing monument, representing the unity of the family and displaying more dignity, strength, and durability than those already standing within the confines of the hallowed place. Pursuant to that desire, a contract was entered into on the 7th of June, 1882, with Evans & Co. of Worcester, mortuary sculptors, by the terms of which they were to construct and put in position a memorial column of a specified design and finish, the whole to be completed early the following autumn. The provisions of the contract were fulfilled, and on the 20th of October the structure was set up in its designated place. It consists of a neat, pyramidal shaft, eighteen inches square at its lower extremity and fourteen feet high, having a base of suitable proportions, with appropriate plinth and die, resting on a massive pedestal, the whole being supported by a solid substructure, making it substantial, firm, and sure. On the front or easterly face of the pedestal is the family designation, BALLOU, in large letters, while above on different sides of the base are inscribed the names of those buried around and beneath, with the proper dates of birth and death affixed. The head-stones formerly standing remain and places of interment more recently occupied are similarly marked. The central structure presents a majestic, commanding appearance, due regard being paid to good taste and artistic requirements, and is eminently typical of him who was the head of the household group sleeping around — erect, calm, dignified, unmoved alike in sun and storm, and ever pointing to the skies.

Essays, Dissertations, and Reviews. In whatever work Mr. Ballou was engaged, his thought, when not otherwise definitely occupied, turned instinctively to his first and most constant love — to the contemplation of great principles of truth and righteousness, and to the devising of ways and means by which those principles could be carried out to practical issues and applied to the various relations and concerns of individual and social life; that so mankind might be benefited and blest and God be glorified. This was manifest not only in his private conversation and public addresses, but in the casual products of his pen. His ever-active mind was making continual sallies into the realm of the infinite wisdom, gaining fresh acquisitions of knowledge or formulating some new plans for doing good in the world, the results of which he was wont to commit to paper and file away for future reference or use. The number of such productions would astonish one not familiar with his life-habit in this particular. Without dwelling upon these, either separately or in the aggregate to any great extent, it yet seems proper that the titles of some of the more important of those prepared during the few last years of his life should be chronicled, and in certain instances the circumstances which called them into being or attended their appearance.

Early in 1883 he wrote an essay upon "The Relation of the Christian Church to Civil Society." This was a concise exposition of his views upon the true mission of the church of Christ in the world, which, in his judgment, was not to conform itself to and sanctify the self-seeking, mammon-serving, war-engendering habits, customs, and institutions of existing civilization, striving to direct, purify, elevate, and regenerate them as an inside factor, pledged from the start to a support of the very things needing reform and supersedence; but to organize and establish an ideal social system on an independent basis, and so illustrate the better way by a consistent example, without demoralizing alliances or crippling entanglements of any sort. Nothing, he believed, was more irrational and futile than to attempt to rectify abuses, remove evils, transcend a low form of moral and social life while consenting to and participating in what was to be rectified, put away, and transcended. And this theory he applied remorselessly to the position of those who, while professing a desire to build up a divine kingdom on the earth, are committed by organic relationship and practical co-operation to the support of institutions and activities in which the spirit and principles of such a kingdom are either ignored or virtually set at naught.

Later in the same year he wrote a review of a work brought out under Spiritualistic auspices and bearing the mystical title of "Oahspe," which its friends claimed was "a new bible," destined to take the place of the Hebrew and Christian scriptures among all enlightened and progressive people. The absurdity of such claims he vigorously exposed, while setting in their true light the real merits of the book. The following year he examined in a paper of considerable length and in searching and depreciative terms Rev. Hosea Ballou's "Treatise on the Atonement," published many years before, with the conclusions of which, calculated to defend the "death and glory" theory of a certain class of Universalists, he had no sympathy, deeming them unscriptural, irrational, and morally illusive and mischievous. He also about the same time prepared a tract upon "The Knighthood of Peace," designed to elucidate the truth of the saying of Milton, "Peace hath her victories no less renowned than war," or, in other words, to show that true courage, heroism, chivalry, can be cultivated and find opportunity to display itself in the innocent, bloodless pursuits and ambitions of life as well as upon the battle-field amid scenes of violence, carnage, and death. Another of these incidental productions of his pen was entitled "The Mistakes of Christ as Discovered by the Wisdom of this World," the object of which was to rescue the name of the Great Teacher from the undeserved reproach of certain classes of so-called advanced thinkers in modern times.

In the latter part of 1885, Mr. Charles K. Whipple, an old-time Abolitionist and Non-resistant, wrote an article for the *Boston Commonwealth*, giving therein his reasons for renouncing his radical peace principles and re-adopting the barbarous maxim, "Peaceably, if we can; forcibly, if we must" — the shibboleth of all the defenders of violence and bloodshed since the world began. A review of the article, setting forth the fallacy and inconclusiveness of the argument therein, was written by Mr. Ballou and sent to the author, who made a reply that called forth a lengthy and exhaustive rejoinder from the reviewer. The original article with subsequent correspondence and supplementary comments, forming a document of considerable size, has been carefully preserved. An essay upon "What is Religion?" another upon "The Union of Church and State in America," and a third upon "Three Spheres of Man's Action and Responsibility in Life," prepared at a later date, have a place in the archives of the household.

It was about the same time that the busy student and author planned a new volume, to be called "The Laconic Expositor." It was evidently designed to be a comprehensive disquisition or statement of views upon "Systematic Theology" and topics germane thereto. The first chapter or article, as he terms it, "Concerning God," seems to have been the only one ever written — the others having been left for that convenient season which never came. Nor was this the only instance in which similar plans and purposes of Mr. Ballou failed of realization. Among the multitude of miscellaneous papers, memoranda, etc., left by him have been found lists of subjects, more or less definitely expressed, upon which he wished to write — a lengthy catalogue involving the labor of his brain and pen for years ahead. Had he been permitted to round out a full century here upon the earth with a good measure of health and strength, he would not have been able to realize all his wishes in this respect — to finish the work he felt himself impelled to do.

In the year 1888 Mr. Ballou prepared a historical sketch of the town of Hopedale for a voluminous "History of Worcester County," published in March, 1889, by J. W. Lewis & Co., Philadelphia. This necessarily included a brief account of the inception, founding, growth, temporary prosperity, and final abandonment of the Hopedale Community, the lineal ancestor of the now incorporated township of Hopedale, and without which the township would never have existed. It is probable that no truer presentation of the spirit, purposes, and aims of the more active participants in that undertaking; of their hopes and disappointments, their trials and triumphs, their transitory success and final failure, with the causes of the latter, was ever given to the public than can there be found. To that authoritative repository of information upon the matter, the interested inquirer may refer while awaiting the publication of the more complete history of the movement by the same author at no very distant day.

Diary Notes. The daily record of current events, personal experiences, incidents from private and public life, etc., kept with much minuteness of detail during Mr.

Ballou's later years, is thickly studded with off-hand comments upon what arrested his attention and awakened a train of consecutive thought in his mind. In order to give the reader some idea of the nature and character of these spontaneous effusions, a few specimen quotations are introduced, with the occasions of them, as they came from his pen.

After listening to a sermon suggested by the death of Ralph Waldo Emerson, in which the preacher indulged in what was deemed a somewhat fulsome panegyric of the illustrious author and philosopher, Mr. Ballou gives his own less adulatory but not unappreciative estimate of him as follows: "I never read his wonderful writings with much pleasure or spiritual profit. His orphic truisms, when interpretable to common sense, are far better expressed in the language of scripture or by plain old poets; other sayings of his are not to me truths at all, or only in some vague, metaphorical sense." "As to Emerson's moral character, it was amiable, harmless, blameless. But I never understood that his practical ethics lifted him much above the surrounding civilistic, social, and scholastic level. He quietly cogitated and elaborated his own transcendental abstractions, many of which, if carried into individual and social practice, would regenerate the world. But the fatal hitch with such moralists is that neither they nor their admirers can sail out of the old ship of society as it is. They are so serene and softly that they live and die content to magnify their own cherished reveries and speculations. I once said to him, 'Mr. Emerson, why cannot you, with your handsome estate and the co-operation of congenial friends, start a community that shall illustrate a true fraternal order of society from which the world may take a pattern?' We had been accordantly deprecating the selfishness and antagonism of the world about us. His reply was: 'Mr. Ballou, I am no builder; if I can only set myself and my own family imperfectly right in these respects, it will be my utmost.' After some further conversation, the topic subsided. He was a very kind-hearted, well-disposed, and thoroughly honest man on his own plane, but powerless to rise above it."

Upon a sermon from Matt. 11: 4, 5, in which Jesus, in proof of his divine mission, says: "The blind receive their sight, the lame walk, etc.," Mr. Ballou observes: "He (the preacher) inserted the word *moral* before blind, lame, etc., and literalized the word 'gospel' into mere good tidings, as if Christ wrought no physical miracles and preached no great religious doctrines or ideas. He went full tilt against creeds, beliefs, and right heart-motives, in glorification of good works, external morality, leaving it to be inferred that outward righteousness has no necessary connection with true religious belief or positive right-heartedness of conviction or principles. I go for a union of the understanding and the outward conduct — no divorce of the one from the other."

The following train of thought was awakened by an article in a Spiritualistic journal, "glorifying modern Spiritualism in contrast with the bible and Christianity." "The chief priests of Spiritualism and the large majority of its adherents are now (1884) undisguisedly anti-Christian. Their genius is radically infidel in every respect excepting that of the fact of human existence after death. This they boast is a matter, not of faith, but of knowledge — with them scientific knowledge. As to scorn and hatred of a religious faith and life, properly so-called, they are hand in hand with Thomas Paine and his adherents. A small minority only grieve and protest, mostly in private. The result of all this will be to break down false traditional religion and prepare the way for the regenerate Practical Christian church. Like all other anti-supernaturalists, anti-religious creedists, these people can pull down but never build up much. They are unconscious axes in God's overruling hand to hew away what must be gotten rid of in order to the incoming of the kingdom of heaven." At a later date he writes upon the same general subject thus: "I am more than ever convinced that neither Swedenborg nor modern Spiritualistic mediums can be accepted as wholly reliable in their teachings. Between them and their spirits there is such a mixture of reality and unreality, of truth and error, that the elective sieve must be used freely." These utterances may be regarded as indicative of his final conclusions concerning the matter to which they refer. Holding to the last a rational belief in the possibility of spirit intercourse, and of its occasional realization under favoring conditions, he yet would accept nothing claiming to come from the unseen world except upon the most trustworthy and incontestable evidence. With him every voice professing to speak of things within the veil must prove itself worthy of credence before hospitable reception could be given to its testimonies.

Concerning a discourse to which he listened upon the subject of "Patience," the general doctrine of which was, "Do not struggle and worry to reform the world and make martyrs of yourselves by running ahead of the multitude; there is a natural growth of truth and righteousness; be patient and wait for nature's law of progress, etc.; things always come round in their season," he remarks: "But when did any great reform ripen without its anxious, self-sacrificing pioneers—its martyrs? What if Jesus and His apostles had taken things easy and waited for nature to establish Christianity in the world, thus avoiding persecution and martyrdom! If nature has anything to do with radical reform and progress, I am pretty certain she always begins by raising up a humble few who dare to outrun the wise and prudent leaders of the multitude and act the part of disliked pioneers and martyrs. But I prefer to think that the Divine Father Spirit manages this business of human progress — not Dame Nature!"

The Town of Hopedale. In the spring of 1885 a movement was started by some of the leading residents of Hopedale village, which had been growing rapidly in population, wealth, and in social and political importance for many years, contemplating its separation from municipal alliance with Milford and the incorporation of it, with considerable contiguous territory and the inhabitants dwelling thereon, as an independent township clothed with all the rights, immunities, and privileges belonging to other townships of the Commonwealth of Massachusetts. The first rumor of this action was received with much incredulity by the people round about and especially by the leading citizens of Milford, who affected to regard the project as too preposterous to be either worthy of serious consideration or within the possibility of successful achievement. But when it was subsequently learned that the persons interested were in earnest and determined to leave no stone unturned that was needful to gain the end in view, a powerful opposition was raised in the mother town equally earnest and determined to prevent the proposed division of its municipal territory and population. A vigorous warfare between the two parties thus formed was inaugurated and waged with tireless activity on both sides during the ensuing autumn in anticipation of the action of the incoming legislature, before which the question at issue was to be presented for final settlement. When the matter came up in that body for consideration and was referred to the committee on towns, who called for a hearing of the case, each party was represented by able counsel and many witnesses. to whose testimony and arguments protracted and respectful attention was given. After due deliberation the committee reported in favor of the petitioners and submitted a bill of incorporation to that effect. The bill was discussed at length in both branches of the General Court, passing through the different stages in each by a decisive majority, and received the approving signature of the governor, George D. Robinson, April 7, 1886. The event was duly celebrated by the people of Hopedale a few days afterward.

With the incipient steps leading to this consummation, Mr. Ballou had nothing whatever to do. He first heard of what was going on by incidental report, but interested himself in it very little until asked to sign the petition praying the legislature to establish a township as proposed. His judgment approving the measure, he decided to give it the benefit of his name and personal influence. Some effort was made on the part of opponents of the measure to induce him to reverse his decision, but he had acted advisedly and was not disposed to yield to solicitations of that sort. He had resolved, however, to maintain an independent position in the matter, and take no active part in the conflict respecting it, even to secure the object which he deemed wise and right. And it was with great reluctance and after much urging that he consented to appear before the legislative committee in behalf of the petitioners for a new town, which he did on the morning of Wednesday, January 27, 1886, in the "green room" of the State House at Boston. He was permitted to present his views upon the matter for the most part in his own way, though subject to considerable questioning by opposing counsel, and the usual cross-examination. So intelligible, full, and exhaustive was his statement, made in such a spirit of candor, conscientiousness, and impartiality, that it without doubt carried great weight with it to unprejudiced minds, and contributed considerably to the final result in the petitioners' favor. For the position assumed in this affair and his general course regarding it, Mr. Ballou had no occasion for subsequent sorrow or regret. His action may, for the time being, have grieved some of his warm personal friends in Milford, but it probably never caused the loss of one of them, and if there was in any direction some transitory feeling of dislike aroused, it soon passed away and the happy relations of former years were restored, never more to be broken or disturbed.

Dedication of the Town Hall. While the agitation of the question of incorporation was going on, Mr. George Draper, who was then at the head of the manufacturing interests of the village, and the virtual father of the town that was to be, caused to be laid the foundations of a substantial, commodious, imposing structure, which he designed to present to the proposed municipality for public use, in case it should become an established fact. The building was to contain a spacious hall with convenient ante-rooms on the second floor, and a store, library-room, post-office, and apartments for other public uses, underneath. The erection of the superstructure went slowly on after the town was incorporated and was approaching completion at the time of the owner's unexpected decease in June, 1887. But this greatly deplored occurrence did not prevent the execution of his original purpose concerning the building, the provisions of his will making everything sure in that particular. It was finished in the succeeding autumn, and appropriate dedicatory services were held in it on the 25th of October. Beautiful floral and other decorations graced the occasion, vocal and instrumental music gave it added interest, prayer was offered, formal addresses were made, a bountiful collation was served, followed by miscellaneous exercises of a more spontaneous character.

The oration, or dedicatory address proper, was delivered by Hon. ex-Governor John D. Long, and was a production of unquestioned merit, replete with eloquent passages and words of wisdom. There were in it however, one or two paragraphs, relating to the Hopedale Community, which reflected somewhat disparagingly and reprehensibly upon the experiment and those engaged in it, contrasting it and them in no favorable light with the existing state of things and the more recent actors upon the stage — the latter of whom the orator eulogized in that graceful, exuberant rhetoric, of which he is an accredited master. Mr. Ballou sat near the eloquent speaker, and listened with attentive interest and becoming patience to the depreciatory and pleasantly sarcastic criticism of the men and women who had toiled and suffered in the former days for truth, humanity, and God, and who, by their labors, as arduous and unremitting as any of later date, had made possible the Hopedale which was now the subject of ornate, unqualified panegyric. When he arose to address the assembled company, which filled every part of the spacious hall, immediately after the distinguished gentleman had taken his seat, every eye was fixed upon him and every ear was eager to hear what he had to say. He began by duly complimenting his predecessor's brilliant and able oration, and proceeded thence, as he felt bound to do in justice to himself, to his co-laborers in the endeavor to illustrate a Christian form of social life forty years before, and to the truth of history, to make a brief reply to the strictures, animadversions, and implications which had fallen from his excellency's lips. The scene has been delineated in part by Mr. Ballou himself in his sketch of Hopedale prepared for the Worcester County History spoken of a few pages back, an extract from which is here given verbatim, as found in that work.

"The writer was the only speaker of the occasion who represented the primary Hopedale of Community days, and he deemed it both a privilege and a duty to revive its memory and show that it had something more to do with preparing the way for subsequent success than appeared on the present surface of things. The honorable and eloquent orator of the day had indeed made one brief reference to it, but in terms of disparaging commiseration rather than commendation. He said:

"'On this spot some forty years ago one of those communities which spring up from time to time and from which so much is anticipated by the enthusiasm of their members, had undertaken, under the sweet guidance of the venerable and beloved pastor who is here today, to solve the problem of a happy, peaceful, industrious Christian brotherhood. It was a joint stock association, sharing capital and profits and run on common account. The result was a practical bankruptcy, avoided only by a change which followed no longer any transcendental lines, but turned to the line of hard, practical, American business; for George Draper took the plant into his vigorous hands, and enlightened and liberal selfishness became, as it usually does, a beneficence to which a weak communism was as the dull and cheerless gleam of decaying punk to the inspiring blaze of the morning sun. The man of affairs was, in temporal things, a better leader than the priest, as he usually is, and as nobody will so emphatically assure you as the priest himself. A meagre manufacturing enterprise that made a few boxes and cotton-spinning temples and employed a dozen hands began that marvelous expansion which in these few years, under George Draper's direction, has come to employ five hundred men, has grown from an annual product of twenty thousand dollars to one of more than twelve hundred thousand, has built and incorporated a Massachusetts town, has erected these trim, convenient homes of skilled and prosperous labor, has enlarged the original industry into four great business houses, constituting one of the largest cotton machinery manufacturing centers in the world.'

"Well, how was the 'venerable and beloved pastor'—the priest—likely to appreciate this rhetorical picture of 'weak communism,' etc? Did he wish to detract from the merits and fame of his lamented friend, the deceased George Draper? By no means. But he did not feel that the honorable reputation of that departed friend needed to be magnified by the unjust disparagement of the Hopedale Community or any member thereof. He was possessed of all the facts in the case and knew that the orator, through some mistake, had radically misrepresented the most important of them. He knew that Ebenezer D. Draper, the elder brother of George, was president of the Community when its joint stock and unitary interests were dissolved; that he was then a much larger capitalist than his brother and wielded much greater power; that he pronounced the condition of the Community eminently harmonious and prosperous less than two months before they decided to withdraw their capital; that there was really no bankruptcy nor any necessitating cause for a dissolution of unitary interests, except their withdrawal of three-fourths of the joint stock; and that 'the plant' was taken into the vigorous hands of the two brothers only to be changed into a successful manufacturing establishment managed on the principles of 'enlightened and liberal selfishness.' Therefore, knowing perfectly the entire history of the Community without whose devoted labors and sacrifices this new town of Hopedale would probably never have attained the importance now being glorified, and knowing that the rising generation was in danger of remaining uninformed on the subject, the aged 'priest' improved the few moments allotted to him in stating the salient facts of the case." "His speech was listened to with respectful attention and he was cordially thanked by many auditors for his exposition. He believes it made a salutary and lasting impression on the assembly."

It is to be regretted that the address of Mr. Ballou on that occasion had not been reported in full as it was delivered, so as to have given it a place here. For the transcriber of the above paragraph, who was present, cannot but feel that while it gives a generally correct idea of what was said, it at the same time but partially and feebly represents the pertinency, vigor, eloquence, and effectiveness which characterized it from beginning to end. It was a severe but merited rebuke of one who had spoken from gross misinformation, or who counted the godliness of gain better than the gain of godliness.

Dr. Richard Eddy and the Restorationist Schism. A circumstance growing out of Mr. Ballou's former connection with the Universalist denomination occurred about this time, giving him great pleasure and satisfaction. Rev. Richard Eddy of Melrose, an able and eminently worthy clergyman of that body, had been for some years engaged in writing a history of the form of faith it represented, to take the place of previously prepared ones nearly if not entirely out of print. The work was to consist of two volumes, the first of which had been already published. The second was mostly written and would soon go to press. It was devoted chiefly to modern Universalism and covered the period of Mr. Ballou's affiliation with its advocates and of the separation of the Restorationist wing from their ultra associates. The editor, an honorable and high-minded man, in treating of the schism referred to, determined to be just to all parties concerned in the controversy which caused it, and to give the whole matter a candid and impartial presentation in his work. In seeking to do this, he applied to Mr. Ballou, the only living person on the Restorationist side who had participated in it, for such information as he was pleased to communicate. The request was cheerfully granted. After the chapter treating of the subject was written, the author visited Mr. Ballou for the purpose of reading it to him in order that he might correct any errors that should have inadvertently been made, or suggest any emendations necessary to render it true to the facts in the case. Of what Mr. Eddy had prepared, Mr. Ballou says: "It was very full, clear, able, well-stated, truthful. I suggested one or two slight additions, which he cheerfully promised to insert in the proper place. The interview was exceedingly pleasant and gratifying." Mr. Ballou, as one of the leaders in the controversy noticed, had always felt that he and his sympathizing brethren had never had their position fairly stated by their opponents and the managers of the Universalist press, nor their motives and aims truly set forth, and it gave him great satisfaction to know that at length in a work that was to go down to posterity as an authentic history of the whole affair, even-handed justice was to be done them, and that they and their cause were to be placed upon their own merits before an enlightened public and the discriminating judgment of coming generations. This was all he had ever desired and this gained he was content and happy.

Count Leo Tolstoi. Upon the appearance in this country of the first of the translated writings of this Russian author and the consequent heralding of him as a new interpreter of the gospel of Christ and as a restorer of primitive Christianity as Jesus taught and exemplified it, Mr. Ballou availed himself of an early opportunity of becoming acquainted with the views and principles upon which such unusual representations were based. From what he learned incidentally through the public press, he hoped to find in this previously unknown author a man after his own heart — a consistent and radical advocate of peace, a friend of all true reform, and a wise counsellor in the work of inaugurating a new order of society from which all injurious force should be excluded and in which all things should be subordinated to and animated by the spirit of pure love to God and man. That his hopes in this direction were not realized — that he was seriously disappointed indeed in both the man and his teachings, the sequel clearly shows.

COUNT TOLSTOI AND HIS THEORIES.   509

The first mention of the new luminary in the religious firmament made by Mr. Ballou was in his journal of Feb. 16, 1886, as follows: "Commenced reading a lately purchased book, Count Tolstoi's 'My Religion.' Found many good things in it on ethics, with here and there an indiscriminating extremeism in the application of Christ's precepts against resisting evil with evil, and in his views of penal judgment and covetousness, or mammonism. But on theology found him wild, crude, and mystically absurd. His ideas concerning the divine nature, human nature, eternal life, Christ's resurrection, humanity's immortality, and the immortality of individuals, etc., are untrue, visionary, chaotic, and pitiably puerile. So it seems to me in this first perusal. But I will read further and think him out more thoroughly."

Further reading and more thorough thinking, however, did not bring him to a more favorable conclusion. "The saying of Christ, 'Resist not evil,' Tolstoi interpreted in its most literal sense, making it inculcate complete passivity not only toward wrong-doers but toward persons rendered insane and dangerous by bad habits, inflamed passions, or unbalanced minds, to the exclusion of non-injurious and beneficent force under any and every circumstance of life." To Mr. Ballou's apprehension this was carrying the doctrine of Non-resistance to an illogical and extravagant extreme, warranted neither by the teachings of Jesus nor by a true regard for the welfare of the evil-doer, the irresponsible maniac, or society at large, which often required wholesome restraint and physical force exercised without accompanying harm or injury to any one. Moreover, the distinctively religious expositions and indoctrinations of Tolstoi, as expressed in the book specified and in subsequent works, met with little favor from Mr. Ballou, whose ideas of God, man, immortality etc., were as definite and pronounced as his ethical principles, and in his estimate as essential to a high type of personal character or a true order of social life.

Some three years after Mr. Ballou began to acquaint himself with the writings of Tolstoi, Rev. Lewis G. Wilson, then pastor of the Hopedale parish and an interested reader of the latter, sent him some of the former's published works, with his photograph and an explanatory letter. On the 5th of July, 1889, he received a responsive communication in which the Count highly commended, in their principal features, the views contained in the publications forwarded to him, though subjecting some of their applications, especially the one relating to the rightful use of uninjurious force as mentioned above, to emphatic protest and denial. This communication Mr. Wilson handed to Mr. Ballou for perusal and a reply if he chose to make one. This he did in due time, taking up the more important points of Tolstoi's dissent — those pertaining to the practical application of Non-resistant principles, the right to hold property, and no-governmentism particularly, and answering them by extended argument and illustration. Thereto were added also some comments upon certain theological and spiritual positions assumed in "My Religion."

On the 26th of March, 1890, the mail brought a rejoinder to this missive, of which the recipient writes: "It relates to some points of difference between us as expressed in a letter sent him some months ago. He declines to argue and refers me to one of his published works, yielding nothing of his extreme Non-resistance even against madmen, but saying, 'I exposed all I think on those subjects.' 'I cannot now change my views without verifying them anew.' The dictum with which the letter opened, 'I will not argue with your objections,' characterized its entire contents and put an end to all discussion. It closed, however, with the statement that 'Two of your tracts are translated into Russian and propagated among believers and richly appreciated by them.'" Tolstoi's communication was answered about two months afterward, but no acknowledgement ever came back, by reason, no doubt, of the writer's death a few weeks later,—an account of which was sent by Mr. Wilson to the distinguished author, whose daughter responded, "Your tidings are very sad, and my father is deeply grieved."

Of the relation between Mr. Ballou and Count Tolstoi, nothing further need be said save that Mr. Wilson embodied the correspondence between them with collateral letters of his own in a sermon read to his congregation on Sunday, April 20, 1890, of which the diary says: "We were all deeply interested, pleased, and enlightened. I never was so much gratified with Brother Wilson's performance. His scripture-reading, prayer, hymns, etc., were all in harmony with Christian Non-resistance, and he dropped not a word or hint that implied reserved dissent from my views." It may be added that the substance of this discourse was subsequently rearranged by the author and published in the *Arena* for December, 1890—a portion of the last letter of Mr. Ballou to Tolstoi being omitted.

Not Lost but Gone Before. The inroad that death was continually making both upon the circle of Mr. Ballou's general acquaintance and that of his more intimate, tried, and trusted relatives and friends, imparted a pathetic and sacred interest to the last years of his earthly pilgrimage. At the obsequies of many of these he had been called upon to minister with words of comfort and consolation, often under a deep sense of personal bereavement and sorrow. Numerous instances of this kind have been already mentioned, with such tokens of esteem and affection as his heart prompted. Others occurred at a date subsequent to that of which his pen bore record for the pages of this work, a few of which may be noted here.

In 1883, Mr. William H. Humphrey, an old member of the Community and a near neighbor for thirty-five years,—a man exemplifying in a marked degree the entire circle of Christian qualities and powers, and one of Mr. Ballou's most steadfast, appreciative, and highly-prized friends, went to join the companion, equally true, faithful, and worthy, who some years before had been translated to the spirit home. Few persons sympathized more fully with him in his peculiar views of truth and duty and in his hopes and struggles for humanity than Mr. and Mrs. Humphrey, and few remained more true to their early professions of loyalty to him and the causes of which he was the trusted champion and promoter. The departure of each of them in turn sent a new pang of loneliness and grief through his breast.

Another death which affected him most sensibly was that of Mr. George Draper, a sometime member of the Community, who, though abandoning it and renouncing its essential principles, yet always held its founder in high regard and veneration, as attested by abundant proofs from time to time. "This lamentable event," to quote from Mr. Ballou's sketch of Hopedale alluded to, "took place in Boston whither he had gone for a temporary sojourn to obtain medical relief from kidney and other ailments, which, though not seemingly dangerous, he was anxious to overcome. Unexpectedly to all, he presently became alarmingly sick under treatment and in a few days expired. His remains were brought home and on the 11th of June his funeral was solemnized with every demonstration that bereaved family affection and public grief could bestow. Thousands appreciated his merits, sympathized in a great public loss, and united in reverential tributes of respect to his memory." On the occasion an appropriate address was made by Rev. Mr. Wilson, but the eulogy proper was pronounced by the old pastor of the departed, who had lived side by side with him for more than thirty years, and who could portray the strong points and many excellencies of his character better than any other living person. A sense of justice and the remembrance of unnumbered expressions of kindly consideration and personal esteem received through so long a period, served to render the testimonial paid the deceased, tender, loving, faithful, and true.

DEATH OF EBENEZER D. DRAPER.

It was only about four and a half months after the demise of George Draper, that his elder brother, Ebenezer D., followed him to the world of spirits. The latter for years had been an intermittent sufferer from the same troubles that caused the former's death, which, in the early summer, had assumed an unusually serious and threatening form. As time advanced they increased in severity and painfulness until they reached a fatal issue on the 19th of October, at the house of his brother-in-law, Mr. Green, in Boston, where he had a short time before taken up his residence. It was while engaged in the ministry at Mendon that this Mr. Draper and his then newly married wife, Anna (Thwing) Draper, a most excellent woman, became religiously interested in Mr. Ballou's preaching, and, though living in Uxbridge, united with his church. They embraced his teachings with a full heart in all their applications, and followed him devotedly through the several stages of practical reform, even to the extent of Non-resistance and Social Reconstruction. They were among the first to subscribe to the Hopedale "Declaration of Principles," as they were among the first to locate upon the territory where those principles were to be brought to the test of actual experiment and made the basis of a new order of society. In fact, Mr. Draper may be regarded as the most important factor, next to Mr. Ballou, in that enterprise, through the entire period of its existence. He was the only one of its original members who had any money to speak of to invest in it, or any recognized standing in the financial world. He had a taste and training for business, and was the most responsible person in the Community's industrial and pecuniary affairs, as Mr. Ballou was in its moral and spiritual concerns. The two were complements of each other, and stood by each other through good and evil report, through prosperous and adverse fortunes, through joy and sorrow, till the great crisis of 1856, when Mr. Draper, yielding to the assumed financial exigencies of the situation and to his brother's pertinacity, united with him in withdrawing their mutual support from the undertaking, thus bringing about its speedy dissolution. The friendship formed under the circumstances named and continuing steadfast through so many years could not be wholly disrupted by the calamitous issue which separated them in many of the particulars in which they had worked so long together, but was continued, though in a modified form, through life. Mr. Draper remained at Hopedale some years after the Community was given up, was prospered in business as senior member of the firm of "E. D. & G. Draper," acquiring a satisfactory competency with which he separated from the partnership in 1868. Two years later his most Christian wife passed on, soon after which he removed to Boston, where, having married again, he spent the remainder of his earthly days.

And now the end had come, and what was mortal of the right-hand man and trusted counselor of Community times was brought back to Hopedale, to receive funeral honors in the house of worship which he, more than any other person, had helped to build, and to be carried thence to its final resting place in the rural cemetery beside the sleeping dust of his first betrothed, who, for a generation had filled his home with music and sunshine, and rendered it attractive and delightful to hosts of appreciative friends by her blessed presence there. At the obsequies, fitting addresses were made by his long-time friend and pastor, and by his adopted son, Rev. Charles H. Eaton, D. D., of New York, interspersed with music and prayer, in the presence of a goodly company of relatives, friends, and acquaintances of other days, assembled to lay upon his bier a wreath of respect and affection sacred to his memory.

Another death that came very near to the subject of this biography and gave him a peculiar sense of loneliness and grief was that of his junior brother, Ariel Ballou, M. D., of Woonsocket, R. I. Though the so closely akin had differed widely from each other in many things, they yet ever held each other in mutual confidence, esteem, and love. In his Ballou history, the elder of the two pays merited honor to the natural ability, high character, and social standing of the younger, testifying to his personal worth "as an intellectual, judicial, self-poised, upright, courageous, high-toned man"; to his professional acquirements, imparting to him "increasing usefulness and fame for more than fifty years"; to his interest in education as "a strong and devoted friend of the public schools"; and to his religious fidelity as "a conscientious, devout, exemplary member of the Episcopal church." It was with a profound feeling of personal loss that the author of these justly commendatory phrases was called to look for the last time upon the face of him to whom they applied, and with unqualified regret that he who was so much interested in and had done so much for the compilation and publication of the "History of the Ballous in America," could not have lived to see the consummation of that great undertaking. But in the order of nature and Providence, it was not so to be. He died while the work was passing through the press, July 15, 1887, aged 81 years.

With the advance of age, Mr. Ballou's labors abroad became less frequent, being naturally less called for, as they were less desired on his part. Yet he had numerous invitations to preach, lecture, or speak on public occasions, but felt impelled to decline the greater part of them. Under existing circumstances, he thought he might be excused from all such efforts save those he could easily perform or that made some special appeal to him. He purposed at one time to refuse all further calls to funerals, but the importunities of surviving relatives and friends and the sympathy of his own heart for the stricken and bereaved, made it difficult for him to carry that purpose into effect. So that, as a matter of fact, the number of such occasions upon which he actually served in some of his later years was as great as at any equal period of his life. His weddings, as a matter of course, diminished toward the last, those at which he officiated occurring in the quietude of his own home. Occasionally he supplied a pulpit at Milford or Upton, or elsewhere not far away, but more frequently at Hopedale, in aid of and as a favor to the regular minister there. At gradually lengthening intervals he attended the meetings of the Worcester Conference, where he frequently had a message to deliver, and where he was always listened to with respect, interest, and acknowledged profit. He was, however, little from home during the last eight years of his life, rarely, if at all, to remain over night; his own work and the uncertain state of his wife's health combining to forbid prolonged absence on his part. He was a regular attendant at church on Sunday unless called elsewhere by a funeral or otherwise, or detained at home by the inclemency of the weather.

Mr. Ballou carried on an extensive correspondence throughout his entire public career. The nature of it changed with the changed conditions of his personal experience. At the outset and far on beyond mid-life, it was of a religious, moral, and reformatory character, but after engaging in historical and genealogical work it took on more of that peculiarity, though never losing the former altogether. He was a free and familiar off-hand writer, the sentences flowing readily from his pen, much of his own genial, affable, courteous, kindly spirit characterizing his letters, of whatever sort they might be — expositional, instructive, advisory, sympathetic, or consolatory — making him a pleasant, much prized, and much enjoyed correspondent.

Some two or three years before Mr. Ballou's decease, a few of his Hopedale friends, under the leadership of Rev. Mr. Wilson, who seemed ever ready to show his veneration and love for his honored predecessor, interested themselves in a project to secure a life-size portrait of him to be presented to the town as a perpetual memorial of his character and career. The object in view was finally gained by calling into requisition the superior skill and exquisite taste of Otto Grundmann, an artist of genius and of excellent standing in Boston and vicinity. By using several of the later photographs of his subject, with the aid of two or three personal sittings, he succeeded in producing a likeness worthy of his reputation and acceptable and gratifying to those employing him. The picture was paid for by private contribution and presented to the town of Hopedale at a regular meeting held Nov. 6, 1888. It was put in charge of the trustees, of the public library, the walls of which institution it now adorns and honors.

During the two years and more that intervened between the conclusion of Mr. Ballou's labors upon the family history and his last illness, all the time and energy he could command were devoted with conscientious fidelity to his auto-biography. Still, the former was so much broken in upon by calls to funerals, by visitation of friends from near and far, by domestic claims, or otherwise, that he found it impossible to accomplish what he desired in furthering his appointed task. He greatly regretted this, nay, was at times impatient at the delay which he seemed powerless to prevent. He realized that the infirmities of age were creeping upon him, that his days on earth at most could not be very many, and that the night was not far away "in which no man can work." He was anxious to complete with his own hand what he had begun and carried so far towards the end, feeling, no doubt, that no one else could do it so well as he — could make it so much what he earnestly desired it to be, a faithful portraiture of himself in all his inner and outer life. In this anxiety his family and friends fully sympathized, sharing with him the regret occasioned by hindrances it seemed impossible to foresee and prevent, or in any way escape. To add to the trying circumstances of the case and increase the delay, his eyesight, which had been remarkably good till he was past eighty years of age, enabling him to read and write without the aid of glasses, had, by reason of over-taxation in deciphering illegible manuscripts while engaged in historical and genealogical researches, become considerably impaired, causing more or less pain and threatening total blindness at no distant day. To such an extent had this trouble increased at length that he was obliged to give up using artificial light and even to cease from labor on dark and stormy days. Nevertheless, he kept up a good heart, was grateful for blessings still enjoyed, patient under the limitations that hemmed him in, and wrought on as best he could, cheerful and brave, till his weary brain and enfeebled hand could no longer respond to the mandates of his strong and earnest will.

On the 23d of April, 1890, the eighty-seventh anniversary of his birth, Mr. Ballou put on record the following outflow of devout and heartfelt meditation, worthy of a St. Francis of Assisi or of his own favorite, Thomas A Kempis:

"My 87th birthday! 'Bless the Lord, O my soul, and forget not all His benefits.' Surely 'His goodness and mercy have followed me all the days of my life.' When I obeyed His voice, He sustained me; when I sinned, He rebuked me in love and forgave me; He encouraged all my repentances and still accepted my services. When I was crushed by disappointment, He revived my despondent spirit. In all my troubles and sorrows, He accepted me. When I lost friends and feared desolation, He bade me trust Him, saying, 'I will never leave thee nor forsake thee.' And He never has. With temporal and spiritual blessings, manifold and innumerable, has He crowned my life. In prosperity and adversity, in judgment and mercy, He has been to me the same 'Father of lights, with whom there is no variableness or shadow of turning.' All my sins have been against His faultless and salutary laws, the ways whereof were death. All my righteousness has been imperfect and profitless to Him, but to me and my fellow-men a granary of unmerited and inestimable good. Therefore will I glorify Him evermore as the Holy Paternal One truly revealed by His son, Jesus Christ, 'of whom, through whom, and to whom are all things.' And now, Father, keep me in Thy bosom and in the guardianship of Thy holy angels during the few remaining days of my mortal pilgrimage, till I finish the work Thou hast given me to do. Then take me to the home Thou deemest suitable for me in the higher life."

THE END DRAWING NEAR.

There is little more to add to this narrative. Few acts or incidents worthy of note occurred during that portion of the 88th year of his age the subject of it was permitted to spend on the earth. His last sermon had been preached in his old pulpit at Hopedale Nov. 3, 1889; his last funeral was attended June 1, 1890; his last marriage was solemnized on the 26th of the same month; and his last public service was rendered on the 29th — a prayer at a Masonic gathering held in Music Hall, Milford, as a testimonial to St. John the Evangelist, instinct with fervor, impressiveness, and spiritual power. Thus ended a ministry of sixty-eight years and eleven months, remarkable for its length, its activity, and its usefulness — for its eminent service of God and man.

During the eight years, three months, and twelve days represented in this chapter, Mr. Ballou participated in 499 funerals, a larger number than ever before in the same length of time, making the aggregate of his life 2606; and presided at the marriage altar of 16 couples, filling out an aggregate of 1199, or of 2398 persons in all. So ends the category of his ministrations in these respects.

Last Illness and Death. The health of Mr. Ballou, which, with rare exceptions, was unusually good from early youth through middle life, continued so till near the end of his earthly pilgrimage. The familiar apothegm, "A sound mind in a sound body," had in him a striking illustration, due, no doubt, to his well-controlled appetites, his regular habits, his even and cheerful temperament, and the simplicity of his whole manner of life. The infirmities of age came upon him with a lingering tread. Until past four-score years his frame was wonderfully erect, and his step correspondingly firm and sure. The glow of his countenance and the vigor of his bodily powers were plainly discernible and subjects of remark far on toward the final hour. Such an example of well-preserved physical endowments, able to discharge their respective functions and free from the ills and pains often accompanying such length of days, is rarely seen.

Nor did his mind seem less vigorous and sound than was his physical system. Its faculties remained singularly acute and active almost to the last. People who met him in private or listened to him in public, commented upon the clearness and energy of his thought and utterance. Happily for him and for his family and friends, no weakening of his intellectual powers manifested itself and no lack of command or balance of the attributes of the understanding, until stricken with the painless illness which brought his earthly labors to an end, and which, not many days afterward, terminated his mortal career.

Nevertheless, his bodily powers had for some time previous to that final attack been slowly giving way, and his hold on the things of earth and time had been growing less and less secure. His neighbors and friends, kindly solicitous for his health and general welfare, and watchful of changes in his personal appearance, had noticed through the spring and early summer of 1890 what they thought and feared were indications of increasing debility on his part. He had himself indeed become aware of loss of strength and vitality, making note of the same, though deeming it nothing more than a little dulness or weariness which by rest would soon pass away. Yet his resolute spirit would not allow him to give up work altogether until absolutely compelled to do so by sheer inability to prosecute it further. His diary shows that during the first days of July he spent a portion of his mornings in the garden, going thence to his writing, which he followed up, only as interrupted by his customary siesta after dinner and incidental intrusions, as long as he could see.

On Saturday, the 12th of the month named, he refers for the last time to his work on his life-history. After noting numerous items which had claimed his attention, he adds: — "Resumed auto-biography at 10.15. On till dinner. Our siestas. Up at 3 P. M. More auto-biography and sundries till supper." The next day, Sunday,

LOSS OF STRENGTH AND ENERGY. 521

he attended church as was his custom, taking a walking stick to support his faltering steps, "the first time," he pleasantly said to a fellow-worshipper, "you ever saw the old gentleman at church with a cane." In the afternoon he wrote his daughter, Mrs. Heywood,— the last letter he ever penned — detailing interesting incidents of family and neighborhood life with characteristic comments, and closing with a few sentences of a personal nature, in which pathos, prophecy, and grateful piety are significantly blended, as shown by a brief extract: "Autobiography crawls slowly along. Another chapter coming down to 1882 is almost finished. But dimness of vision greatly hinders progress. There is no improvement. The smoke grows gradually more dense, with little hope of betterment. But we must be patient and thankful for the good that remains. Dissolution must come to us both ere long and all will be right. The Heavenly Father doeth all things well. With ever-abiding love to you all, we remain, affectionately yours, ADIN and LUCY H. BALLOU."

Alas, dissolution came to *him* sooner than he thought, no doubt,— sooner than any of his friends dared to anticipate. On Monday he was in the garden again, but only for a short season, doing little else through the day except to assist in some trifling domestic matters, most of the time being spent upon the lounge. Tuesday he helped the carpet-cleaners and his wife put the house to rights for the summer. At night was "tired." The next day his final entry in his journal was made. Brief extracts reveal his condition at that date: "I, shiftless and languid, helped (wife) what I could. My blindness worse than any time yet. Lounged and lazied away most of the forenoon, feeling rather cheaply in body and mind. Dinner; siestas until three. Brought up diary until six p. m. Sundries. Eyesight sadly dim." The remainder of the week he kept quiet, getting all the rest he could, hoping thereby to regain his lost strength and revive his exhausted energies; but all in vain.

The Sunday following, July 20, he rose early and at the proper hour began to prepare for church, but his caretaking wife, who knew how weak he was better than he knew himself, dissuaded him from attempting to go. As the day wore on, his power of vision failed rapidly, and before evening it was lost to him forever. When he realized that he could no longer see, his heart for the time being sank within him and he bewailed the sadness of his lot. But sustained and encouraged by the cheerful words of his wife and by voices from the invisible world, which had comforted him in many a trying hour before, he became calm and resigned, saying, "Light comes to me. The heavens are once more opened; all is right and well," and no expression of murmuring or disquietude afterward escaped his lips.

The next day he spoke of his auto-biography, regretting that it was not finished and asking his wife if he could not dictate to her what she could write out for him. Upon being told that he was too ill to do anything of that kind and must be quiet in order to promote recovery, he readily acquiesced, but soon after proceeded to mention certain things he wanted to have noted by whomsoever might complete the work, provided he should not be able to do it himself. He was told that all should be done as he desired and it would be right, which seemed to satisfy him, putting his mind at rest, and he never mentioned the matter again. That night he went to the bed from which he never rose.

The following morning it was deemed advisable to call a physician, and Dr. Jerome Wilmarth, mentioned before, who was then residing in Milford, was summoned. He found the patient suffering from a slight pulmonary trouble and prescribed remedies which brought apparent relief. On Wednesday the daughter, Mrs. Heywood, and her husband, who had been informed of her father's illness, arrived by an afternoon train, finding him seriously but they hoped not dangerously sick, free from pain, and able to converse intelligently and with little difficulty. He greeted them cordially and affectionately and had a somewhat lengthy interview with them, giving directions much in detail in anticipation of his possible approaching departure, with accompanying assurances of love, gratitude, and pious trust.

On Thursday he asked his daughter to read to him favorite passages in the bible and also his own account of a highly gratifying seance with Rev. T. L. Harris, an eminent Spiritualistic impressionist and seer, enjoyed many years before. Her doing so gave him evident satisfaction, comfort, and peace. His physician, at his evening visit, said he was "holding his own" and saw grounds for hope that he would rally from the attack and be about again in a few days. But a slight paralytic shock before morning, affecting his entire left side, foreclosed all further expectation of such a devoutly-to-be-wished-for issue.

After this new feature of the case appeared, his difficulty of speaking, declining strength, and waning consciousness precluded all continued conversation, and foreshadowed, beyond all peradventure, the not-far-distant fatal result. He, however, continued able to recognize those about him, answer questions in brief terms, and respond to expressions of interest and affection by intelligent signs and tokens, almost to his last expiring breath. Gradually, with no show of suffering, peacefully he sank away, the thread of life becoming manifestly attenuated day by day as time went on. He was tenderly and lovingly watched over by the members of his household, conscientiously and effectively cared for by his physician and a skilfully trained nurse, Mrs. Belle A. Varney of Worcester, until the morning of the fifth of August, when, in the presence of his family and of a neighbor watcher, Mrs. Sarah Jane Hatch, at 4.45 o'clock, just as the rising sun began to fleck with golden hues the surrounding hills, he passed without a struggle to the more immediate companionship of the dear ones gone before, and to the rest and reward "of the people of God."

Funeral Services. On the afternoon of Friday, August 8, appropriate burial rites in honor of the departed were duly solemnized in the Hopedale church. A large concourse of people was present, coming from near and far to pay their tribute of respect, veneration, and love to the relative and friend whose earthly labors had now come to an end, and to mingle their sorrow and tears sympathizingly with each other under a sense of one common bereavement — of one profound, heartfelt grief. The exercises of the occasion had been arranged for the most part by the deceased and were carried out in accordance with his wishes. The pall-bearers were of his own selection and the several speakers had been named by him as among the truest and best of his much prized friends. It was his request that his Masonic brethren should have his body in charge and render the beautiful and impressive burial service of the Order at the grave, and this was done. In the unavoidable absence of Gen. William F. Draper, whom he had personally asked to act as conductor at his obsequies whenever they should take place, Mr. Eben D. Bancroft was invited to the position, the duties of which were discharged with gratifying quietude, system, and efficiency. A Masonic quartette interspersed the exercises with most appropriate and admirably executed selections of vocal music.

Everything pertaining to the sacred occasion was as simple and unostentatious as, in the nature of the case, it well could be. The usual emblems of distress and gloom were dispensed with, and a hopeful, cheerful, but subdued and reverent spirit prevailed. The body was encased in a massive broadcloth covered casket, heavily but not gorgeously mounted, and flowers in abundance, wrought into chaste and expressive forms, testified to the thoughtful love of earthly friends, as well as to the fatherly kindness of the great Giver of All Good.

At 12.45 o'clock, prayer was offered at the house, where the family and other near relatives were convened, by an almost life-long friend, Rev. William H. Fish of

Dedham, preliminary to the more public services at the church. These were introduced by an organ voluntary, effectively given by Prof. Origin B. Young while the funeral cortege was passing in. A brief invocation was followed by singing and readings from the scriptures and from Whittier's "Eternal Goodness."

Rev. George S. Ball of Upton spoke most feelingly and impressively of Mr. Ballou as one called by God to a great and noble work, which he had most conscientiously and faithfully performed, in a spirit of self-consecration, animated by a living faith in the eternal realities and an all prevailing love of God and man. Rev. Samuel May of Leicester said that the lesson of the hour was "the worth of a life, and how much can be accomplished in a single life," as illustrated in the career of the departed, who had exemplified the highest type of faith, hope and charity, and whose translation to the company of the great cloud of witnesses by which we are compassed about, made heaven seem nearer and the spiritual life more real and abiding. Rev. Carlton A. Staples of Lexington paid an earnest and tender tribute to his early pastor and always revered friend, reviewing briefly his Mendon ministry and the wonderful success he achieved therein as a preacher of a large and noble Christian faith, as a champion of all good causes, and as a winner of human hearts to himself and to a better life. Rev. Mr. Fish, referring to his early acquaintance with the deceased, expressed profound gratitude that at the outset of his professional experience he came under the influence of so enlightened and noble a mind, and so able a preacher of pure Christianity, breathing "peace on earth and good will to men." He also alluded to the calm and happy close of his earthly pilgrimage and of the undoubted joy with which he had already been greeted by his beloved Adin Augustus and other dear ones gone before in the spirit home, whence had descended blessed ministrations in days gone by, and where he would welcome all the loved ones left behind in days to come.

At the conclusion of the address of Mr. Fish, the present writer, by special request of his father-in-law, read portions of the sermon he had himself prepared some years before for his own funeral, the full text of which may be found in the appendix. Of this part of the service, the *Milford Journal* said: "It was most affecting. Through it (the discourse) pulsed the old-time fervor of devotion to others, of lofty ideals, of generous self-effacement, so significant of the writer. The power and beauty of the periods — of a voice literally 'from out of the grave' — was indescribably touching. The tall, kindly form, the saintly, benevolent face, the modestly courageous but eloquent speech, all stood out visibly as the beautiful sentences fell from the reader's lips. At the tender farewell close, the mourning in the hearts of those present well nigh broke restraint, and grief was uncontrollably visible."

Rev. Mr. Staples followed this reading with a prayer full of fervor and tender feeling, overflowing with Christian hope and trust, thanking the Giver of All Good for the noble life now closed and for all the benefits resulting from it, and invoking upon the immediately bereaved and all sorrowing with them, the blessing of the Heavenly Father and all needed heavenly comfort, encouragement, consolation, and peace. After the singing of another sacred hymn, Rev. Mr. Ball pronounced the benediction, bringing this part of the service to a close.

Then came the leave-taking, when the assembled multitude, filling not only the auditorium of the church but the stairway and vestibule with much of the vestry below, passing by the coffined form, looked for the last time upon the familiar face — benignant, kindly, expressive, saintly, in death as in life — the relatives and family following all the rest. When the last lingering look of bereaved affection was given, the casket was reverently closed and borne forth from the place where the voiceless sleeper had so long and devotedly ministered in holy things to the burial carriage awaiting it outside, in which, followed by a long procession in vehicles of various kinds and on foot, it was conveyed to the rural cemetery across the river clothed in all the loveliness and glory of nature's midsummer garniture, as if to welcome a royal inhabitant to its peaceful abodes. And there in the family lot, already consecrated by the dust of loved ones sleeping beneath its turf of living green, the wearied frame was laid to rest. The impressive burial service of the Masonic brotherhood was feelingly rendered by Master Frank E. Matherson of Montgomery Lodge, Milford, and Chaplain Whitney, accompanied by further singing on the part of the quartette, whose deep, rich voices, blending in perfect harmony and floating aloft and away on the gentle air, seemed like echoes or preludes of the anthems of heaven. A sprig of green dropped from the hands of brethren of the mystic tie upon the casket already deposited in its lowly bed, a tender, tear-dimmed glance into the place of sepulture by each one of the passing throng, and all was over.

> "And now he rests; his greatness and his sweetness
>   Blend without jar or strife;
> And death has moulded into calm completeness
>   The story of his life.
>
> "Where the dews glisten and the song-birds warble
>   His dust to dust is laid;
> In nature's keeping, with no pomp of marble
>   To shame his modest shade.
>
> "Around his grave are quietness and beauty
>   And the sweet heaven above;
> The fitting symbols of a life of duty
>   Transfigured into love."

APPENDIX A.

TRIBUTES AND TESTIMONIALS.

The foregoing pages present in distinct outline and with sufficiency of detail a portraiture of the man whose life-history they rehearse, drawn from the standpoint of his own personal consciousness and considerate judgment of himself and of his work in the world. It seems most desirable that this delineation should be accompanied by an additional one representing him as he was seen by others — by those who knew him well and whose mental and moral discernment and sense of justice fitted them to render a trustworthy verdict concerning the distinguishing and meritorious features of his character and career. Hence it is that a few tributes and testimonials derived from various sources are introduced as an appropriate supplement to what has gone before.

I. FUNERAL VOICES.

REV. GEORGE S. BALL, UPTON.

"Our brother, our father in Israel, has been long spared to us. He has 'come down to the grave in full age, like as a shock of corn cometh in its season.' Far back in his youth a great vision opened to him, changing the whole tenor of his life. Like Paul, he was not disobedient thereto. Though he went forth bearing his seed weeping, he has gathered great sheaves into God's garner, and could repeat in retrospect eth apostle's words, 'I am ready to be offered; the time of my departure is at hand. I have fought a good fight, I have finished my course, I have kept the faith. Henceforth there is laid up for me a crown of righteousness.' . . . .

"But let us not forget that even the grave bears not away all. There is a life of soul above its reach. Let memory hold its living power still. Let souls commune and even the dead shall speak.

"And first there rises, at the recall, a beautiful simplicity that marked his life. How great was the impulse that sent forth this character on its mission! How luminous the vision that consecrated that long life of love in his chosen profession! Simplicity marks God's work. We can believe all that Paul portrays as the result of faith. The call came. The vision opened such a view of the character of God, such ineffable beauty, that he was ever afterward drawn to Him as the All-Father. Not far away but present, for 'in Him we live and move and have our being.' The Father of all, hence one family tie binds all spirits together. It was this Christian idea of the mutual relation between God and man that entranced and inspired his soul; from this came his consecration. How from this central thought he reasoned, argued, and led men! Christ became real to him — the elder brother and master, 'the way, the truth, the life.' His ideal, so grand, was taken into life, became a power for the uplifting of humanity, for the salvation of the world here and now. His philosophy took in all men, high and low, rich and poor. How he sought to inaugurate this life of God among men as practical Christianity, that they might make it real here and now, and be prepared for the living, loving work of eternal growth! He saw through the Great Master's eyes that which ever drew him on, called him to advocate every reform, and to labor for every class and condition of mankind.

"How was he thus consecrated to the anti-slavery work! What blows he struck at all those evils and sins that degrade men and lead them into bondage, that imbrute them and take away that peace and happiness which come only from obedience to the higher law of their being! His broad soul could welcome all working to the same great ends. How faithful in all these relations! How various his calls! What tasks he performed! And through all his soul has grown and the love that inspired him has illumined his face, given sweetness to his smile, fervor to his voice, and warmth to the grasp of his hand, that we shall bear on the tablet of our hearts as long as affections remain.

"Perhaps more marked than all has been the practical outcome of his great mind and faith. Ever active, he never outran his conscience and so has shown an example we all may welcome as a height of greatness rarely attained. He held fast the good while aspiring for the better, showing to us the sources of that power whose loss we now mourn. All this culminated in a spiritual habit that made his later life a walk with God — a commerce with the sky. Often thwarted and apparently failing as he worked with men, he has felt a divine presence upholding him if for a moment cast down.

"His own experience prepared him to speak directly to hearts overwhelmed in affliction. To him the veil of death had been pierced, the light of God shone through, the voice of Him who had brought life and immortality to light was heard proclaiming the mansions of the Father's house open to our feet. Night was changed to morning, and the eternal day for all souls dawned."

REV. SAMUEL MAY, LEICESTER.

"The lesson of this hour is of the worth of life and how much may be accomplished in a single life. I am almost awestruck in the presence of this long-protracted, now finished life — a life devoted with such singleness of purpose, such unintermitting industry, such uniform gentleness, yet such manifest force, to the highest and noblest human ends. Compare it with lives we daily look upon, spent aimlessly and weakly — still more with those spent viciously and injuriously. Compare its wise and generous activities with the self-seeking and frivolous course of many; its wealth of thought and purpose with their emptiness; its precious product with their waste. Can these so different lives all come into one category and be classed as *human* lives — one so full, the others so barren; one so positive and high, the others so negative and low? We understand why it is asked of the latter, 'Is life worth living?' We cannot imagine its being asked of the well-ordered, high-principled, consecrated life which has just come to its close. . . . .

"A life well spent! Can there be any truer, better eulogy? Could human life have a more perfect crown than to be thus sealed? An honorable life too and a happy life,— and both because it was well spent, because it was filled with the service of truth, of man, and of God. What cause of human good did he ever refuse? What service to humanity has he turned from? What divine truth has he ever feared to accept and to proclaim both by word and deed? Is a deep, living faith in those high ideas and principles which take hold of the very throne of God, in itself a rich possession, a pearl of great price? Such faith he had. Is a hopeful trust in men, in their power of progress and attainment, and in their larger and nobler future,—a hope stronger than all doubts and fears,— to be desired? Such hope was his. Is a generous sympathy, taking in all sorts and conditions of men, ministering gladly to all sorrows and needs, encouraging all hearts,—which has patience for weakness, pity for failure, which refuses to despair of those whom God cares for, which brings its own human love to work with God's to turn the sinful from the error of their ways,—is such wide charity to be revered and sought? We can truly say, it lived in his bosom. Yes, he had all these graces,—this faith, this hope, this charity; and which of them were greatest in him it were hard to tell.

"I do not know the precise time when Mr. Ballou first declared himself to be of the grand army of anti-slavery workers,—grand not in numbers, but in its principles, in its aims, in the spirit of moral courage and self-sacrifice, which inspired it and held it together. I *do* know that it was in the very early years that he took his place in that warfare, standing strong and firm as a good soldier of God, in line with its most outspoken advocates, its most earnest friends, giving to that cause, though then 'everywhere spoken against,' his unqualified adherence, the influence of his pulpit, the force of his mental training and of his earnest, searching speech, and, better than all beside, of his high personal character, his generous sympathy, his clear and true conscience. . . . Had the American pulpit, with a proper loyalty to the gospel it professed to teach, with a general accord, and with a courage and Christlike mind such as Mr. Ballou manifested, lifted up its voice against slavery, we should have been saved a thousand evils, and, in all human probability, the long and destructive war, with its costly sacrifice of life and substance, would have been averted."

"The departure of this dear friend enlarges that 'cloud of witnesses' by which 'we are compassed about.' As he passes out of sight and joins that 'innumerable company' of which the sacred writers tell us in so many a glowing figure, with so many a lofty and inspiring phrase, we feel sensibly that it becomes of greater personal interest to ourselves; that heaven is nearer; that this brief earthly life is really far less substantial and sure than we have regarded it, the spirit's life more vivid and infinitely more worthy. New motives come to us. Our purpose to lay aside every weight which holds us down is quickened. Oh, how greatly should it be quickened, till we wholly understand what manner of men we ought to be, seeing that we have had such companionship as his, seeing that we may hope for it again, seeing that we are ever surrounded by this 'so great a cloud of witnesses!'

"May a portion of his spirit fall on us who remain. His witness for God and truth does not cease with his mortal breath. He lives to God, who will not forget his promises, and who will visit the bereaved, the lonely, the stricken, with his comforting spirit. So may his kingdom come, and his will be done 'on earth as it is in heaven.'"

REV. CARLTON A. STAPLES, LEXINGTON.

Mr. Staples was a native of Mendon, belonging to one of the families connected with the parish of which the deceased was for eleven years pastor, and grew up to manhood largely under his guidance and influence. He ever held him in sincere esteem and reverence, and his tribute on the occasion under notice was most earnest, tender, and affectionate. The substance of it, much amplified and illustrated, was embodied in a "Memorial Sermon," preached in the old Mendon church shortly afterward, extracts from which appear on a subsequent page.

REV. WILLIAM H. FISH, DEDHAM.

"I have probably known him (the departed) intimately and associatively longer than almost any other person present, which is nearly sixty years. For fifty-three years I have been in ministerial fellowship with him, he introducing me to my first society in Millville, and taking an important part there in my ordination, which was effected by a friendly union of Restorationists and Unitarians. And to-day I certainly have good reasons for gratitude that I early came under the helpful influence of so enlightened and noble a mind, and so able and efficient a teacher of that pure gospel of Christ which breathes only 'peace on earth and good will' to all mankind. It is fifty-six years since I first visited him in his hospitable home in Mendon, and our parishes were so near to each other for several years that he was of great assistance to me by frequent pulpit exchanges and in various other fraternal ways. And very pleasant to me is the memory of those opening days of my public ministry—among the happiest of my life. . . .

"And that was a blessed close of a consecrated life,—a life consecrated to God and humanity in the Christ faith and spirit. The messenger which we call Death seemed to approach him in the best possible way for both himself and his beloved and devoted companion of sixty years. The first shock that came to him, rendering him helpless, and turning the light of day into darkness, was sudden, indeed, but after this prostration his life ebbed so slowly, so peacefully away, and the heavens opened so clearly and brightly to him, that the two weeks interim thoroughly fortified his afflicted and anxious wife for the change, and comforted and sustained by the divine presence and, as she believed, by the ministry of angels, she was able to say in her trusting heart, 'Even so, Father, for so it seemeth good in thy sight,' and now she only patiently and hopefully waits,

'Till the shadows are a little longer grown,'

to rejoin him in the heavenly home, which has for so many years been their mutual anticipation and their constant consolation and encouragement. As they have lived so long together in the spiritual as well as in the material world, confident that their dear, long-ago departed Adin Augustus was with them as a ministering presence, there must now seem to her to be but a thin veil between her and them, and that soon they will be brought together to realize their highest dearest hopes, and the fulfillment of all the promises made to them by the various revelations of the universal Father received in filial faith and trust. So this great light, which has just ceased to shine upon us through that noble form that is presently to be laid away in the beautiful cemetery planned originally by him, will shine henceforth in some more glorious form, wherein the pure spirit will enjoy a happiness that 'eye hath not seen, nor ear heard, nor the heart of mortal man conceived.' May we, dear friends, make this our hope, by living the faith which our elder and departed brother so long preached in your midst and so tenderly and impressively brought home to you in your hours of bereavement and sorrow, and may that hope be fully realized by us all, when we also shall be summoned hence."

II. TRIBUTES OF FRIENDS.

REV. CHARLES H. EATON, D. D., NEW YORK.

"I can sincerely say that in my moral and spiritual nature I owe more to Mr. Ballou than to all the ministers and men with whom I have ever come in contact. His superior allegiance to the truth, his boldness and humility, his wisdom and love, excited my admiration as a boy and have been my constant inspiration in later life. We may say of him what Tyndall said of Faraday, 'Surely, here was a strong man; but let me not forget the union of strength with sweetness in his character.' We cannot regret the going home after so long, rich, holy, and helpful a life. For *him*, certainly, 'to die is gain.' May God help us to love him so much that we may grow to be like him, and if we may not realize his power we may attain something of his spirit."

HON. LATIMER W. BALLOU, WOONSOCKET, R. I.

"Brother Ballou was one of my earliest school-teachers, a near neighbor of my father, and though afterward separated by our varied callings, we have been warm friends more than seventy years. I am grateful for the noble life, the warm friendship and the blessings the dear departed has conferred, and the bright hope and faith he proclaimed to so many sorrowing hearts."

GEN. WILLIAM F. DRAPER, HOPEDALE.

"It is with the most profound regret that I read in the papers here (in Europe) of the death of Mr. Ballou. Notwithstanding his extreme age, the news came like a shock to me. I admired and respected — nay, revered him more than any other man I ever met. To me he combined a perfectly blameless life with most extraordinary reasoning powers. I feel that he has done much to develop the best that there is in me."

REV. LEWIS G. WILSON, HOPEDALE.

Closing paragraphs of a sermon from the text, "The strength of the hills is his also," delivered Sept. 14, 1890.

"What a great good fortune it has been to us all that we have so long dwelt near him whose vacant place fills us with grief, even in the midst of our gratitude! How like some great mountain of spiritual strength he has been these many years! Like a white-crowned hill, he towered above us, and to be near him was to feel safe, and in our trouble to gain courage to go on our way cheerfully, trusting in the Father in whom he trusted.

"The strength of the hills was his, but it was his because he went up to their summits, as his Master did. There he prayed; there he labored with the hard and knotted problems of life; there he received and brought down to hundreds of waiting and expectant hearts the consolation of a changeless love.

"If such a life, filled with such a power, does not have its weight with us and linger in our memory as a constant inspiration of faith and reminder of duty, then are we pitifully weak and thoughtless. But such will not be the case. We shall go forth and labor to realize his ideal of brotherly love and peace — the fundamental principles of Christianity.

"'Those bright summits which he saw in his prayers, those angels with whom he communed across the silent sea, those star-fretted heavens into whose realm his spirit has been welcomed — we will think on these things and tell them to our children while we do good service in the name of God, in the name of Christ, and in the name of a glorified humanity.''

REV. CARLTON A. STAPLES, LEXINGTON.

Extracts from a discourse given in the Unitarian Church, Mendon, Aug. 24, 1890, and afterwards printed at the request of his hearers.

In Memoriam.

" When the ear heard me, then it blessed me; and when the eye saw me, it gave witness to me. . . . The blessing of him that was ready to perish came upon me."—*Job* XXIX, 11, 13.

" It is now nearly sixty years since Adin Ballou, then a young man less than thirty years of age, was installed in this house as the minister of the society worshipping here. He had been preaching then for ten years, having entered his profession when barely eighteen, and had already attained popularity as an interesting and eloquent preacher. . . .

"Into the town life he entered heartily; he was in sympathy with its people in their struggles, sufferings, and sorrows, and their friend and counselor in all the experiences of life. He soon won their confidence and their love. He delighted to talk with them upon their affairs, their opinions, and their hopes. He made himself one with them in their homes, at their work, in their afflictions and their joys. A kindly, genial, courteous man who never held himself above anybody — black or white, saint or sinner, poor or rich — who had a cordial greeting for every one whom he met on the street, and who was as ready to stop and talk with a bronzed, rugged farmer or his son and daughter as with the finest gentleman and lady of the town; it is no wonder that the whole population was drawn to him and gave him their sincere respect and affection. His beaming face, his pleasing manner, his soft, musical voice, his interest in the humblest people, and his readiness to help and encourage all who were in want and trouble, opened the way to everybody's heart. The children and the young men and women were his sincere friends, drawn to him and held fast by his friendly spirit toward them and his devotion to their good. He impressed their minds with moral and religious truths. He awakened an ambition in them to do and to be something worthy of their opportunities, an honor and a blessing to their fellowmen and their country. The influence of his teaching and of his spirit did much to mould their characters and cheer and elevate their lives. To many of them he has been a power for good in all the subsequent journey of life, and to their dying day they will remember him as the gentle, persuasive teacher and faithful friend who first turned their thoughts toward God as our loving Father, Jesus as our faithful Guide, and Heaven as our eternal home.

"Mr. Ballou soon became popular with the society and influential in the town. As a preacher, he was interesting, forcible, practical, and often eloquent. Of a logical mind, strong reasoning powers, tender feelings, and a devout spirit, he moved, convinced, and uplifted his congregation. This meeting house was usually filled with interested worshipers, who came from all parts of the town and from neighboring towns, attracted by the fervor and power of his pulpit services. . . . He was a preacher who brought home to his hearers the great truths of religion and the duties of life in a way that people understood, illustrated them with facts and stories often homely but pungent and moving, appealed to the reason, the conscience, and the heart with convincing power. His themes were not far removed from the common experience; they touched the great issues of life and questions of individual and social well-being. He had an impressive manner, a fine, commanding presence, a voice of singular pathos and sweetness. It was a pleasure to look at the man and follow his discourse. I suppose the first five years of his ministry here were the period of his greatest popularity as a preacher. The congregation was large, united, proud of its minister; and he was winning new admirers and friends in the adjoining towns. Through his paper, his lecturing and preaching, he gained a wide influence in this portion of the State, and made a reputation as a controversialist, writer, and preacher, which might well have satisfied his ambition. Thus the prospect of a long, prosperous, and peaceful pastorate seemed open before him. Few ministers at his age had achieved so enviable a reputation. . . .

"Forty-eight years of life remained to him after his connection with this society as pastor came to an end. Of this long period of work and care, of heavy responsibilities, of bitter disappointments, yet of useful labors and of large achievements, I can speak only very briefly. . . . What good cause, however unpopular, what cause founded on justice, on purity, on Christian truth and love, did he not engage in and help forward by word and deed and influence? None such ever appealed to him in vain. He was a brave, fearless soldier in the battle for truth and righteousness; and he never shrank from any sacrifice of personal advantage to do his duty toward God and man. Of untiring industry, he accomplished an amount of difficult and disagreeable literary work such as few ever attempt and fewer ever finish; and he ceased not until almost fourscore and ten years had been reached. Nothing could turn him aside from his purpose and the task before him. Of firm Christian faith, he sought to embody its principles and its spirit in the institutions of society, and make them the guide of human conduct and the basis of character. The gospel of Christ and above all the spirit of Christ were to him the final court of appeal, before which all institutions, all enterprises, all lives, must be brought for judgment, and approved or condemned as they harmonized or antagonized them. He rested in the faith that the immutable right and good were brought to men in the Christian revelation, and before it man should bow in obedience and love.

"But one word more needs to be spoken. He was a man of large and tender sympathies, of a kind and generous heart, and that brought him near to other hearts. Few men ever won the love of so many people, in all classes and in all conditions. They knew him to be their friend, they found him to be their helper and comforter. He spake to the heart, because he spake from the heart, of God, and heaven, and eternal life. Invisible things were real to him; he lived much with them and in them, and when he spoke of them it strengthened human faith and comforted human sorrow. There are few homes in this town and in many adjoining towns where he was not known, and where his voice and presence are not associated with the most solemn and the most joyous occasions of life, and where he is not remembered gratefully and lovingly; and many there are, scattered far and wide in our country, who remember words of his that touched their hearts and kindled some higher purpose, some nobler ambition, or some kinder feeling. And many there are who have forgotten his words, but are conscious, nevertheless, that his influence has given their lives a worthier aim, and made their characters brighter and better. 'Let me die the death of the righteous, and let my last end be like his,' was the prayer of an ancient man, as recorded in the bible. It is a beautiful prayer. So we would all meet death at last. But to die in the peace and assurance of the righteous, man must live in his faith, in his devotion to what is right and good, loving and serving God, walking in the sweet ways of charity and holiness. Thus I believe Adin Ballou lived,—a righteous man, a Christian man, the faithful servant of God, the friend and helper of his fellow-beings. He died in peace, honored and loved; and his name and influence will long remain to bless the world."

GEORGE L. CARY.

President of Meadville Theological School.

"More than any other individual, (he) was instrumental, without being aware of it, of arousing and strengthening in me that interest in a rational and practical Christianity, which, as I grew older, deepened into an earnest desire to devote my life to some form of helpful human service. He was such a warm friend of my father and his name was such a household word in our family, that when a boy I used to think of him as a sort of thirteenth apostle, and from the beginning of the publication of the *Practical Christian* to the end I doubt if there was a column of it I did not read. This and his 'Christian Non-Resistance' exerted such a powerful influence over me that, until I was twenty years old, I was most thoroughly and completely his disciple.

"In two directions I can most clearly trace Mr. Ballou's influence upon my mind and character. How wonderfully strong he was on the ethical side of his nature! Whether it was his moral enthusiasm which first kindled the same flame in my own life or whether it was only his breath which fanned the spark that nature had placed there, my indebtedness to him in this direction was beyond price. Later years and wider experience naturally modified to some extent the opinions formed in those early years concerning the various relations of man to man, but the spirit I imbibed from his teachings has never ceased to be my inspiration.

"Mr. Ballou's New Testament expositions in the *Practical Christian* laid the foundation of whatever success I have since had as an interpreter of the scriptures. It was only the planting of the germs, and yet I can distinctly trace, even in some of my present opinions, the development of ideas which first came to me as I read that series of articles."

III. TESTIMONIES OF RELIGIOUS AND PHILAN= THROPIC BODIES.

THE HOPEDALE PARISH.

"*Whereas*, In the Providence of God, the Hopedale Parish has, in the deeease of the Rev. Adin Ballou, lost the founder of this community, a valued friend, a wise counselor, a comforter in bereavement, and in all things a spiritual father, therefore be it

"*Resolved*, That his life has always been, and the memory of it must continue to be, to ourselves and to our children, an example of noble allegiance to the truth, of unequivocal integrity, and of the faith which knows neither fear nor doubt; that his presence for many years has been an inspiration to the highest life and thought; that in his decease we have lost one who merited the love which thousands were glad to accord him; and that while we are deeply grieved at his departure into that realm where all who loved and knew him shall seek his presence again, we can never cease to be grateful that such a life has been spent in our midst."

THE UNIVERSALIST CHURCH, WOONSOCKET, R. I.

By its Pastor, Rev. CHARLES J. WHITE.

"At a meeting of our church held Monday evening, July 28, the severe and possibly final illness of Rev. Adin Ballou was reported. At the mention of the fact, all our hearts were touched with deep sorrow, for his name has been a household word in our homes for three-quarters of a century, and none knew him but to respect and love him. Many were the kind words spoken and many the sacred memories of the past rehearsed.

"It was voted to spread upon our records the expression of our loving esteem for and our deep sympathy with the faithful servant of God and our dear friend lying so very ill at his home in Hopedale, with the prayer that, if it were possible, he might yet longer be spared to us and to the world; but, if not possible, then God's will be done; commending him to the Father whom he loved and to the great company in the immortal life whom he had blessed. The pastor was requested, if he could make it convenient, to carry this expression and message of love in person to Mr. Ballou.

"We have inscribed in our records a brief biography with an account of his funeral. We feel that we owed it to him and that the whole community owes it to him to recognize the great service to a reasonable religion and a righteous life he rendered in his long years of residence in the vicinity. We congratulate the widow and all your family that you have such precious memories of your departed one. Surely, if ever the words of the psalmist were appropriate, they are in his case: 'Precious in the sight of the Lord is the death of his saints.' 'They go down to the grave in a full age, like as a shock of corn cometh in its season.' He had made royal all of this life and was ripe for the better world beyond. My field of labor for these twenty years has been especially fragrant with the

names of Rev. John Boyden and his beloved neighbor and life-long friend, Rev. Adin Ballou. I shall never cease to be grateful to them. 'They labored and we are entered into their labors.'
'Only the actions of the just
Smell sweet and blossom in the dust.'"

THE WORCESTER CONFERENCE.

At a meeting of this body held in Templeton, Oct. 2, 1890, the opening session was devoted to an appropriate service in appreciative and grateful memory of Rev. Adin Ballou. Tender and impressive tributes to the disinterested spirit, eminent virtues, and noble work of him whose recent decease touched with a sacred grief so many hearts, were rendered by Revs. Alvin F. Bailey of Barre, George W. Stacey of Milford, Austin S. Garver of Worcester, and Grindall Reynolds of Boston, secretary of the American Unitarian Association; after which the following declaration, with an accompanying resolution of sympathy for the afflicted and bereaved, was unanimously adopted:

"The recent departure of our revered brother, Rev. Adin Ballou of Hopedale, to mansions of glorious rest, is indeed remembered with widespread grief. His was a well-spent life — a life devoted to the cause of practical Christianity, based on the enthusiasm of humanity; a life ever helpful in advancing righteousness as required by the precepts and illustrated by the example of Jesus Christ, our Lord and Master."

WORCESTER CO. COMMANDERY, K. T.

"He was widely known and where best known was loved and respected. His life was long, peaceful, busy, and useful — kind in action, gentle in speech, and agreeable in manner, never making enemies, but always gaining friends. He was a man of commanding presence and his pleasant smile and kindly words greeted every one and won all to a mutual friendship. This is but a faint picture of a noble man and a Christian gentleman and Knight Templar, who was honored and respected in life and now sincerely lamented in death."

THE UNIVERSAL PEACE UNION, PHILADELPHIA, PENN.

"His long life of nearly eighty-eight years has been devoted to the purest principles of true peace, and he has left us a legacy of more worth than can be computed in silver or gold. As one of the founders of the Universal Peace Union, having been present at the preliminary meeting in 1865 and at the organization of the society in 1866, and continuing with us in spirit ever since, sending us occasional letters of encouragement and always living the very incarnation of peace — we testify to his high worth and feel we have cause of thankfulness that we had so faithful an officer to labor with us."

IV. EULOGIES OF THE PRESS.

MILFORD JOURNAL.

" ' His life was gentle, and the elements so mixed in him that nature might stand up and say to all the world, *This is a man.*' "

" It is doubtful if in all New England there is another clergyman who has entered so many homes as a comforter, to whom it was given to personate so becomingly the loveliness of eternal truths. About his ministrations clustered the spiritual lives of thousands; under his tender offices grew the solemn links of life,—the hours of birth, the hours of christening, of marriage, and of mourning, until his mild presence breathed a perpetual benediction and his steps brought peace. Few in all this section there are but have known his tender offices, whether the hour was of nuptial joy, of tremulous rejoicing for nativity, of life dedication in uprightness, or binding up the hearts of bereaved mourners in the hour of desolation.

" A gentle minister to all grief, a partaker of all homely joy, he is a part of the innermost life of thousands like a sacred experience, something to remember and revere."

MILFORD GAZETTE.

" Early Tuesday morning, Rev. Adin Ballou, widely known for his many virtues, died at his home in Hopedale, after an illness of only two weeks' duration. . . . His was a busy life. Aside from his ministerial duties, he devoted considerable attention to literature, was the author of several books, including a history of the town of Milford and a genealogy of the Ballou family in America, besides various pamphlets and tracts.

" He was a man of simple habits and quiet tastes, large-hearted and full of sympathy, rejoicing with the happy, comforting the sorrow-stricken. His friends are legion, and to those in whose joys and griefs he has shared, his departure is a heavy loss."

BOSTON HERALD.

"The late Adin Ballou . . . grew up with such scanty advantages as could be secured in a plain New England home and at the district school. . . . From the first he was a person of mark. He was large for his age, uncommonly advanced in thoughtfulness, and reached at a bound the mature decisions which belong to people of ripe years. His tendency from the first was toward religious thinking and living. . . .

"He had in him the self-confidence, the burning enthusiasm, the fearless self-assertion, the irresistible impulse, which constitute a natural leader of society, and though he exercised his gifts without the aid of a distinguished position, he was early known as one of the strongest agitators in a community that was as full of reform ideas as an egg is full of meat. . . .

"Mr. Ballou was one of the interested believers in the new form of associationism, and he had seen too little of the practical development of Christian communism in the Christian church to feel that, within its existing limits, the higher forms of social life could be developed and maintained. He wished to try the experiment for himself, and in the spring of 1842, he secured an extensive domain in the town of Milford in this state, and there, with the aid of others, organized what has since been known as the Hopedale Community. . . . He had matured his plan after long and constant study of the different systems for renewing civil society which were in vogue at that time, and he had such an original mind, and had gone so far into the foundation of things, that his own social scheme took shape from his own liberal and devising brain. . . . What he contemplated was nothing less than a new incarnation of the spirit of Jesus Christ in community life. What he aimed at was to institute and consolidate a true order of human society, in which all individual interests should be harmonized for the common good, and be controlled by divine principles as their supreme law. . . . In the statement of these principles, Mr. Ballou was a happy optimist. He inculcated the existence of one Infinite God, his mediatorial manifestation through Jesus Christ, the doctrine of a perfect divine retribution, the necessity of spiritual regeneration, and the final universal triumph of good over evil.

"What is remarkable in Mr. Ballou's work is that he gave it a distinctive religious purpose and character. He did not expect to reform people unless he controlled their spiritual life, and the religious direction of the community was the principle to which everything else was subordinated. He also insisted that the family life should be maintained in its purest and best possible forms. . . .

"Adin Balllou was one of the most remarkable self-made men that New England has ever produced. He belonged to the century. . . . He was the product of the spirit of associationism or community life, permeated and guided by Christian principles, which was in its day an attempt to realize the larger mission of the Christian church through a social unity.

"He was a man of charming simplicity of manner, of firm yet childlike faith, of keen and natural intellectual force, and of unusual contentment of mind and spirit. . . . He was a Christian Socialist more than a decade before Maurice and Kingsley and Hughes began that movement in England, and one of a high and pure tpye which men are attempting to realize to-day. . . . It was his misfortune to live and think at a time when the world was not yet ready for his services in the form in which he desired to render them, but as one of the strong personal forces in our practical yet speculative New England life, he was as distinct an incarnation of the spirit of the forefathers as Cotton Mather, or Sam. Adams, or Ralph Waldo Emerson."

BOSTON JOURNAL.

"Rev. Adin Ballou, who died at his home in Hopedale, Mass., Tuesday morning, was widely known and where best known was loved and respected. His life was long, peaceful, busy, and useful, and he probably leaves not an enemy behind, as he had not one in life. He was kind in action, gentle in speech, agreeable in manner. . . . His kindly words of wisdom and advice have truly gained for him the title of Father Ballou. Entering so many families in time of trouble and in time of joy, he has gained the hearts of many people who in his death will feel a personal loss. . . .

"He was a strong anti-slavery man, a firm advocate of temperance, and a man of peace in all the walks of life. . . . He was of commanding presence, benignant countenance, and his kindly smile greeted every one and won all hearts."

BANNER OF LIGHT.

"Rev. Adin Ballou, whose pilgrimage of eighty-seven years on earth terminated on the fifth of this month, commenced when quite young to work out the mission of his life, which was evidently to enlighten his fellowmen on spiritual things.

". . . When seventeen he preached a sermon to his young companions and at eighteen formally adopted the ministry as his profession.

"From 1831 to 1842 he was pastor of a church in Mendon, where his literary and controversial labors may be spoken of as incessant, for aside from his theological warfare he assailed every species of society evil — intemperance, war, slavery, business dishonesty, etc., — with all the vigorous ability of voice and pen.

"As might be expected of a man of his liberal views and honesty of purpose in his profession, Mr. Ballou availed himself of the earliest opportunities that presented themselves to investigate the claims of Modern Spiritualism. The result was that he soon received indubitable evidence that those claims rested on a sure foundation and that the veil which had long been suspended between this and the life beyond, had indeed been rent asunder, and immortality had become to mankind an assured fact."

THE CHRISTIAN LEADER.

"The death of Adin Ballou, at venerable years, takes from earth as white a soul as ever animated a human form. . . . In various ways he sought to make immediately practical the unselfish life enjoined by the Divine Master; and in pursuing this end, no personal sacrifice could be large enough to dull his ardor or shake his endeavor. His memory will ever be sacred to all who knew him or shall know of him. Every righteous cause found a champion in Adin Ballou.

"He was a man of great intellectual gifts and no theory or rule satisfied his heart that did not accord with his reason.

"Mr. Ballou sought by original devices to give practicality to the doctrine of doing as we would be done by. He originated the 'Christian Socialism' that was embodied in the Hopedale Community. It did not succeed, but only a man of great force and originality could have even started such a movement. It certainly had a *moral* success; it witnessed to the power of the doctrine of Christian brotherhood when that doctrine was lodged in an earnest and consecrated soul.

"Mr. Ballou was by instinct a believer in universal salvation. His faith in the power of Divine Goodness was implicit. His logical mind could see no possibility of failure in the plan of God — in the outcome of His saving grace. . . .

"Mr. Ballou reached venerable years. He passed from earth loved and honored by all who knew him, and literally reverenced by the few who knew him intimately. Peace be to the ashes of the sainted dead."

THE CHRISTIAN REGISTER.

"Rev. Adin Ballou was a marked figure among the men of the present generation. Though he did not hold so conspicuous a place in the church as the Rev. Hosea Ballou, still he must be regarded as a force in the religious and social life of New England. His bent, even in early years, was toward religious thinking. He worked his way out of the popular religious creed and became a devoted minister of the Universalist church. Here he soon engaged in theological discussions, taking ground against the view then taught by Thomas Whittemore and others — known as 'death and glory'— and advocated the doctrine of restoration. This controversy resulted in an ecclesiastical break and he afterwards became identified, for a time, with the Unitarians. He was an earnest Abolitionist and was associated with Garrison and other pioneers of this great struggle. He was deeply impressed with the evils of intemperance and entered with his wonted vigor and enthusiasm into the efforts to remove this curse from the land and also to plead for the cause of universal peace. But the chief point of interest in his life was his organization of the Hopedale Community on the basis of Christian Socialism. Kingsley, Thomas Hughes, and Maurice were at work in London, in their efforts to apply this theory, but as Mr. Ballou was an independent thinker, he wrought out his own plan. He was fully steeped in the spirit of Christian philanthropy, and he designed to make his society a practical Christian republic on the basis of the teachings of Jesus. . . . The leading idea of his life was to make of the community a true Christian Church,—the kingdom of God on earth.

"Mr. Ballou was a man of striking personal features. He had a kindly eye and a genial face. . . . His old age was serene and beautiful. He had consecrated his life to noble ends. So when the angel voice of death came, to few would the words of Jesus, whom he loved and whose spirit was the guide of his life, more fitly apply: 'Inasmuch as ye have done it unto the least of these my disciples, ye have done it unto me. Enter thou into the joy of thy Lord.'"

APPENDIX B.

SERMON.

BY ADIN BALLOU.

Prepared as a part of the service at his own funeral.

"Moreover, I will endeavor that ye may be able, after my decease, to have these things always in remembrance."—*II Peter 1, 15*.

PETER clearly anticipated his decease — the time when he must put off his mortal tabernacle and be clothed upon by his immortal one. So have I, these many years. He was not so much concerned to be personally remembered after he had passed away as to have the things remembered which he had taught; for he was deeply sensible of his personal frailties and shortcomings, but knew that the doctrines, truths, and duties he had made known to men were divine. Hence the endeavor expressed in the text. And as with the Apostle in this respect, so has it been with me. With a similar endeavor I prepared this discourse while I was yet in the flesh and in the full possession of my mental powers, in order that it might be read at my funeral. It may seem strange to my relatives, friends, and former hearers that I should have done so. But I felt moved to it by influences from the spiritual world as more likely to do justice to the proper demands of the occasion than might otherwise be done. Attend then to the words I have left you.

1. I thank my Heavenly Father for the hosts of kind friends he raised up to me through a long life, besides those of my loving and precious family. He knoweth their innumerable ministrations to my comfort and wel-

fare under all the changing vicissitudes through which I have passed — ministrations of the near and dear within the home circle — ministrations of personal associates and friends more or less intimately connected with me in social relations — and ministrations of a more casual and general nature from thousands who knew me as a public teacher. I always desired to appreciate gratefully every favor, token of affection, and expression of respect thus conferred on me. Doubtless I fell short in many instances of doing so. But I regarded them all as flowing out, through whatever channels, from the Giver of every good and perfect gift. I know they are all in the book of His remembrance and that whoever bestowed them at His prompting will not go unrequited. Therefore, I need not enter into specifications.

2. Notwithstanding general good intentions toward God and my fellow-creatures, I have often sinned against both in ways of commission and omission. It has pleased God to make me very sensible of all these sins, to give me a humble, penitent, and contrite heart, and to assure me a thousand times of his forgiving grace. So of my fellow-creatures, one and all, whom in any manner I have harmed or neglected, I this day entreat their forgiveness, as they themselves implore human and divine forgiveness. And I tenderly conjure my friends who think I have done any good in the world, not to eulogize me as a sinless man or as one inherently excellent in any respect, or as being anything at best but an instrument in the Divine Hand, acted upon and through by a measure of wisdom and goodness above my own. For this is the absolute truth to my highest and inmost consciousness. If I had done my whole duty and come up to my best ideal of Christlike excellence, I should have had no self-sufficiency to boast of, and only reason for profound thankfulness to the one infinite Fountain of All Good. But instead of such complete dutifulness, I take to myself shame for my many sins, faults, and follies. I credit all good to God and charge all evil to the frailty of the creature. This

is the light in which I stand, and thus I wish to be represented by the friends who may remember me. Here I end what is strictly personal to myself.

3. I come now to the doctrines, principles, and duties which I have been privileged to preach and teach. These are "not mine, but His that sent me." They are distinct from and incomparably above my mere personality. It is these that, now I am gone, I would have you keep always in remembrance. You may forget me, but do not forget them. For though I failed to work them out and illustrate them in social institutions or in the individual character of many receivers, I am sure they are from Heaven and will finally prevail. What are they? They are all both theoretical and practical. I have endeavored to preach no theological doctrine as essential to religious faith, but what legitimately required of its believers great duties of essential righteousness in strict accordance with it. And on the other hand, I have preached no duty as essential to absolute righteousness which was not dictated by some great theoretical principle plain to the understanding as a sufficient ground for it. Thus I have been careful never to divorce reason and religion, the understanding and moral sentiment, faith and practice, the head and heart.

I have preached the existence of one infinite, all-perfect God — the supreme Divine Mind — a self-existent, omnipresent Spirit and the Father of all intelligent finite spirits, whose love, wisdom, and power are illimitable, faultless, and unchangeable from and to eternity. I have not confounded this God with mindless nature, fate, or law, but held him up to the awe, confidence, and adoration of rational moral agents as perfect in all the attributes of mental personality, — governing all worlds, beings, and things by intelligent will-power as the infallible, supreme, free, moral agent. And I have carefully avoided ever representing Him as willing, purposing, or treating any one of his intelligent offspring — friend or foe, good, bad, or indifferent — otherwise than as a just, benevolent, merciful, and wise Father, in time or eternity. I have, therefore, steadfastly rejected and protested against all forms of the doctrine of endless punishment, and also of every kind of vindictive or unbenevolent punishment whatsoever as morally impossible under the Divine Government, — uncompromisingly affirming that all God-given law and God-administered retribution must be in perfect accordance with His supreme and inerrable Fatherhood. On this basis I have built the whole superstructure of my ethics, accepting as unquestionable the duties of piety toward God and fraternal treatment of all fellow moral agents in the universe, according to the two great commandments — love to God and the neighbor. I have, therefore, always faithfully insisted on supreme love toward the All-Father with the whole heart, mind, and strength, as a duty and privilege absolutely indispensable to the highest good of each individual soul, of human society, and the universal whole of moral intelligences. And in harmony therewith, I have preached the duties and privileges of worshiping that Father "in spirit and in truth," praying to Him, thanking Him as the source of all good, trusting implicitly in His providence, reverencing His laws of order, opening the soul to His inspirations, accepting His spiritual revelations, exercising repentance toward Him for all sin, relying on His pardoning grace, being led by His spirit, ever striving to put on His moral character, and by His help to be holy as He is holy, just as He is just, merciful as He is merciful, and perfect as He is perfect. Then, under the second comprehensive commandment, I have urgently insisted on the brotherhood of man and the vast neighborhood of all moral natures, and taught that each should love every other as himself and do unto every other as he would be done unto; that love to God can be proven only by love to one another; that this love must not only be exercised toward those who love us, but toward them that hate us — toward the unthankful and evil, as God's love is — toward our enemies and injurers to the extent that refrains totally from rendering evil for evil, resisting evil with evil, and that consummates itself by overcoming evil with good; and also that whatsoever in us it be that hates, or seeks to harm, or knowingly does harm, even the worst fellow moral agent, is contrary to pure love toward either God or man. I have preached and insisted on this perfect righteousness toward God and fellow moral agents, not only as an indispensable duty but as the grandest privilege and crowning glory of the holiest souls.

I have steadfastly preached Jesus Christ and His gospel as set forth in the scriptures of the New Testament — not according to the scholastic theology of the degenerate Church — as the highest and most authoritative revelation of the All-Father's nature, will, law of order, grace, truth, regenerating dispensation, and purposed destiny of the human race. In so doing, I have placed Jesus of Nazareth where He Himself claimed to have been placed by the Father, neither below nor above, ordained before the foundation of the human world, predictively promised, through the best of ancient prophets, as the Christ-man, born in the fulness of time, plenarily anointed with the Father's holy communicable spirit for the accomplishment of His mission, and so rendered preeminently the Son of God and Saviour of the world. I have held Him up as the model man, the moral and spiritual head of the human race, saying and doing nothing of His mere selfhood, in virtue of His own inherent human attributes, but all officially as the chosen organ of God, in virtue of the indwelling Spirit of the Father, constantly inspiring and directing Him. Therefore I have insisted that He has shown us the Father's moral perfections, His true character, will, law, and purposes; so that "God was in Him reconciling the world to Himself"; to which end he said, did, and suffered all that distinguished Him as the Christ, and entered into the heavenly existence where He will reign in glory until "God shall be all in all." Thus placing Jesus Christ where he claimed that the Father placed Him, I ascribe to Him a name and authority above every other name, unto which every creature in heaven, earth, and the spirit world must bow and " every tongue confess that He is Lord to the glory of God the Father." I have not held him up as an ordinary man. Nor as one among many other Christly men, speaking and acting from His own partially developed intuitions and aspirations, and so, at best, a fallible religious teacher, sometimes right and sometimes wrong; but as invested by the Father with infallible spiritual and moral authority over human souls in this world and the next, during his mediatorial reign. I have not ranked Him with Plato, Pythagoras, Socrates, Confucius, or any of the ancient sages, or with any of the famous philosophers, poets, scientists, and literati of later times, firmly believing that by divine endowment, He outranks all other human beings. With me His thoughts were God's thoughts, His will God's will, His wisdom God's wisdom, His controlling spirit God's spirit, His word God's word, His righteousness God's righteousness, His example God's example, and His authority God's authority, to be reverenced and conformed to accordingly.

In preaching concerning the veneration due to the scriptures of the Old and New Testaments, I have placed them above all other human writings as intrinsically more divinely inspired and religiously excellent than any others, but I have not claimed for them anything diviner than they purport to claim for themselves on a fair interpretation. I have not put them on a level of superhuman perfection, nor confounded their higher testimonies with their evidently lower and ordinary ones, nor made the Old Testament co-equal with the New, nor construed their mere letter and verbalism to be the word of God, but have insisted that they ought to be interpreted and understood in strict accordance with their essential spirit and highest fundamental principles—never otherwise. No mere literalism of sound or sense, no mere figurative words, phrases, or texts, have been held up by me as divine truth against declared fundamental objects, principles, and spiritual essentials, clearly ascertainable. On this ground I have, for myself, studied, understood, and expounded the scriptures of both Testaments in respect to faith and practice, never sacrificing the spirit to the letter, nor a great principle of truth and duty to the mere literal phraseology of a text. Consequently, I have carefully avoided placing Moses above Christ, or the patriarchs and prophets above His chosen apostles, or the law above the gospel, or a threatening against a promise, or a lower form of righteousness against a higher, or retribution against a destined end, or temporarily permitted evil against its final overrulement for good, or a dispensation of pain against an eternity of blessedness. After this method, I have searched, understood, and explained the scriptures. After this method I have ascertained to my satisfaction who and what Jesus Christ claimed to be, what His mission and authority really were, what He taught as the highest truth and righteousness, how He exemplified that truth and righteousness in the flesh, and how He still more gloriously exemplifies them in the heavens. My theology, piety, and ethics — my entire religion — have thus been determined, defined, preached, and established harmoniously.

I have not belonged to the indefinite, creedless school of religionists, always seeking and never finding the truth, groping my way through a maze of uncertainties and doubtful speculations, with unsettled convictions about this world and the future world. I have indeed been a free inquirer, but not a schooled doubter, on the gravest questions of religious concern. I have tried not to be a self-sufficient, traditional Pharisee on the one hand, nor on the other, a self-sufficient Sadducee, too learned and proud to feel the force of evidence in support of immortality or the existence of angels and manifestable spirits. I was and am a rational Christian Spiritualist, accepting all the reliably proven spiritual phenomena of ancient and modern times as belonging to one continuous succession of manifestations. But I have never embraced any form of spiritualism that ignored or belittled Christ or reduced Him to the grade of a mere medium for the communication of departed spirits, nor allowed myself to trust to spirit-mediums beyond good evidence of their reliability, nor to accept the teachings of the departed as infallible, nor to receive any so-called spiritual philosophy which conflicted with or set at nought the teachings, example, and spirit of Christ. On the contrary, I held it my duty, and also my privilege, to "try the spirits" out of the flesh as well as those still in it, whether they were of God or mere self-deifiers. For I had no doubt that the spirit spheres are peopled with good and evil angels, with good, bad, and indifferent departed human beings corresponding to those that inhabit the realm of flesh and blood.

You know, too, that I have not been any more of an indefinitist in ethics than in theology. Non-organizationism and non-committalism were never agreeable to my reason, conscience, or taste. Having satisfied myself as to the great truths of religious faith and the great duties of practical righteousness, I declared them and bound myself to them by unmistakable pledges. I could not preach the Fatherhood of God and go on just as if He might sometime, somewhere, treat His creatures like a cruel despot; nor as if mankind might excusably treat Him with habitual filial contempt, as millions do. I could not preach the brotherhood of man and all moral agents, and then teach them to kill, oppress, wrong, and trample one another under foot, as if only beasts. I could not apologize for chattel slavery, war, and the various customs of general society whereby the strong, cunning, and favored classes flourish at the expense of their underlings. I could not preach that mankind were immortal spirits, all governed by their Heavenly Father by law, justly and graciously, as destined to immortal blessedness; and then look on their cruelty to each other, their intemperance, licentiousness, and all manner of debasing practices with indifference, with tacit fellowship, and no confrontment of reproof and counter-example. I could but point out their sins, call them to repentance, and above all show them by my own practice the right way — yea, the most excellent way. And this I must do whether they would bear or forbear, whether they would heed my counsel and example, or rush like the war-horse into the battle.

And I call you to record this day, as you look for the last time on my earthly tabernacle from which I have ascended, that these things have been my chief concern during the major portion of my long life. The trumpet of my testimony has given no uncertain sound, either in precept or example. When the cause of total abstinence from intoxicating beverages came up for serious consideration, did I hide myself from responsibility or burrow among the sophistries of apology, non-action, and non-committalism? Or was I in the front of the battle? And ever since, where have I stood but on the safe ground of unswerving fidelity to my pledge? If I have withheld my hand from attempting to drive others into temperance by penal laws, nevertheless no one mistook which way my precept and example besought him to go. So in the anti-tobacco reform, have the old or the young mistaken my position? Have they seen me waver in my theoretical or practical testimony? If I refrained from words, did any one ever suspect my course?

When the anti-slavery agitation summoned every inhabitant of the land to protest against that horrible abomination, I could do no otherwise than respond. Yea, though all but one in a thousand were so drugged with pro-slavery as to be utterly indifferent to the wails of the downtrodden, or so maddened against the Abolitionists as to jeopardize their very lives by mobocratic outrages. The millions in bondage were no less my brethren and sisters than their oppressors. Truth was truth, justice was justice, and I could not refrain from uncompromising denunciation of such utter wrong inflicted by the strong against the weak. So I took my stand with the few against the many in those dark days.

The bloody theme of war loomed up for consideration, and I was summoned by the voice of God to decide whether I would stand for or against it. I saw that it was a vast system of manslaughter, even in its most excusable form — unfraternal, savage, and barbarous; anti-Christian, irrational, and full of monstrous evils. I saw that it was based on the assumed rightfulness of resisting evil with evil and overcoming deadly force with deadly force, which Christ both by precept and example unqualifiedly forbade His disciples to do, even toward their worst enemies. He had laid His great regenerative axe at the root of this upas-tree, and it must be destroyed, trunk and branches. I was fully convinced of this and took my stand accordingly. Beginning where the Son of God did, I left no room for compromise with the least of its rootlets or sprigs. Starting from the divine fundamental principle of pure, universal good will, absolute love, I felt bound to go with that principle wherever it carried me, for all that it dictated, against all that it condemned. I did not allow myself to be sophisticated into any excuses for defensive war or resorts to so-called justifiable deadly force in extreme cases, but committed myself to total abstinence from all war, preparations for war, glorifications of war, commemorations of war, and organic action involving any resorts whatsoever to deadly force against my fellow-men. I would neither be an officer nor private in any warlike organization, nor in any social, political, religious, or governmental organization by which I made myself responsible for the infliction of death or injurious force on any human being. I would neither fight, vote, pray for, nor give any approval of any custom, practice, or act which contravened the law of perfect love toward God, toward my fellow moral agents, or the universal highest good. I would have no deadly weapon on my person or in my habitation, and held all resorts to their use (except for the destruction of animal life in proper cases) to be a hateful abomination. Thus I was an unmistakable peace man from the crown of my head to the soles of my feet. And I died without a doubt of my Christlikeness in these respects, yea, without a doubt that all men must come up to this plane of righteousness, in order to perfect safety and blessedness.

In respect to worldly property, power, and distinction, I long ago learned of Christ and became fully convinced that they ought to be entirely subordinate to the law of pure fraternal good will, perfect love toward God and fellow moral agents; that property should neither be acquired, used, nor expended contrary to the Golden Rule, nor to the degradation, neglect, or unhappiness of any human being; that no one should consume for personal or family gratification, more than would be his equitable share in well-ordered human society, whilst his surplus beyond this should be devoted in some rational way to the relief, elevation, and welfare of his needy fellow-creatures; that riches and poverty are both great evils which ought to be done away with by the voluntary concurrence of all right minds, and that until this shall be accomplished property will be grossly abused, to the misery of the human race. I learned also that all power and preeminence of one human being over another, however rightful or justifiable, ought to be exercised and manifested in conscientious conformity to Christ's unequivocal injunction, "He that is greatest among you, let him be as the younger, and he that is chief as he that doth serve," — which exactly reverses the carnal ambition of superiors in the world, who aggrandize themselves more and more at the expense of their inferiors and exalt themselves to their degradation. Not so Christ himself; not so His true followers; and not so ought it ever to be among human beings. The law of perfect love imperatively requires that the more talented, or wise, or rich, or gifted in any respect one is, so much the greater is his obligation to serve and help the less favored. And until this law is voluntarily and conscientiously obeyed, the strong will continue to take advantage of the weak, and superiors to prey on their inferiors to an abhorrent extent.

I have faithfully preached the ethics of this doctrine, and no less faithfully exemplified it in my practice. I have never acquired, used, or consumed property contrary to the Golden Rule. I have never exacted a high price for my services. I have never made merchandise of the gospel, nor received anything for my ministrations but what was voluntarily contributed by those who enjoyed them. I have sued no man at the law to obtain my dues. I have occupied no finer house, kept no better equipage, eaten no costlier food, worn no richer clothing, nor consumed any more for the gratification of myself and family than would be my equitable share with all others in a well-ordered state of society. Nor in any respect wherein I was superior to others or moved as a leader, have I ever exacted deference, or assumed airs of importance, or taxed others to support my dignity, or shirked hard labors of body or mind for the common good; but have willingly served rather than be served. What I did to found and establish a fraternal order of society in Hopedale, in which these sublime virtues might be illustrated, but in which I succeeded so poorly, I need not remind you. My aspirations, convictions, and principles never changed in respect to the fraternalization of the social conditions of men. I girdled them firmly about my heart even unto death, and they live in my bosom as a spirit forevermore. They will yet be realized in their highest excellence on earth by devoted disciples who will rejoice in the sacrifices necessary to insure their blessings to suffering millions. The last, best labors of my head and pen have done all in my power to prepare the way for this grand Social Reform, and my small pecuniary savings have been consecrated to its promotion. I have left the world under a very strong assurance from Heaven that a regenerate Christlike form of the Church will ere long be developed to prosecute this work, and now leave you a solemn prophecy that the coming century will witness a glorious practical consummation of the cardinal principles in behalf of which God made it my high privilege to bear testimony.

Having thus indicated the principal things which I desire you to have in remembrance, and for which I wish to be personally remembered by all my survivors, I now draw to a close. In doing so, I sincerely repeat that I claim no merit or credit for any of the truth and good illustrated through my instrumentality. God has inspired and wrought it through me. I have at best done merely my indispensable duty, and am but an unprofitable servant with no reasons for boasting, though unspeakable ones for gratitude to the Most High Father. On the other hand, I take shame and humiliation to myself for all my shortcomings. I am profoundly sensible of my unworthiness. Though my sins have mainly sprung from passional frailty, aberration of temper, misdirected appetites, and weak judgment, they have filled me with pungent sorrow and prostrated me in the dust of contrition before the throne of my Heavenly Father. I have never confirmed or excused myself in evil in His presence, but constantly confessed that His law was holy and just and good, and thanked Him for all His faithful rebukes. And he has graciously responded to all my penitent confessions, "Whom I love I correct"; "Go, and sin no more."

I wish it also to be remembered and understood that while I have strictly and uncompromisingly claimed that the Christ-plane of truth and righteousness on which I planted myself was absolutely the highest in the moral universe, I have never denied that there was more or less truth and righteousness on lower moral planes, nor taught that those who occupied those lower planes were void of conscientiousness and worth in acting up to their light. I have tried to judge all by their own acknowledged moral standard, or left them to the infallible judgment of the All-perfect God. Nor have I ever allowed myself to withhold due credit for right feelings, intentions, or conduct in any human being, whatever his general moral character, knowing that on every moral level there are good, better, and best; or contrariwise, bad, worse, and worst. Thus I have humbly endeavored, without sacrifice of truth, to be just and charitable to all mankind, always considering the force of circumstances and making the best I could even of the worst. My prayer, in the language of the great practical poet, has been

> "Teach me to feel another's woe
> To hide the faults I see;
> The mercy I to others show,
> That mercy show to me."

And now farewell to you all; to the nearest and dearest of kin that sit as mourners today; to my religious and sympathizing friends; and to all of every relationship and class who have known me during my long earthly life. I have "finished my course" and "the ministry which I received of the Lord Jesus, to testify the gospel of the grace of God." I have commended my spirit to the disposal of infinite love and wisdom, and am at rest in my appropriate mansion of the All-Father's vast house. I shall meet you again in due time on the immortal shore. Until then, I invoke on you all the richest benedictions of Heaven, and thenceforth will invoke them on you forevermore. *Amen.*

APPENDIX C.

The Adin Ballou Lectureship of Practical Christian Sociology.

IT was the long-cherished desire of Mr. Ballou that whatever property he might be in possession of at the time of his decease should be used to promote the same philanthropic and noble objects to the attainment of which the crowning aspirations and efforts of his life had been directed. That desire was embodied in the several clauses of his *Last Will and Testament*, and with it detailed requisitions in regard to the ways and means of accomplishing the end it had in view. After providing for the payment of funeral expenses and all just claims against his estate, and making a few private bequests of inconsiderable amount, the testator ordered that there be set apart, as a Publication Fund, a sum sufficient for printing certain specified volumes already prepared or to be prepared by him and to be left in manuscript, together with one or more others composed of selections from his miscellaneous writings, if his executors deemed it expedient, and for distributing the same, free of expense, to theological schools, libraries, and educational institutions, where they would be accessible to those of coming generations desirous of learning how to make the world better; and that the residue be held in trust until a church should be organized upon the ethical and religious basis set forth in his treatises on Primitive Christianity, and should have entered practically upon the work of reconstructing the existing social system along the lines presented in the same series of volumes, — a consummation which he was confident would be reached within fifty years, — when it should be paid, with all its accumulations, in full and without restriction, to such church, to be used at its discretion in carrying its purposes and plans into effect.

The legally appointed administrators of the estate, deeming the contemplated achievement exceedingly problematical, especially within the period stated, and fearing that the money appropriated to its aid would be frittered away and lost, so far as the ends proposed were concerned, petitioned the court in authority to set aside the clause of the will relating to this particular matter and issue a decree assigning the amount of property involved to the only surviving heir thereto, Mrs. Abbie B. Heywood, wife of Rev. William S. Heywood of Sterling, Mass., to be used or expended as her best judgment might dictate. The petition received favorable consideration and an order was issued accordingly. Whereupon Mrs. Heywood, conjointly with her husband, neither of whom wished to gain any personal advantage or profit from the decision of the court, but rather to employ the means thus put at their disposal for purposes in harmony with the general spirit and design of the Will, began to institute inquiries in respect to some method or agency by which that result could be accomplished. Numerous schemes were suggested and considered with conscientious deliberation, but the one which commended itself most unqualifiedly to the judgment and moral sense of those immediately concerned, and which secured their final acceptance, was that indicated in the following copy of a communication, the meaning and purpose of which are expressed with so much clearness and precision that they require no comment or elucidation.

" *To the President and Trustees of the Meadville Theological School:* —

"Gentlemen: — Having come into possession of what may remain of the estate of my revered father, Rev. Adin Ballou, late of Hopedale, Mass., deceased, when the several obligations specifically mentioned in his Last Will and Testament have been fully met and cancelled, I desire in grateful honor of his name and memory to devote the same, amounting to about sixteen thousand dollars ($16,000) now in hand, to the promotion of those great objects of Christian beneficence and philanthrophy in which he was deeply interested when upon the earth, and to the advancement and realization of which he consecrated the best energies and efforts of his long and active life. After careful and mature deliberation upon various means and methods of accomplishing the end in view, I have at length decided upon the plan embodied in the following proposition, which I am pleased to submit to you for consideration and for such action on your part as your best judgment may dictate, to wit:—

"I propose to give to the Institution of which you have charge or to its properly authorized representatives, the aforesaid sum of sixteen thousand dollars ($16,000), to be held in trust as a permanent fund for the establishment and maintenance of a department of instruction therein to be called *The Adin Ballou Lectureship of Practical Christian Sociology.* The purpose of this offer is to secure the annual delivery of a course of lectures, by the most satisfactory talent that can be obtained, upon the social aspects of the religion of Christ and the consequent duty and importance of applying the principles and spirit of that religion to the intercourse of man with man, in all the actions and relations of life. In these lectures special attention shall be paid to such subjects, for example, as 'The Barbarism of War' and the consequent 'Claims of the Cause of Peace'; 'The Extinction of the Evils of Intemperance'; 'The Proper Relation of the Sexes,' including 'The True Doctrine of Marriage and Divorce'; 'The Higher Education and Complete Enfranchisement of Woman'; 'The Adjustment and Harmonization of the Relation between Capital and Labor'; 'The Prevention of and Remedy for Poverty'; 'The Care and Reformation of Criminals'; 'The Amelioration and Improvement of the Condition of the Unfortunate and Perishing Classes'; including in their full range all topics calculated to enhance the well-being and happiness of mankind and to fashion human society after the Christian ideal of the kingdom of heaven on earth. These lectures, or such of them as shall be deemed most valuable by the president and board of instruction, shall be published from time to time and sent, free of expense, to other theological schools and to leading educational institutions, libraries, etc., throughout the land, to the end that their usefulness may be extended as far and wide as possible.

"It is furthermore my express wish and desire that the contemplated lectureship shall be based upon the distinct and positive recognition of the eternal excellency of the religion of Christ in its fundamental truth and essential spirit, as taught and exemplified in the scriptures of the New Testament and as interpreted by the advancing intelligence of mankind, and that its administration shall be absolutely impartial and free, regardless alike of denominational peculiarities and limitations, and of all artificial distinctions of race, sex, or nationality.

"This offer is made with the full expectation and assurance that, if accepted, the endowment involved will be held sacred to the purposes for which it is designed, and in the earnest hope that the work of human improvement and social regeneration, so dear to the heart of my beloved father, will be advanced by the instrumentality it provides for and ordains, and that his name and influence for good in the world may be conserved and perpetuated unto many generations.

"Sincerely and respectfully yours,
(Signed) "ABBIE B. HEYWOOD.

"Heartily concurring in the above proposition, I indicate the same over my own proper signature.
(Signed) "WILLIAM S. HEYWOOD."

This proposition was formally accepted by the Trustees of the Meadville school at a meeting held soon after it was received, January 31, 1891, when a resolution was passed, thanking the donor for her generous gift and assuring her "that the objects which the said donation is intended to promote meet with the cordial approval of the Board as being in harmony with the work of the school." Three months later the money was paid into the treasury of the institution and steps were immediately taken to provide means of improving the opportunity thus opened to its students during the then coming academic year. Those steps proved effectual, and the lectureship was inaugurated and started out on its mission of usefulness the following winter. Its work to this date (1896) has been highly satisfactory and gratifying to its founder, so far as she has been made acquainted with it, as it seems to be with others interested in the principles and purposes it was designed to foster and carry forward in the world. Numerous testimonials from students, alumni, and members of the faculty of the school have been received, assuring her of the great good already done through its instrumentality and of the rich promise of good it gives for the days and years to come; leading her to believe and feel that her action in regard to the money assigned her was timely and judicious; that the cause of Practical Christian truth and righteousness is to be permanently subserved thereby; and that the name and memory of her father are to be correspondingly preserved and honored with the advancing years of time.

The first course of lectures upon the foundation thus established was given during the winter of 1892-3 by Rev. Washington Gladden, D. D., of Columbus, Ohio, a most profound, conscientious, and reverent student of the problems that enter into the organization and improvement of human society. His addresses were subsequently published by Houghton, Mifflin & Co., Boston, under the somewhat enigmatical title, "Tools and the Man," which had a wide circulation, five hundred copies of it having been distributed by the authorities at Meadville, agreeably to the specifications of the communication quoted above.

The principal course for the year 1893-4, consisting of seven lectures, was delivered by Rev. Francis G. Peabody, D. D., Plummer professor of Christian morals in the Harvard Divinity School, which was supplemented by two lectures from Rev. Edward E. Hale, D. D., of Boston. The course for 1894-5 was by Rev. E. B. Andrews, D. D., President of Brown University, and consisted of ten lectures, of which five were given in the autumn of the first-named year and five the following spring.

Rev. Lyman Abbot, D. D., the widely known pastor of Plymouth Church, Brooklyn, N. Y., and editor of the *Outlook*, gave the fourth course, during the scholastic year 1895-6. His lectures, which were delivered extemporaneously, have been written out in an amplified form, and, with some correlative matter, have been embodied in a volume of three hundred and seventy pages entitled, "Christianity and Social Problems," just issued from the press of Houghton, Mifflin & Co. This also will be in part circulated, as was the work of Dr. Gladden, in accordance with the conditions upon which the lectureship was established.

The lectures for the current year, 1896-7, it is expected, will be by Rev. Samuel W. Dike, LL.D., upon "The Family"; by Rev. John Graham Brooks on "The Organization of Charity"; and by Benjamin Trueblood, LL.D., secretary of the American Peace Society, upon "International Arbitration."

APPENDIX D.

Mrs. Lucy Hunt Ballou.

THIS estimable woman, the second wife of the subject of the narrative contained in this volume and for more than sixty years his household companion and helper in manifold ways, belonged to one of the oldest and most substantial of New England families, and possessed in large measure those sterling qualities of mind, heart, and character which have distinguished the New England name from the beginning and clothed it with lustre and renown throughout the civilized world. Her paternal immigrant ancestor was William Hunt, a native of the mother country, born about 1605, who, under the leadership of the celebrated Rev. Peter Bulkley, came to these shores in 1637 with Capt. Simon Willard, the Wheelers, and other notable men, and assisted in founding the historic town of Concord, Mass. He was made freeman in 1641, and is represented as an upright, God-fearing man, a good citizen, earnestly devoted to the principles of the Puritan faith, exemplary in the discharge of his domestic duties, training up his children "in the nurture and admonition of the Lord." From him, in the line of Isaac of Concord, Isaac of Sudbury, Abidah of Holliston, and Daniel of Holliston and Milford, descended Pearley of Milford, the father of the subject of this sketch. He was an enterprising merchant and leading citizen of the town, "a man of superior natural abilities, aptitudes, and qualifications to make a respectable mark in society." He was a Democrat in politics, and in religious faith a Universalist. For twenty-one years he held the office of postmaster, and that of justice of the peace during all the later part of his life. Much interested in public education, he was repeatedly chosen a member of the school committee, serving with skill and efficiency. "He lived beloved and esteemed in domestic and social circles for his kindness, urbanity, generosity, hospitality, and kindred virtues, and died in honor and peace."

Lucy Hunt was the daughter of Pearley Hunt, Esq., and his wife, Chloe (Albee) Hunt, and was born Oct. 31, 1810. She inherited from her parents good intellectual capabilities and a personality marked by unusual independence of opinion and action, great power of will, and resolute perseverance in whatever she undertook to execute. In her childhood and youth she manifested a gentle nature and a disposition characterized by thoughtfulness, cheerfulness, kindness, and amiability. These qualities not only made her an agreeable associate and companion, gaining for her a large circle of devoted friends as she grew up to womanhood, but rendered her susceptible to those moral and spiritual influences and tuitions which afterward brought into prominence the best that was in her and nurtured those attributes and graces of character which crowned and glorified her maturer life. An apt and diligent scholar, she profited exceedingly by the educational opportunities accessible to her in her native town, meagre and poor indeed compared with what are now offered there, and by a brief term of instruction at a higher institution of learning in Providence, R. I., from which, however, she was unexpectedly summoned home to minister at the bedside of Mr. Ballou, her future husband, who had been stricken down with a well-nigh fatal illness, and to whom she was already affianced, as narrated in its proper place in the body of this work. A few months after his recovery, on the 3d of March, 1830, they were married, she being not far advanced in the 20th year of her age. But though so young, she was yet unusually mature, both in womanly qualities and executive ability, which, brought, it would seem, prematurely into requisition, vindicated themselves most fully by the wisdom, tact, and efficiency with which she met the responsibilities and discharged the duties of wife and mother at the very outset, as she did thenceforward to the end of her mortal pilgrimage. By her conscientious, painstaking fidelity in the performance of the tasks imposed upon her in the home, which were increased in number and in burdensomeness for some years by reason of the circumstances and exactions incident to her husband's calling and career, she so overtaxed her energies that they at length gave way in part, seriously impairing her health and power of endurance and causing her to suffer a sort of semi-invalidism during the remainder of her earthly days. Yet by a constant, watchful care of herself and the prudent use of the resources left to her, she was able in her quiet, leisurely way to bring more to pass than many with much greater strength and vitality than she, attending to the cares and labors of the household and performing other duties of a various nature, with such occasional help as could easily be called in and only a single interruption of a few weeks, through a life lengthened out far beyond the Psalmist's allotted period of three score years and ten.

Nor was she competent and efficient in the strictly domestic concerns of the household alone. Her clear-seeing intellect, practical good sense, and literary accomplishments enabled her to render substantial aid in many ways to her husband in the varied phases of the work to which he devoted his life. She assisted him greatly in his labors as editor and author, especially in his later years, and by her suggestion, counsel, and criticism contributed largely to the success of those labors. Moreover, she did much to cheer and strengthen him in the midst of the trials and disappointments which at times, as he repeatedly confessed, almost overwhelmed him, and to encourage him to continued efforts for the enlightenment, uplifting, and redemption of mankind. Her faith in the eternal verities — in God and immortality — was unwaveringly sure and steadfast and served to reinvigorate and stimulate his when, for any cause, it grew faint within him. For many of the last years of her life, it was her great care, as it was her joy also, to do for him and make him comfortable and happy, and her prayer was that she might live to minister to him to the very last — to smoothe his dying pillow, to close his eyes in the sleep that knows no waking here below, and to see his physical frame properly prepared for its sepulture and laid away tenderly in the family burial lot which they had planned together and fitted up as the final resting-place of all that was mortal of themselves and of those they held most dear.

That prayer was graciously answered; and when it was answered she was ready to follow on and be forever with him and all the loved ones gone before, in some higher mansion of the Father's house towards which for many years their united thought and heart had been turned with unfailing, triumphant hope and trust. The two were not long separated. She survived him a year and two days only, passing peacefully away after a two weeks' illness on the 7th of August, 1891, at the age of 80 years, 9 months, and 8 days.

Mrs. Ballou was a most hearty and earnest sympathizer with her husband in all his religious convictions, principles, and ideas, as she was in his manifold labors of philanthropy and reform. Her conceptions of duty toward God included love and good will to men, which she exemplified in a disposition to help and bless them in all possible ways, according to her ability. Many were they in her immediate neighborhood who shared her kindness and her benefactions, and her ear and hand were ever open to the appeals of the poor, needy, suffering sons and daughters of men. All good causes enlisted her interest and received her cordial encouragement and support — the cause of peace being especially near to her heart, as attested by repeated contributions to its treasury while she lived, and by a bequest of two thousand dollars to the Universal Peace Union of Philadelphia, of which that eminent philanthropist, Alfred H. Love, is president, provided for in her Last Will and Testament. She was most emphatically

> "One who, calm and true,
> Life's highest purpose understood;
> And like the Blessed Master, knew
> The joy of doing good."

To the high character, marked ability, effective service, and genuine worth of his household companion and helpmeet for so many years, Mr. Ballou himself pays appreciative and grateful tribute in his "History and Genealogy of the Ballous in America," as follows:—

"In my marriage to my present wife, who has grown old in my companionship, I have been greatly blessed. Solomon well said, 'A prudent wife is from the Lord.' Mine is such — a model of discretion, domestic order, executive industry; a constant minister of good under all circumstances in her family and neighborhood; an intelligent counselor in all emergencies, and a sympathetic companion in all high principles and endeavors. Though not robust in health and physical strength, she excels in actual accomplishment through mental judgment and persistent will-power. . . . We have shared our joys, sorrows, labors, and trials together for more than fifty-seven years. We are now nearing their completion and preparing for our summons to the higher life."

The *Milford Journal*, in noticing the death of Mrs. Ballou, bore the following testimony concerning her:

"Mrs. Ballou, throughout her entire life, admirably co-operated with her husband in all his work, ardently supplementing his efforts to promote the social and religious growth of his fellow beings. It is not too much to say that she was a great help to him; she was most loyal and unwavering. Her life was always kindly and by those to whom she was best known she was most highly esteemed. Many will regret her departure as the cessation of a gentle, lovable, charitable influence from their visible midst."

Rev. Lewis G. Wilson, the pastor of the Hopedale parish, who knew her well in her later years, prepared a brief obituary of her for the *Christian Register*, in which he most appropriately and expressively says:

"Her life was beautiful and saintly. Her nature was an earnest of the pure devotion and perfect faith of an exalted humanity. As the needle to the star, so was her spirit to the Father. In her ways as simple and unpretentious as a child, in her belief as sure and steadfast as an apostle, and in her practical piety an example for all who knew her. For more than sixty years she entered deeply into all the great spiritual aspirations and achievements of her husband, and by a well-nigh infallible intuition, sympathized and counseled with him in the perplexing emergencies of his remarkable life. Almost unconsciously to herself, she became an influence to inspire love and peace, to engender the sense of spiritual serenity, and to yield an inestimable blessing to the community in which she lived. Her mission, so well accomplished, cannot fail to be the source of pure motives, noble efforts, and blessed memories for many years to come.

"The blessing of thy presence
   And all thy tender care
Was like the peaceful sunlight
   That enters everywhere.

It cheered us in our sorrow,
   And strength of soul it gave;
It lifted high the spirit
   Above life's troubled wave.

O, blessed spirit, visit
   And teach us as of yore,—
A presence be to guide us
   Where thou hast gone before."

APPENDIX E.

Published Works of Adin Ballou.

BOUND VOLUMES.

Christian Non-Resistance, 1846.
Hopedale Hymn Book: Compilation, 1849.
Spirit Manifestations, 1852.
Memoir of Adin Augustus Ballou, 1853.
Practical Christian Socialism, 1854.
The Monitorial Guide, 1861.
Primitive Christianity, Vol. I, 1870.
History of Milford, Mass., 1882.
History of the Ballous in America, 1888.

PAMPHLETS, TRACTS, ETC., WITH DATES.

Review of Hosea Ballou's Sermon on *The New Birth*, 1820.
The Furious Priest Reproved, 1823.
Fourth of July Oration at Milford, 1827.
Sermon on *The Inestimable Value of Souls*, 1830.
Fourth of July Oration at Blackstone, 1830.
Discussion with Rev. Daniel D. Smith, 1834.
Sunday School Manual, 1836.
Address on Slavery at Mendon, July 4, 1837.
The Touchstone, 1837.
Conference Hymn-Book: — A Compilation, 1839.
Non-Resistance and Human Governments, 1839.
Constitution of The Fraternal Communion, 1843.
Scriptural Doctrine of the Second Advent, 1843.
Superiority of Moral to Political Power, 1845.
Constitution of The Practical Christian Ministry, 1848.
Constitution of The Hopedale Community, 1849.
What Entitles One to the Christian Name, 1849.
Endless Punishment Rejected, 1849.
The Bible; its Principles Divine, its Language Human, 1849.
The Hopedale Community: an Exposition, 1851.
Lecture on Capital Punishment, 1851.

THE HOPEDALE COMMUNITY: HISTORICAL SKETCH, 1853.
THE PRACTICAL CHRISTIAN REPUBLIC, 1854.
CONSTITUTION OF THE PRACTICAL CHRISTIAN REPUBLIC, 1854.
LECTURE ON THE BIBLE, 1859.
PRACTICAL CHRISTIANITY AND ENDLESS PUNISHMENT, 1860.
VIOLATIONS OF THE FEDERAL CONSTITUTION, 1861.
REVIEW OF A SERMON BY HENRY WARD BEECHER, 1862.
HUMAN PROGRESS IN RESPECT TO RELIGION, 1867.

ALSO THE FOLLOWING, WITHOUT DATES.

FUNDAMENTAL PRINCIPLES THE ONLY AUTHORITY IN RELIGION.
DIFFERENT CHRISTS AND CHRISTIANITIES.
CHRISTIAN NON-RESISTANCE: QUESTIONS ANSWERED.
LEARN TO DISCRIMINATE, ETC.
INSPIRATION OF THE BIBLE.
NON-RESISTANCE IN EXTREME CASES.
PRACTICAL CHRISTIANITY IN RELATION TO VOTING.
PRACTICAL CHRISTIANITY IN RELATION TO HUMAN GOVERNMENT.
PRACTICAL CHRISTIANITY IN RELATION TO MARRIAGE AND DIVORCE.
PRACTICAL CHRISTIANITY IN RELATION TO EDUCATION AND AMUSEMENTS.
REPLY TO PARSON HOR ON WAR.
AN INQUIRER ANSWERED.

Numerous minor productions of the author's pen appeared in tract form during the more active portion of his life, of which no record has been made. He was editor of the *Dialogical Instructor* for six months; of the *Independent Messenger*, eight years; and of the *Practical Christian*, twenty years. He prepared a "Sketch of the Town of Hopedale" for a voluminous "History of Worcester County" in 1889; and an indefinite number of articles written by him from time to time were published in the columns of religious and reformatory papers and periodicals with whose spirit, principles, and aims he was more or less in sympathy.

INDEX.

Abolitionists and the John Brown raid 416
Achievement, A happy 435
Address, Valedictory as President of The Hopedale Community 367
Aldrich, Dea. Nathaniel, Interview with 87
American Anti-slavery Society and its peace principles . 417
Amusements in the paternal home 13
Ancestry and lineage 3
Announcement, Startling 67
Anti-slavery espousal 277
           Sermon 281
           Oration 283
Apthorp, Rev. W. P., Discussion with 264
Aspirations for a collegiate education thwarted 40
Attacked at a funeral service 166
Authorship, First attempt at 71
Auto-biography, End of work upon 476

Bachelor, Origin, Call from 151
           Discussion with 152, 370
Ball, Rev. George S., Address at funeral 529
Ballou, Elder Abner, Pastor of "Six Principle Baptist" Church 6
Ballou, Ariel, father of Adin 1
           Residence with son 269
           Death 315
Ballou, Ariel, M. D., brother of Adin, married 228
           Relation to Ballou History . . 490, 491
           Death 514
Ballou, Arnold, brother of Adin, Death of 38
Ballou, Cyrus, brother of Adin, Death of 37
Ballou, Edilda Tower, mother of Adin, Death of . . . 258
Ballou, Hosea, Relationship to Adin 3
           Characteristics of 93
           Call to New York city 140

INDEX.

Ballou, Hosea, Result 142
               Reflections on his course 145
Ballou, Hosea, 2d, First meeting with 80
               Official services of, at second marriage 164
Ballou, James, great-great-grandfather of Adin 4
Ballou, Hon. Latimer W., Relation to Ballou History 490, 491
Ballou, Lucy Hunt, Severe labors of 361
               Serious illness of 485
               Sketch of 567
Ballou, Maturin, Immigrant ancestor of American Ballous 3
Ballou, Family, History of 490, 491, 492
Ballou Meeting-house 5, 6
Ballou Neighborhood, Description of 4
               Religion in 12
Ballou & Stacey, name of printing firm 183
Baptism and reception to the church 32
             Administered by immersion 305
Baptists of Bellingham, Collision with 97
Belief in theological doctrines formulated 45
             Change of 84
Bellingham, Exciting Sunday scenes in , ... 97, 98
Bible, Views upon the 409-431
Birth, Place and date of 1
Blind Tom, a negro, Wonderful performances of . . . 452
Books and reading, Early love for 18
Boston, First visit to 70
      Second visit to 93
      Candidacy in 101
Brook Farm 326
Brothers and sisters 2, 3
Brownson, Rev. Orestes A., Installation of, at Canton . 254
Burial lot, Family, at Hopedale 494
Burying ground at Cumberland 11
Business venture and its unfortunate results 59

Call to the work of the Ministry 62
Capron, Edmund, Theological student 253
             Ordained 289
             Death of 290
Casualties in early life 8
Celebration of American Independence at Milford . . . 126
                           At Blackstone . . 187
Centennial of American Independence at Milford, Address
    at 477
Chambré, Rev. A. St. John, Criticism by 464
Chandler, Seth, Theological student 157

INDEX. 577

Chandler, Seth, installed at Oxford 234
Change of theological belief announced 85
                                Results 85–88
Channing, William Ellery, D. D., Friendly letter from . 335
Chaplain of Regiment of Mass. Militia 109
Child lost in New York city 135
Children, Death of two 231
Christian, The Practical, a semi-monthly paper started . . 317
                            Suspended 422
Christianity and Civilization 111
Christianity, Practical, Standard of 309–313
Christianity, True 296
Christmas, First Celebration in Mendon 305
Church, The, joined 32
        Disowned by 88
        At Hopedale 414
        The world's need of 458
        Views upon 470
Cincinnati, Visit to 394
Commentary on the New Testament 422
Commune No. 1 404
Communion, Fraternal 324
Community, The Hopedale . 325, 341, 342, 362, 396, 400, 429
Conferences, Quarterly 315, 333
Conscription, Case of 449
            Protest against 450
Constitution, Violations of the Federal 428
Controversy with ultra Universalists opened 172
                           Closed 262
Crisis in Community affairs 400
Crisis in ministerial career 175
Crossman, Elder Zephaniah 29
                Fell from grace 46
Cutler, Rev. Stephen, Experience with 236

Daughter, Birth of 153
Dean, Rev. Paul 260
          Letter of 336
Declaration of Principles 327
Dedication of Town Hall, Hopedale 503
Destiny of the wicked, Views upon 45
Destruction of the wicked, Favoring texts upon 82
                     Belief in tested 83
Destructiveness in childhood 9
Dialogical Instructor, a semi-monthly paper 136
Diary extracts 159–161, 226–230, 298–302

INDEX.

Discussion, Oral, with Rev. D. D. Smith 247
" Mr. Follett 351
" Rev. M. W. Burlingame 352
" Origin Bachelor 370
" Rev. Thomas Williams 371
" Miles Grant 428
Domestic life begun 76
Doubts concerning theological views 79
Douglas, Frederic, First visit to Hopedale 338
Dow, Lorenzo, Recollections of 48
His eccentricities 49
Dr. Nathaniel Emmons and his members 118
Draper, Ebenezer D., Death of 513
Draper, George, Death of 512

Eddy, Rev. Richard, upon the Restorationist schism . . 507
Editorship, First experience in 136
Educational Home contemplated 377
Project abandoned 385
Edwards, Rev. Thomas, ordained 289
Emerson, Ralph Waldo, Notes upon 499
Employes, Pleasant relations with 10
Endless Punishment, Favoring texts upon 82
England, War with, 1812–1815 25
Ernst, Andrew H., Gift of 355
Hospitality . . . . , ... 394
Death 415
Error of Hosea Ballou exposed 71
Essays, Dissertations, and Reviews 495, 497, 499
Exchanges with noted Universalist ministers 108
Expositor, The Laconic, planned 24
Experiment, Unfortunate 325
Experiments, Various social 497

Family burial lot at Hopedale 494
Farr, Rev. Jonathan, Discussion with 238
Father's government 9
Farm 13
Opposition on religious grounds 86
Estate settled 259
Residence at Mendon 269
Death 315
Field of labor enlarging 157
First religious impressions 12
Fish, Rev. Wm. H., Ordination 301
Address of, at funeral 533

INDEX. 579

Fisher, Rev. Abial, Encounter with 99
Fletcher, E. F., Post G. A. R., Sermon before 482
Fraternal Communion organized 324
                   Basis of 327
Free Masonry espoused 108
              Views of 109
Funeral experiences 118–123, 165–167
Funeral services 524, 529–534
Furious priest reproved 100
Future retribution, Belief in 79
              Bible teachings upon 82

Gale, Memorable, September, 1815 35
Garrison, Wm. Lloyd, Peace declarations of 420
                Discourses at Hopedale 438
                Review of the same 442
                Letter from 480
Gloomy premonition concerning wife 149
Granddaughter, Lucy Florence Heywood, born 430
Grandparents, sketch of 2
Granny Grant, a childhood terror 20
Grant, Miles, Oral discussion with 428
Groton Convention, A mottled gathering 319

Hare, Prof. Robert, a noted spiritualist, Interview with . 398
Harris, Rev. Thomas L., a spiritualist seer, Vision of . . 407
Hastings, Hon. William, elected to Congress 305
Hawkins, John H. W., a Washingtonian lecturer . . . 338
Henry, Rev. Samuel, a Christian reformer, Death of . . 415
Heywood, Abbie Ballou 375
Heywood, Rev. William S. 375, 438
Historical sketch of the town of Hopedale 498
History of the Ballous in America 490, 491
History of the Hopedale Community 473
History of Milford, Mass. 474
Home, provision for 116
      Established 125
      A public hostelry 296
Home School started 408
        Its reputation 409
        Given up 437
Hopedale named 329
      Taken possession of 330
      Removed to 337
      Progress at 340, 355, 396
      Trials 342

580 INDEX.

Hopedale, changes 346
           Meetings 356
           Radical change 402
Hopedale Community founded 331
                   Virtually given up 402
Hopedale, Town of, incorporated 501
Hudson, Rev. Charles, a prominent Restorationist, Letters of 147
Huidekoper, H. J., Tracts on Destruction of the wicked reviewed 238
Humphrey, William H., a valued friend, Death of . . . 511
Hunt, Mrs. Chloe Albee, wife's mother, Death of . . . 382
Hunt, Pearley, Esq., wife's father, Death of 358

Illness, Sudden and serious 161
       Of wife 485
       Final 519
Immigrant ancestor, Maturin Ballou of Providence . . .   3
Immaculate Conception, Dogma of, rejected 465
Immortality, Faith in 156
Independence, American, celebrated 126, 187
              Centennial of 477
Independent Messenger started 182
              Suspended 316
Inductive Communion 389
Intoxicating liquors, Early training concerning 16
Introduction to future wife, Abigail Sayles 57

Johnson, Oliver, an active reformer 381
Joke practiced on a colored man 105

Kneeland, Rev. Abner 129
           Popularity of 136
           Bound to atheism 148

Lamson, Rev. David R., ordained 255
             Troublesome 345
             Later life 348
Last letter to daughter, Abbie B. Heywood 520
Learning, Intense desire for 40
Leaven of the better faith working 50
Lectureship of Practical Christian Sociology founded . . 561
Leighton, Andrew, of Liverpool, England, Surprised by . 453
Lesson from Lorenzo Dow 50
Letters from notable men on Community life 328
Life at the paternal homestead 14, 39

INDEX.

Light from on high sought and found 84, 85
Livermore, Rev. Abiel Abbot, of Cincinnati 394
Locality for a Community selected 329
Long, Ex-Gov. John D., Dedicatory address at Hopedale
    and response 504
Lovejoy, Rev. Elijah P., an anti-slavery editor, murdered 295

Man, a moral and religious being 339
Marriage, First consummated 74
    Second 164
Marriages, First, officiated at in Boston 102
    Singular ones in New York 149
May, Rev. Samuel, Address at funeral 531
May, Rev. Samuel J., at Mendon installation 215
    Visited 399
Meadville, Penn., Lectureship in theological school . . . 561
Meditation on 87th birthday 518
Medway, Engaged to preach in 168
    Memorable sermon 172
    Result 173
Memoir of Adin Augustus Ballou 379
    Butler Wilmarth, M. D. 388
Mendon, Call to 186
    Installed there 215, 216
    Farewell 337
Messenger, Independent, prospectus of 183
    Suspended 316
Milford, Call to 103
    Left for New York 133
    Return to 139
    Discharged from 186
Milford, Town of, much divided 104
Milford Society, Religious condition of 112
Military chaplaincy, Appointed to 109
    Views of 110
Minister of Hopedale parish 456
    Resigned the position . . . 468
    Left it 475
Morse, Cyrus, a student for the ministry 267
    Death of 268
Morse, Rev. William, installed at Marlboro' 256
Mother, Edilda Tower Ballou, deceased Dec. 27, 1834 . . 258

New Communities proposed 396
New York, Call to 132
    Removal thither 134

INDEX.

New York, Return from, to Milford 144
No-future-punishment dogma 170
                          Controversy upon opened . . 179
                          Continued 199
                          Closed 262
Non-resistance, Christian, espoused 308
                       Treatise on 370
                       Pure 420
Non-resistance Society, Meeting of 316
                       Speech at 316
                       President 357
Non-resistant, The, organ of society revived 380
                   Merged in Practical Christian . . . 381
Non-resistants, War-approving 421
North American Phalanx, a Fourierite Community . 325, 393
Northampton Community at Florence, Mass. 325
Notable statesmen, Interview with 393
Novel punishment at school 112
Nuptial festivities interrupted 74

Oahspe, an assumed-to-be new bible, Review of 496
Omega with ultra Universalists 262
Opponents, Distinguished Orthodox 254
Oration July 4, 1827 126
            1830 187
            1837 283
            1876 477
Orthodox controversialists numerous, persistent, and unrelenting 263
Orthodox opinion of the Independent Messenger 185
Owen, Robert Dale, a noted English socialist, at Hopedale 363

Parents and their characteristics 1, 2
Parish at Hopedale organized 455
Parish party and Town party in Milford 104
Parker, Theodore, Preaching for, under difficulties . . . 382
Parochial Christian Union formed 467
Partridge, Emmons, licensed to preach 287
Pawtucket, R. I., Dedication at 151
Peace, Claims of 306
        Argument for 307
        Organized agencies 462
Pernicious errors withstood 389
Perry, Rev. J. M. S., in an unenviable position 220
Personal religion indispensable 294
Phalanx, North American, in Monmouth Co., N. J. . . 325

INDEX. 583

Phalanx, North American, visited 393
Phelps, Rev. Amos A., Discussion with 209
Philadelphia, Visit to 393, 398
Pickering, Rev. David, an eloquent Restorationist . . . 268
Place, Rev. Stephen, a "Six Principle Baptist" minister 6, 11
Plans of father for the future 44
Portrait by Otto Grundmann 516
Practical Christian Republic 390
Primitive Christianity, Vol. 1 460
      Vol. 2 469
      Vol. 3 470
Prince St. Society, N. Y., Call to and ministry therein . 129
Promulgation Society instituted 425
Providence Association joined 182
     Temperance action of 225
Providential provision 186
Public affairs, Interest in 27, 51
Publications, List of 573
Public worship, First attendance at 11
Publishment of a cousin under difficulties 55
Punishment, Endless, abhorrent 244

Raid of John Brown to free slaves 416
Reaction, Monarchical, in 1815 35
Recorder, Boston, Opinion of Independent Messenger . . 185
     Restorationist ministers . . 188
Religion in Ballou neighborhood 12
Religion mixed in youthful mind 33
Religious experiences, Personal 31
Religious Reformation in Cumberland 29
      Effects of . . . 30
Religious susceptibility in childhood 12
Remarkable visitation 62
Reply to Trumpet's attack on the Restorationist Association 200
Restorationism assailed by numerous antagonists . . . 209
Restorationism, Texts proving it 82
    Faith in it established 85
Restorationism vs. Ultra Universalism openly avowed . . 182
Restorationist Association founded 197
     Assailed 199
     Defended 200
Restorationist Association and Moral Reform 292
    Harmony disturbed by its action 292
    The breach widening 314
    Its demise 333

INDEX.

Restorationist secession, Errors concerning it corrected 460, 507
Restorationists little known 46
                Prejudice against 94
                Timid 175
Review of Hosea Ballou's Sermon on the New Birth . . 71
Ripley, Rev. Dr., of Concord, Visit with 272
Russell, Rev. Philemon R., installed 255

Salary, Rule regarding 212
School reminiscences 16, 17, 52, 53
Schools in Rhode Island 16, 17
Second Advent, Discussion upon 351
                Scriptural doctrine of 354
Sermon, First 67
        First as a Universalist 93
        After severe illness 162
        Before G. A. R. Post 482
        For own funeral 547
Sin, Danger of, real and great 68
Singing School, Privileges of denied 42
Situation respecting ultra Universalism canvassed . . . 177
Smith, Rev. Daniel D., Discussion with 248
Smith, Rev. Elias 47
Smith, Hon. Gerritt, visited at his home, Peterboro', N. Y. 399
Son, First born 100
     Second 188
     Third 235
Spirit manifestations 372
              Work on 380
Spirit seances, Remarkable 427, 431
Spiritualists, Attitude towards 387
           Opinion of 462, 500
Stacey, Rev. George W., ordained 271
           Withdrew from the Community 362
Staples, Rev. Carlton, Services of, at funeral 526
              Sermon 536
Stone, Rev. Edwin M., ordained 251
Stone, Rev. Richard, ordained 256
Stroke of good policy 107

Tavern of William Ballou 15
Teacher, Trouble with 21
Teaching, First attempt at 72
Temperance Reform espoused 219
            Indebtedness to 222
Temperance meeting, Address at, under peculiar circumstances 221

INDEX. 585

Theological belief 45
     Questionings 77, 79
     Change 84
Tobacco, Use of, renounced 159
Tolstoi, Count Leo 508
Total Abstinence adopted and proclaimed 275
Touchstone, The, a theological pamphlet 294
Tour to the West 392
Tributes of friends 534
    Associations 540
    The press 542
Troublesome townsman 284
Trumpet and Recorder . . . . , ... 188
Trumpet columns never open to Restorationists . . . 209
Trying experience 485

Unfortunate incident in school 73
Union Convention at Groton 319
Unitarian controversy inaugurated 45
Unitarians, Attitude of, towards Universalists 217
    Opinion concerning 461
Universal holiness and happiness, Belief in precious . . 176
Universalism, its repugnant features 89
    State of, in New York 148
Universalism, Ultra, once dominant in the denomination . 175
Universalist doctrine of punishment in early days . . . 170
Universalist leaders and their policy 175
Universalist Ministry, Ordained to 102
Universalists, Challenge to 246
    Response 247
    Result 248
Universalists, Change of belief among them concerning
  punishment 263
Unusual ceremonial at South Wilbraham 305

Violations of the Federal Constitution 428
Vision, A memorable one 62
Vision of Rev. Thomas L. Harris 407

Washington, D. C., Visit to in 1854 393
Watertown, Call to 236
Weak point in the argument for the destruction of the
  wicked 79
Western journey and its incidents 392
Whipple, Charles K., Review of his argument for abandon-
  ing peace principles 497

38

INDEX.

Whitman, Rev. Bernard, Sermon of 217
                        Letters 235
                        Death 257
Whitney, Rev. Daniel S., licensed to preach 287
                        Ordained 314
                        Withdrawal from the Community 365
Whittemore, Rev. Thomas, Cordial notice by 424
Williamson, Passamore, Visited in prison 398
Wilmarth, Butler, M. D., Tragic death of 388
                    Memoir of 388
Wilson, Rev. Lewis G., Tribute of 535
Winchester's dialogues on Universal Restoration read . . 77
Women's Rights, Position regarding 463
Worcester Conference joined 457
                 Sermon before 458
Worcester, South, Anti-slavery Society, Notable meeting
  of 418
Work for the future 456, 459
Workingmen's movement 463
Wrentham school, Interesting incidents connected with it 19
Wright, Henry C., and his work 381
Wright, Rev. Nathaniel, a Restorationist clergyman . . . 257